ISLAMIC DESK REFERENCE

ISLAMIC
DESK REFERENCE

Compiled from
The Encyclopaedia of Islam
by

E. VAN DONZEL

E.J. BRILL
LEIDEN · NEW YORK · KÖLN
1994

The paper in this book meets the guidelines for permanence and durability of the Committee on Production Guidelines for Book Longevity of the Council on Library Resources.

Library of Congress Cataloging-in-Publication Data

Islamic desk reference / compiled from The Encyclopaedia of Islam by E. van Donzel.
    p.   cm.
    Based on: The Encyclopaedia of Islam. New ed. 1960-[i.e. 1954]
-<1993   >
    ISBN 9004097384 (alk. paper)
    1. Islamic countries—Dictionaries.   2. Civilization, Islamic-
-Dictionaries   3. Islam—Dictionaries.   I. Donzel, E.J. van.
II. Title: Encyclopaedia of Islam.
DS35.53.I83   1994
908'.097671'003—dc20   94-31619
                                   CIP

Die Deutsche Bibliothek – CIP-Einheitsaufnahme

Donzel, Emeri van:
Islamic desk reference : compiled from The Encyclopaedia of
Islam / by E. van Donzel. - Leiden ; New York ; Köln : Brill,
1994
    ISBN 90-04-09738-4
NE: HST

ISBN 90 04 09738 4

dedicated to the memory of
Charles Pellat

PREFACE

It was Frans Pruijt, the late director of the House of E.J. Brill who, early in 1992, suggested the compilation of the present work. He saw the first draft, but his untimely death on 5 December 1993 prevented him from seeing the final result. The Editors of the *Encyclopaedia of Islam* remember with respect and gratitude the unremitting support, in every possible form, which they enjoyed from him during his directorship, which unfortunately lasted only four years.

The aim of the present work is to present the reader with a condensation of the subject-matter of the *Encyclopaedia of Islam* in brief, orderly, and intelligible form. This, however, is a hazardous task. Such a work is supposed to contain the essentials of the *Encyclopaedia*, but the definition of what the essentials are is a ready subject of discussion, and brevity easily comes in conflict with them. Yet, the growing demand for concise and factual information about the history and culture of Islam justifies an endeavour to try to compile a reference book based on the *Encyclopaedia of Islam*.

The first edition of the *Encyclopaedia* was published in English, French and German between 1915 and 1936, followed by a Supplement in 1938. The articles relating in particular to the religion and law of Islam were republished, with certain revisions, in 1941 by A.J. Wensinck and J.H. Kramers in the *Handwörterbuch des Islam*, an English edition of which was published by H.A.R. Gibb and J.H. Kramers in 1961 under the title *Shorter Encyclopaedia of Islam*. An unrevised reprint of the entire first edition appeared in 1987 under the title *E.J. Brill's first Encyclopaedia of Islam 1913-1936*, and again, in paperback, in 1993.

The second edition, in English and French, began to be published in 1954, Volume I being dated 1960. So far, seven volumes (A – al-Naẓẓām), three double fascicules of Volume VIII (Nedīm – Rafʿ), three double fascicules of a Supplement to Volumes I-III (al-ʿAbbās b. Aḥmad b. Ṭūlūn – al-ʿIrāḳī), and Indexes of Proper Names and of Subjects have appeared.

For the present work, use has been made of the second edition in so far as it has been published, the remaining part of the alphabet being based on the first edition. C.E. Bosworth, *The Islamic Dynasties*, re-

vised edition, Edinburgh 1980, has in particular been used for the sur-
veys of the greater dynasties, and the *Encyclopaedia Britannica* for the
spelling of a number of names which have found their way into English, as well as for factual information. The spelling of place names is
in general that of *The Times Atlas of the World*, 6th edition, London
1980, but without the diacritical marks. For the rest, the *Encyclopaedia
of Islam* is the only source for the present work. An attempt has been
made to remain as close as possible to the original texts. The names of
the authors of these texts can be found in the *Encyclopaedia*. Sometimes elements of one article have been used for another.

Except for where Arabic, Persian and Turkish names appear after an
English entry, and for the ʿ (A. *ʿAyn*) and the ʾ (A. *Hamza*) in proper
names, diacritical marks have been omitted in the present work. The
most important difference with the spelling used in the *Encyclopaedia*
is that *dj* and *ḳ* have been replaced by *j* and *q*. These changes obviously
entail a deviation from the alphabetical order of the *Encyclopaedia*, but
they do not pose a real problem for the reader who wants to consult the
parent work, to which he is referred for further and more substantial information. If a word or term is not found under *k*, it may appear under
q, or vice-versa.

In the *Encyclopaedia* not only proper names, but also general terms
appear under their Arabic, Persian or Turkish forms. However, since
the present work is meant for the general reader, the English alphabet
and, as far as possible, English concepts are the starting point, the Arabic, Persian or Turkish terms being given between brackets, so that the
term in question can easily be found in the *Encyclopaedia*, for instance
Slave (A. *ʿAbd*). Names or words of Arabic, Persian or Turkish origin
which in the West were corrupted to another spelling, for instance *Ibn
Sīnā* to *Avicenna*, *al-Kuḥl* to *alcohol*, are as a rule found under their
westernized form, with reference to the original ones. When a person is
not known by his *kunya*, *ism*, *nasab* or *laqab* (see under "Name"), he is
indicated with the adjective indicating his origin (A. *Nisba*), e.g. *Abu
Jaʿfar Muhammad al-Khwarazmi* is found under *al-Khwarazmi, Abu
Jaʿfar*.

For the benefit of the reader who is not familiar with the Islamic
calendar, dates are given according to the Christian calendar only. If no
date of death is known, the century in which the person in question

lived is added in Roman numerals. For rulers, the last date given coincides with that of their death, unless otherwise indicated.

Both the article *al-* and the *b.* (= son of) and *bint* (= daughter of) in a name are disregarded in the alphabetical sequence.

Names and terms which do not appear in this *Desk Reference* may be looked up in the Indexes of the *Encyclopaedia*.

I am grateful to my colleagues of the Editorial Committee of the *Encyclopaedia of Islam* C.E. Bosworth, W. Heinrichs and G. Lecomte, for their assistance in preparing the present work. A special word of thanks goes to V.L. Ménage, a former editor of the second edition, who also suggested corrections for the text and the English language. It is a pleasure to express gratitude to H. Halm, Tübingen, who very generously allowed me to make a selection from his photographical collection of Islamic monuments. All the photographs but one, for which I am grateful to M. Kurpershoek, Leiden, were made by him. Finally, I am, as always, indebted and grateful to Peri Bearman for her advice. Needless to say that I alone am responsible for any shortcomings in both text and language.

The work is dedicated to the memory of Charles Pellat who, between 1956 and 1992, devoted his extraordinary qualities as an Arabist and Islamologist to the *Encyclopaedia of Islam*. During all these years he was the editor of the French edition, and indeed one of the pillars of the entire enterprise.

Leiden, January 1994   E. van Donzel

SIGLA

A.	Arabic
b.	born; as part of a name: son of
Banū	"tribe", see under following name
bint	daughter of
c.	century/centuries
d.	died
P.	Persian
pl.	plural
r.	reigned
s.	singular
S.	Supplement
Sp.	Spanish
T.	Turkish
the Prophet	the Prophet Muḥammad

name between parentheses: the name by which the person, place etc. is also, or better, known .

LIST OF MAPS

A

Aaron (A. *Hārūn b. 'Imrān*): one of the prophets of Islam. The Qur'an associates him with Moses at the time of the flight from Egypt and gives him a role in the making of the Golden Calf.

Ababda (A. *'Abābda*): Arabic-speaking tribe of Beja origin in Upper Egypt with branches in the northern Sudan. They claim Arab descent but certain wide-spread customs are of Hamitic origin. They venerate Shaykh Abu 'l-Hasan al-Shadhili, whose tomb in the Atbai desert is a place of pilgrimage.

Abadan (A. *'Abbādān/Ābādān*): town on an island of the same name on the Shatt al-'Arab.

Aban b. Abd al-Hamid al-Lahiqi (al-Raqashi): Arabic poet in Baghdad; d. ca. 815. He was a court poet of the Barmakids, wrote panegyrics in praise of the 'Abbasid Caliph Harun al-Rashid and versified popular stories of Indian and Persian origin.

'Abbad b. Sulayman al-Saymari (al-Daymari): Mu'tazili from Basra who emphasized the difference between God ("the other") and man; d. ca. 864.

'Abbadids (Banu 'Abbad): dynasty of Arab origin which ruled over the southwest of al-Andalus from 1023-1091 during the age known as that of the Muluk al-Tawa'if; its capital was at Seville.

'Abbas I (the Great): shah of Persia of the Safawid dynasty; b. 1571, r. 1587-1629. He enforced his authority over the Qizil-Bash amirs with the help of a cavalry corps created from Georgian prisoners. He also recruited a standing army of some 37,000 men. Having pacified the provinces of Iraq, Fars, Kirman and Luristan, and subjugated the rulers of Gilan and Mazandaran, he defeated the Özbegs in 1598 and the Ottomans in 1605, from whom he took Baghdad in 1623. Bahrain was annexed in 1601, Shirvan conquered in 1607, Hormuz taken from the Portuguese in 1620 and bitter wars were waged with the Georgians. Shah 'Abbas maintained diplomatic contacts with European countries, with Mughal India, with the princes of Muscovy and the Tatar khans of the Crimea. He also admitted foreign Christian monastic orders, had roads, bridges, and caravanserais constructed, and built mosques, palaces and gardens at Isfahan, the new capital since 1597, at Kazvin, at Ashraf and at Farahabad on the Caspian Sea.

al-'Abbas b. 'Abd al-Muttalib (Abu 'l-Fadl): half-brother of the Prophet's father 'Abd Allah. He joined the Prophet in 630 and died ca. 653. The 'Abbasids took their name from him, being descended from his son 'Abd Allah Ibn 'Abbas.

al-'Abbas b. al-Ahnaf: amatory poet of Iraq; ca. 750-after 808. He became a favourite of the 'Abbasid caliph Harun al-Rashid and was connected with the Barmakids. He cultivated only the genre of erotico-elegiac poetry, known as ghazal, using simple and fluent language. His poems became ready-made material for composers and singers.

al-'Abbas b. 'Amr al-Ghanawi: general and governor of the 'Abbasid caliphs about 900, known for his battle against and release by the Carmathians; d. 917.

'Abbas b. Firnas b. Wardus: Andalusian scholar and poet of Berber origin at the court of Córdoba; d. 887. The invention of the making of crystal is attributed to him.

'Abbas Hilmi I: viceroy of Egypt; b. 1813, r. 1848-1854. A grandson of Muhammad 'Ali Pasha, he succeeded his uncle Ibrahim Pasha. He showed great hostility to foreigners and considered previous reforms as blameworthy innovations. As a result, French influence declined in Egypt. Great Britain offered its support in the conflict with the Ottoman government regarding the Reforms (T. *Tanzimat-i Khayriyye*). He was succeeded by his uncle Muhammad Sa'id.

'Abbas Hilmi II: khedive of Egypt; b. 1874, r. 1892-1914, d. 1944. Son of Muhammad Tawfiq, whom he succeeded, he came into conflict with Lord Cromer, later with Lord Kitchener. In December 1914 he was deposed by the British.

'Abbas Mirza: son of the Qajar shah of Persia Fath 'Ali Shah; 1789-1833. He was known for his bravery and generosity. Devoted to military art, he was for many years governor-general of Azerbaijan.

al-'Abbas b. al-Walid: Umayyad general who fought against the Byzantines; d. 750. He was thrown into prison by the last Umayyad Caliph Marwan II and died there.

'Abbasa: daughter of the 'Abbasid caliph al-Mahdi and sister of the caliphs Harun al-Rashid and al-Hadi. Her name is connected with the fall of the Barmakids in 803, because of a love-affair in which she was allegedly involved.

'Abbasids (Banu 'Abbas): dynasty of caliphs who replaced the Umayyad dynasty in 750 and first ruled, then reigned, over the greater part of the Islamic world for almost eight centuries, with capitals at Baghdad (750-1258) and Cairo (1261-1517). The period of their sovereignty covers the great epoch of classical Islamic civilization. The authority of the caliphs gradually declined, individual military leaders rising to power. From 945 to 1258 the caliphs, with the exception of al-Nasir li-Din Allah, retained a purely nominal suzerainty, real power, even at Baghdad itself, being exercised by dynasties of secular rulers. In 1258 Baghdad was conquered by the Mongols, and an 'Abbasid shadow-caliphate was established in Cairo by the Mamluk sultan Baybars I. The last caliph, al-Mutawakkil III, was deposed by the Ottoman sultan Selim I in 1517, and the shadow-caliphate was abolished.

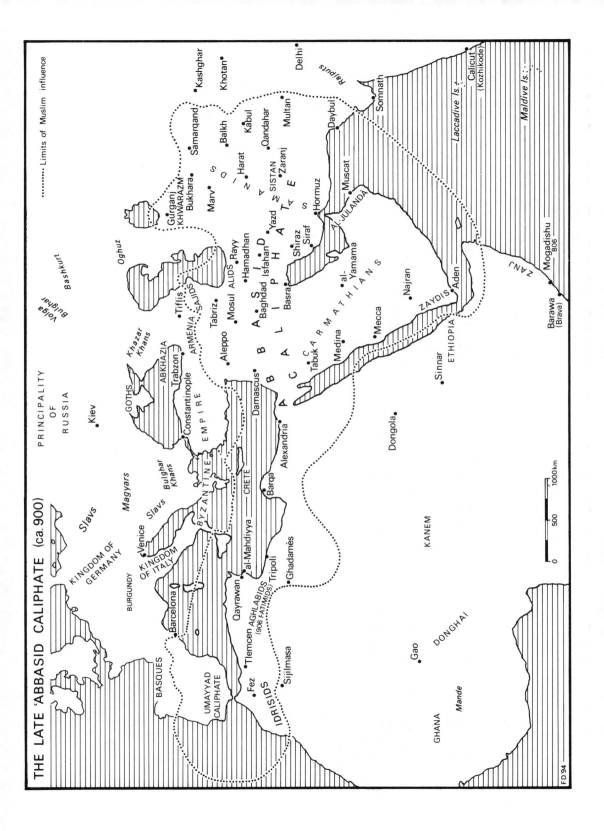

THE LATE 'ABBASID CALIPHATE (ca. 900)

······ Limits of Muslim influence

PRINCIPALITY OF RUSSIA

KINGDOM OF GERMANY

BURGUNDY

Slavs

Magyars

Bulghar Khans

Slavs

Venice

KINGDOM OF ITALY

BASQUES

UMAYYAD CALIPHATE

Barcelona

Fez

Sijilmasa

IDRISIDS

Tlemcen

Qayrawan

AGHLABIDS
(906 FATIMIDS)

al-Mahdiyya

Tripoli

Ghadamès

GHANA

Mande

DONGHAI

Gao

KANEM

GOTHS

Khazar Khans

Oghuz

Bashkurt

Volga Bulghar

ABKHAZIA

Trabzon

Constantinople

BYZANTINE EMPIRE

CRETE

Barqa

Alexandria

Damascus

Aleppo

ARMENIA

Tiflis

Tabriz

Mosul

Rayy

Hamadhan

ALIDS

SAJIDS

Baghdad

Isfahan

Yazd

Basra

Shiraz

Siraf

C A L I P H A T E

A B B A S I D

KHWARAZM

Gurganj

Bukhara

Samarqand

Marv

Harat

Balkh

Kabul

Qandahar

Zaranj

SISTAN

Multan

Daybul

Kashghar

Khotan

Delhi

Rajputs

Somnath

Laccadive Is.

Calicut
(Kozhikode)

Maldive Is.

Hormuz

Muscat

AL-JULANDA

C A R M A T H I A N S

al-Yamama

Najran

Mecca

Medina

Tabuk

ZAYDIS

Aden

ETHIOPIA

Sinnar

Dongola

Kiev

ZANJ

Mogadishu
806

Barawa
(Brava)

0   500   1000 km

F.D.'94

The following is a list of the 'Abbasid caliphs:

In Iraq and Baghdad (749-1258):

749	al-Saffah
754	al-Mansur
775	al-Mahdi
785	al-Hadi
786	Harun al-Rashid
809	al-Amin
813	al-Ma'mun
817-9	*Ibrahim b. al-Mahdi, in Baghdad*
833	al-Mu'tasim
842	al-Wathiq
847	al-Mutawakkil
861	al-Muntasir
862	al-Musta'in
866	al-Mu'tazz
869	al-Muhtadi
870	al-Mu'tamid
892	al-Mu'tadid
902	al-Muktafi
908	al-Muqtadir
932	al-Qahir
934	al-Radi
940	al-Muttaqi
944	al-Mustakfi
946	al-Muti'
974	al-Ta'i'
991	al-Qadir
1031	al-Qa'im
1075	al-Muqtadi
1094	al-Mustazhir
1118	al-Mustarshid
1135	al-Rashid
1136	al-Muqtafi
1160	al-Mustanjid
1170	al-Mustadi'
1180	al-Nasir
1225	al-Zahir
1226	al-Mustansir
1242-58	al-Musta'sim

Mongol sack of Baghdad

In Cairo (1261-1517):

1261	al-Mustansir
1281	al-Hakim I
1302	al-Mustakfi I
1340	al-Wathiq I
1341	al-Hakim II
1352	al-Mu'tadid I
1362	al-Mutawakkil I (*first time*)
1377	al-Mu'tasim (*first time*)
1377	al-Mutawakkil I (*second time*)
1383	al-Wathiq II
1386	al-Mu'tasim (*second time*)
1389	al-Mutawakkil I (*third time*)
1406	al-Musta'in
1414	al-Mu'tadid II
1441	al-Mustakfi II
1451	al-Qa'im
1455	al-Mustanjid
1479	al-Mutawakkil II
1497	al-Mustamsik (*first time*)
1508	al-Mutawakkil III (*first time*)
1516	al-Mustamsik (*second time*)
1517	al-Mutawakkil III (*second time*)

Ottoman conquest of Egypt

'Abd Allah b. al-'Abbas (Ibn 'Abbas): the father of Qur'anic exegesis and ancestor of the 'Abbasids; 619-686. He gathered information about the Prophet by questioning the latters' Companions. He was also one of the signatories of the treaty of Siffin, but later fell out with the fourth caliph 'Ali. After the latters' death, he established contact with the Umayyad caliph al-Mu'awiya and opposed the anti-caliph 'Abd Allah b. al-Zubayr.

'Abd Allah b. 'Abd al-Qadir (Munshi'): innovative Malay author; 1796-1854. His principal work is his Memoirs, in which he emphasized the advantages of a European administration over an Indian one, even though he sharply criticized the administrative measures of the English and the Dutch.

'Abd Allah b. Buluggin b. Badis: ruler of the Zirid dynasty in Granada; b. 1056, r. 1064-1090. His reign was marked by armed conflicts with his Muslim neighbours and by compromises with Alfonso VI, king of Castile. He is known for his Memoirs.

'Abd Allah al-Ghalib bi-'llah: sultan of the Sa'did dynasty in Morocco; b. 1527, r. 1557-1574. He sought an alliance with the Spanish against the Ottomans.

'Abd Allah b. Hammam al-Saluli: Arab poet who played a political role under the Umayyads; d. after 715. He had contacts with the Kharijite agitator al-Mukhtar b. 'Awf and with the anti-caliph 'Abd Allah b. al-Zubayr.

'Abd Allah b. Hanzala al-Ansari: leader of the revolt at Medina against the Umayyad caliph al-Yazid I; d. 683.

'Abd Allah b. al-Husayn: Emir of Transjordan, in 1946 king of the Hashemite kingdom of Jordan; d. 1951. Born in Mecca as the second son of the Sharif al-Husayn b. 'Ali, king of the Hejaz, he was proclaimed constitutional king of Iraq in 1920, but the British gave the throne to his brother Faysal who had been expelled from Damascus by the French. In 1921 'Abd Allah became head of a national Arab government in Transjordan, and in 1946 the independent state of Transjordan was recognized by Great Britain. 'Abd Allah was assassinated in Jerusalem in 1951 before being able to accomplish his ideal of Greater Syria.

'Abd Allah II b. Iskandar: greatest ruler of the Shaybanid dynasty; b. 1533, r. 1557-1598. In 1557 he conquered Bukhara and ruled from there as khan of all Özbegs. He subjugated Balkh, Samarqand, Tashkent, Farghana, West Khurasan, Gilan and Khwarazm.

'Abd Allah b. Isma'il: Filali Sharif of Morocco; r. 1729-1757. His reign was several times interrupted in a period marred by internal strife.

'Abd Allah b. Ja'far b. Abi Talib: nephew of the Prophet's son-in-law 'Ali; d. ca. 699. He was known for his generosity.

'Abd Allah b. Mu'awiya: 'Alid rebel; d. 746. Great-grandson of Ja'far, a brother of the Prophet's son-in-law 'Ali, he asserted that both the godhead and the prophetic office were united in his person. He ruled for a while in al-Jibal, Ahvaz, Fars and Kirman, where the Kharijites and some 'Abbasids, opponents of the caliph, joined him. Abu Muslim had him executed in Khurasan.

'Abd Allah Muhammad al-Ta'a'ishi ('Abdullahi): successor of Muhammad Ahmad b. 'Abdallah, the Sudanese Mahdi; d. 1899. He assumed control of the Mahdist state in 1885, lost the battle of Omdurman in 1898 and met his death at Umm Dubaykarat in Kordofan.

'Abd Allah b. Saba': reputed founder of the Shi'a. It is not clear what historical person or persons lay behind this figure.

'Abd Allah Sultanpuri (Makhdum al-Mulk): leading Indian theologian; xvith c. He is said to have issued a legal advice (A. *fatwa*) to the effect that the pilgrimage to Mecca was not obligatory for the Muslims of India because the journey by sea could not be undertaken without European passports and the land route lay through Shi'ite Persia.

'Abd Allah b. Tahir: member of the Tahirid dynasty; 798-844. He was a poet, general and virtually independent ruler of Khurasan, a man of wisdom, of wide culture and an accomplished musician.

'Abd Allah b. 'Umar b. al-Khattab: authorized transmitter of traditions and son of the second caliph; d. 693. He was a man of high moral qualities who refused three times to become caliph.

'Abd Allah b. Wahb al-Rasibi: Kharijite leader; d. 658. He was known for his bravery and piety, and died in the battle of Nahrawan.

'Abd Allah b. al-Zubayr: anti-caliph; 624-692. On caliph Mu'awiya's death in 680, 'Abd Allah, together with the Prophet's grandson Husayn, refused allegiance to caliph Yazid at Damascus and fled to Mecca, where he proclaimed himself Commander of the Believers, the title adopted by 'Umar b. al-Khattab on his election as caliph in 634. After a six months' siege, during which the Ka'ba came under bombardment, Mecca was taken by Yazid's general al-Hajjaj b. Yusuf in 692 and 'Abd Allah slain.

'Abd al-'Aziz b. 'Abd al-Rahman Al Sa'ud; founder king of Saudi Arabia; b. ca. 1880, r. 1902-1953. In 1902 he took Riyadh from the Rashid dynasty, and by 1912 he had restored Sa'udi rule in Najd. He then started settling Bedouins in Wahhabiyya-centred agricultural colonies whose members were known as "The Brothers" (A. *al-Ikhwān*). In 1914 he expelled the Ottomans from Eastern Arabia and in the following years subdued the Jabal Shammar area in northern Najd and annexed Asir. In 1924 he entered Mecca, in 1925 Medina and Jidda and in 1926 he was proclaimed king of the Hejaz. In 1934 the dispute with Yemen was settled by a military victory followed by a treaty, and the government unified as the Kingdom of Saudi Arabia. After World War II he joined the United Nations and the Arab League. The first commercial find of oil was made in 1937.

'Abd al-'Aziz al-Dihlawi: noted Indian theologian; 1746-1824. He is the author of several religious works in Arabic and Persian.

'Abd al-'Aziz b. al-Hasan: Filali Sharif of Morocco; b. 1878, r. 1894-1908, d. 1943. Increasing European pressure as, for instance, shown at Algeciras in 1906, which was interpreted as an act of surrender to the European powers, made 'Abd al-'Aziz unpopular. In 1907 his brother Mawlay 'Abd al-Hafiz was proclaimed sultan and 'Abd al-'Aziz abdicated.

'Abd al-Ghani b. Isma'il al-Nabulusi: mystic, theologian, poet and traveller; 1641-1731. A prolific author, he was the leading figure in the religious and literary life of Syria.

'Abd al-Hamid b. Yahya b. Sa'd: founder of Arabic epistolary style; d. 750. He was employed in the Umayyad secretariat and wrote epistles which are influenced by Sasanian tradition.

'Abd al-Karim al-Jili: mystic; 1365-ca. 1428. He lived in Zabid and visited India. Among other works, he wrote *The Perfect Man* in which he shows himself an adherent of Ibn al-'Arabi.

'Abd al-Malik b. Abi 'Amir: son and successor of Almanzor; b. 975, r. 1002-1008. He was the real master of Muslim Spain from 1002 until his death.

'**Abd al-Malik b. Marwan**: Umayyad caliph; b. 646, r. 685-705. He succeeded in restoring the unity of the Arabs under Syrian leadership. The administration was centralized, Arabic substituted for Greek and Persian, and
Islamic coinage issued. Also during his reign the 'Uthmanic text of the Qur'an
was re-edited with vowel-punctuation, and the Dome of the Rock built in
Jerusalem.

'**Abd al-Mu'min b. 'Ali**: successor of the Mahdi Ibn Tumart in the leadership of the Almohad movement; r. 1133-1163. In 1147 he conquered the
Almoravid capital of Marrakesh. In Spain, Granada and Seville surrendered
to him.

'**Abd al-Muttalib b. Hashim**: paternal grandfather of the Prophet, who negotiated with Abraha, the leader of an Abyssinian army invading Mecca. He
traded with Syria and Yemen and is credited with having dug the Zamzam
well at the Ka'ba. On the death of the Prophet's mother, Amina, he took the
boy of six into his own house.

'**Abd al-Qadir b. Ghaybi**: the greatest of the Persian writers on music,
whose works are of great importance in the history of Persian, Arabian and
Turkish music; d. 1435.

'**Abd al-Qadir al-Jilani** (al-Jili): Hanbalite theologian, preacher and Sufi;
1077-1166. He gave his name to the mystical order of the Qadiriyya. His
tomb in Baghdad has remained one of the most frequented sanctuaries of
Islam.

'**Abd al-Qadir b. Muhyi al-Din** (Amir Abd el-Kader): Algerian leader in
the revolt against the French between 1832 and 1847; 1808-1883. Later he
became their loyal subject, saving the French consul and several thousand
others when the Druzes tried to massacre the Christian population in Damascus in 1860.

'**Abd al-Qays** ('Abd Qays): old Arabian tribe in Eastern Arabia, which
gave a cordial reception to the Prophet's envoys. During the period of apostasy (A. *ridda*) under Caliph Abu Bakr, part of the 'Abd al-Qays proclaimed a
Lakhmid as their ruler.

'**Abd al-Rahim Khan**: general, statesman and scholar in Mughal India;
1556-1627. He translated Babur's autobiography into Persian, and was a patron of arts and letters.

'**Abd al-Rahman I** (al-Dakhil): founder of the Umayyad amirate in Córdoba; b. 731, r. 756-788. In 750, after the victory of the 'Abbasids, he fled
from Medina to Qayrawan. He disembarked at Almuñecar in August 755 and
entered Seville in 756. In the same year he was proclaimed amir of al-Andalus in Córdoba, the traditional residence of the Arab governors. Until 769
he suppressed rebellions by the Spanish neo-Muslims, the Berbers and the
Arabs. A coalition of Arab chiefs sought the aid of Charlemagne, who in 778
laid siege to Saragossa but had to return to the Rhine. In the pass of Roncevaux he suffered the famous defeat associated with the memory of Roland. In

780 'Abd al-Rahman subdued the Basques, and occupied Saragossa for a short time. In 796 he went to negotiate with Charlemagne at Aix-la-Chapelle and offer him support in a campaign against Barcelona and the region of the Ebro delta. This campaign took place in 801, when Barcelona fell to Charlemagne's Franks and Louis the Pious was able to organize the Spanish Marches. 'Abd al-Rahman's long reign was spent in consolidating his position.

'Abd al-Rahman II: Umayyad amir of Córdoba; b. 792, r. 822-852. He dealt with the revolt of Mozarab Christians of Toledo and Córdoba and with the raiding Northmen. He was a builder and patron of letters and arts.

'Abd al-Rahman III: the greatest of the Spanish Umayyad amirs and first caliph of Córdoba; r. 912-961. The first period of his reign was spent in internal pacification, which led to political unity in the emirate of Córdoba. The second, longer period was devoted to an offensive against Christian Spain, and to a struggle with the Fatimid empire for influence in North Africa. Seville and Cremona submitted in 917, Bobastro was captured in 928 and Toledo surrendered in 932. The amir checked the advance of the Christian prince Ordoño II of León (d. 951) in 920, and built a powerful fleet against the Fatimids, whose invasion was foreseen. In 929 he assumed the title of "Commander of the Believers", thus restoring in Spain the Umayyad caliphate of Damascus. In 923 Ceuta was captured and the whole of the central Maghrib subdued, with the exception of the region of Tahert. This period also saw the formation of parties which were in the end to cause the greatest disorder: the Slav party and the Berber party. The Slavs were prisoners from eastern Europe, Italy and northern Spain and soon formed a large class in Córdoban society. The Berber party was to play a part in the early ixth c. About 955 the caliph's help was invoked by King Sancho and Queen Tota of Navarre against Ordoño IV, an event without precedent in the annals of Muslim Spain. In 954 the Fatimids made a raid on the Spanish shore near Almería; as a reprisal Marsa 'l-Kharaz on the North African coast was burned. 'Abd al-Rahman built near Córdoba the town of Madinat al-Zahra' for his own residence.

'Abd al-Rahman b. Abi 'Amir (Sanchuelo): son of Almanzor; d. 1009. He is known as Sanchuelo, "the little Sancho", for being a grandson of King Sancho of Navarre. He succeeded his elder brother 'Abd al-Malik al-Muzaffar as "major domo". In 1008 he obtained from the Spanish Umayyad Hisham II his designation as heir presumptive to the throne, but was executed shortly afterwards.

'Abd al-Rahman b. 'Awf: early Muslim convert; d. 652. On 'Umar b. al-Khattab's death, he was one of the counsel of six who had to choose the new caliph.

'Abd al-Rahman b. Hisham: Filali Sharif of Morocco; b. 1789, r. 1822-1859. He had to repress several tribal revolts. During his reign a number of European powers renewed, or completed, their commercial treaties with Morocco.

'Abd al-Rahman Khan: amir of Afghanistan; b. 1844, r. 1880-1901. During his reign the country became a buffer state between Britain and Russia whose boundaries were demarcated where possible.

'Abd al-Rahman b. 'Umar al-Sufi: eminent astronomer at the court of the Buyids; 903-986. His best known work is a description of the fixed stars.

'Abd al-Ra'uf al-Fansuri al-Sinkili: religious leader in Sumatra; ca. 1620-ca. 1693. He wrote directions for recitation (A. *dhikr*) as practised by the Shattariyya order, into which he had been initiated in Arabia. He also translated the Qur'an into Malay.

'Abd al-Razzaq al-Qashani: Sufi author in Persia; d. 1329. He followed the school of Ibn al-'Arabi.

'Abd al-Razzaq al-Samarqandi: Persian historian; 1413-1482. He served several Timurid rulers in Samarqand and left a historical work which is an important source of information.

'Abd al-Salam b. Mashish: popular mystic in Morocco; d. 1227. He became famous in the northern part of Morocco in the xvth c.

'Abd al-Wadids (Zayyanids): Berber dynasty which reigned over Central Maghrib from their capital Tlemcen between 1236-1554. The dynasty was founded by Yaghmurasan (Yaghamrasan) in 1236. The kingdom was twice conquered by the Marinids, but restored in 1348 and remained independent till the Turkish conquest in 1554.

'Abd al-Wahhab, Hasan: polygraph and scholar of Tunisia; 1884-1968. He occupied a number of administrative posts and became a historian of Tunisia, writing in Arabic and in French.

'Abdan: brother-in-law and lieutenant of Hamdan Qarmat; d. 899. He soon became the leading spirit of the Carmathian movement and conducted the propaganda quite independently. He was killed at the instigation of Zikrawayh b. Mihrawayh for having fallen away from the policy of the Isma'ili headquarters in Salamiyya.

al-'Abdari: North African author of the xiiith c. He wrote a travelogue which is of interest for the state of Muslim scholarship in the period.

Abdülaziz: Ottoman sultan; b. 1830, r. 1861-1876. Revolts in the Balkan provinces brought about the intervention of foreign powers. Notwithstanding the policy of reforms, the government had to declare itself bankrupt, and the sultan was deposed. He committed suicide a few days later.

Abdülhak Adnan Adivar: Turkish author, scholar and politician; 1882-1955. He was a prominent member of the Committee of Union and Progress (T. *Ittihad we Teraqqi Jem'iyyeti*), and later joined the Nationalist Movement, but then founded the Progressive Republican Party which represented the main opposition to Mustafa Kemal Atatürk. In 1940 he became chief editor of the Turkish Encyclopaedia of Islam. His principal work is a history of science in Turkey.

Abdülhak Hamit: Turkish poet and author of the first Turkish play; 1852-

1937. His use of new metres and a sort of blank verse deeply influenced Turkish poetry between 1885 and 1905 and his early works recorded the first clash between Western science and Muslim faith.

Abdülhamid I: Ottoman sultan; b. 1725, r. 1774-1789. He was forced to sign the Treaty of Küčük Qaynarja with Russia, which was dictated by the Russians. Despite his benevolent nature and love of peace, Abdülhamid's reign was marked by war with Persia, again with Russia, mainly over the Crimea, and with Austria.

Abdülhamid II: Ottoman sultan; b. 1842, r. 1876-1909, d. 1918. In order to put a stop to the intervention of the European powers, he initiated an international conference in Istanbul and promulgated the first Constitution, which introduced a two-Chamber parliamentary system. The parliament, however, was prorogued in 1878 until 1918. Wars were waged with Russia in 1877 and with Greece in 1897. The Macedonian imbroglio led to interventions by the European Powers which precipitated the Young Turk revolution. The sultan was deposed by the National Assembly in 1909. His reign was marked by absolutism, which in its turn led to fear and suspicion, and by Pan-Islamism which, among other things, prompted the sultan to build the Hijaz Railway, connecting Turkey to the Holy Cities of Islam.

Abdülmecid I: Ottoman sultan; b. 1823, r. 1839-1861. During his reign the Crimean War (1853-1856) and a whole series of troubles and insurrections in various regions of the Empire took place. He is known for his legislative work and for important reforms in administration, army, education and coinage.

Abdülmecid II: the last Ottoman sultan and caliph; b. 1868, r. 1922-1924, d. 1944. After the sultanate had been abolished on November 1, 1922, Abdülmecid was elected caliph on November 18. On October 29, 1923, however, the Republic was proclaimed and on March 3, 1924, the caliphate abolished, whereupon Abdülmecid left Istanbul. He died in Paris.

Abenguefith (A. *Ibn Wāfid, Abu 'l-Muṭarrif*): Andalusian physician, pharmacologist and agricultural theorist; 1007-1074. One of his works was translated into Latin by Gerard of Cremona with the title *Liber Albenguefith philosophi de virtutibus medicinarum et ciborum*.

Abenragel/Albohazen (A. *Ibn Abi 'l-Rijāl, Abu 'l-Ḥasan*): famous astrologer at the Zirid court of Qayrawan; xith c. He wrote an important scientific work on astrology, which was translated into Latin, Old Castilian and Old Portuguese.

Abha: capital of the province of Asir in Saudi Arabia.

Abkarius (A. *Iskandar Agha b. Yaʿqūb*): Armenian man of letters from Beirut; d. 1885. He composed anthologies of Arabic literature, and is the author of a narrative of the events in Lebanon from 1860-1869.

Abkhaz: minor people of Western Caucasia on the Black Sea. They were attacked by the Muslims in the early part of the viiith c. but won their independence towards 800. By 1010 their land was united to Georgia. From about 1325 till 1864 Abkhazia was ruled by the House of Sharvashidze. After the Ottomans had settled on the east coast of the Black Sea in the xvith c., the Abkhaz came under the influence of Islam, although Christianity was but slowly supplanted. In 1801 Georgia was incorporated into the Russian Empire, and Abkhazia followed in 1864. In 1866 an attempt to impose taxation led to a considerable emigration to Turkey. Soviet power was proclaimed in 1921, and in 1930 Abkhazia became part of Georgia as an autonomous republic. In recent times ethnic conflicts have broken out and the Abkhazians are struggling for independence from Georgia.

Ablution (A. *ghusl/wuḍū'*): *ghusl* is the term for the general ritual ablution, in ritually pure water, of the whole human body. This ablution is required for a person who finds himself in a state of major ritual impurity (A. *janāba*), caused by marital intercourse, to which religious law assimilates any *effusio seminis*. *Wuḍū'* is the term for the minor ritual ablution, consisting of washing the face, the hands and the forearms, of rubbing the head with the wet hand, and of washing the feet, in this sequence. The intention of performing the *wuḍū'* must be duly formulated. The simple ablution is to be performed after incurring a minor ritual impurity which is caused by contact with an unclean substance or by certain facts, explained in Muslim religious law.

Abraha: Christian king of South Arabia in the middle of the vith century C.E. In Islamic literature his fame is due to the tradition that he led a Yemeni expedition against Mecca, referred to in Qur'an CV, in the year of the birth of the Prophet (ca. 570 C.E.). He left a long inscription on the dam of Marib.

Abraham (A. *Ibrāhīm*): the Abraham of the Bible plays an important role in Islamic religious history as the founder of the monotheistic Ka'ba. The Qur'an, which mentions him often, refers to him as a "speaker of truth" and as a prophet, calls Islam "the religion of Abraham", and gives him the epithet "monotheist" (A. *ḥanīf*).

Abstention (A. *'idda*): the Arabic term indicates the period of abstention of three months from sexual relations, imposed on a widow or divorced woman, or on a woman whose marriage has been annulled, before she may re-marry.

Abstinence (A. *zuhd*): the Arabic word means abstinence from sin, from what is superfluous, from all that estranges from God in the first place. As a technical term in Muslim mysticism, it indicates complete asceticism, i.e. renunciation of dress, lodging, pleasant food and women. The Arabic term *istibrā'* indicates the period of sexual abstinence imposed on an unmarried female slave whenever she changed hands or her master set her free or gave her away in marriage. This period was imposed in order to avoid confusion over paternity since female slaves often were concubines of their master. Voluntary celibacy is called *tabattul*, but is not approved by the Prophet.

Abu 'l-'Abbas al-Saffah: first 'Abbasid caliph, r. 749-754. He was proclaimed caliph in the Great Mosque at Kufa in November 749. During his reign the 'Abbasid movement not only passed from the revolutionary to the legal phase, but also consolidated itself.

Abu 'Abd Allah al-Shi'i: Shi'i propagandist and the founder of Fatimid rule in North Africa; d. 911. He was a native of San'a' in Yemen.

Abu 'Amr b. al-'Ala': "reader" of the Qur'an; d. ca. 770. He is regarded as the founder of the grammatical school of Basra.

Abu 'Amr al-Shaybani: one of the most influential philologists of the school of Kufa; ca. 719-ca. 825.

Abu 'l-'Anbas al-Saymari: famous humorist of the 'Abbasid court; 828-888. He was also a jurist, astrologer, oneiromancer, poet and man of letters.

Abu 'l-'Atahiya: Arabic poet; 748-825. He is known for the freshness and unconventionality of his style.

Abubacer (A. *Ibn Ṭufayl, Abū Bakr Muḥammad*): celebrated philosopher and physician of Guadix (A. *Wādī Āsh*); d. 1185. He advised Averroes to write a commentary on the works of Aristotle, and was succeeded by the former as court physician of the Almohad Abu Ya'qub Yusuf (r. 1163-1184). He is famous for his philosophical allegory called *The Tale of Hayy b. Yaqzan*, which bears the same title as the work by Avicenna.

Abu Bakr (al-Siddiq): the first caliph; b. ca. 570, r. 632-634. He was one of the first male followers of the Prophet, his constant companion and chief advisor. At the Prophet's death in 632, he became the leader of the community, taking the title "Deputy of the Messenger of God". During his caliphate, he had to deal with what became known as the "apostasy" (A. *ridda*).

Abu 'l-Barakat: philosopher and physician in Iraq; 1077-1164. His main work deals with logic and metaphysics.

Abu Dawud al-Sijistani: famous transmitter of traditions of the Prophet; 817-889. He is said to have submitted his work, known as *al-Sunan*, to Ahmad b. Hanbal, who gave it his approval.

Abu Dhabi (A. *Abū Ẓabī*): name of an emirate and its capital on the Persian Gulf. The town is said to have been founded about 1761 by the Banu Yas. The ruling family, a clan of the Banu Yas, is called Al Bu Falah. In 1795 Shakhbut b. Dhiyab came to the throne. Under Khalifa b. Shakhbut, the Banu Yas came under Wahhabiyya influence. Zayid b. Khalifa (r. 1855-1908) made Abu Dhabi the leading power on what was then called the Trucial Coast. Shakhbut b. Sultan, a grandson of Zayid, came to the throne in 1928. In 1971 Britain cancelled its earlier treaties with the Trucial States and Abu Dhabi became a member of the United Arab Emirates.

Abu 'l-Faraj al-Isfahani: author of the well-known *Book of Songs*; 897-967. It is a collection of songs chosen by famous musicians, to which Abu 'l-Faraj added rich information about the poets who were the authors of the songs and about ancient Arab tribes.

Abu 'l-Faraj b. Mas'ud Runi: Persian poet of the Ghaznawid period;

xith c. The scene of his career was mainly at the court of Lahore. He had great influence on Persian poetry.

Abu 'l-Fida: Syrian prince of the Ayyubid dynasty; 1273-1331. He is mainly known as a historian and geographer. His fame rests on a universal history covering the pre-Islamic period and Islamic history down to 1329, and on a descriptive geography.

Abu 'l-Ghazi Bahadur Khan: ruler of Khiva and a Chagatay historian; b. 1603, r. 1644-1663. He wrote a history of the Mongols and another of the Shaybanids.

Abu Hamid al-Gharnati: Andalusian traveller; 1080-1169. He collected stories known as *Marvels*.

Abu Hanifa al-Nuʿman: theologian and religious lawyer; ca. 699-767. He is the eponym of the school of the Hanafites.

Abu Hayyan al-Tawhidi: man of letters and philosopher; xth c. He compiled a record of 37 sessions, held by Ibn Saʿdan, the vizier of the Buyid Samsam al-Dawla Abu Kalijar, on the most varied topics. Another work of his is a collection of 106 conversations on various philosophical subjects. He was a master of Arabic literary style.

Abu 'l-Hudhayl al-ʿAllaf: the first speculative theologian of the Muʿtazila; 752-840. His theology is essentially polemical and is opposed to the anthropomorphism of popular Islam. He also became an apologist of Islam against other religions.

Abu Hurayra: Companion of the Prophet and a well-known transmitter of traditions; d. 678.

Abu ʿInan Faris: sovereign of the Marinid dynasty; b. 1329, r. 1349-1358. He had a passion for building, the Bu ʿInaniyya at Fez being his most monumental *madrasa*.

Abu ʿIsa al-Warraq: Muʿtazili at first, he became one of the arch-heretics of Islam; ixth c. He was accused of Manichean sympathies.

Abu Kalijar al-Marzuban b. Sultan al-Dawla: ruler of the Buyid dynasty; b. 1009, r. 1024-1048. He reigned in Fars and Khuzistan, but had to constantly preserve his rule against several other members of the dynasty as well as the Saljuqs.

Abu Kamil Shujaʿ: one of the greatest mathematicians of the Islamic Middle Ages; ixth c. Next to Abu Jaʿfar Muhammad al-Khwarazmi, he is the oldest Islamic algebraist of whose writings some remains have survived.

Abu 'l-Khattab al-Maʿafiri: the first Imam elected by the Ibadis of the Maghrib; d. 761. He was one of the five missionaries sent from Basra to preach the Ibadi creed in the West.

Abu 'l-Khayr: founder of the Shaybanid dynasty; b. 1412, r. 1429-1468.

Abu Lahab: half-brother of the Prophet's father, mentioned in Qurʾan CXI; d. after 624.

Abu Lu'lu'a: Christian Persian slave of al-Mughira b. Shu'ba who in 644 killed the Caliph 'Umar b. al-Khattab.

Abu Madyan: famous Andalusian mystic; ca. 1126-1197. His fame rests on the memory of him handed down by his disciples and on the maxims attributed to him.

Abu Mahalli: jurist and mystic of Morocco; d. 1613. He played a part in the final years of the Sa'did dynasty.

Abu 'l-Mahasin b. Taghribirdi: Arab historian; 1409-1470. He wrote biographies of the Burji Mamluk sultans, and a history of Egypt covering the period from 641 down to his own time.

Abu Ma'shar al-Balkhi: Arab astrologer, known in the West as Albumasar.

Abu Muslim: leader of the revolutionary 'Abbasid movement in Khurasan; d. 754. He was put to death by the second 'Abbasid Caliph al-Mansur.

Abu Nuwas: famous Arab poet; ca. 747-ca. 813. He is known for his poems on wine and pederasty, his panegyrics and hunting poems. He was connected with the Caliph Harun al-Rashid, and his name occurs in the Thousand-and-One Nights.

Abu Qurra, Theodore: Melkite bishop of Harran; ca. 740-ca. 820. He is known for his polemic writings against Islam.

Abu Sa'id b. Abi 'l-Khayr: Persian mystic; 967-1049. He is known for his extreme ascetic practices and his service to the poor.

Abu Sa'id b. Timur: sultan of the Timurid dynasty; b. 1424, r. 1449-1469. Taking advantage of the desperate situation of Ulugh Beg, he succeeded in extending his power, but was unable to prevent the Özbegs from raiding the south of the Oxus. His campaign of 1468 to help the Qara Qoyunlu against the Aq Qoyunlu ended in disaster. Abu Sa'id had a great interest in agriculture.

Abu Shama: Arab historian in Damascus; 1203-1268. Among other works he wrote the history of the Zangid Nur al-Din Mahmud and of Saladin.

Abu Shuja', Ahmad b. Hasan: famous Shafi'ite jurisconsult; 1042-after 1106. He is the author of a short compendium of Shafi'ite law, which acquired a considerable number of commentaries.

Abu Sufyan: prominent Meccan merchant; d. ca. 653. Having at first resisted the Prophet, he submitted to Islam in 630. His daughter Umm Habiba was married to the Prophet. The first Umayyad Caliph Mu'awiya was one of his sons.

Abu 'l-Su'ud (Khoja Čelebi): famous Ottoman Shaykh al-Islam; 1490-1574. He succeeded in bringing the administrative law of the Ottoman Empire into agreement with the sacred law of Islam.

Abu Talib: full brother of the Prophet's father; d. ca. 619. Though he protected the Prophet, he did not become a Muslim.

Abu Tammam: Arabic poet and anthologist; 804-845. He collected fragments by lesser known poets in a work called *Ḥamāsa*, and was the most celebrated panegyrist of his time.

Abu 'Ubayd al-Bakri: the greatest geographer of the Muslim West, theologian, philologist and botanist; d. 1094. He was one of the most characteristic representatives of Arab Andalusian erudition in the xith c.

Abu 'Ubayda Ma'mar b. al-Muthanna: Arabic philologist in Basra; 728-824. He composed some dozens of treatises on points of Arab and early Islamic history, and on tribal traditions.

Abu 'l-Wafa' al-Buzajani: one of the greatest Arab mathematicians, who further developed trigonometry; 940-998.

Abu Ya'qub Yusuf I: ruler of the Almohad dynasty; r. 1163-1184. Considered as the most gifted of the Almohad rulers, he was a friend of scholarship. He perished before Santarém.

Abu Yazid (Bayazid) **al-Bistami**: one of the most celebrated Islamic mystics; d. 874. Some five hundred of his sayings have been handed down.

Abu Yazid al-Nukkari: Kharijite leader; 883-947. He shook the Fatimid realm in North Africa to its foundations.

Abu Yusuf al-Kufi: religious lawyer; d. 807. He was one of the founders of the Hanafite school of law.

Abu Yusuf Ya'qub al-Mansur: ruler of the Almohad dynasty; r. 1184-1199. His reign marked the apogee of the Almohad empire. He finished the minaret of the Kutubiyya mosque in Marrakesh and built the Giralda of Seville and the ensemble of the mosque of Hassan in Rabat.

Abulelizor/Albuleizor (A. *Ibn Zuhr, Abu 'l-'Alā'*): famous physician of Seville; d. 1130. Some nine works of his are known, but he owed his reputation to his skill as a practising physician.

Abulpharagius Abdalla Benattibus (A. *Ibn al-Ṭayyib, Abu 'l-Faraj 'Abd Allāh*): Nestorian monk, physician, philosopher and theologian of Baghdad; d. 1043.

Abumeron/Abhomeron Avenzoar (A. *Ibn Zuhr, Abū Marwān b. Abi 'l-'Alā'*): famous physician of Seville, son of Abulelizor; d. 1161.

Abyssinia/Ethiopia (A. *Ḥabash, Ḥabasha*): the name Habash, said to be of South Arabian origin, is applied in Arabic usage to the land and peoples of Ethiopia, and at times to the adjoining areas in the Horn of Africa. Muslim traditions mention friendly relations between the Prophet and the Negus (A. *al-Najāshī*), but the Muslim conquests severed Christian Ethiopia from its ally Byzantium and from the Patriarchate of Alexandria, its spiritual source. Islam was established gradually in the ports on the Red Sea and the lowlands, and the nomadic groups living between the sea and the eastern slopes of the escarpment became Islamicized. The slave trade accelerated conversion to Islam because a Muslim could not be enslaved. Between the xivth-xvith c. a war of attrition was waged between the sultanates of Adal, Ifat, Dawaro, Harar, Bali, Hadya, Arababni, Sharkha and the Christian kingdom on the high plateau. The Ethiopian king Amda Tsion defeated Hadya and Ifat, and his victories caused mass conversions to Christianity. In the xvith c. Ahmad b. Ibrahim (nicknamed *Grāñ* "the left-handed") almost brought Ethiopia to its knees. With the help of Portuguese troops under Christovao da Gama, he was defeated and slain in 1543. Despite some isolated Muslim successes, Ethiopia was not to be confronted with Islamization until the xixth c. In 1875 Egyptian troops invaded the country but were defeated by Emperor Yohannes. The Sudanese Mahdists were defeated in the battle of Metemma in 1889, in which the emperor lost his life. Since then religious toleration has prevailed in general between the Christians and the important minority of Muslims. Islam is spreading slowly in the south-western lowlands. Of the four law schools, the Hanafites, the Malikites and the Shafi'ites are represented.

After the revolution of 1974, which brought an end to imperial power, Ethiopia was officially laicized. At that date, the number of Muslims was estimated at 35 % of the population of ca. 30 million. President Mengistu Haile Maryam fled the country in 1991 and Meles Zenawi, chairman of the Ethiopian People's Revolutionary Democratic Front, became interim president.

Academies: Arab authors use the term "house of wisdom" (A. *Dār al-Ḥikma*) to indicate the academies which, in pre-Islamic times, spread knowledge of the Greek sciences. The term is specifically used for the institute of this name, founded in Cairo by the Fatimid Caliph al-Hakim in 1005, which lasted until 1171. For modern academies the terms "Academy of science" (A. *Majma' 'ilmī*) and "Academy of 'Arabic' language" (A. *Majma' al-lugha*) are used. The rise of the latter is connected with the Arabic renaissance of the xixth c. Apart from private academies in Beirut and Cairo, official ones were established in Damascus (1919), Cairo (1932) and in Baghdad (1947). In Morocco, a "Bureau Permanent de l'Arabisation" was established in Rabat in 1961. In 1957 a Union of Arab Academies was founded in Cairo.

In Iran, attempts to write in a Persian devoid of Arabic words go back at least to the xth c. The first academy (P. *Farhangistān*) was established in 1935 but was active only until the abdication of Reza Shah Pahlavi in 1941. The second academy was formed in 1970, but has been inactive since 1979.

In Turkey, Mustafa Kemal Atatürk founded the Turkish History Society and the Turkish Language Society. Together with the Atatürk Culture Centre, they are now united in the Atatürk Culture, Language and History Higher Organisation (T. *Atatürk Kültür, Dil ve Tarih Yüksek Kurumu*).

In India, the Indian academy (A. *al-Majma' al-'ilmī al-hindī*) was founded in 1976, aiming mainly at expanding knowledge of Arabic.

Aconite (A. *aqunitun*): the Arabic term is derived from the Greek *akoniton* and appears frequently in Arabic medical writings as a particular deadly poison originating from a plant root. It can denote a substance either from the Mediterranean region or from India.

Acre (A. *'Akkā*): port in northwest Israel. Captured by the Arabs in 634, it was rebuilt by Mu'awiya I. Under the Fatimids, it became one of the naval bases in Syria. In 1104 Baldwin I of Jerusalem succeeded in gaining possession of Acre, which became the central point in the Christian possessions. After Saladin's victory at Hattin, the port surrendered to him, but it was retaken by Philippe Auguste and Richard I the Lion-Heart. The port became known in the West as Saint-Jean d'Acre after the name of the church built there by the Knights of St. John. Its capture in 1291 by the Mamluk Khalil al-Ashraf put an end to the crusade period. From 1526 to 1918 Acre was under Ottoman rule, except for the period between 1832 and 1840, when it was in the hands of Ibrahim Pasha of Egypt. In 1799 the port successfully withstood Napoleon's siege. It has been part of Israel since 1948.

Acrobat (P. *jānbāz*): the Persian term, which means "playing with one's life", was adopted in Ottoman Turkish and is especially used for a rope-dancer.

Adana: town in southern Turkey. It was occupied by the Arabs around 650, but was off and on held by the Byzantines, the Armenians, the Rum Saljuqs and the Mamluks. In 1516, it came under Ottoman suzerainty. In 1832, Adana became the headquarters of the Egyptian army under Ibrahim Pasha, but it was restored to the Ottomans in 1840. Occupied by French troops in 1918, the city was returned to Turkey in 1922.

Aden (A. *'Adan*): town and seaport on the southwestern coast of Arabia on the Gulf of Aden. Legend usually ascribes its foundation to Shaddad b. 'Ad, and according to an old tradition, Cain, having killed his brother Abel, fled from India to Aden, where his grave is reported to be. After Badhan, the last Persian governor, had submitted to the Prophet, Aden was allegedly visited in 631 by the Prophet's son-in-law 'Ali, who is said to have preached there. The port was conquered in 1062 by 'Ali b. Muhammad al-Sulayhi, a missionary of the Fatimids of Egypt and founder of the Sulayhid dynasty. It passed into the hands of the Ziyadids, then into those of the Zuray'ids, and was taken by Saladin's brother Turan-Shah in 1173. The periods of the Ayyubids, the Rasulids and the Tahirids were a golden age for the trade of Aden. The Portuguese having failed to take it in 1513, Aden was in Turkish hands between 1538 and 1568, when it passed to the Zaydi Imams of San'a'. In 1735 it was taken by the 'Abdali sultan of Lahj, and in 1839 by the British. In 1967 Aden became part of the independent Republic of South Yemen and was made the national capital in 1968. In 1990, when the Yemen Arab Republic (North Yemen) and the People's Democratic Republic of Yemen (South Yemen) were united into the Republic of Yemen, San'a' became the state capital.

al-'Adid li-Din Allah: the last Fatimid caliph of Egypt; b. 1151, r. 1160-1171. He died a few days after Saladin had the Sunni Caliph of Baghdad, al-Mustadi, proclaimed in Cairo.

'Adil-Shahs: designation of the Muslim dynasty which ruled over Bijapur from 1489-1686. They were great patrons of art and literature.

Adivar, 'Abd al-Haqq 'Adnan: Arabic spelling of the name of Abdülhak Adnan Adivar.

'Ajman (A. *'Ajmān*): the smallest of the seven shaykhdoms of the United Arab Emirates.

Administration (A. *dīwān*): the first governmental department in Islam, that of the army, was instituted by the Caliph 'Umar b. al-Khattab in order to organize the pay, register the fighting forces, and put the treasury in order. Under the Umayyads, the central governmental office was the *dīwān* of the land tax (A. *kharāj*). In the 'Abbasid period, *dīwān* denoted first the treasury and then the whole civil administration which was in its turn divided into various *dīwān*s.

In Egypt the history of administration can be divided into three periods: the time when the country was a province of the great Muslim Empire (649-969), the Fatimid caliphate (969-1171), and the Ayyubid and Mamluk period (1171-1517).

In the Muslim West the *dīwān* consisted of a Chancellery, a State Secretariat and Ministries of Finance and of the Army.

In Iran, administration was concerned primarily with the issue of diplomas and decrees, financial administration and the administration of justice.

In Mughal India, from the time of the Mughal emperor Akbar, administration was chiefly associated with finance.

In the Ottoman Empire, the central organ of the government was the so-called *dīwān-i Humāyūn* which was headed by the Grand Vizier. It dealt with the whole range of government business. By the xviiith c. the *dīwān-i Humāyūn* had dwindled into insignificance because of the growing importance of the Grand Vizierate against the palace.

The term *dīwān* was early extended to mean the audience chamber of important government officers which was furnished with mattresses and cushions along the walls. The meaning of *dīwān* thus was extended to sofa.

'Adnan: the name of the ancestor of the Northern Arabs.

Adrianople (T. *Edirne*): town in Eastern Thrace, Turkey. It became the capital of the Ottomans after Bursa. Turks from Asia Minor appeared before Edirne in 1342, and it surrendered in 1362. The forward base of Ottoman expansion in Europe, it was from here that sultan Bayezid I started the blockade of Constantinople in 1394, which lasted seven years. After the conquest of Constantinople in 1453, Sultan Mehemmed II again held court in Edirne, as did other rulers after him. During the Russian-Ottoman war of 1828-1829, the city was occupied by the Russians, and again in 1878-1879. The hostilities in the Balkan wars and following the First World War led to further devastations.

'Adud al-Dawla: the greatest amir of the Buyid dynasty; b. 936, r. 949-

983. He ruled in Iraq and Iran, and was a builder and patron of the learned and of poets.

al-Afdal b. Badr al-Jamali: Fatimid vizier in Egypt for twenty-seven years; 1066-1121. During his office, the country enjoyed internal tranquillity, although 1103 Acre fell to the Crusaders.

Afghan: Persian designation applied to the western tribes of Afghanistan, the eastern ones being called Pathan, the Indianized form of the native name Pashtun. For the language and the literature of the people of Afghanistan the term Pashto is generally used.

Afghanistan ("the land of the Afghans"): the name of the country of Central Asia came into being only after the supremacy of the Afghans had been assured in the middle of the xviiith c. The population consists of the following main groups: Afghans, Tajiks and other Iranians, Turko-Mongolians, Hindu Kush Indo-Aryans and Kafirs. The majority of the inhabitants speak either Pashto or Persian. Other languages used are Indo-Aryan, Kafiri, and Turkish dialects. Practically the entire population is Muslim, and the great majority are Sunnis. Until the reign of Ahmad Shah Durrani (1747-1773), the territories that form modern Afghanistan did not constitute a separate entity but were parts of different provinces subject to many rulers from outside the actual country.

Afghanistan became a republic in 1973, when Muhammad Zahir Shah of the Barakzay line of Afghan kings (r. 1933-1973) was deposed. The Soviet Union intervened in 1980, but its troops left again in 1989, having failed to defeat the Muslim rebels. President Muhammad Najibullah's Communist regime collapsed in 1992, but inter-Muslim strife has continued.

Afrasiyab: legendary king of the Turanians according to Iranian tradition. It is also the name of the founder of a line of governors of Basra (r. 1612-1668).

Afrasiyabids: minor dynasty of Mazandaran; r. 1349-1503. The eponym of the clan, Afrasiyab b. Kiya Hasan, put an end to the rule of the Bawandids. In 1503 Shah Isma'il I forced the last ruler to surrender.

Afridi: name of a large Pathan tribe on the northwest frontier of Pakistan. Their territory straddles the Khyber Pass.

Afsharids: Oghuz dynasty which ruled in Persia from 1736-1795. It was founded by Nadir Shah Afshar.

Afyon (Afyun Qara Hisar): town in western Turkey. Its name comes from the rich production of opium (A. *afyūn*) in the district. The town came into Turkish hands in 1209.

Aga (T. *Agha*/*Āqā*): title given in the Ottoman Empire, up to the Reform Period, to persons employed in a military post, and as such contrasted with Efendi.

Aga Khan: title applied to the Imams of the Nizari Isma'ilis, originally an honorary title at the court of the Qajar Shahs of Persia. Aga Khan I (1800-

1881), whose personal name was Hasan 'Ali Shah Mahallati, fled to Sind in 1840. Internal conflicts among the Khojas concerning the leadership of the Imam led to a lawsuit in 1866, which elicited much information about the Nizari Isma'ilis. Aga Khan II 'Ali Shah ruled the community from 1881 till 1885, when he was followed by Aga Khan III. The latter, born in 1877, ruled from 1885 till his death in 1957. He acquired a leading position among the Muslims of India, and in 1937 became president of the League of Nations. His son Aga Khan IV, formerly Prince Karim, was born in 1936.

Agadir: one of the names for a fortified enclosure among the Berbers. It is also the name of a Moroccan town on the Atlantic coast, which was occupied by the Portuguese from 1505-1541, when it was captured by the Sa'di Sharif Muhammad al-Shaykh al-Mahdi (r. 1517-1557).

Agha Muhammad Shah: founder of the Qajar dynasty of Persia; b. 1742, r. 1779-1797. In 1785 he made Teheran his capital, and in the following year he re-established Persian authority over Georgia. He was crowned shah in 1796.

Aghlabids (Banu 'l-Aghlab): a Muslim dynasty which throughout the ixth c. held Ifrīqiya in the name of the 'Abbasids and reigned at Qayrawan.

Agra: town in the Indian state of Uttar Pradesh, for a long time seat of the residence of the Mughal emperors and renowned for its remarkable monuments, especially the Taj Mahal.

Agrigento (A. *Jirjent*): town on the south coast of Sicily, which fell into the hands of the Arabs in 829. It went through Fatimid, Kalbid, Zirid and Hammudid rule before it was captured by the Normans in 1087.

Ahl al-Bayt (Al al-Bayt) ("People of the House"): the name for the family of the Prophet. The phrase occurs twice in the Qur'an. According to one tradition, it is opposed to the Emigrants and the Helpers. Among the Shi'a it is applied to the Prophet, his son-in-law 'Ali and to the latter's sons al-Hasan and al-Husayn.

Ahl-i Hadith: designation used in India and Pakistan for the members of a Muslim sect who claim to be the true followers of the Prophetic tradition.

Ahl-i Haqq: secret religion in western Persia. It has its own dogmas, believes in metempsychosis and has a number of quite original rites.

Ahl al-Kitab: the term means "People of the Book" and denotes in the Qur'an the Jews and the Christians, who are the recipients of the Torah, the Psalms and the Gospel, which were revealed before the Qur'an. The term was later extended to the Sabaeans, to the Zoroastrians, and, in India, even to the Hindus and others.

Ahmad Amin: Egyptian scholar and writer; 1886-1954. His most important production was a history of Islamic civilisation to the end of the xth c.

Ahmad al-Badawi: the most popular saint of the Muslims in Egypt, venerated at Tanta; 1199-1276.

Ahmad Bey: bey of Tunis; r. 1837-1855. He resisted the claims of Turkey, which was supported by Britain, and sought the aid of France. In 1846 he abolished slavery.

Ahmad b. Hanbal: famous theologian, jurist, transmitter of traditions and founder of the Hanbali school of law; 780-855. His most celebrated work is a collection of traditions, known as *Musnad*.

Ahmad al-Hiba: religious leader of southern Morocco, and ephemeral pretender to the Sharifian throne; 1876-1919.

Ahmad al-Mansur: Sa'di Sharif of Morocco; b. 1549, r. 1578-1603. He turkicised his court and administration and showed real diplomatic talents in foreign affairs.

Ahmad al-Nasiri al-Salawi: Moroccan historian; 1835-1897. His major work is a general history of Morocco.

Ahmad Shah Durrani: founder of the Durrani Empire in Afghanistan; r. 1747-1773. He led six expeditions against India, conquering the Marathas at Panipat in 1761, and the Punjab Sikhs near Gujarwal in 1762. At his death the empire extended from the Oxus to the Indus and from Tibet to Khurasan.

Ahmad Sirhindi, Shaykh: eminent divine and mystic of Muslim India; 1564-1624. He contributed in a considerable measure towards the rehabilitation of orthodox Islam after the heterodoxies of the Mughal Emperor Akbar.

Ahmad b. Tulun: Turkish slave who founded the Tulunid dynasty of Egypt and Syria; b. 835, r. 868-884.

Ahmadabad: city in the state of Gujarat, west central India. It was founded in 1411 by sultan Ahmad I of Gujarat (r. 1411-1442), and captured by the Mughal Emperor Akbar in 1572.

Ahmadiyya: religious movement founded in the Punjab in the xixth c. by Mirza Ghulam Ahmad. His aim was to synthesize all religions under Islam. His centre was at Qadiyan in the Punjab, and is now at Rabwa, Pakistan. In 1914 a son of the founder seceded from the main body and established his centre at Lahore.

Ahmed I: Ottoman sultan; b. 1590, r. 1603-1617. He constructed in Istanbul the magnificent mosque which bears his name.

Ahmed III: Ottoman sultan; b. 1673, r. 1703-1730, d. 1736. He was forced by the Janissaries to abdicate in 1730.

Ahmed Jewdet Pasha: Ottoman writer and statesman; 1822-1895. He was five times Minister of Justice. The most important of his numerous works are historical, covering the xixth c.

Ahmed Khan, Sir Sayyid: educational reformer and founder of Islamic modernism in India; 1817-1898.

Ahmed Midhat: Ottoman Turkish writer; 1844-1913. He played an important role in the development of Turkish journalism and wrote an enormous amount of books.

Ahmed Pasha Bonneval (Claude-Alexandre Comte de Bonneval): French count who turned Muslim and entered Ottoman military service; 1675-1747.

Ahmed Rasim: prolific Turkish writer; 1864-1932. His work comprises novels, carefully prepared historical compilations, and textbooks.

Ahmed Wefiq Pasha: Ottoman statesman and leading turcologist; 1823-1891. He published the first Turkish dictionary in Turkish worthy of the name and adapted sixteen comedies of Molière.

Ahmedi, Taj al-Din Ibrahim: the greatest Ottoman poet of his time; ca. 1330-1413. Among other works he wrote poems on the life and deeds of Alexander the Great, on the love of Jamshid and Khurshid and on medicine. He also composed panegyrics, among others on prince Süleyman Celebi, a son of Sultan Bayezid I.

Ahrar, Khwaja 'Ubayd Allah: shaykh of the Naqshbandiyya order; 1404-1490. Under his guidance the order became firmly rooted in Central Asia.

'A'isha bint Abi Bakr: third and favourite wife of the Prophet; ca. 614-678. In 627, while waiting in a camp from which the caravan had moved off, she was found by a young man who escorted her to Medina. This led to gossip, which was countered by a revelation to the Prophet. After the murder of the Caliph 'Uthman b. 'Affan in 644, she joined the anti-'Ali party, but 'Ali was victorious in what became known as the Battle of the Camel.

Akbar: the greatest of the Mughal emperors; b. 1542, r. 1564-1605. At his death, the Mughal Empire comprised fifteen large provinces, the result of his numerous annexations within India to his empire. He centralized the government by suppressing the unlimited vizierates. He is also known for his administrative policy. Although illiterate, he was genuinely interested in Comparative Religion.

Akhbariyya: term which, in the Twelver Shi'a, denotes those who rely primarily on the traditions (A. *akhbār*) of the Imams as a source of religious knowledge, in contrast to the Usuliyya.

Akhund-zada: the first writer of original plays in Azeri Turkish; 1811-1878.

Alamut: name of a fortress in the Alburz mountains north of Qazvin in Iran. It was the centre of the Nizari Isma'ilis, known as the Assassins, between 1090 and 1256. The fortress was destroyed in 1256 by the troops of the Mongol Il-Khan Hülegü.

Alarcos, Santa Maria de ~ (A. *al-Arak*): small citadel near Ciudad Real in southern Spain where the Almohad Abu Yusuf Ya'qub al-Mansur defeated Alfonso VIII of Castile in 1195.

Alawites (A. *'Alawiyya*): next to Filali, another name under which the reigning dynasty in Morocco is known. It was established in 1631 by Muhammad I al-Sharif of Tafilalt. Filali is derived from the latter name.

In the Syrian context, the word 'Alawi has come to replace that of Nusayri, which had been in usage since the Middle Ages.

Albacete (A. *al-Basīṭ*): Spanish town in the province of Murcia where in 1146 the battle took place between the Hudid Sayf al-Dawla ("Zafadola") al-Mustansir bi-'llah and the Castilian Counts sent by Alfonso VII.

Albania (T. *Arnawutluq*): country in Eastern Europe. Anatolian Turks first arrived in 1337 as allies of the Byzantine emperor. In 1385 the Albanian lords recognised the overlordship of the Ottoman sultan, and in 1415 the country was conquered by the Ottomans. Throughout the history of the Ottoman Empire, Albanians occupied an outstanding place in the ruling class. At least thirty Grand Viziers are identified to have been of Albanian origin.

Albatenius/Albategni (A. *al-Battānī, Abū ʿAbd Allāh Muhammad*): one of the greatest Arab astronomers; ca. 858-929. His only work that has survived is an astronomical treatise with tables (A. *al-zīj*), which was translated into Latin in the xiith c., but this version has not survived. An edition of the text without the tables was published in Nuremberg in 1537 under the title *De motu stellarum*.

Albohali (A. *al-Khayyāt, Abū ʿAlī Yahyā*): Arab astrologer; d. ca. 835. His fame in medieval Europe stems from his work on judicial astronomy.

Albubather (A. *Ibn al-Khasīb, Abū Bakr*): astrologer of Persian origin; ixth c. His fame rests on an extract from a sort of astrological encyclopaedia.

Albumasar (A. *Abū Maʿshar al-Balkhī*): Arab astrologer from Balkh; ca. 790-886. He wrote several works on astrology, some of which were translated into Latin with such titles as *Introductorium in astronomiam Albumasaris Abalachii*, *De magnis coniunctionibus*, and *Flores astrologiae*.

Alcabitius (A. *al-Qābisī, ʿAbd al-ʿAzīz*): Arab astrologer; xth c. His main work is an exposition of some of the fundamental principles of horoscopy.

Alcantara (A. *al-qantara*, pl. *qanātir)*: the Arabic word means a bridge of masonry or stone, an aqueduct (or dam), and a high building. Al-Qantara and al-Qanatir are frequently found as names for places. Worthy of mention are: al-Qantara in Algeria and in Egypt; Alcántara in Spain; al-Qantara Zaynab and Qanatir Firʿawn ("Pharaoh's aqueduct") in Syria, and the diminutive Qunaytira (Qunetra) in the Golan district.

Alchemy (A. *al-kīmiyāʾ*): the term, derived from Greek through Syriac, was used by the Arabs to indicate the process by which base metals are transmuted into gold and silver. There exist a great number of Arabic alchemic writings, fragments and quotations, of which only an extremely small part has been disclosed through catalogues or published. Translations into Latin were made in the Middle Ages and led to modern chemistry. Arabic alchemy thus holds a key position in the development of chemical thinking as a whole.

Alcira (A. *Jazīrat Shuqr*): the Arabic name denotes the island of Júcar, situated between two channels of the river of the same name, near Valencia in Spain.

Alcohol (A. *al-kuhl*): the Arabic word, the origin of our word alcohol, was used in medieval Arabic and Persian texts to indicate both an eye cosmetic, an eye unguent and a lead mineral found at Isfahan. From the fine powder used to stain the eyelids, the word was applied to an essence obtained by distillation. The process needed for the production of alcohol itself was probably introduced into the Islamic world from Europe, where it was first discovered in the xiith c.

Alcolea (A. *al-qulay'a*): the Arabic word is the diminutive of *al-qal'a* and means "little castle". In Muslim Spain it was the name of a number of small places whose importance lay in the military purpose they served. In Algeria there is the oasis town of El-Goléa, some 900 km. south of Algiers, and the small town of Koléa west of the capital.

Alcove (A. *al-qubba*): the word is derived from the Arabic, meaning "cupola, dome".

Alembic (A. *al-anbīq*): name for that part of the distilling apparatus in alchemy which is also called "head" or "cap". The Arabic word was borrowed from Greek *ambix*.

Aleppo (A. *Ḥalab*): town in Syria. First mentioned in the xxth c. B.C., Aleppo was conquered by Muslim troops under Khalid b. al-Walid in 636. The monumental Great Mosque was constructed in the viiith c. In 944 the town became the capital of the Hamdanid amir Sayf al-Dawla, whose court was a centre of great literary activity. In 962 it was destroyed by the Byzantine Emperor Nicephorus Phocas. During the xith c. Aleppo, ruled by the Mirdasids, had to resist the Byzantines and the Fatimids, and in 1086 it was annexed to the empire of the Great Saljuqs.

In 1103 Aleppo was forced to pay tribute to the Crusaders, but in 1129 'Imad al-Din Zangi's son Nur al-Din Mahmud rebuilt the walls, the citadel, the Great Mosque and the markets (A. *sūq*), and repaired the canals. He also founded the first *madrasa*, which was to support his efforts to restore Sunni orthodoxy against Shi'ism. In 1183 the town surrendered to Saladin. Saladin's son Ghazi was able to resist his uncle al-Malik al-'Adil and Aleppo, again a centre of intellectual life, became the capital of a strong and prosperous state which concluded commercial treaties with the Venetians until it was ruthlessly sacked by the Mongol Il-Khan Hülegü in 1260. After the defeat of the Mongols at 'Ayn Jalut, Aleppo came under Mamluk domination, but did not recover its earlier position. Only at the beginning of the xvth c., after the destruction of the Armenian kingdom of Cilicia and of the Genoese factories on the Black Sea, did the town embark upon a new period of prosperity. It became the starting point for the caravans which fetched silk in Gilan to resell to the Venetians in exchange for Italian cloth. The suqs grew, large caravanserais were constructed and many great mosques built.

After the defeat of the Mamluks at Marj Dabiq in 1516, Aleppo passed under Ottoman rule for the next four centuries. Internal strife between Janissaries, petty artisans and tradesmen, and the Ashraf, the higher social groups, marked this period. Nevertheless, Aleppo became the principal market of the whole of the Levant, Western consulates being opened and the famous Ottoman caravanserais built. In many respects, the xvith-xviiith centuries constituted the crowning point in Aleppo's history.

At the end of the First World War, Aleppo was joined to Syria. It became an industrial town and a political and intellectual centre second only to Damascus.

Alessio (T. *Lesh*): this minor port, military stronghold and administrative centre in northern Albania was part of the Ottoman empire between 1478 and 1912. Skanderbeg, rebel against the Ottomans and national hero of Albania, died here in 1468. His tomb was discovered in 1978.

Alexander the Great: it is generally agreed that the epithet "the two-horned" in Qur'an XVIII, 82-98, is to be identified with Alexander the Great. There it is said that he was given power on earth and that he built a wall or rampart of iron and brass against the incursions of Gog and Magog.

Alexander of Aphrodisias (A. *al-Iskandar al-Afrūdīsī*): as was the case in mediaeval Europe and at the time of the Renaissance, the Peripatetic philosopher (fl. about 200) was regarded in Islamic countries as the most authoritative of the ancient commentators of Aristotle. His materialistic arguments against the immortality of the human soul gave rise to wide discussions which spread from Islamic to Christian learned circles. A major theme in the correspondence between Emperor Frederick II Hohenstaufen and the Sufi Ibn Sab'in is the difference between Aristotle and Alexander over this question.

Alexander Romance (A. *Iskandar-nāma*): the Arabs have known of the Alexander Romance (pseudo-Callisthenes) from early times, since what is said about Moses in Qur'an XVIII, 59 ff. is in fact derived from this romance.

In Persian literature Alexander is found in Firdawsi's Shah-nama and in the fifth poem of Nizami's Khamsa.

In classical Ottoman literature the one famous and very popular poem on the subject is the Iskender-name of Ahmedi.

Adaptations exist also in Hindustani, Malay, Javanese and Buginese.

Alexandria (A. *al-Iskandariyya*): the main seaport of Egypt, named after Alexander the Great. It came into Arab hands in 642 and, though its glory had diminished by then, it was still a great city. The well-known story of the burning of the great library by order of the second caliph 'Umar b. al-Khattab, which is related by a xiiith c. Arabic author, cannot be accepted as historical.

There are a great many other towns of the same name, of which Alexander was the reputed founder, or for which he was chosen as eponymous protector.

Alfarabius/Avennasar (A. *al-Fārābī, Abū Naṣr*): one of the most outstanding and renowned Muslim philosophers; d. 950. Of Turkish origin, he was known as "the second teacher", the first being Aristotle. He was influenced by the Aristotelian teaching in Baghdad and the late Alexandrian interpretation of Greek philosophy. He had a great impact on authors such as the Ikhwan al-Safa', al-Mas'udi and Miskawayh. Avicenna, Averroes and Maimonides appreciated him highly.

Alfraganus (A. *al-Farghānī, Abu 'l-'Abbās Aḥmad*): astronomer from Farghana; ixth c. His work was translated into Latin by John of Seville and

Gerard of Cremona, and is known under the title *Elementa astronomica*. There also exists a Hebrew translation.

Algarve (A. *Gharb al-Andalus*): the southwest coast of Portugal. The Arabic expression, which means "the West of Andalusia" and from which the Portuguese word is derived, was applied by Arab historians and geographers to the territory lying to the southeast of Lisbon. Towns like Mérida, Niebla and Béja were centres of Berber revolts against the Spanish Umayyad 'Abd al-Rahman I. Around 860 a certain Ibn al-Jilliqi ("son of the Galician") founded the dynasty of the Banu Marwan, which survived till 930. In the xiith c. Ibn Qasi established himself at Mértola but later summoned the Almohads who subdued all of the Algarve. Ca. 1200 the Portuguese began to retrieve the cities, Faro being conquered by Alfonso III in 1249.

Algebra (A. *al-jabr*): the Arabic word became the term for the theory of equations and was adopted in Western languages. In the oldest Arabic work on algebra, composed by Muhammad b. Musa al-Khwarazmi ca. 850, the word means eliminating quantities. Research into Babylonian mathematics has shed new light on al-Khwarazmi's sources and their relation to Greek, Hebrew and Indian works. A considerable influence on the development of algebra was exercised by Abu Kamil Shuja'. New methods were learnt from the translations of Greek mathematical works, culminating in the studies of Abu Ja'far al-Khazin and especially of 'Omar Khayyam.

Algeciras (A. *al-Jazīra al-Khaḍrā'*): seaport in southern Spain. The Arabic name is a translation of the name of the offshore Isla Verde ("the Green Island"). Muslim expeditions from and to the Iberian Peninsula took place, among others, from this port. The international meeting held at Algeciras in 1906 authorized French designs of intervention in Morocco, whose independence Germany sought to uphold.

Algeria (A. *Barr al-Jazā'ir*): country in North Africa. The frontiers of the modern state date only from the xvith c., when the Turkish regency of Algiers was established. From the beginning of the Islamic conquest of North Africa until Turkish times, the future Algeria was part of what the Arab writers called Central Maghrib and Ifrīqiya. Algeria is almost entirely Muslim, following mainly the Malikite school of law. The national language is Arabic, but Berber is still spoken by an important minority.

Algeria became independent in 1962, after 130 years of French occupation. In December 1991, the Front Islamique du Salut won a majority of the vote in the first round of the elections. However, before the second round could take place, the Algerian armed forces forced President Chadli Bendjedid to resign, and the elections were cancelled in January 1992. Since then, unrest prevails in the country.

Algiers (A. *al-Jazā'ir*): capital city of Algeria. The Arabic name indicates the islets off the northwest coast of Algiers Bay. It was then applied to the town, founded in the xth c. by the Zirid Yusuf Buluggin I b. Ziri (r. 972-984).

Only in the xixth c. was the name transformed by the French into Algiers ("Alger"). In the xiith c. the Almoravids erected a large mosque. From the xvth c. onwards, Sidi ʿAbd al-Rahman al-Thaʿalibi has been the patron saint of the city. At that time the population consisted in part of refugees who had fled from the Christian reconquest of Andalusia, many of whom established themselves as corsairs. After the Spanish had imposed a levy in order to suppress the corsairs, the inhabitants summoned the Turkish corsair and admiral Khayr al-Din Pasha, known as "Barbarossa", who in 1529 captured the fortress, known as Peñon, built by the Spanish on the largest of the islets. The fortress was pulled down, and the material used to construct the breakwater which henceforth connected the islets with the mainland, thus forming the port of Algiers. The Ottomans now were in the possession of an important naval base in the Western Mediterranean. Emperor Charles V attempted in vain in 1540 to capture the port, which was turned into a stronghold by the Ottomans. Privateering remained profitable, and the Spanish, the Danish, the English and especially the French several times tried to check it. In 1830 the city surrendered to the French. In 1962 it became the capital of independent Algeria.

Alhagiag bin Thalmus (A. *Ibn Ṭumlūs, Abu ʾl-Ḥajjāj*): physician and philosopher of Alcira; ca. 1164-1223. He succeeded Averroes as personal physician to the Almohad Muhammad al-Nasir (r. 1199-1214).

Alhambra (A. *al-Ḥamrāʾ* "the red ʿfortressʾ"): name of the fortress and palaces in Granada. The Arabic name appears at the end of the ixth c. and was first applied to a small fortress where the Arabs, pursued by rebel peasants, took refuge during the revolts that took place under the Spanish Umayyad ʿAbd Allah b. Muhammad al-Marwani. Work on the actual Alhambra began under the founder of the Nasrid dynasty, Muhammad I al-Ghalib called Ibn al-Ahmar (r. 1237-1273)

Alhazen/Avennathan (A. *Ibn al-Haytham, Abū ʿAlī al-Ḥasan*): one of the principal Arab mathematicians and their best physicist; 965-1039.

Alhidade/Alidad(e) (A. *al-ʿiḍāda*): the movable part on the back of an astrolabe.

Al-i Ahmad, Sayyid Jalal: Iranian prose writer and ideologist; 1923-1969. He wrote literary fiction, essays and reports, and regional monographs.

ʿAli, Mustafa: one of the most outstanding representatives of Turkish literature of the xvith c.; 1541-1600. He owes his fame to a history of Islam, extremely valuable for the century in which he lived.

ʿAli b. Abi Talib: cousin and son-in-law of the Prophet, married to the latter's daughter Fatima, and fourth caliph; b. ca. 596, r. 656-661. Whether he was the second after Khadija to believe in the Prophet's mission, or the third after Khadija and Abu Bakr, was much disputed between Shiʿis and Sunnis. In the Prophet's lifetime he took part in almost all the expeditions and his courage became legendary. He at first refused to recognise Abu Bakr's

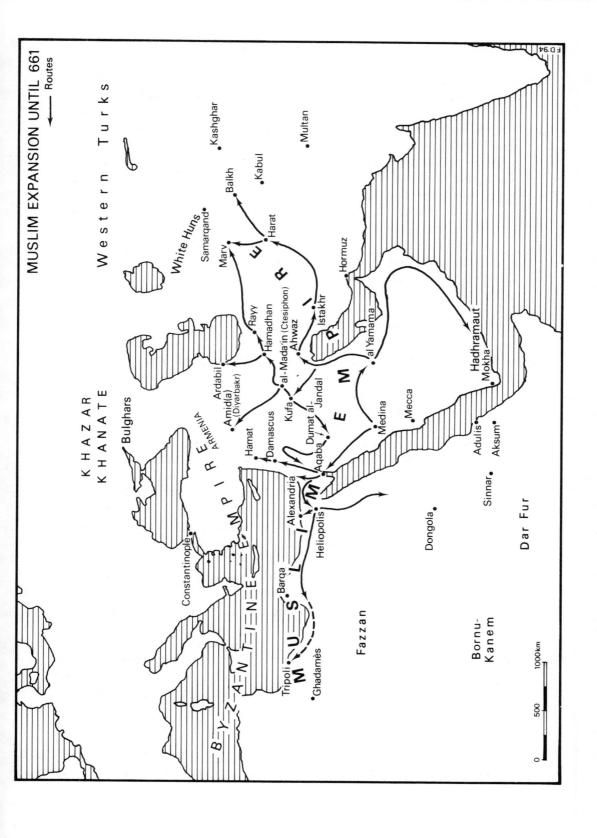

MUSLIM EXPANSION UNTIL 661

→ Routes

Western Turks

Samarqand•
Kashghar•
• Balkh
• Kabul
• Multan

White Huns

• Harat
E M P I R
Marv•
• Hormuz

Rayy•
Hamadhan•
al-Mada'in (Ctesiphon)•
Ahwaz
• Istakhr

KHAZAR KHANATE

Bulghars

Ardabil•
Amid(a) (Diyarbakr)•
ARMENIA

Hamat•
Damascus•
Kufa•
Dumat al-Jandal
al Yamama•

E M P I R E

Hadhramaut
Mokha•

• Medina
• Mecca

Constantinople•

B Y Z A N T I N E

Alexandria•
Heliopolis•
Aqaba•

M U S L I M

Barqa•
Tripoli•
Ghadamès•

Fazzan

Dongola•

Adulis•
Aksum•
Sinnar•

Dar Fur

Bornu-Kanem

0   500   1000km

F.D.94

election as caliph. Although regarded as a valued counsellor, it is doubtful whether his advice was accepted by the second caliph 'Umar b. al-Khattab. During the caliphate of 'Uthman b. 'Affan, 'Ali accused the caliph of innovation (A. *bid'a*) in religious matters, and on political questions he joined 'Uthman's opponents.

After the killing of 'Uthman, 'Ali allowed himself to be nominated caliph also by the rebels who had the former caliph's blood on their hands. This provoked strong reactions in Mecca, Syria and Egypt. Mu'awiya, governor of Syria and cousin of 'Uthman, accused 'Ali of complicity with the murderers and refused to pay homage to him.

The Prophet's widow 'A'isha engaged in Mecca in active propaganda against the new caliph, and was soon joined by Talha b. 'Ubayd Allah and al-Zubayr b. al-'Awwam. In the famous Battle of the Camel of 656 Talha and al-Zubayr lost their lives, and 'A'isha was peremptorily ordered by 'Ali to return to Medina under escort.

Mu'awiya demanded the surrender of the murderers of 'Uthman, in the meantime still refusing to pay homage to 'Ali. The deeper cause of the struggle was whether pre-eminence lay with Syria or with Iraq. 'Ali took the offensive, and the two armies met on the plain of Siffin. Mu'awiya, about to lose the battle, had his soldiers hoist copies of the Qur'an on their lances. 'Ali was forced to submit the difference to consultation of the Qur'an, i.e. to arbitration. Already at Siffin a group of individuals rejected arbitration with the cry "there is no decision save that of God". After 'Ali's return to Kufa in Iraq, they learned that he had sent his arbitrator Abu Musa al-Ash'ari to meet 'Amr b. al-'As, Mu'awiya's arbitrator. The group then secretly left Kufa and were joined by dissidents from Basra at al-Nahrawan on the eastern bank of the Tigris river. These dissidents, those who had "departed", were thereafter called Kharijites. 'Ali's troops attacked and massacred them at al-Nahrawan, but as a consequence many more defections from 'Ali's cause followed and he had to give up the campaign against Mu'awiya.

The arbitrators met at Adhruh. Abu Musa and 'Amr agreed to declare both 'Ali and Mu'awiya deposed, but in the public discourses that followed, 'Amr declared 'Ali deposed and confirmed Mu'awiya's nomination. In the end, no decision on the caliphate was taken.

'Ali continued to be regarded as caliph by his partisans, though their numbers were daily diminishing, and Mu'awiya by his. 'Ali remained passive at Kufa when Mu'awiya made small incursions into Iraq, Arabia and Yemen. In 661 the Kharijite Ibn Muljam, in revenge for the men slain at al-Nahrawan, struck 'Ali with a poisoned sword before the door of the mosque at Kufa. Over his tomb outside Kufa, a sanctuary arose in the time of the 'Abbasid Caliph Harun al-Rashid, around which the town of al-Najaf grew.

'Ali b. 'Isa: the best known oculist of the Arabs; xith c.

'Ali al-Rida: the eighth Imam of the Twelver Shi'a; 765-818. The 'Abbasid Caliph al-Ma'mun appointed him in 816 as heir to the caliphate, but in Iraq a revolt was started against the caliph, who made a gradual change of policy.

'Ali b. Yusuf b. Tashufin: amir of the Almoravid dynasty; b. 1084, r. 1106-1143. He ruled over a large part of North Africa and of southern Spain.

Alicante (A. *Laqant*): according to al-Idrisi, there was a great mosque and a minbar in the xiith c. The town passed under the control of James I of Aragon (1208-1276), on condition that the local Muslims retain their lands.

'Alids: the descendants of 'Ali b. Abi Talib. It was to 'Ali's three sons al-Hasan, al-Husayn and, for a time, Muhammad b. al-Hanafiyya al-Nafs al-Zakiyya and their descendants that the loyalties of the different groups of the Shi'a were given. Many dynasties, known as Hasanids and Husaynids, claimed to be of 'Alid descent.

Allah (A. *Allāh*): God the Unique one, the Creator and Lord of the Judgement.

'Allal al-Fasi: Moroccan statesman and writer; 1907-1974. He took part in the diffusion of the progressive movement of the Salafiyya.

Almada, Almadén (A. *al-Ma'din*): town in the Spanish province of Ciudad Real, known for its mercury. The name is derived from the Arabic word which means mine, ore, mineral.

Almagest (A. *al-Mijistī*): the current name for the astronomical and mathematical encyclopaedia compiled by Ptolemy consists of the Arabic definite article al- and the Greek word *megistè* "the greatest".

Almanzor (A. *al-Manṣūr bi-'llāh (Ibn Abī 'Āmir al-Ma'āfirī)*): vizier of the Spanish Umayyad Hisham II al-Mu'ayyad; b. 938, r. 978-1002. He was *de facto* the real master of al-Andalus. He purged the splendid library of the Spanish Umayyad Caliph al-Hakam II and conducted 52 expeditions against the Christian states.

Almería (A. *al-Mariyya*): chief town of the province of the same name in eastern Spain on the Mediterranean coast. The name may be connected with the notion of "watch-tower". The town was conquered in 713-715 and populated by Yemenis and Berbers. It reached its fullest economic potential under the Almoravids.

Almicantarat (A. *Muqanṭarāt*): Arabic technical term to denote the parallel circles at the horizon, normally called parallels of height.

Almodovar (A. *al-Mudawwar*): the Arabic word, meaning "that which is round", is the name given to a small river in the province of Cadiz, in Spain, and to several places in Spain and Portugal.

Almohads (A. *al-Muwaḥḥidūn*): name of a reformist movement founded by the Mahdi Ibn Tumart, that ruled over North Africa and in Spain from 1130 till 1269. Its principal element was the divine Oneness (A. *tawḥīd*). The Almohad Empire attained its highest point of material and cultural success between 1163 and 1213. Its army, consisting of Berber troops of the Masmuda and Zanata tribes and complemented by a large and powerful fleet, was invincible. The intervention in Spain began under 'Abd al-Mumin, but Almohad authority was never completely established there. The second period of the political history of the Almohads was characterised by military weakness and anarchy. They introduced monetary reform, exchanged letters with several Popes but did not accept Christian missionaries, and persecuted the Jews. They were patrons of architecture, and in general economic life thrived during their reign.

Almoravids (A. *al-Murābiṭūn*): dynasty of Berber origin which ruled in North Africa and then Spain, ca. 1050-1147. The name is usually assumed to be derived from a type of "warrior-monk" who inhabited a fortified convent on the frontiers of Islam (A. *ribāṭ*). The dynasty unified Morocco, and their legacy was to survive in Mauritania, in Mali, in the Niger Republic and in parts of northern Nigeria. The last Almoravid ruler in Marrakesh, Ishaq (r. 1146-1147), was killed.

Alms (A. *ṣadaqa*): the term is frequently employed as synonymous with alms-tax (A. *zakāt).* The proper use of the term is in the sense of voluntary almsgiving. According to the Qur'an, alms may be given openly, as long as this is not done ostentatiously, but those given in secret are better.

Alms-tax (A. *zakāt*): tax levied on definite forms of property. It is one of the principal requirements of Islam. In the Qur'an stress is laid on the practice of benevolence as one of the chief virtues of the true believer. The first Caliph Abu Bakr made the alms-tax as a regular tax a permanent institution, which, through the establishment of a state treasury, contributed greatly to the expansion of Muslim power.

Almuñecar (A. *al-Munakkab*): small port on the Mediterranean coast of Spain in the province of Granada. The Spanish Umayyad 'Abd al-Rahman I disembarked here on August 14, 755.

Alp Arslan: Great Saljuq; b. 1030, r. 1063-1073. He conducted campaigns against the Armenians and the Georgians and defeated the Byzantines in the battle of Malazgird.

Alp Takin (Alp Tigin): Turkish slave commander who ruled in Ghazna; d. 963.

Alpuente (A. *al-Bunt*): this small town in the province of Valencia in Spain gained some renown when Abu Bakr Hisham, brother of the Spanish Umayyad caliph 'Abd al-Rahman IV al-Murtada (r. 1018) who had been killed at Cadiz, sought refuge here. He was proclaimed caliph in 1027, returned to Córdoba but was deposed in 1031. The town passed into the hands of the Almoravids, then into those of the Almohads, and was subjected to the jurisdiction of the bishop of Segorbe in the xiiith c.

Aman Allah (Amānollāh Khān): amir of Afghanistan; b. 1892, r. 1919-1929, d. 1960. In 1919 Britain recognised, by implication, Afghanistan's independence, and Aman Allah started administrative and legal reforms, but he was denounced as an infidel and was forced to abdicate in 1929. He was succeeded by Nadir Shah (r. 1929-1933).

Ambergris (A. *'anbar*): probably a secretion of the gall-bladder of the sperm-whale, highly valued in the East as a perfume and as a medicine.

al-Amin: 'Abbasid caliph; b. 787, r. 809-813. His father Harun al-Rashid, in the so-called "Meccan documents", had designated his two sons al-Amin and al-Ma'mun as his successors. Open hostility broke out between the two brothers in 811, al-Amin having his base in Iraq, al-Ma'mun in Khurasan. The fraternal war has been viewed by some as an aspect of the conflict between Arabism and Iranism, but in fact it was primarily a dynastic dispute. Al-Amin was captured by al-Ma'mun's general Tahir b. al-Husayn and put to death.

Amin al-Husayni: Palestinian leader; 1893-1974. An avid anti-Zionist, he was appointed Great Mufti by the British. In 1931 he convened a Pan-Islamic conference and attempted to prohibit further sale of Arab land to Jewish settlers. In 1937 he went to Italy and lived in Nazi Germany between 1941 and 1945. His part in the Nazi extermination policy of the Jews is not clearly established, but he actively tried to prevent the emigration of Jews to Palestine from Nazi-occupied countries. After the proclamation of the State of Israel, Egypt allowed him to settle in Gaza. In 1951 he chaired a World Muslim Conference, but at the Bandung Afro-Asian Conference, he was forced to accept President Nasser's predominance. His influence having diminished, he moved about and died in Beirut.

Amina: the Prophet's mother; d. ca. 576 when the Prophet was six years old.

Amir al-Hajj: the leader of the caravan of pilgrims to Mecca. In 630 the pilgrimage was conducted by Abu Bakr, in 631 by the Prophet himself. Thereafter this duty belonged directly to the caliphs, who either undertook it themselves or nominated an official to act in their place.

Amir Kabir, Mirza Muhammad: the most prominent reformist statesman of xixth c. Persia; ca. 1807-1852. He took part in diplomatic missions to Russia and Turkey and, as a consequence, made strenuous efforts to introduce modernising measures. He met with hostility at the court, and was executed in Kashan.

Amir Khusraw Dihlawi: great Indo-Persian poet; 1253-1325. He enjoyed favour under the Khalji sultans of Delhi.

Amir al-Mu'minin: "Commander of the Believers", a title adopted by 'Umar b. al-Khattab on his election as caliph in 634, later employed exclusively as the protocollary title of a caliph.

Amir Nizam: high official of Kurdish origin in Iran; 1820-1899. He protected the interests of the Russians and was hostile towards modernization.

Amir b. Sa'sa'a: large group of tribes in western Central Arabia.

'Amirids: name of the descendants of Almanzor, who ruled in Valencia from 1021-1065, when they were conquered by the Dhu 'l-Nunids.

Amman (A. *'Ammān*): capital of the Hashemite Kingdom of Jordan. It was captured by the Muslims in 635. The town did not play a role in Islamic history until 1921, when 'Abd Allah b. al-Husayn made it the capital of Transjordan.

'Amr b. al-'As: one of the most wily politicians of his time; ca. 573-663. First sent by the Prophet to Oman, he then conquered Palestine in 633 and Egypt in 640. He played an important role in the arbitration between the Prophet's son-in-law 'Ali and Mu'awiya at Siffin in 657.

'Amr b. Kulthum: pre-Islamic poet; vith c. He resisted the domination of the kings of al-Hira and was seen as an incarnation of the virtues of pre-Islamic times.

'Amr b. 'Ubayd: one of the first of the Mu'tazila; d. ca. 761.

Anatolia (T. *Anadolu*): name of the mountainous peninsula proceeding from the southern part of the Asiatic continent towards Europe. Arab geographers in the Middle Ages, and Turks until far into Ottoman times, called the region "Country of the Rhomaeans" (A. *bilād al-rūm*). The main part of Anatolia remained untouched by the conquests of the Muslim Arabs. The Saljuqs began a Holy War against Byzantium in the xith c. and after the conquest of Constantinople in 1453 Anatolia was firmly in Ottoman hands.

al-Andalus (A. *Jazīrat al-Andalus*; Sp. *Andalusia*): term used in the Islamic world up to the end of the Middle Ages to denote the greater part of the Iberian peninsula. A connection of the name with the Vandals is probably to be rejected. Muslim occupation of the Iberian Peninsula lasted for seven centuries. The conquest started in 711 under Tariq, lieutenant of Musa b. Nuṣayr, governor of Ifriqiya and the Maghrib. Until 756, al-Andalus was ruled by governors responsible to the Caliphs of Damascus, and after that date until 912 by Umayyads from Córdoba who called themselves amirs. 'Abd al-Rahman III adopted the titles of Caliph and of Amir al-Mu'minin. His reign was the most flourishing period in the Muslim history of al-Andalus. The Córdoban caliphate collapsed in 1031 and Muslim Spain was split up into a multitude of small states. During this period of the Muluk al-Tawa'if, political blocs of some importance were formed by the kingdoms of Seville, Badajoz, Granada, Toledo and Saragossa. In 1086, al-Andalus was occupied by the Almoravids, later by the Almohads. In the xiith c. territory was won back each year by the Christians from the North during the so-called Reconquista. After the battle at Las Navas de Tolosa in 1212, Córdoba fell in 1235, Valencia in 1238 and Seville in 1248, the "Kingdom of Granada" remaining the only territory under Muslim rule. The dynasty of the Nasrids lasted there until 1492, when the city surrendered to Ferdinand and Isabella. Al-Andalus, in contact with the Orient between the viiith and xvth centuries, produced and preserved some of the most beautiful monuments of Islamic art.

Angels (A. *malā'ika*; s. *malak*): the word is frequently used in the Qur'an for beings who are in absolute submission and obedience to Allah. The

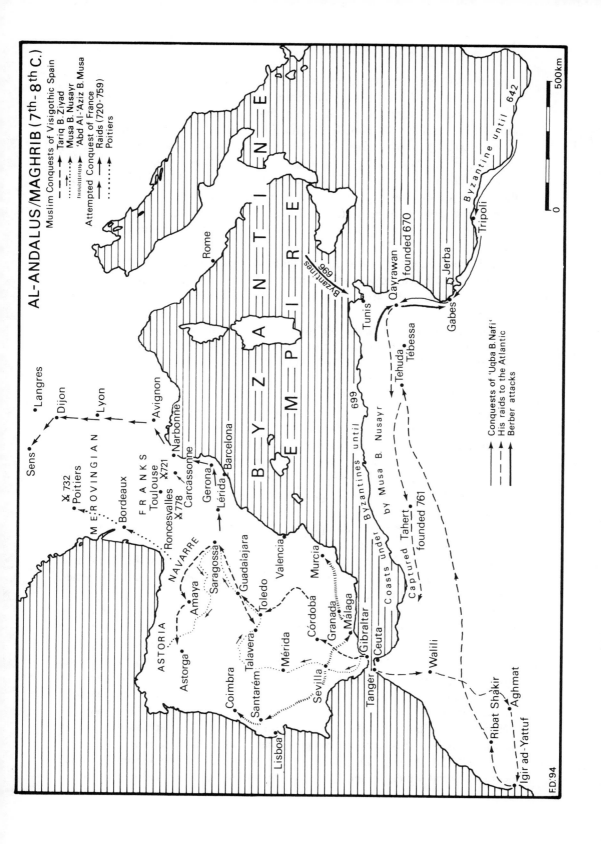

AL-ANDALUS/MAGHRIB (7th-8th C.)

Muslim Conquests of Visigothic Spain
------- Tariq B. Ziyad
········· Musa B. Nusayr
ıııııııı 'Abd Al-'Aziz B. Musa
—— Attempted Conquest of France
      Raids (720-759)
········· Poitiers

500km

—— Conquests of 'Uqba B. Nafi'
----- His raids to the Atlantic
—— Berber attacks

B Y Z A N T I N E   E M P I R E

Byzantine until 642

Byzantines 696

Byzantines until 699

Coasts under Byzantines until 761 by Musa B. Nusayr

Captured Tahert founded 761

Tripoli
Jerba
Gabes
Qayrawan founded 670
Tunis
Tébessa
Tehuda
Walili
Ribat Shakir
Aghmat
Igir ad-Yattuf

Rome

Langres
Dijon
Sens
Lyon
Avignon
Narbonne
Carcassonne
Barcelona
Gerona
Lérida
Toulouse
X721
Roncesvalles X778
Bordeaux
X 732 Poitiers
M E R O V I N G I A N
F R A N K S
Poitiers

NAVARRE
Saragossa
Guadalajara
Valencia
Murcia
Toledo
Amaya
Astorga
ASTORIA
Coimbra
Santarém
Talavera
Mérida
Córdoba
Granada
Málaga
Sevilla
Lisboa
Gibraltar
Ceuta
Tanger

F.D.'94

Qur'an also mentions two fallen angels, Harut and Marut. The *Fiqh Akbar I*, the Hanafite creed which may date from the middle of the viiith c., mentions Munkar and Nakir, two angels who examine the dead and if necessary punish them in the tomb. In Shi'ism, the Imams are guided and aided by angels.

Animals (A. *hayawān*): the word is attested only once in the Qur'an, where it means "the true life" and is used of the other world. However, the Qur'an enumerates on several occasions the dietary prohibitions concerning the eating of the flesh of an animal that has not been ritually slaughtered, concerning spilt blood, and the pig. In Muslim art, representations of animals occupy only a restricted place in view of a disapproval of the depiction of living forms.

Ankara (Ancyra): capital of the Turkish Republic since 1923. The town came under Turkish supremacy after the battle of Malazgird in 1071. In the battle of Ankara of 1402, the Ottoman Sultan Bayezid I was defeated by Tamerlane.

Ansari, Shaykh Murtada: Shi'ite *mujtahid* of Iran; 1799-1864. His widely-recognised religious leadership in the Shi'ite world has not yet been surpassed.

'Antar, Sirat: the romance of 'Antar, the model of Arabic chivalry. The numerous legendary stories are taken from Arab paganism, Islam, Persian history and epic, and the Crusades.

'Antara: name of several pre-Islamic warrior-poets, the best-known among them being 'Antara b. Shaddad; vith c.

Anthologies (A. *hamāsa*): they generally include brief extracts chosen for the literary value they have in the eyes of the anthologists, and are classified according to the genre to which they belong. They are found in Arabic, Persian, Turkish, Central Asian, Urdu and Swahili literature.

Apollonius (A. *Balīnūs*): the Arab name is used for both the mathematician Apollonius of Perge in Pamphylia (ca. 200 B.C.E.) and for Apollonius of Tyana in Cappadocia (first c. C.E.).

Apostasy (A. *ridda*): the Arabic term is given to the period of defection from Islam and of the rise of some prophets among several recently converted tribes during the caliphate of Abu Bakr.

Apostate (A. *murtadd*): in the Qur'an, the apostate is threatened with punishment in the next world only, but in Tradition the Prophet is said to have prescribed the death penalty as punishment for apostasy. Traditions differ on the question whether the apostate should be given an opportunity to repent. In the law books there is unanimity that the male apostate must be put to death, but only if he is an adult, of sound mind, and has not acted under compulsion. About the death penalty for a woman, the law schools differ. Apostasy deprives the apostate of burial with Muslim rites, and has certain civil consequences, such as suspension of property and annulment of marriage.

Apostle (A. *hawārī*; pl. *hawāriyyūn*): the word, borrowed from Ethiopic, occurs several times in the Qur'an with the meaning of helpers of Jesus.

"Apostle of God" is sometimes used in translations for "Messenger of God" (A. *Rasūl Allāh*), to describe the Prophet, but this is a misnomer.

Aq Qoyunlu: "those of the White Sheep", a federation of Turkmen tribes which rose in the region of Diyarbakr in the xivth c. and lasted till 1502.

Aqa Khan Kirmani (Bardasiri): modernist thinker of Iran; 1853-1896. He was a Pan-Islamic activist, but was nevertheless anti-religious and quite hostile to many traditional practices.

Aqa Najafi: a member of an important clerical family of Isfahan and himself an influential and wealthy religious authority; 1845-1931.

al-ʿAqqad, ʿAbbas Mahmud: Egyptian littérateur, journalist, educator, polemicist and critic; 1889-1964.

Arab League, The (A. *al-Jāmiʿa al-ʿArabiyya*): established at the end of the Second World War, the League reflects the desire to renew the national homogeneity, based on a common language and on a similar way of life and culture. At the first meeting in Alexandria in October 1944, a protocol was signed, and in 1945 the Pact of the Arab League was ratified by Egypt, Iraq, Lebanon, Saudi Arabia, Syria, Transjordan and Yemen. Subsequently, the League has been joined by Libya (1953), Sudan (1956), Tunisia and Morocco (1958), Kuwait (1961), Algeria (1962), South Yemen (1967), the United Arab Emirates, Qatar, Bahrain and Oman (1971), Mauritania and Somalia (1974) and Jibouti (1977). The Palestine Liberation Organisation (P.L.O.) has been admitted, first as an observer (1965), then as a full member (1976). The object of the League is the forging of links between the Member States and the coordination of their policies. The supreme body is the Council of the League, which can meet at the level of Heads of State, Prime Ministers or Foreign Ministers. The Secretary General is elected by a two-third's majority.

Arabian Peninsula (A. *Jazīrat al-ʿArab*): commonly called Arabia, the peninsula in extreme southwest Asia comprises Saudi Arabia, the Republic of Yemen, the sultanate of Oman, the United Arab Emirates, Qatar, Bahrain and Kuwait. The Arabic term means "Island of the Arabs".

Arabic language and literature (A. *ʿarabiyya*): the Arabic language can be distinguished in: 1. pre-classical Arabic, usually divided into three sections: a. Arabic as a Semitic language; b. Old Arabic ("Proto-Arabic"); c. Early Arabic (iiird-vith c. A.D.); 2. the literary language, consisting of a. Classical Arabic; b. Early Middle Arabic; c. Middle Arabic; d. Modern written Arabic; 3. the vernaculars i.e. the Eastern or Arabian (Egypt and Syria) and North Arabian (the Arabian Peninsula, the Syrian desert and Iraq) dialects, and the Western dialects.

The various periods of Arabic literature are indicated as follows: 1. early Arabian i.e. pre-Islamic poetry and prose and viist c. poetry; 2. viiith c. poetry and prose; 3. ixth-xth c. poetry and prose; 4. xith-xviiith c. literature; 5. modern Arabic literature a. to 1914; b. since 1914.

Arabs, The (A. *al-ʿArab*): they first appear in the light of history in 854

B.C.E. during the reign of the Assyrian king Salmanassar III as camel-breeders and traders. Their expansion at the beginning of Islam came about through enlistment in the armies that were sent to the Euphrates, to Transjordania, Southern Palestine, Iraq, Syria, al-Jazira, Iran, Egypt, North Africa and Spain.

'Arafa (*'Arafāt*): plain to the east of Mecca, on the road to Ta'if. It is the site of the central ceremonies of the annual pilgrimage to Mecca.

Aragon (A. *Araghūn*): as a geographical term, the word refers to a river of Navarre, in Spain. In its political sense, it refers to the Christian mediaeval kingdom in northeastern Spain which, during the xith-xiiith c., was constantly expanding at the expense of the neighbouring Hispano-Arab states. The royal house of Aragon was more tolerant than Castile towards the conquered Muslims. For the Arab historians, Aragon also included Catalonia, the Balearic Islands and Valencia.

Architecture: building as an artistic activity started under the Umayyads with the Great Mosques at Basra and Kufa and quickly reached an extraordinary high level with the famous Dome of the Rock at Jerusalem, completed in 691. The Great Mosque of Damascus, the audience hall and bath known as Qusayr 'Amra in Jordan, and many palaces, among them that of Mshatta south of Amman, were all built before 750. With the 'Abbasids the centre of gravity was transferred to Baghdad, founded in 762, where Hellenistic culture was replaced by influences from Sasanian Persia. There, in the "circular city", a new mosque and the palace of caliph Abu Ja'far al-Mansur were built. At Ukhaydir near Karbala' another palace arose, and at Jerusalem the Aqsa mosque was partly rebuilt. At Ramla in Palestine the well-known Cistern was built and Fustat in Egypt saw the construction of the Mosque of 'Amr. The Great Mosque of Qayrawan in Tunisia dates from the ixth c., as do the famous palace at Samarra in Iraq and the Great Mosque of Susa in Tunisia. The Mosque of Ibn Tulun at Cairo was built in 876.

Ardabil (T. *Erdebīl*): district and town in eastern Azerbaijan. It was made a provincial capital during the caliphate of 'Ali, and was the domain of the Sajids. In 1220 it was destroyed by the Mongols. Shaykh Safi al-Din made Ardabil the centre of the Safawids, and his shrine is found there.

'Arif, Mirza Abu 'l-Qasim: Persian revolutionary poet and satirist; ca. 1880-1934. His poetry is full of social satire, attacks on corruption, and of nostalgia for Persia's great past.

Aristotle (A. *Aristū(tālīs)*): the writings of the Greek philosopher, with a very few exceptions, became known to the Arabs in translation. Most Arabic philosophers regard him as the outstanding and unique representative of philosophy. Averroes (A. *Ibn Rushd*) calls him "the example of what nature invented to show final human perfection".

Armenia (A. *Armīniya*): landlocked region south of the Caucasus, southeast of the Black Sea and southwest of the Caspian Sea. It was invaded by the

Arabs as early as 639, but they were not able to implant themselves solidly. The princes of the Bagratid dynasty enjoyed some form of independence between 861-1064, when Armenia was annexed by Byzantium. In the xith c. the Armenian territories on the borders of Azerbaijan were incorporated into the Saljuq empire, while those in the centre and west took shape as different principalities. In the beginning of the xiiith c. Diyarbakr was annexed by the Ayyubids of Egypt and Syria. The land suffered under the savage assault of Tamerlane and the establishment of the dynasty of the Aq Qoyunlu did not restore Armenian strength. Western Armenia was conquered by the Ottomans in the xivth c., eastern Armenia in the following two centuries, but difference of religion prevented assimilation.

After the massacres and deportations under the Young Turk government in 1915, Armenia, Georgia and Azerbaijan formed the Transcaucasian Federal Republic in 1918, but very quickly split into separate republics. In 1920 Armenia was recognized by Turkey as a free and independent state, but Mustafa Kemal Atatürk repudiated the treaties and seized Kars. In 1922 Armenia again joined Georgia and Azerbaijan to form the Transcaucasian Soviet Federated Socialist Republic. The Nakhichevan enclave was awarded to Azerbaijan and remained a constant cause of friction between the two republics. In 1988 Armenians in Nagorno-Karabakh, a mountainous region in Azerbaijan, demanded that the territory be transferred to Armenia, and the enmity between the Christian Armenians and the Muslim Azerbaijanis erupted into violence.

Artuqids: Turkmen dynasty which reigned over the whole or part of Diyarbakr, either independently or under Mongol protectorate. One line ruled in Hisn Kayfa and Amid (1102-1408), another in Mardin and Mayyafariqin (1104-1408). They were removed from power by the Qara Qoyunlu.

ʿAruj: Turkish corsair who, together with his brother Khayr al-Din Barbarossa, seized possession of Algiers at the beginning of the xviith c.

Ascension (A. *al-maṭāliʿ*, s. *maṭlaʿ*): an important concept in medieval spherical astronomy and astronomical timekeeping.

Ascetic (A. *mujāwir*; *zāhid*): the Arabic word *mujāwir* means "neighbour" but is used in the restricted sense for those persons who, for a shorter or longer period of time, settle in a holy place in order to lead a life of asceticism and religious contemplation and to receive the blessings (A. *baraka*) of that place. Such places are the Kaʿba in Mecca, the Haram in Jerusalem, and the Prophet's tomb in Medina, but also tombs of highly venerated Muslims.

Ashab al-Kahf: "those of the cave", the name given in the Qurʾan to the youths who in the Christian West are usually called the "Seven Sleepers of Ephesus".

al-Ashʿari, Abu ʾl-Hasan: theologian and founder of the Ashʿariyya; 873-935. He left the Muʿtazila for the orthodox traditionists, the Sunnis, but defended his new beliefs by the type of argument which the Muʿtazila employed.

Ashʿariyya (*Ashāʿira*): the school of orthodox theology founded by al-

Ash'ari. It was attacked by the Hanbalites for their use of rational arguments and by the Maturidiyya for being too conservative. The Ash'ariyya became the dominant school in the Arabic-speaking parts of the 'Abbasid caliphate.

'**Ashiq Čelebi**: Ottoman man of letters; 1520-1572. His most important work is his *Biography of the Poets*.

'**Ashura**': name of a voluntary fast-day which is observed on the 10th of Muharram, the first month of the Muslim year. In the Maghrib alms-giving on that day is a usual practice.

'**Asim, Abu Bakr**: head of the Kufan school of Qur'an "readers"; d. 745. His system of pointing and vowelling the Qur'anic text has become the *textus receptus* in Islam.

Asir (A. *'Asīr*): region in western Saudi Arabia with the capital Abha. In 1934 it became part of Saudi Arabia.

al-'Askari, Abu al-Hasan 'Ali (al-Naqi/al-Hadi): tenth Imam of the Twelver Shi'a; 829-868. He lived peacefully in Medina until the accession of the 'Abbasid Caliph al-Mutawakkil, who kept him under surveillance but whose respect he seems to have won.

al-'Askari, Abu Muhammad al-Hasan: eleventh Imam of the Twelver Shi'a; 844-873. At his death, dissension arose on the question whether or not he had left a child named Muhammad al-Qa'im.

al-Asma' al-Husna ("The most Beautiful Names"): the words indicate the 99 Names of God, which the pious Muslim repeats and on which he meditates, usually with the help of the 99 beads of the rosary (A. *subha*). The Wahhabis object to this custom and consider it reprehensible.

al-Asma'i: Arab philologist; 740(?)-828. Later Arabic philologists owe most of their knowledge about Arabic lexicography and poetry to this scholar and to his contemporaries Abu 'Ubayda and Abu Zayd al-Ansari (d. 830). All of them were disciples of Abu 'Amr b. al-'Ala'.

Assassins: term originally referring to the Nizari Isma'ilis, who were also known as Hashishiyya. From the xith c. until the Mongol conquest, they considered the murder of their enemies a religious duty. The name, which derives from the Arabic *hashishi* "hashish-taker", was carried to Europe by the Crusaders.

Astrolabe (A. *asturlāb*): the earliest Arabic treatises on this instrument of astronomy were composed in the ixth c. The earliest specimens preserved date from the second half of the xth c.

Astrologer (A. *munajjim*): an important dignitary among the Muslims, the astrologer answered questions concerning everyday activities, distinguished auspicious and inauspicious astrological signs with regard to important events, and studied the omens at the moment of birth.

Astronomy (A. *'ilm al-hay'a*) : for Muslim astronomers after about 800, the "science of the figure (of the heavens)" coincided by and large with that expounded by Ptolemy in his *Almagest*. The earliest translation of a Sanskrit astronomical text into Arabic was made in Sind around 735. Other translations were made from Pahlavi, Greek and Syriac. Of particular interest are the so-called Sindhind tradition, the "Toledan Tables" and the School of Maragha in Azerbaijan, where Nasir al-Din al-Tusi founded an observatory in 1259.

'**Atabat**: the Arabic name, which means thresholds, indicates the Shi'i shrine cities of Iraq: Najaf, Karbala', Kazimayn and Samarra.

Atabeg (T. *Atabak*): title of a high dignitary under the Saljuqs and their successors. The atabegs were Turkish slave commanders who were appointed as tutor-guardians to Saljuq princes, but soon established hereditary governorships and even dynasties, like the Zangids, the Ildeñizids and the Salghurids.

Atatürk, Mustafa Kemal: founder and first President of the Turkish Republic; 1881-1938. From 1899 on he took an active part in the secret movements that opposed the reign of the Ottomans. They had been brought into being by the despotism of Sultan Abdülhamid II. Mustafa Kemal took part only from a distance in the activities of the "Union and Progress" movement. He distinguished himself in the defence of Tripolitania, when it was invaded by the Italians in 1911, at the Dardanelles in 1915, in the Caucasus in 1916 and in Palestine in 1917. He did not agree with the draconian terms of the Armistice, and in 1919 landed at Samsun with his mind made up to fight for the total independence of Turkey. He organised congresses at Erzurum and Sivas and assembled in 1920 the first Great National Assembly in Ankara. The struggle against the Allies, in particular the Greeks, was won in 1922, and against the Government at Istanbul in the same year, when the sultanate was abolished. In 1923 he was elected President, and at the Lausanne Conference Turkey was given complete independence and national frontiers. The caliphate was abolished in 1924.

Mustafa Kemal was fiercely determined to modernise the country, to free it from foreign economic tutelage and to secularise it. Relying on the absolutely devoted People's Party, he suppressed the religious courts, the Qur'anic schools and dervish orders, prohibited the wearing of the fez and abolished the article of the Constitution declaring Islam the state religion. Foreign companies were nationalised, agriculture and industry stimulated, and national banks created. He further reformed the alphabet, introduced the vote for women and new civil, criminal, and commercial codes. In 1934 a law required all citizens to use family names. In that year the National Assembly accorded Mustafa Kemal the name of Atatürk "Father of the Turks". In foreign policy, he showed himself to be pacific, though determined to protect the independence of his country.

Atay, Falih Rifqi: Turkish writer, journalist and politician; 1894-1971. He was a great master of modern Turkish prose.

Atsiz b. Uvak: Turkmen chief; d. 1079. At the appeal of the Fatimids he occupied Jerusalem, Palestine and southern Syria, conquered Damascus in 1076 and attacked Egypt itself in 1077, but was defeated. He appealed to the

Great Saljuq Malik-Shah, who decided to make Syria an appanage for his own brother Tutush b. Alp Arslan, who had Atsiz killed.

Avars: name of an Ibero-Caucasian people, inhabiting the mountainous part of Dagestan and the northern part of Azerbaijan.

Avempace (A. *Ibn Bājja, Abū Bakr Muḥammad*): celebrated philosopher and vizier at Saragossa in Muslim Spain; d. 1139. Ibn Khaldun ranked him, with Averroes in the West and Alfarabius and Avicenna in the East, as one of the greatest philosophers of Islam. He was also a poet, musician, and composer of popular songs, and studied mathematics, astronomy and botany. He became a vizier under the Almoravids. His works survive in their original Arabic in a few manuscripts and in Hebrew translations. His most celebrated work, *Rule of the Solitary*, is of a Neo-platonic character.

Averroes (A. *Ibn Rushd, Abu 'l-Walīd Muḥammad*): the "Commentator of Aristotle" of Córdoba; 1126-1198. In 1153 he was engaged in astronomical observations at Marrakesh, where he may have met Ibn Tufayl. In 1169 he was judge of Seville, and later of Córdoba, and in 1182 he succeeded Ibn Tufayl as chief physician of the Almohad ruler Abu Ya'qub Yusuf, but fell into disgrace during the last years of the reign of Abu Yusuf Ya'qub. He died at Marrakesh, from where his body was later brought to Córdoba. His fields of study were the Qur'anic sciences and the natural sciences, including physics, medicine, biology and astronomy, as well as theology and philosophy. Only a small number of his works in Arabic survive, the majority having been preserved in Latin and Hebrew translations.

Avicenna (A. *Ibn Sīnā, Abū 'Alī al-Ḥusayn*): one of the greatest Muslim scientists and philosophers; 980-1037. He was born near Bukhara, probably with Persian as his native language. At the age of eighteen he had mastered all the then known sciences. After the death of his father, an official of the Samanid administration, and the overthrow of the Samanids by the Ilek-Khans in 1005, he first wandered through Persia and then, from 1021 until shortly before his death, he lived at Isfahan as court physician of the Buyid rulers Shams al-Dawla and Sama' al-Dawla, who by then had come under Kakuyid suzerainty. Avicenna died at Hamadhan, where a monument was erected to celebrate the millennium of his birth.

Known primarily as a philosopher and physician, Avicenna contributed also to all the sciences that were accessible in his day: natural history, physics, chemistry, astronomy, mathematics and music. He wrote on economics, politics, moral and religious questions, Qur'anic exegesis, and poetry. In 1954, 131 authentic and 110 doubtful works were listed in his bibliography. Among his most famous works are the *Book of Healing* 'of the Soul', a vast philosophical and scientific encyclopaedia, the *Canon of Medicine*, one of the most famous books in the history of medicine, and the *Tale of Hayy b. Yaqzan*, a philosophical allegory. Avicenna's influence on medieval European philosophers such as Michael Scot, Albertus Magnus, Roger Bacon, Duns Scotus and Thomas Aquinas is undeniable.

Awadh (Oudh): tract of country comprising the Lucknow and Faydabad divisions of the Indian State of Uttar Pradesh. The Muslim invaders established themselves in Awadh in the last decade of the xiith c. and annexed it to the Dehli Sultanate. The weakness of the central government after the death of the Mughal Emperor Awrangzib in 1707 gave the Nawwabs of Awadh an opportunity to assert their independence, although nominally they still acknowledged the authority of the Mughal emperor. The Awadh dynasty reigned from their capital Ayodhya from 1722 until the annexation of the territory by the British in 1856.

Awrangzib: Mughal emperor; b. 1618, r. 1658-1707. The war of succession in 1658 showed him at his best as a general and an administrator; he was never to attain that standard again. Under his long reign the empire was ruined by a series of wars, many of which were of his own seeking. The reasons for the failure of the Mughal Empire were increasing corruption, harassment of the peasantry, neglect of government orders by officers in charge and failure of the state's financial resources.

Aya Sofya: known in Greek as *Hè Hagía Sophía*, the church was turned into a mosque at the conquest of Constantinople by the Ottomans in 1453. In 1934 Atatürk decreed it to be a museum.

Ayatollah (P. *Āyatullāh*): title with a hierarchical significance used by the Twelver Shi'is and meaning literally "(miraculous) sign of God". According to the doctrine of the Twelver Shi'a, all political power is illegitimate during the occultation of the Hidden Imam, but from the Safawid period (1501-1722) onwards, political theories have taken shape and a hierarchy within the top ranks of the *mujtahids* has been formed. In the course of the xixth c. the Usuliyya elaborated the theory according to which at every given moment there can only be one unique "source of imitation" (P. *marja'-i taqlīd*). The Ayatollah Burujirdi (d. 1961) was recognised as such by the mass of the Twelver Shi'is. After his death the number of "sources of imitation" spread widely. However, from 1963 onwards, a certain consensus seems to have grown up around the Ayatollah Ruhollah Khomayni, the main religious opponent of the Pahlavi régime.

Aydin-oghlu: Turkmen dynasty which reigned from 1308 to 1425 over the emirate of the same name in western Anatolia.

'Ayn Jalut ("Spring of Goliath"): village near Nazareth in Israel. It is famous in Islamic history for the battle of 1260, in which the Mongols of the Il-Khan Hülegü, led by the Christian Turk Kitbuga Noyon, were defeated by the Mamluks of Sultan Qutuz (r. 1259-1260), led by the future Mamluk Sultan Baybars I. The Arabic chronicles regard the battle as a decisive victory, which saved the Syro-Egyptian Empire and indeed Islam itself from the

Mongol menace. In fact, the ebbing of the Mongol tide was due to events in the East at least as much as to Mamluk resistance.

Ayyam al-'Arab ("Days of the Arabs"): name which in Arabian legend is applied to the wars which the Arabian tribes fought amongst themselves in the pre-Islamic era.

Ayyubids: name of the dynasty founded by Saladin which ruled Egypt, Muslim Syria-Palestine, the major part of Upper Mesopotamia and the Yemen from 1169 until the Mongol conquest in 1260. There were minor branches in Baalbek, Homs, Karak, Hamat, Baniyas, Subayba and al-Busra.

The following is a list of the Ayyubid rulers:

In Egypt:

1169	al-Malik al-Nasir I Salah al-Din (Saladin)
1193	al-Malik al-'Aziz 'Imad al-Din
1198	al-Malik al-Mansur Nasir al-Din
1200	al-Malik al-'Adil I Sayf al-Din (Damascus; Aleppo)
1218	al-Malik al-Kamil I Nasir al-Din (Damascus)
1238	al-Malik al-'Adil II Sayf al-Din (Damascus)
1240	al-Malik al-Salih Najm al-Din Ayyub (Damascus)
1249	al-Malik al-Mu'azzam Turan-Shah (Damascus; Diyarbakr/ Hisn Kayfa)
1250-2	al-Malik al-Ashraf II Muzaffar al-Din

Bahri Mamluks

In Damascus:

1186	al-Malik al-Afdal Nur al-Din 'Ali
1196	al-Malik al-'Adil I Sayf al-Din (Egypt; Aleppo)
1218	al-Malik al-Mu'azzam Sharaf al-Din
1227	al-Malik al-Nasir Salah al-Din Dawud
1229	al-Malik al-Ashraf I Muzaffar al-Din (Diyarbakr)
1237	al-Malik al-Salih 'Imad al-Din (*first reign*)
1238	al-Malik al-Kamil I Nasir al-Din (Egypt)
1238	al-Malik al-'Adil II Sayf al-Din (Egypt)
1239	al-Malik al-Salih Najm al-Din Ayyub (Egypt; Damascus; Diyarbakr/Hisn Kayfa) (*first reign*)
1239	al-Malik al-Salih 'Imad al-Din (*second reign*)
1245	al-Malik al-Salih Najm al-Din Ayyub (Egypt) (*second reign*)
1249	al-Malik al-Mu'azzam Turan-Shah (Egypt)
1250-60	al-Malik al-Nasir II Salah al-Din (Aleppo)

Mongol conquest

In Aleppo:

1183	al-Malik al-'Adil I Sayf al-Din (Egypt; Damascus; Diyarbakr)

1186	al-Malik al-Zahir Ghiyath al-Din
1216	al-Malik al-ʿAziz Ghiyath al-Din
1237-60	al-Malik al-Nasir II Salah al-Din (Damascus)

Mongol conquest

In Diyarbakr (Mayyafariqin and Jabal Sinjar):

1185	al-Malik al-Nasir I Salah al-Din (Saladin; Egypt)
1195	al-Malik al-ʿAdil I Sayf al-Din (Egypt; Damascus; Aleppo)
1200	al-Malik al-Awhad Najm al-Din Ayyub
1210	al-Malik al-Ashraf I Muzaffar al-Din (Damascus)
1220	al-Malik al-Muzaffar Shihab al-Din
1244-60	al-Malik al-Kamil II Nasir al-Din

In Diyarbakr (Hisn Kayfa and Amid):

1232	al-Malik al-Salih Najm al-Dīn Ayyub (Egypt; Damascus; Diyarbakr/Mayyafariqin)
1239	al-Malik al-Muazzam Turan-Shah (Egypt; Damascus)
1249	al-Malik al-Muwahhid Taqi al-Din
1283	al-Malik al-Kamil III Muhammad
?	al-Malik al-ʿAdil Mujir al-Din
?	al-Malik al-ʿAdil Shihab al-Din
?	al-Malik al-Salih Abu Bakr
1378	al-Malik al-ʿAdil Fakhr al-Din
?	al-Malik al-Ashraf Sharaf al-Din
1433	al-Malik al-Salih Salah al-Din
1452	al-Malik al-Kamil IV Ahmad
1462	Khalil (?)
?	Sulayman
?	al-Husayn

Aq Qoyunly conquest

In Yemen:

1174	al-Malik al-Muʿazzam Shams al-Din Turan-Shah
1181	al-Malik al-ʿAziz Zahir al-Din Tughtigin
1197	Muʿizz al-Din Ismaʿil
1202	al-Malik al-Nasir Ayyub
1214	al-Malik al-Muzaffar Sulayman
1215-29	al-Malik Masʿud Salah al-Din

Rasulids

Azad, Abu 'l-Kalam: reviver of Muslim thought in India; 1888-1958. He was an ardent opponent of Sir Sayyid Ahmad Khan.

Azerbaijan: name of a province in northwestern Iran, conquered by the

Arabs around 640. It is also the name of a republic on the western shore of the Caspian Sea of which Baku is the capital. The parliament of the republic of Azerbaijan formally voted the republic out of the Commonwealth of Independent States in 1992.

Azeri: name of a Turkic people as well as of their language and literature in Azerbaijan.

al-Azhar: one of the principal mosques of Cairo founded under the Fatimids in the ixth c. and a seat of learning throughout Islamic history.

al-Azhari: Arab lexicographer; 895-980.

al-'Aziz bi-'llah: Fatimid caliph; b. 955, r. 975-996. He was the first whose reign began in Egypt.

B

Ba (Bu): genealogical term used especially among the *sayyids* and *shaykhs* in Hadramaut, Yemen, to form individual and collective proper names, as in Ba 'Alawi, a large and influential clan of Sufis living in Hadhramaut.

Baalbek (A. *Ba'labakk*): small town in inland Lebanon, with most impressive ancient monuments, annexed by the Muslims under Abu 'Ubayda al-Jarrah in 637. Held successively by the Burids, the Zangids, the Ayyubids and the Mongols, the town passed into Mamluk control in 1260, and into that of the Ottomans in 1516. Apart from its ancient ruins, the site is one of the most interesting relics of Arab military architecture of mediaeval Syria.

Bab (A. *bāb*): the Arabic term, meaning "gate", denotes the monumental entrance of mosques and the gateways of fortified enclosures. In early Shi'ism the term was applied to the senior authorised disciple of the Imam. The term is also used as an appellation of Sayyid 'Ali Muhammad of Shiraz, the founder of the Babis (d. 1850).

Babis: followers of the religion founded in 1844 by the Bab, known as Babism. At the convention of Badasht in 1848, the Babis openly declared their total secession from Islam.

Babur: soldier of fortune, and the first of the Mughal rulers in India; b. 1483, r. 1526-1530. He was also a poet. Among other works he wrote an autobiography in Chagatay Turkish.

Bacchic poem (A. *khamriyya*): the Arabic term for a wine poem is known in modern critical terminology at least since Taha Husayn used it in 1923. The theme, however, was known to pre-Islamic poets such as Labid b. Rabi'a, 'Antara and 'Amr ibn Kulthum. Bacchism constituted a dominant characteristic of a group of poets of al-Hira such as al-Aswad b. Ya'fur and Tarafa b. 'Abd al-Bakri. One may speak of Hejazi and Iraqi Bacchism, the first being represented by Ibn Sayhan (viith c.), the second by al-Akhtal (d. 710) and al-Mughira b. 'Abd Allah (al-Uqayshir al-Asadi). A conspicuous group was gathered around the Umayyad Caliph al-Walid II, who is recognised as the master of modern Bacchism. One may also speak of a school of Kufa in the viiith c. and of the Pre-Nuwasians, Abu Nuwas being the glory of the genre. Paradoxically, a new impetus was given to Bacchism by the mystics. It found its full extent in Muslim Spain in the xith c.

Badakhshan: mountainous region in northeastern Afghanistan, situated on the left bank of the upper reaches of the Oxus river. In the Middle Ages Badakhshan was famous for its lapis lazuli.

Badham/Badhan: Persian governor of Yemen towards the end of the Prophet's lifetime. He is said to have become a Muslim in 631.

Badr: a small town southwest of Medina, where the Prophet defeated the Meccans in 624.

Badr al-Jamali: Armenian slave who became a Fatimid commander-in-chief and vizier in Egypt; ca. 1010-1094. With great though brutal vigour he brought order into affairs and inaugurated a second period of splendour to the Fatimid Empire.

Badusbanids: minor Caspian dynasty, noteworthy for its longevity, which lasted from 665 till 1599.

Baghdad: the capital city of Iraq on both sides of the river Tigris. The origins of the pre-Islamic name are not clear. The actual city, founded by the second 'Abbasid Caliph Abu Ja'far al-Mansur, continued to be the centre of the 'Abbasid caliphate and the cultural metropolis of the Muslim world until it was conquered by the Mongols in 1258. After that date it was a provincial centre until 1921, when it became the capital of modern Iraq.

Baha' Allah: founder of the Baha'is; 1817-1892. He was one of the first disciples of the Bab Sayyid 'Ali Muhammad of Shiraz. Arrested in 1852, he lived in Kurdistan and was then exiled to Istanbul. He declared his prophetic mission openly in Edirne. In 1868 he was banished to Acre, where he wrote the *Most Holy Book*, the fundamental work of his religion.

Baha' al-Dawla wa-Diya' al-Milla, Abu Nasr Firuz: Buyid supreme amir; b. 979, r. 998-1012. He ruled in Iraq and southern Persia.

Bahadur Shah I: Mughal emperor; b. 1643, r. 1707-1712. The second son of Emperor Awrangzib, he reduced the Rajput raja of Jodhpur to submission but found himself confronted with a Sikh rebellion and had to make a compromise with the Rajputs.

Bahadur Shah II: the last Mughal emperor; b. 1775, r. 1837-1857, d. 1862. He was in fact a pensionary of the British East India Company, and was exiled to Rangoon in 1857.

Baha'is: adherents of the religion founded by Baha' Allah. According to Baha'i doctrine, the Bab Sayyid 'Ali Muhammad of Shiraz was the forerunner of the Baha'i religion. It is opposed to dogma, but nevertheless teaches theological, philosophical, and social doctrines and has its own forms of worship. The administrative centre is in Haifa.

Bahmanids: line of eighteen Muslim sultans who ruled in the Deccan from 1347-1527. They left monuments in Gulbarga and Bidar.

Bahrain (A. *al-Baḥrayn*): Arab emirate on an archipelago in the Persian Gulf. Islam was introduced at the time of the Prophet. In the viith c. the Kharijites maintained a bastion of their power in Bahrain, and in 930 the Carmathians brought here the Black Stone from Mecca for two decades. During the xvith c. the island was under Portuguese rule for about eighty years, and from 1602 till 1750 under Persian sovereignty. The rule of the present dynasty of Al Khalifa was inaugurated in 1783. In 1970 the Persian government renounced its claim to sovereignty over Bahrain, and in 1971 Britain withdrew from its special position in the Gulf. In 1973 the ruler 'Isa b. Salman promulgated a constitution which declared Bahrain to be an Islamic state with the Canon Law of Islam as the principal source of legislation.

al-Baladhuri, Ahmad b. Yahya: Arabic historian of the ixth c., well known for his *History of the Muslim Conquests*.

al-Balawi: Egyptian historian of the xth c. His biography of Ahmad b. Tulun, the founder of the Tulunids (r. 868-884), is the most important source for the period.

Balban, Ghiyath al-Din: the most prominent of the Mu'izzi or Slave Sultans of Delhi; r. 1266-1287.

Balinus: Arab name for Apollonius of Perge and Apollonius of Tyana.

Balkh: important city in ancient and medieval times in northern Afghanistan.

Baluchistan "land of the Baluch": arid and mountainous country between southeastern Iran and western Pakistan. Its population is predominantly nomadic. The two important towns are Zabol and Zahedan.

Bamiyan: town in central Afghanistan north of the main range of the Hindu Kush. It is a commercial centre and was an important fortress in the Islamic Middle Ages. Down to the xviiith c. Bamiyan belonged to the Mughal empire, and afterwards to the newly formed Afghan kingdom.

Bandar 'Abbas: Persian port on the Strait of Hormuz, named after Shah 'Abbas I, who established it in 1623 to replace Hormuz, which had been captured by the Portuguese in 1514.

al-Banna', Hasan: the founder and director-general of the "Muslim Brethren" (A. *al-Ikhwān al-Muslimūn*); 1906-1949. Convinced that Islamic society should return to Qur'an and Tradition, he founded the Brotherhood in 1927. He was arrested several times, and assassinated in 1948 after the Brotherhood had been suppressed.

al-Baqi, Mahmud 'Abd: Turkish poet; 1526-1600. He was a court poet of the Ottoman Sultans Süleyman II, Selim II, Murad III and Mehemmed III and is recognised as the greatest *ghazal* poet in Turkish literature.

al-Baqillani (Ibn al-): Ash'arite theologian and Malikite jurisprudent; d.

1013. He is said to have been a major factor in the systematising and popularising of Ash'arism.

Barakat: name of four Sharifs of Mecca: Barakat I (r. 1418-1455), Barakat II (r. 1473-1525), Barakat III (r. 1672-1682), Barakat IV (r. 1723).

Barakzays: clan in Afghanistan which ruled the country from 1826, when Dust Muhammad assumed power in Kabul, until 1973, when Muhammad Zahir Shah was removed from the throne by his brother-in-law General Muhammad Dawud Khan.

al-Baranis: name of one of the two confederations of tribes which, together with the al-Butr, constitute the Berbers.

al-Barbahari: Hanbalite theologian, traditionist, jurist and preacher; xth c. He played a role in the struggle of Sunnism against Shi'ite missionaries.

Barber (A. *hallāq*): a person of very humble status, who could only marry within his own social group. He worked at market places and in the public baths on specific days of the week.

Bar Hebraeus (A. *Ibn al-'Ibrī, Abu 'l-Faraj*): Christian author and translator from Malatya, and the last classical author in Syrian literature; 1225-1286. He owes his nickname "son of the Hebrew" to the Jewish descent of his father. Having been a monk, he was ordained a Jacobite bishop, became Metropolitan of Aleppo in 1253 and in 1264 head of the Jacobite church. He owes his fame to his *Compendium of the Dynasties*, written in Arabic, which is an abbreviated translation of the first part of his Syriac *Chronography*, in which he treats political history from the Creation down to his own time.

Barid Shahis: dynasty founded at Bidar in India by Kasim Barid, originally a Turkish slave. The dynasty, which ruled from 1527-1619, left important monuments in Bidar.

Barmakids (A. *al-Barāmika*): Iranian family of secretaries and viziers of the early 'Abbasid caliphs; viiith c. Khalid b. Barmak (d. 781) was entrusted by the first 'Abbasid caliph Abu 'l-'Abbas al-Saffah with the administration of the army and land-tax, and with the governorships of Fars and Mosul by the Caliph Abu Ja'far al-Mansur. His son Yahya was chosen as vizier by the caliph Harun al-Rashid in 786 and remained in office until 803. Yahya's two sons, al-Fadl and Ja'far, also held high positions at the court, but in 803 Harun al-Rashid had Ja'far executed and al-Fadl arrested.

Barsbay: Burji Mamluk sultan of Egypt, r. 1422-1438. He invaded Cyprus, which had to pay tribute. His siege of the Turkmen capital of Diyarbakr was unsuccessful and he was forced to enter into negotiations with the Aq Qoyunlu. He had a diplomatic struggle with the Timurid Shahrukh over the right to cover the Ka'ba with a palanquin (A. *mahmal*). Barsbay fell a victim to the plague.

al-Barudi: Egyptian statesman and poet; 1839-1904. He is considered to be one of the most effective pioneers of the renaissance of Arabic poetry.

al-Baruni: Tripolitanian Ibadi scholar and politician; d. 1940. He inspired his countrymen in their struggle against Italy.

al-Basasiri, Arslan: Turkish slave who became one of the chief military leaders at the end of the Buyid dynasty; d. 1060. He rebelled against the 'Abbasid Caliph al-Qa'im bi-Amr Allah.

Bashkurt (Bashkir/Bashjirt): name of a Turkish people living in Bashkurdistan in the southern Urals.

Bashshar b. Burd: famous Arabic poet of Iraq; viiith c. He was considered one of the glories of Basra.

Basra/Bassora (A. *al-Baṣra*): town on the Shatt al-'Arab in Iraq, consisting of Old Basra, at present the village of Zubayr, and New Basra, founded in the xviiith c. The town reached its zenith in the viiith-ixth c. Here Arab grammar and prose were born, Mu'tazilism was developed and great scholars and poets flourished. After the ixth c. Basra was supplanted by Baghdad.

al-Batiha ("the marshland"): name applied to the swampy area in Iraq on the lower course of the Euphrates and Tigris.

Batiniyya: name given (a) to the Isma'ilis in medieval times, referring to their stress on the "inner" meaning (A. *bāṭin*) of the literal wording of sacred texts; (b) to anyone accused of rejecting the literal meaning of such texts in favour of the "inner" meaning.

al-Battani, Abu 'Abd Allah Muhammad: outstanding Arab astronomer, known in the West as Albatenius or Albategni.

Batu b. Juči: Mongol prince; d. 1255. A grandson of Genghis Khan, he conquered Russia and founded the Golden Horde.

Batu'ids: the descendants of Batu b. Juči, who formed the ruling house of the Golden Horde.

Bawandids (Bawend): Iranian dynasty which ruled in three different branches in Tabaristan from 665-1349.

Bayazid Ansari: founder of a religious and national movement of the Afghans; 1525-1572. He fought the Mughals, and wrote several works, among which an autobiography.

Baybars I al-Bunduqdari: Bahri Mamluk sultan; b. 1233, r. 1260-1277. He reorganised the state, fought the Ayyubid princes and the Mongols and defeated the Crusaders. He also received the 'Abbasid caliph al-Mustansir bi'llah in Cairo after the Mongols had conquered Baghdad in 1258.

Baybars, Sirat: extensive Arabic folk-tale purporting to be the life-story of the Mamluk sultan Baybars I.

al-Baydawi: well-known commentator of the Qur'an; d. ca. 1290. His commentary is largely a condensed and amended edition of the famous work of al-Zamakhshari.

Bayezid I (Yildirim "the Thunderbolt"): Ottoman sultan; b. 1354, r. 1389-1403. He succeeded to the throne when his father Murad I fell in the battle of

Kosovo. He centralized the Ottoman Empire, but was defeated by Tamerlane in the battle of Ankara in 1402, and died in captivity.

Bayezid II: Ottoman sultan; b. 1447, r. 1481-1512. Under his rule, the Ottomans became a formidable power at sea.

Bayhaqi, Abu 'l-Fadl Muhammad Katib (P. *Dabīr*): famous Persian historian; 995-1077. He is the author of a voluminous history of the Ghaznawid dynasty.

al-Bayhaqi, Zahir al-Din: Persian author from Sabzawar; 1100-1168. Among other works he wrote a history of his native district of Bayhaq.

Bayhaqi Sayyids: religio-political group active in the political life of early Islamic Kashmir.

Bayram: in Turkey *büyük bayram* denotes "the major festival" (A. *'īd al-aḍḥā*), celebrated on 10 *Dhu 'l-Hijja*, whereas *küçük bayram* indicates "the minor festival" (A. *'īd al-fiṭr*), celebrated on 1st *Shawwal* and the following days.

Bedouin (A. *badw*): the English word for desert dwellers is derived from the Arabic word, which means desert.

Beg (bey): Turkish title meaning "lord". Under the Saljuqs and other subsequent Turkish regimes, the title came to be employed as the equivalent of the Arabic amir. Under the Ottomans, it remained in wide use for tribal leaders, high civil and military functionaries, and the sons of the great. Turkish *beglerbegi* (*beylerbey*) means "commander of the commanders".

Begum (begam): feminine form of beg, used in particular in Muslim India.

Beirut (A. *Bayrūt*): capital of the Lebanese Republic. Berytus, destroyed by an earthquake in 551, was taken by the Muslims in 635. Caliph Mu'awiya I had colonists brought from Persia to repopulate the town. In the xth and xith c. it was in the hands of the Fatimids, but in 1110 it was taken by the Crusaders. In 1187 Beirut capitulated to Saladin, but was retaken by the Crusaders in 1197. In 1291 it was taken on behalf of the Mamluk Sultan al-Malik al-Ashraf Khalil. The town saw a brilliant period under the Druze amir Fakhr al-Din II. Occupied by the Russians for a short time in 1773-1774 during the Russo-Turkish war, the flourishing commerce was ruined during the campaigns of Ibrahim Pasha in 1840. The massacre of the Christians in Syria in 1860 led to a major exodus towards Beirut, which acquired a deep Christian imprint. In 1943 the city became the capital of independent Lebanon. The city witnessed heavy fighting between 1974-1990.

Bektashiyya: dervish order in Turkey, whose patron is Hajji Bektash Wali from Khurasan; xiiith c. The Bektashis, who in their secret doctrines are Shi'is, show the general features of popular mysticism and disregard Muslim ritual and worship.

Belgrade: capital of Serbia since 1867 and of Yugoslavia since 1927. After sieges in 1440 and 1456, the Ottoman army entered the city in 1521. It developed quickly as a fortress, but economy and commerce lagged behind. After the middle of the xvith c. Belgrade took on the character of an Oriental town and prospered until it was taken by Maximilian of Bavaria in 1688. In the xviiith c. it was a mere border garrison for the Janissaries. After two Serbian revolts in 1804 and 1815, the town remained in Turkish hands until it became in 1867, after lengthy negotiations, the capital of Serbia.

Ben Gesla/Byngezla (A. *Ibn Jazla, Abū ʿAlī Yaḥyā*): Arab physician of Baghdad; d. 1100. He described 352 maladies, indicating the appropriate diets for them.

Benin (former Dahomey): Muslim penetration probably began in the xvith c. from the northeast through merchants who founded families. A second wave of Islamic influence took place in early xviith c., and a third one during the xviiith c., reaching the present capital of Porto Novo. The greater part of the Muslims belongs to the Tijaniyya order.

Berbers: name of the populations who, from the Egyptian frontier to the Atlantic Ocean and the great bend of the Niger, speak local forms of the Berber language. The name is probably derived from Greek Barbaroi and Latin Barbari. They were converted to Islam in the beginning of the viiith c. and were the nucleus of the armies which subjugated the Maghrib and Spain. The Almoravids and Almohads were Berber dynasties. They have a deep feeling of belonging to the Islamic community, but retain many practices which are in direct opposition to Islamic precepts. An anonymous compilation was put together in 1312 to the greater glory of the Berbers of Morocco and al-Andalus.

Berke: ruler of the Golden Horde; r. 1257-1266. He was a son of Juči and was converted to Islam. He waged war with his cousin Hülegü and therefore formed an alliance with the Mamluk sultan Baybars I.

Berkyaruq, Rukn al-Din: Great Saljuq; b. 1079, r. 1094-1105. He ruled in Iraq and Persia, but in his time the visible decline of the regime began.

Bethlehem (A. *Bayt Laḥm*): the town is venerated by the Muslims as the birthplace of Jesus.

Bey (Bay): title derived from the Turkish beg and applied to the ruler of Tunisia from 1705-1957.

Bhopal: the second most important Muslim State in India, next to Haydarabad. In 1949 it was merged with the Indian Union. Bhopal is also the name of the capital of the Indian province of Madhya Pradesh.

Bidar: district and town in the Deccan, in India. The town was the capital city of the Bahmanids, and is known for its monuments.

Bihbihani, Aqa Sayyid Muhammad Baqir: Shiʿite *mujtahid* of Persia and proponent of the Usuliyya; ca. 1705-1791. He was commonly regarded by his contemporaries as the "renewer" (A. *mujaddid*) of the xviiith c. (xiith c. A. H.). By the end of his life he had been able almost completely to uproot the influence of the Akhbariyya from the Shiʿite shrines in Iraq and to establish the Usuliyya as normative for all of the Twelver Shi'is. He was in effect the ancestor of all those *mujtahids* who have sought since his time to assert a guiding role in Iranian society.

Bijapur: district and town in Bombay State, in India. The Muslim kingdom of Bijapur was founded in 1485 and ruled by the dynasty of the 'Adil Shahs until 1686.

Bihar: province of eastern India to the south of Nepal, known for the mausoleum of the Afghan sultan of Delhi Shir Shah Sur.

Bihzad, Kamal al-Din: the most famous Persian miniature-painter; ca. 1450-1536. His patrons were the poet Mir 'Ali Shir Nawa'i, the Timurid ruler in Khurasan Husayn Bayqara (r. 1470-1506) and the Safawid Shahs Isma'il I and Tahmasp I.

Bilal b. Rabah (Ibn Hamama): Ethiopian slave who was born in Mecca and became the *muezzin* of the Prophet; d. ca. 640.

Bilawhar wa-Yudasaf: Arabic work deriving from the traditional biography of Gautama Buddha, and subsequently providing the prototype for the Christian legend of Barlaam and Josaphat.

Al-Biruni (al-Khwarazmi): one of the most original and profound scholars of medieval Islam; 973-ca. 1050. Of Iranian origin, he was equally versed in the mathematical, astronomic, physical and natural sciences and also distinguished himself as a geographer and historian, chronologist and linguist and as an impartial observer of customs and creeds.

Bitriq: Arabicised form of Latin Patricius, an honorary dignity, not connected with any office, conferred for exceptional services to the State.

Black Sea (T. *Qara Deñiz*): large inland sea between southeastern Europe and Asia, connected to the Mediterranean by the Bosporus, the sea of Marmara, and the Aegean Sea. The Saljuqs of Rum occupied Tokat, Sinop and Samsun at the end of the xiith c. In the xvth c. the Black Sea became an Ottoman lake, access of foreign ships being forbidden. After Azov was captured by the Russians in 1696, the Black Sea gradually became accessible to foreigners. The Conference of Lausanne of 1921 made it practically a free sea, but at the Conference of Montreux of 1936 Turkey received the right to fortify the Straits, to restrict freedom of passage to the fleets of the powers bordering on the Black Sea and to close the Straits in the event of war in which she remained neutral.

Black Stone (A. *al-ḥajar al-aswad*): stone built into the outside wall of the Ka'ba at Mecca, in the eastern corner, about 1,50 m above the ground. Formerly broken into three pieces and several fragments, it is now held together by a ring of stone mounted in a silver band. The surface is hollowed out irregularly. Its diameter is around 30 cm., and its colour is reddish black with red and yellow particles. In 930 it was carried off by the Carmathians who sent it back in 950. According to popular Islamic legend, the stone was given to Adam on his fall from paradise and was originally white but has become black by absorbing the sins of the pilgrims who have kissed and touched it. The stone is sometimes described as lava or basalt, but its real nature is difficult to determine, because its visible surface is worn smooth by touching and kissing.

Blessing (A. *baraka*): the word, used in the Qur'an only in the plural, means beneficent force, of divine origin, which causes prosperity and happiness as well as superabundance. The Prophet and his descendants are especially endowed with it.

Bohoras (Bohras): Muslim community in western India, who are Isma'ili Shi'is of Hindu descent. They uphold the claims of the Fatimid Caliph al-Musta'li bi-'llah (d. 1101) to succeed his father al-Mustansir against his brother Nizar. They are therefore also known as Musta'lis, Nizar's adherents being known as Nizaris. Up to 1539, the head of the Bohoras resided in Yemen.

Book (A. *kitāb*): the Arabic word was used, until Napoleon arrived in Egypt with the printing-press in the xviiith c., for manuscripts. According to traditions, these manuscripts were originally sheets with verses of the Qur'an put between wooden covers. With the rise of the 'Abbasid caliphate, books and book knowledge became a general aim of Islamic society. They were multiplied in writing rooms. Titles, simple and short in the past, became ornate and flowery. Tens of thousands of volumes are kept in libraries all over the Islamic world. The upright quarto size was widespread, other sizes being reserved for special occasions. The well-known flap, often pentagonal, to protect the edge appears at an early period. Rag paper was used in general, parchment for copies of the Qur'an and other de luxe editions. Quires, which usually consisted of five double sheets, were marked by consecutive numbers written out in words. Several quires combined together, sometimes by chain-stitches, made a sewn book. Many books ended with a colophon containing the name of the scribe, often the date and sometimes the place. In the post-Mongol period, the sizes and the writing became smaller, the paper thinner, stronger and smoother. Splendid, calligraphic specimens of large size were produced at the courts of the Timurids, the Safawids, the Mughals and the Ottomans; magnificent copies of the Qur'an were also produced at the court of the Mamluks. The bookbinders formed their own guild from the time of the Ottoman sultan Bayezid II onwards.

Bosnia and Hercegovina: the mostly mountainous region in former Yugoslavia was first invaded by the Ottomans in 1386. After the battle of Kosovo in 1389, the Bosnian kings had to recognize Ottoman suzerainty. The sultan's sovereign rights ended in 1908, when Bosnia and Hercegovina was annexed by Austria-Hungary. In 1918 it was annexed to Serbia, and in 1946 it became one of the six republics of Yugoslavia. In 1991 Bosnia and Hercegovina, together with Slovenia, Croatia and Macedonia applied for international recognition as independent states, Serbia and Montenegro re-forming into a new

Yugoslavia, which was not recognized by Western governments. In 1992 fighting broke out in Bosnia and Hercegovina between Bosnian Muslims and Serb nationalists, who were backed by the new rump Yugoslavia. Bosnian Serb leaders proclaimed the creation of a Serbian republic of Bosnia and Hercegovina, with a constitution that declared it to be a constitutive part of the new Yugoslavia. Islamic countries declared themselves ready to help Bosnia. At the time of writing, the Serbian policy of ethnic cleansing against the Bosnian Muslims is in full swing.

Bornu (Barnu): emirate and province in northeastern Nigeria. Its early history is linked with that of the Kanem Empire, which had received Islam by the xith c. In the xvith c., when Fulani settlers are first mentioned, the Bornu Empire expanded greatly. This process was helped by the conquest by Morocco of Bornu's rival, the Songhay Empire. At the beginning of the xixth c., the Fulani intervened repeatedly, but in 1835 peace was made with them by Shehu 'Umar (r. 1835-1880), the son and successor of Shehu Muhammad al-Amin al-Kanemi. The Shehu is Nigeria's second most important Muslim leader after the Fulani sultan of Sokoto.

Bosphorus (T. *Boghaz-îčî*): the strait which unites the Black Sea and the Sea of Marmara and separates parts of Asiatic Turkey from European Turkey. It has a length of about 30 km and a width which varies from 700 m to about 3,550 m. There is a strong current and an undercurrent. The lands bordering on it came under Muslim rule in the xivth-xvth c. At the narrowest part are, on the Asiatic side, the fortress of Anadolu Hisari, on the European side that of Rumeli Hisari.

Bow (A. *qaws*): the ancient Arabs used the bow more for hunting than for warfare. Archery having been an ancient tradition among the Persians of Khurasan, new techniques were introduced under Abu Muslim. The practice of the Turks from Central Asia to fight on horseback was intensified under the Saljuqs. The union of horse and bow may well have inspired the graphic shape of the *tughra*. Many treatises on archery date from the time of Saladin and the Mamluk period.

Bread (A. *khubz*): the economy of ancient Arabia was such that the Arabs could not make bread the basis of their diet, so that the expression "bread-eater" was a laudatory epithet implying considerable wealth. The nomads occasionally ate a kind of pancake cooked on a heated stone. Sedentary people did not eat it regularly either. They used to crumble it to make a broth. According to tradition, the Prophet placed it above all other foods.

Bribes (A. *marāfiq*): the inducements given to a potential bestower of benefits were institutionalised during the caliphate of the 'Abbasid caliph al-Muqtadir by his vizier Ibn al-Furat (Abu al-Hasan). Bribes and money from commissions collected from aspiring candidates were placed in a special office.

Bridal gift (A. *mahr*): in the Qur'an the bridal gift is a legitimate compensation. It is the property of the wife and therefore remains her own if the marriage is dissolved. According to Muslim law books, a marriage is null without a bridal gift.

Brigand (A. *fallāq*): the Arabic word is used particularly to indicate the rebels in Tunisia and Algeria. In Ottoman Turkish the term *jelali* is used to describe companies of brigands, led usually by idle or dissident Ottoman army officers. They were widely spread throughout Anatolia from about 1590 but diminished in the early xviith c.

Bu Saʿid, Al: name of the ruling dynasty of Oman. The sultan of Zanzibar, of the same dynasty, was deposed in 1964. The dynasty was founded by Ahmad b. Saʿid, the governor of Suhar in Oman under the Yaʿrubid Imam, who assumed the title of Imam in 1749. The greatest ruler of the united empire of Oman and Zanzibar was Saʿid b. Sultan.

Buda (T. *Budīn/Budūn*): the part of present Budapest, the capital of Hungary, which is situated on the right bank of the Danube. It was conquered by the Ottomans in 1526, in 1529 and finally in 1541, when it became the centre of that part of Hungarian territory which was converted into an Ottoman province.

al-Buhturi, Abu ʿUbada: Arab poet and anthologist; 821-897. He had a brilliant career as court poet under the ʿAbbasid caliph al-Mutawakkil and maintained his position in the troubled period which followed.

Bukhara (Bukhārā): city in a large oasis in present day Uzbekistan. The first Arab army is said to have appeared before Bukhara in 674. After the fall of the Tahirids in 873, a governor was appointed by the Samanids, who ruled Khurasan and Transoxiana between 819-1005 from Samarqand. New Persian literary renaissance bloomed in Bukhara. On the fall of the Samanids, the city was governed by governors of the Ilek-Khans. In the xiith c., the Al-i Burhan family came to prominence. In 1220 Bukhara submitted to Genghis Khan. During the xiiith and xivth c., the city was several times destroyed and rebuilt. In 1500 it was taken by the Özbegs and remained in their hands till the Russian revolution, except for two brief periods after 1510 and in 1740.

al-Bukhari, Muhammad b. Ismaʿil: famous traditionist; 810-870. He is known for his collection of Prophetic traditions, called *al-Ṣaḥīḥ*.

Bulgaria: East-European country which took its name from the Bulghars, who invaded the Dobruja in 679. The Ottomans came into contact with the Bulgarians in 1352, and during the xvth c. Bulgaria became strongly Ottomanised. In the xixth c. one-third of the population was said to be Muslim. After the great insurrection of 1876, Bulgaria became the main field of operations of the Ottoman-Russian war of 1877. At the time of the revolution of 1908 in Istanbul, Prince Ferdinand declared the independence of Bulgaria and assumed the title of Czar. In 1989 some 300,000 ethnic Turks left Bulgaria for Turkey, under pressure of the assimilation policy persued by the Communist party leader Zhivkov.

Bulghars: name of a Turkic people by whom two states, one on the Volga, the other on the Danube, were founded in the early Middle Ages.

al-Buraq: the fabulous beast on which the Prophet is said to have ridden when he made his miraculous night-journey (A. *isra*) to the "remote place of worship", which tradition has always understood as a reference to Jerusalem.

Burda: piece of woollen cloth worn as a cloak and used as a blanket. The *burda* of the Prophet was burned by the Mongol Il-Khan Hülegü on his conquest of Baghdad in 1258, but it was afterwards claimed that the real one was saved and is still preserved in Istanbul.

Burda is also the name of a poem by al-Busiri, certainly the most celebrated in Arabic literature, whose verses are supposed to have supernatural powers.

Burids: dynasty of Turkish origin which reigned in Damascus from 1104-1154. It was founded by the atabeg Tughtigin, and endured until the city was captured by the Zangid Nur al-Din Mahmud.

Burma: republic of Southeast Asia. Islam came to the country in the xvth c. and was intensified when Prince Shuja', brother of the Mughal Emperor Awrangzib, fled to Arakan in 1660. The 1931 census gave a Muslim population of some 585,000, out of a total of more than fourteen million. The greater part of the Muslims were of Indian origin. Burma was separated from India in 1937 and became an independent republic in 1948. In 1945 the Burma Muslim Congress was formed as a political organisation. In 1970 religious affiliation to other than Buddhism was less than 15%.

Bursa (T. *Brusa/Burusa*): town in Turkey on the northern foothills of the Mysian Olympus. It was the main capital of the Ottoman state between 1326-1402, when Edirne (Adrianople) became the principal capital.

Burtuqal: name given by the Arabs to the ancient town Cale (Calem), the modern Oporto, at the mouth of the Douro. It became later the name of the kingdom of Portugal.

Burujirdi, Hajji Aqa Husayn Tabataba'i: the greatest religious authority of the Shi'i world in his time; 1875-1961. Under his guidance, the Qum Circle for Religious Studies became the most important clerical centre of Shi'ism. He was also concerned with Sunni-Shi'i relations and entered into correspondence with Azhar rectors such as Shaykh Mahmud Shaltut (d. 1963). In the arena of politics, Burujirdi remained rather inactive, but at times he favoured the shah of Iran.

al-Busiri, Sharaf al-Din: Egyptian poet of Berber origin; 1212-ca. 1294. He was a skilled calligrapher, a traditionist and a celebrated reciter of the Qur'an, but his name has been immortalised by the *burda* ode, a poem in praise of the Prophet.

al-Bustani: Lebanese family distinguished in the field of Arabic literature during the xixth and xxth c. They represent the various stages of the renaissance of Arabic literature.

al-Butr: name given to one of the two confederations of tribes who constitute the Berbers, the other being the al-Baranis.

Buyids (Buwayhids): Shiʿite dynasty of Daylam origin which marked the so-called "Iranian intermezzo" between the Arab domination of early Islam and the Saljuq occupation of Baghdad in 1055. There was a line in Fars and Khuzistan, one in Kirman, one in Jibal, with branches in Hamadan, Isfahan and Rayy, and one in Iraq. The recognised ʿAbbasid caliph was only a figurehead. The Buyids patronised literature and science of a traditionally Arabic character, but also showed a genuine interest in neo-Persian literature.

The following is a list of the different lines of the dynasty:

In Fars and Khuzistan (934-1062):

934	ʿImad al-Dawla ʿAli (Jibal)
949	ʿAdud al-Dawla Fana-Khusraw (Kirman)
983	Sharaf al-Dawla Shirzil
990	Samsam al-Dawla Marzuban (Kirman; Iraq)
998	Bahaʾ al-Dawla Firuz (Kirman)
1012	Sultan al-Dawla
1021	Musharrif al-Dawla Hasan
1024	ʿImad al-Dawla Marzuban (Kirman)
1048	al-Malik al-Rahim Khusraw-Firuz
1055-62	Fulad-Sutun (in Fars only)

Power in Fars seized by the Kurdish chief Fadluya

In Kirman (936-1048):

936	Muʿizz al-Dawla Ahmad (Iraq)
949	ʿAdud al-Dawla Fana-Khusraw (Fars/Khuzistan)
983	Samsam al-Dawla Marzuban (Fars/Khuzistan; Iraq)
998	Bahaʾ al-Dawla Firuz (Fars/Khuzistan)
1012	Qiwam al-Dawla
1028-48	ʿImad al-Dawla Marzuban (Fars/Khuzistan)

Saljuq line of Qawurd

In Jibal (932-977):

932	ʿImad al-Dawla ʿAli (Fars/Khuzistan)
947-77	Rukn al-Dawla Hasan

In Hamadan and Isfahan (977-1028):

977	Muʾayyid al-Dawla Buya
983	Fakhr al-Dawla ʿAli (Rayy)

997   Shams al-Dawla
1021-28   Sama' al-Dawla (under Kakuyid suzerainty)

In Rayy (977-1029):

977   Fakhr al-Dawla 'Ali (Hamadan/Isfahan)
997   Majd al-Dawla Rustam
Ghaznawid conquest

In Iraq (945-1055):

945   Mu'izz al-Dawla Ahmad (Kirman)
967   'Izz al-Dawla Bakhtiyar
978   'Adud al-Dawla Fana-Khusraw (Fars/Khuzistan; Kirman)
983   Samsam al-Dawla Marzuban (Fars/Khuzistan; Kirman)
987   Sharaf al-Dawla Shirzil (Fars/Khuzistan)
989   Baha' al-Dawla Firuz (Fars/Khuzistan; Kirman)
1012   Sultan al-Dawla (Fars/Khuzistan)
1021   Musharrif al-Dawla Hasan (Fars/Khuzistan)
1025   Jalal al-Dawla Shirzil
1044   'Imad al-Din Marzuban (Fars/Khuzistan; Kirman)
1048-55 al-Malik al-Rahim Khusraw-Firuz (Fars/ Khuzistan)
Saljuq occupation of Baghdad

C

Čač-nama: name of a Persian history of the Arab incursions into Sind in the viith and viiith c. Its most meaningful part is the extensive account of the relationship that developed between the Arab conquerors and the local population.

Cadiz (A. *Qādis*): seaport in southwestern Spain. Captured by the Muslims in 711, the town is occasionally mentioned by Arab historians and geographers because of the famous pillars of Hercules.

Caesar (A. *Qayṣar*): the Arabic term, which represents the Greek *Kaisar*, is not found in the Qur'an but occurs frequently in the biography of the Prophet. It was considered as a proper name. Hisham b. 'Abd Manaf, great-grandfather of the Prophet, is said to have received from *Qayṣar* a letter of safe conduct for merchants visiting Syria. This letter is said to have been sent by the Prophet to the Byzantine emperor Heraclius. In the Meccan period, the Prophet's sympathies were with Heraclius against the Sasanian emperor Khusraw (II) Parwiz, but in the Medinan period Byzantium and its *Qayṣar* become the enemy of Islam.

Caesarea (A. *Qayṣariyya*): the Arab sources know of only two of the at least seventeen places of this name in the Roman territories of the Near East and North Africa. One is the town on the Israeli coast, classical Caesarea Maritima, south of Haifa, the other is Kayseri in central Anatolia.

Cain and Abel (A. *Hābīl wa-Qābīl*): the two sons of Adam are mentioned in Qur'an CV, on which the prohibition of murder in Islam is based.

Cairo (A. *al-Qāhira* "the Victorious"): one of the most important centres of religious, cultural and political life in the Muslim world. The foundations of the city were laid in 643, when 'Amr b. al-'As established a permanent encampment on the strategical point between the Muqattam Mountain and the river Nile. The present-day name of the city is derived from Misr al-Qahira, a town established in 970 by the Fatimid Caliph al-Mu'izz.

Calabria (A. *Qillawriya*): peninsula in southern Italy, the so-called "toe" of the Italian "boot". The first serious Arab operation against Calabria took place from Sicily in 839. Notwithstanding Byzantine intervention under Nicephorus Phocas in 885, Arab raids continued until Calabria was occupied by the Normans towards 1050.

Calcutta (A. *Kalikātā*): capital of West Bengal in India. Founded in 1690, the modern city dates from 1757. It is a centre of Muslim culture, with an important library, holding a large number of Arabic and Persian manuscripts.

Caliph (A. *khalīfa*, pl. *khulafā'*): the Arabic word means "deputy". The full title of the leader of the Muslim community is "deputy of the Messenger of Allah". After the first four caliphs: Abu Bakr, 'Umar b. al-Khattab, 'Uthman b. 'Affan and 'Ali b. Abi Talib, known as "the Rightly Guided Caliphs", the title passed to the Umayyads, then to the 'Abbasids. But it was also assumed by the Spanish Umayyad 'Abd al-Rahman III and his successors as well as by the Shi'i Fatimids, the Hafsids and the Marinids. On the other hand, the title was never officially transferred to the Ottoman sultans. Only in 1922, after the abolition of the sultanate, did the Grand National Assembly at Ankara ask Abdülmecid II to consider himself as the caliph of all Muslims. But this same National Assembly abolished the caliphate in 1924.

In Islamic mysticism, the term carries the idea of vicarship.

Call (invitation) (A. *da'wa*): term used in the Qur'an for the call to the dead to rise from the tomb on the Day of Judgement, and for the invitation, addressed to men by God and the prophets, to believe in the true religion, Islam. In the politico-religious sense, the term is the invitation to adopt the cause of some individual or family claiming the right to civil and spiritual authority over the Muslims. It has been one of the means of founding a new empire, used by the 'Abbasids and the 'Alids. The term was specifically used for the Carmathian movement and for the establishment of the Fatimid dynasty.

Call to prayer (A. *adhān*): the Arabic word, which means "announcement", is used to indicate the call to the divine service of Friday and to the five daily prayers. The call to prayer of the Sunnis consists of the following seven formulas: Allah is most great; I testify that there is no god besides Allah; I testify that Muhammad is the messenger of Allah; Come to prayer; Come to salvation; Allah is most great; There is no god besides Allah. The call to prayer of the Shi'is has an eighth formula: Come to the best of works, inserted between the fifth and the sixth.

Calligraphy (A. *khatt*): Arabic script lends itself to practise writing as an aesthetic and decorative art. Calligraphy is one of the outstanding performances of Islamic culture and has reached remarkable peaks in the Arab heart-lands as well as in Persia, Turkey and Muslim India.

Cambay (A. *Khambāyat*): port in Gujarat, western India, which was important during the medieval period. It was famous for its sandals.

Camel, Battle of the (A. *al-Jamal*): name of a famous battle which took place in December 656 near Basra between the Prophet's son-in-law Caliph 'Ali on the one hand and the Prophet's widow 'A'isha and the Companions Talha b. 'Ubayd Allah and al-Zubayr b. al-'Awwam on the other. The battle, in which 'Ali was victorious, was particularly fierce round 'A'isha's camel, hence its name. 'A'isha was taken prisoner, was shown great respect but ordered by 'Ali to return to Medina.

Cameroon: united republic of West Africa on the Gulf of Guinea of the Atlantic Ocean with the capital Yaoundé. Until 1919 the German colony of Kamerun, the republic is a federation consisting of the former United Nations Trust Territory of Cameroun under French administration, which became independent in 1960, and the southern half of the former Trust Territory of Cameroon under British administration, which voted to join Cameroon in 1961. The northern half of British-administrated Cameroon joined the Republic of Nigeria. Islam seems to have penetrated the area about the xiith c., but experienced its period of great expansion at the beginning of the xixth c. under the influence of the Fulani Ahmadu Lobbo and Modibbo Adama (d. 1847). The north is predominantly Muslim, whereas the southern peoples adhere to animism and Christianity. Among the Muslims the Qadiriyya order is the oldest one, but the Tijaniyya order is the most numerous, while the Sudanese Mahdiyya order also has many adherents. In 1958, a Fulani Muslim was appointed Premier of the newly-formed State.

Čamlibel, Faruq Nafidh: Turkish poet and playwright; 1898-1973. He wrote patriotic and epic-historic poems, eulogizing Anatolia. His easy style made him one of the most popular poets of the 1920s.

Camomile (A. *bābūnaj*): plant of the genus *Anthemis* the blossoms of which were used by the Arabs, in a manner similar to the practice in antiquity and to present-day practice, for infusions ("camomile tea"), for baths and as a medicine for relaxing spasms and for stimulating the peristaltic motion.

Camphor (A. *Kāfūr*): the white, translucent substance which is distilled together with camphor oil from the wood of the camphor tree. According to Marco Polo, the Indonesian kind, to be distinguished from that of China, Japan and Formosa (Taiwan), was worth its weight in gold. According to Qur'an LXXVI,5, devout Muslims are refreshed in paradise with a drink flavoured with camphor. Its main significance for the Arabs lay in its use as medicine and perfume.

Canton (A. *Khānfū*): main port of South China at the head of the Pearl River Delta. Muslims are known to have settled in the port before 758 and to have perished at the capture of the town by a Chinese rebel general in 877.

Capitulations (A. *imtiyāzāt*): the earliest documentary evidence of commercial and legal privileges dates from the xiith c. These privileges, emanating from Muslim chanceries in Muslim Spain, Egypt and Syria, were unilateral and represented decrees rather than documents of certification. They included provisions with respect to the status of non-Muslim merchants. In the Ottoman Empire, the non-Muslims needed to make an application for a safe conduct with a promise of friendship and peace. Privileges were granted to a representative of foreign merchants and to individuals and dealt with safe conduct by sea and with guarantees for the free transport and sale of goods. The period of the Italian maritime states (1300-1569) was followed by that of the predominance of the states of Western Europe (1569-1774), during which time the capitulations became an instrument of European imperialism and led to abuses. From the end of the xviiith c. onwards, attempts were made to abolish them. Complete abolition was agreed upon in the Treaty of Lausanne in 1923.

During the xviith and xviiith c. European trade in Persia was carried out under the protection of edicts (P. *farmān*) given by different Shahs to the Dutch, the English and the French. The privileges were abolished in 1928.

In Egypt, privileges were granted to foreigners under Muhammad ʿAli Pasha, Saʿid Pasha and the khedive Ismaʿil. They dealt with taxation, customs, individual liberty, inviolability of domicile, legislative immunity and jurisdiction. Reforms began in 1875, and the privileges were abolished in 1937.

Caravan (A. *kārwān*): word ostensibly of Iranian origin. The oldest feature in the history of the western Asiatic caravan is the so-called "Silk Route", connecting China and Central Asia. In the Islamic Middle Ages, Baghdad was the point of departure, northwards via Mosul to Aleppo and Cairo, westwards to Damascus, and eastwards via Hamadhan and Samarqand to Farghana and China.

In the Ottoman empire, the most important caravan route across Anatolia, mainly a silk route, was that between Bursa and Tabriz. Regular journeys were also made between Istanbul and Belgrade.

Carlowicz (T. *Qarlofça*): this town in the north of former Yugoslavia was the site of the peace negotiations in 1699 between the Ottoman empire and Austria and her allies, after the Ottoman defeat at Mohácz in 1687.

Carmathians (A. *Qarmaṭī*, pl. *Qarāmiṭa*): the name given to the adherents of a branch of the Ismaʿiliyya. The central theme of the rebellion of Hamdan

Qarmat and his brother-in-law 'Abdan against Isma'ili leadership in 899 was that the appearance of the Mahdi Muhammad b. Isma'il, the seventh Imam and seventh messenger of God, was at hand, ending the era of the Prophet, the sixth messenger. The term Carmathians was generally used for those Isma'ili groups which joined the revolt and repudiated the claim to the Imamate of 'Ubayd Allah, the later Fatimid Caliph al-Mahdi. Their missionaries were active in Syria, Bahrain, Yemen, Khurasan and Transoxiana but lacked united leadership. In the first decade of the xth c. the Carmathian movement appears to have regained its ideological unity. Damascus was subdued, and Hamat, Ma'arrat al-Nu'man, Baalbek and Salamiyya were sacked before the 'Abbasid troops, sent against them, were victorious in 906. In 923 the Carmathians of Bahrain, under the leadership of Abu Tahir al-Jannabi began a series of devastating campaigns in southern Iraq. In 930 they conquered Mecca during the pilgrimage, committed a barbarous slaughter among the pilgrims and the inhabitants and carried off the Black Stone of the Ka'ba. In 951 Abu Tahir's brothers returned the Black Stone for a high sum paid by the 'Abbasid government, having rejected an earlier offer by the Fatimid Caliph al-Mansur bi-'llah. The fourth Fatimid Caliph al-Mu'izz succeeded in regaining partly the support of the dissident Isma'ili communities, but failed to win the allegiance of the Carmathians of Bahrain, who clashed openly with them. Towards the end of the xth c. the Carmathian state declined and, outside Bahrain, their communities were rapidly absorbed into Fatimid Isma'ilism or disintegrated. In 1077 a definite end was put to the Carmathian reign in Bahrain.

Cartography (A. *kharīṭa*): the Arabic word means "map", not cartography. With the advent of Islam, cartography received a new impetus. The first detailed world maps drawn in Arabic date from the xith c. They had been made possible through the introduction of Greek, Indian and Iranian astronomical and geographical works in the viiith and ixth c. The first Islamic world map was constructed in Baghdad under the 'Abbasid caliph al-Ma'mun. The xth and xith c. saw great cartographers like Muhammad al-Khwarazmi, Thabit b. Qurra, Ibn Yunus, Abu Zayd al-Balkhi, al-Istakhri and Ibn Hawqal. In Persia an anonymous cartographical work, called "the limits of the world", was produced in 982, while al-Biruni introduced new concepts in physical geography. In Sicily, the well-known geographer al-Idrisi produced a series of world and sectional maps at the order of Roger II.

Ottoman cartographers like Piri Re'is and Katib Čelebi made some very significant contributions to Islamic cartography.

Casablanca (A. *(al-)Dār al-Bayḍā'*): principal port of Morocco. The name is a Spanish transformation of the Portuguese Casabranca, the Arabic name being a literal translation. The Portuguese had destroyed the former Anfa, a small corsair republic, in 1468. The town was rebuilt by the Filali Sharif of Morocco Muhammad III b. 'Abd Allah. In the xxth c. it became the principal port.

Caspian Sea (A. *Baḥr al-Khazar* "the Sea of the Khazars"): world's largest inland sea, east of the Caucasus Mountains. In the xivth c. the Turks called it Baḥr Qurzum, "Beaver Sea". The prevailing designation refers to the kingdom of the Khazars, who in the early Middle Ages occupied the shores to the north of the Caucasus.

Castrogiovanni (Enna) (A. *Qaṣryānnih*): medieval place in Sicily, named Castrum Ennae. The Arabised form gave rise to Castrum Iohannis, from which the Italian name is derived. This highest town of the island was a Byzantine stronghold, which surrendered to the Muslims in 859 after a siege of thirty years. The rule of the Kalbid amirs, which ended ca. 1040, was followed by a period of anarchy. The stronghold was captured by the Norman Count Roger ca. 1090.

Catalogues (in Muslim Spain) (A. *fahrasa*): in these works scholars listed their masters and the subjects or works studied under their direction.

Categories (A. *al-maqūlāt*): the Arabic term is the translation of the title of the work of Aristotle on that subject. The earliest work in Arabic is a version of a Greek compendium attributed to 'Abd Allah Ibn al-Muqaffa'. The full translation that we possess is attributed to Ishaq b. Hunayn. Avicenna wished to remove the work completely from the syllabus of the study of logic.

Caucasus (A. *al-Qabq*): mountainous region between the Black and Caspian Seas, politically divided in the republics of Georgia, Armenia and Azerbaijan. After overrunning Azerbaijan and Armenia, the early Muslims were able initially to cross the mountains but, prevented by the Khazars and the Turks, made no permanent conquest north of their bastion of Darband. During the viiith and ixth c. Arab control over the Caucasus remained weak, and in the xth c. local Caucasian, Daylami and Kurdish dynasties came to power. The Saljuq and Mongol periods saw the beginning and development of a gradual process of turkicisation in many parts of the Caucasus and Transcaucasia. The spread of Islam, however, was a slow process. The rise of the Ottomans, together with pressure from the Muslim powers in Arran and Azerbaijan, brought about the end of Christianity in Dagestan, probably towards the end of the xvth c.

Čelebi: title given in Turkey between the xiiith and xviiith c. to poets and men of letters, but also to princes and heads of an order.

Cemetery (A. *maqbara*): Muslim cemeteries vary from places where the dead lie in anonymity to veritable necropolises. The stringent regulations of Sunni Islam require that a tomb should be simple and made of transient material. For the majority of authors and the consensus of believers, the cemetery is a holy place because it contains the tombs of individuals venerated in Islam. In the Maghrib, ceremonial visits and meals, usually accompanied by prayers, are made at gravesides. In pre-Ottoman and Ottoman Turkey, funerary monuments often are made of durable material. The Ottoman gravestone has an anthropomorphic shape, with a reproduction on top of some kind of headgear. It carries inscriptions which underwent very few alterations. In India the Arabic term is used for both graveyard and mausoleum.

Ceramics (A. *fakhkhār/khazaf*): ceramic wares and pottery are the glories of Islamic art. The city of Rayy was a very active centre of ceramic production until the xiiith c. Nishapur in Transoxiana showed ceramic activity between the viiith-xith c., Chinese influence asserting itself during the Mongol period. In the xiith c. Konya, the capital of the Saljuqs of Rum, became an important centre, to be replaced in the xivth c. by Bursa, the capital of the Ottomans. The real centre, however, became Iznik (Nicaea). Egypt, with its very old tradition of ceramics, underwent a remarkable development under the Fatimids. North Africa and al-Andalus did not lag behind in producing beautiful works of art. By producing on-glaze painting, lustre painting, tile mosaics, *cuerda seca* and underglaze painting, the Islamic artist has contributed fundamental glazing techniques in the field which, in turn, have made certain European developments possible.

Ceuta (A. *Sabta*): maritime town in Morocco on the Strait of Gibraltar. The Arabs entered the town peacefully round 680. Having almost been destroyed by the Kharijite revolt in the middle of the viiith c., Ceuta became part of the Idrisid kingdom. In the ixth-xth c. the town was ruled by a Berber dynasty. The Spanish Umayyad ʿAbd al-Rahman III took the town in 931, and later it was in the hands of the Almoravids, the Almohads, the Hafsids and the Marinids. In 1415 Ceuta was taken by the Portuguese and the annexation of Portugal by Philip II of Spain in 1580 transferred it to this country, which retained it after Portugal became independent again in 1668. From 1693 to 1721 it was besieged by the Filali Sharif Ismaʿil al-Samin. The British held the town between 1810 and 1814, when they restored it to Spain.

Chagatay Khan: founder of the Chagatay khanate; d. 1241. He was the second son of Genghis Khan, and the greatest authority on the tribal laws of the Mongols. He reigned over the Uyghur territory between Bukhara in the east and Samarqand in the west. Nothwithstanding his intimate relations with his Muslim minister Qutb al-Din Habash ʿAmid, he was not favourably inclined towards Islam, since certain Islamic prescriptions like slaughtering an animal by cutting its throat and ablutions in running water constituted infringements of Mongol law.

Chagatay khanate: this khanate in Central Asia was not really founded till some decades after the death of Chagatay Khan. The first Chagatay convert to Islam was Mubarak Shah, proclaimed *khān* in 1266. His cousin Baraq Shah (r. 1266-1271) also adopted Islam, but Muslim culture became victorious only several decades later. Till 1370, real power was in the hands of Turkish amirs.

Chagri Beg, Dawud: Oghuz leader who, with Tughril Beg, founded the Saljuq dynasty; d. 1060. In 1040 they defeated the Ghaznawid Masʿud I, and

Chagri Beg established Saljuq power in Khurasan. In 1060 peace was concluded between the Saljuqs and the Ghaznawids.

Chaks: tribal group in Kashmir which ruled from 1561-1588, when they were crushed by the Mughals.

Chaldiran: plain in northwestern Persian Azerbaijan, the scene of the decisive victory of the Ottoman Sultan Selim I over the Safawid Shah Isma'il in 1514.

Chamberlain (A. *hājib*): originally, the Arabic term indicated the person responsible for guarding the door of access to the ruler. It then came to mean master of ceremonies, superintendent of the palace and even chief minister or head of government.

Charity (A. *khayr*): in Islam, to make gifts in money or kind to needy persons is a religious act. Charity by individual Muslims is still widespread.

Chechaouen (A. *Shafshawān*): town in northwest Morocco, south of Tétouan. It was founded about 1471 as a place of refuge against the Portuguese.

Cheetah (A. *fahd*): the animal was used for hunting purposes and was a source of inspiration for Muslim poets.

Cherchel (A. *Shershel*): town in Algeria which dates back to Phoenician times. During the Muslim period, it was held by the Almohads, the 'Abd al-Wadids and the Marinids. In the xvth c. numerous Muslim fugitives from Spain settled there. In 1528 the town came under Turkish rule, during which the Marabout family of the Ghobrini was influential. In 1840 it was occupied by the French.

Chess (P. *shatranj*): according to Muslim authors this game came to the Islamic world from India, but it seems more probable that it came from Persia. In the xth c. the game was not yet fixed, al-Mas'udi knowing six main forms. Al-Biruni describes as one of the commonest forms in India a game of chance, played with dice, in which it is the dice, not the skill of the player, which determine the movements of the pieces. Firdawsi describes the game in poetical language. The famous legend about the summation of the successive powers of 2 is given by Abu 'Ali al-Sadafi (xiith c.): an inventor asked a king, as his reward, to place a grain of wheat on the first square, two on the second, four on the third and so on, doubling each time. The result is a number in 20 figures beyond possibility of fulfilment. Chess was a noble game in the Middle Ages both in east and west. Harun al-Rashid is said to have sent a chessboard as a present to Charlemagne and one of the last Nizari Isma'ilis of Alamut presented a very handsome one to St. Louis, King of France. The word chess itself allegedly derives from Persian *yā shāh* "O king", said when the king is threatened; but this etymology is not very satisfactory.

Child custody (A. *hadāna*): in the majority of the law schools, the guardianship ends at the age of seven for a boy, for a girl at pre-puberty. Though exercised as a rule by the mother or a female relative in the maternal line, custody may in certain circumstances devolve upon the father or other male relative.

Chios (T. *Saqiz*): Greek island off the western coast of Turkey. In the early xivth c. the island was raided by Saljuq princes of Anatolia. From 1329 till 1566 it was ruled by the Genoese Giustiniani, who paid tribute to the local Turkish dynasts of Anatolia, and later to the Ottoman sultans. In 1566 the Ottoman admiral Piyale Pasha took it without a blow being struck. In 1694 the Venetians temporarily occupied the island. During the Greek War of Independence Chios was ravaged.

China (A. *al-Sīn*): already in pre-Islamic times contacts with China were almost exclusively based on the silk-trade, the Persians being the traders and consumers, the Turks the carriers. The early Arab geographer Ibn Rusta knew only of South China, while al-Masʿudi was better informed. For both of them China was only reached by sea. The roads leading to northern China were described by Ibn Khurradadhbih and Gardizi. Ibn Battuta first stepped ashore on Chinese soil at Zaytun (Chüan-chou-fu) from where he set out on his journeys to the interior. After the coming of Islam, the existing trade was continued by the peoples of the South Arabian coast and the Persian Gulf, but the merchants remained on the coast. The first direct contacts with the interior began during the Mongol period. It is remarkable that from that time onwards the Persian language has been regarded by the Muslims of China as the language of polite speech, and that the popular Chinese written by these Muslims is strongly mixed with Persian words. Genghis Khan took as one of his officers Shams al-Din ʿUmar, known as Sayyid-i Ajall, who was said to come from Bukhara and claimed to be a descendant of the Prophet. According to the usual statements, Sayyid-i Ajall governed Yunnan from 1273 till his death in 1279. The main credit for the dissemination of Islam in Yunnan is ascribed to Sayyid-i Ajall's son, Nasir al-Din (the Nescradin of Marco Polo; d. 1292). A further descendant was Ma Chu (ca. 1630-1710) who published a famous work, called "The Magnetic Needle of Islam". The Muslims were particularly known for being hirers of animals for riding and transport purposes.

Chirognomy (A. *ʿilm al-kaff*): the art of deducing the character of a person according to the shape and appearance of the hands. The Arabic term also covers chiromancy, the study of the lines of the hand, dactylomancy, prognostications drawn from the observation of the finger joints, and onychomancy, divination from the finger nails. The Islamic tradition is based on the Indian and the Hellenistic ones, and is represented by a very small number of writings.

Christians (A. *naṣārā*, s. *naṣrānī*): early Islam had to deal mainly with the Copts (A. *Qibṭ*) of Egypt, the Maronites of Lebanon, the Melkites of Byzantium (A. *Rūm*), the Nestorians (A. *Nasṭūriyyūn*) or eastern Syriacs who were numerous in what are now Iraq and Iran and owed allegiance to the Catholicos of al-Madaʾin (Seleucia-Ctesiphon), and the "Jacobites" or western

Syriacs, suspected of Monophysitism and belonging to the patriarchate of Antioch. The Christians (and the Jews) had to pay a poll-tax (A. *jizya*) but were protected by the *dhimma*, a sort of indefinitely renewed contract through which members of other revealed religions were accorded hospitality and protection, on condition of their acknowledging the domination of Islam. They therefore were called *dhimmī*s or *ahl al-dhimma*. They were forbidden to insult Islam and to seek to convert a Muslim. On the other hand, they did take part in government. Although their condition was sometimes unstable, due to measures of individual caliphs or to outbursts of popular anger, it was essentially satisfactory until the Mongol invasions and the coming to power of the Mamluks.

Chronogram (A. *ḥisāb al-jummal*): this method of recording dates consists of grouping together, in a word or short phrase, a group of letters whose numerical equivalents, added together, provide the date of a past or future event.

Church (A. *kanīsa*): the eastern church, whether in Mesopotamia, Syria, Palestine or Egypt, is rectangular in form, always oriented towards the east, and is divided into the sanctuary and the nave. After the Muslim conquest, Christians were prohibited from building any new churches but were, in theory, permitted to keep the existing buildings. In fact, however, over the centuries numerous churches were confiscated and converted into mosques, or even destroyed.

The word *kanīsa* also designates the synagogue of the Jews and the pagan temple.

Cid, El (A. *al-Sīd*): the popular name for Rodrigo Diaz da Vivar; ca. 1030-1099. He is the most celebrated of the heroes of Castilian chivalry. The name is derived from Arabic *sayyidī* "my master", in vulgar Spanish *sidi* "mio Cid", given to him by the Muslim soldiers of Saragossa. From 1081 onwards he led the life of a "condottiere", fighting, as occasion arose, the Muslims or his own co-religionists on behalf of a third person or on his own behalf. He offered his services to the Hudids of Saragossa, and received tribute from the Count of Barcelona, the Muslim princes of Tortosa and Valencia and several Arab lords. He forced King Alfonso VI of Castile to lift the siege of Valencia and, after a revolt in the town led by the judge Ibn Jahhaf against his Muslim lieutenant Ibn al-Faraj, El-Cid took the town in 1094, of which he remained absolute master until his death.

Cilician Gates (T. *Gülek Boghaz*): the narrowest defile in the Cilician Taurus near Tarsus in Turkey, at an altitude of 1,160 m. It dominated the route from Anatolia to Syria.

Cinnamon (A. *dār sīnī*): spice with a fragrant aroma and sweet flavour, consisting of the dried inner bark of the bushy evergreen tree, native to Sri Lanka, the Malabar coast of India, and Burma. It was used by the Arabs as spice for food and taken as medicine.

Cipher (A. *al-ṣifr*): the Arabic word, which means "the empty" and as such is a translation from Sanskrit, is the origin of the western words cipher and zero.

Circassians (A. *Jarkas*, pl. *Jarākisa*; T. *Čerkes*): group of peoples who form, with the Abkhaz, the Abaza and the Ubykh, the northwestern branch of the Ibero-Caucasian peoples. Islam was brought to them in the xvith c., but only imposed in the xviiith c., replacing Christianity. They are Sunni Muslims of the Hanafi school. Between the end of the xivth c. till 1517, they constituted the predominant element of Mamluk military society. The Mamluk Sultan Barquq, a Circassian himself, became the founder of what is called the Circassian line of the Mamluk sultans, known as Burjis, which lasted until 1517.

Circumcision (A. *khafḍ/khitān*): the term *khitān* is used indifferently for males and females, while *khafḍ* is used in particular for female excision. The practice is not mentioned in the Qur'an, but must have been common in early Arabia. It does not take a prominant place in the books of law, but much value is attached to it in popular estimation.

Čishtiyya: one of the most popular and influential mystical orders of India. It was founded by Khwaja Mu'in al-Din Čishti (1141-1236).

Cistern (A. *ḥawḍ*): storing water was a necessary feature of the mosque in view of the ablutions. Islamic architecture paid great attention to the cistern.

Clan (A. *āl*): a genealogical group between the family (A. *ahl*) and the tribe (A. *ḥayy/qabīla*). The Arabic term also means the dynasty of the ruler, e.g. Āl Fayṣal Āl Sa'ūd, the official title of the Saudi Arabian dynasty.

Client (A. *mawlā*, pl. *mawālī*): in the Qur'an, the term is applied to Allah with the meaning of Tutor, Trustee, and Lord. In historical and legal usage it indicates a person linked by proximity (A. *walā'*) to another person. In early Muslim law the client was a non-Arab freedman, convert or other newcomer in Muslim society. All non-Arabs who aspired to membership of Arab society had to procure a patron. His role, and that of his agnates, was to provide the client with the payment of compensation for bodily harm, in cash or in kind. In return, the patron acquired a title to the client's estate. In Umayyad society, clients, very often prisoners of war who were enslaved, were felt to be unsuitable for positions of authority, but their education, skills and sheer number was such that they rapidly made administrative and military careers. Although the 'Abbasid revolution deprived the Arabs of their social and political privileges, they yet continued to be regarded as a superior people. This led to the so-called Shu'ubiyya movement. In Spain, the relationship between Arab and non-Arab Muslims differed from that of the east. There was no purely Arab conquest élite, no Shu'ubiyya movement, and there were armed conflicts between Arabs and indigenous Muslims. In political terms, however, the institution of *walā'* played much the same role as it did in the 'Abbasid East.

Clock (A. *sā'a*): apart from the so-called "hour machines" to measure the course of the hours of day and night, the quadrant and the astrolabe to measure astronomical time, the Muslim Arabs knew sand and water clocks, described in works by Isma'il b. al-Razzaz al-Jazari (xith c.), Ridwan b. Muhammad al-Khurasani (xiiith c.) and Taqi al-Din b. Ma'ruf (d. 1565).

Clothing (A. *libās*): many of the garments worn by the Prophet continued as the basic clothing of villagers and Bedouins, while since Umayyad times the urban dweller has been constantly modifying his wardrobe. Early Islam had certain laws and customs regarding clothing, "embroidery" (A. *ṭirāz*) becoming a standard feature of medieval Islamic material culture. Specific clothing was imposed on Christians, Jews and Magians, who wore a special belt, called *zunnār*, at present used to indicate the locks of hair worn by Jews, the sacred thread of the Brahmans and, in Sufi poetry, the external practices of religion. The Umayyad Caliph 'Umar II b. 'Abd al-'Aziz forbade the Christians to ride on saddles, to wear turbans or to copy the dress of the Muslims in any way. The 'Abbasid Caliph Harun al-Rashid introduced special badges for them, and yellow became their distinctive colour. Many new garments and fabrics came into use in the 'Abbasid period. Central Asian styles were brought to the Near East by the Turkish dynasties of the Saljuqs, the Ayyubids and the Mamluks, and were rather continued than changed by the Ottomans. In 1004 the Fatimid Caliph al-Hakim bi-Amr Allah ordered the Christians and Jews to wear black belts and turbans, and in 1009 the Christians were forced to wear in the baths a cross, the Jews a small bell. Clothing in the Muslim West, influenced by Berbers, native Iberians, not by the Persians and only at a late stage by the Turks, had its own particular style in dress.

Clove (A. *qaranful*): the dried flower-buds of the tropical evergreen tree, believed indigenous to the Moluccas, were used by the Arabs in cooking as a spice, but above all in pharmacy. The very costly spice was imported via the Red Sea.

Coffee (A. *qahwa*): originally a name for wine, the Arabic term was transferred towards the end of the xivth c. in Yemen to the beverage made from the berry of the coffee tree. The beverage was probably introduced from Ethiopia, where it is called *būn*, and 'Ali b. 'Umar al-Shadhili, the patron saint of Mokha (d. 1418), is said to have started using it.

Coimbra (A. *Qulumriya*): town in central Portugal, occupied in 714 by 'Abd al-'Aziz b. Musa b. Nusayr, governor of al-Andalus. Conquered by Ferdinand I in 1064, it was one of the Mozarabs' most lively centres.

Coinage (A. *sikka*): the Arabic term, related to Italian *zecchino*, has given the word "sequin", formerly current at the ports of India. It found its way into Anglo-Indian vocabulary in the form "chick".

Colour (A. *lawn*): white is the colour of brightness, authority and virtue, but also of grief and mourning. Black evokes darkness and mystery and demands respect; the Black Stone of the Ka'ba is a pillar of spiritual influence. Blue is magical, inauspicious and disturbing, while green is the symbol of joy, gaiety or success. The green standard of the Prophet and the green cloak of his son-in-law 'Ali have become the very emblems of the Religion. White was the colour of the Umayyads, and later of the Fatimids, black that of the 'Abbasids and green that of the Shi'ites. Yellow can refer just as easily to cowardice or treason as to royal power and glory, and red is the colour of fire and of blood, of passion, of impulse and of danger.

Comans (T. *Qūmān*): important branch of the Turkish Qipčaq (Kipchak) confederation who, fleeing before the Mongol invasion of 1237, sought asylum in Hungary. The famous Codex Comanicus of the xivth c. is a collection of texts brought together in South Russia by Italian and German missionaries.

Community (A. *umma*): in the Qur'an, the term always refers to ethnic, linguistic or religious bodies of people who are the objects of the divine plan of salvation. God has sent to each *umma* a messenger or admonisher to guide them on the right path. The ultimate reason for the plurality of communities lies in God's inscrutable decree. In the first period of his prophetic activity, the Prophet regarded his Meccan countrymen or the Arabs in general as a closed community, to which he had been sent, just as the earlier messengers had been sent to their community, in order to show it the way of salvation. After the Hijra, he created a new *umma* in Medina, formed by the citizens of the town, including the Jews. After the Prophet had successfully attacked the Meccans, he excluded from his politico-religious community the Medinans, especially the Jews, who had not yet adopted his religion. As time went on, his community became more and more to consist only of his proper followers, the Muslims. The community of the Arabs now was transformed into that of the Muslims. This community very soon spread far beyond the bounds of Arabia.

Comoro Islands (A. *Qumr*): group of islands at the northern end of the Mozambique Channel between Madagascar and the southeast African mainland. Arab merchants may have settled on the islands before the xvth c., but Islamic culture was in fact introduced by the Shirazis in the xvth-xvith c. At present, most of the population, estimated in 1970 at 290,000, are Arabic-speaking Muslims.

Companions of the Prophet (A. *aṣḥāb/ṣaḥāba*): in earlier times the term was restricted to those who had been close to the Prophet. Later it also included those who had met him during his life, or who had seen him even if only for quite a short time. After the Qur'an, the Companions were the sources of authentic religious doctrine. Tradition is based on the utterances handed down by them as authentic. The highest place among them is taken by the first four caliphs: Abu Bakr, 'Umar b. al-Khattab, 'Uthman b. 'Affan and 'Ali. Other categories are the Emigrants, the Helpers and the Badriyun, i.e. those who cooperated with him at the battle of Badr. The Shi'a in general hold a different attitude towards the Companions, because with their approval the first three caliphs took away the rights of 'Ali and his family.

Conakry: capital of the Republic of Guinea. The majority of the population is Muslim. The main Sufi order remains that of the Qadiriyya, which resisted the penetration of the Tijaniyya in the xixth c.

Concubine (T. *khāṣṣekī/qîz*): the concubines who were the especial favourites of the sultan, and whose number varied between four and seven, were honoured by the title of *qadîn*, and those who bore him a child were called *khāṣṣekī sulṭān*. The word *qîz*, basically "girl, unmarried female", was often used in the meaning of "slave girl, concubine". The term "aga of the girls" (T. *qîzlar aghasî*) was generally used to denote the chief of the black eunuchs in the imperial palace.

Congo (Brazzaville): republic which lies astride the Equator in west central Africa. Muslim slave and ivory traders from East Africa, especially from Zanzibar, began to reach the borders of the Congo River Basin in the xixth c. The great majority of the Congo Muslims, estimated at 200,000 in 1960, are Shafi'ites and belong to the order of the Qadiriyya.

Constanta (T. *Köstenje*): port on the Rumanian shore of the Black Sea. It was conquered by the Ottoman Sultan Bayezid I, and again in 1419 by Mehemmed I. During the Russo-Turkish war of 1806-1812, the port was captured by the Cossacks, but was returned to the Ottoman Empire by the Treaty of Bucharest. In 1878 it was ceded to Rumania.

Constantine the African (*Constantinus Africanus*): the first to introduce Arab medicine into Europe; d. 1087. Born in Tunisia, he infused new life in the medical school of Salerno, where he translated into Latin the best works of Arab medicine which had appeared so far.

Constantinople (A. *(al-)Qusṭanṭīniyya*): old name for Istanbul, capital of the Ottoman Empire. According to tradition the Prophet had foretold the conquest of the city. In 644 'Abd al-Rahman b. Khalid advanced as far as Pergamon, and the admiral Busr b. Abi Artat is said to have reached the city itself. In 653 a fleet was equipped in Tripolis, which defeated the Greek fleet at Phoenix (A. *Finika*) on the Lycian coast, but it did not reach the city. Another attack was made in 666, and in 672 a strong fleet cast anchor off the European coast of the Sea of Marmara under the walls of the city. The Arabs attacked it from April to September, spent the winter in Cyzicus and renewed their attacks in the following spring. A great part of the fleet was destroyed by Greek fire and many ships were wrecked on the return journey. This siege has acquired particular renown in the Arab world, as the Helper of the Prophet Abu Ayyub Khalid b. Zayd fell in it and was buried before the walls; during the final siege in 1453 his tomb was found.

There was a truce for over 40 years between the Byzantines and Arabs until the Umayyad Caliph Sulayman in 715 equipped a great expedition against Constantinople. His brother Maslama surrounded the city and had the Golden Horn barred by a chain. The siege lasted a whole year but then Maslama found himself forced to retreat.

In 782 the Umayyad prince Harun, the later caliph, encamped at Scutari. The Empress Irene hastened to make peace and agreed to pay tribute. Apart from prisoners of war, numerous Muslim merchants and envoys sojourned in the city, as did later Saljuq sultans. The name of Constantinople was changed into that of Istanbul when the city, at its conquest by the Ottomans in 1453, became the capital of the Ottoman Empire. In 1923, when the Turkish republic was founded, the capital was transferred to Ankara.

Constitution (A. *dustūr*): the Arabic term, of Persian origin, has come to mean constitution or constitutional charter. Constitutions were introduced in Tunisia, Turkey, Egypt, Iran, Afghanistan, Iraq, Saudi Arabia, Yemen, Syria, Lebanon, Jordan, Indonesia, Libya, Sudan, Pakistan, Mauretania and Kuwait.

Consultation (A. *mashwara*): consultation by the ruler of his advisers, mentioned in the Qur'an, is considered a necessity in Islamic political literature.

Copts (A. *Qibṭ*): the native Christians of Egypt. The Arabs did not distinguish between the Melkites and the Monophysites when they arrived in Egypt in 640. The Christians were well treated by the Tulunids, the Ikhshidids and the Fatimids, with the exception of the reign of al-Hakim bi-Amr Allah, nor did they suffer continuously under the Ayyubids. Under the Mamluks, the Copts continued to work in the Muslim administration, although occasionally harassed by Muslim mobs. These outbreaks diminished under the Ottomans. During the period of the dynasty founded by Muhammad 'Ali Pasha, which ruled until 1953, the position of the Copts improved, except for some occasional incidents. The Christian population of Egypt numbers about 200,000; of these the majority are Copts.

Córdoba (A. *Qurṭuba*): Spanish city on the Guadalquivir River. It was occupied by the Muslims in 711, and was made the capital of al-Andalus in 716 instead of Seville. Work on the Great Mosque began in 787. After the earthquake of 880, the minaret was rebuilt under 'Abd al-Rahman III, who also built the governmental city (A. *Madīnat al-Zahrā'*). The town was conquered by Ferdinand III of Castile in 1236. Great Arab scholars like Ibn Hazm, Averroes and Maimonides belong to the history of the city.

Corfu (T. *Körfüz/Körfüs*): Greek island in the Ionian Sea, between northwestern Greece and Italy. Notwithstanding two major attempts to occupy the island, the Ottomans never succeeded in dislodging the Venetians, who controlled it from the opening of the xvth c. until the dismemberment of the Venetian republic in 1797. The island was incorporated into the Napoleonic Empire, but became a British protectorate in 1815. In 1864 it was ceded to Greece.

Corinth (T. *Qordos*): the ancient city on the Peloponnesus in Greece remained under Byzantine rule up to 1210, when it was conquered by the Crusaders. Having passed into the hands of several rulers, it was finally conquered by the Ottoman Sultan Mehemmed II in 1458. It was taken by the Greeks in 1822.

Coromandel (A. *Ma'bar*): the eastern shores of the Indian Deccan were dominated by the Muslims between 1310 and 1336, and again during the short-lived conquest of the Mughal emperor Awrangzib.

Coron (T. *Qoron*): fortress in the southwest of the Peloponnesus in Greece. In the hands of the Venetians from 1209 until 1500, it then fell to the Ottomans. It was retaken by the Genoese admiral Andrea Doria, but reconquered by Khayr al-Din Barbarossa in 1533. Between 1684 and 1715 it was again in Venetian hands, when it was recovered by the Ottomans. Coron was taken by the Greeks during the War of Independence.

Corpse-washer (A. *ghassāl*): according to Muslim law, washing the corpse, putting a shroud on it, attending the funeral prayers and burying the deceased is an obligation on all Muslims. It became a profession which tended to become hereditary in some countries of the Middle East.

Corsair (A. *qursān*): the fact that the Arabs, probably from the ixth c. onwards, use a loanword, derived from Italian *corsale*, indicates that they made a distinction between piracy and privateering, as indeed should be done. They call a pirate "sea-robber". Piracy indeed is a purely private enterprise, while privateering consists of attacking enemy ships with the more or less explicit connivance of the authorities. In the Western Mediterranean and the Atlantic, piracy and privateering were practised by the Muslims from the viith c. onwards. In the Turkish waters they can be dated as far back as the xith c. In the Persian Gulf, piracy and privateering have been endemic since ancient times. In the xviiith c. the southern shore of the Gulf was known as "the Pirate Coast".

Cossack (T. *Qazaq*): in the Turkic language the term originally meant independent, vagabond. Under the Timurids, it signified the pretenders in contrast to the actual rulers. It also began to be applied to nomad groups which separated from their prince and kinsmen and thus came into conflict with the state. The word became the name of a political unit and later an ethnic designation for the Özbegs who migrated to northestern Turkestan and gave their name to present-day Kazakhstan. In the xviith c. the Kalmuks forced some groups to make an approach to Russia and to accept Russian supremacy.

Cotton (A. *qutn*): in the period of the Arab conquests cotton had already been propagated from India to eastern Persia and the neighbouring lands. It played an important role in Upper Mesopotamia and Palestine, but especially in Syria. A substantial part of the cotton imported into Europe in the xivth and xvth c. came from the Ottoman empire, where production and marketing were highly organized.

Court (A. *mahkama*): the judicial functions of the Prophet were taken over by the first caliphs in Medina. Under the Umayyads, the judges (A. *qādī*, pl. *qudāt*) as a rule were appointed by the governors. The 'Abbasids, however, made a point of assuming directly the exercise of this function of the sovereign, as did the Spanish Umayyads, the Fatimids and the Ottoman sultans. In the Ottoman Empire the jurisdiction of the courts was reformed at the end of the xviiith c. In Persia, the Shi'a considered the ultimate source of the judge's authority to be the Imams. In modern times, the courts in all Islamic lands underwent substantial reforms.

Court ceremonies (A. *marāsim*): they were presided over by the caliph seated on a throne, surrounded by the insignia of sovereignty, and veiled by a curtain.

The 'Abbasid caliph wore a black outer garment with full-length sleeves, a black turban, and red boots, and girded himself with the sword of the Prophet. The protocol for caliphal audiences was much the same for both 'Abbasids and Fatimids, though the latter's colour was white. The ceremonies required keen attention to rank and dignity.

In Persia, the ceremonial was designed to emphasise both the awe in which the ruler was held and his separation from the rest of the population. The insignia of sovereignty like the throne, the parasol, the standard and the musical instruments were symbols of old. The grant of robes of honour, the scattering of coins, jewels and precious objects, and keeping open table were practiced by all rulers.

In the Ottoman Empire ceremonial, protocol and etiquette were in general held more or less along the same lines as in Persia.

Ceremonial at the Muslim courts in India, while deriving much from Islam elsewhere, especially Persia, has also continued and adapted indigenous traditions.

Couscous (A. *kuskusū*): the culinary preparation containing semolina is the national dish of the peoples of North Africa. The Arabic word is probably of Berber origin.

Crac des Chevaliers (A. *Ḥiṣn al-Akrād* "Fortress of the Kurds"): strategic castle to the northwest of Homs in Syria, seized by the Crusaders in 1099 and conquered by the Mamluk sultan Baybars I in 1271.

Creed (A. *'aqīda*): the main dogmas of Islam may be summarized as follows: God is one; His existence is rationally proved from the originated character of the world; He is eternal, has eternal qualities and is characterized by active attributes, such as creating and giving sustenance; He is different from created things; although not being corporeal, He will be seen by the faithful in the world to come; the Qur'an is the eternal and uncreated speech of God; His will is supreme and always effective; man's acts are created by God, but are nevertheless properly attributed to man; He will judge all men on the Last Day, on which certain persons, and notably the Prophet, will be permitted by Him to intercede for others; Paradise and Hell already exist, and will continue to exist eternally; He has sent to mankind messengers (A. *rusul*; s. *rasūl*) and prophets, of whom the Prophet is the seal.

Crescent (A. *hilāl*): the new moon is important in Islamic religious law because it determines the date of the pilgrimage and the beginning and end of the month of Ramadan. In Islamic art, it is found as an emblem on coins, on royal horses, in jewelry, in symbolical personifications of the planets and on flags.

Crete (A. *Iqrīṭish*): Greek island in the Mediterranean between Asia Minor and mainland Greece. The first Arab incursions took place under the Umayyad caliph Muʿawiya I. After a revolt in 818 in Córdoba against the Umayyad amir al-Hakam I which was ruthlessly suppressed, the inhabitants fled to Alexandria and from there to the island. The amirs of Crete, belonging to the family of Abu Hafs ʿUmar, reigned from 828-961, when the island was conquered by the Byzantine Nicephorus Phocas. In 1204 it fell to the Franks who sold it to the Venetians. In 1669 it was conquered by the Ottomans. After several uprisings, notably during the Greek revolution of 1821, and another of 1866, the Turks were finally ejected in 1898 and the island was granted autonomous status under Prince George, a younger son of the King of Greece. Crete was officially united with Greece in 1913.

Crimea (T. *Qîrîm*): peninsula jutting out into the Black Sea south of the Ukraine. One of the main factors facilitating the rise of an independent khanate in the Crimea was the movement westwards of the tribes upon whose support the rulers of the Golden Horde relied. The first contact of the peninsula with Islam dates from a campaign of the Rum Saljuq sultan Kayqubad I in the early xiiith c. In 1238 it was occupied by the Mongols of the Golden Horde. From 1426-1792 the peninsula was ruled by the Giray Khans, descendants of Genghis Khan, who were allies of the Ottomans against Russia. In 1783 the Crimea was annexed by Catherine the Great.

Crow (A. *ghurāb*): in the Qur'an, the bird is sent by God to show Cain how to bury his brother Abel whom he had just killed.

Crusades: it cannot be maintained that the Crusades helped to increase the interpenetration of peoples, the knowledge of Islam in the West, or of the West in Muslim countries. Where the West has acquired knowledge of Muslim civilization, it has done so mainly through Spain and Sicily and not through the Crusaders. The few accurate ideas that the West finally acquired are due to the efforts of missionaries, who worked in an entirely different spirit from that of the Crusaders. Muslim historians, geographers and anti-Christian polemists for their part, although showing a certain curiosity about the Franks in the East, in particular about such an exceptional Western leader as Frederick II of Hohenstaufen, still had after the Crusades the same few notions about the European West, gleaned from their co-religionists in the West, that they had before.

Ctesiphon (A. *al-Madā'in*): the Arabic term, which means "the Cities", refers to the Sasanian metropolis on both banks of the Tigris, about 30 km. southeast of Baghdad. The oldest city on the east bank was Ctesiphon, which fell to the Muslims in 637 and which they called "the Old City". Al-Mada'in declined in political and commercial importance after the foundation of Baghdad in 762.

Čubanids (*Chūpānids*): family of Mongol amirs in Persia, who served the Il-Khans between 1289-1343. They were overcome by Hasan Buzurg, the founder of the Jalayirids.

Cubit (A. *dhirāᶜ*): the Arab term originally indicates the part of the arm from the elbow to the tip of the middle finger. In fact, there were a considerable number of different cubits in common use in Islam.

Cuenca (A. *Qūnka*): a town in Castile, Spain. During the period of the Muluk al-Tawa'if, it passed to the Dhu 'l-Nunids. After Alfonso VI had taken Toledo in 1085, Cuenca passed under Castilian rule. In 1108 it was occupied by the Almoravids, but surrendered to Alfonso VIII in 1177.

Cupper (A. *ḥajjām*): he is a much-satirised character in Arabic tales, and had a very low status, although cupping was generally believed to have medicinal value. The cupper practised blood-letting on parts of the body other than veins.

Customary law (A. *ᶜāda*): although influenced, to a greater or lesser degree, by Muslim law, customary law continued to survive in various Muslim regions, as in the Berber-speaking regions of North Africa, in India, where it was revived after the establishment of the British legal system, and in Indonesia.

Cyprus (A. *Qubrus*; T. *Qîbrîs*): island in the Mediterranean, south of Turkey. The Muslims made their first expedition against the island in 647, which was the beginning of a form of joint-rule by the Byzantine emperor and the caliph. In 1191 the Emperor Isaac II Angelus was dethroned by Richard the Lion-Heart, after which the island was ruled by the House of Lusignan until 1489. To safeguard Cyprus from the Ottoman Turks' expansion, it was taken over by the Venetians, who ruled until 1571. By a treaty in 1573 Venice formally ceded the island to the Ottoman sultan. From 1878 until 1959, Cyprus was ruled by the British, and it became independent in 1960.

Cyrenaica (A. *Barqa*): peninsula in Libya. It was occupied by the Arabs in 642, and became a major thoroughfare from Egypt westwards. Like the latter, it was dependent in turn on the Umayyads, the 'Abbasids and the Fatimids. It was occupied by the Turks in the xvith c. The Italians landed in 1911, but became masters only by the end of 1931. In 1951 the British placed Idris, the leader of the Sanusiyya confraternity, on the throne. His government was overthrown in 1969.

Czechoslovakia (T. *Čeh*): the Ottoman term indicated the inhabitants of Bohemia and Moravia, but partly also of Slovakia, until recently parts of the federated republic in central Europe. Some southern regions were occupied by the Ottomans after the battle of Mohács in 1526. After losing the larger part of the region during the so-called Fifteen-Years' War (1593-1606), Ottoman rule was re-established between 1663-1685, but dwindled after that date. The frontiers between the Ottomans and the Habsburg monarchy remained unstable and underwent many changes.

D

Dacca (*Dhākā*): the capital of Bangladesh. Muslim presence can be traced back to the xiiith c. The city served as the Mughal capital of the province of Bengal between 1608-39 and 1660-1706 under the name of Jahangirnagar, after the Mughal emperor Jahangir.

Dactylonomy (A. *ḥisāb al-ʿaqd*): the art of expressing numbers by the position of the fingers was already known to the ancient Arabs.

Dagestan (*Dāghistān*): republic at the eastern end of the northern flank of the Great Caucasus Range, bounded on the east by the Caspian Sea. The Muslims entered the north of "the land of the mountains" in the viiith c. Islam, however, seems to have made but slow progress. In the xiiith and xivth c. the Laks or Lezgians were regarded as the champions of Islam against the pagan peoples around them. The Timurid conquest and the Ottoman occupation (1461-1606) marked the further advance of Islam. From the xvith c. onwards, Dagestan was claimed by Persia, Russia and Turkey. Persia renounced her claims in 1813 by the peace treaty of Gulistan. Having fought the Russians off and on for several centuries, Dagestan had to surrender to the Soviet regime in 1920. It is now a multi-national republic with ten official literary languages.

Dahlak Islands: group of islands off the west coast of the Red Sea. The largest island was occupied by the Muslims in the viith c. and used as a place of exile or prison by the Umayyads and the ʿAbbasids. About the ixth c. the islands passed under the dynasty of the Ziyadids, ruling from Zabid in Yemen. In the xiith c. they achieved independence as an amirate, allied to the Mamluks. In the xvith c. they came under Turkish suzerainty and, in the second half of the xixth c., temporarily under Egyptian rule. Occupied by the Italians in 1885, the islands came under Ethiopian rule in 1952.

Dakar: capital of Senegal, almost entirely Muslim, is a centre of the Tijaniyya, Muridiyya, Qadiriyya and Laye orders.

Dalmatia: region of Croatia in former Yugoslavia. It was raided by the Arabs in the ixth c., by the Mongols in the xiiith c., and by the Ottomans from 1417 onwards. Between the Cyprus War (1570-1573) and the Cretan War (1645-1669), Dalmatia was divided into a Turkish and a Venetian territory. The Ottoman presence was ended after their defeat before Vienna in 1683. By 1718 Dalmatia came under Venetian control which lasted until 1797. It was subsequently ruled by Austria (1797-1805), France (1805-1809), was then one of the Illyrian provinces (1809-1813), and returned to Austria (1815-1918). The Muslim religious community of Dalmatia was officially recognised by Austria in 1912.

Damascus (A. *Dimashq*): capital of Syria. The town, an outpost of Byzantium, surrendered to the Muslims in 635 and was made the capital of the

Umayyad caliphate by Muʿawiya in 656. The Great Mosque of the Umayyads was built by caliph al-Walid I in 706. Taken by the ʿAbbasids in 750, Damascus was reduced to the level of a provincial town, but continued to resist the ʿAbbasids. Between 868 and 968, the town was ruled by the Tulunids, sieged by the Carmathians and held by the Ikhshidids, who were replaced by the Fatimids. A century of political anarchy and decadence followed. From 1104-1154 it was ruled by the Burid Tughtigin, and then by the Zangid Nur al-Din Mahmud, who made it again the capital of a vast Muslim state, opposed to the Shiʿi Fatimids and the infidel Franks. Under the Ayyubids, Damascus remained a great centre of cultural and religious life. Occupied for a short time by the Mongol Il-Khan Hülegü in 1260, the town came under Mamluk suzerainty but was pillaged by Tamerlane in 1399. Ottoman rule began in 1516 and lasted till 1831, when Ibrahim Pasha, the son of Muhammad ʿAli Pasha, ruled the town until 1840. Ottoman domination returned, but Damascus became one of the centres of Arab nationalism. In 1918 the Turkish troops evacuated the town, which was occupied by the French in 1918 until 1946, when Damascus became the capital of independent Syria.

Damietta (A. *Dimyāṭ*): town of Lower Egypt on the eastern arm of the Nile, near its mouth. Damietta was besieged by Amalric I of Jerusalem in 1169, captured by the Franks in 1218 but reconquered by the Ayyubid al-Malik al-Kamil. Taken by Louis IX in 1249, the town was restored to Muslim rule on Louis' subsequent capitulation. The Mamluk sultan Baybars I had the walls and town, except for the mosque, demolished and the river-mouth blocked.

Danishmendids: Turkmen dynasty which reigned in central and eastern Anatolia from ca. 1071-1177. Its founder, Amir Danishmend, became the hero of an epic romance.

Danqali (pl. *Danāqil*): tribe on the western Red Sea coast, inhabiting a territory of extreme heat and desolation. The Danqali sultan of Aussa in northeastern Ethiopia is the only potentate commanding more than sub-tribal or group prestige.

Daqiqi, Abu Mansur Muhammad: Persian poet; ca. 930-980. He composed the oldest-known text of the *Book of Kings*, the national epic of Persia.

Dar Fur (Darfur) ("the land of the Fur"): province of the Republic of the Sudan. The region was ruled by a dynasty of sultans, whose origin goes back to the xviith c. In 1916 Dar Fur was annexed to the Anglo-Egyptian Sudan and kept its administrative structure when the Sudan became independent in 1956.

Dar al-Harb ("the Land of War"): traditionally, the term is used to indicate those territories where the faith of Islam does not reign, i.e. where Muslim law is not in force, or which are not covered by agreements and regulations about payment of poll-tax.

Dar al-Islam ("the Land of Islam"): term indicating the whole territory in which Muslim law prevails. It thus is the opposite of *Dar al-Harb*.

Dar-es-Salaam: capital of the Republic of Tanzania, situated on the Indian Ocean. The first settlement was made in the xviith c. from Barawa, south of Mogadishu. In 1862 Sultan Majid of the Al Bu Sa'id dynasty built a palace there. In 1888 it became a station of the German East Africa Company and served as capital of German East Africa, 1891-1916, of British-ruled Tanganyika, 1916-1964, and subsequently of Tanzania. Islam is the majority religion.

Dar al-Sulh ("the House of Truce"): term used for territories not conquered by Muslim troops but which, by paying tribute, bought a truce or armistice. Two historic examples are Najran and Nubia.

Dara Shukoh: Mughal prince, general, Sufi and prolific writer; 1615-1659. He was the eldest son of Shah Jahan and challenged Awrangzib's rights to the throne.

al-Daraqutni, Abu 'l-Hasan 'Ali: scholar of Muslim tradition; 918-995. He is highly praised by his biographers.

al-Darazi, Muhammad b. Isma'il: one of the founders of the Druze religion; xith c. He is said to have been the first to proclaim the divinity of the Fatimid al-Hakim bi-Amr Allah.

Dardanelles (T. *Çanak-kale Boğāzî*): strait in northwest Turkey, which links the Aegean Sea with the Sea of Marmara, known to the Greeks as the Hellespont. The Ottomans came to dominate both sides of the strait in 1335, but their control remained insecure as long as they lacked an efficient fleet. The fortifications along the shores fell into disrepair during the xvith-xviith c. but were restored during the Cretan War (1645-1669). The Gallipoli campaign was fought in 1915-1916.

Dardic and Kafir languages: term for a number of languages and dialects of the Indo-Aryan linguistic area in Afghanistan, Pakistan and Kashmir.

Dardistan: area between the Hindu Kush and Lamghan in eastern Afghanistan. Islam is the prevailing religion, but pockets of paganism still exist.

Dareios (Darius): Achaemenid king whose Persian names are Dara or Darab.

al-Darimi, 'Abd Allah b. 'Abd al-Rahman: scholar of Muslim tradition; 797-869. His collection of traditions is commonly known as *al-Musnad*.

al-Darjini, Abu 'l-'Abbas: Ibadi jurist, poet and historian; xiiith c. He was the author of a historical and biographical work on the Ibadis.

al-Dasuqi, al-Sayyid Ibrahim b. Ibrahim: trusted collaborator in the preparation of E. W. Lane's *Arabic-English Lexicon*; 1811-1883.

Date palm (A. *nakhl*): it is often cited in the Qur'an as an example of the beneficence of Divine Providence towards humanity, along with the vine, the olive, the pomegranate and cereals.

David (A. *Dāwūd/Dā'ūd*): the Biblical David is mentioned in several places in the Qur'an. Muslim tradition stresses his zeal in prayer, in fasting and his gift in singing psalms.

Dawaro: Muslim trading state of southern Ethiopia, which included the great Islamic centre of Harar.

al-Dawasir (s. *Dawsari*): name of a large tribe in central Arabia. About 1689 they forced the Al Sabah and the Al Khalifa to migrate to the Persian Gulf, where the latter in time became the rulers of Kuwait and Bahrain.

Dawlat Giray I: khan of the Crimea; r. 1551-1577. He was supported by the Ottoman sultan against Russia.

Dawlatabad: hill fort in Maharashtra State in India to the northwest of Awrangabad, also known as Deogiri. The place was reported to possess immense wealth and was taken by a member of the dynasty of the Khalji Sultans of Delhi in 1294. The earliest Muslim monument is perhaps the mosque of the Khalji Sultan Qutb al-Din Mubarak Shah (r. 1316-1320).

Dawn and Twilight (A. *al-ṣubḥ/al-fajr* and *al-shafaq*): these terms are of special importance in the Muslim world and in Muslim astronomy because they determine two of the five times for the daily prayer. The legal time for the morning prayer begins with the so-called "true dawn", i.e. with the faint white light in early morning, and ends with the moment of sunrise. The legal time for the late evening prayer begins at the moment when the "red dusk" after sunset is gone, and ends when dawn appears in the East.

Dawr: Arabic term indicating the periodic movement of the stars. In the doctrines of the extreme Shi'i sects, the term is used for the period of manifestation or concealment of God or of the secret wisdom.

Dawraq: formerly a town in southwestern Khuzistan, replaced by Fallahiyya, now Shadagan. The swampy area between Shadagan and the coast of the Persian Gulf is still known as Dawraqistan.

Dawsa (*Dōsa*): ceremony during which the shaykh of the Sa'di order in Cairo rode on horseback over members of the order lying down with their faces to the ground. It was abolished in Egypt by the khedive Muhammad Tawfiq in 1881.

Dawud b. Khalaf: Imam of the school of the Zahiriyya (Dawudiyya); d. 884. The school is hostile to human reasoning and relies exclusively on Qur'an and Tradition.

Dawud al-Fatani: Malay author from Patani, in Thailand; xixth c. He wrote popular tracts and extensive handbooks on Shafi'i law, theology and orthodox mysticism.

Dawudpotras: dynasty who ruled at Bahawalpur in Pakistan from 1723-1956. In this last year Bahawalpur was merged with West Pakistan.

Daylam: the highland of Gilan in Iran. Towards the end of the viiith c. the mountains served as places of refuge for the 'Alids fleeing from the 'Abbasids. Under the rule of the Justanids (ca. 800-927), the Daylamites became strongly opposed to the caliphate in Baghdad. Since the beginning of the ixth c. Fatimid Isma'ili propaganda had been rampant among them. Daylam was the region of origin of such dynasties as the Buyids, the Hasanwayhids, the Kakuyids, the Kurdish Marwanids, the Musafirids, the Shaddadids and the Ziyarids. In the xith c. the Daylamites adhered to the teachings of Hasan-i Sabbah who, in 1090, seized the fortress of Alamut.

Dayr al-ʿAqul: town in Iraq where, in 876, the ruler of Sistan Yaʿqub b. al-Layth al-Saffar was defeated by Caliph al-Muʿtamid's brother al-Muwaffaq.

Dayr al-Jathaliq: monastery in Iraq where, in 691, governor Musʿab b. al-Zubayr, brother of the anti-caliph ʿAbd Allah b. al-Zubayr, was defeated by the Umayyad caliph ʿAbd al-Malik.

Dead Sea (A. *Baḥr Lūṭ* "Lot's Sea"): salt lake between Israel and Jordan into which the Jordan river flows. Arab geographers usually call it "the Dead Sea", "the stinking Sea" or "the overturned Sea" because it is situated in "the land that has been overturned".

Death (A. *mawt/wafāt*): the term *wafāt* is in origin Qurʾanic. It is connected with a verb which means "his term was brought to an end (by God)", carrying the sense of God's predetermining a man's lifespan or executing His decree concerning a man's term of life. In modern Arabic, *wafāt* has a more delicate and euphemistic sens than the stark word *mawt*, something like English "demise, decease".

Death-penalty (A. *qatl*): Muslim law contains special regulations regarding the punishment of death for sorcerers, highway robbers and renegades from Islam.

Deccan (A. *Dakhan*): high triangular tableland comprising most of peninsular India. In 1294 the Muslims marched into the Deccan arriving from Delhi, and in 1318 the region was annexed to the Delhi empire. In 1345 the Deccan nobles revolted against the Tughluq Sultan Muhammad Shah II (r. 1325-1351), bringing the Bahmanids to power. In the xviith c. Deccan fell to the Mughal emperor Awrangzib, but his authority was undermined by continuous raids of the Marathas. In 1724 the dynasty of the Asafjahids came to power and ruled until 1948 when the Haydarabad State was integrated into the Indian Union. In 1956 the State was partitioned between Andhra Pradesh, Bombay State and Mysore State more or less according to linguistic affinities.

Decree of God (A. *al-qaḍāʾ wa-ʾl-qadar*): when combined into one expression, these two words mean both the eternal Decree (*al-qaḍāʾ*) and the Decree giving existence in time (*al-qadar*).

Dede: Turkish term of reverence, given to the heads of dervish communities. It usually follows the name.

Dede Qorqut: Turkish collection of twelve tales in prose which is the oldest surviving specimen of the Oghuz epic and a monument of the Turkish language.

Delhi (A. *Dihlī*): capital of India. The city in north central India served as the capital of the Muslim rulers of India from 1211-1858, from 1911 as the capital of British India. In 1947 it became the capital of independent India.

The buildings of Delhi present the earliest monuments of a settled Islamic power in the sub-continent.

Delhi Sultanate: the establishment of the principal Muslim kingdom in northern India was made possible by the campaigns of the Ghurid Muʿizz al-Din (r. 1173-1206) and his lieutenant Qutb al-Din Aybak, who was the first ruler of the Muʿizzi or Slave Kings of Delhi. Iltutmish, a Turk of the Ilbari clan, is considered as the real founder of an independent sultanate. Other dynasties were the Khaljis, the Tughluqids, the Sayyids (1414-1451), the Lodis and the Sur or Afghans. In 1555 the Mughal Emperor Humayun entered Delhi and put an end to the sultanate.

Derebey: Turkish name, meaning "valley lord", and indicating the virtually independent rulers in Asia Minor from the early xviiith c. They were vassal princes, ruling over autonomous and hereditary principalities and exercising good government. The best-known Derebey families were the Qara ʿOthman-oghlu of Aydin, the Čapan-oghlu of Bozok and the family of ʿAli Pasha of Janik in Trabzon.

Dervish (P. *Darwīsh*): the term is used broadly through Islam in the sense of a member of a religious fraternity, but in Persian and Turkish more narrowly for a mendicant, called *faqir* in Arabic. The Mawlawis, founded by Jalal al-Din Rumi, stimulate their ecstasies by a whirling dance. Under the Mamluks, the standing of the dervishes was much higher than it is now in the eyes of canon lawyers and professed theologians. Women dervishes have their own religious services.

Devil (A. *Iblīs*): in the Qur'an, Iblis refuses to bow down before Adam and is accursed by God. He also tempts Adam and Eve in the Garden. His punishment is deferred until the Day of Judgement and he is allowed to tempt men, but not the true believers. At the end of time he is to be thrown into the fire of hell. Muslim tradition remains undecided as to whether Iblis was an angel or a jinn, but does not hesitate to consider him as the enemy of God and mankind.

Devshirme: Ottoman term for the periodical levy of Christian children for training to fill the ranks of the Janissaries and to occupy posts in the palace service and in the administration. The earliest reference to the institution known so far dates back to 1395. The levy seems to have ended in the xviiith c.

Dey (T. *Dayî*): the Turkish word, which means "maternal uncle", probably began to be used as a sort of honourific title, and later designated bearers of official functions in the Regencies of Algiers and Tunis.

al-Dhahabi, Shams al-Din: Arab historian and theologian from Damascus; 1274-1348. He was a compiler, but his works are distinguished by careful composition and constant references to his authorities. They have become very popular. His greatest work is a History of Islam, which begins with the genealogy of the Prophet and ends with the year 1300.

Dhakir, Qasim Bey: foremost Azerbaijani poet and satirist; ca. 1786-1857. He relentlessly criticised the religious fanaticism of the mollahs, the corruption of the local aristocracy and the Czarist administration officials.

Dhikr: the Arabic word indicates the act of reminding, then the oral mention of the memory, especially the tireless repetition of an ejaculatory litany, and finally the very technique of this mention. In mysticism it is possibly the most frequent form of prayer. In the Muslim brotherhoods, the *dhikr* may be uttered aloud or in a low voice, solitarily or collectively. The sessions generally take the form of a kind of liturgy, and the formula chosen may vary according to tradition and the spiritual advancement attained by the Sufi. The duration of the experience is regulated either by the *shaykh*, or, in solitude, by numbers, with or without the help of a rosary. The three main stages are the *dhikr* of the tongue, the *dhikr* of the heart, and the *dhikr* of the inmost being.

Dhimma: term used to designate the sort of indefinitely renewed contract through which the Muslim community accords hospitality and protection to members of other revealed religions, on the condition that they acknowledge the domination of Islam. The beneficiaries of the *dhimma* are called *dhimmi*s, and are collectively referred to as *ahl al-dhimma* or simply *dhimma*. The essential distinction with the Muslims consisted in the paying of the *jizya* or tax, later a precise poll-tax, which expressed subjection. The *dhimmi*s had also to wear a distinctive mark in their garb (A. *ghiyār*), described as a piece of cloth of a stipulated colour (red, blue, yellow) placed over the shoulder. Originally only Jews and Christians were seen as *dhimmi*s, but soon Zoroastrians and other minor faiths in Central Asia had to be considered as people possessing a Holy Book. When Islam grew numerically, the Muslims sought to delimit more clearly the rights of the non-Muslims. Under circumstances, the policy towards the *dhimmi*s may have hardened, but in general they were not persecuted. The only exception in this respect was the Fatimid caliph al-Hakim bi-Amr Allah. Under the Saljuqs, too, the condition of the Christian community deteriorated only very marginally. The period of the Mongols was of temporary advantage to the Christians, as the latter were found in their ranks, and because the Mongols held the balance between the various faiths. Under the Mamluks, the Christians suffered the repercussions of the struggle against the Mongols. In the West, an intolerant policy towards Christians and Jews was adopted by the Almoravids and even more by the Almohads because of the suspicions of complicity with the Spanish Reconquista.

Dhofar (A. *Ẓafār/Ẓufār*): region in the Sultanate of Oman on the Indian Ocean, which abuts on the Republic of Yemen. Its most important port is that of Salala from which Sultan Sa'id b. Taymur (r. 1932-1970) ruled Oman, then called Muscat and Oman. The Arabic word means "aromatic plant" and the region indeed is known from ancient times as the land of frankincense. In 1265 amir Mahmud b. Ahmad al-Kusi, lord of Hormuz, conquered and plundered Dhofar. In 1378 Salim b. Idris, ruler of Dhofar, surrendered to the Muzaffarids. In the xixth c. the region belonged only nominally to the sultanate of Oman; it was ruled by the Wali of al-Hafa.

Dhū: the Arabic word means "possessor of" or "who has", and is used to provide surnames or nicknames.

Dhu 'l-Faqar: name of the famous sword which the Prophet obtained as booty in the battle of Badr. The term has often been inscribed on finely engraved swords.

Dhu 'l-Himma (*Dhāt al-Himma*): name of the principal heroine of a romance of Arab chivalry. The main subject is the Arab war against the Byzantines during the first three centuries of Islam. The edition of 1909 in 7 volumes covers a total of 5,084 pages in 8vo with 27 lines to the page.

Dhu 'l-Khalasa: name of the sacred stone which was worshipped by several tribes in a place some 190 km south of Mecca.

Dhu 'l-Nunids: prominent family of Berber origin who ruled in Toledo from the early xith c. till 1085 during the period of the Muluk al-Tawa'if.

Dhu Nuwas: pre-Islamic king of the Yemen; vith c. After his conversion to Judaism he took the name Yusuf. He persecuted the Christians of Najran, perhaps in 523, and his name is connected with the invasion of Yemen by Ethiopian troops under Abraha. After his defeat he threw himself into the sea.

Dhu 'l-Qadr: Turkmen dynasty which ruled from Elbistan, in Turkey, over the region Mar'ash-Malatya between 1337-1522 as clients first of the Mamluks, then of the Ottomans.

Dhu Qar: name of a watering-place near Kufa, in Iraq, where a skirmish (or battle) took place around 610 in which the Bakr b. Wa'il tribe put other Arabs to flight. Among the latter were regular Persian troops and so the skirmish showed that the Persians were not as invincible as had been supposed.

Dhu 'l-Rumma: nickname of the famous Arab poet Ghaylan b. 'Ukba; d. 735. His prestige was high with the grammarians of the Basra school, and with the lexicographers, for the profuse richness of his descriptions of the camel, the onager, the oryx, and the desert in general.

Diatribe (A. *hijā'*): the Arab poet took the adversary's honour as his target, dishonouring and humiliating him. The genre has been widely cultivated by the Arabs ever since the pre-Islamic period.

In Persia, to obtain humorous effects, a poem by another author was taken as the basis for a satire and inserted in one's own poem. One of the oldest Persian specialists was Suzani of Nasaf (d. 1173).

In Turkey also the satire was blended with humour. The earliest example in Ottoman Turkish literature is "the Book of the Donkey" by Sheykhi of Germiyan (d. ca. 1430).

The greatest writer of satire in Urdu is Mirza Rafi' Sawda (1713-1780).

Di'bil: nickname of Abu 'Ali Muhammad al-Khuza'i, a satirical poet; 765-

860. A Shi'i, who was famous for his poems praising the eighth Imam 'Ali al-Rida, he generally attacked the 'Abbasid caliphs.

Dictionary (A. *mu'jam*; *qāmūs*): medieval Arabic dictionaries may be classified as those arranging roots anagramatically, those arranging roots primarily under the final radical, and those arranged, more or less, on the modern European pattern. Dictionaries were compiled from the viiith through the xivth c., and again in the xviiith c. and later.

The normal Persian word for "dictionary" is *farhang* and the oldest surviving Persian dictionary was compiled between 1058-1068. The next one is recorded at the beginning of the xivth c. Afterwards the centre of Persian lexicography moved to India, and in the xvith c. Turks, writing in Persian, also made efforts to interpret Persian writers. Other dictionaries were compiled in the subsequent centuries.

In Turkey, lexicographers maintained the arrangement of Arabic and Persian dictionaries. The first Turkic dictionary, dealing with the standard language of the Ilek-Khan Empire, was written in Baghdad in 1074. Dictionaries in Chagatay Turkish were compiled from the xvith c. onwards. Systematic investigation into the (non-Ottoman) Turkic languages in the former Soviet Union began after World War I.

Dienné: town in southern Mali, which adopted Islam at about 1300 and became an entrepôt at about 1500 because of its direct communication with Timbuktu. In 1591 it was occupied by the Moroccans of Jujar, after 1818 by the Fulani Shehu Ahmadu Lobbo, in 1861 by the Tukulor al-Hajj 'Umar and in 1893 by the French.

Dihqan (P. *Dehkān*): name for the head of a village and for a member of the lesser feudal nobility of Sasanian Persia. As the representatives of the government, the *dihqan*s were an important class. In the xith c. their influence diminished.

al-Dihlawi, Shah Wali Allah: revolutionary Indian thinker, theologian, pioneer Persian translator of the Qur'an and traditionist; 1703-1762. He is considered the founder of Islamic modernism.

Dinar: the name of the gold unit of currency in early Islam, derived from Greek *dènarion*, Latin *denarius*.

Dinawar: important town in western Persia during the Middle Ages, in Caliph Mu'awiya's reign renamed Mah al-Kufa. It surrendered to the Muslims in 642 and prospered under the Umayyads and the 'Abbasids. It was completely destroyed by Tamerlane, never to be rebuilt.

al-Dinawari, Abu Hanifa: Arab scholar of Iranian origin; d. 894. Among other works he wrote a well-known history from a Persian point of view.

Dinet, Alphonse: French painter of oriental subjects and writer; 1861-1929. He assumed the name Nacir Ed Dine (Nasir al-Din) when he became a convert to Islam.

Din-i Ilahi ("Divine Faith"): the heresy promulgated by the Mughal emperor Akbar in 1581. It derived its essential tenets from various streams of orthodox and heterodox Sufism and reflects Akbar's eclecticism.

Dioscorides (A. *Diyusquridīs*): after Galen, the physician most quoted by Muslims. His work has been the foundation of Muslim pharmacology.

Diplomacy (Diplomat/Ambassador = A. *safīr*; T. *elči*): from an early date the Ottoman sultans exchanged occasional diplomatic missions, for courtesy or negotiation, with other Muslim rulers and also sent a number of missions to various European capitals. From the xvith c., European states established permanent missions in Istanbul. The Ottoman government, however, made no attempt to respond to this practice until the end of the xviiith c., preferring to rely, for contact with the European powers, on the foreign missions in Istanbul.

Diplomatic: Arabic material for this science is found in papyri and manuals for secretaries. The introductory protocol is followed by the text and the concluding protocol. Documents consist mainly of letters of appointment, contracts and business or legal material. The first chancellery is said to have been set up by the caliph ʿUmar b. al-Khattab. In Umayyad times, the official language, hitherto Persian in the east and Greek in the west, became Arabic. Under the ʿAbbasids, Persian became important again. In Egypt, a chancellery was introduced ca. 872 under Ahmad b. Tulun. For Mamluk times, al-Qalqashandi is the best source.

In the Muslim West the external characteristics of documents appear to have been simpler than in the East.

The origins of Persian diplomatic date from the times of the Ghaznawid Mahmud b. Sebüktigin, while diplomatic in Ottoman Turkey can be traced back to the beginnings of the Empire in the xivth c.

Dirham: the name, derived from Greek *drachmè*, indicates both a weight and the silver unit of the Arab monetary system, used from the rise of Islam down to the Mongol period.

al-Dirʿiyya (al-Darʿiyya): oasis in Najd, Saudi Arabia, northwest of Riyadh. The capital of the Al Saʿud in the early xixth c., it surrendered to Ibrahim Pasha of Egypt in 1818, was retaken by Turki b. ʿAbd Allah Al Saʿud but destroyed by the Egyptian commander Husayn Bey in 1821. In 1824 Turki chose Riyadh as the new capital.

Ditch (A. *al-khandaq*)**, Battle of the**: in 627 the Prophet foiled a Meccan attempt to storm Medina by digging a moat or trench at those parts of the oasis which were open to attack by cavalry.

Diu: island with a good harbour, lying off the Saurashtra coast of Gujarat, India, in the Gulf of Cambay of the Arabian Sea. It was taken by the Khalji sultan of Delhi Muhammad Shah I (r. 1296-1316) about 1300, but fell to the Portuguese in 1537 and remained a Portuguese colony until 1961.

Divination (A. *kihāna*): notwithstanding the dictum "there is no divination after the prophetic mission", divination was legitimised by Muslim encyclopaedists and bibliographers by including it in the mainstream of prophecy. It is divided into physiognomancy, magic and judicial astrology. Special books were in use in order to know if not the future, at least the signs or circumstances that are auspicious for some decision.

The Arabic term *firāsa* indicates the technique of inductive divination which permits the foretelling of moral conditions and psychological behaviour from external indications and physical states.

Divorce (A. *ṭalāq*): the Arabic term indicates the sending away of a wife by her husband. Qur'an, Tradition and juridical schools deal in detail with this form of divorce.

Diyarbakr (A. *Diyār Bakr*): capital of the province of the same name in southeastern Turkey, formerly called Amid. It was taken by the Arab Muslims ca. 639 and by the Ottomans in 1527. The city is remarkable for its basalt walls.

Dizful: capital of the district of the same name in Khuzistan, Iran. The town was known for a bridge of Sasanian times and for the cultivation of indigo.

Dobruja: plateau between the Danube to the west and the Black Sea to the east, called Scythia Minor in the Graeco-Roman period. Until the advent of the Ottoman Turks, the Cumans appear to have played the most important part in the history of the region. Anatolian Turks settled in Dobruja after 1263, and in 1393 the region was taken under direct Ottoman control, being made into a frontier for irregular cavalry. Dobruja preserved this character throughout its history, attracting warlike elements, dissidents and sectarians. After Sultan Mehemmed I's expedition in 1419, the Ottomans were firmly established in the region. From 1575 onwards Cossack attacks became a constant threat to Dobruja. In the xixth c. the region became a battlefield between the Ottoman and Russian armies. By the treaty of Berlin of 1878 the Southern Dobruja was annexed to Rumania, while the rest was made part of Bulgaria under Ottoman suzerainty.

Dog (A. *kalb*): the dog is regarded in Islam as a fundamentally unclean animal and therefore forbidden food. In Arabic, the word is a biting insult. Dogs, however, were indispensable scavengers in cities like Istanbul, Cairo, Alexandria and in the Muslim West. Rabies was endemic in all Islamic countries at all periods.

Dolmabahçe (Dolma Bahçe): palace on the Bosporus in Istanbul, built in 1853 by Sultan Abdülmecid I.

Dome of the Rock (A. *Qubbat al-Ṣakhra*): at times called the Mosque of 'Umar, the monument in Jerusalem was constructed by the Umayyad caliph 'Abd al-Malik in 691. According to Muslim tradition, it is the place whence the Prophet went on his journey to heaven (A. *mi'rāj*).

Dongola: name of two towns in Nubia, Republic of Sudan, and, more generally, of the riverain territory dependent on these towns.

Donkey (A. *ḥimār*): the Prophet is said to have owned one, but Arabs of high rank do not ride it. Its flesh is forbidden food.

Dönme : the Turkish word, which means convert, is used to indicate a sect formed by Jews in the xviith c. upon their conversion to Islam.

Drač (It. *Durazzo*; Alb. *Durrës*): Slavonic and Ottoman name for the principal port of Albania. It was conquered by the Ottomans in 1501.

Drinking (A. *sharāb*): according to tradition, blessings should be uttered before and after drinking and the cup should be held in the right hand. Opinions differ on the question whether it is permitted to drink standing. It is considered forbidden to drink out of the mouth of the water-skin, and one should not blow or snort into the drink, and not drink the whole at one draught. If one is drinking in company, the cup should be passed to the right.

Drinks (A. *mashrūbāt*): the Qur'an prohibits the consumption of wine (A. *khamr*). Consequently, the problem of the distinction between "permitted" and "forbidden" in relation to drinks is a subject of great interest to Islamic religious literature.

Druggist (A. *al-ʿaṭṭār*): the Arabic word primarily means a perfume merchant, but as most scents and drugs were credited with some healing properties, the word also came to mean chemist and homeopath, whose activities combine commerce with science and medicine. In general, druggists have been known for their cheating in measures and general quackery.

Drum (A. *ṭabl*): the Arabic term indicates two classes of the drum family, the cylinder type and the bowl type.

Druzes (A. *Durūz*, s. *Durzī*): a numerically small religious group of people living in southern Syria, Lebanon, Israel, and Jordan. They profess an initiatory faith derived from the Ismaʿiliyya and originated around the Fatimid caliph al-Hakim bi-Amr Allah. The Druzes live in expectation of al-Hakim's return and form a closed community, keep their doctrines secret, frown on intermarriage and permit neither conversion nor apostasy. Under the Jumblat, they caused trouble to the Ottomans until the beginning of the xxth c.

Dualism (A. *thanawiyya*): to Islam with its striving after monotheism, the doctrine that light and darkness are the two equal eternal creative principles means the abolition of the very idea of God. It thus is considered one of the worst forms of heresy and Islam never has known a regular Thanawiyya sect or school. As the characteristic name of a school of thought, the term is limited to three non-Muslims and their adherents: Bardesanes (A. *Ibn Dayṣān*, d. 201), Mani b. Fattik (d. 274) and Mazdak (vith c.).

Dubai (A. *Dubayy*): name of one of the United Arab Emirates and of its capital. Dubai became an independent principality in 1833 and an independent State in 1971.

Dubrovnik (Ragusa): port of Dalmatia in Croatia. The town was first besieged by the Arabs from Apulia in the ixth c. From the end of the xivth c., it entertained excellent relations with the Ottomans. Incorporated by Napoleon into the "Illyrian Provinces" in 1808, Dubrovnik passed to Austria in 1815 and became part of former Yugoslavia in 1918.

Dumat al-Jandal: oasis on the most direct route between Medina and Damascus. The Prophet undertook three expeditions to conquer it. In 1921 'Abd al-'Aziz Ibn Sa'ud added it to his domains.

Durayd b. al-Simma: ancient Arabic poet and one of the most powerful Bedouin opponents of the Prophet; ca. 530-630.

Durranis: name carried by an Afghan tribe, known as Abdali, until it was changed by Ahmad Shah Durrani. They ruled in Afghanistan from 1747-1819.

Dürrizade: patronymic of a family of Ottoman scholars of the xviiith-xixth c., five members of which attained the office of Shaykh al-Islam.

Dürrizade 'Abd Allah Bey: the last Shaykh al-Islam of the Ottoman Empire; 1869-1923. He is known for his legal opinions (A. *fatwā*) condemning the Turkish nationalist movement under Mustafa Kemal Atatürk.

Dust Muhammad: founder of Barakzay rule in Afghanistan; r. 1826-1863. He took the title of amir in 1835 and made the country into a geographically compact unit.

Dynasty (A. *dawla*): the Arabic term is often used as the second element in titles, e.g. Mu'izz al-Dawla "Fortifier of the Dynasty". *Dawla* titles were especially used by the Hamdanids, the Ayyubids, the Ghaznawids, the Ilek-Khans, and bestowed by the Fatimids upon high officials.

E

Edict (T. *fermān*): any order or edict of the Ottoman sultan was called *fermān*, but in a more limited sense the term means a decree of the sultan headed by his cipher (*tughra*). At the Mughal court the formalizing of the discourse of the emperor into a state document could also be elaborate.

Efendi: an Ottoman title of Greek origin, common as a designation of members of the scribal and religious, as opposed to that of the military classes, which was *čelebi*. In the xixth c. it was used, following the personal name, as a form of address or reference for persons possessing a certain standard of literacy and not styled Bey or Pasha. The title was abolished in Turkey in 1934, but in the form *efendim* it remains in common use.

Egypt (A. *Miṣr*): Egypt was conquered by 'Amr b. al-'As in 640 and ruled by the Umayyads from Damascus, from Baghdad by the 'Abbasids. In 969 the country was conquered by the Shi'i Fatimids, who ruled from the new capital Cairo until 1171. Saladin inaugurated the period of the Sunni Ayyubids, which lasted until 1250 and was followed by the Mamluks. Ottoman rule, which began in 1517, was interrupted by the French occupation (1798-1805) and in name re-established by Muhammad 'Ali Pasha, whose dynasty reigned until 1952. The British Protectorate lasted from 1882 until 1936, when Egypt became independent.

Ekrem Bey: Turkish writer, poet and critic; 1847-1914. He was one of the leading personalities in the victory of the modern school of poetry over traditional poetry.

Elbistan: name of a town and a plain in southeastern Anatolia. The Ulu Jami' mosque was built in 1241.

Elegy (A. *marthiya*): a poem to lament the passing of a beloved person and to celebrate his merits. The genre occupies a position of importance in Arabic, Persian, Turkish, Urdu and Swahili literatures.

Elephant (A. *fīl*): the Arabs were barely aquainted with the animal, but the name, derived from Persian *pīl*, became well known to them since it appears in the title and first verse of Sura CV of the Qur'an which alludes to the Ethiopian expedition of Abraha. As a beast of war, it was mainly used by the Ghaznawids. The animal appears with increasing frequency in Mughal painting.

Elisha (A. *Alīsaʿ*): the Biblical prophet is mentioned in the Qur'an under the name Alisaʿ or Alyasaʿ.

Elite and commonalty (A. *al-khāṣṣa wa-'l-ʿāmma*): Islam preaches equalitarianism but the existence of social classes within the community is indisputable.

Elijah (A. *Ilyās*): the Biblical prophet is mentioned in the Qur'an in connection with the worship of Baal. In Muslim legend there is confusion of Ilyas with al-Khadir (al-Khidr) and Idris.

Elixir (A. *al-iksīr*): originally the term for externally applied dry-powder or sprinkling-powder used in medicine. At an early date the name was transferred to the substance with which the alchemists believed it possible to effect the transformation of base metals into precious ones.

Eloquence (A. *balāgha*): next to purity and euphony of language, the Arabic term includes the knowledge of the proper connection and separation of the phrase, clarity, and appropriateness to the occasion. The demand for skill in improvisation originated in the Arabian milieu. When referring to clarity of speech in particular, the Arabs use the terms *bayān* and *faṣāḥa*.

Elvira (A. *Ilbīra*): the Arab governors of the region of Granada first resided in the Roman town of Iliberri. About 747 they founded a new capital called Qastalla or Qastiliya, which soon became known by the name of its predecessor Elvira. The original Elvira in time came to be known as Granada.

Embalming (A. *ḥināṭa*): the practices described in law books and historical works have more to do with some form of preservation of the dead body than with embalming proper.

Embroidery (P. *ṭirāz*): the Persian term denotes a robe adorned with elaborate embroidery, especially one ornamented with embroidered bands with writing upon them, worn by a ruler or person of high rank. It also means the workshop in which such materials are made.

Emigrants (A. *muhājirūn*): term primarily applied to those Meccan Muslims who made the Hijra or emigration from Mecca to Medina either just before the Prophet himself or in the period up to the conquest of Mecca in 630.

In Turkey the term *muhājir* was used for those Muslim populations who became exposed to the imposition of unfavourable Christian administrations, notably in Russia and in the Balkans, and who emigrated to Anatolia and Thrace as the refuge of Islam.

In Muslim India, the term has been used to describe those Muslims who left British India for Afghanistan in the early decades of the xxth c., and those who migrated to Pakistan after the partition of British India in 1947.

Emin Pasha: born in Prussian Silesia as Eduard Schnitzer; 1840-1892. He entered Ottoman service as a medical officer in Albania in 1865 and became an African explorer and governor of the Equatorial province of Egyptian Sudan.

Emir (A. *amīr*): the Arabic word indicates a commander, a governor or a prince.

Emir Sultan: patron saint of Bursa in Turkey; 1368-1429. His mausoleum is a place of pilgrimage.

Empedocles (A. *Anbaduqlīs*): the historical philosopher plays no role in Islamic philosophy, but his figure was appropriated by late Neoplatonic circles. Treatises in which Neoplatonic speculations were put into his mouth were translated into Arabic.

Encampment (A. *dawār*): the Arab Bedouins arranged their tents in a circle or an ellipse, forming a sort of enceinte around the open space in the middle where the animals passed the night.

Encyclopaedia (A. *mawsū'a*): the Arabic term is a neologism which emerged only in the xxth c., but already in the ixth c. the Arabo-Islamic world undertook encyclopaedic activity.

In Persia, the first encyclopaedia was composed in the xith c.

Endowment, Pious (A. *waqf*): a pious endowment is created by a legal process. Its object can be defined as a thing which, while retaining its substance, yields a usufruct and of which the owner has surrendered his power of disposal with the stipulation that the yield is used for permitted good purposes. The law specifies regulations about the founder (A. *wāqif*), the object itself (A. *mawqūf*), the purpose – which must be a work pleasing to God –, the form, the conditions necessary for the completion of a valid endowment, the administration, and the extinction.

Enoch (A. *Idrīs*): the person whom the Qur'an mentions twice under the name Idris is most frequently identified with the seventh patriarch in the book of Genesis, more rarely with Elijah or al-Khidr. Astrologers and alchemists identified him with Hermes (A. *Hirmis*).

Enver Pasha: Young Turk soldier and statesman; 1881-1922. He joined the *Ittihad we Teraqqi Jem'iyyeti* and was the most consistent advocate of a close alliance with the Central Powers. In 1918 he fled to Berlin, and in 1921 he went to Bukhara where he was engaged in efforts to mobilize various Özbeg factions into common resistance against Soviet rule. He lost his life in action near Dushanbe in Tajikistan.

Ephesus (T. *Aya Solūk*): ancient town in Turkey. It was occupied temporarily by the Arabs in 798, and taken by the Turks in 1071. It became part of the Ottoman Empire in 1425.

Epic (A. *ḥamāsa*): the Arabic word, which means "bravery, valour", is in fact the title of a certain number of poetic anthologies which generally include brief extracts chosen for their literary value.

In Persia, the word was used to denote the heroic and martial epic.

In Turkey, and especially in Central Asia among the Turkic-speaking peoples, oral heroic poetry has been very popular.

The earliest epic in Urdu dates from the xviith c.

Eritrea: independent country in Northeast Africa, bordering on the Red Sea. It was thus named by the Italians in 1890 after the Mare Erythraeum (Red Sea) of the Romans. The first contacts with Islam date from the time of the Prophet, when a number of his followers emigrated to Ethiopia during the so-called "First Hijra". From the xvith-xixth c. the Ottoman Turks ruled in the port of Masawwa', but the mainland remained virtually independent. In the xixth c. the Egyptians tried to gain a permanent foothold in the region, but they were decisivily defeated by Negus Yohannes in 1875. The territory was occupied by the Italians in 1889, came under British Military Administration in 1941, and was federated as an autonomous unit to Ethiopia in 1952. After becoming a province within the Ethiopian Empire in 1962, the war of independence started in the same year and was brought to a successful end in 1991.

Erzincan: town in eastern Turkey which has always been an important meeting point for caravan routes between Sivas and Erzurum. After the battle of Malazgird in 1071, it came under the rule of the Saljuqs. In 1243, the town was taken by the Mongols and administered by Il-Khanid governors. After the Ottoman sultan Bayezid I had been defeated by Tamerlane in 1402, Erzincan passed to the Qara Qoyunlu and the Aq Qoyunlu. In 1514 the town was finally incorporated in the Ottoman Empire. Erzincan has frequently suffered destruction by earthquakes.

Erzurum: town in eastern Turkey and capital of the province of the same name. Situated on the caravan route from Anatolia to Iran, Erzurum has always been an important commercial and military centre. Taken by the Arab Muslims in 653, its possession fluctuated between Byzantines and Arabs until the Saljuq conquest in 1201. The native Armenian princes in the area played an important role in all these changes. The town was taken by the Mongols in 1242, and in 1502 by the Safawid Shah Isma'il from the Aq Qoyunlu. After his victory over the Safawids at Chaldiran, the Ottoman Sultan Selim I conquered the town in 1514. The convention of Turkish nationalists met at Erzurum in 1919 to organize resistance to the partition of Anatolia by the Allied Powers.

Es'ad Efendi, Mehmed: Ottoman official historiographer and scholar; 1789-1848. His library is one of the most important private collections in Turkey.

Eschatology: in theological works the subject is dealt with under the general title of "the Return" (A. *al-ma'ād*), to which belong also the concepts of "the Reckoning" (A. *al-ḥisāb*), of "the Resurrection" (A. *al-qiyāma*), of "the Hour" (A. *al-sā'a*) and of "the Day of Judgement" (A. *yawm al-dīn*).

Esztergom: fortress town in Hungary on the right bank of the Danube, taken by the Ottomans in 1543, recaptured by the Hungarians in 1595, and again taken by the Ottomans in 1605. In 1683 it passed definitively into the hands of the Habsburgs.

Eternity (A. *qidam*): essentially, eternity consists in the fact of needing absolutely nothing other than the self in order to exist. This implies the necessity of the being and in this sense the Eternal is the necessary Being. On this point all the Islamic philosophers and theologians are in agreement. There are differences of opinion on the question of the eternity of the attributes of God.

Eternity of the world (A. *abad*): directly following the systems of thought of the Greek thinkers, the philosophers of Islam upheld the view of the eternity of the world, because that which has a beginning must have an end and what has no beginning cannot have an end. According to them, it is impossible to conceive a temporal beginning to the world, a moment of time in which it was created, in such a way that an empty time preceded the creation. The theologians believe in the temporal creation of the world; at the end of the world, there remain Paradise and Hell which are eternal, as is said in the Qur'an in a number of places.

Ethics (A. *akhlāq*): the preaching of the Prophet produced a radical change in moral values. Fear of God and of the Last Judgement, kindness and equity, compassion and mercy, generosity, self-restraint, sincerity and moral fellowship among the Believers became the new bases of conduct.

In the classification of the various branches of philosophy, ethics is considered, together with politics and economics, as a part of practical philosophy.

Euboea (T. *Eğriboz*): Greek island in the Aegean Sea. It was conquered by the Ottomans in 1470. In 1833 it became a part of Greece.

Eunuch (A. *khaṣī*): from the juridical point of view, prohibition in Islam of practising emasculation appears to have been evaded by a sort of tacit consensus.

Euphrates (A. *al-Furāt*; T. *Fîrat*): rising in Turkey, the river crosses Syria and enters Iraq where it unites with the Tigris to form the Shatt al-'Arab. From the confluence of its two principal arms, the Qara-su and the Murad-suyu, the river measures 2,233 km. to Basra.

Eve (A. *Ḥawwā'*): her name does not appear in the Qur'an, which speaks only of the spouse of the First Man.

Evliya Čelebi: famous Turkish traveller; 1611-1684. His long journeys within the Ottoman Empire and in the neighbouring lands are described in his ten-volume work called *Seyahat-name*. He is an imaginative writer with a marked penchant for the wonderful and the adventurous, but, in spite of these reservations, his work offers a wealth of information.

Eye, evil (A. *'ayn*): belief in the evil eye is well established in Islam. According to a tradition, the Prophet considered it as a reality, but orthodoxy makes him condemn this belief.

F

Fadli, Mehmed (Qara Fadli): Turkish poet; d. 1563. He owes his fame to his *mathnawi* "the Rose and the Nightingale". Unlike most of his contemporaries, he does not follow any particular Persian model.

Faith (in God) (A. *īmān*): in the Qur'an the word means sometimes the act and sometimes the content of faith, sometimes both together. The Qur'an continually teaches the necessity of faith and proclaims its demands.

Fakhkh: locality near Mecca, now called al-Shuhada' "the Martyrs", where the 'Alid al-Husayn b. 'Ali Sahib Fakhkh was killed in 786 in battle against the 'Abbasid forces.

Fakhr al-Dawla: member of the Buyid dynasty, who ruled in Hamadan and Isfahan; b. ca. 952, r. 983-997.

Fakhr al-Din I: Druze amir of the Banu Ma'n, ruler of the Shuf in Lebanon; d. 1544.

Fakhr al-Din II b. Qurqumaz: grandson of Fakhr al-Din I; b. ca. 1572, r. 1591-1635. Under his rule the Druze and Maronite districts became united for the first time.

Fakhri: famous silhouette-cutter in Turkey; d. ca. 1618. The art was brought from Persia to Turkey in the xvith c., and to the west in the xviith c.

Fakhr-i Mudabbir: Persian author in India; d. ca. 1236. He is known for his extensive genealogical tables, extending from the Prophet to the Ghurids, and for his treatise on kingship and statecraft and a rather idealised consideration of the art of war.

Fakir (A. *faqīr*): in the Qur'an the word indicates a needy person. In mystic terminology it means a person who lives for God alone. In popular parlance the term is used for a poor man, a pauper or a beggar.

Fallata: although strictly signifying the Fulani, the term is used for Muslim immigrants from the western Sudan, and in particular for those from northern Nigeria.

Falconry (A. *bayzara*): this sport won the favour of caliphs and high Muslim dignitaries after the great Muslim conquests which brought them into contact with the Persians and the Byzantines. It was also known to the Ottomans, and became an inspiration for poets.

Famagusta (A. *Maghōsha*; T. *Magusa*): port of Cyprus. It was raided by the Muslims in the viith c. The town passed to Guy de Lusignan in 1192, to the Genoese in 1383 and to the Venetians in 1489. The Ottomans conquered it in 1572.

Faqir of Ipi: name of a Pathan mollah and agitator along the Northwestern Frontier of the Indo-Pakistan subcontinent; d. 1960.

al-Farabi, Abu Ibrahim: lexicographer; d. 961. He owes his fame to a dictionary, whose arrangement was adopted by his nephew Abu Nasr al-Jawhari.

al-Farabi, Abu Nasr: the great Muslim philosopher became known in the West under the names Alfarabius and Avennasar.

Fara'idiyya: Muslim sect in Bengal established at the beginning of the xixth c. by Hajji Shari'at Allah.

Farangi Mahall: family of prominent India Hanafi theologians and mystics flourishing from the xviiith c. to the present day.

al-Farazdaq ("the lump of dough"), properly Tammam b. Ghalib: famous Arab satirist and panegyrist; after 640-ca. 728. He nursed an implacable hostility for Jarir b. 'Atiyya.

Farghana (Fergana): valley on the middle Iaxartes, in Uzbekistan. It was reached by Qutayba b. Muslim in 712. Ruled subsequently by the Samanids, the Ilek-Khans, the Mongols, the Timurids, and the Shaybanids, the valley was the centre of the khanate of Khoqand between 1709-1876. In 1876 the khanate was annexed by the Russians.

al-Farghani, Abu 'l-'Abbas Ahmad: astronomer from Farghana, known in the West as Alfraganus.

Farhad and Shirin: Shirin was the favourite Christian wife of the Sasanian king of Iran Khusraw (II) Parwiz. The love of the king and Shirin, as well as the latter's love for the royal architect Farhad, became the subject of a series of romances in verse in Turkish and Kurdish, but above all for the Persian poets Nizami and Amir Khusraw Dihlawi.

Farid al-Din Mas'ud "Ganj-i-Shakar": one of the most distinguished of the Indian Muslim mystics; 1175-1265. He was a member of the Čishtiyya order, which he transformed into a powerful movement.

Farighunids: dynasty which ruled Juzjan in eastern Khurasan, now in northwest Afghanistan, during the xth c.

al-Farisi: outstanding Arab grammarian; d. 987.

Farouk (A. *Fārūq*): king of Egypt; b. 1920, r. 1936-1952, d. 1965. The last ruler of the Muhammad ʿAli dynasty, he was deposed by the Free Officers, led by Muhammad Neguib.

Farrukhi-Sistani, Abu ʾl-Hasan: celebrated Persian poet; d. 1037. He was attached to the court of Mahmud b. Sebüktigin of Ghazna, singing his poems to his own accompaniment on the lute. The collected edition of his poems contains more than 9,500 lines of verse.

Farrukh-Siyar: Mughal emperor; 1683, r. 1713-1719. He broke with emperor Awrangzib's policies in a number of spheres and granted the English East India Company the right to carry on trade free of duties in several districts and ports.

Fars: province in southwestern Iran. The first attempt of the Muslim Arabs to conquer Fars was made under the caliphate of ʿUmar b. al-Khattab, and the subjugation was completed in 648. Later it was ruled by the Saffarids, the Buyids, the Saljuqs, the Salghurids and the Muzaffarids. In 1503 the Safawid Shah Ismaʿil I established his authority in Fars.

Faruqids: dynasty of sultans who established and ruled the semi-independent Muslim principality of Khandesh in the Northern Deccan, in India, from 1370-1601. It was extinguished by the Mughal Emperor Akbar.

Farwan: district of Afghanistan, conquered by the Arabs ca. 792. The Khwarazm-Shah Jalal al-Din defeated the Mongols there in 1221.

Fasaʾi, Hajji Mirza Hasan: Persian scholar; 1821-after 1895. He was the author of a historical-geographical work on his native province of Fars.

Fasanjus, Banu: a family which hereditarily occupied high administrative offices under the Buyids.

al-Fashir: capital of Dar Fur in the Sudan. The Furawi sultanate was established there in 1791 and lasted until the annexation of Dar Fur to the Egyptian Sudan in 1874. The sultanate was revived in 1898 but finally annexed to the Anglo-Egyptian Sudan in 1916.

Fashoda: royal village of the Shilluk, lying near the west bank of the White Nile in the Sudan. It became notorious through the so-called Fashoda Incident between Great Britain and France in 1898.

al-Fasi ("the one from Fez"): name of origin of the members of a prominent family of Moroccan scholars who have contributed most actively to religious, intellectual and literary life from the xviith-xixth c.

al-Fasi, Taqi al-Din: outstanding historian of the city of Mecca; 1373-1429. The subject had virtually been neglected since the ixth c.

Fasting (A. *ṣawm*): the first regulations concerning the manner of the Muslim fasting are given in the Qurʾan. The Muslim law books describe in great detail the essentials of the fast, the relaxations permitted and the circumstances under which voluntary fasting is meritorious. Fasting in the month of Ramadan is the fourth pillar of Islam.

al-Fath b. Khaqan: member of the Turkish ruling family at Farghana; ca.

817-861. He was the chief of the Turkish contingent of the guard of the ʿAbbasid Caliph al-Muʿtasim.

Fath ʿAli Shah: ruler of the Qajar dynasty; b. 1771, r. 1797-1834. Much of his long reign was spent in military expeditions against internal rebels, against Russia, the Ottoman sultan, and against Afghanistan.

Fath-name: term used by the Ottomans and other dynasties to indicate an official announcement of a victory.

Fathpur-Sikri: city near Agra, in India, built by the Mughal emperor Akbar in 1570. He resided there until 1586, when he abandoned it. Shortly after his death in 1605, the city began to fall into ruin. Many of the buildings, however, still remain in an excellent state of preservation.

Fatiha: "the sura which opens the Scripture of Revelation", the designation of the first sura of the Qurʾan. It is an indispensable component of the prayer-ritual and is often said at other occasions, too.

Fatima: daughter of the Prophet and Khadija, wife of ʿAli and mother of al-Hasan and al-Husayn. She became the object of great veneration by all Muslims. It is customary to add to her name the honorific title "the Shining One".

Fatimids: Shiʿi dynasty, connected with the Ismaʿilis, which traced their origin to ʿAli and Fatima. They reigned in North Africa from 909-973 and then in Egypt until 1171. Syria was subdued, but was never a solidly Fatimid possession. Relations with North Africa were strained, and Sicily became virtually independent. With Byzantium, the Fatimids in general maintained good relations. In Baghdad, the ʿAbbasid caliph and the *de facto* rulers, the Ayyubids, contested the authenticity of the ʿAlid genealogy of the Fatimids, who sent missionaries as far as Sind. The Sunni Saljuqs had no sympathy for them either. In Yemen, however, they found fervent supporters in the Sunni Sulayhids. The Fatimids were less interested in the struggle against the Crusaders than were the Turkish amirs of Syria. In 1171, Saladin put an end to the Fatimid caliphate and re-established Sunnism and ʿAbbasid sovereignty in Egypt.

Under the Fatimids, the viziers occupied a place of gradually increasing importance while there was a progressive decline of the caliphs from power to impotence, causing disturbances, rebellions and revolutions. Sunni practices were in general forbidden, but there were some periods of tolerance and some of strictness. On the other hand, Fatimid Egypt in general enjoyed great prosperity, industry and trade flourished and there was an intense intellectual, literary and artistic activity.

The following is a list of the Fatimid caliphs:

909	al-Mahdi ʿUbayd Allah
934	al-Qaʾim
946	al-Mansur
953	al-Muʿizz
975	al-Hakim

1021 al-Zahir
1036 al-Mustansir
1094 al-Mustaʿli
1101 al-Amir
1130 interregnum; rule by al-Hafiz as Regent but not yet as Caliph
1131 al-Hafiz
1149 al-Zafir
1154 al-Faʾiz
1160-71 al-ʿAdid
Ayyubid conquest

Fatimid Art: during the North African period, the first Fatimid al-Mahdi ʿUbayd Allah founded al-Mahdiyya, "the city of the Mahdi", in modern Tunisia. Apart from the ruins of the fortifications, a mosque and traces of the palace of the second caliph al-Qaʾim are preserved.

At the gates of Qayrawan there is the palace of Sabra Mansuriyya, dating from the time of the third caliph al-Mansur. Cairo shows the mosques of the caliph al-Hakim bi-Amr Allah, of vizier Talaʾiʿ b. Ruzzik, and many mausoleums. The all-powerful vizier Badr al-Jamali gave Cairo a new city wall and the well-known Bab Zuwayla, Bab al-Nasr and Bab al-Futuh. The artistic creations of the Fatimid epoch above all in Egypt but sometimes also in Spain are the glory of European museums and church treasures.

Fattahi: Persian poet of the Timurid period; d. 1448. His most famous work is a *mathnawi* of about 5,000 distichs, entitled "the Rule of Lovers" or "Beauty and Heart".

Fatwa: the Arabic term for an opinion on a point of law, given by a *muftī* or legal advisor. Requirements for this profession are: being a Muslim, integrity, legal knowledge and the ability to reach, by personal reasoning, the solution of a problem.

Faydabad (Fyzabad): town in the district of the same name near Ayodhya in Uttar Pradesh, India, known for its monuments.

Faysal b. ʿAbd al-ʿAziz Al Saʿud: king of Saudi Arabia; b. ca. 1906, r. 1964-1975. In 1958 his elder brother Saʿud b. ʿAbd al-ʿAziz surrendered power to Faysal while remaining king nominally, but in 1964 the latter was proclaimed as such. He opposed Israel and communism, headed the conservative Muslim bloc, and maintained friendship with the United States. He was shot down during an assembly (A. *majlis*).

Faysal I b. Sharif (later king) Husayn b. ʿAli: king of Syria and of Iraq; b. 1883, r. in Syria 1918-1920, then in Iraq 1921-1933. In 1912 he was elected to the Turkish parliament but, resentful of Turkish severity against Arab dissidents in Syria, he took command of the Mecca-based "Arab Revolt". His efforts to consolidate an Arab monarchy in Syria failed in the face of French opposition. British favour and Iraqi election then secured him a throne in Iraq. He was able to hold a balance between British requirements and local patriotism.

Faysal II b. Ghazi b. Faysal I: king of Iraq; b. 1935, r. 1953-1958. He ruled effectively, accepting the guidance of Nuri al-Saʿid, his Prime Minister, but was killed during the revolution of 1958.

al-Fayyum: geographical region in the Libyan desert of Middle Egypt, east of the Nile valley. After the Arab conquest of Egypt, al-Fayyum remained an important centre of Coptic Christianity.

Fazughli: region of the upper Blue Nile in the Republic of the Sudan, near to the Ethiopian border, known for its alluvial gold.

Fazzan (Fezzan): an entirely desert region in the Republic of Libya. Though conquered by ʿUqba b. Nafiʿ in 666, Fazzan long remained outside the sphere of Arab expansion. In 1190 the dynasty of the Banu Khattab fell before the attacks of Qaraqush al-Ghuzzi, a Turcoman adventurer from Armenia. From the xiiith-xvith c. it passed under the domination of the kings of Kanem. After that it was ruled by the dynasty of the Awlad Muhammad, who had their capital in Murzuq, a busy caravan centre. In the xvith c. the Turks did not succeed in imposing an effective rule, nor did the Qaramanli dynasty, which governed Tripolitania from 1710 until 1835. The Turks returned to Tripolitania in 1835 and ruled Fazzan until 1911, considering it a convenient place of exile for the Young Turks. The Italians occupied Fazzan for a few months in 1914, and again from 1929 until 1943, when it came under French authority. In 1951 it became an autonomous province of the United Kingdom of Libya.

Fejr-i Ati ("the coming dawn"): Turkish literary group, active after the Young Turk Revolution of 1908.

Fehim Pasha: chief of the secret police under the Ottoman sultan Abdülhamid II; 1873(?)-1908.

Fener: name of a quarter of Istanbul. The church of St. George is still the seat of the Greek patriarch.

Fennec (A./P. *fanak*): in the Muslim west, the word is commonly applied to the fennec-fox, in the eastern countries to the so-called Corsac (T. *qūrsāq*) fox. But the Arab writers, naturalists, encyclopaedists and poets undoubtedly mean the mink. Its pelt was greatly esteemed in the luxury fur-trade and imported to the Muslim lands, at great expense, from central Europe and Asia.

Ferhad Pasha: Ottoman Grand Vizier of Albanian origin; d. 1595. He was successful in the war against Persia.

Feridun Beg: private secretary of the Ottoman Grand Vizier Mehmed Pasha Soqollu; d. 1583. As the head of the chancery he compiled a collection of state-papers.

Festival (A. *ʿīd*): the Muslim year has two canonical festivals, the "sacrificial festival" (A. *ʿīd al-aḍḥā*), also called the "major festival" (A. *ʿīd al-kabīr*) – known in Turkey as *büyük bayram* or *kurban bayrami*, and the "festival of breaking the fast" (A. *ʿīd al-fiṭr*), also called the "minor festival" (A. *al-ʿīd al-ṣaghīr*) – known in Turkey as *kuçük bayram* or *sheker bayrami*. The first is celebrated on 10 Dhu 'l-Hijja, the days on which the pilgrims sacrifice in the valley of Mina, the second on 1st Shawwal and the following days.

Fez (A. *Fās*): town of Northern Morocco, said to have been founded in 789 on the site of the old Roman town of Volubilis, by Idris b. ʿAbd Allah, father of Idris I, the founder of the Idrisid dynasty. Idris I is said to have founded the twin town on the left bank of the wadi, which was given the name al-ʿAliya. Fez was conquered by the Almoravid Yusuf b. Tashufin ca. 1070. In 1145 it was taken by the Almohad ʿAbd al-Muʾmin, and in the xiiith c. it came under the authority of the Marinids, who made it into their capital. In 1559 the Saʿdi Sharifs, masters of Marrakesh, conquered the town and held it until 1666 when the Filali Sharif al-Rashid took possession of it. Under his successor Ismaʿil, Meknès became the new capital, but Fez regained its position towards the end of the xviiith c. In 1912 the town was taken by the French. At present, Fez ranks as the third city of Morocco after Casablanca and Marrakesh. It rightly remains famous for its monuments, among which should be mentioned the Qarawiyyin mosque, begun in 857 as the mosque of Fatima.

Fez (A. *fās*): name for the traditional Turkish headgear, which took its name from Fez in Morocco. It is a brimless red felt cap shaped as a truncated cone, with a flat crown to which a tassel is often attached. It was abolished by Mustafa Kemal Atatürk in 1925. It is a synonym for the red tarboosh.

Fidaʾiyyan-i Islam: small politico-religious terrorist group based in Teheran, active between 1943-1955. They tried to enforce Muslim law and attacked politicians with foreign connections.

Fijar, Harb al ("the sacrilegious war"): name of a war waged towards the end of the vith c. between a number of important Arabian tribes for the control of the trade routes in the Najd in Arabia. It is admitted that the Prophet was present at the war, but there is much controversy about the particulars.

Fighani (Baba): pseudonym of a celebrated Persian poet from Shiraz; d. 1519. His patronymic, like his first name, is unknown.

Fighter for the faith (A. *mujāhid*): the Arabic word is connected with "Holy War" (A. *jihād*). In the Indian subcontinent, the term has been associated with Islamic revivalist movements from the late xviiith c. onwards in response to threats to the waning power of the Mughals in Delhi and other Muslim sultanates from the increased pressures of the Marathas, the Sikhs and the British. The duty to fight for the faith was stressed by Shah Wali Allah Dihlawi.

In the contemporary Arab world many Muslims have come increasingly to regard all rulers who do not exercise power according to Islamic law as unbelievers (A. *kāfirūn*). Thus, when born as Muslims, they are considered as apostates from Islam (A. *murtaddūn*) who, according to Islamic law, merit the death penalty. A member of the group that assassinated President Anwar al-

Sadat in 1981 wrote a memorandum, called *al-Farida al-Ghariba*, which is the best primary source for modern Islamic activism and extremism. The most often quoted authority is the Hanbalite jurist Ibn Taymiyya.

Fikri, 'Abd Allah Pasha: Egyptian statesman, poet and prose-writer; 1834-1890. He is regarded as one of the authors who have helped to give a simpler character to Arabic literary style.

Filali: name of the dynasty of Sharifs (*Shorfa'*) from Tafilalt, reigning in Morocco from 1659 till the present day.

Findiriski: Persian scholar and philosopher; d. 1640. He was respected by both the Safawid Shah 'Abbas and the Mughal court in India.

Fine (A. *jurm*): fines are unknown to Muslim criminal law, but some jurists admitted monetary penalties in certain cases. In Ottoman law they were prescribed for a large number of offences.

Firdawsi (Ferdowsi): one of the greatest Persian poets, author of the epic *Book of Kings*; 940-1020. He was not on good terms with the monarch of his time, the Ghaznawid sultan Mahmud b. Sebüktegin, not only because he was a Shi'i, Mahmud being a Sunni, but also because the sultan showed lack of interest in his work and because the poet was dissatisfied with the inadequacy of the reward. The *Book of Kings*, amounting in several manuscripts to some 60,000 verses, speaks of the beneficiary activities of the first kings of Iran on behalf of humanity and of their struggle against the demons which infest the world. The assassination of the son and successor of one of these mythical kings by two brothers started an endless cycle of wars of revenge between the Iranians and the nomadic Turanians of Central Asia. The exploits of the heroes, among whom the famous Rustam, are interwoven with love-stories, by which Firdawsi became the founder of the romantic narrative poem which was to have such a brilliant future in Persia. The last part of the poem is more historical and recounts the reigns of the Sasanian kings. Firdawsi has had a profound and lasting influence on Persian literature and indeed on the spirit of the people of Iran.

Firdewsi (Rumi/Uzun): Turkish poet and polymath; b. 1453, d. at an unkown date. He is the author of *The Book of Solomon*.

Fire-arms: the Arabic term for gunpowder (*bārūd*) appears for the first time in the xiiith c. In the Maghrib it was the name given to the "snow of China" or saltpetre, a substance with medicinal properties. In the Muslim West fire-arms seem to have been used for the first time at the siege of Huescar in Spain in 1324.

The Mamluks employed fire-arms for the first time about the 1460s.

The Ottomans began to use them during the reign of Sultan Mehemmed I.

The Persians were familiar with the use of fire-arms long before the time in which they are said to have been introduced by the brothers Sherley during the reign of the Safawid Shah 'Abbas I.

In India, fire-arms may have been introduced in the xivth c.

Firishta (Muhammad Qasim Hindu Shah): Indo-Muslim historian and writer on Indian medicine; ca. 1570-ca. 1625. He served the Ahmadnagar and Bijapur sultanates and wrote the history of the Muslim sultanates of the Deccan.

Firman (P. *farmān*/T. *fermān*): the basic meanings of the Persian term are both command and edict or document. The Turkish term denotes any order or edict of the Ottoman sultan. In a more limited sense it means a decree of the sultan headed by his cipher (*ṭughrā*).

Firuz Shah III Tughluq: Delhi sultan of the Tughluqid dynasty; b. 1307, r. 1351-1388. He founded the cities of Firuzabad (Delhi) and Jawnpur.

Firuzabad (Piruzabad, "the town of victory"): town to the southeast of Shiraz in Iran, originally known as Gur or Čur.

al-Firuzabadi: lexicographer, who lived in Jerusalem, Mecca and in Yemen; 1329-1415. He compiled an extensive dictionary of Arabic, known as *The Ocean*.

Firuzkuh (Ferozkoh): capital of the Ghurids to the east of Harat in Afghanistan, identified with the present Jam. It also is the name for a castle in Tabaristan, in Iran, which was a stronghold of the Khwarazm-Shahs. Taken by the Mongols in 1227, it came into the possession of the Isma'ilis of Alamut, but was conquered again by the Mongols under the Il-Khan Hülegü in 1256.

Firuzpur (Ferozpur): district and town in the Punjab. The town was reputedly founded in the time of Firuz Shah III Tughluq. The Muslim population of the city, and of the district, emigrated to Pakistan in 1947.

Fitna: the Arabic word, which means "trial, test", appears frequently in the Qur'an with the meaning of external test of faith. It generally refers to the series of events which included the murder of caliph 'Uthman, the designation of 'Ali as his successor, the battle of Siffin, the development of the Shi'a and of the Kharijite movement, and the seizing of power by the Umayyad Mu'awiya I. This first major struggle within the Muslim community is often called the first, or the great, trial.

Fitrat (Fitra): inspirer and theorist of the reform movement in Turkestan; xxth c. In his works he studied the causes of the spiritual and temporal decay of the Muslim world, as seen in the example of Bukhara.

Flag (A. *'alam*): the Prophet is known to have used both a black and a white flag. The Umayyads adopted white, the 'Abbasids black, and the Shi'is green.

Flower poetry (A. *nawriyya*): as a genre, the description of flowers is closely connected with the descriptions of gardens or of the spring. It was especially appreciated in al-Andalus.

Food (A. *ghidhā'*): the Qur'an insists on the beneficial nature of food in general. Of the many prohibitions existing before Islam, only a limited number were retained.

Fornication/Adultery (A. *zinā'*): Qur'an, Tradition and Muslim law forbid any sexual intercourse between persons who are not in a state of legal matrimony or concubinage.

Frankincense (A. *lubān*): it formed the wealth of the old South-Arabian states of the Minaeans and Sabaeans. It was used as a medicine and is until now still of great importance in popular medicine and magic.

Franks (A. *Ifranj/Firanj*): this name was originally used for the inhabitants of the empire of Charlemagne, and later extended to Europeans in general. The first definite report of a Frankish embassy to Baghdad dates from 906. During the xith c., the advance of Christendom against Islam brought Franks and Muslims in close and regular contact, but it is remarkable that the Muslims showed so little interest in the internal affairs of the Crusading states. Muslim knowledge of Europe came not from the Levant but from Spain, Sicily and North Africa. Ottoman interest in Christian Europe, on the other hand, was noticeably greater than among earlier Muslim peoples. Between the xvith-xixth c. the word "Frank" did not include the Orthodox, but was limited to Catholics and Protestants.

Fraxinetum (La-Garde-Freinet): village in the Mt. des Maures (Var, France), from 891-972 occupied by Muslim pirates.

Freemasonry (A. *Farmāsūniyya*): freemasonry first penetrated the Ottoman Empire via lodges established by Europeans in the xviiith c. Membership figures were generally modest, but the importance of freemasonry was enhanced by such important persons as Jamal al-Din al-Afghani and Muhammad 'Abduh. Though Tal'at Pasha was an active freemason, there is no conclusive evidence that freemasonry as such played a role in the preparation and implementation of the Young Turk Revolution. It was proscribed during sultan Abdülhamid II's reign, is discredited in Republican Turkey, prohibited in Syria and Egypt and severely limited in several other Arab states.

Friday (A. *yawm al-jum'a* "the day when people come together"): the weekly day of communal worship in Islam. Attendance at the Friday service is a duty incumbent on all male, adult, free, resident Muslims; if feasible, it should be held in the Great Mosque (A. *jāmi'*) only, and a minimum attendance of at least a sizeable number is required.

Frunze (formerly Pishpek): capital of Kirgizistan, founded in 1878 near the fortress of Pishpek which had been built by the khan of Khoqand. It was captured by the Russians in 1860.

Fu'ad I of Egypt: b. 1868, sultan 1917-1922, king 1922-1936. Under his reign the nationalist movement launched the open struggle against the British occupation. Fu'ad founded schools, encouraged the new university at Gizeh and the reform of al-Azhar, and promoted numerous cultural institutions.

Fu'ad Pasha, Kečeji-zade: five times Ottoman Foreign Minister and twice Grand Vizier; 1815-1869. He was a convinced westernizer, and tried to preserve the Ottoman empire through diplomacy and reform.

Fujairah (A. *al-Fujayra*): constituent emirate of the United Arab Emirates since 1971. The port of Khawr al-Fakkan, occupied by the al-Qawasim as early as 1775 and now part of the Sharjah emirate, divides Fujairah into two portions, Fujairah town lying in the southern part. Fujairah became virtually independent in 1902 and was recognized as such by Great Britain in 1952.

Fuduli (Fuzuli): one of the most illustrious authors of classical Turkish literature; 1480 (?)-1556. He was a Shi'i, and never left his native Iraq. He also wrote in Arabic and Persian. In his literary Azeri, he treats the themes of love, suffering, the impermanence of this world, the emptiness of worldly favours and riches, and the theme of death.

Fulani (Fulbe; Fr. *Peuls*): Muslim pastoral people, living between Lake Chad and the Atlantic Ocean. Their origin has been the subject of hot dispute. They are first mentioned in the xvth c. by al-Maqrizi and have played an important role in the establishment of various African kingdoms.

Funeral (A. *janāza/jināza*): traditionally, the body, having been washed several times except that of martyrs who have fallen in battle, was carried to the grave on an open bier with a cloth thrown over it, and with an extra covering for a woman. Burial, which took place on the day of death or the following day, was usually in a cemetery and prayers were said by the grave, which was a pit with a narrower trench at the bottom. Coffins were not used at first but were common by the xiith c.

Funj: the Funj appear in the early xvith c. as a nomadic cattle-herding people in the Nilotic Sudan. They gradually extended their range down the Blue Nile. The Muslim dynasty of the Funj kings reigned from 1533-1762 and their capital Sinnar is said to have been founded in 1504.

Fuqaha' (s. *faqīh*): the Arabic term came to indicate a specialist in religious law and its branches (A. *fiqh*).

Fuqaha' al-Madina al-Sab'a: the seven jurists of Medina, to whom tradition attributes a significant role in the formation of Muslim law. They all died between 709 and 724.

Furqan: a soteriological expression used in the Qur'an. From the many translations given in the West: "discrimination", "criterion", "separation", "deliverance", "salvation", it is clear that for Western scholars the interpretation remains a problem.

al-Fustat (Old Cairo): the first town to be founded in Egypt by the Muslim conquerors. It grew from the permanent encampment established by 'Amr b. al-'As in 643 on the east bank of the Nile, alongside the Greco-Coptic township of Babylon (A. *Bābalyūn*). The Great Mosque, called Jami' 'Amr or al-Jami' al-'Atiq, attained its present dimensions in 827. The mosque of Ahmad b. Tūlūn was completed in 879. In 969 the general of the Fatimids Jawhar al-Siqilli entered al-Fustat and began to build a new capital, Cairo.

Futa (Fouta) **Jallon**: mountainous region of west central Guinea. In 1694 the Fulani formed an empire which was to last for two centuries, one of its characteristic political features being a permanent state of Holy War. In 1881 it was placed under French protection.

G

Gabès (A. *Qābis*): town in Tunisia on the gulf of the same name (the Little Syrte of Antiquity). The town was taken by the Muslims between 654 and 670. It was not spared the violent Kharijite storm which racked the whole of Ifriqiya from 740-772. In the xth c. it passed into the hands of the Fatimids, then into those of the Zirids of Ifriqiya. In the xith c. Gabès came to terms with the Banu Hilal, but suffered from the expansionist policy of the Normans of Sicily. It was finally acquired by the Almohads in 1205. Ruled by the Banu Makki from 1282 until 1394, the town, along with the whole of Tunisia, came under Turkish domination in 1574 and under French Protectorate in 1881.

Gabon: republic on the west coast of Africa. Islam was introduced in the xixth c. by Senegalese soldiers who were stationed with the garrison of Fort d'Aumale, but the number of Muslims have remained very limited.

Gabriel (A. *Jabrā'īl/Jibrīl*): the archangel Gabriel was the bearer of the revelations to the Prophet.

Gafsa (A. *Qafsa*): town in Tunisia, taken by 'Uqba b. Nafi' in 667. After being under the authority of the Fatimids and then the Zirids, Gafsa, for more than a century (1053-1159), became the capital of an independent little state including present-day Jerid. In 1159 the town was taken by the Almohad 'Abd al-Mu'min, conquered by the Banu Ghaniya of Mallorca but in 1187 re-taken by the Almohad al-Mansur. During the Hafsid period (1228-1574), life was no more tranquil. In 1556 the town was taken by the governor of Tripoli, but Turkish occupation failed to restore prosperity. In 1881 it came under French Protectorate.

Gagauz: small Orthodox Christian Turkic tribe in Bessarabia, in south Ukraine, in the district of Rostov and in some areas of Central Asia.

Gakkhar: war-like Muslim tribe inhabiting mostly the Hazara district in Pakistan and parts of the district of Rawalpindi.

Galata (T. *Beyoğlu*): district of Istanbul between the northern shore of the Golden Horn and the Bosphorus. Before the conquest of Constantinople in 1453, it was the walled Genoese colony known as Pera, afterwards the area of largely Frankish and Greek settlements known to the Ottomans as Beyoğlu, "the bey's son", i.e. Luigi Gritti, son of a doge of Venice. The concession granted to the Genoese in 1267 developed into a self-governing district under the authority of a *podestà* sent out annually from Genoa. Its major landmark was, and is, the Torre di Christo, i.e. the Galata Külesi. From the middle of the xivth c., the Genoese acted as political allies of the Ottomans against

Venice and Byzantium, but on the day following the fall of Constantinople, Galata surrendered also.

Galatasaray: name of a palace school at Galata, founded ca. 1490, and, later, of a modern lycée.

Galen (A. *Jālīnūs*): the Arabs came to possess translations of every work of Galen (d. about 199), still read in Greek centres of learning during the viith-ixth c. They thus knew a number of Galen's works which disappeared in the late Byzantine period. These works became an integral part of Arab medical learning. The translations into Arabic, among others by Hunayn b. Ishaq, have greatly influenced medieval and renaissance medicine in Europe.

Galicia (A. *Jillīqiyya*): the northwest region of the Iberian peninsula. Arab rule lasted for only a short time.

Gallipoli (T. *Gelibolu*): town on the European coast of Turkey and at the Marmara end of the Dardanelles. Its occupation in 1352 made it possible for the Ottomans to install themselves in Europe. Taken by the Crusaders in 1366, it was handed over to the Byzantines in 1367, but returned to the Ottomans in 1376. It then became the principal base for the Ottoman fleet. In the xvth c. the Venetians, notwithstanding great efforts, were not able to conquer the fortified town. Before the capture of Constantinople in 1453, Gallipoli was one of the principal customs-houses of the Ottoman Empire. It was also the principal control-point for traffic between Rumeli and Anatolia, and a centre for the slave-trade. During the Gallipoli Campaign of World War I, it was the scene of determined Turkish resistance to the Allied forces.

Gambia, The: country in West Africa. Islam was introduced from the xith c. onwards, but conversion remained superficial until the so-called "marabout" wars in the xixth c. At least four-fifths of the indigenous population are Muslims of the Maliki school of law, and most of them are attached to the Qadiriyya or Tijaniyya orders.

Gambling (A. *al-maysir*; *qimār*): according to Muslim law, gambling is strictly forbidden. Backgammon, played with six-sided dice, chess and draughts, horse racing, archery, pigeon flying, footracing, swimming and wrestling as well as fighting games of animals, when played for stakes, fall into the category of gambling. The jurists considered legal the establishment of stakes by a non-participant, or by one of the participants. Stakes by both or all participants were illegal. The Qur'an strictly forbids casting lots by arrows (A. *al-maysir*).

Gao: town in the Republic of Mali, situated on the left bank of the Niger. Probably referred to by Abu 'Abd Allah al-Khwarazmi before 833 and much frequented by traders from the Maghrib, its king was converted to Islam at the end of the ixth c. The town was visited by Ibn Battuta in 1352. In the xvith c. it was the centre of the Gao empire. Leo Africanus describes it as a very large city without walls.

Garden (A./P./T. *bustān*): a Persian word, used in Persian and Turkish in the sense of "kitchen-garden", in Arabic in the sense of "garden" in general. Horticulture flourished in Persia long before the birth of Islam, and was continued in Baghdad, in Egypt, Ifriqiya, Morocco, and by the Mughals in India.

Gardiz: town of Afghanistan, said to be founded (or re-founded) by the Kharijite leader Hamza b. ʿAbd Allah in about 797. In the xth c. it fell into the hands of the Ghaznawids.

Gardizi, Abu Saʿid: Persian historian; xith c. He wrote histories of the pre-Islamic kings of Persia, of the Prophet and the caliphs up to the year 1032, and a detailed history of Khurasan from the Arab conquest to 1041.

Gaspirali (Gasprinski), **Ismaʿil**: prominent ideological writer of the Russian Turks; 1851-1914. He advocated Pan-Turkism, preaching unity in language, thought and action.

Gawilgarh: fortress in Berar, Central India. A former stronghold of the Gawali chiefs, its fortifications were probably strengthened by the Bahmanid Ahmad I Wali (r. 1422-1436) in 1425. Much of the walling still remains.

Gawur Daghlari ("the Mountains of the Unbelievers"): name given by the Turks to the mountainous massif to the north of Erzurum, and to that of the Amanus, the south-western extremity of the eastern Taurus.

Gaykhatu: ruler of the Mongol Il-Khanid dynasty; r. 1291-1295. Though adopting a Buddhist (Tibetan) name, he was in no way hostile to the Muslims.

Gaza (A. *Ghazza*): the largest city of the Gaza Strip, in southwest Palestine. From ancient times it was an agricultural and caravan centre, lying on the route leading from Palestine to Syria and at the junction of the caravan-routes coming from Arabia. Merchants from Mecca visited it regularly, and the Prophet's great-grandfather Hashim b. ʿAbd Manaf is said to have died there. In early Islam, the town was conquered by ʿAmr b. al-ʿAs. Al-Shafiʿi was born there in 767. In the xth c. it was in the hands of the Fatimids and in the xiith c. occupied by the Crusaders. After the fall of Jerusalem in 1187, it was surrendered to Saladin by the Grand Master of the Templars, recaptured by Richard the Lion-Heart, but restored to the Muslims in 1229. Witnessing two serious defeats of the Crusaders in 1239 and 1244, the town was occupied by the Mongol armies of Hülegü, marking the furthest limit of their advance. In the Mamluk period, the town was very prosperous. Occupied by the Ottomans in 1516, the town of Gaza enjoyed a period of particular prosperity at the end of the xviith c. under Husayn Pasha who put a stop to the periodic raids of the Bedouins. Since June 1967, the city has been under Israeli military administration.

Gazelle (A. *ghazāl*): the meat of the gazelle is permitted by the Qurʾan. "The daughter of the sand" was an important source of inspiration for Arabic literature.

Gaziantep (A. *ʿAyntāb*): town in southeastern Turkey, strategically situated on the junction of the roads running from Marʿash to Aleppo and from

Diyarbakr to Adana. In 1151 Gaziantep was taken by the Great Saljuq Mas'ud b. Muhammad and in 1153 by the Zangid Nur al-Din Mahmud. Later it was an advance post for the Ayyubids and the Mamluks against the Saljuqs and the Armenians. Taken in 1400 by Tamerlane and then by Qara Yusuf of the Qara Qoyunlu (r. 1389-1420), it passed to the Turkoman dynasty of the Dhu 'l-Qadr, who surrendered it to the Ottomans.

Geber (A. *Jābir b. Aflaḥ*): astronomer of Seville; xiith c. His astronomic work, which sharply criticizes certain views held by Ptolemy and contains a chapter on trigonometry, was translated into Latin by Gerard of Cremona.

Gedi/Gede: late medieval Arab-African town, built on a coral ridge south of Malindi, Kenya. Excavations have produced large quantities of Chinese porcelain and Islamic faïence.

Genghis Khan: founder of the Mongol world-empire; 1167-1227. His original name Temüjin was changed into that of Genghis Khan or "Universal Ruler" when he was acclaimed *khan* by the Mongol princes. In 1215 he captured and sacked Peking. The conquest of East Turkestan (Sinkiang) by the Mongol general Jebe in 1218 gave the Mongols a common frontier with the Khwarazm-Shah 'Ala' al-Din Muhammad (r. 1200-1220). Hostilities broke out in 1219 and Utrar surrendered. Bukhara and Samarqand were conquered in 1220, Balkh in 1221. Genghis Khan's generals Jebe and Sübetey crossed the Caucasus and defeated the Russians and the Qipčaq (Kipchak) Turks in the Crimea, while his sons Chagatay and Ögedey razed Gurgan to the ground. Genghis Khan's youngest son Toluy laid waste to Khurasan and captured Harat, Marw al-Shahijan and Nishapur. 'Ala' al-Din's successor Jalal al-Din Mingburnu was defeated on the Indus in 1221.

Genie (A. *jinn*: spirit, sprite): the Qur'an teaches that the genies were created of smokeless flame, while mankind and the angels, the other two classes of intelligent beings, were created of clay and light. They are capable of salvation. They play an important role in Arabic, Turkish, Indian and Indonesian folklore. The Arabic term *zār*, a loanword from the Amharic language of Ethiopia, indicates spirits who may temporarily become incarnate in particular human beings. Belief in the existence of such genii is spread in Ethiopia itself, in Somalia, Egypt, the Hejaz and in Oman.

Geniza (Cairo Geniza): a term which refers to writings coming from the store-room of the "Synagogue of the Palestinians" in al-Fustat. Most of the documentary material, such as letters, accounts, court records, contracts etc., comes from Fatimid and Ayyubid times, between 965 and 1265. The major part of this material is written in Arabic, though in Hebrew characters. In addition to Egypt itself, Tunisia and Sicily are conspicuously represented in the Geniza. The documents are highly important for the economic, social and cultural history of medieval Islam, as well as for the history of the Arabic language.

Geography (A. *jughrāfiyā*): the Arabs began acquainting themselves with scientific geography under the 'Abbasid Caliph al-Mansur, the founder of Baghdad. The process of acquiring and assimilating Indian, Iranian and Greek geographical, astronomical and philosophical knowledge resulted in completely revolutionizing Arab geographical thought. By the ixth c. a considerable amount of geographical literature had been produced. For the sake of convenience one might use the term Iraqi School for the authors who tend to consider Baghdad as the centre of the world, or treat Mecca as such, and the term Balkhi School for those who followed Abu Zayd al-Balkhi (d. 934) and confined their accounts to the world of Islam. The apogee of Arab geography can be said to have been reached in the xith c. with al-Biruni. Between the xiith and the xvith c. Arab geography displayed, with some exceptions, signs of decline. The literature of this period comprises world geographical accounts, cosmological works, geographical dictionaries, travel accounts, maritime, astronomical and regional geographical literature.

The Ottoman Turks seem to have begun to write geographical works about the middle of the xivth c., starting with small cosmographies and translations from Arabic and Persian. Original works were produced in the fields of marine geography and navigation, especially by Piri Re'is. The most important comprehensive geographical work is that of Katib Čelebi, also known as Hajji Khalifa, while the major work in the field of travel description is the "Travel Book" of Ewliya Čelebi.

Geometry (A. *'ilm al-handasa*): in the evolution of geometry among the Arabs, two important periods may be distinguished. The first is that of translations and of initiation (ixth c.), in which works of Euclid, Apollonius, Menelaus, Pappus, Archimedes and Hero of Alexandria were translated by famous translators like Ishaq b. Hunayn and Thabit b. Qurra. The second period is that of creativity (xth-xvth c.). Among the great Arabic names should be mentioned al-Khwarazmi, al-Jawhari, Muhammad b. Shakir, al-Mahani, al-Battani (ixth c.); al-Nayrizi, al-Buzjani, al-Sijzi (xth c.); Ibn al-Haytham (xith c.); 'Omar al-Khayyam (xiith c.); Nasir al-Din al-Tusi and Shams al-Din al-Samarqandi (xiiith c.); al-Kashi (xvth c.). The Muslims developed and codified in particular a sister science of geometry, sc. trigonometry.

George, St. (A. *Jirjīs*): Islam honours the Christian martyr as a symbol of resurrection and renovation.

Georgia (A. *al-Kurj; Gurj; Gurjistān*): republic in Western Caucasia. Arab expeditions penetrated into Transcaucasia in 643. After Habib b. Maslama had conquered Armenia in 645, he turned to Tiflis. He guaranteed the inhabitants the exercise of their religion, but they were soon converted to Islam, and after 654 an emirate was established in the town. In 830-853 Ishaq b. Isma'il carved himself out a principality in Georgia, but Tiflis was taken by Bugha al-Kabir al-Sharabi, the Turkish commander of the 'Abbasid Caliph al-Mutawakkil. This was the beginning of the decline of Arab power in the Caucasus.

Between 980-1072 the lands inhabited by the Georgians were united by the Christian Bagratids of Armenia, although the Great Saljuq Alp Arslan invaded their lands in 1068. On the complaints of the Muslims of Tiflis, ruled by a dynasty called Banu Jaʿfar, the Great Saljuq Mahmud b. Muhammad sent an expedition into Georgia, but Tiflis was stormed by the Bagratid Dawid II in 1121. During the reign of Queen Tamar (r. 1184-1211), the Christian kingdom of Georgia assumed the offensive and surrounded itself with Muslim vassals. In the end, however, Tamar could only retain the town of Kars. The Georgians were several times defeated by the Mongols, and in 1225 by the Khwarazm-Shah Jalal al-Din Mingburnu, who took Tiflis and, according to one account, massacred all those who did not accept Islam. In 1236 the Mongols returned, burned the town, sent the people of note to the Great Khan in Mongolia and broke up the political organisation of the country. After the death of the Il-Khan Öljeytü, the Bagratid King Giorgi V drove out the Mongols, but Tamerlane captured Tiflis in 1386, laid the country waste in 1400 and again in 1403.

In 1466 Georgia came under the control of the Aq Qoyunlu Uzun Hasan. In 1501 the Safawid Shah Tahmasp I sent four expeditions against Georgia. In 1578 Tiflis was seized by the Ottomans, whose rule lasted till 1603 when the town was retaken by the Safawid Shah ʿAbbas I. Persian manners and customs now became the fashion. King Erekle I (r. 1688-1691, 1695-1703) became a convert to Islam. The defeat of Georgian forces, sent to eastern Persia by the Safawid Shah Husayn I against the Afghans, paved the way to the Afghan invasion of Persia.

At the Russo-Turkish Treaty of Istanbul in 1724, Turkey obtained the Georgian territory. In 1734 Tiflis was surrendered by the Ottomans to Nadir Shah Afshar, but after the latter's death, Georgia enjoyed a respite under their own kings, the Bagratids of Kakhetʿi (1744-1790), who followed a policy of rapprochement with Russia. In 1795, however, Aga Muhammad Shah took Tiflis, pillaging it dreadfully. In 1800 Czar Paul I signed the manifesto of annexation of Georgia and, after a Georgian revolution in 1812, Russia was confirmed in the possession of the country in the Gulistan Treaty. During the Crimean War (1854-1856), Georgia was the base for Russian attacks on Turkey. In 1918 Transcaucasia declared itself an independent federative republic, comprising Christian Georgia and Armenia and Muslim Azerbaijan, but shortly afterwards an independent Georgian Republic was set up. Peace was made with Turkey, which regained Batum and Kars, but the new state had to fight off the Armenians, the Turks and the Bolsheviks, who took Tiflis in 1921. The Transcaucasian Soviet Federated Socialist Republic was installed, which was replaced in 1936 by the Georgian Soviet Socialist Republic. Georgia became an independent republic in 1991.

Germiyan-oghullari: Germiyan, at first the name of a Turkmen tribe, was afterwards applied to a family, then to an emirate. The Germiyan appeared for the first time in 1239 in the region of Malatya. In 1299 the emirate was founded by Ya'qub b. 'Ali Shir with its capital at Kütahya. At the battle of Ankara 1402, one of Ya'qub's successors, Ya'qub Čelebi, pointed the Ottoman sultan Bayezid I out to Tamerlane and thus contributed to his capture. After 1411, the Germiyan amir reigned under the protection of the Ottomans until the emirate was bequeathed to the Ottoman sultan Murad II in 1428.

Ghadamès (A. *Ghadāmis*): little oasis in the Libyan Sahara, occupied by 'Uqba b. Nafi' in 667. Between the viiith and the xth centuries it was Ibadi, and maintained its independence until 1860, when it had to recognize the authority of the Turks of Tripoli. Its essential activity was trans-Saharan trade.

Ghadir Khumm: name of a pool, or a marsh, situated in an area called Khumm, between Mecca and Medina. The place is famous in the history of Islam because of a sentence (or some sentences) uttered by the Prophet in favour of his son-in-law 'Ali on 18 Dhu 'l-Hijja 10/16 March 632. This date is celebrated in Iran and among the Nusayris.

al-Ghafiqi, Abu Ja'far Ahmad: Spanish-Arabic pharmaco-botanist; xiith c. He wrote a work on drugs, quoting the best-known sources and adding personal observations.

al-Ghafiqi, Muhammad: Spanish-Arab scholar and oculist; xiith c. His *Guide of the Oculist* is regarded as a summary of all the knowledge of ophthalmology possessed by the Arabs of both the Islamic East and West in the author's time.

Ghafuri, Mejid: one of the best-known national poets of the Bashkurt and Tatars; 1881-1934.

Ghalib, Mirza Asad: one of the greatest Muslim poets of the Indo-Pakistani subcontinent; 1797-1869. His letters reveal his keen interest in Persian grammar, lexicography and stylistics. He can be regarded as the father of modern Urdu prose.

Ghalib Dede: Turkish poet; 1757-1799. He was the last great exponent of the so-called *dīwān* poetry. He owes his great fame mainly to his allegorical romance of mystic love, called "Beauty and Love".

Ghalib b. Sa'sa'a: father of the poet al-Farazdaq, famous for his generosity; viith c.

Ghalzay (Ghalji, Ghilzay): large western Afghan Pashto-speaking tribe between Qandahar and Ghazna.

Ghāna (Ancient): name of a trading empire, and of its capital, in the Nigerian Sudan. Known to Muslim geographers before 800 as "the land of gold", it was destroyed in 1240.

Ghana: West African Republic, formerly known as the Gold Coast. Islam first spread in the xivth c. from Mali, later, in the xvth c., from the Hausa states. By the early xviiith c., the three major states of northern Ghana, Gonja, Dagomba, and Mamprusi, each had a Muslim ruler. Throughout the xixth and into the xxth c., Muslim immigration increased in volume. Both the Qadiriyya and the Tijaniyya orders are established in Ghana. When the Gold Coast attained independence in 1957, the country was named after Ancient Ghana.

Ghanimat Kunjahi, Muhammad Akram: poet of Mughal India and exponent of the "Indian style" in the Persian poetry of the subcontinent; d. about 1695.

Ghaniya, Banu: family of the Sanhaja Berbers who, in the Almohad epoch, attempted to restore the Almoravids in North Africa.

Gharb: name of a part of the coastal plain of northwestern Morocco. Its population is almost entirely of Arab origin.

al-Gharbiyya: province of Lower Egypt, with the capital Tanta, lying within the Nile Delta.

Ghardaïa (A. *Ghardāya*): chief town of the Mzab region in Algeria, founded in 1053 by the Ibadis and growing over the centuries owing to Ibadi immigration.

Gharjistan (Gharshistan): territory in the mountains of Afghanistan east of Harat. Islam was introduced in the viiith c.

al-Gharid: nickname meaning "the fresh [voice]", given to Abu Zayd ʿAbd al-Malik, a renowned singer of the Umayyad era; viiith c.

Ghasil al-Malaʾika: nickname of Hanzala b. Abi ʿAmir, a Companion of the Prophet; d. 623. He was mortally wounded in the battle of Uhud.

Ghassanids (A. *Ghassān*): division of the great Arabian tribal group al-Azd. They settled in Syria, became Monophysite Christians and, at the eve of Islam, were allies of Byzantium against Sasanian Persia and against the Persia-oriented Lakhmids of al-Hira. They were swept away by the Muslim conquest of Syria. Some of the Arab Christian families of the contemporary Near East trace their descent to the Ghassanids.

Ghatafan: name of a group of northern Arabian tribes, belonging to the Qays ʿAylan. They played a role in the Prophet's time and in early Islam.

Ghazal: Arabic term, also used in Persian, Turkish and Urdu, to denote a love-poem.

al-Ghazal, Yahya b. Hakam: poet at the court of the Spanish Umayyads, known for his satires and avarice; ixth c. In 840 the amir ʿAbd al-Rahman II sent him on a diplomatic mission to the Byzantine emperor Theophilus.

al-Ghazali, Abu Hamid Muhammad (Algazel): outstanding Muslim theologian, jurist, original thinker, mystic, and religious reformer; 1059-1111. His great work *Revival of the Religious Sciences* made Sufism an acceptable part of orthodox Islam.

al-Ghazali, Ahmad b. Muhammad: brother of the more renowned Abu Hamid; d. 1126. He was a Sufi and a popular preacher.

Ghazan, Mahmud: ruler of the Il-Khanid dynasty; b. 1271, r. 1295-1304. Brought up as a Buddhist, he became a Muslim shortly before his accession. In his reign Islam was recognized as the state religion, but Ghazan also took a great interest in the history and traditions of his own people. It was at his suggestion that his minister, the famous Rashid al-Din Tabib, compiled his *History of the Mongols*, in which his source for much of the information about the Mongols was the khan himself.

Ghazi (pl. *ghuzāt*): Arabic indication of those who took part in a razzia, later in a *ghazwa*, i.e. a "raid against the infidels". The word later became a title of honour.

Ghazi b. Faysal I: king of Iraq; b. 1912, r. 1933-1939. His short reign was marked by the short-lived coup of General Bakr Sidqi in 1936.

Ghazi Čelebi: ruler of Sinop on the Black Sea in Turkey; r. 1300-1330 (?). He is known for his piratical exploits against the Genoese, making sometimes alliance with and sometimes against the Greeks of Trabzon.

Ghazi 'l-Din Haydar: Nawwab-Wazir of Awadh; b. 1774, r. 1814-1827. Supported by Lord Hastings, he declared his independence from the Mughal emperor in 1819, assuming the royal title under which he is known.

Ghazi Giray II (Bora): one of the greatest khans of the Crimea; b. 1554, r. 1588-1607. He managed to steer a course between the Ottoman sultan and the Crimean aristocracy, which was seeking independence from Istanbul.

Ghazi Miyan (Sipah Salar Mas'ud): one of the earliest and most celebrated of Indo-Muslim saints; d. 1033. His tomb at Bahraič in Uttar Pradesh is visited by Hindus and Muslims.

Ghazna: town in eastern Afghanistan on the Kabul-Qandahar road. In this area, then basically Iranian, but with a considerable admixture of Turkish and other Central Asian peoples, Islam was introduced during the reign of the Umayyad Caliph 'Abd al-Malik. In 977, under the slave commander Sebüktigin (r. 977-997), the founder of the Ghaznawid dynasty, Ghazna became the capital of a vast empire and a frontier fortress town on the edge of the pagan Indian world. In the xiith c. the town was twice occupied by the Saljuqs, sacked in 1150 by the Ghurid 'Ala' al-Din Husayn (r. 1149-1161), and passed into Ghurid hands in 1163. In 1215 it came into the possession of the Khwarazm-Shahs, but the sack by Genghis Khan's Mongols in 1221 marked the end of Ghazna's period of glory. The town successively fell into the hands of Tamerlane, the Mughal emperors Babur and Awrangzib, Nadir Shah Afshar and the ruler of Afghanistan Ahmad Shah Durrani.

Ghaznawids: Sunni Turkish dynasty which ruled in Khurasan, Afghanistan, and northern India, with its centre at Lahore, from 977 to 1186. Cultivating a Persian civilization, the Ghaznawids executed works of art in towns like Ghazna, Bust, Balkh, Harat and Nishapur. Archaeological remains provide an insight into the art that flourished under the aegis of the Ghaznawids.

Ghifar, Banu: small Arab tribe to whom the Prophet guaranteed in one of his earliest letters the protection of Allah and His messenger for their lives and goods.

al-Ghitrif b. 'Ata': 'Abbasid governor of Khurasan; viiith c. He introduced a new coinage into Bukhara, the so-called Ghutrifi or black *dirham*.

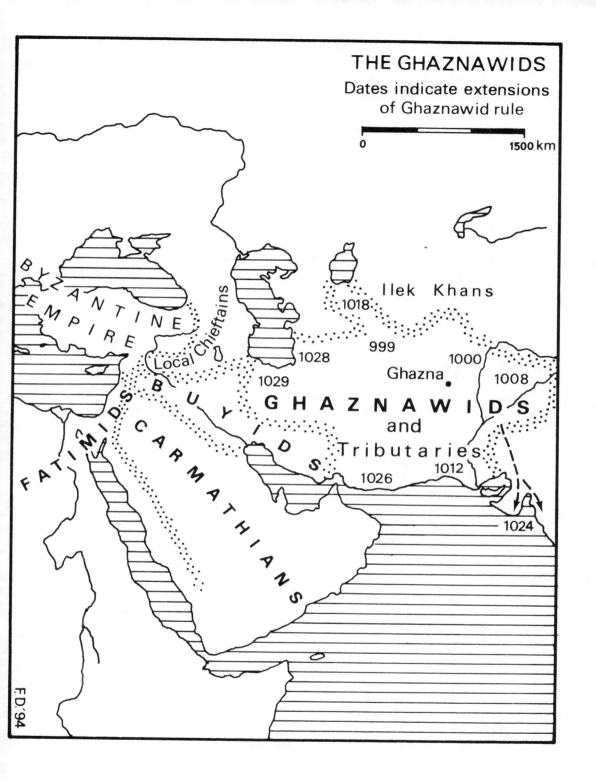

THE GHAZNAWIDS

Dates indicate extensions
of Ghaznawid rule

0   1500 km

BYZANTINE EMPIRE

Ilek   Khans
1018

Local Chieftains

999

1028

Ghazna

1000

1008

1029

GHAZNAWIDS
and
Tributaries

FATIMIDS

BUYIDS

CARMATHIANS

1026

1012

1024

F.D.'94

Ghiyath al-Din Tughluq I Shah (Ghazi Malik): founder of the Tughluqid dynasty and ruler of India; r. 1320-1325. A Turk by origin, he became governor of Dipalpur in the Punjab, held the Mongols at bay for fifteen years, and defeated Khusraw Khan, a Khalji general of Hindu origin who had apostatized from Islam and begun a reign of terror in Delhi. Contemporary Muslim historiography eulogises him as the saviour of Islam in India.

Ghiyath al-Din Tughluq Shah II: grandson of Ghiyath al-Din Tughluq I; r. 1388-1389. His reign led to the rapid disintegration of the Delhi sultanate.

Ghoul (A. *Ghūl*): fabulous being believed by the ancient Arabs to inhabit desert places and, assuming different forms, to lead travellers astray, to fall upon them unawares and devour them. It appears in many stories.

Ghulam (pl. *ghilmān*): in Arabic and Persian the word indicates a young man or boy, a servant, or a bodyguard. The word is specifically applied to slave *ghilmān*, attendants or guards who played a role in the running of various eastern and western Muslim states. The ʿAbbasid Caliph al-Muʿtasim bi-Allah (833-842) caused to be bought at Samarqand about three thousand Turkish slaves who were to form the nucleus of his new guard and of the new army. Their commanders began to occupy important positions and occasionally interfered in political affairs, under the ʿAbbasids in Samarra and Baghdad and in Egypt under the Tulunids, the Ikhshidids and the Fatimids.

In Persia, the institution of the *ghilmān* began with the Turkish prisoners-of-war who fell into the hands of the Arab governors of Armenia and Khurasan. Military slavery was practised under subsequent dynasties up to the reign of the Qajar Fath ʿAli Shah.

In India, the Muslim conquest was mainly the achievement of Turkish *ghilmān*, known as the Muʿizzi or Slave Kings, who ruled from 1206 to 1290. Military slaves continued to become high officers under the Khalji and Tughluq sultans. Under the Mughals, however, slaves played a very minor part in administration and in the army, although they occasionally became subordinate commanders.

In the Ottoman Empire, administration was based upon the training of young slaves for the palace service and the service of the state. The practice was inherited from the Saljuq Sultanate of Rum and continued until about 1700.

Ghulam Husayn Khan Tabatabaʾi: political negotiator and soldier in India; 1727-ca. 1815. He is the author of a detailed history of India for the period 1707-1781.

Ghulam Qadir Rohilla: eunuch, known for his cruel treatment of the Mughal emperor Shah ʿAlam (r. 1759-1806) and his family; d. 1789. He deposed the Shah in 1788, had him blinded, and every conceivable cruelty perpetrated on the royal family. He was put to death by the Marathas.

Ghulam Thaʿlab: nickname of an Arab philologist; d. 957. His fame rests on his extraordinary erudition in matters of Arabic vocabulary.

Ghumara, Banu: Berber tribe of the western Maghrib, in what is now northern Morocco, who adopted Kharijite doctrines and caused difficulties to the Marinids.

Ghumdan: the castle of San'a' in Yemen. It is said to have been destroyed by the Abyssinian conquerors in 525 but to have been rebuilt after the Persian occupation in 570. It was destroyed during the Muslim conquest of Yemen.

Ghurids: strongly Sunni eastern Iranian dynasty with its base at Ghur, the mountainous territory in northwestern Afghanistan. Its capital was at Firuz-kuh; fl. ca. 1000-1214. Having been vassals to the Ghaznawids and the Sal-juqs, the Ghurids became a major power in Khurasan, Afghanistan and nor-thern India in the xiith c., reaching their apogee between 1163 and 1206. The Ghurids were generous patrons of art and literature. Sultan 'Ala' al-Din Muhammad was deposed in 1214 by the Khwarazm-Shah, also called 'Ala' al-Din Muhammad (r. 1200-1220).

Ghuta: name given in Syria to abundantly irrigated areas of intense cul-tivation surrounded by arid land, in particular to the area of gardens and orchards around Damascus.

Giaour (A. *Gabr*/T. *Gāvur*): *gabr*, derived from Arabic *kāfir* "infidel", is generally applied in Persian literature – with rather depreciative implications – to Zoroastrians and only secondarily to "unbelievers". Turkish *gāvur* was used contemptuously for Christians.

Gibraltar (A. *Jabal Ṭāriq*): town on the northeastern entrance of the Strait of Gibraltar, which connects the Atlantic Ocean and the Mediterranean. It is called after Tariq b. Ziyad who landed there in 711. During the entire Arab period the port was a sure base for vessels. In 1462 it was conquered by the duke Guzmán de Medina Sidonia and in 1704 it fell into British hands.

Gilan: historic region in Iran near the Caspian Sea, with the capital Rasht. The doctrines of the Zaydis penetrated into the region from Tabaristan and Mazandaran. Apart from a short-lived rule of the Il-Khan Öljeytü Khuda-banda in 1307, Gilan remained independent until it was incorporated into Per-sia by the Safawid Shah 'Abbas I in 1592.

Giray: cognomen borne by the members of the dynasty which ruled in the Crimea from the beginning of the xvth c. until 1783. The family was de-scended from a grandson of Genghis Khan.

Gisu Daraz, Sayyid Muhammad: celebrated Čishti saint, scholar and au-thor of India; 1321-1422. He knew several languages, was a prolific writer and fully conversant with Hindu folklore and mythology.

Gog and Magog (A. *Yājūj wa-Mājūj*): two peoples who belong to Muslim eschatology. They are mentioned in the Qur'an.

Gökalp, Ziya (Mehmed Diya'): Turkish author and poet, sociologist and national leader from Diyarbakr; 1875-1924. After the revolution of 1908 he became a member of the Union and Progress Committee and preached Pan-Turanism. In 1921 he joined the movement led by Mustafa Kemal Atatürk.

He stressed the need of reforms in all aspects of life and after his death was recognised as the father of Turkish nationalism.

Golconda (Golkonda): a hill fort west of Haydarabad in southern India, renamed Muhammadnagar by Sultan Quli Qutb al-Mulk, the founder of the Qutb Shahi dynasty. It was the most important trade-center for diamonds in Asia.

Gold (A. *dhahab*): the Qur'an warns against hoarding. Along with silver, gold constituted the basis for the official Muslim monetary system. It was studied by Muslim alchemists and used as a medicine.

Golden Horde: name given by the Russians to the western division of the Mongol Empire, which ruled from 1227-1502. It was created by Batu b. Juči on the lower Volga, with its centre at Old, later New, Saray. In eastern literature, the country is usually referred to as the Qipčaq (Kipchak) Steppe. Batu's brother Berke was the first Mongol prince to become a Sunni Muslim, and thereby he began the incorporation of the Tatars into Islam. His death did not altogether put an end to Islamic influence, although his immediate successors were again Shamanists. Özbeg Khan (r. 1313-1341), a Muslim himself, definitely strengthened the position of Islam. The Golden Horde became more and more at the mercy of Poland-Lithuania and Muscovy. After 1419, the formation of independent khanates in Qazan, Astrakhan and in the Crimea started the disintegration of the Golden Horde. In 1502 it was vanquished by the Crimea and Muscovy.

Goletta (A. *Ḥalq al-Wādī*; Fr. *La Goulette*): township in Tunisia on the coastal strip enclosing the lagoon of Tunis. Captured in 1534 from the Hafsids by Khayr al-Din Barbarossa, it was seized by the Emperor Charles V, but in 1574 by the Turks. Until the end of the xviiith c. Goletta remained a haunt of corsairs. After 1893 it became the outer harbour of Tunis.

Gondeshapur (A. *Jundaysābūr*): town in Khuzistan, southwestern Iran, founded by the Sasanian king Shapur I. It was taken by the Muslims in 638 and became well known in Islam because of its medical school.

Gospel(s) (A. *Injīl*): the word is found in the Qur'an and refers to the Revelation transmitted by Jesus. In the present state of knowledge it cannot be asserted that the Prophet and his first Companions could have had a direct knowledge of the Gospels in Arabic. On the other hand, it is probable that the passages in the Qur'an which reflect the canonical or apocryphal Gospels derive from Christian communities in Syria and in Yemen. There is an important influence of the New Testament on Tradition and, because of growing contact between Muslims and Christians, the former gained a deeper knowledge of the Gospels. This closer contact very soon gave rise to polemic about the basic dogmas of Christianity, such as the Trinity, the Incarnation and the Redemption. Muslim mystic literature contains many references to the Gospels.

Granada (A. *Gharnāṭa*): city in southern Spain. It came into prominence through the Sanhaja Berber tribe of the Zirids. The amirs Habus (r. 1019-

1038) and Badis (r. 1038-1073) gave their capital a strong surrounding wall which still exists. The bath, known as Bañuelo, dates also from this period. Under the African dynasties of the Almoravids and the Almohads Granada did not undergo great changes. In 1238 the city was taken over by the Nasrids, and remained till 1492 the capital of the last Muslim state in Spain. Of the religious buildings of this period hardly any remains, while of the secular buildings, next to the Alhambra, a public bath, an inn and a few other much restored constructions are left. The Alhambra remained the residence of the Nasrids until the capture of the city by the Christians in 1492.

Grand Vizier (A. *ṣadr aʿẓam*; Ott. T. *ṣadr-i aʿẓam*): title which means "the greatest of the high dignitaries" and which, from the time of Süleyman II, was borne by the "first minister". He was appointed at the sultan's pleasure. As a sign of his dignity, he received and always kept with him a gold ring with the sultan's seal. He presided over the central administration, known as *dīwān-i Humāyūn*, held monthly audiences, received the principal officials twice a week, made rounds periodically and rendered assistance in the case of fire. He had the right to eight guards of honour, twelve led horses and a barge with thirteen pairs of rowers, with a green canopy. He wore a white hat, shaped like a truncated pyramid with rounded corners and adorned with an oblique band of gold. In case of war, he could become commander-in-chief and carried with him the standard of the Prophet, being replaced in the capital by a deputy, the *qāʾim maqām*. The office was insecure and ephemeral. The dismissed Grand Vizier handed over his seal at an audience and went into exile, if he was allowed to live. The office disappeared with the sultanate in 1922. The last Grand Vizier was Damad Ferid Pasha (d. 1923).

Greece: Ancient Greece was known to the Arabs as Yunan. The Byzantine Empire is called Rum in Arabic, Persian and Turkish, although this term is also used for Konya, the capital of the sultanate of the Rum Saljuqs. Occasionally it also indicates Ancient Greece. In the early Ottoman period the word indicated the districts of Amasia and Sivas, and in Central Asia it was used for the Roman Empire. From the conquest of the peninsula of the Peloponnesus from around 1360 onwards, the Turks used the word Mora (Morea) as a *pars pro toto*. Turkish domination lasted from 1460-1821, Greece becoming independent after the Greek War of Independence (1821-1833).

Greek fire (A. *nafṭ*/P. *naft*): the mixture of Mesopotamian bitumen with fats, oil, sulphur and, later, saltpetre constituted the basic ingredient of a liquid incendiary hurled at the enemy. The Muslims made use of it against the Crusaders and the Mongols.

Guinea: republic on the west coast of Africa. The name probably is of Berber origin. Islam began to be spread in the xith c. Since independence was gained from France in 1958, a strict neutrality in religious matters has been imposed, although the Fulani are Muslim-born and the Mandingos are adopting Islam.

Gujar (Gujjar, Gurjjar): name of an ancient tribe, wide-spread in many parts of the Indo-Pakistan subcontinent, akin to the Rajputs, the Jats, and the Ahirs. They were a source of great trouble to the Mughal Emperor Babur and to Shir Shah Sur, the Afghan Sultan of Delhi. They were finally forced to a settled life by the Mughal Emperor Akbar. It is not known when they adopted Islam.

Gujarat: constituent state on the northwestern coastline of India. Islam was introduced after the conquest of the region by the Delhi sultan Muhammad Shah I Khalji in 1298. During the xivth c. Gujarat was ruled by governors sent out by the Tughluq sultans of Delhi. In 1391 the governor Muzaffar Khan made himself independent and in 1407 assumed the insignia of royalty. His dynasty remained in power till 1583 when Gujarat fell to the Mughals. Under their rule the region remained largely peaceful and was famous for silk weaving, velvet, fine cotton cloth and indigo. Mughal rule was extinguished by the Marathas in 1758.

Gujarati: language spoken in Gujarat and in Gujarati communities elsewhere. It belongs to the Indo-Aryan branch of the Indo-European language family.

Gujrat: town and district in Punjab province, Pakistan.

Gülbaba: Turkish title, with the sense of head of a Muslim cloister (*tekke*) of the Bektashi order. It is also the name of *tekke*s at Buda and Edirne, and the name of a legendary personality.

Gulbadan Begam: daughter of the Mughal Emperor Babur; 1523-1603. She wrote her memoirs under the title *Humayun-nama*.

Gulbang: Persian word meaning the song of the nightingale. In Turkish usage it is applied to the call of the muezzin. In the Ottoman Empire it was used specifically for the acclamations of the Janissaries.

Gulbarga: town and district in the north of Mysore state in India, capital of the Bahmanids. The town is known for its monuments.

Gulshani (*Gülsheni*), **Ibrahim**: Turkish mystic and prolific poet; ca. 1435-1534. He wrote in Arabic, Persian and Turkish, and built a convent in Egypt for the order named after him, which is a branch of the Khalwatiyya.

Gurani, Sharaf al-Din (Molla Gurani): Ottoman scholar and Shaykh al-Islam; 1410-1488. He wrote commentaries on the Qur'an and on the *Ṣaḥīḥ* of al-Bukhari.

Gurgan (A. *Jurjān*): town and province in Iran at the southeastern corner of the Caspian Sea. The country was conquered by the Muslims in 716. During the ixth and xth c. it must have been very prosperous. Ja'far al-Sadiq, the last Imam recognized by both Twelver and Isma'ili Shi'is, was buried in Gurgan. It was the capital of the Khwarazm-Shahs, but razed to the ground at the time of the Mongol invasion.

Gurgani, Fakhr al-Din As'ad: author of the first-known courtly romance in Persian, called *Wīs and Ramīn*; xith c.

Gurkhan: title borne by the non-Muslim rulers of the Karakhitai or Western Liao, who governed Central Asia between 1128 and 1212. The victory of the Chinese prince Yeh-lü Ta-shih (d. 1143) over the Great Saljuq Sanjar b. Malik Shah, north of Samarqand in 1141, i.e. of a non-Muslim ruler over one of the most powerful rulers of Islam, may have provided the foundation for the legend of Prester John.

Gwadar: town and district on the Makran coast, Pakistan. It was an Omani possession until ceded to Pakistan in 1958.

Gwalior (Gwaliyar): town and district in Madhya Pradesh state, India. The town was captured by the Ghaznawid Mahmud b. Sebüktigin in 1022, but the history of the Muslim occupation of Gwalior is a chequered one. In the xvith c. it was known for its music performances.

Gwandu: town and emirate in north-western Nigeria. It was taken by Usman dan Fodio in 1805 and ruled by the Dan Fodio dynasty until the British occupation in 1903.

Gypsies: gypsy communities are indicated by a variety of names. It is suggested that the name *Čingane* (T. *Čingene*) comes from Čangar or Zingar, said to be the name of a people formerly dwelling on the banks of the Indus. *Luli* is one of the names for gypsies in Persia, while the terms *Nuri* and *Zutt* are also found. In Muslim countries the gypsies usually are said to profess Islam, but they have in fact their own form of religion. The Arab historian al-Baladhuri relates that the Zutt had been settled in the ports of the Persian Gulf since before Islam. The Arab historian Hamza al-Isfahani and the Persian poet Firdawsi relate that Bahram Gur, king of Persia (r. 420-438), asked the king of India to send him 10,000 *Luri*, men and women, expert at playing the lute. The Zutt, who had settled in the marshes between Wasit and Basra in great numbers, rose in rebellion during the reign of the 'Abbasid Caliph al-Ma'mun, but submitted in 834 on condition that their lives and property were spared.

H

Habash al-Hasib al-Marwazi: early Muslim astronomer in Baghdad; ixth c. He possessed a perfect mastery of trigonometrical functions and their application to the problems of spherical astronomy.

Habashat: term found in several Sabaean inscriptions with apparent reference to Aksumite Abyssinia, and probably also to a South Arabian tribe related to it.

Habesh: Ottoman name of a province covering the African coastlands of the Red Sea south of Egypt as far as the Gulf of Aden, including Jidda in Arabia. The area corresponded approximately to the coastal districts of the present-day Sudan, Ethiopia, Jibuti and the Zayla' district of Somalia. The

African parts of the province were transferred to Muhammad ʿAli Pasha of Egypt in 1830.

Habib b. ʿAbd al-Malik: cousin and confidant of ʿAbd al-Rahman I, the founder of the Umayyad amirate in al-Andalus; viiith c. He was the founder of the line of Habibis, which provided al-Andalus with some notable men of learning and of letters.

Habib Allah (Habibullah) Khan: ruler of Afghanistan; b. 1872, r. 1901-1919. He adopted a pro-British policy and in internal affairs introduced needed reforms.

Habib b. Maslama: military commander of the Umayyad caliph Muʿa-wiya I; 617-662. He served as a representative of Muʿawiya in the negotiations with the fourth Caliph ʿAli after the battle of Siffin.

Habshi: term derived from the Arabic-Persian word Habashi, meaning Abyssinian, and used in India to indicate slaves of Abyssinian but certainly also of Nilotic and Bantu origin. Many of them rose to positions of power and eminence as early as the xiiith c. They are found among the Khaljis and the Tughluqids, in Gujarat, in Bengal and, perhaps most conspicuously, in the Deccan. The most prominent of the Habshis in Ahmadnagar in the xviith c. was the vizier Malik ʿAmbar. Habshis were also prominent in the navies of Gujarat and the Deccan powers.

Habsiyya: name used in Persian literature for a poem dealing with the theme of imprisonment. The model for prison-poetry was set by Masʿud-i Saʿd-i Salman.

al-Haddad, al-Tahir: nationalist and reformist Tunisian writer, considered the pioneer of the movement for the emancipation of women in his country; ca. 1899-1935.

al-Hadi ila ʾl-Haqq: regnal name of the ʿAbbasid caliph Musa b. al-Mahdi; r. 785-786. His attitude of frank hostility to the ʿAlids led to the massacre of Fakhkh.

al-Hadi ila ʾl-Haqq, Yahya: the real founder of the Zaydi imamate in Yemen; r. 893-911. His tomb in the mosque of Saʿda became a place of pilgrimage for the Zaydis.

al-Hadr: Arabic name of ancient Hatra, to the southwest of Mosul. It was destroyed by the Sasanian king Shapur I (241-272). The Arab authors of the first centuries of Islam have preserved the legend of the capture of Hatra, in which al-Nadira, the daughter of the ruler of the town, plays a part. The theme of the legend is repeated in Hans Andersen's fairy tale "The Princess and the Pea".

Hadhramaut (A. *Ḥaḍramawt*): in its strictest sense the name of the deep valley (*wādī Ḥaḍramawt*) which runs parallel to the southern coast of Arabia; in a larger sense the region of the valley in central Yemen. First contacts with Islam were made directly with the Prophet, who was in correspondence with the local Kinda leaders. Kharijite ideas penetrated in 685 and in 747 Ibadi doctrines were introduced by al-Mukhtar b. ʿAwf. The region was ruled successively by the Ziyadids, the Sulayhids and by the latter's clients, the Zurayʿids. The Ayyubids, who came to Yemen in 1174, also ruled Hadhramaut, though without firm control. In 1229 began the peaceful administration of the Rasulids, which lasted until 1454. After a short intermezzo of the Tahirids, the Kathiris, a tribal group originating from Dhofar, came to power in the latter half of the xvth c. One faction brought in the large tribal unit of the Yafiʿis, and the political history of Hadhramaut down to the xxth c. is the chronicle of the disputes between these groups. During the British Protectorate, Hadhramaut was divided between the Kathiri sultanate with its capital in Sayʾun and the Kuʿayti sultanate, originally a Yafiʿi group, centred on al-Mukalla. The whole of South Arabia became independent in 1967.

Hafiz: the Arabic word means "one who knows the Qurʾan by heart". It was formerly used as an honorific epithet.

al-Hafiz: regnal name of a Fatimid caliph of Egypt; b. 1073, r. 1131-1146. His rule was marked by continuous internal troubles.

Hafiz, ʿAbd al (Moulay Hafid): Filali Sharif of Morocco; b. 1880, r. 1907-1912, d. 1937. The Agadir Incident, provoked by a German attempt to challenge French rights in Morocco by sending a warship to the Moroccan port of Agadir, took place in 1911. The Sharif abdicated in 1912 after the French General Lyautey had been appointed Resident Commissioner General.

Hafiz Ibrahim: Egyptian poet and writer; ca. 1870-1932. His poetry is the echo of the sufferings and hopes of the Egyptian people.

Hafiz, (Khwaja) Shams al-Din Muhammad Shirazi: Persian lyric poet and panegyrist, commonly considered the pre-eminent master of the *ghazal* form; ca. 1325-ca. 1390.

Hafiz Tanish (Nakhli): historian of ʿAbd Allah Khan II, the Shaybanid ruler of Bukhara (r. 1583-1596).

Hafiz-i Abru: nickname of a Persian historian of the Timurid period recording part of the reign of Shahrukh Mirza; d. 1430.

Hafs al-Fard: theologian from Egypt; ixth c. He taught that on the Day of Resurrection God will create the sixth sense in order to enable His creatures to see Him.

Hafs b. Sulayman: transmitter of al-ʿAsim's "reading" of the Qurʾan; 709-796. The "reading" passed down by his efforts was adopted for the establishment of the text of the Qurʾan published in Cairo in 1923.

Hafsa bint ʿUmar b. al-Khattab: a wife of the Prophet, who married her in 625; d. 665.

Hafsids (Banu Hafs): Berber dynasty in Ifrīqiya, which ruled from 1228-1574. The founder of the dynasty, amir Abu Zakariyyaʾ Yahya (r. 1228-1249), had commercial treaties with Provence, Languedoc, Sicily and Aragon. His son and successor Abu ʿAbd Allah (r. 1249-1277) adopted the caliphal title of al-Mustansir bi-ʾllah. The good relations with Christendom suffered a temporary setback after the crusade of Louis IX, who died at Carthage in 1270. Tunis was temporarily occupied by the Marinids in 1348 and in 1357, but the prestige of the Hafsids was restored by Abu 'l-'Abbas Ahmad II (r. 1370-1394) and his son and successor Abu Faris (r. 1394-1434). The Ottomans conquered Tunis in 1534, again in 1569, and definitively in 1574.

Hagiography (A. *manāqib*, s. *manqaba*): the Arabic term features in the titles of a quite considerable number of biographical works of a laudatory nature, which have eventually become a part of hagiographical literature in Arabic, Persian and Turkish.

Haha: Moroccan confederation of Berber tribes belonging to the sedentary Masmuda and inhabiting the plateaux of the Western Atlas as far as the sea.

Haifa (A. *Hayfā*): city and port in northeastern Israel. In early Islam the port at the foot of Mount Carmel was overshadowed by Acre. It is first described in the xith c. The port was conquered and reconquered by Crusaders and Muslims until 1291, when it finally fell into the hands of the Mamluk sultan al-Ashraf Khalil. In 1761 Shaykh Zahir al-'Umar, who had founded a principality in Galilee, built Hayfa al-Jadida, the new Haifa, which became the nucleus of the present town.

al-Ha'ik, Muhammad: compiler of the texts of songs deriving from Andalusian Arabic music; viiith c. A great number of these texts have been transmitted orally down to the present day.

Ha'il/Hayil: chief town in the district of Jabal Shammar in central Arabia, former capital of the Rashid dynasty of Najd.

Ha'iri, Shaykh 'Abd al-Karim Yazdi: Persian religious leader; 1859-1937. He argued that politics in the Muslim world were being controlled by Western powers and were consequently hostile to Islam. In order to prevent the extinction of Islam, therefore, a responsible religious leader must not interfere in politics. He trained many disciples who later on became religious leaders and who, unlike their master, undertook political activities, the best-known example being Ruhollah (A. *Rūh Allāh*) Khomayni.

Hajj: the Arabic term for the pilgrimage to Mecca.

al-Hajj 'Umar Tal: celebrated Tukulor conqueror, who founded a short-lived kingdom in west Sudan; 1797-1864. He became the khalifa of the Tijaniyya order for the Sudan and established himself in Futa Jallon in 1838, preaching Holy War against the Bambara kingdom of Segu and the Kaarta. He was defeated by the French in 1857. In 1861 he took the town of Segu, and Hamdallahi, the capital of the Fulani of Masina, and had the latter's king Ahmadu-Ahmadu killed in 1862.

al-Hajjaj b. Yusuf al-Thaqafi: the most famous general and governor of the Umayyads; ca. 661-714. He besieged the anti-caliph 'Abd Allah b. al-Zubayr at Mecca, had the Holy City bombarded and took it after seven months in 692. He then became governor of the Hejaz, the Yemen and the Yamama and had the Ka'ba restored. In 694 he was entrusted with the governorship of

Iraq, in turmoil because of the intrigues of the Kharijites. The sermon with which he installed himself in Kufa has found its place in Arabic literature. Having removed the Kharijite danger in Iraq, he was appointed governor of Khurasan and Sijistan. When he was beleaguered in Basra by Ibn al-Ash'ath, Syrian troops came to his rescue and the Iraqi Arabs were defeated. Having pacified the Kurdish and Daylami brigands, he built the fortified town of Wasit to isolate the Syrians from the Iraqis. The conquests of Transoxiana by Qutayba b. Muslim, of Oman by Mujja'a b. Si'r, and of India by Muhammad b. al-Qasim al-Thaqafi during the caliphate of the Umayyad Caliph al-Walid I were the results of al-Hajjaj's efforts. He sponsored a new text of the Qur'an, began to strike purely Arabic coins, and made efforts to improve agriculture. Al-Hajjaj is considered one of the greatest statesmen, not only of the Umayyads, but of the whole Islamic world.

Hajji Bayram Wali: patron saint of Ankara and founder of the order of the Bayramiyya; 1352-1429.

Hajji Giray; founder of the Giray dynasty of khans of the Crimea; d. 1466.

Hajji Pasha, Jelal al-Din: Turkish physician and author of several medical texts; xvth c.

al-Hakam I b. Hisham: Umayyad amir of Córdoba; b. 770, r. 796-822. After one of the numerous rebellions by the neo-Muslims in Córdoba, he banished over 20,000 families from the country. About two-thirds of them went to Egypt and later to Crete, the remainder going to Fez.

al-Hakam II al-Mustansir b. 'Abd al-Rahman III: Umayyad Caliph of Córdoba; b. 915, r. 961-976. He enlarged and embellished the Great Mosque of Córdoba, and gradually became the suzerain of all the Christian princes of the north. In 966 the Normans made a new attempt to land in Spain. Al-Hakam's reign was one the most peaceful and fruitful of the Córdoban dynasty.

Hakim Ata: Turkish saint of Khwarazm and author of popular poems on mystic life; d. 1186. His works are very popular down to modern times in Turkestan and in the Volga basin.

al-Hakim bi-amr Allah: Fatimid caliph; b. 985, r. 996-1021. He was famous because of his excesses, his cruelty and his persecutions, particularly of the Christians. The divine character which certain of his supporters attributed to him is an article of faith with the Druzes. His end has always been a mystery.

Hakkari: name of a Kurdish tribe and of a Turkish province in the extreme southeast of Turkey.

al-Halabi, Burhan al-Din: famous Hanafi scholar from Aleppo; d. 1549. His handbook on Hanafi law met with great success. It was translated into Turkish and became authoritative in the Ottoman Empire.

al-Halabi, Nur al-Din: Arabic author; 1567-1635. He wrote a biography of the Prophet which found a wide circulation and was translated into Turkish.

Halet Efendi: Ottoman statesman; 1761-1822. He used the Janissaries as an instrument to maintain his influence over the sultan, and for a time controlled nominations to the posts of Grand Vizier and Shaykh al-Islam. He played a part in the expedition against ʿAli Pasha Tepedelenli, the governor of Jannina, which provoked the Greek revolt in the Morea in 1821.

Haleti, ʿAzmi-zade Mustafa: Ottoman poet and scholar; 1570-1631. He is considered the master of the quatrain in Turkish literature.

Hali, Khwaja Altaf Husayn: Urdu poet; 1837-1914. He revolutionized Urdu poetry by introducing the dynamics of Pan-Islamism and paved the way for Urdu and Indo-Persian political poems.

Haliqarnas Baliqčisi (Cevat Shakir Kabaağaçli): Turkish novelist and short story writer; 1886-1973. He laboured inceasingly to develop the seaport of Bodrum where he had been banished for one of his publications.

Halima bint Abi Dhuʾayb: foster-mother of the Prophet.

al-Hallaj, Abu ʾl-Mughith: Arabic-speaking mystic theologian of Persian origin; 857-922. A monogamist and profoundly faithful to Sunnism, he led a fervently ascetic life. He made the pilgrimage to Mecca three times and travelled far and wide in the Islamic world. The main aim of his preaching was to enable everybody to find God within his own heart, but he was accused of deception, false miracles, magic and sorcery by Muʿtazilites, Sufis and Shiʿis. According to a hostile account of the grammarians of Basra, he proclaimed: "I am (God) the Truth". Having been imprisoned in Baghdad for nine years, he finally was executed.

Hamadhan (Hamadan): a very old city in central Iran, taken by the Arabs in 645. It was successively conquered by the Daylamis, the Turkmen, the Saljuqs and the Mongols. After 1503 the Safawids established their rule there, but the town was occupied several times by the Ottomans. It reverted to Persia in 1732.

al-Hamadhani, Ahmad Badiʿ al-Zaman ("the Prodigy of the Age"): Arabo-Persian author and letter-writer; 968-1008. His name is perpetuated by his *Sessions*, sketches which represent keen observations of everyday life. They were to serve as a model for almost a thousand years.

Hamaliyya (Hamallism): African-Islamic movement which made its appearance in Mali at the beginning of the xxth c. as an attempt to reform the teaching of the Tijaniyya.

Hamat: town in central Syria on the Orontes river, taken by the Arabs in 636. In the xiith c. it was in the hands of the Ayyubids, the well-known historian Abu ʾl-Fidaʾ being its governor in the first quarter of the xiiith c. In the xivth c. it was administered by Mamluk governors and from the xvith c. onwards by the Ottomans. It passed to Syria after World War I.

Hamd Allah al-Mustawfi al-Qazwini: Persian historian and geographer from Qazvin; ca. 1281-after 1339. His work is important for the period of the Il-Khans.

Hamdala: the Arabic word means the saying of the formula *al-ḥamdu li-'llāh* "Praise belongs to Allah", quite frequent in Muslim usage.

Hamdan, Banu: large Arab tribe of Yemen. They joined in the attack made on Abraha when he marched against Mecca. Many of them are said to have been in 'Ali's army at Siffin.

Hamdan Qarmat: leader of the Carmathian movement in Kufa; ixth c.

al-Hamdani, Abu Muhammad (Ibn al-Ha'ik): South-Arabian scholar, most famous as antiquarian, genealogist, geographer and poet; 893-945 (?). His magnum opus is the encyclopaedic *The Crown*.

Hamdanids: name of three families of the Banu Hamdan who ruled over San'a' and its dependencies from 1088-1175.

Hamdanids: name of two minor dynasties whose members ruled as amirs in Mosul (905-991) and in Aleppo (945-1004).

Hamdi, Hamd Allah: Turkish poet; 1449-1503. Among other works he wrote a *mathnawī* on the story of Joseph and Potiphar's wife, treated in a mystical manner. It became immensely popular.

al-Hamidi, Ibrahim b. al-Husayn: the second head of the Tayyibi Isma'ilis in Yemen; d. 1162. He was succeeded by his son Hatim (d. 1199) and his grandson 'Ali (d. 1209).

Hammadids (Banu Hammad): dynasty in the Central Maghrib (1015-1152) collateral with the Zirids in Ifriqiya and eastern Algeria. The founder, Hammad b. Buluggin I b. Ziri (r. 1015-1029), severed his relations with the Fatimids of Cairo and transferred his allegiance to the 'Abbasids of Baghdad.

Hammudids: dynasty of the period of the Muluk al-Tawa'if, which reigned over various towns in Muslim Spain from 1016 till 1058.

Hamza b. 'Abd al-Muttalib: the paternal uncle of the Prophet; d. 625. He became the central figure of a popular romance, called *The Romance of Amir Hamza*, known in Persia, Turkey and Indonesia.

Hamza b. 'Ali: founder of the Druze religious doctrine; xith c. Of Persian origin, he played a role in the proclamation of the divinity of the Fatimid Caliph al-Hakim bi-Amr Allah.

Hamza b. Habib: one of the "Seven Readers" of the Qur'an; d. 772. He was a pupil of Abu Bakr 'Asim.

Hamza Beg (Imam): Imam of Dagestan, leader of the popular politico-religious movement which disturbed the northern Caucasus from 1832 to 1859; d. 1834.

Hamza Fansuri: Indonesian Sufi; xvith c. Originating from the west coast of Sumatra, he was the author of treatises and poems in Malay.

Hamza al-Isfahani: Persian philologist and historian; ca. 893-after 961. He is the author of a well-known chronology of pre-Islamic and Islamic dynasties. He is also described as a Persian nationalist with strong prejudices against the Arabs.

Hanafites (A. *Ḥanafiyya*): the followers of the Sunni school of theology, law and morality which grew up from the teachings of Abu Hanifa al-Nuʿ-man. Like the other three Sunni schools of law (Hanbalites, Malikites and Shafiʿites), the Hanafites acknowledge the Qurʾan and the deeds, utterances and unspoken approval (A. *sunna*) of the Prophet as the primary sources of law. In the absence of precedent, however, they accept personal opinion (A. *raʾy*). The Hanafi school originated in Iraq and spread to Syria, Khurasan, Transoxiana, Afghanistan, the Indian subcontinent, Turkish Central Asia and China. It later became the favourite school of the Saljuqs and of the Ottomans and, as a legacy of Ottoman rule, it has retained official status even in those former Ottoman provinces where the majority of the native Muslim population follows another school, e.g. in Egypt, Sudan, Jordan, Israel, Lebanon and Syria.

Hanbalites (A. *Ḥanābila*, s. *Ḥanbalī*): the followers of the Sunni school of theology, law and morality which grew up from the teaching of Ahmad b. Hanbal. Hanbalism recognizes no other sources than the Qurʾan and the Sunna of the Prophet. It is hostile to speculative theology (A. *kalām*) and to esoteric Sufism. Under the Shiʿi Buyids, Hanbalism became a politico-religious opposition party in Baghdad, contributing decisively to Sunni restoration, as is clear from the works of many Hanbali theologians of this period. The final two centuries of the caliphate in Baghdad (1061-1258) are the golden age of Hanbalism. One of the great Hanbalites of this epoch was ʿAbd al-Rahman Ibn al-Jawzi. Under the Bahri Mamluks, Hanbalism remained very active in Syria and Palestine, the most famous Hanbalite then being Ibn Taymiyya. It lost some of its importance in Syria and Palestine under the Circassian Mamluks, and was not favoured by the Ottomans, who gave pre-eminence to Hanafism. In the xviiith c., under Ottoman rule, shaykh Ibn ʿAbd al-Wahhab won over to Hanbalism the amir Muhammad b. Saʿud, the founder of the Al Saʿud dynasty of Saudi Arabia.

Haniʾ b. ʿUrwa al-Muradi: Yemeni chief who lost his life during the attempt made by ʿAli's son al-Husayn to seize power; d. 680.

Hanif (A.): the term means in Islamic writing one who follows the original and true (monotheistic) religion. In the Qurʾan it is used especially of Abraham as the type of this pure worship of God.

Hansawi, Shaykh Jamal al-Din: Sufi mystic of the Indian Čishtiyya order; 1184-1260. His Persian *dīwān* is the earliest known poetical work of a Čishti mystic, important for the history of North India in the early xiiith c.

Hansi: town of the Indian Punjab. It was an important forward position in the Ghaznawids' Indian province. Gateways and lengths of bastioned walls of the old fort are parts of its monuments.

al-Haram al-Sharif ("the Noble Sanctuary"): the well-known Muslim sanctuary of Jerusalem, after Mecca and Medina the acknowledged third holiest one. It is a large, totally artificial, trapezoidal platform, surrounded with walls on its southern and eastern ends, which were built by the Ayyubids, the Mamluks and the Ottomans and which are now pierced by fifteen gates. In the centre of the Haram is a smaller platform reached by eight sets of stairs, on which is found the Dome of the Rock. On the Haram are further found the Masjid al-Aqsa, from where the Prophet's ascension to heaven (A. *mi'rāj*) took place, and a number of other sanctuaries.

al-Haramayn ("the two Holy Places"): the word usually refers to Mecca and Medina and occasionally, in both Mamluk and Ottoman usage, to Jerusalem and Hebron.

Harar: important commercial centre in eastern Ethiopia, and one of the main Muslim cities in East Africa. The inhabitants follow the Shafi'i school of law and adhere to the Qadiriyya order.

Harat (Herat): city and district in western Aghanistan. Taken by the Arabs during the conquest of Khurasan around 652, the city, strategically located on trade routes from the Mediterranean Sea to India and China, was noted for its textiles during the 'Abbasid caliphate. It flourished especially under the Ghurid dynasty in the xth c. Twice captured and destroyed by the Mongols, it was rebuilt and became flourishing again under the Kurt dynasty (xiiith c.). Harat reached its greatest glory under the Timurid Husayn Bayqara (r. 1469-1506). In the xviiith c. it came under Afghan rule.

Harem (A. *ḥarīm*): the Arabic word means "an inviolable place" and is applied to those parts of the house to which access is forbidden, and hence more particularly to the women's quarters.

al-Hariri, Abu Muhammad: Arabic poet and philologist; 1054-1122. His best-known work is the *Sessions*, which imitate very closely those of al-Hamadhani, but of which they are no more than a pale reflection. On the other hand, al-Hariri possessed an unequalled mastery of the Arabic language and a perfect command of its inexhaustible vocabulary.

al-Harith b. Jabala: the most famous king of the Ghassanids; 529-569. He was an ally of Byzantium and fought the Persians and their Arab allies, the Lakhmids.

al-Harith b. Kalada: traditionally considered as the oldest known Arab physician; d. 634. His personality is surrounded by a host of legends.

al-Harithi, Salih b. 'Ali: Ibadi leader; 1834-1896. He was the shaykh of the confederation of tribes of eastern Oman known as the Sharqiyya Hinawis.

Harra: name for a basalt desert. The al-Harra par excellence is the Harrat Waqim on the northeastern side of Medina, where Muslim b. 'Uqba al-Murri defeated in 683 the Medinese who had rebelled against the Umayyad Caliph Yazid I.

Harran: ancient city, now a village, near Urfa in Turkey. It was occupied by the Muslims in 640 and became the capital of the Umayyads under Marwan II b. Muhammad. After the latter's defeat against the 'Abbasids in 750, the city was destroyed, but became later a centre of translation under the guidance of Thabit b. Qurra. Ruled between 990 and 1063 by the Numayrids, a nomad petty dynasty, it flourished under the Zangid Nur al-Din Mahmud and under Saladin. After having been governed for the Ayyubids, the city was destroyed by the Mongols in 1271 and not rebuilt after the Mamluk victory over them in 1303. Of the ruins of its monuments may be mentioned the Citadel, the Great Mosque, called Jami' al-Firdaws, the mausoleum of Shaykh Hayat and the city gates.

Harun al-Rashid: 'Abbasid caliph; b. 766, r. 786-809. Thanks to the "Thousand-and-One Nights", he is almost a legendary figure which obscures his true historic personality. In fact, his reign initiated the political disintegration of the Islamic empire. Syria, inhabited by tribes with Umayyad sympathies, remained the bitter enemy of the 'Abbasids and Egypt witnessed risings due to maladministration and arbitrary taxation. The Umayyads had been established in Spain in 755, the Idrisids in the Maghrib in 788 and the Aghlabids in Ifriqiya in 800. Besides, unrest flared up in Yemen, and the Kharijites rose in rebellion in Daylam, Kirman, Fars and Sistan. Revolts also broke out in Khurasan. A great part of Harun al-Rashid's fame was due to his interest in Holy War against the Byzantines, in which he occasionally participated personally. He also paid attention to naval power. Arabic sources do not substantiate the allegation that embassies and gifts were exchanged between Harun al-Rashid and Charlemagne. The caliph virtually dismembered the empire by apportioning it between his two sons al-Amin and al-Ma'mun.

Harut and Marut: name of two angels, mentioned in the Qur'an, who are a reminiscence of the "fallen angels" of Genesis VI, 1-4.

al-Hasa (al-Ahsa'): group of oases in eastern Saudi Arabia, with al-Hufuf as capital. According to one version of the story, it was here, and not in Bahrain, that the Carmathians kept the Black Stone between 930 and 950. The Ottomans occupied the oases in 1872, but were expelled in 1913 by 'Abd al-'Aziz Ibn Sa'ud.

al-Hasan I b. Muhammad: Filali Sharif of Morocco; b. 1836, r. 1873-1894. On his initiative and that of Britain the first international conference concerned with Morocco was held at Madrid in 1880. It initiated the process which was to lead to the French Protectorate of 1912.

(al-)Hasan b. 'Ali: son of 'Ali and the Prophet's daughter Fatima; 624-669. After 'Ali was murdered in 661, al-Hasan half-heartedly claimed the caliphate but was persuaded by Mu'awiya, the governor of Syria, to renounce all rights to the caliphate. This was done in the mosque at Kufa in 661. In the eyes of the Shi'is, al-Hasan is the second Imam and in the Persian religious dramas he is one of the principal characters.

al-Hasan al-A'sam: famous Carmathian leader of Bahrain; 891-977. He took Damascus and fought the Fatimids.

Hasan al-Basri: famous preacher of Basra; 642-728. The fragments of his sermons which have been preserved are among the best surviving specimens of early Arabic prose.

Hasan Bey-zade: Ottoman historian; d. 1636. His *History of the Ottomans* is of great importance since it depends on his own experiences. He also left a collection of maxims of government.

al-Hasan b. Muhammad b. al-Hanafiyya: grandson of the Prophet's son-in-law 'Ali; d. ca. 710. He is the author of the two earliest texts so far known of Islamic theology.

Hasan Pasha b. Khayr al-Din: commander in Algiers in the years 1544-1551, 1557-1561 and 1562-1567. He fought the Spaniards and tried to enroll the Kabyles in his service against the Moroccans.

Hasan b. Ustadh-Hurmuz: leading figure of the Buyid regime; ca. 960-1011. He is praised for the impartial energy of his administration, which restored order and established a sound financial system.

Hasan al-Utrush: ruler in Tabaristan; 844-917. The Zaydis in Yemen recognize him as Imam under the official name al-Nasir al-Kabir.

al-Hasan b. Zayd b. Muhammad: descendant of the Prophet's son-in-law 'Ali; d. 884. He founded the Zaydiyya in Tabaristan, which ruled there from 864-928.

Hasan-i Sabbah: the first chief propagandist (A. *dā'ī*) of the Nizari Isma'ilis at Alamut; d. 1124. He seized the fortress in 1090 and held it against many Saljuq attacks. His exposition of the Shi'i doctrine that absolute authority in religious faith must be accepted greatly affected Abu Hamid al-Ghazali.

Hasani (pl. *Ḥasaniyyun*): name of the 'Alid Sharifs descended from 'Ali's son al-Hasan. In Morocco the Hasani family have given birth to the Sharifian dynasties of the Sa'dids and of the Filalis.

Hasanwayhids: name of a Kurdish chieftain, and of the dynasty descended from him. Between 960 and 1014 they maintained more or less autonomous principalities in Western Persia.

Hashid wa-Bakil: large confederation of tribes in the highlands of northern Yemen between San'a' and Sa'da, which has played a role since dawn of history.

Hashim b. 'Abd Manaf: great-grandfather of the Prophet. He had made the tribe of Quraysh dominant in Mecca and had reorganized the pilgrimage. He is said to have died at Gaza on a journey to Syria.

Hashimids (al-Hawashim): collective name of the four main branches of Hasanid Sharifs, who ruled Mecca from 960-1924. The name al-Hawashim is used to distinguish them from the Hashimites of the Hejaz, Iraq and Jordan. The eponym of the Hashimids was Hashim b. 'Abd Manaf. They were descended from Musa I al-Jawn, a great-grandson of 'Ali's son al-Hasan. Musa I's son 'Abd Allah al-Shaykh al-Salih was the sire of the Meccan Sharifs, and from the latter's son Musa II sprang the four main branches of the dynasty – the Musawids, the Sulaymanids, the Hashimids and the Qatadids.

Hashimites: name of the royal family of the Hejaz (1908-1925), of Iraq (1921-1958) and of Jordan (1921-the present day). The family belongs to the Dhawu ʿAwn, one of the branches of the Hasanid Sharifs of Mecca. In 1908 the Ottoman sultan appointed Husayn b. ʿAli as sharif and amir of Mecca and of the Hejaz. In 1916 he became king of the Hejaz, but was forced in 1924 by ʿAbd al-ʿAziz Al Saʿud to abdicate. His eldest son ʿAli, nominated king, left the country in 1925. Al-Husayn's second son ʿAbd Allah, the grandfather of king Husayn of Jordan, became amir of Transjordan in 1923, and his third son Faysal I became king of Iraq in 1921.

al-Hashimiyya: name of the administrative capital of the ʿAbbasids before the building of Baghdad in 763. The word refers not to a single place but to wherever the caliph chose to establish his residence.

Hashimiyya: in Umayyad times the term was applied to a religio-political faction who believed that the Imamate had passed from the ʿAlid Muhammad b. al-Hanafiyya to his son Abu Hashim (d. 716). The ʿAbbasids inherited Abu Hashim's party and organisation, the Hashimiyya, which was the main instrument of the ʿAbbasid propaganda and movement in Khurasan. The term was then applied to members of the ʿAbbasid house, and understood as denoting the descendants of Hashim b. ʿAbd Manaf, the common ancestor of the Prophet, of the latter's son-in-law ʿAli and of al-ʿAbbas.

Hassan b. al-Nuʿman al-Ghassani: Umayyad general who played a decisive part in the consolidation of the conquest of Ifriqiya by storming Carthage; d. 699.

Hassan b. Thabit: traditionally known as the "poet laureate" of the Prophet, he is the most prominent of several poets who were associated with the rise of Islam; d. 659.

Hausa: name of a people, now predominantly Muslim, dwelling mainly in the northern region of Nigeria. Islamic rites of slaughter and prayer were introduced in Kano by Mandingo missionaries in the xivth c. A further stage in the establishment of Islam was the arrival of the North African divine ʿAbd al-Karim al-Maghili in the xvth c. Islamic literature, written in Hausa, is almost entirely in verse and religious in character.

Hawran: region of southern Syria, conquered by the Muslims in 634 after the battle of the Yarmuk which halted the Byzantine counter-offensive. The region suffered from the incursions of the Carmathians, the pillage of the Crusaders and the ravage of the Khwarazmians and the Mongols. During the xviiith and xixth c. the Druzes settled in Jabal Hawran.

Hawwara: name of a Berber people, who spread from Tripolitania to Fazzan, Morocco, Tunisia, Algeria, Spain, Sicily, Egypt and the Sudan.

Haydar-i Amuli: early representative of Persian theosophy and commentator of Ibn al-ʿArabi; 1320-after 1385.

Haydarabad: city in the Deccan of India, founded in 1589 by the Qutb Shahid Muhammad Quli Qutb Shah (r. 1512-1687), when North India was in the hands of the Mughal emperors. Some of its finest buildings were erected in the xviith c. In 1724 the city became the capital of Haydarabad State, founded by Nizam al-Mulk, who gave his name to the dynasty of the Nizams. The State was integrated into the Indian Union in 1948.

Haydarabad (Sind): city in Sind Province, Pakistan. It is built on the site of the ancient Nirunkot, which was conquered by Muhammad b. Qasim al-Thaqafi at the time of the first Muslim conquest of Sind in the viiith c.

Hayy b. Yaqzan: name of the principal character of two philosophical allegories, one by Avicenna and the other by Ibn Tufayl.

Hazaras: group of peoples inhabiting the central mountains of Afghanistan. They are mainly Twelver Shi'is.

Hazaraspids: local dynasty in Persia with its capital at Idhaj. They ruled over parts of Luristan from 1148-1424, when the Timurids put an end to the dynasty.

Hazmiriyyun: Moroccan religious brotherhood; xivth-xvth c. Its main object was to islamize the Berbers who were inclined to form their own and even local brand of Islam.

Heart (A. *qalb*): according to the Qur'an, where the word is very frequently employed, man understands with his heart, and it is from there that his awareness or ignorance of God originates. In Sufi terminology, it is both the source of man's good and evil aspirations and the seat of learning of religious apprehension and of divine visitations.

Hebron (A. *al-Khalīl*): town on the West Bank of the river Jordan, south-southwest of Jerusalem, since 1968 under Israeli administration. The Arab word is a reference to Abraham who, according to the Qur'an, was taken by God as a friend (A. *khalīl Allāh*). Immediately after the Islamic conquest in 635, his tomb became sacred to the Muslims. The sanctuary of the Ibrahim al-Khalil Mosque contains, besides Abraham's tomb, those of Adam, Sarah, Isaac, Joseph, Leah and Rebecca. According to a legend of the viiith c., the Prophet bestowed Hebron on his companion, the oil-merchant Tamim b. Aws al-Dari, and the rights of the Daris have been recognised down the ages. From 1100-1260 the town was controlled by the Crusaders.

Hejaz (A. *al-Ḥijāz*): name of the northwestern part of the Arabian Peninsula, the birthplace and the spiritual centre of Islam. The areas surrounding the Two Holy Cities Mecca and Medina are sacred preserves which only Muslims are allowed to enter. From the beginning of Islam, the region was under control of Muslim rulers, first the Four Rightly-Guided Caliphs, then the Umayyads and, until 1258, the 'Abbasids. It then fell to the Egyptians and, in 1517, to the Ottomans. King al-Husayn b. 'Ali reigned from 1916 to 1924, and since 1925 the region belongs to the territory of Saudi Arabia.

Hejaz Railway: the purpose of this major railway project was to facilitate the pilgrimage to the Holy Cities, to further Pan-Islamic policies and to establish Ottoman control over often turbulent Arabian provinces. The main line, from Damascus via Darʿa and Maʿan to Medina, was constructed in 1900-1908. The major branch line from Darʿa to Haifa was completed in 1905. During World War I parts of the section between Maʿan and Medina were successfully damaged by raids, largely inspired by T.E. Lawrence. Restoration of this section was started in the 1960s.

Hell (A. *jahannam*): the word is very often used in the Qurʾan as a synonym of fire (A. *nār*). Islamic descriptions show hell as a place made up of concentric layers of increasing depth. The Jahannam proper, generally put in the higher zone, is reserved for members of the Muslim community who have committed grave sins for which they have not repented and whom God, in accordance with His threats, decides to punish for a time with infernal torments. Even those Muslims who uphold the eternity of hell admit that Jahannam will cease to exist when the last repentant sinner leaves it to enter paradise.

Helmand (Hilmand): important river which, with its five tributaries, drains all of southwest Afghanistan.

Helpers (A. *al-Anṣār*): the term denotes those men from Medina who supported the Prophet, in distinction from the Emigrants, i.e. his Meccan followers.

Hemerology/Menology (A. *ikhtiyārāt*): the astrological procedure whose aim is to ascertain the auspicious or inauspicious character of the future, was entrusted to the court astrologer. This task, already practised in the Umayyad period, became increasingly important under the ʿAbbasids as a result of the adoption of Iranian customs and Sasanian calendars. In Iranian and Turkish milieus, special attention is paid to the first day of the Iranian year, the Nawruz.

Henna (A. *ḥinnāʾ*): the name of a shrub whose leaves possess medical properties and are used as a dye.

Herald (A. *munādī*): in the Qurʾan, the word is used for the one who will proclaim the Last Day and give the summons to Judgement, in popular Islam usually identified with the angel Israfil. In the towns of the pre-modern Islamic world, the town crier performed a vital function of communication.

Heretic (A. *mulḥid/zindīq*): in the Qurʾan, the word is used with the meaning of "deviator". In the Umayyad age, the term denoted desertion of the community of the faithful and rebellion against the legitimate caliphs. In the early ʿAbbasid age, theologians began to use the term for someone who is a religious sceptic inclining to atheism, and in particular for someone who critizises the Qurʾan and teaches deviation from it.

Hermes Trismegistus (A. *Hirmis*): for Islamic authors, the author of philosophical, scientific and magical works appears divided into three individuals. The first Hermes was identified with Enoch and Idris, who lived in Egypt before the Flood and built the Pyramids. The second lived in Babylon after the Flood and revived the study of the sciences. The third wrote in Egypt after the Flood about various sciences and crafts.

Hidayat, Sadiq: revolutionary writer of modern Iran; 1903-1951. His daring experiments in technique and in thought have exercised a powerful influence on the development of modern Persian fiction.

Hijra (latinized as Hegira): the emigration of the Prophet from Mecca to Medina in September 622. The term connotes primarily the breaking of the ties of kinship or association. On the death of 'Ali's father Abu Talib about 619 and his replacement as chief of the clan by Abu Lahab, the Prophet lost support in Mecca. He negotiated successfully with representatives of all the main Arab clans of Medina and concluded an agreement with them at al-'Aqaba during the pilgrimage of June-July 622. In the company of Abu Bakr he arrived at Medina on 24 September 622.

Muslim dates are normally given according to the era of the Hijra. This era does not begin on the date of the Prophet's arrival at Medina, but on the first day of the lunar year in which that event took place, which is reckoned to coincide with 16 July 622.

Hilal, Banu: tribe of Arabia who, in the viiith c., emigrated to Egypt, joined the Carmathians in the xth c. and were given Ifriqiya by the Fatimids in the xith c. to invade. Their movement into North Africa and the battles they fought there form the historical basis for the saga known as *Sirat Bani Hilal*.

Hindi: the national language of the Republic of India. It is now generally regarded as that form of the central north Indian speech which draws its erudite vocabulary from Sanskrit and its culture from Hinduism. For literary purposes it includes the standard dialect and several other dialects. As late as the xixth c. it was also used to describe the speech of north Indian Muslims. The relevance of Hindi to Islam is threefold: there is a small but important corpus of Hindi works by Muslim writers; Muslim rulers and nobles have been active patrons of Hindi poetry; and there has been a considerable Muslim influence on Hindi vocabulary.

Hindu Kush: extensive range of mountains in northern Afghanistan. Although presenting substantial difficulties to north-south communications, the range has never been found insuperable. The main routes are all open for six months of the year. The routes between Kabul and the north via the Panjshir valley and the Khawak Pass, and up the Bamiyan valley over the Aq Ribat Pass, were used by Genghis Khan and Tamerlane.

Hindustani: term which has been used, confusingly, in India for: a synonym for Urdu as spoken in North India, i.e. the Muslim speech of Hindustan as opposed to the Deccan; a name for that sort of language in which a Muslim villager might converse with a Hindu villager and in which common Persian loanwords are used freely; a conscious attempt, made in the 1930s and 1940s but now abandoned, at a language acceptable to both Muslims and Hindus.

Hintata: famous Berber confederation in the central Moroccan High Atlas. They were the first to support the Mahdi Ibn Tumart, the founder of the Almohads.

al-Hira: capital of the Lakhmids, located to the southeast of present day Najaf in Iraq.

Hisham b. ʿAbd al-Malik: caliph of the Umayyad dynasty; b. 691, r. 724-743. His reign marks the final period of prosperity and splendour of the Umayyad caliphate.

Hisham I, Abu ʾl-Walid al-Rida: Umayyad ruler of Muslim Spain; b. 757, r. 788-796. During his reign expeditions were sent regularly against the Christians, and Narbonne was attacked in 793.

Hisham II, al-Muʾayyad bi-ʾllah: Umayyad caliph of Córdoba; b. 966, r. 976-1009, 1010-1013. He was held under permanent tutelage of the vizier Almanzor.

Hisham III, al-Muʿtadd bi-ʾllah: the last of the Umayyads caliphs of Córdoba; b. 974, r. 1027-1031, d. 1036. He was deposed in 1031, after which followed the period of the Muluk al-Tawaʾif.

Hisham b. al-Hakam: the most prominent Imami theologian in the times of the Imams Jaʿfar al-Sadiq and Musa al-Kazim; d. 795. The theory of the imamate which he elaborated has remained at the basis of Imami doctrine.

Hisn Kayfa (Hasankeyf): town in Turkey on the right bank of the Tigris. The present ruins bear witness to its importance in the Middle Ages.

Hit: town in Iraq on the right bank of the Euphrates. Occupied by the Arabs in 629, Hit was a flourishing transit centre, famous for its asphalt and naphtha, its cereals and its wine.

Hittin/Hattin: village at the southwest end of the Sea of Galilee (Lake Tiberias) in Israel near which Saladin in 1187 won a great victory over the Crusaders, led by Guy de Lusignan, king of Jerusalem.

Hmad u-Musa, Sidi: great saint of southern Morocco and patron saint of Sus; ca. 1460-1563.

Holy War (A. *jihād*): the Arabic word, which signifies an effort directed towards a determined objective, is used for military action with the object of the expansion of Islam and, if need be, of its defence. The notion stems from the fundamental principle of the universality of Islam, according to which this religion, along with the temporal power which it implies, ought to embrace the whole universe, if necessary by force. This principle, however, must be partially combined with another which tolerates the existence, within the Islamic community itself, of the adherents of "the religions with holy books", i.e. Christians, Jews and Zoroastrians. For them Holy War ceases as soon as they agree to submit to the political authority of Islam and pay the poll tax (A. *jizya*) and the land tax (A. *kharāj*). At present times there is a thesis according to which Islam relies for its expansion exclusively upon persuasion and other peaceful means.

Homosexuality (A. *liwāṭ*): Lot and his people are condemned in the Qurʾan. Muslim Tradition prescribes that the agents be subjected to death by stoning.

Homs (A. *Ḥimṣ*/T. *Humus*): town in Syria on the eastern bank of the Orontes, taken by the Muslims without bloodshed in 637. The town is known for its gates, its citadel, the Great Mosque of the Zangid Nur al-Din Mahmud, its baths, and several places of pilgrimage.

Homs witnessed the first great trial of strength between the Mamluks and the Mongols in a battle which took place in 1281 and in which the Mamluks were victorious.

Hoopoe (A. *hudhud*): in the Qur'an the bird plays a prominent role in the story of king Solomon and the Queen of Sheba.

Horde: the term, originating from the Turkish *ordu*, indicates the administrative centre of great nomad empires, in particular the highly adorned tent of the ruler, and then such nomad confederacies themselves.

Hormuz (Hurmuz): the original town, or Old Hormuz, was situated on the mainland of Persia on the east side of the entrance to the Persian Gulf. In 1300 the inhabitants moved to the small island of Jarun where an exceedingly flourishing town, called New Hormuz, came into being. The name Jarun was transferred to the small port of Suru, became corrupted to Gamru and was further corrupted by Europeans into Gambrun, Gombrun and Gom(b)roon. The island was occupied by the Portuguese in 1514, and reconquered by the Persians in 1622.

Hospital (P. *bīmāristān, māristān*): the Persian word was adopted by the Arabs. In modern usage the word is applied especially to a lunatic asylum.

Hospitallers, Knights (A. *Isbitāriyya*, from Latin *hospitalis*): the religious military order is first mentioned by Ibn al-Qalanisi. They were known to 'Imad al-Din al-Katib al-Isfahani, the chief source of Saladin's reign, who describes the latter's massacre of Templar and Hospitaller prisoners after the battle of Hittin in 1187. After the fall of Acre in 1291, the Hospitallers retreated to Cyprus, in 1309 to Rhodes and, after the Ottoman conquest of the island, to Malta.

Houris (A. *Ḥūr*): the term is used in the Qur'an for the virgins of Paradise promised to the Believers.

Hubaysh b. al-Hasan al-Dimashqi (al-A'sam): translator of Greek medicinal writings; ixth c. With the exception of the Hippocratic oath and the herb-book of Dioscurides, he translated 35 of Galen's works from Arabic into Syriac, and three from Syriac into Arabic. He also wrote additions to a work of his uncle Hunayn b. Ishaq, which won extremely wide diffusion.

Hud: name of the earliest of the five "Arab" prophets mentioned in the Qur'an, the others being Salih, Ibrahim, Shu'ayb and the Prophet himself.

al-Hudaybiya: village on the edge of the sacred territory of Mecca where the Prophet, arriving from Medina, negotiated a treaty with the Meccans in 628.

Hudids (Banu Hud): Muslim Arab dynasty that ruled Saragossa in Spain from 1039 till 1146 during the period of the Muluk al-Tawa'if. The last ruler, Abu Ja'far Ahmad III al-Mustansir bi-'llah, was killed in a battle with the Christians.

Hudud al-ʿAlam ("The limits of the World"): important anonymous Persian geography of the world, Islamic and non-Islamic, composed in the xth c. in northern Afghanistan.

Hujja: the Qurʾanic term for "proof" is used in Shiʿi terminology to indicate that person through whom the inaccessible God becomes accessible. For the Twelver Shiʿis the present *hujja* is the hidden twelfth Imam. Among the Ismaʿilis, the term usually refers to a particular figure in the religious hierarchy, thought of as fulfilling a function in revelation.

Hujr b. ʿAdi al-Kindi: Shiʿi agitator in early Islam, put to death by the Umayyad Caliph al-Muʿawiya I.

Hülegü/Hüleʾü (A. *Hūlāgū*): Mongol conqueror and founder of the Il-Khanid dynasty of Persia; b. 1217, r. 1256-1265. This grandson of Genghis Khan was sent by his brother the Great Khan Möngke against the Ismaʿilis and the ʿAbbasid Caliph al-Mustaʿsim. He conquered Alamut in 1256, took Baghdad in 1258 and Aleppo and Damascus in 1260, but returned to Persia at the news of the death of the Great Khan. The army he had left behind was destroyed by the Mamluks at ʿAyn Jalut in 1260.

Hulwan: town to the south of Cairo, known for its mineral springs.

Humayun: the word, which means "royal", became widely used in Persian chancery style during the Safawid period. With the spread of Persian culture and especially Persian chancery practice, the concept reached Asia Minor with the Saljuqs, and India with the Mughals. It is found as early as the beginning of the xvth c. among the Ottomans, who in chancery practice were linked firmly to Saljuq traditions.

Humayun, Nasir al-Din: son of Babur and the second Mughal ruler of Hindustan and Kabul; b. 1508, r. 1530-1540, 1555-1556. His first period of rule was a long struggle against his family, most of all his half-brother Kamran, and against the Afghan chief Shir Shah Suri, who took over Bengal and used it as a base from which to eject Humayun from India. In 1543, Humayun was obliged to seek the hospitality of Shah Tahmasp I of Persia, who forced him to sign papers professing Shiʿism. In 1555 he was able to return to Delhi. He was a keen patron of mathematics and astronomy, wrote Persian verse, and carried books on his travels.

Hunayn: a valley situated a day's journey from Mecca where the Prophet, soon after the conquest of Mecca in 630, defeated the confederate tribe of the Hawazin.

Hunayn b. Ishaq al-ʿIbadi: the most important mediator of ancient Greek science to the Arabs; 808-873. He is credited with an immense number of translations from Greek into Syriac and Arabic, among them those of Hippocrates and Galen. He also composed numerous original works, mainly on medical subjects, and had a special interest in ophthalmology.

Hungary (T. *Majar/Majaristān*): republic of central Europe. Arabic and

Persian authors of the ixth-xivth c. knew the Hungarians as al-Majghariyya. The first written information telling of Muslims living among the Hungarians in historical Hungary dates from the xth c. Arab geographers designated the Hungarians also with the name Bashkirs, who were in fact a Turkish tribe. The most ancient Muslim elements appeared as early as the second half of the ixth c.

Buda and Esztergom were occupied by the Ottoman sultan Sülayman II in 1541. The upkeep of Turkish forces in Hungary was very costly. Cattle-breeding was prosperous but many vineyards were lost. A large number of Hungarians escaped to territories which had not passed under Turkish rule. No deliberate efforts were made to settle large numbers of Turkish families in Hungary, nor did Islam gain any ground.

Hunting: falconry, and hunting with the cheetah were very popular in the Muslim east and west.

al-Hurmuzan: a Persian ruler and general; d. 644. He was killed at Medina by 'Ubayd Allah b. 'Umar under the suspicion of being involved in Caliph 'Umar b. al-Khattab's murder by the Persian slave Abu Lu'lu'a.

Hürriyyet we I'tilaf Firqasi (Freedom and Accord Party): liberal political party in Turkey, formed in November 1911. The Liberals assumed power in 1912 but were overthrown by the Unionists in 1913. A second party of the same name was formed in 1919 but was rejected in the elections of that year.

Hurufiyya: unorthodox Muslim sect of gnostic-cabalistic tendencies founded by Fadl Allah Hurufi (1340-1394) of Astarabad in Persia.

Husayn I b. Shah Sulayman I: Safawid monarch; b. 1668, r. 1694-1722; d. 1726. During his reign, Persia was attacked by Mahmud of Qandahar and by Turkey and Russia. The Shah was deposed in 1722.

al-Husayn b. 'Ali: Bey of Tunis; r. 1705-1735. Recognised by the Ottoman sultan, he was the founder of the Husaynid dynasty, which reigned over Tunisia until 1957.

Husayn b. 'Ali: amir and sharif of Mecca and the Hejaz from 1908-1916, king of the Hejaz from 1916-1924; b. 1853, d. 1931. Appointed by the Ottoman sultan, he at first showed loyalty to the sultan, but prevented the extension of the Hejaz Railway southward from Medina. In 1916 he proclaimed the Arab revolt and expelled the Turks from Mecca, but the Allied military occupation of Syria and Iraq precluded effective Arab rule. In 1924 he adopted the title of caliph, but did not find support for his assumption of the caliphate. 'Abd al-'Aziz Ibn Sa'ud forced him to abdicate in the same year.

(al-)Husayn b. 'Ali: grandson of the Prophet and son of 'Ali and Fatima; 626-680. Though pressed by the Shi'is, he did not resist the Umayyad Caliph Mu'awiya I after his father's death in 661. In 680, however, when Mu'awiya died, he refused to recognize the latter's son and successor Yazid I. From Medina he fled to Mecca and then tried to make his way to Kufa, the majority of whose inhabitants were Shiʿis. He made his camp at a place called al-Ghadi-riyya near Karbalaʾ, where he was attacked by the troops of ʿUmar b. Saʿd b. Abi Waqqas and finally beheaded by Sinan b. Anas b. ʿAmr al-Nakhaʿi. Among the Shiʿis Husayn holds an exalted position. Legend speaks of the marvels connected with his birth and childhood, his death, his severed head, the punishment of those who had insulted and wounded him and of his supernatural attributes which caused marvels.

al-Husayn b. ʿAli, Sahib Fakhkh: an ʿAlid; d. 786. He led a revolt at Medina during the caliphate of the ʿAbbasid Caliph al-Hadi ila ʾl-Haqq and was killed at Fakhkh.

(al-)Husayn b. al-Dahhaq (al-Khaliʿ): poet from Basra at the ʿAbbasid court; d. 864. He can be regarded as the perfect type of court poet, at least at a court dominated by the taste for pleasure.

Husayn b. al-Husayn: the last dey of Algiers; r. 1818-1830, d. 1838. In 1830 he set his seal upon the capitulation proposals formulated by the French government.

Husayn Jahid (Hüseyin Cahit Yalçin): Turkish writer, journalist and politician; 1874-1957. In 1930, in the presence of Mustafa Kemal Atatürk, he publicly opposed the project of a government-sponsored language reform.

Husayn Kamil: sultan of Egypt; b. 1853, r. 1914-1917. With the declaration of a British Protectorate in 1914, Turkish sovereignty over Egypt was terminated.

Husayn Nizam Shah I: ruler of the Nizam Shahi sultanate of Ahmadnagar, western India; r. 1554-1565. His reign was spent in almost continual warfare, mostly with Bijapur.

Husayn Pasha (Küčük Hüseyin Pasha): Ottoman Grand Admiral; 1758-1803. He is accounted the founder of the new Ottoman fleet.

Husayn Pasha, Aga: Ottoman vizier; 1776-1849. He is known for having suppressed the Janissaries in 1826.

Husayn Pasha, Hajji (Mezzomorto): Algerian corsair and Ottoman general; d. 1701. He owes his Italian nickname "half-dead" to the fact that as a young man he had been wounded, apparently fatally, in a sea-fight with the Spaniards.

Husayn Rahmi (Hüseyin Rahmi Gürpinar): Turkish novelist and short story writer; 1864-1944. He wrote about the everyday life of families and individuals and their development within the disintegrating Ottoman society.

Husayn Shah, al-Makki: founder of the Husayn-Shah dynasty of Bengal; d. 1519. He claimed descent from the Sharifs of Mecca.

Husayn Shah Arghun: founder of the Arghun dynasty of Sind; b. 1490, r. 1521-1555.

Husayn Shah Langah I: founder of the Langah dynasty of Multan, western India; r. 1469-1502.

Husayn Shah Langah II: son of Mahmud Langah (r. 1498-1524) and the last ruler of the Langah dynasty of Multan; r. 1524-1526. In 1526 Multan became a dependency of the Mughal Empire.

Husayn Shah b. Mahmud Shah Sharqi: the last of the line of the Sharqi sultans of Jawnpur; r. 1458-1479. He was a great musician.

Husayni Dalan: Shi'i shrine in the old city of Dacca, Bangladesh, built in 1642. From the first to the tenth day of the month Muharram many pilgrims gather here.

Husaynids: dynasty of Beys of Turkish origin, which reigned in Tunisia from 1705 until 1957. Having been reigned by the Beys under Turkish sovereignty until 1881, Tunisia became a French Protectorate in 1883. Under Ahmad Bey (1919-1942), Habib Bourguiba founded the Néo-Destour party. A republican regime was proclaimed in 1957.

Hushang Shah Ghuri: ruler of Malwa; 1405-1432. He extended the Malwa territories northwards and southwards. He had a fine taste for architecture, which made Mandu a magnificent town.

Hutaym: pariah tribe in northwestern Arabia. At times, the name is used as a designation for any of the pariah tribes in the eastern Arab lands.

Huwa Huwa: literally "he is he" or "it is it". In logic it means entirely identical, e.g. "Muhammad b. 'Abd Allah" and "the Prophet". In mysticism the expression means the state of the saint whose perfect personal unity testifies to divine unity in the world.

Hypocrites (A. *al-munāfiqūn*): the Qur'anic term covers a wider semantic range than the translation usually given in western languages. The English word that comes nearest to *munāfiqūn* in its totality of use in the Qur'an is "dissenters", the *munāfiqūn* being clearly dissenters within the Muslim community, whether openly or in secret. The English word "hypocrite" most closely fits post-Qur'anic Muslim usage of the term.

I

Iaxartes (Sir-Darya): large river in Central Asia, flowing like its sister stream, the Oxus (Amu-Darya), into the Aral Sea.

Ibadan: town in the Western region of Nigeria, originated during the 1820s. Islam penetrated into the town from the north through the activities of Muslim traders. The massive conversion to Islam in the city began in 1893, when the British imposed their control. By far the most of the Muslims of the city are Sunnis who follow the Maliki school of law. Some have adopted the Qadiriyya order but many more have joined the Tijaniyya order.

al-Ibadiyya (Abadiyya): one of the main branches of the Kharijites, representatives of which are today found in Oman, East Africa, Tripolitania and southern Algeria. The name is derived from 'Abd Allah b. 'Ibad (viiith c.) of Basra, who broke away from the Khariji extremists. The chief scholar and organizer of the Ibadis was Jabir b. Zayd al-Azdi from Oman (ca. 639-ca. 711). His scholarly pupil Abu ʿUbayda Muslim at first hoped to win the caliphs to Ibadism, but later made Basra into the centre of missionary activities. Outside Basra there were Ibadi centres at Kufa, Mosul, the Hejaz, even at Mecca and Medina, in Central Arabia, Hadhramaut, Yemen and Oman, where the town of Nizwa was their capital. The first to preach Ibadism in East Africa in the ixth c. were probably merchants from Oman. The movement also spread to Persia (Khurasan), Egypt, Ifriqiya, the Maghrib, western and central Sudan, and to Spain and Sicily.

Unlike the Khariji extremists, represented by the Azraqis, the Ibadis do not regard a non-Khariji Muslim as an infidel and a polytheist, and thus reject assassination for religious reasons. Marriage with non-Ibadis is also permitted. If circumstances were unfavourable, it was not necessary to have an Imam. The latter was elected by a council of important lay persons or by shaykhs, and proclaimed before the people. He was also leader in war, judge and theologian. He could be deposed if he did not observe the Qurʾan, the Sunna of the Prophet and the example of the first Imams. In general, the dogma and the politico-religious theories of the Ibadiyya resemble those of the Sunnis.

Among the several Ibadi sects should be mentioned the Nukkaris in North Africa.

Ibn ʿAbbad, Abu ʾl-Qasim (al-Sahib): vizier and man of letters of the Buyid period; 938-995. Of Persian origin, he was an arabophile and wrote on dogmatic theology, history, grammar, lexicography, literary criticism and composed poetry and belles-lettres.

Ibn ʿAbd al-Hakam: name which refers to the son and the four grandsons of ʿAbd al-Hakam, a wealthy and influential family of legal scholars and historians in ixth c. Egypt.

Ibn ʿAbd al-Munʿim al-Himyari: author of an important Arabic geographical dictionary. He used the works of al-Bakri and al-Idrisi. His dictionary acquired a great popularity in the Maghrib.

Ibn ʿAbd al-Wahhab: Hanbali theologian from Najd and the founder of Wahhabism; 1703-1792. Already as a young theologian, al-Wahhab began his teaching against the cult of saints, paganism among the Bedouins, sacred trees and some sacred tombs. In 1744 amir Muhammad b. Saʿud of al-Dirʿiyya and Ibn ʿAbd al-Wahhab swore an oath of mutual loyalty to strive, by force if necessary, to make the kingdom of God's word prevail. Ibn ʿAbd al-Wahhab's doctrine was very strongly influenced by that of Ibn Taymiyya and opposed to sects which were considered as incompatible with Sunnism, such as Shiʿism, the Muʿtazila and the Kharijiyya.

Ibn Abi ʾl-Rijal, Abu ʾl-Hasan: astrologer of Qayrawan, known in the West as Abenragel or Albohazen.

Ibn Abi ʾl-Rijal, Ahmad b. Salih: historian, jurisconsult and poet from

Yemen; 1620-1681. He is known for his alphabetically arranged collection of about 1300 biographies of famous Zaydis of Iraq and Yemen.

Ibn Abi ʾl-Shawarib: name of the members of a family of traditionists, jurists and judges which played an important role at Baghdad during the ixth and xth c.

Ibn Abi Tahir Tayfur: littérateur and historian of Persian origin; 819-893. He is famous for his *History of Baghdad*, continued down to the reign of the ʿAbbasid Caliph al-Muhtadi.

Ibn Abi Tayyiʾ: important Shiʿi historian from Aleppo; 1180-ca. 1228. He is particularly known for his *Universal History*, which is even used by Sunni writers. It is valuable for the history of northern Syria in the time of the Crusades.

Ibn Abi Usaybiʿa: physician and bibliographer of Damascus; 1194-1270. He owes his fame to a collection of 380 biographies which are of inestimable value for the history of Arabic science.

Ibn al-ʿAdim: historian of Aleppo; 1192-1262. He wrote a biographical dictionary of men connected with Aleppo, and a history of the city.

Ibn ʿAjiba: Moroccan Sufi of Sharifian origin; 1746-1809. He was one of the most distinguished representatives of the mystical order of the Darqawa.

Ibn Ajurrum: Moroccan grammarian; 1273-1323. He wrote a summary syntax, called the *Muqaddima*, which has enjoyed to the present day great popularity in all the Arabic-speaking countries. Since the xvith c., it was one of the first treatises available to European Arabists for the study of the Arabic grammatical system.

Ibn ʿAliwa: Sufi and poet of Mostaganem in Algeria; 1869-1934. His intellectual amplitude went hand in hand with a profound conservatism and an implacable orthodoxy. By the time of his death, he was said to have very many disciples, from North Africa to Damascus, Addis Ababa and Europe.

Ibn al-ʿAmid, Abu ʾl-Fadl: vizier of the early Buyids and man of letters of Qum; d. 970. His reputation was due to his prodigious memory, to his generosity and to his friendly character. He is praised for his correspondence.

Ibn ʿAmir: "reader" of the Qurʾan; d. 736. His "reading" is counted among the seven canonical ones.

Ibn al-ʿArabi, Muhammad b. Ziyad: philologian of the school of Kufa; 767-846. About twenty works are attributed to him.

Ibn ʿAqil, Abu ʾl-Wafaʾ: Hanbali jurist and theologian of Baghdad; 1040-1119. Because of his interest in the Muʿtazila, he was forced into exile in another quarter of the city. In 1072 he publicly retracted his writings in favour of al-Hallajj and of certain Muʿtazili doctrines.

Ibn al-ʿArabi, Muhammad b. Ziyad: philologian of the school of Kufa; 767-846. About twenty works are attributed to him.

Ibn al-ʿArabi, Muhyi ʾl-Din al-Taʾi (al-Shaykh al-Akbar): one of the greatest, and certainly the most prolific, Sufis of Islam; 1165-1240. Born in Murcia, Spain, he impressed his father's friend Averroes, who was then judge in Seville. He travelled far and wide in the Muslim countries, and in 1230 settled in Damascus where he died and was buried. There seems little doubt that he is the author of some 400 works, among which are a full exposition of the author's Sufi doctrine, and a summary of the teaching of 28 prophets from Adam to the Prophet. His ideas had their most profound influence in Anatolia. It has been suggested that his description of his "ascension to heaven" (A. *mi'rāj*) from the world of being to the station in God's presence influenced Dante.

Ibn 'Arabshah, Ahmad b. Muhammad: Arab historian and writer of Damascus; 1392-1450. He had learned Persian, Turkish and Mongol and in his chief work describes the conquests of Tamerlane and the conditions under his successor Shah Rukh.

Ibn 'Asakir: name of the members of a family who, between 1077 and 1261, held important positions in Damascus and produced a dynasty of Shafi'i scholars. The best-known among them is 'Ali Ibn 'Asakir; 1105-1176. Having travelled to many cities in the eastern Islamic world, he settled in his native town and was befriended by the Zangid Nur al-Din Mahmud, who occupied Damascus in 1154. His *History of the city of Damascus* is a biographical dictionary in 18 volumes.

Ibn al-Ash'ath: descendant of a noble Kindi family of the Hadhramaut, who became famous for his rebellion against al-Hajjaj, the governor of Iraq; d. 704.

Ibn 'Ashir: Sufi of Muslim Spain and patron saint of the town of Salé; d. 1362.

Ibn 'Ashur: patronymic of a family of Idrisid descent and Moroccan origin which settled in Muslim Spain; xviith-xxth c.

Ibn 'Askar, Abu 'Abd Allah: Idrisid sharif and Moroccan author of a highly esteemed hagiographic dictionary; 1529-1578.

Ibn 'Askar, Muhammad b. 'Ali: Andalusian jurist, philologist, poet and man of letters; ca. 1188-1239. He wrote a history of Málaga.

Ibn al-'Assal: name of a Coptic family of Egypt, also named Awlad al-'Assal, whose members rose to wealth and high station at the Ayyubid court during the xiiith c. Their position reveals the loyalty of the Copts to the reigning dynasty and their hostility to the Crusaders, who considered them schismatics. The literary figures were al-Safi, al-As'ad and al-Mu'taman.

Ibn 'Ata' Allah: Arab mystic of Egypt; d. 1309. He was a follower of Abu 'l-Hasan al-Shadhili and one of the foremost adversaries of the Hanbalite Ibn Taymiyya.

Ibn al-Athir: name borne by a number of apparently unrelated families, which was given great lustre by three brothers from Jazirat Ibn 'Umar: 1) Majd al-Din; 1149-1210. Living at Mosul, he was the author of a collection of Traditions which became a much used standard reference work, and of a dictionary of less common words and meanings in the Prophetic traditions, which has been incorporated in Ibn Manzur's famous dictionary *The Language of the Arabs*; 'Izz al-Din; 1160-1233. He also lived at Mosul, and became famous for his annalistic history from the beginning of the world to the year 628, called *al-Kāmil*; Diya' al-Din; 1163-1239. He obtained the title of vizier, and lived mainly at Mosul. His works are all concerned with literary criticism.

Ibn Babawayh(i), Abu Ja'far Muhammad: known as al-Saduq, he is regarded among the Twelver Shi'is as one of their foremost doctors and traditionists; 923-991. He was a prolific author.

Ibn Badis, 'Abd al-Hamid: founder of an orthodox reformist movement in Algeria; 1889-1940. He founded a newspaper and a monthly review which, from 1930 onwards, propagated reform and nationalism, strongly tinged with Arabism, and attacked marabout societies and gallicization.

Ibn Bajja, Abu Bakr Muhammad: famous Muslim philosopher and vizier at Saragossa, Spain, known in the West as Avempace.

Ibn al-Banna': Qur'anic scholar, traditionist and jurisconsult of the Hanbali school at Baghdad; d. 1079. He kept a diary of day-to-day socio-religious life in Baghdad from an unkown date until 1077.

Ibn Banna' al-Marrakushi: versatile Moroccan scholar of mathematics, astronomy, astrology and occult sciences; 1256-1321. His knowledge was highly esteemed by Ibn Khaldun.

Ibn Baraka: Ibadi author from Oman; xth c. He wrote several historical and juridical works, among them a book on the state of Oman in the time of the Imam al-Salt b. Malik (ixth c.).

Ibn Barrajan: Andalusian mystic theologian who taught in Seville; xiith c. In Marrakesh he is still known by the name Sidi Berrijal (Sidi Abu 'l-Rijal).

Ibn Barri, Abu Muhammad 'Abd Allah: Arab grammarian of Egypt; 1106-1187. He was said to have the greatest knowledge of his generation of Arabic grammar and vocabulary.

Ibn Bashkuwal, Abu 'l-Qasim: Andalusian scholar; 1101-1183. In his *The Continuation* he continued the *History of the scholars of al-Andalus* by Ibn al-Faradi (d. 1013), and gathered 1400 biographies of men of letters.

Ibn Bassam al-Shantarini: Andalusian poet, native from Santarém; d. 1147. He owes his fame to an anthology, compiled with a sound judgement on the quality of the works thus collected.

Ibn Batta (al-'Ukbari): Hanbali theologian and jurisconsult in Baghdad; 917-997. He is an example of the Sunni opposition to the Buyid regime and, to a lesser degree, to Mu'tazilism and philosophy.

Ibn Battuta: one of the world's most renowned travellers and authors of travel books; 1304-1368. Between 1325 and 1353, his journeys brought him from his native Tangiers to Egypt, Syria, Mecca, Iraq, the Red Sea and

Yemen, Oman, Istanbul, Transoxiana, Afghanistan, the Indus, the Maldives, Ceylon, Bengal, Sumatra and the Chinese port of Zaytun (*Ts'üan-chou*), Sardinia, Granada, and across the Sahara to the country of the Niger. His "Travel-book" is in fact a description of the then known world, and has been translated into many languages.

Ibn al-Bawwab (Ibn al-Sitri): famous calligrapher of the Buyid period; d. 1022. He perfected the style of writing invented by the vizier Ibn Muqla.

Ibn al-Baytar: botanist and pharmacologist of Málaga; d. 1248. In one of his works he lists some 1400 simples. This work had a considerable influence both outside and within the Islamic world.

Ibn Bazzaz al-Ardabili: son and first successor of Shaykh Safi al-Din al-Ardabili, the founder of the Sufi order of the Safawiyya and, as ancestor of Shah Isma'il I, the eponym of the Safawids. One of his works was used for the genealogy of the Safawids, who claimed descent from the seventh Imam Musa al-Qazim.

Ibn Bibi, al-Husayn b. Muhammad: historian of the Saljuqs of Rum; xii-ith c. His work, written in Persian and covering the period from 1192 till 1280, can be classed as memoirs in that he handed down what he himself had heard and seen at the court of the Rum Saljuqs.

Ibn al-Biklarish: physician and pharmacist of Almería; xiith c.

Ibn Burd: name of an Andalusian family, two representatives of whom enjoy some fame: 1) Ibn Burd al-Akbar; d. 1027. As the head of the chancellery under the Spanish Umayyad Hisham II al-Mu'ayyad, he drew up the act of investiture for the "major domo" 'Abd al-Rahman b. Abi 'Amir (Sanchuelo) in 1008; 2) Ibn Burd al-Asghar: author and poet; ca. 1005-1054.

Ibn Butlan: Christian physician and theologian of Baghdad; d. 1066. His main work is a synopsis of hygiene and macrobiotics, to which al-Ghazali refers in the preface of his *The Revival of Religious Sciences*.

Ibn Daniyal: Arab writer in Egypt; ca. 1248-1310. He was the author of the earliest shadow-plays in medieval Egypt.

Ibn Darraj al-Qastalli: Andalusian poet of Berber origin; 958-1030. He is considered one of the greatest poets of Muslim Spain and the main representative of the golden age of Arabo-Andalusian poetry.

Ibn Dawud: famous Zahiri jurist and the first codifier of Arabic "courtly love"; d. 909.

Ibn al-Daya: historian from Baghdad; ixth c. He wrote a biography of Ahmad b. Tulun and a work containing stories about rewards for good deeds, punishment for evil deeds, and timely escape from difficult situations.

Ibn al-Dayba': historian and religious scholar of Zabid in Yemen; 1461-1537. His history of the town of Zabid is brought down to 1518.

Ibn Dirham: seldom-used patronym of an eminent family of Maliki jurists and judges, originally from Basra. They flourished between 717 and 971.

Ibn al-Dubaythi: Iraqi historian; 1163-1239. He is known for his *History of Baghdad*, containing biographies of people who died after 1166. His *History of Wasit* is not preserved.

Ibn Durayd: Arab philologist and lexicographer; 837-933. He wrote a monumental work, called *al-Jamhara*, in which he included a large number of loanwords, tracing as far as possible their origins.

Ibn Fadl Allah al-'Umari: distinguished author and administrator of the Mamluk period; 1301-1349. He was a writer and expert on a wide variety of subjects related to politics and administration.

Ibn Fadlan: Arabic writer of the xth c. He left an account of the embassy sent by the 'Abbasid Caliph al-Muqtadir to the king of the Bulghars of the Volga in 921.

Ibn Fahd: name of an important Meccan family who, through four successive generations (xivth-xvith c.), boasted of productive historians whose chief interest lay in local history and biography.

Ibn al-Faqih: Persian author of a geography written in Arabic; ixth c. In his only surviving work *The Book of the Countries*, he describes his native town Hamadan and the countries of Iran, Arabia, Iraq, Syria, Egypt, Rum, Jazira, Central Asia, Nubia and Abyssinia. North Africa, al-Andalus and Sudan are given merely a brief résumé.

Ibn Faraj al-Jayyani: poet, anthologist and historian of Muslim Spain; xth c. He is the author of a remarkable anthology of Andalusian poetry.

Ibn al-Farid: celebrated Sufi poet of Cairo; 1181-1235. His tomb beneath al-Muqattam is still frequented. His *dīwān* is one of the most original in Arabic literature.

Ibn Farighun: author from the upper Oxus lands; xth c. He wrote a concise Arabic encyclopaedia of the sciences.

Ibn Faris: Arab philologist of Persia; d. 1004. He wrote some 40 works, but lexicography was his favourite domain. To the Arab world he remained "the grammarian".

Ibn al-Furat: name of a number of persons who held the offices of secretary or vizier under the 'Abbasid caliphs or the Ikhshidid amirs in the ixth-xth c. The members of this Shi'i family worth mentioning are: 1) Abu 'l-'Abbas; d. 904. He was commissioned to restore the state finances; 2) Abu 'l-Hasan; 855-924. Several times vizier of the 'Abbasid Caliph al-Muqtadir, he was a prominent financier and politician and a man of great culture, but too often concerned primarily with increasing his own wealth; 3) Abu 'l-Fath (Ibn Hinzaba); d. 938. He was vizier for a few months in 932; 4) Abu 'l-Fadl; 921-1001. He was vizier of the Ikhshidids of Egypt and facilitated the entry of the Fatimid troops into that country. He had the reputation of a patron of poets and scholars but also that of an eccentric.

Ibn al-Furat, Nasir al-Din: Egyptian historian; 1334-1405. He was the author of a vast *History of the Dynasties and Kings*, of which only the volumes covering the years after 1106 were finished completely. Its value rests on its being very detailed and on the wide range of its sources.

Ibn al-Fuwati: historian and librarian from Baghdad; 1244-1323. He did much copying of manuscripts and wrote large works on history and biography, most of which have been lost. Preserved are his large biographical dictionary arranged according to nicknames and honorary titles, a first-class reference tool, and a centennial history which is of very great interest for everyday life in Baghdad.

Ibn Ghalbun: ruler of Molina de Aragón; xith c. He was the son of a convert and brought up in Islam. He became a loyal subject of El Cid.

Ibn Ghalib: historian and geographer living in Granada; xiith c. In his geographical work he gives details about the habitats of the Arab tribes in Spain.

Ibn Ghannam, Abu Tahir: author of a treatise on oneiromancy; d. 1294. He led this discipline away from the traditional paths by renouncing the plan inspired by that of the *Book of Dreams* of Artemidorus of Ephesus.

Ibn Ghannam, Shaykh Husayn: chronicler of the Wahhabiyya; d. 1810. He wrote a theological exposition of the Wahhabiyya and a chronicle of the expansion of the movement in Arabia.

Ibn Gharsiya: Andalusian writer and poet; xith c. Of Basque origin, he was a fervent Muslim but wrote a violent, insulting and bitter treatise against the Arabs, glorifying the Slavs, the Rum and all the non-Arabs.

Ibn Ghidhahum (Ben Ghedahem): leader of the 1864 revolution in Tunisia; ca. 1815-1867. The revolt against the Khaznadar government was started in 1864 as a result of a doubling of taxes. It was crushed in the same year and Ibn Ghidhahum died in prison.

Ibn al-Habbariyya: Arab poet; d. 1115. A great poetic talent, he rendered the *Kalila wa-Dimna* into verse.

Ibn Habib, Badr al-Din: scholar and jurist; 1310-1377. He wrote a history in rhymed prose of the Mamluk Empire from its beginning in 1250 down to his own time.

Ibn al-Haddad: Andalusian poet from Cadix; d. 1088. One of his love poems is dedicated to a Coptic Christian nun in Egypt, whom he had seen while about to embark for the pilgrimage.

Ibn Hajar al-ʿAsqalani: Egyptian scholar of Tradition, judge and historian; 1372-1449. He is one of the greatest and most typical representatives of Muslim religious scholarship. He wrote a great commentary on the *Ṣaḥīḥ* of al-Bukhari, and some large biographical dictionaries.

Ibn Hajar al-Haytami: famous scholar and prolific writer of the Shafiʿi school of law; 1504-1567. His main work is a commentary on Muhyi al-Din al-Nawawi's *Path of the Students*.

Ibn al-Hajj: name of several persons, in particular of the Maliki jurist Abu ʿAbd Allah al-Fasi; b. 1336. The name also refers to four grammarians (xith, xiiith and xixth c.), two Andalusian men of letters (xivth c.) and a poet and theologian who wrote a commentary on al-Sanusi. Another Ibn al-Hajj al-Fasi (1760-1817) was one of the most outstanding scholars of the reign of the Filali Sharif of Morocco Mawlay Abu 'l-Rabi' Sulayman.

Ibn al-Hajjaj: Arab poet of Baghdad in the time of the Buyids; ca. 941-1001. A wealthy man of affairs, he shows a dual personality in his work. On the one hand he wrote traditional panegyrics, on the other he did not respect anything, neither Islam, nor the most honourable persons, nor himself.

Ibn al-Hajib, Jamal al-Din: Maliki jurist and grammarian; ca. 1174-1249. He owes his reputation to two short works on morphology and syntax.

Ibn Hamdis: Arab poet of Muslim Sicily; ca. 1055-1132. He exulted in the failure of the expedition mounted by Roger II of Sicily against al-Mahdiyya in Tunisia in 1123.

Ibn Hamdun: name of the members of the Banu Hamdun family in Baghdad who were "boon-companions" of the caliphs and who flourished mainly in the first half of the ixth c.

Ibn Hamid: one of the most prominent Hanbali scholars of Baghdad under the Buyids; d. 1012.

Ibn Hani' al-Andalusi: famous court poet of the Banu Hamdun, rulers of Masila, and of the last Fatimid Caliph of Ifriqiyya al-Mu'izz li-din Allah; ca. 934-ca. 973. He is considered the first great poet of the Muslim West.

Ibn al-Hannat: Andalusian poet; d. 1045. He is considered one of the greatest scholars of the early xith c. in the field of Arabic language and literature.

Ibn Hatim: state official and historian under the Rasulid sultan of Yemen al-Muzaffar Yusuf (r. 1249-1295).

Ibn Hawqal: Arab geographer of Nisibis in Upper Mesopotamia; xth c. With his contemporary al-Muqaddasi, he is one of the best exponents of geography based on travel and direct observation. He began his series of journeys in 943 and was engaged in the activities of a merchant and a supporter of Fatimid policy. His journeys brought him to North Africa, Spain, and the southern edge of the Sahara (947-951), Egypt, Armenia and Azerbaijan (955), al-Jazira, Iraq, Khuzistan and Fars (961-969), Khwarazm and Transoxiana (ca. 969), and finally Sicily (973). His main work is called *Configuration of the Earth*, which is more original than that of his senior and predecessor al-Istakhri, whom he met.

Ibn al-Hawwas: one of the commanders in Sicily; d. ca. 1064. He managed to remain lord of Agrigento, Castrogiovanni and Castronuovo and defeated his brother-in-law Ibn al-Maklati.

Ibn al-Haytham, Abu 'Ali al-Hasan: great Arab mathematician, known in the West as Alhazen or Avennathan.

Ibn Hayyan: the greatest historian of the Middle Ages in all Spain, both Muslim and Christian; 987-1076. His history of al-Andalus is an assemblage of earlier writings. His original work covers the history of his own times.

Ibn Hazm: patronymic of an Andalusian family, several members of which played an important role during the Spanish Umayyad caliphate. Apart from Abu Muhammad ʿAli Ibn Hazm, there are the latter's father Abu ʿUmar; d. 1012; his elder brother Abu Bakr; 989-1011; his son Abu Rafiʿ al-Fadl; d. 1086, and his cousin Abu 'l-Mughira (d. 1046), who was vizier to the petty kings of Saragossa.

Ibn Hazm, Abu Muhammad ʿAli: Andalusian poet, historian, jurist, philosopher and theologian; 994-1064. Born at Córdoba, he was one of the greatest thinkers of Arabo-Muslim civilization. He can be studied as a psychologist and moralist, as a theoretician of language, as a jurist – he is the most outstanding representative of the Zahiri school – and as a historian of religious ideas.

Ibn Hijja: one of the most famous poets and prose-writers of the Mamluk period; 1366-1434. In 1389 he witnessed the great burning of Damascus during the siege by the Burji Mamluk Barquq, which gave him the theme for his first literary work. His most valuable contribution is his collection of official letters, diplomas and private correspondence written while he was working at the Mamluk chancery.

Ibn Hisham, Abu Muhammad: scholar of Basra, best known for his work on the biography of the Prophet; d. 833. He edited the *Life of the Prophet* of Ibn Ishaq, which is not preserved as a single work. Comparison with passages from Ibn Ishaq's work, which have been preserved by others but have been omitted by Ibn Hisham, shows that the material omitted was not directly relevant to the Prophet's career.

Ibn Hisham, Jamal al-Din; jurist and grammarian from Cairo; 1310-1360. Ibn Khaldun recognised him as one of those very rare men who, in the history of Arabic grammar, have succeeded in mastering the whole of their subject.

Ibn Hubayra: the name of two persons, ʿUmar b. Hubayra and his son Yusuf b. ʿUmar, who were both governors of Iraq under the Umayyads; viiith c. Yusuf was unable to defend the Umayyad cause against Abu Muslim, the leader of the ʿAbbasid movement in Khurasan. He had to abandon Caliph Marwan II to his fate in 750.

Ibn Hubayra, ʿAwn al-Din: scholar from Baghdad; 1106-1165. He served for sixteen years as vizier under the ʿAbbasid Caliphs al-Muqtafi and al-Mustanjid. He brought the influence of the last Saljuqs to an end, and had a hand in the conquest of Fatimid Egypt by the Zangid Nur al-Din Mahmud.

Ibn Hubaysh: traditionist of Muslim Spain; 1110-1188. Among other works, he wrote an account of the victorious expedition under the Caliphs Abu Bakr, ʿUmar b. al-Khattab and ʿUthman b. ʿAffan.

Ibn Hudhayl: man of letters and writer of Granada; xivth c. He wrote a treatise on the Holy War, aimed at convincing the Andalusian Muslims of the need to resume the profession of arms and to establish a cavalry worthy of their ancestors. This work is of the greatest importance for the knowledge of the equestrian and military arts in medieval Islam.

Ibn 'Idhari, Abu 'l-'Abbas: historian from the Maghrib. He left an account of the history of Ifrīqiya from the conquest of Egypt in 640 to the capture of al-Mahdiyya by the Almohads in 1205. The work is a basic source for the history of the Maghrib and of al-Andalus.

Ibn Idris, Abu 'Abd Allah: vizier and man of letters in Morocco; 1784 (?)-1847. The renaissance of the fine official epistolary style is due to him.

Ibn Idris, Abu 'l-'Ala': son of the previous; d. 1879. He was sent on a diplomatic mission to Napoleon III, of which he left an account.

Ibn 'Iraq: astronomer and mathematician; xith c. He was the teacher of al-Biruni.

Ibn-i Isfandiyar: Persian historian, known for his *History of Ṭabaristān*; xiiith c.

Ibn Ishaq, Muhammad: one of the main authorities on the biography of the Prophet; ca. 704-767. His work, known as *Life of the Prophet* was edited by Ibn Hisham. Malik b. Anas fostered enmity against him.

Ibn Iyas: Egyptian historian; 1448-1524. He has been recognised as a prime source of the decline and fall of the Mamluk rule in Egypt and of the first years of the dominion of the Ottomans.

Ibn al-Jadd: a family which was famous and influential at Seville and Niebla; xith-xiith c. Worth mentioning are Abu 'l-Qasim, d. 1121, and Abu Bakr Muhammad (1102-1190).

Ibn Jama'a: distinguished Shafi'i family of the Mamluk period in Syria and Egypt.

Ibn Jami' (Jumay'): Jewish physician who entered the service of Saladin; d. 1198. He wrote a compendium of medicine, and a commentary on Avicenna.

Ibn al-Jawzi, 'Abd al-Rahman: Hanbali jurisconsult, traditionist, historian and preacher in Baghdad; 1126-1200. He was one of the most influential persons in the 'Abbasid capital, as much through his activity in the university as through his preaching, especially during the reign of the 'Abbasid Caliph al-Mustadi' bi-Amr Allah. He fell in disgrace during the reign of the Caliph al-Nasir li-Din Allah, who sent him in exile to the town of Wasit in 1194. In 1199 he made a triumphant return to the capital. He was one of the most prolific writers of Arabic literature. As a historian, he is especially known for his history of the caliphate from 871 to 1179, an exceptionally rich source, for his history of Sufism, and for his laudatory biographies.

Ibn al-Jawzi, Sibt: famous preacher and historian; 1185-1256. A grandson of 'Abd al-Rahman Ibn al-Jawzi, he abandoned Hanbalism for Hanafism. He is the author of an immense universal history. The work is of inestimable value not only for his own period but also for the xth-xith centuries because he preserves *in extenso* and without criticism the versions of sources which often no longer survive.

Ibn Jazla, Abu 'Ali Yahya: Arab physician of Baghdad; d. 1100. Of Christian origin, he embraced Islam and wrote several works, one of which was translated into Latin in 1280 by the Sicilian Jewish physician Faraj b. Salim (Magister Farachi) under the title *Tacuini aegritudinum*.

Ibn Jinni: Arab grammarian; ca. 913-1002. He founded the science of Arab etymology.

Ibn Jubayr: famous Andalusian traveller and writer; 1145-1217. His journey to Mecca, executed between 1183 and 1185, brought him to Sardinia, Sicily, Crete, Alexandria, Cairo, Jidda, Mecca, Medina, Kufa, Baghdad, Mosul, Aleppo and Damascus. A second journey lasted from 1189 to 1191, but of this he left no account. The *Travel-book* of the first journey is the first and one of the best of its kind. It served as a model to many other pilgrims, and many later authors have borrowed from it. The work has been translated into English, French and Italian.

Ibn Juljul: Arab physician from Córdoba; 944-994. Among other works, he wrote a history of physicians, probably one of the oldest collections of biographies on this subject in Arabic, and the earliest example of the use of Arabic translations from Latin.

Ibn Kathir, 'Imad al-Din: Syrian historian and traditionist; ca. 1300-1373. His history of Islam in 14 volumes is one of the principal historical works of the Mamluk period. He also wrote a monumental compilation of Traditions, and was interested in jurisprudence.

Ibn Kaysan: Arab grammarian of Baghdad; d. 911. He was a representative of the so-called eclectic school of Baghdad, refusing to take sides between the opposed grammatical doctrines of Basra and Kufa.

Ibn Khafaja: famous Andalusian poet; 1058-1139. He is best known as a poet of nature.

Ibn Khalawayh: famous Arab grammarian and man of letters; d. 980. Like Ibn Kaysan he was, in grammatical doctrines, an eclectic between the Basrans and the Kufans. He became famous already during his lifetime.

Ibn Khaldun, 'Abd al-Rahman: historian, sociologist and philosopher of Tunis; 1332-1406. He is one of the strongest personalities of Arabo-Muslim culture in the period of its decline. Carefully educated, and having escaped the Black Death, he went to Fez in 1350, then the most brilliant capital of the Muslim West. He was put in prison for two years for having changed his loyalty in the disturbed political situation around 1360. His friendship with the vizier Ibn al-Khatib ensured him an honourable reception in Granada in 1362, from where he also came in contact with the Christian world. Abu 'Abd Allah, the amir of Bougie (A. *Bijāya*), meanwhile had regained his amirate and appointed Ibn Khaldun as his chamberlain. After the death on the battlefield of the amir, Ibn Khaldun handed over the town to the conqueror, Abu 'Abd Allah's cousin Abu 'l-'Abbas, amir of Constantine, and entered his service. But he resigned in time and went to Biskra where he attempted to lead the life of a man of letters. But, not able to resist intrigue, he was continuously on the move, trying to back the winner although there was no winner in the Muslim West of the xivth c. By now he was regarded with mixed feelings never entirely free from suspicion. He left for Tlemcen, where the sultan once again wanted his services. Pretending to accept, he fled to live in the castle of Ibn Salama (1375-1379), near the present-day Frenda in Algeria. In 1379 he returned to Tunis where he lived as a teacher and scholar. But enmity from Ibn 'Arafa, the representative of the Maliki school in Hafsid Tunisia, made Ibn Khaldun decide to leave the Muslim West. The sultan granted him permission for the pilgrimage, and in 1382 he left for Cairo. Here he taught at al-Azhar and was appointed Maliki chief judge, but intrigues made him resign. After his pilgrimage, he was placed at the head of the khanqah of Baybars, the most important Sufi convent in Egypt. Appointed judge again, and dismissed after a year, he was obliged to accompany the Burji Mamluk al-Nasir Faraj on his expedition to relieve Damascus, which was threatened by Tamerlane. Left in the besieged town, he played a certain part in its surrender. Having witnessed the horrors of the burning and sacking of Damascus, he returned to Cairo where he was well received. He died during his sixth office as judge.

Ibn Khaldun's fame rests primarily on his *Introduction*. It was the author's intention to write an introduction to the historian's craft and present it as an encyclopaedic synthesis of the methodological and cultural knowledge necessary to produce a truly scientific work. The central point is the study of the symptoms and of the nature of the ills from which civilizations die. His *Moralistic Examples* (from History) is important for the xiiith and xivth c., especially for the Muslim West and particularly for the Berbers.

Ibn Khaldun's changes of allegiance should be judged according to the standards of his time. The very concept of "allegiance" to a country scarcely existed, the only treason being apostasy.

Ibn Khaldun, Abu Zakariyya': brother of the above, poet and man of letters; 1333-1378. He wrote a history of the kingdom of Tlemcen, whose literary value is superior to that of his brother 'Abd al-Rahman.

Ibn Khallikan: Arabic biographer from Iraq; 1211-1282. He wrote a famous biographical dictionary which contains only persons whose year of death he could ascertain. He omitted on purpose the Companions of the Prophet, the transmitters of the second generation and all caliphs, because information about these persons was easily available.

Ibn al-Khasib, Abu Bakr: astrologer of Baghdad, known in the West as Albubather.

Ibn al-Khatib (Lisan al-Din): vizier and historian of Granada; 1313-1375.

He was the greatest Muslim writer of Granada, distinguishing himself in almost all branches of learning.

Ibn Khatima: man of letters, poet, historian and grammarian of al-Andalus; d. 1369. He was an intimate friend of Ibn al-Khatib.

Ibn Khayr al-Ishbili: philologian and traditionist of Seville; 1108-1179. He owes his fame to the catalogue of the works which he had read and of the teachers with whom he had studied.

Ibn al-Khayyat, Abu 'l-Hasan: Arab poet in Sicily; xith c. He was the panegyrist of the Kalbis.

Ibn Khayyat al-ʿUsfuri (Shabab): chronicler and genealogist; d. 854. His *History* is the oldest known complete Islamic survey of events and gives special attention to the Umayyad Caliphate of Damascus and to the extension of the Islamic Empire. In his *Classes* he provides a biographical dictionary of early Islamic Tradition, with especial attention to the genealogy of tribes, groups and families.

Ibn Khurradadhbih: one of the earliest geographical writers in Arabic; ca. 820-ca. 911. Of Iranian origin, he was a familiar and friend of the ʿAbbasid Caliph al-Muʿtamid. Among other works he wrote *The Book of Itineraries and Kingdoms*.

Ibn Killis: Fatimid vizier; 930-991. By origin a Jew, he embraced Islam in 967 and entered the service of al-Muʿizz li-Din Allah, the last caliph of the Fatimid dynasty of Ifrīqiya, whom he encouraged to conquer Egypt. He was an able administrator and the Fatimid Caliph al-ʿAziz appointed him vizier in 977. Under his tenure of office, the Fatimid Empire saw its greatest territorial expansion.

Ibn Kullab: theologian of Basra; d. 855 (?). He was a foremost representative of a compromising theology during the period in which there was an Inquisition over the question whether the Qurʾan had been created or not (A. *mihna*).

Ibn al-Labbana (al-Dani): Andalusian poet; xith c. He is famous for his loyalty to the poet-king al-Muʿtamid Ibn ʿAbbad.

Ibn Maʾ al-Samaʾ, Abu Bakr ʿUbada: Andalusian poet; d. after 1030. He is famous as the author of the poetic genre known as *muwashshaḥāt*.

Ibn Maja, Abu ʿAbd Allah: author of the last of the six canonical collections of Tradition; 824-887. His work contains some 4,000 traditions in about 150 chapters. It was criticized, because many of them are weak.

Ibn Majid, Shihab al-Din: one of the greatest Arab navigators in the Middle Ages; xvth c. Improving the works of his father and grandfather, who were both "master of navigation", Ibn Majid acquired during his lifetime the reputation of an expert navigator of the Indian Ocean. He had studied the works of the three Arab navigators of the ʿAbbasid period Muhammad b. Shadan, Sahl b. Aban and Layth b. Kahlan, even though he was doubtful about the value of their writings. In Arabic geographical writings of the

Middle Ages, the description of the east coast of Africa usually stopped at Sofala because Arab ships did not sail beyond this point for fear of being wrecked by the strong currents and winds there. Moreover, according to the Ptolemaic concept, the east coast of Africa, to the south of Sofala, turned towards the east instead of the west, and extended latitudinally as far east as China, leaving only a channel that connected the Indian Ocean with the Pacific, thus giving the Indian Ocean the shape of a lake. Thus, the Arab geographers and cartographers drew maps which covered the whole of the southern hemisphere with land.

Ibn Majid was the first Arab navigator to describe in more positive terms the coast of Africa south of Sofala, although he conceived Africa as being much smaller than it actually is. Ibn Majid's contribution to geography lies mainly in the field of navigation. His description of the Red Sea has never been surpassed or even equalled, apart from the inevitable errors in latitude. He used sea-charts and several instruments of navigation, but it is doubtful if he was the inventor of the compass. On the other hand, he was fully aware of the several attempts made by the Portuguese to enter the Indian Ocean. In his extant works, he does not record the fact of his having guided Vasco da Gama from Malindi to Calicut, but the fact is proved by the contemporary Arabic and Portuguese sources.

Ibn Malik, Abu 'Abd Allah: Arab grammarian of al-Andalus; 1203-1274. He owed his great reputation to his philological knowledge and because he versified Arabic grammar.

Ibn Mammati: name of three highly-placed officials of the same Coptic family from Asyut, who flourished under the later Fatimids and early Ayyubids. They were 1) Abu 'l-Malih, d. ca. 1100; 2) al-Muhadhdhab Abu 'l-Malih, d. 1182, who embraced Islam because of the imminent danger of an invasion of Egypt by the Crusaders under Amalric, the Latin king of Jerusalem, and the worsening of the situation of the Copts; 3) al-As'ad b. Muhadhdhab; 1147-1209. He versified the life of Saladin and the *Kalila wa-Dimna*, and wrote a work including a complete record of all Egyptian townships with their taxable acreage for the land-tax.

Ibn Manda: famous family of scholars of Tradition and historians from Isfahan; xth-xith c. The reputation of Yahya b. 'Abd al-Wahhab, a member of this family (1043-1118), is based on his *History of Isfahan*.

Ibn Mangli: author of several works on the art of war and of a treatise on hunting; xivth c.

Ibn Manzur (Ibn Mukarram): author of the famous dictionary called *The Language of the Arabs*; 1233-1311. The work is based on five earlier dictionaries and was used by Muhammad Murtada.

Ibn Mardanish (*Rey Lobo* or *Lope*): Spanish Muslim leader; 1124-1172. He made himself master of Valencia and Murcia and contended with the Almohads for the territories in the centre of al-Andalus.

Ibn Maryam, Muhammad b. Muhammad: North African hagiographer; d. 1605. He compiled a catalogue of local saints, mainly of Tlemcen.

Ibn Marzuq (pl. *Maraziqa*): family of clerics at Tlemcen, who in varying degrees made their mark in the religious, political and literary life of the Maghrib; xiiith-xvith c. The best known of the Maraziqa is Shams al-Din Muhammad IV (1311-1379).

Ibn Masarra: philosopher and mystic of Córdoba; 883-931. His work is connected with the doctrine of pseudo-Empedocles and was known to Ibn Hazm and Ibn al-'Arabi. The latter can be considered a member of Ibn Masarra's school.

Ibn Masawayh (Mesue): famous physician; d. 857. He contributed to the translation of Greek scientific works but was known particularly in his capacity as court physician and as a specialist on diet. His influential protectors were convinced Nestorians, who did not abandon their religion when they were at the caliph's court and kept in touch with Greek learning. He wrote a collection of medical aphorisms and a sort of description of the seasons of the year, based on the twin theories of the humours and the "qualities". As late as the xvth c. he was held in high esteem in the West.

Ibn Mas'ud: famous Companion of the Prophet, and "reader" of the Qur'an; d. 652. He received the Qur'an directly from the Prophet and is thought to have been the first to have attempted reading it in public in Mecca, which earned him insults from some of the pagans.

Ibn Miqsam: one of the most learned experts in the "reading" of the Qur'an; 878-965.

Ibn Misjah: one of the greatest singers of the early Hejaz school of Arabic music; viiith c.

Ibn al-Mudabbir: name of two brothers, who played an important part as high officials, courtiers and men of letters at Samarra and in Egypt and Syria during the middle of the ixth c. Abu 'l-Hasan Ahmad (d. 883) was director of finance in Egypt and became the most powerful man of his time. Abu Ishaq (Abu Yusr) (d. 892) is probably the author of one of the earliest treatises on administration and the civil service.

Ibn Muflih: family of Hanbali jurisconsults who can be traced from the xivth to the xviith c.

Ibn Mujahid: "reader" of the Qur'an; 859-936. He was influential in persuading the authorities to proscribe the Qur'an versions of the Prophet's son-in-law 'Ali, Ibn Mas'ud, Ibn Shanabudh and Ubayy b. Ka'b. Seven "readers" were recognized by him as authorities for the "reading" of the Qur'an.

Ibn al-Mujawir, Yusuf b. Ya'qub: geographer and historian from Damascus; 1204-1291. He is the reputed author of an important work on the geography, history, and customs of western and southern Arabia. It is a collection of itineraries which contains miscellaneous information on towns and tribes, and describes in detail Jidda, Zabid, Aden, Qalhat, Muscat, Suhar, the island of Qays (Kish) and Bahrain.

Ibn Muljam, 'Abd al-Rahman: Kharijite who murdered Caliph 'Ali in 661.

Ibn Munadhir: satirical poet of Aden; d. ca. 813. He also wrote panegyrics of the Barmakids.

Ibn al-Mundhir: grand master and chief veterinary surgeon of the stables of the Bahri Mamluk al-Nasir Muhammad b. Qalawun. He wrote a treatise on hippology.

Ibn al-Muqaffa', 'Abd Allah: Arabic author and translator of Persian origin; 720-756. He was one of the first translators into Arabic of literary works of the Indian and Iranian civilizations, and one of the creators of Arabic literary prose. Under the title *Kalila wa-Dimna* he translated into Arabic the Pahlavi version of the celebrated collection of Indian fables, which go back to the Pañcatantra. He also translated from Pahlavi into Arabic a royal chronicle composed under the Sasanids, a picture of the institutions, customs and hierarchy of the court in the same period, and a biography of the Sasanian kings Khusraw Anushirwan (r. 531-579) and Khusraw (II) Parwiz (r. 579-628). Ibn al-Muqaffa' further composed one of the earliest "Mirror for Princes" and a series of reflections on certain political, religious and social problems, addressed to an unnamed caliph who without doubt is the 'Abbasid al-Mansur. He probably is also the author of a Manichaean apologia. His works soon became classic in the great 'Abbasid civilization and exerted a very great influence on the following generations.

Ibn al-Muqaffa', Severus (A. *Sawiris*): Coptic bishop of Ashmunayn; xth c. The first Copt to adopt the Arabic language in ecclesiastical literature, he is best known for his history of the patriarchs.

Ibn Muqla: vizier of the 'Abbasid period and a famous calligrapher; 885-940.

Ibn al-Muslima: by-name given to a family of Baghdad, whose most important member was Abu 'l-Qasim 'Ali b. al-Husayn, vizier to the caliphate; d. 1058. He introduced to Baghdad the Saljuq Tughril I, who entered the city in 1044.

Ibn al-Mu'tazz: 'Abbasid prince and poet; 861-908. A son of the 'Abbasid Caliph al-Mu'tazz bi-'llah, he was proclaimed caliph in December 908 but killed shortly afterwards.

Ibn al-Muwaqqit: Moroccan author; 1894-1949. He was a reformist and wrote some biographies. He kept up a relentless struggle against the confraternities, the marabouts and the judges.

Ibn Muyassar: Egyptian historian; 1231-1278. His *Annals of Egypt* cover the years 1047-1158, while two extracts exist for the years 973-976 and 991-997.

Ibn al-Nadim: Shi'i of Baghdad and author of an *Index* of Arabic books;

ca. 936-995. The work, which exists in a larger and a shorter recension, is intended to be an index of all books written in Arabic either by Arabs or non-Arabs.

Ibn al-Nafis: distinguished physician and many-sided author from Damascus; d. 1288. He wrote an encyclopaedia of medicine, a comprehensive record of the whole knowledge of the Arabs in ophthalmology, which was also translated into Hebrew and Turkish, a medical commentary on the Aphorisms of Hippocrates, and an extensive commentary on the *Canon* of Avicenna, part of which was translated into Latin. His most important achievement in the field of medicine is his theory of the lesser or pulmonary circulation of the blood, boldly contradicting the accepted ideas of Galen and of Avicenna and anticipating part of William Harvey's discovery.

Ibn al-Najjar: historian and leading Shafi'i transmitter of Prophetic traditions; 1183-1245. He wrote a history of Medina and one of Baghdad.

Ibn Naqiya: poet and man of letters of Baghdad; 1020-1092. Among other works, he wrote a collection of *Sessions* which reflect an attitude of denigration and sarcasm.

Ibn al-Nattah: traditionist, genealogist and historian; d. 866. He is possibly the author of an important extant work on the 'Abbasids.

Ibn Nubata, Abu Bakr: poet and prose writer; 1287-1366. He was the favourite poet of the Ayyubid ruler al-Malik al-Mu'ayyad Abu 'l-Fida' in Hamat.

Ibn Nubata, Abu Yahya: preacher at the court of the Hamdanid Sayf al-Dawla 'Ali I; d. 984. His sermons, written to exhort the population to support the ruler in the war against the Byzantines, aroused great enthusiasm.

Ibn al-Qadi, Shihab al-Din: Moroccan polygraph of Fez; 1553-1616. He composed two collections of biographies of great documentary value.

Ibn al-Qalanisi: historian from Damascus; 1073-1160. His history of his native town is of great importance for the events in central Syria during the first half-century of the period of the Crusades.

Ibn Qalaqis: Arab poet, author and letter-writer of Alexandria; 1137-1172. He visited Aden, Zabid and 'Aydhab and wrote a description of his travels in Sicily.

Ibn Qasi, Abu 'l-Qasim: rebel in the Algarve; d. 1151. He created a fragile kingdom, but when hard-pressed, approached the Almohads who landed at Cadiz in 1146 and caused his fall as well as that of the Almoravids.

Ibn al-Qatta', 'Ali b. Ja'far: anthologist, historian, grammarian and lexicographer of Sicily; 1041-1121. He wrote an anthology of Arabo-Sicilian poetry.

Ibn al-Qattan, Abu 'l-Qasim: poet, traditionist, and oculist of Baghdad; 1086-1163. He is known for his vigorous satires.

Ibn Qays al-Ruqayyat, 'Ubayd Allah: Arab poet of the Umayyad period. His verses were set to music by the great singers of Medina and later by those at the court of the 'Abbasids.

Ibn Qayyim al-Jawziyya: Hanbali theologian and jurisconsult of Damascus; 1292-1350. He was the most famous pupil of Ibn Taymiyya but, unlike his master, much more strongly influenced by Sufism. He also was less of a polemicist and much more a preacher, and a writer of great talent. He is still today an author very highly esteemed among the Wahhabiyya, the Salafiyya and in many circles of North African Islam.

Ibn al-Qifti: versatile Arab writer from Egypt; 1172-1248. While exercising the office of director of finance in Aleppo, he gave shelter to Yaqut al-Rumi, who had fled from the Mongols. Of his many works, two biographies are known to have survived, one of physicians, philosophers and astronomers, the other of scholars.

Ibn al-Qitt: by-name of the Spanish Umayyad prince Ahmad b. Muʿa-wiya; d. 901. Persuaded by the Andalusian missionary Abu ʿAli al-Sarraj who had gathered many supporters, Ahmad, who was a devotee of astrology and aspired to the throne, laid siege to Zamora but was killed.

Ibn al-Quff: Christian physician and surgeon; 1233-1286. He was the first known military physician-surgeon and composed a manual on surgery.

Ibn Qutayba: one of the great Sunni polygraphs, being both a theologian and a man of letters; 828-889. The some sixteen authentic works of Ibn Qutayba show the influence of a number of teachers in all fields of extant scholarship. He also borrowed from existing, and remarkably faithful, translations of the Torah and the Gospels. In his theological works, he put his literary talents at the service of the restoration of Sunnism, undertaken by the ʿAbbasid Caliph al-Mutawakkil after the latter had put an end to the disputation whether the Qurʾan was created or not (A. *mihna*). He also wrote two chronologically arranged anthologies, one on poetic themes and the other on the poets themselves.

Ibn al-Qutiyya: grammarian and, in particular, historian of Muslim Spain; d. 977. He wrote a history of the conquest of the Iberian peninsula.

Ibn Quzman: name of a Córdoban family, of which the following five men of letters are worthy of mention: 1) Abu ʾl-Asbagh, a poet of the xth c.; 2) Abu Bakr Muhammad al-Akbar, a famous stylist and poet (d. 1114); 3) Abu Marwan b. Abi Bakr, a scholar and jurist (d. 1169); 4) Abu ʾl-Husayn b. Abi Marwan, a jurist and poet (d. 1196), and 5) Abu Bakr Muhammad al-Asghar, the famous poet of the popular Arabic poem in strophic form, called *zajal*, which is written only in the Arabic dialect of Spain (d. 1160).

Ibn Raʾiq (Muhammad b. Raʾiq): the first commander-in-chief of the army of the ʿAbbasid caliphate in Baghdad; d. 942.

Ibn al-Raqiq: man of letters and chronicler of Qayrawan; xth c. He was regarded by Ibn Khaldun as the best specialist on the history of Ifriqiya. His *History*, which has not yet been traced, was the basis for the works of many famous Muslim historians.

Ibn Rashiq, Abu ʿAli Hasan: one of the most illustrious men of letters of Ifriqiya; 1000-1063. His poetry is characterized by its conscious artistic elegance.

Ibn al-Rawandi (al-Rewendi): a Mu'tazili and heretic; xth c. His heterodox doctrine, which includes a biting criticism of prophecy in general and of that of the Prophet in particular, has been refuted by several generations of Muslim theologians.

Ibn Ridwan: renowned physician, medical author and polemicist of Egypt; 998-1061. His commentaries on Ptolemy and Galen were translated into Latin, Turkish and Hebrew. Another work of his contains important information on the transmission of Greek science to the Arabs.

Ibn Rushd, Abu 'l-Walid Muhammad: famous Muslim philosopher, known in the West as Averroës.

Ibn Rusta: historian and geographer from Isfahan; d. 912. The one volume which is left of what must have been a very voluminous work may be defined as a short encyclopaedia of historical and geographical knowledge.

Ibn al-Sa'ati: physician of Damascus; d. 1230. He wrote a book on clock-making.

Ibn Sab'in (Ibn Dara): philosopher and Sufi of Murcia, Spain; 1217-1269. His life consisted of controversies, quarrels and persecutions.

Ibn Sa'd: traditionist of Basra; 784-845. The fame of this secretary to al-Waqidi is based on his *Book of the Classes*, which provides information on some 4,250 persons who, from the beginning of Islam down to the author's time, had played a role as transmitters of traditions about the Prophet's sayings and doings.

Ibn Sahl al-Isra'ili: poet of Seville; 1212-1251. The poems of this convert from Judaism to Islam belong to the finest specimens of Andalusian poetry.

Ibn al-Salah: Iraqi author of a standard work on the sciences of Tradition; 1181-1245.

Ibn Sarabiyun (Suhrab): geographer of Persian origin; xth c. In his *Book of the Marvels of the Seven Climates*, mainly based on Abu Ja'far al-Khwarazmi's *Configuration of the Earth*, he describes in detail the technique of constructing a map on a cylindrical projection.

Ibn al-Sarraj: Arab grammarian of Baghdad; d. 929. He took part in the wide-spread movement which led the Arab grammarians to base their work on *The Book* of Sibawayhi.

Ibn al-Sayrafi, Abu Bakr: Andalusian poet, historian and traditionist from Granada; 1074-1162. His fame rests on a history of the Almoravids.

Ibn Sayyid al-Nas: biographer of the Prophet; 1273-1334. His biography makes use of a number of sources now lost or imperfectly known. It was eminently successful in its time.

Ibn Shaddad, Abu Muhammad: chronicler of Zirid descent; xiith c. His history of the Maghrib, probably lost, was used by well-known Arab historians.

Ibn Shaddad, Baha' al-Din: biographer of Saladin; 1145-1235. From 1188 until Saladin's death in 1193, he was in constant attendance of the Ayyubid ruler. His *Biography of Saladin* is considered to be without parallel in the historical literature of medieval Islam.

Ibn Shaddad, 'Izz al-Din: geographer and historian from Aleppo; 1217-1285. He wrote a historical topography of Syria and the Jazira.

Ibn Shahin al-Zahiri: high official at the court of the Mamluk sultans Barsbay and Jaqmaq; xvth c. He left a vivid picture of Egypt under the Mamluks and also wrote an oneirocritical treatise which was widely circulated.

Ibn Shanabudh: "reader" of the Qur'an; d. 939. The vizier Ibn Muqla had him flogged because he had introduced in the public prayer Qur'anic readings which varied from the recension of Caliph 'Uthman.

Ibn Shahrashub (Zayn al-Din): Imami theologian, preacher and jurist of Mazandaran in Persia; d. 1192. He had the reputation of being the greatest Shi'i scholar of his time and was highly thought of even by the Sunnis.

Ibn Sina, Abu 'Ali al-Husayn: great Muslim scientist and philosopher, known in the West as Avicenna.

Ibn Sirin: renowned Muslim interpreter of dreams; 654-728. He was also a traditionist, renowned for his piety and for the reliability of the information which he handed on.

Ibn Suda (Sawda): name of a number of Maliki scholars and judges of Fez, flourishing from ca. 1550-1903.

Ibn Sulaym al-Aswani: Fatimid propagandist; xth c. His work on Nubia is one of the principal medieval sources on the eastern Sudan.

Ibn Taymiyya: Hanbali theologian and jurisconsult from Harran; 1263-1328. Persecuted and imprisoned for his convictions, he aimed to integrate and harmonize tradition, reason and free-will in a solidly constructed doctrine which might be defined as a conservative reformism. In the field of dogma, his main intention was to follow the Qur'an and the Tradition. He considered individual reasoning (A. *ijtihād*) as necessary for the interpretation of the Law, but attempted to define the rules which every *mujtahid* ought to follow. Consequently, he attached much importance to reasoning by analogy (A. *qiyās*). In the xviiith c. his ideas were adopted by Muhammad b. 'Abd al-Wahhab, gave rise to Wahhabism and to the state of the Al Sa'ud dynasty. With al-Ghazali and Ibn al-'Arabi, Ibn Taymiyya remains one of the writers who have had the greatest influence on contemporary Islam, particularly in Sunni circles.

Ibn al-Thumna: lord of Syracuse in Sicily; r. 1052-1062. He gave support to the Normans when they invaded the island.

Ibn Tilmidh (Amin al-Dawla): Christian Arab physician from Baghdad; 1073-1165. He was gifted for languages, skilled in poetry and music, and was also an excellent calligrapher. Although a priest, he enjoyed the favour of the caliphs.

Ibn al-Tiqtaqa: Iraqi historian; xivth c. He is known for an enjoyable history of the caliphs down to al-Musta'sim and of their viziers.

Ibn Tufayl, Abu Bakr Muhammad: known in the West as Abubacer.

Ibn Tulun, Shams al-Din: scholar and prolific writer from Damascus; 1473-1546. His historical writings, among them an autobiography, deal with the end of Mamluk rule and the beginning of Ottoman domination of Syria.

Ibn Tumart: Berber who founded the Almohad movement in Morocco; 1078-1130. Having visited Córdoba, Alexandria, Mecca and Baghdad, he returned in 1116 to the Maghrib. His uncompromising insistence on the punctilious observance of religious obligations, his piety and learning won him many followers. In 1121 he openly revolted against the Almoravid 'Ali b. Yusuf b. Tashufin and had himself proclaimed as the Mahdi or restorer of religion and justice. The siege of Marrakesh by the Almohads in 1130 failed, but did not in fact much hinder the progress of the movement.

Ibn Tumlus, Abu 'l-Hajjaj: Muslim physician of Spain, known in the West as Alhagiag bin Thalmus.

Ibn Umayl, al-Hakim al-Sadiq: one of the representatives of the allegorical and mystagogical type of alchemy; xth c. He had a special interest in the old Egyptian temples and their wall-paintings and actually visited an ancient temple at Busir al-Sidr in the province of al-Jiza, where he saw a statue of Imhotep.

Ibn Wafid, Abu 'l-Mutarrif: Andalusian author, known in the West as Abenguefith.

Ibn Wahshiyya: name of a person of whose existence there is as yet no reliable historical proof. Among the many works attributed to him is the *Book of the Nabataean Agriculture*, which is the subject of vigorous debate among orientalists.

Ibn al-Wannan: poet from Fez; d. 1773. His fame is based on a poem which is a résumé of the traditional culture of the Arabs. It is known as *al-Shamaqmaqiyya* and is used as a textbook to be learned by heart.

Ibn Wasil: historian, judge and man of letters of Hamat; 1208-1298. One of his works, which reaches the year 1263, is the most valuable source for the history of the Ayyubids.

Ibn Yunus (Yunis): one of the most prominent Muslim astronomers; d. 1009. His sets of astronomical tables have been treated extensively by modern scholars.

Ibn Zafar: Arab scholar and polygraph from Sicily; 1104-1170. His biography of illustrious individuals was translated into Italian, English and Turkish.

Ibn al-Zaqqaq: one of the great poets of Muslim Spain; ca. 1100-1133. His *dīwān* acquired great fame.

Ibn Zamrak: poet and statesman from Granada; 1333-ca. 1393. In his panegyrics he celebrates the beauty of Granada's gardens and palaces.

Ibn Zaydan: Moroccan official and historian of Meknès; 1873-1946. His works may be considered as the best source for the history of Meknès and of the Sharifs of Morocco.

Ibn Zaydun: famous poet of Córdoba; 1003-1070. His romantic and literary life was dominated by his stormy relations with the poetess Wallada, the daughter of the Spanish Umayyad Muhammad III al-Mustakfi (r. 1024-1025).

Ibn Zayla: pupil of Avicenna, mathematician and excellent musician; d. 1048.

Ibn al-Zayyat: man of letters and jurist from Morocco; d. 1230. He is known and esteemed as a hagiographer of the saintly personages of the country, among them the great Moroccan saint Abu 'l-'Abbas al-Sabti.

Ibn Ziba'ra: noted poet of the Quraysh who satirized the Prophet and his followers; viith c.

Ibn al-Zubayr, Abu Ja'far: transmitter of traditions, "reader" of the Qur'an, man of letters and historian of Jaén, south central Spain; 1230-1308.

Ibn Zuhr: patronymic of a family of scholars in Spain; xiith-xiiith c. The physician Abu 'l-'Ala' Ibn Zuhr (d. 1130) was known to medieval western scholars as Abulelizor or Albuleizor. Another physician of this family, Abu Marwan Ibn Zuhr (1092-1161), was known as Abhomeron Avenzoar.

Ibn Zur'a: Jacobite Christian philosopher, apologist and translator of Baghdad; 943-1008. Among other works of Aristotle, he translated the *Historia Animalium*.

Ibn-i Yamin: the most important Persian poet of epigrams; 1287-1368. He was one of the earliest poets to write on the Shi'i Imams and the tragedy of Karbala'.

Ibrahim I b. al-Aghlab: founder of the Ifriqiyan dynasty of the Aghlabids; r. 800-812. In 801 he received the envoys of Charlemagne at Qasr al-Qadim (al-'Abbasiyya) near Qayrawan.

Ibrahim II, Ahmad b. Muhammad: after Ibrahim I, the most outstanding personality of the Aghlabid dynasty; b. 850, r. 875-902. He is distinguished for his exceptional qualities but, affected by a mental illness, he very soon built up a system of complete despotism and thus prepared the way for the triumph of the Fatimids. During his reign the conquest of Sicily was completed in 901. He abdicated in 902, became an ascetic and died in the same year under the walls of Cosenza in southern Italy.

Ibrahim: Ottoman sultan; b. 1615, r. 1640-1648. Until about 1644, Ibrahim concerned himself with his empire, establishing peaceful relations with Persia and Austria. Afterwards, however, he came increasingly under the influence of concubines and favourites. In 1645 he embarked on a war with Venice, which was to last for 24 years.

Ibrahim b. 'Abd Allah: rebel against the 'Abbasid Caliph al-Mansur; 716-763. He was a full brother of Muhammad b. 'Abd Allah al-Nafs al-Zakiyya.

Ibrahim b. Adham: prominent Sufi of Balkh in Khurasan; 730-777. Legends about his life spread to Persia, India and Indonesia.

Ibrahim b. 'Ali b. Hasan al-Saqqa': teacher and preacher from Cairo; 1797-1881. He gave an oration at the ceremony of the opening of the Suez canal.

Ibrahim Bey al-Kabir: with Murad Bey he occupied the beylicate of Egypt in a duumvirate between 1768 and 1798; d. 1816.

Ibrahim Edhem Pasha: Ottoman Grand Vizier; 1818-1893. He is held responsible for the disastrous Turco-Russian war of 1877, but contributed to the modernization of Turkey.

Ibrahim Haqqi Pasha: Ottoman statesman, diplomat and Grand Vizier; 1862-1918. He was a moderate influence in the conflict between the Committee of Union and Progress and the opposition.

Ibrahim Lodi: the last of the Lodi Sultans of Delhi; r. 1517-1526. He indulged in acts of capricious tyranny. The Punjab rose in rebellion under Dawlat Khan Lodi, who invited the Chagatay Turk Babur, the founder of the Mughal dynasty, to attack India. The battle of Panipat of 1526, in which Ibrahim was killed, marked the beginning of Mughal rule in india.

Ibrahim b. al-Mahdi: 'Abbasid prince; 779-839. He was a son of the 'Abbasid Caliph al-Mahdi and was proclaimed caliph in 817 against the reigning al-Ma'mun, but had to resign in 819. Afterwards he led the life of a poet-musician.

Ibrahim al-Mawsili: one of the greatest musicians and composers of the early 'Abbasid period; 742-804. Having learned the Persian style of singing at Rayy, he reached the summit of his career under the Caliph Harun al-Rashid. With his colleagues Ibn Jami' and Fulayh b. Abi 'l-'Awra' he made a selection of 100 songs which form the framework of the *Book of Songs* of Abu 'l-Faraj al-Isfahani.

Ibrahim b. Muhammad (Ibrahim al-Imam): leader of the 'Abbasid propaganda against the Umayyads; 701-749.

Ibrahim Müteferriqa: Ottoman statesman, diplomat, and founder of the first Turkish printing press; 1670-1745. He wrote a passionate condemnation of Catholicism and of the temporal power of the Papacy. The work seems to have been written to prove the link between the author's early Unitarianism and his passage to Islam. The printing press was opened in 1727 to promote Islamic learning.

Ibrahim Pasha: general and viceroy of Egypt; 1789-1848. The eldest son of Muhammad 'Ali Pasha, he fought on behalf of his father against the Mamluks in Upper Egypt, the Wahhabis in Arabia, the Greeks in the Morea and the Turks in Syria. Owing to Muhammad 'Ali's senility, Ibrahim formally assumed the governorship of Egypt but predeceased his father.

Ibrahim Pasha (*Maqbūl* "the favourite; *Maqtūl* "the executed"): Ottoman Grand Vizier; 1493-1536. Having been appointed Grand Vizier and beylerbey of Rumeli by Sultan Sülayman II at the very early age of thirty, he reached the zenith of his power after having occupied Tabriz and Baghdad in 1534. In 1536 he quite unexpectedly was strangled.

Ibrahim Pasha, Damad: Ottoman Grand Vizier of Bosnian origin; ca. 1550-1601. He took command of the Ottoman armies engaged in the Hungarian war.

Ibrahim Pasha, Nevshehirli: Ottoman Grand Vizier; 1662-1730. His vizierate began in 1718 and is known as "The Tulip Period".

Ibrahim Shah Sharqi: ruler of the dynasty of the Sharqi Sultans of Jawnpur; r. 1402-1440. He was a patron of art and letters and graced his capital with many fine buildings.

Ibrahim b. Shirkuh: Ayyubid prince of Aleppo and Damascus and cousin of Saladin; r. 1240-1246. He several times defeated the Khwarazmians.

Ibrahim b. al-Walid I b. 'Abd al-Malik: Umayyad Caliph in 744; d. 750. After the death of his brother Caliph Yazid II, who reigned for a couple of months in 744, Ibrahim was recognized as caliph in the southern part of Syria but he soon submitted to the new Caliph Marwan II and became a member of the latter's suite.

(al-)Ibrahimi: Algerian reformist scholar and writer; 1889-1965. He propagated the separation of the Muslim religion from the state, the independence of the Muslim judicial system, and the official recognition of the Arabic language.

al-Ibshihi: Egyptian author of one of the most famous anthologies of Arabic literature; 1388-ca. 1446.

Idol (A. *ṣanam*; pl. *aṣnām*): the term occurs in the Qur'an and is explained as "an object which is worshipped besides God", made of stone, wood or metal. The Arabic term *wathan* is almost synonymous with "picture or painting". The Prophet is said to have the idols at Mecca destroyed by fire.

Idris I (al-Akbar): founder of the Idrisid dynasty; r. 789-791. Of 'Alid descent, he escaped the massacre at Fakhkh in 786 and settled at Walila (Volubilis), from where he consolidated his authority in the valley of the Wargha. He is said to have founded the town of Fez.

Idris II (al-Asghar/al-Azhar): ruler of the Idrisid dynasty; b. 791, r. 803-828. He wished to end the Berber predominance near Fez. His tomb in the mosque of the Chorfa remains the object of veneration.

al-Idrisi, Abu 'Abd Allah (al-Sharif al-Idrisi): famous geographer; 1100-1165. He owes his fame to *The Book of Roger*, which he produced in 1154 on the orders of Roger II, the Norman king of Sicily. The work is a key to a large silver planisphere which the author himself had made.

Idrisids (Adarisa): Moroccan dynasty of descendants of the Prophet's son-in-law 'Ali and thus connected with the line of Shi'i Imams; r. 789-985.

Yahya I b. Muhammad (r. 849-863) founded in 859 the two great mosques of Fez, that of the Qarawiyyin and that of al-Andalus.

Ifran, Banu: the most important branch of the large Berber tribe of the Zanata, whose presence in Tripolitania, Wargla, Ifrīqiya, the Maghrib and Spain is recorded from the viith c. onwards.

Ifriqiya: the Arab term, borrowed from the Latin *Africa*, indicates the eastern part of the Maghrib. In modern Arabic use, *Ifriqiyā* mainly indicates the African continent, whereas *Ifrīqiya* refers to the medieval Arabo-Muslim territory which bore its name. In the texts the latter term is sometimes confused with the whole of the Maghrib and sometimes considered as a greographically separate region. The exact meaning can only be found in relation to the context and the period.

'Ifrit: epithet used for a class of rebellious beings which possess power and cunning and show insubordination. The word, found only once in the Qur'an, became widely used in popular tales, especially in the Thousand-and-one Nights.

Ihram: technical term for the state of temporary consecration of someone who is performing the pilgrimage (A. *ḥajj*) or the little pilgrimage (A. *'umra*) to Mecca. This holy state is entered into by the statement of intention, accompanied by certain rites and, for men, by the donning of the ritual garment, consisting of two pieces of white seamless cloth. Certain places are traditionally stipulated for the assumption of the state of consecration.

al-Ikhwan ("the Brothers"): term for the Arab tribesmen who joined a religious and military movement between 1912 and 1930 under the rule of 'Abd al-'Aziz Al Sa'ud. The movement, which was inspired by the resurgence of Wahhabism and spread rapidly, was characterised by religious fervour and the settlement of nomadic tribesmen in military cantonments. 'Abd al-'Aziz' intention was to supersede the tribal tie with that of religion. Thanks to the prowess of the Ikhwan, most of the Arabian Peninsula was brought under the sway of 'Abd al-'Aziz. However, they at last revolted against their sovereign who checked and confined them.

al-Ikhwan al-Muslimun ("the Muslim Brethren"): Muslim movement, both religious and political, founded in Egypt by Hasan al-Banna' in 1928. Dedicated to the service of Islam, the Brethren's main objective was the struggle against western invasion in all its forms and the creation of an authentically Muslim state. Their ideas are still widely spread.

al-Ikhwan al-Safa': name under which the authors of the so-called *Epistles of the Brethern of Purity* conceal their identity. Of Isma'ili inspiration, the Epistles were composed in Basra ca. 960, and should be regarded as an attempt to reunite the non-Fatimid Isma'ilis on a common doctrinal basis countering the ideological offensive of the Fatimids.

'Ikrima: a Successor and one of the main transmitters of the traditional interpretation of the Qur'an, attributed to Ibn 'Abbas; 643-723.

Ilahi: term used in Turkey of a genre of popular poetry of religious inspiration, consisting of poems sung – without instrumental accompaniment – in chorus or solo during certain ceremonies.

Ilat (s. *Il*): Turco-Persian term denoting nomadic or semi-nomadic tribes.

Ildeñiz, Shams al-Din: a Qipčaq (Kipchak) Turk who, by 1146, made himself the virtually independent ruler of Azerbaijan and founded the dynasty of the Ildeñizids; d. 1175.

Ildeñizids/Eldigüzids: line of Turkish slave commanders who governed most of northwestern Persia and Azerbaijan from 1150 to 1225. They were patrons of poets and scholars.

Ilek-Khans/Qarakhanids: Turkish dynasty which ruled in both Western Turkestan (Transoxiana) and in Eastern Turkestan (Kashgharia or Sinkiang), from the xth to the early xiiith c. The Ilek-Khans gradually assimilated themselves to the Perso-Islamic cultural and governmental traditions and were patrons of scholars and literary men.

Ileri, Jelal Nuri (Celal Nuri Ileri): Turkish modernist, writer, publicist and journalist; 1877-1938. He wrote about the legal system, the emancipation of women, the causes of Ottoman decline, the alphabet and language reform and reform in Islam.

Ilghazi I, Najm al-Din: Saljuq ruler and founder of the Mardin and Mayyafariqin branch of the Artuqid dynasty; r. 1104-1122.

Ilghazi II, Qutb al-Din: member of the Artuqid dynasty in Mardin and Mayyafariqin; r. 1176-1184.

Ili: large river in Central Asia. In the xiiith c. it was regarded as marking the farthest boundary of Islam.

Il-Khans: a Mongol dynasty founded by Hülegü which ruled in Persia from 1256 to 1355. They showed a tendancy toward Buddhism and Christianity, Nestorianism in particular, and were tolerant of the Shi'a until Arghun (r. 1284-1291) embraced Sunni Islam, which set the seal on the fusion of Mongols and Turks in Persia. Öljeytü Khudabanda, however, embraced Shi'ism in 1310 but his son and successor Abu Sa'id (r. 1316-1335) reverted to Sunni Islam. Of particular interest are Il-Khanid architecture, ceramics, metalwork and textiles. Their art reflects Far Eastern influence in miniature painting and in the use of new iconographic themes of Chinese derivation, such as the lotus, the phoenix and square Kufic script, which was probably inspired by Chinese seal characters.

Iltutmish b. Elam Khan, Shams al-Din: the greatest of the Mu'izzi or Slave Kings in Northern India; r. 1211-1236. He laid the foundations of Muslim rule in India.

'Imad al-Dawla, 'Ali b. Buwayh: the eldest of the three Daylami brothers who became the founders of the dynasty of the Buyids (Buwayhids); r. 934-949. He seized Baghdad in 945 and brought the 'Abbasid caliph under his control.

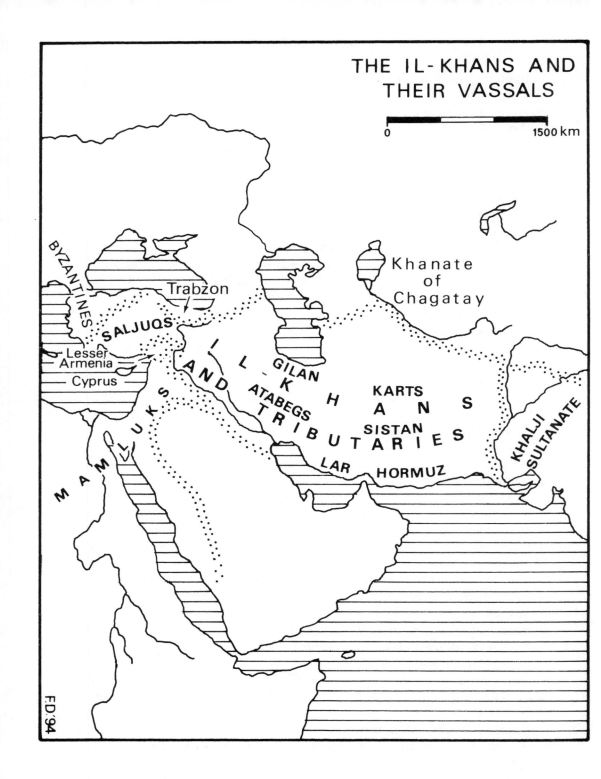

THE IL-KHANS AND
THEIR VASSALS

0   1500 km

BYZANTINES

Trabzon

Khanate
of
Chagatay

SALJUQS

Lesser
Armenia

Cyprus

M A M L U K S

I L - K H A N S

GILAN

ATABEGS

A N D   T R I B U T A R I E S

KARTS

SISTAN

LAR   HORMUZ

KHALJI
SULTANATE

F.D.'94

'Imad al-Din al-Katib al-Isfahani: famous stylist and historian; 1125-
1201. His most remarkable work is *Qussian eloquence on the conquest of
Jerusalem* (of 1187). The term Qussian is related to the name of Quss b.
Sa'ida al-Iyadi.

'Imad al-Din Zangi I b. Aq Sunqur: member of the line of the Turkish
Zangid dynasty in Mosul and Aleppo; b. 1084, r. 1127-1146. In 1127 he was
appointed governor of Mosul, and received the title of atabeg. He took possession of Jazirat Ibn 'Umar, Nisibis, Sinjar, Harran, Aleppo and Hamat. His
attack on Baghdad, however, was unsuccessful, as was that of the 'Abbasid
Caliph al-Mustarshid bi-'llah on Mosul. 'Imad al-Din approved of the deposition of the 'Abbasid Caliph al-Rashid (r. 1135-1136) and paid homage to the
latter's successor al-Muqtafi (r. 1136-1160). In 1137 he routed King Fulk of
Jerusalem, took the fortress of Ba'rin (Monsferrandus), and pursued the Emperor John II of Constantinople on his return to Antioch after an unsuccessful
attack on Shayzar. He received Homs and in 1139 conquered Baalbek. He
then laid siege to Damascus, whose commander Mu'in al-Din invoked the
support of the Crusaders. 'Imad al-Din then raised the siege and returned to
Mosul. In 1144 he took Edessa from the Crusaders, which set off the Second
Crusade.

'Imad Shahi: title of a ruling family, founded by a Hindu convert to Islam,
which ruled over Berar, the eastern districts of what is now Maharashtra
State, western India, from 1490 until 1574.

Imamiyya: the term indicates the Twelver Shi'a, and as such is distinguished from the Isma'iliyya, which branched off from the Imamiyya after
the death of Imam Ja'far al-Sadiq. Imami is an adjective derived from
Imamiyya.

Immolation (A. *dhabīḥa*): Muslim law contains strict rules for the immolation of a victim in fulfilment of a vow, on the seventh day after the birth
of a child, on the occasion of the feast of the 10th Dhu 'l-Hijja or in atone-
ment for certain transgressions committed during the pilgrimage.

Immunity from error and sin (A. *'iṣma*): the Arab term and the concept
do not occur in the Qur'an or in canonical Sunni Tradition. In early Islam
moral failures and errors of the Prophet were freely mentioned, although there
was an inconsistent tendency to minimize his shortcomings, in particular to
deny that he had ever participated in the worship of idols. Immunity from
error and sin is attributed by Sunnis to the prophets and by Shi'is to the
Imams. The doctrine that the Imam, as the divinely appointed and guided
leader and teacher of the community, must be immune from error and sin has
always remained a cardinal dogma of the Imamiyya.

'Imran (Hebrew *'Amrām*): Muslim authors mention two persons of this
name, the first of whom appears in the Bible but not in the Qur'an, the second
vice versa. The first is the father of Moses, Aaron and Maryam (Exodus, VI,
20), the other the father of Maryam, the mother of Jesus (Qur'an, III, 31). The

last mentioned is also, according to the historians, the father of Elizabeth (A. *Ashba'*), the mother of John the Baptist.

'Imran b. Shahin: bandit-lord of the swampy area on the lower course of the Euphrates and Tigris between Kufa and Basra (A. *al-baṭā'iḥ*); d. 979.

Imru' al-Qays: by-name, meaning "slave of (the god) Qays", of several Arab poets. The most famous of them is Imru' al-Qays b. Hujr, generally considered to have died circa 550. Although remaining an obscure and semi-legendary personality, he has acquired a great reputation. Some of his admirers in Basra credited him with the creation of the *qaṣīda*. Among his poems the so-called *Mu'allaqa* has aroused the most interest.

Imzad (Berber): name of a musical instrument in use among the Touareg and generally compared with a violin.

In sha' Allah: Arabic expression which means "if God wills", "if it pleases God". It indicates that God alone is the master of all that happens, as well as of the thoughts, acts and plans of man. In Islamic countries in ordinary speech it is used to qualify anything in the future.

Inal (Aynal) al-Ajrud: Mamluk sultan of Egypt and Syria; b. 1381, r. 1453-1461. During his reign Mamluk troops intervened in dynastic troubles of the Lusignan in Cyprus, but suffered many losses.

Inal, Ibn al-Emin (Ibnülemin Mahmud Kemal Inal): Turkish biographer and writer; 1870-1957. He was probably one of the last outstanding representatives of traditional Ottoman scholarship and erudition, ignoring the changes which were taking place around him. In 1940 he became an adviser to the Editorial Board of the Turkish edition of the Encyclopaedia of Islam.

'Inan: famous poetess in Baghdad; d. 841. She is considered the first woman to have won literary fame under the 'Abbasids. She played an important role as the centre of a literary circle.

'Inayat Allah Kanbu: author of a history of the Mughal emperor Shah Jahan I; 1608-1671.

Independence (A. *istiqlāl*): the Arabic term refers to independence from foreign political control of Arab territories after World War I.

Indian National Congress: it was a gathering of English-educated, middle class Indians, including Hindus, Parsis and Muslims, who formed themselves into an All-India political organization. Its first session was held in Bombay in December 1885. Most Muslims saw in it a Hindu movement and claimed special minority rights. The Muslim League was founded in December 1906 and the gulf with the Congress gradually widened. The schism reached its climax in 1947 in the partition of India and the foundation of Pakistan.

Indonesia: the earliest known record of probable Muslim settlement in the Malay-Indonesian Archipelago is a Chinese report of 674 which mentions the existence of an Arab settlement in east Sumatra. In the ixth c. large numbers of Muslim merchants fled from Canton and sought refuge on the west coast of the Malay Peninsula. Islam was introduced into the northern tip of Sumatra

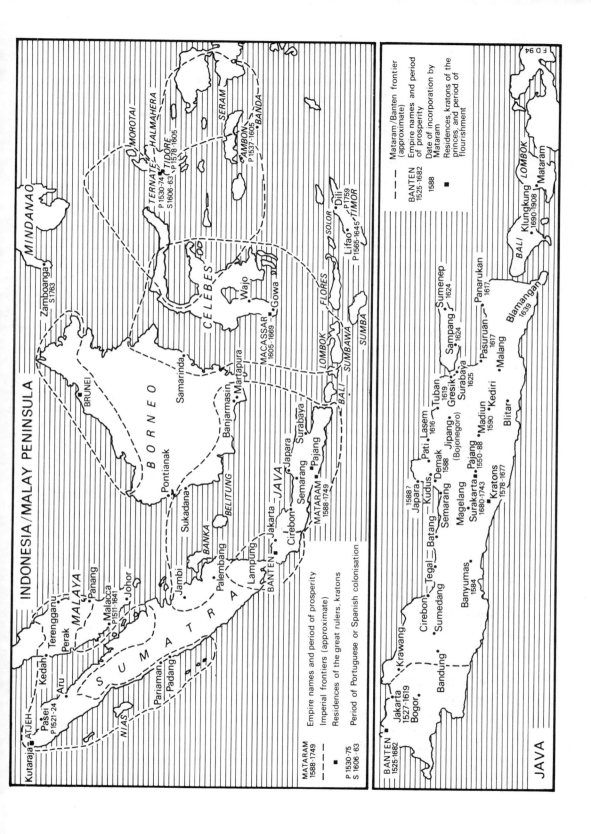

INDONESIA/MALAY PENINSULA

MINDANAO

Zamboanga•
S 1763

MOROTAI

TERNATE• •HALMAHERA
P 1530-74 •TIDORE
S 1606-63 P 1578-1605

SERAM

AMBON•
P 1537-1605

BANDA

BRUNEI

B O R N E O

Pontianak•

Samarinda•

Banjarmasin•
Martapura•

Sukadana•

CELEBES

Wajo

MACASSAR
1605-1669
Gowa•
1510

SOLOR

FLORES

Dili•

Lifao•
P 1759

P 1565-1645 TIMOR

SUMBA

LOMBOK

SUMBAWA

BALI

Kutaraja• ATJEH
Pasei•
P 1521-24

Kedah
Terengganu

Aru•

Perak

M A L A Y A

Panang•

Johor•

Malacca•
P 1511-1641

N I A S

S U M A T R A

Pariaman•
Padang•

Jambi•

Palembang•

BANKA

BELITUNG

Lampung

Jakarta• J A V A

BANTEN• Cirebon•
1525-1682

Semarang•

Japara•

Surabaya•

Pajang•

MATARAM
1588-1749

MATARAM
1588-1749

MATARAM
1588-1749
Empire names and period of prosperity

Imperial frontiers (approximate)

■ Residences of the great rulers, kratons

P 1530-75
S 1606-63
Period of Portuguese or Spanish colonisation

F D 94

Mataram/Banten frontier
(approximate)

BANTEN Empire names and period
1525-1682 of prosperity

1588 Date of incorporation by
Mataram

■ Residences, kratons of the
princes, and period of
flourishment

BALI Klungkung
1690-1908
Mataram•

LOMBOK

Sumenep•
1624

Sampang•
1624

Panarukan
1617

Pasuruan
1617

Blamangan
1639

Tuban•

Gresik•
1619

Surabaya•
1625

Malang•

Pati• Lasem
1616

Jipang•
(Bojonegoro)
1588

Madiun•

Kediri
1590

Blitar•

Japara•
1588?

Demak•
Kudus•

Semarang•

Magelang•

Surakarta•
1680-1743

Pajang•
1550-88

Kratons
1578-1677

Cirebon• Tegal Batang

Sumedang•

Banyumas•
1584

Jakarta
1527-1619
Bogor•

Krawang•

Bandung•

BANTEN
1525-1682

J A V A

sometime around 1112. When Ibn Battuta visited Pasai in 1345, the sultan was zealous in propagating Islam. On Java, Arab and Persian missionaries propagated Islam from 1400 onwards, while Islam came to the southern region of Sumatra, to south Kalimantan and to the Moluccas in the xvth c. Sulawesi (Celebes) was islamicised in the beginning of the xvith c. Indonesia declared its independence from the Netherlands in 1945, but its struggle for independence continued until 1949.

Infidel (A. *kāfir*, pl. *kāfirūn*): in most passages of the Qur'an, the term refers to unbelievers, who are threatened with God's punishment and hell. Tradition reflects the great controversy in early Islam on the question whether a Muslim should be considered an infidel for committing a major sin. Eternal damnation for the infidel has remained an established dogma in Islam. Down to the time of the Crusades there prevailed in Islam a tolerance towards the unbeliever, especially "the people of the Book", the Christians and the Jews. Religious fanaticism against them was aroused and nourished by the repeated wars with unbelievers.

Innovation (A. *bidʿa*): in strict sense, the word indicates a belief or practice for which there is no precedent in the time of the Prophet. According to al-Shafiʿi, any innovation which runs contrary to the Qur'an, the deeds, utterances and tacit approval of the Prophet (A. *sunna*) and to a Tradition traced to a Companion or a Follower is erroneous.

Inscriptions (A. *kitābāt*): the oldest known inscriptions written in the Arabic language have been discovered in Syria. Inscriptions are known from all great Muslim dynasties in the Near East: the Umayyads, the ʿAbbasids, the Fatimids, the Saljuqs and the Mamluks. Inscriptions are also found in Muslim Spain, in North, West and East Africa, Turkey, South-East Asia, Persia, Transoxiana and India.

Institut d'Égypte: the first French institute was founded by Bonaparte in Cairo in 1798. After the French had left Egypt, the large collections which had been gathered were made known in the famous "Description de l'Égypte". The second institute was founded in Alexandria in 1859 and transferred to Cairo in 1880.

Intention (A. *niyya*): the religious practices, obligatory or not, require to be preceded by a declaration, pronounced audibly or mentally, that the performer intends to perform such an act. Without it, the act is invalid (A. *bāṭil*). The intention thus is required before the performance of washing, bathing, prayer, alms, fasting, pilgrimage and sacrifice. Yet, a survey of the opinions of the jurists regarding the intention in connection with each of the religious practices would show that there is only unanimity as far as the ritual prayer (A. *ṣalāt*) is concerned.

Intercession (A. *shafāʿa*): the term is usually found in eschatological descriptions. As such it already occurs in the Qur'an, and the principle of intercession has been adopted unrestrictedly in Islam. The Prophet's intercession at the Day of Judgement is described in an often quoted tradition.

Interpreter (T. *terjumān*): the activity of these indispensable functionaries began to enter into clearer historical light only in the xiith c. Used in the commercial chancelleries and for concluding and interpreting treaties, they were originally appointed by the local authorities. Under the Ottoman Empire the most common name for them in European sources is the Italian form "drogman" or "dragoman", the French "truchement" remaining also a long time in use. The most important post was that of dragoman of the Ottoman government, the first being ʿAlī Beg, who brought the peace treaty of 1502 to Venice. These dragomans were largely Greeks, Germans and Hungarians, and almost without exception Christians. In the xviiith c. the function became almost hereditary in certain Greek families. The dragomans of the embassies and consulates were often no less powerful international mediators. They represented the consuls in the actions before Ottoman tribunals and with time their interference in Ottoman affairs became insupportable to the Porte. In 1914 the capitulations were abolished, and with them foreign diplomatic or consular functionaries with the title of dragoman.

Investiture (A. *bayʿa*): investiture was the act by which one person was proclaimed and recognised as head of the Muslim State. The title of a new caliph was either established by the testamentary designation of his predecessor or by a body of electors, made up of the high dignitaries and notables of the State. Neither *manumissio* nor confirmation by oath was required as condition of validity. From early ʿAbbasid times onwards, the investiture acquired a religious character, the ruler being held to receive his from God.

Iqbal, Muhammad: Indian poet and philosopher; 1877-1938. Writing in English, Persian and Urdu, he taught the Muslims how to regain strength by developing their personality, be it as individuals or as nations. He also insisted on the necessity of forming a separate Muslim state in Northwest India, which eventually was realized in the nation of Pakistan in 1947.

Iran or **Persia** (P. *Īrān*): Islamic republic of western Asia. The name Iran is of Pahlavi origin, i.e. of the so-called Middle Persian language, which existed from the iiird to the xth c. and was the official language of the Sasanian Empire (226-652). The name Persia is derived from a region of southern Iran formerly known as Persis, modern Fars. The Islamic conquest, preceded by a series of raids, began with the victory of the Muslim Arabs over the Sasanian king Yazdagird III at the battle of al-Qadisiyya in 635. The final defeat of the Persian army took place at Nihawand in 642.

The subsequent history of Iran is that of the many dynasties who ruled over various large areas, whose boundaries extended far beyond modern Iran. As far as the modern country is concerned, the Bawandids reigned in Tabaristan and Gilan, the Tahirids and the Samanids in Khurasan, the Saffarids in

Sistan, the Buyids in Fars, Khuzistan and Kirman, the Ghaznawids in Khurasan, the Saljuqs in western Iran and Kirman, the Khwarazm-Shahs over parts of northeastern Iran, the Ildeñizids in northwestern Iran, the Il-Khans over most of modern Iran, the Muzaffarids in southern Iran, the Timurids in Khurasan and western Iran. The Safawids, the Qajars and the Pahlavis ruled over regions which more or less coincided with modern Iran.

For the history of Iran the Safawid period is of supreme importance because Imami Shi'ism was imposed as the state religion in a country which up till then had been, at least officially, predominantly Sunni.

The rightly famous Persian literature can be said to comprise the poetry and belletristic prose works composed in the New Persian literary language produced by the Muslim population from the ixth c. onwards. An important aspect of a poet's life was his being dependent, in one way or the other, on patronage, a situation which lasted until the end of the xixth c. The most important lyrical form of poetry until the Mongol invasion in the xiiith c. was the *qaṣīda*. The Persian quatrain (P. *rubā'ī*) occurs in the sermons and the biographies of Sufi shaykhs and in mystical treatises, while the rich epic poetry uses the so-called *mathnawī*.

Persian literary history can be divided in four periods: a. from the Samanids to the Mongol invasion (xth-xiiith c.); b. from the Mongol period to the rise of the Safawids (xiiith-xvth c.; c. from the Safawids to the late Qajar period (xv-xixth c.); d. The modern period.

To the first period belong, among others, Rudaki, Firdawsi, 'Unsuri, Farrukhi and Sana'i. During the xiiith-xvth c., Shiraz, which had escaped the devastations of Mongol warfare, was the centre for such poets as Sa'di and Shams al-Din Hafiz. During the Safawid period, religious poetry was greatly cultivated, while secular Persian poetry and prose flourished under the Mughal emperors in India. The modern period is characterized by the propagation of new ideas on political, social and scientific issues. The historical novel and the short story achieved great popularity.

Iraq (A. *'Irāq*): Arab republic of the Middle East. The Muslim conquest of the fertile land began with the decisive battle against the Sasanian general Rustam at al-Qadisiyya in 637. Fortified camps were established at Basra and Kufa and the conquest was assured by the victory at Nihawand in 642. The 'Abbasids established their capital first at Kufa and later at Baghdad. Iraq then became the centre of trade for the whole Orient as well as an intellectual and artistic centre. In the political complex controlled during the xth c. by the Shi'i Buyids, Iraq ceased to be the centre of the empire. The Sunni Saljuqs dominated the land during the xith-xiith c.

After the revival under the 'Abbasid caliph al-Nasir li-Din Allah, the country was conquered by the Mongols in 1258. Iraq now came under the rule of Mongol dynasties such as the Il-Khanids, the Jalayirids and the Timurids, and of Turkmen dynasties such as the Qara Qoyunlu, the Aq Qoyunlu and the Safawids.

The Ottomans captured Baghdad in 1534. Under their domination, which lasted until 1918, Iraq was primarily a bastion against the Safawid rulers of Persia, the Kurds in the north-east and the Arab tribesmen on the Tigris-Euphrates plain. The country was occupied by the British in 1918, became a constitutional monarchy under Faysal I in 1921 and was given formal independence in 1930.

The monarchy came to an end in 1958 with the revolutionary coup led by 'Abd al-Karim Qasim. The civil war with the Kurds, which broke out in 1961, was brought to a temporary end by an agreement in 1966 under President 'Abd al-Salam 'Arif. A coup d'état of 1967, followed by a second one in 1968, brought General Ahmad Hasan al-Bakr to the presidency. He resigned in 1979 because of ill health and was succeeded by Saddam Husayn al-Takriti.

'Isa b. Dinar: one of the founders of Islamic theology in Spain; 771-827. He wrote a large work of Maliki jurisprudence.

Isaac (A. *Ishāq*): the Biblical Isaac is mentioned several times in the Qur'an.

Isaf wa-Na'ila: a pair of gods worshipped at Mecca before Islam.

'Isami: Persian poet in India; xivth c. His fame rests on his *Conquests of the Sultans*, dedicated to 'Ala' al-Din Hasan Bahman Shah (r. 1347-1358), the founder of the Bahmanid dynasty.

'Isawa ('Isawiyya): mystical order founded by Shaykh Muhammad b. 'Isa (1467-1534), who became the patron saint of the town of Meknès.

Isfahan: town and province in Persia. The town was conquered by the Muslims in 642. Under the Buyids Isfahan became a flourishing and extensive city. In the xith c. the town was taken by the Saljuqs, who made it into their capital and into an important Sunni centre. In 1240 it fell to the Mongols and afterwards changed hands several times. In 1502 the town was finally taken by Shah Isma'il I. By the xviith c. Isfahan had become the political, administrative and commercial centre of the Safawids and Shah 'Abbas I made it his capital. European visitors like Chardin praised its splendour. In 1722 the Afghans conquered the city, which became only a shadow of its former self. Isfahan played a prominent role during the Constitutional Revolution of 1906. The city is rightly famous for its splendid Islamic monuments.

Isfendiyar-oghullari: Turkmen dynasty at Kastamonu, northern Anatolia; r. ca. 1290-1461. Also known as Candar, the dynasty was renowned for their patronage of men of letters and contributed to the development of Turkish as a literary language. The principality was annexed by the Ottoman Sultan Mehemmed II, but members of the dynasty continued to serve as governors under the Ottomans.

Ishaq b. Hunayn: like his father Hunayn b. Ishaq, an eminent translator of ancient science and philosophy; d. 910. Well versed in Greek, Syriac, Arabic and Persian, he made many translations of Aristotle, Plato and other Greek philosophers as well as of many standard works on mathematics and astronomy. His own writings were mainly on medical and pharmacological subjects.

Ishaq b. Ibrahim al-Mawsili: the greatest musician of his time; 767-850. He showed a predilection for ancient poetry, and is mentioned in the *Sessions* of al-Hariri and in the "Thousand-and-One Nights".

Ishaq Efendi, Khoja: Ottoman mathematician and engineer; 1774-1835. He wrote the first work in Turkish on the modern physical and natural sciences.

Ishmael (A. *Ismāʿīl*): the Biblical figure is mentioned several times in the Qur'an, but he is not linked directly to Abraham.

Iskandar Agha b. Yaʿqub: Armenian man of letters, known in the West as Abkarius.

Iskandar Beg al-Shahir bi-Munshi: Persian historian; ca. 1560-ca. 1632. His work, one of the greatest in Persian historiography, deals with the origins of the Safawids and the period between Shah Ismaʿil and Shah Safi.

Islam: the word means "submission, total surrender (to God)" according to the message of the Prophet. A Muslim, therefore, is "one who submits to God" while following the teachings of the Qur'an and the Muslim Tradition. In European languages, Islam often also denotes the whole body of Muslim peoples, countries, and states, in their socio-cultural or political as well as in their religious sphere. Finally, the word denotes the ideal Muslim community.

After the death of the Prophet in 632, Islam spread very quickly to Syria/Palestine, Egypt, North Africa, Spain, and, in the east, to Iraq, Armenia and Iran, as far as Transoxiana and Chinese Turkestan, all within the viith c. Expansion continued to India, Indonesia, sub-Saharan West Africa, East Africa and the Nile valley. The Ottomans brought Islam to Eastern Europe. Although almost confined to Asia and Africa, Islam was introduced in North and South America by immigrants, while migrant and transient workers spread it in western Europe. Present-day statistics lead to an estimate of ca. 600 million Muslims, thus representing about one-sixth of all human beings.

Islam Giray: name of three Khans of the Crimea: Islam Giray I (r. 1532), Islam Giray II (r. 1584-1588) and Islam Giray III (r. 1644-1654).

Ismaʿil I: shah of Persia and founder of the Safawid dynasty; b. 1487, r. 1501-1524. He defeated the Aq Qoyunlu in 1501, gained control of Azerbaijan and extended Safawid power over great parts of modern Iran. He proclaimed the Twelver Shiʿa as the official religion of the Safawid state, which was an important factor in making Iran a national unit for the first time since the Arab conquest in the viith c. He thus decisively differentiated his dominions from those of the Sunni Ottomans. In 1514 Sultan Selim I invaded Persia and inflicted a crushing, but not decisive, defeat on Isma'il at Chaldiran. Isma'il now began exploring the possibilities of an alliance with European powers and received envoys from Louis II, King of Hungary, and from Emperor Charles V.

Under the pseudonym of Khata'i, Isma'il wrote poetry in the Turkish language of Azerbaijan.

Isma'il b. Ahmad: first member of the Samanid family to rule effectively all Transoxiana and Farghana as an independent sovereign; b. 849, r. 892-907.

Isma'il Haqqi: Turkish scholar, mystic and poet of Bursa; 1652-1725. Writing in Turkish and Arabic, he was one of the most prolific Ottoman scholars.

Isma'il Pasha: khedive of Egypt; b. 1830, r. 1863-1879, d. 1895. Through education, journeys and appointments, he had first-hand experience of Europe, mainly France, and of the politics and administration of Istanbul. His reign brought Egypt material prosperity, but also financial bankruptcy. At the insistence of the European powers he was deposed by his suzerain the Ottoman Sultan Abdülhamid II.

Isma'il Sabri Pasha: Egyptian poet and statesman; 1854-1923. Drawing upon his knowledge of classical Arabic and French, he contributed to the awakening of national consciousness in Egypt.

Isma'il Sidqi: Egyptian politician and statesman; 1875-1948. Having joined the Wafd movement in 1918, he became the moving spirit of the anti-Wafdist element in Egyptian politics. He played a leading role in the drafting and implementation of the Declaration of 1922 which granted Egypt its independence, as well as in that of the Constitution of 1923.

Isma'ilis (A. *Ismā'īliyya*): a major section of the Shi'a, also known, not quite accurately, as the "Seveners".

Isra'il, Banu ("the Children of Israel"): term used in the Qur'an and in Islamic Tradition for the Jewish people.

Isra'iliyyat: Arabic term covering narratives, regarded as historical, edifying tales and fables belonging to folklore, allegedly borrowed from Jewish and other sources. They are found in commentaries on the Qur'an, on mystics, and were popular with compilers of edifying stories and other writers.

Istakhr (modern Takht-e Jamshid): town in Fars, Iran, north of the Achaemenid capital Persepolis, which opposed a stubborn resistance to the advance of the Muslims in 643.

al-Istakhri, Abu Ishaq Ibrahim (al-Farisi): Arab geographer; xth c. He was one of the first and most important representatives of the new trends adopted by Arabo-Muslim geography in the xth c.

Istanbul: capital of the Ottoman Empire from 1453 to 1923. The name is derived from the Greek *eis tèn polin*. The city of Constantinople was known

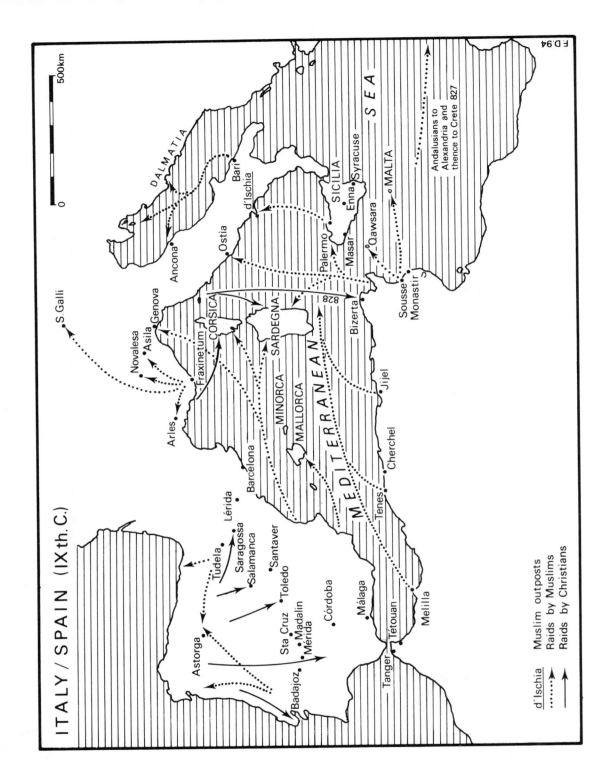

ITALY/SPAIN (IXth.C.)

S. Galli

DALMATIA

Bari

d'Ischia

Ancona

Ostia

Novalesa
Asila
Genova

Arles

CORSICA

Fraxinetum

SARDEGNA

MINORCA

MALLORCA

Barcelona

Lérida

Tudela
Saragossa
Salamanca
Santaver

Sta Cruz
Madalin
Toledo
Mérida

Córdoba

Astorga

Badajoz

Málaga

Tanger
Tétouan

Melilla

Cherchel

Tenes

Jijel

Bizerta

828

Sousse
Monastir

Qawsara

Masar

Palermo

SICILIA

Enna
Syracuse

MALTA

M E D I T E R R A N E A N   S E A

Andalusians to
Alexandria and
thence to Crete 827

d'Ischia   Muslim outposts
··········▸   Raids by Muslims
———▸   Raids by Christians

500km
0

F.D.94

to the Arabs as (al-)Qustantiniyya. It was conquered in 1453 by the Ottoman Sultan Mehemmed II.

Italy (A. *Īṭaliya*): the earliest information provided by the Arab chroniclers about the Saracen attacks on continental Italy concerns the defeat of the Venetian fleet off Taranto in 840 and the accompanying attacks on Bari where, for a quarter of a century, an emirate was established. In 846 Saracen contingents sacked the basilica of St. Peter, but in 849 a large Muslim fleet was defeated at Ostia. Taranto was occupied between 846 and 880, and in 902 the Aghlabid emir Ibrahim II landed in Calabria. Under the Fatimid al-Qa'im Genoa was conquered. Raids in Apulia and Calabria continued under the Kalbid dynasty of Sicily. After the conquest of the island by the Normans in 1072, Italy was seen as finally lost to Islam.

Ithna 'Ashariyya: name of that branch of Shi'i Islam that believes in twelve (A. *ithnā 'ashar*) Imams and is therefore also known as the "Twelvers".

Ittihad-i Muhammedi Jem'iyyeti ("Muhammedan Union"): name of a politico-religious organization which acquired notoriety as the instigator of the insurrection in Istanbul in 1908.

Ittihad we Teraqqi Jem'iyyeti ("Committee of Union and Progress" or C.U.P.): the conspirational nucleus of the Young Turk movement, which was responsible for the destinies of the Ottoman Empire from the revolution in 1908 to its destruction in 1918.

Iyad b. Musa: Maliki scholar in the Muslim West; 1088-1149. His existence coincided almost exactly with that of the Almoravid dynasty to whom throughout his life he remained inflexibly attached.

Izniq: town in present-day Turkey, the ancient and Byzantine Nicaea. It was besieged in vain by the Arabs in 717 and 725. In 1081 Nicaea fell into the hands of the Rum Saljuq Sulayman b. Qutlumish, but was recaptured by the Byzantines and the Crusaders in 1097. It was taken by the Ottomans under Orkhan in 1331. The town was once a flourishing pottery centre, known for its tiles.

'Izra'il ('Azra'il): name of the angel of death. Next to Gabriel, Michael and Israfil, he is one of the four archangels.

'Izzet Molla: Turkish poet; 1785-1829. He was the last great representative of *dīwān* poetry.

'Izzet Pasha (Ahmed Izzet Furgaç): Ottoman soldier and statesman; 1864-1937. He was an aide to Colmar Baron von der Goltz-Pasha and, having served in Yemen, he became chief of the Ottoman general staff after the 1908 revolution. He was Ottoman military delegate to the peace conferences at Brest Litovsk and Bucharest. In 1921 he re-entered the cabinet under Ahmed Tewfiq Pasha as foreign minister and remained in function until the dissolution of the sultan's government in november 1922.

'Izzi (Süleyman Efendi): Ottoman official historiographer; d. 1755. His history covers the years 1744-1752.

J

Jabal Nafusa: a limestone escarpment running from the Libyan Mediterranean coast slightly to the west of the Tripolitanian town of al-Khums in a west-southwestern direction to Nalut. Berbers and Jews took refuge there. At the time of the Italian occupation of Libya immediately preceding the First World War, many of the Arabs were nomadic or semi-nomadic while the Berbers and the Jews were sedentary. In 1948 the Jews fled. Population grew rapidly in the period after the exploitation of oil in 1961.

Jabal Says: name of a volcanic mountain in Syria, ca. 100 km southeast of Damascus, known for its ruins which consist of a number of houses, a mosque, a church, a bath and a palace.

Jabart: name of the Muslims of Ethiopia, originally the name of a region in the territories of Zaylaʿ and Ifat.

al-Jabarti, ʿAbd al-Rahman: Arab historian; 1753-1825. He is famous for an important chronicle of the Arab countries, of Egypt in particular, which covers the years 1688 to 1821.

Jabir b. ʿAbd Allah: Companion of the Prophet; d. 697. He is noted as a most prolific narrator of traditions from the Prophet.

Jabir b. Hayyan: one of the principal representatives of earlier Arabic alchemy; viiith c. All later Arab writers quote his work, and several of his books were translated into Latin.

Jabir b. Zayd: famous Ibadi transmitter of traditions and jurist of Basra; 642-711. He enjoyed an enormous prestige as a man of learning and as an authority on the Qurʾan.

Jabran Khalil Jabran: Lebanese writer, artist and poet; 1883-1931. Having stayed off and on in Boston and Paris, he settled in New York in 1912. He wrote in Arabic and English. His *The Prophet* is considered his masterpiece.

Jacob (A. *Yaʿqūb*): the patriarch is mentioned in the Qurʾan, where he is numbered among the prophets.

Jaén (A. *Jayyān*): capital of the Andalusian province of the same name. The Muslims built a fortress here which was considered to be impregnable.

Jaʿfar b. Abi Talib: cousin of the Prophet and elder brother of ʿAli; d. 629. He took part in the so-called first Hijra to Abyssinia, and fell in the battle of Muʾta.

Jaʿfar b. Abi Yahya: Zaydi scholar and judge of Yemen; d. 1177. He played the most conspicuous role in the introduction in Yemen of the religious literature of the Caspian Zaydi community.

Jaʿfar Čelebi: Ottoman statesman and man of letters of Amasya; 1459-1515. He was also a famous calligrapher and patron of poets.

Jaʿfar al-Sadiq: the last Imam recognized by both "Sevener" and "Twelver" Shiʿis; 700-765.

Ja'far Sharif: author of an authoritative account of Indian popular Islam; xixth c.

Jaffa (A. *Yāfā*): port on the Mediterranean coast, now known as Tel Aviv-Yafo, Israel. It was taken by 'Amr b. al-'As in 636. During the Crusades its possession was hotly disputed.

al-Jaghmini: well-known Arab astronomer; d. 1344. He wrote an epitome of astronomy which was frequently commented upon.

Jahangir: Mughal emperor of India, son of Akbar; b. 1569, r. 1605-1627. In 1599 he revolted against his father, but was nevertheless confirmed as his successor. His eldest son Khusraw, who revolted in 1606, had been supported by his Sikh guru Arjun, who was then put to death by the emperor. This punishment laid the foundations of the deep-rooted hostility which has continued to embitter the relations between the Indian Muslims and the Sikhs over the centuries. Jahangir was a patron of art and literature and above all of painting and he encouraged Persian culture in Mughal India. In his memoirs he shows himself to be an accomplished prose-writer.

Jahan-suz, 'Ala' al-Din: Ghurid ruler and poet; r. 1149-1161. He is notorious for his burning of Ghazna in 1151.

Jahiliyya: Arabic term which refers to the state of affairs in Arabia before the mission of the Prophet. In general it has the connotation of ignorance and paganism.

Jahirids (Banu Jahir): name of a dynasty of viziers during the protectorate of the Great Saljuqs between 1150 and 1240.

al-Jahiz, Abu 'Uthman: famous Arab prose writer of Basra; 776-869. A real master of the Arabic language, he wrote on literature, Mu'tazili theology and politico-religious polemics, showing an invincible desire for learning, a remarkably inquisitive mind and a great sense of humour. Among his main works are *The Book of the Animals*, *The Book of Elegance of Expression and Clarity of Exposition* and *The Book of Misers*.

al-Jahshiyari, Abu 'Abd Allah: scholar of Kufa; xth c. He wrote a work on the history of the secretaries of state and viziers until 908.

Jajarmi, Muhammad b. Badr: Persian poet; xivth c. He is known for his extensive anthology of poetry, the autograph of which attracted the attention of art historians for its miniatures.

Jakarta: capital of Indonesia. In 1527 the sultan of Bantam defeated the Portuguese in that region and called the place Jajakarta. During the Dutch colonial times (1619-1949) the city was called Batavia.

Jalal al-Dawla, Abu Tahir: member of the Buyid dynasty; 993-1044. He was governor of Basra and fought the Buyid ruler Abu Kalijar al-Marzuban and, in the end, left the Buyid kingdom in a state of the deepest degradation.

Jalal al-Din 'Arif (Celāleddin Arif): Turkish lawyer and statesman; 1875-1930. In 1920 his differences with Mustafa Kemal Atatürk became apparent.

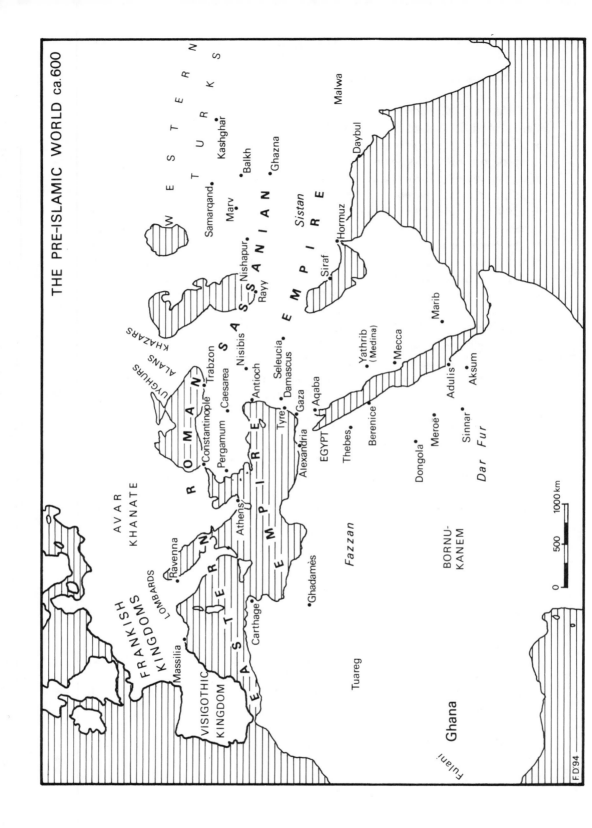

THE PRE-ISLAMIC WORLD ca.600

WESTERN TURKS

KHAZARS

ALANS

UYGHURS

AVAR KHANATE

FRANKISH KINGDOMS

LOMBARDS

VISIGOTHIC KINGDOM

ROMAN

EASTERN EMPIRE

SASSANIAN EMPIRE

Sistan

Malwa

Daybul

Kashghar

Balkh

Ghazna

Samarqand

Marv

Hormuz

Nishapur

Rayy

Siraf

Marib

Yathrib (Medina)

Mecca

Nisibis

Trabzon

Constantinople

Caesarea

Pergamum

Antioch

Seleucia

Damascus

Tyre

Gaza

Aqaba

Alexandria

EGYPT

Thebes

Berenice

Adulis

Aksum

Sinnar

Dar Fur

Meroé

Dongola

Athens

Ravenna

Massilia

Carthage

Ghadamès

Fazzan

BORNU-KANEM

Tuareg

Ghana

Fulani

0   500   1000 km

F D'94

Jalal al-Din Khwarazm-Shah (Mingburnu/Mangubirti): the last ruler of the dynasty of the Khwarazm-Shahs; r. 1220-1231. Pursued by the Mongol Genghis Khan, he escaped across the Indus, fought in Azerbaijan and Georgia and met his death near Mayyafariqin.

Jalal al-Din Rumi (Mawlana/Mevlana): the greatest mystic poet in the Persian language and founder of the Mawlawiyya order of dervishes ("The Whirling Dervishes"); 1207-1273. He is famous for his lyrics and for his didactic epic *Spiritual Couplets*.

Jalalabad: town of eastern Afghanistan, said to have been founded by the Mughal Emperor Akbar in 1570.

Jalali (P. *Ta'rīkh-i Jalālī*): name of an era and of a calendar used often in Persia and in Persian books and literature from the last part of the xith c. onwards. The era was founded by the Saljuq ruler Malik Shah I and named after his regnal title Jalal al-Dawla. It began on Friday, 9 Ramadan 471/15 March 1079. The new calendar was instituted in 1075.

Jalayirids: name of one of the successor-dynasties that divided up the territories, in Iraq and Azerbaijan, of the defunct Il-Khanid empire of Persia; r. 1336-1432. It was founded by Hasan Buzurg (r. 1336-1356).

Jallab (Jallaba): an outer garment used in certain parts of the Maghrib, that is very wide and loose with a hood and two armlets.

Jalula (Qizilrobat): town in Iraq, where the Arabs inflicted a severe defeat on the army of the Sasanian king Yazdigird in 637.

Jamal al-Din al-Afghani: philosopher, writer, orator and journalist; 1838-1897. He is known as the founder of modern Muslim anti-colonialism. With him began the reform movement which gave rise to the Salafiyya and, later, the Muslim Brothers. He preached the necessity of a Muslim revival. His ultimate object was to unite Muslim states (including Shi'i Persia) into a single caliphate. The Pan-Islamic idea was the great passion of his life.

Born in either Persia or Afghanistan, he travelled to India, made the pilgrimage, was welcomed in Turkey, lectured in Cairo from where he was expelled by the British, and defended Islam against Ernest Renan in Paris. When the Qajar Shah of Persia Nasir al-Din had him forcibly removed from a place near Teheran, regarded as affording an inviolable sanctuary (P. *bast*), Jamal al-Din developed feelings of hatred and a desire of vengeance towards the shah. At first well received in Istanbul, his relations with Sultan Abdülhamid II became extremely frigid.

Jamal Qarshi: scholar and administrator in Turkestan during the Mongol era; b. ca. 1230. He composed a Persian commentary on the lexicon of Abu Nasr al-Jawhari, adding to it an important historical and biographical supplement.

Jami, Mawlana Nur al-Din: great Persian poet and mystic; 1414-1492. The depth and variety of his knowledge, and his perfect mastery of language and style, also had great influence on Turkish literature.

Jamil b. 'Abd Allah al-'Udhri: Arab poet; 660-701. He died for love of his tribeswoman Buthayna. In literary tradition he is considered as the most famous representative of the 'Udhri school of poetry, with its chaste and idealized form of love.

Jamil Nakhla al-Mudawwar: Arab journalist and writer; 1862-1907. He acquired fame with a work on early 'Abbasid times.

al-Jamra: name of three halts in the valley of Mina, where pilgrims returning from 'Arafat during their annual pilgrimage stop to partake in the ritual throwing of stones.

Jamshid (Jam): Iranian hero who has remained alive in popular and literary tradition, from Indo-Iranian times until the present day.

Janab Shihab al-Din (Cenap Şehabettin): Turkish poet and writer; 1870-1934. He made a remarkable contribution to the modern school of Turkish poetry.

al-Janadi, Abu 'Abd Allah: Shafi'i jurist and historian from Yemen; d. 1332. He is the author of a biographical dictionary of the learned men of Yemen, preceded by a political history from the time of the Prophet to 1323.

Jandarli: name of an Ottoman family of statesmen, prominent from ca. 1350 to 1500.

Jangali: a nationalist and reformist movement in Persia which came into being in 1915 and collapsed in 1921 against the forces of Reza Khan (later Shah) Pahlavi.

Janikli Hajji 'Ali Pasha: Ottoman soldier and founder of a Derebey family; 1720-1785. In 1776 he presented a memorandum to the government on the reforms that were needed in the Empire.

Janids: Özbeg dynasty which ruled Bukhara from 1599 to 1785. Under the Janids Bukhara was one of the centres of Sunni orthodoxy, which played a leading role in defensive struggles against Shi'i Persia.

Janissaries (T. *Yeñi-čeri* "New Troops"): name given to the regular infantry created by the Ottomans in the xivth c. Their ranks were filled by periodical levy of Christian children (T. *devshirme*). They played an important role in Ottoman politics from the time of the assassination of Sultan 'Othman II in 1622. The corps was abolished by Sultan Mahmud II in 1826.

Janjira: name of a former native state on the west coast of India, not far from Bombay. The Sunni Muslim rulers, known as Sidi, withstood the determined onslaughts of the Marathas and other challengers from ca. 1500 until 1870, when the state was forced to conclude a treaty with the British. In 1947 Janjira became part of the Maharashtra state of India.

al-Jannabi, Abu Sa'id: founder of the Carmathian power in East Arabia; d. 913.

al-Jannabi, Abu Tahir: one of the most famous chiefs of the small Carmathian state of Bahrain; 907-943. For several years he was the terror of the pilgrims to Mecca and of the inhabitants of lower Iraq. In 930 he spent eight days pillaging and massacring in Mecca and took away the Black Stone.

Japheth (A. *Yāfith*): the Biblical figure is not mentioned in the Qur'an, but Qur'an exegesis and legend are familiar with the sons of Noah.

Jaqmaq (Čaqmaq): Mamluk sultan of Egypt; r. 1439-1453. He made peace with the Knights of St. John on Rhodes, and was on good terms with all Muslim rulers, including the Ottoman sultan. He was a frugal and pious man, liberal to the learned, although Christians and Jews were harassed with strictly enforced petty regulations.

Jarir b. 'Atiyya: one of the most important satirical poets of the Umayyad period; d. 728. Ca. 683 he began his famous forty-year-long dispute with al-Farazdak.

Jariya b. Qudama: Companion of the Prophet and staunch supporter of the latter's son-in-law 'Ali; d. after 661.

Jarrahids (Banu 'l-Jarrah): family of Yemenite origin which settled in Palestine and attained some importance in the xth and xith c. by following a policy of vacillation between the Fatimids and the Byzantines.

Játiva (A. *Shātiba*): town in Spain near Valencia. In the Middle Ages the Muslim town was celebrated for its manufacture of paper, still recognizable in old Arabic manuscripts, on account of the watermarks bearing the name of its place of origin. In Morocco the name "Játiva paper" (A. *shātibī*) is still given to a kind of coarse grained paper. In 1239 the town was conquered by Jaime I, King of Aragon.

Jaunpur (Jawnpur): city on the Gumti river in Uttar Pradesh, India, founded in 1359 by Firuz Shah III Tughluq of Delhi, whose fort still stands. Between 1394 and 1479, the city was the capital of the independent kingdom of the Sharqi sultans. In 1489 it was absorbed in the Delhi empire. In 1526 it was taken by the Mughal Humayun for his father Babur, but was lost to the Afghan Shir Shah Sur. Emperor Akbar I made his temporary residence there. In the early xviiith c. the city passed into the possession of the Nawwabs of Awadh, and into British hands in 1775. It was long celebrated for its learning, and it is known for its monuments.

al-Jawaliqi: Arab philologist and calligrapher from Baghdad; 1073-1144. His works played a part in raising the cultural level in the Arabic language from the depths to which it had fallen in the Saljuq period.

Jawan, Mirza Kazim 'Ali: one of the pioneers of Urdu prose literature; d. ca. 1815.

Jawdhar: eunuch and slave who played an important part under the first Fatimid caliphs. His biography, compiled by his private secretary al-Mansur, is historically important for the collection of documents it contains.

Jawf (Jaww): topographical term denoting a depressed plain, applied to many locations. Jawf Ibn Nasir in northwest Yemen abounds with archeological sites. It is described by al-Hamdani and several travellers.

al-Jawf: district and town in north-central Saudi Arabia. It was taken by the Ikhwan levies of ʿAbd al-ʿAziz Ibn Saʿud in 1922.

Jawhar Aftabači: author of valuable memoirs of the reign of the Mughal Emperor Humayun; xvith c.

Jawhar al-Siqilli: general and administrator of the fourth Fatimid Caliph al-Muʿizz li-Din Allah; d. 992. He entered al-Fustat in 969, built a new town – Cairo – to house his troops and laid the first stone of the al-Azhar mosque in 970.

al-Jawhari, Abu Nasr: celebrated Arabic lexicographer of Turkish origin; d. 1002. He made linguistic investigations among the Arabs of the desert and seems to have been the last lexicographer of fame to maintain that tradition. His reputation is based on his dictionary, commonly known as *al-Ṣiḥāḥ*.

Jawhari, Tantawi: modernist Egyptian theologian; 1862-1940. He was the official Egyptian candidate for a Nobel Prize in 1939.

Jawi (pl. *Jāwa*): name used in Mecca to denote the Muslims from southeast Asia.

Jawid, Mehmed: Young Turk economist and statesman; 1875-1926. A member of the *Ittihad we Teraqqi Jemʿiyyeti* and several times minister of finance, he was arrested following the 1926 assassination attempt on Mustafa Kemal Atatürk and hanged.

Jayn (Jain): community of followers of Mahavira, called the Jina, in Gujarat. The personal beliefs and habits of the Mughal Emperor Akbar I seem to have been much influenced by the Jayn leaders.

al-Jazari, Badiʿ al-Zaman: engineer of al-Jazira; xiith c. His reputation rests upon his *Book of knowledge of ingenious mechanical devices*.

al-Jazari, Shams al-Din: Arab historian from Damascus; 1260-1338. He owes his fame to his historical work commonly known as *The History of al-Jazari*, of which only the last volume is preserved.

al-Jazari, Shams al-Milla wa 'l-Din: composer of *Sessions*; d. 1301. He was a native of Jazirat Ibn ʿUmar and imitated the *Sessions* of al-Hariri.

al-Jazira (Jazirat/Iqlim Aqur): name used by Arab geographers to denote the southern part of the territory situated between the Tigris and the Euphrates (Upper Mesopotamia). But the term also includes the regions and towns which are across the upper Tigris in the north, and a strip of land lying to the west, along the right bank of the Euphrates.

Jazirat Ibn ʿUmar (T. *Cezire-i Ibn Ömer/Cizre*): town in Turkey on the frontier with Syria, said to have been founded by al-Hasan b. ʿUmar b. al-Khattab al-Taghlibi (d. ca. 865).

Jazirat Shariq: name given to the small peninsula projecting from the eastern coast of Tunisia between the two gulfs of La Goulette and Hammamat.

al-Jazuli, Abu ʿAbd Allah: Sufi from Morocco; d. 1465. He wrote a well-known collection of prayers for the Prophet.

al-Jazuli, Abu Musa: grammarian from Morocco, known for his Introduction to the study of Arabic grammar; d. 1209.

al-Jazzar Pasha, Ahmad: the dominant political figure of his time in southern Syria; ca. 1722-1804. He set up a regime of remarkable stability, based on fear.

Jelal-zade Mustafa Čelebi (Qoja Nishanji): Ottoman civil servant and historian; 1490-1567. Of his projected description of the whole empire, a very full history of Sultan Süleyman II up to 1555 is known to exist.

Jem: Ottoman prince; 1459-1495. Son of Sultan Mehemmed II, he opposed his elder brother Bayezid II but was defeated and fled to the Mamluk Sultan Qa'it Bay in Cairo, and then to Pierre d'Aubusson, the Grand Master of the Knights of St. John in Rhodes. A valuable hostage, he was interned in France, and then in Rome where he met Pope Innocent VIII. The French King Charles VIII took him to Naples where he died. Jem composed poems in Persian and Turkish.

Jemal Pasha (T. *Cemal Paşa*): Young Turk soldier and statesman; 1872-1922. From 1913 until the end of World War I he formed, together with Enver Pasha and Tal'at Pasha, the informal dictatorial triumvirate which ruled the Ottoman Empire. From his headquarters in Damascus, he reacted severely against political disaffection among the local Arab leaders. In 1918 he fled to Berlin and Switzerland. From Moscow, he facilitated the diplomatic contacts between the Bolshevik and Kemalist regimes.

Jerba (Jarba): Tunisian island in the Gulf of Gabès. It was conquered by the Muslims in 665, and for the next few centuries came under the rule of Qayrawan and Mahdiyya, becoming attached to Kharijism. From the xiith-xviith c. it was off and on in the hands of Christians from Sicily and the Muslim dynasties in Ifrīqiya. In the xviith c. it came under Turkish rule and was variously administered by the Deys and Beys from Algiers and Tunis.

Jeremiah (A. *Irmiyā*): the Biblical prophet is not mentioned in the Qur'an, but Muslim legend makes use of the details found in the Bible.

Jerez de la Frontera (A. *Sharīsh*): town in Spain, north of Cadiz, taken from the Muslims by Alfonso the Wise in 1264.

Jericho (A. *Rīḥā/Arīḥā*): town on the west side of the Jordan Valley, north of the Dead Sea. It is alluded to in Qur'an V, 23.

Jerusalem (A. *al-Quds*): as the scene of the Prophet's night journey (A. *isrā'*) and of his ascension to Heaven (A. *mi'rāj*), and as the domicile of the ancient prophets and saints, Jerusalem ranks as the third central sanctuary in Islam after Mecca and Medina.

The city fell into the hands of the Muslims after the battle of the Yarmuk in 638. The conditions of the surrender safeguarded to the Christians the use of their churches. The Temple area, which was largely or entirely unoccupied, served as a place of prayer to the Muslims from the very beginning. On the so-called al-Haram al-Sharif, a large trapezoidal platform, the Dome of the Rock, the Aqsa Mosque and other sanctuaries were erected during the Umayyad period. Some of the early 'Abbasid caliphs visited the city, but Harun al-Rashid and his son al-Ma'mun never went there. In 1009, under the Fatimid Caliph al-Hakim bi-Amr Allah, the Holy Sepulchre was destroyed and the earthquake of 1016 left the city in shambles. Nevertheless, great caravans of Christian, Muslim and Jewish pilgrims continued to arrive. Jerusalem again suffered greatly in 1071 under the Turkmen Atsiz b. Uvak. Under the Saljuq Sultan Malik Shah I the city was incorporated into the great Saljuq empire. But its economic situation remained unsatisfactory, and despite its holiness for the three monotheistic religions, it did not become for any of them a great spiritual centre.

The Crusaders took Jerusalem by assault in 1099 and made it into a Christian city, where no Muslim or Jewish cult was permitted.

In 1187 Jerusalem surrendered to Saladin, and soon assumed the character of a predominantly Muslim city. Saladin's nephew al-Mu'azzam Sharaf al-Din ordered in 1219 the destruction of the city with the exception of the Temple area, the Holy Sepulchre and the citadel. His brother al-Kamil concluded a treaty with the Emperor Frederick II Hohenstaufen in 1229, ceding to him the city for ten years. The emperor, being under papal ban, crowned himself without clerical assistance – the last time that a monarch was crowned in Jerusalem. With the exception of the Haram al-Sharif, which remained in Muslim hands, Muslims and Jews were not permitted access to the city. In his struggle with the Ayyubids in Damascus, al-Malik al-Salih enlisted the Khwarazmians, who had been driven to the West by the Mongols. They took Jerusalem in 1244.

After the victory of the Mamluks over the Mongols at 'Ayn Jalut in 1260, Jerusalem came under the rule of Egypt and remained so until the Ottoman conquest in 1516. The Ottoman sultan Sülayman II built the city wall, renovated the Dome of the Rock and created the four public fountains. However, during almost the entire Ottoman period, the city's development was impeded by lack of security.

The conquest of Palestine by Ibrahim Pasha in 1831 and the ensuing new policy of the Ottoman sultan favoured the Christians. The British entered the city in 1917, and their mandate ended in 1948, when the state of Israel was proclaimed.

Jesus (A. *'Īsā*): the Qur'an refers to him in 15 Suras and devotes to him 93 verses which are the foundation for Muslim Christology. The latter has been enriched by traditions from the apocryphal gospels and from mystic Christian literature. Islamo-Christian polemic has tended through the years to harden the positions, most of which have become classic and are to be found unchanged in present-day Muslim writers. The Prophet had a great veneration for the Son of Mary, but he is quite clear that Jesus is in no sense divine.

Jewdet, 'Abd Allah (T. *Abdullah Cevdet*): Turkish poet, translator, politician, free-thinker and publicist of Kurdish origin; 1869-1932. He made the study of psychology known to his compatriots.

Jewelry (A. *jawhar*): the word does not appear in the Qur'an, though references are made to both jewelry (gold and silver bracelets, bracelets of pearls) and precious stones. There are very few extant pieces of Islamic jewelry datable to before the first half of the xith c., but there are pictorial or sculptural representations in addition to literary descriptions. The history of jewelry in Islam can be divided into three periods: early medieval (xith-xiiith c.), late medieval (xivth-xviith c.), and the final phase of the tradition (xviiith and xixth c.)

Jews (A. *Yāhūd*): the Qur'an speaks of them as "those to whom the scripture was given", as "the Children of Israel" (A. *Banū Isrā'īl*) and as "the descendants of Abraham". Revelation is considered to have been granted them through Moses, and they have been given many clear signs, but, as the Christians, they have distorted the sense of the words of the scriptures. They were invited to believe in Allah, in the Last Judgement and in the Prophet's mission, but they refused and finally were regarded, with the idolaters, as the greatest enemies of the Believers.

Jeza'irli Ghazi Hasan Pasha: Grand Vizier and one of the most famous Grand Admirals of the Turkish navy; d. 1790.

al-Jibal: name formerly given by Arab authors to that portion of Arabia Petraea which dominates the depression of the Jordan Fault. Islamic geographers also gave the name to the mountainous part of western Persia, which was also called 'Iraq-i 'Ajami.

Jibuti: town and port on the African coast of the Gulf of Aden, at the mouth of the Gulf of Tajoura. The territory was given to France by the 'Isa, a Somali-speaking tribe, in 1885. It became independent in 1977. The town and the port were built up by France and became one of the leading ports on the east coast of Africa.

Jijelli: coastal town in Algeria, to the west of Bougie. It retained its independence when the Arabs conquered the Maghrib but was taken in the xith c. by the Hammadids.

Jidda (A. *Judda*): city and major port on the Red Sea in central Hejaz, Saudi Arabia. In 646 Caliph 'Uthman chose it as the port of Mecca in place of the older port of al-Shu'ayba. After the Saudi occupation of Mecca in 1924, Jidda became the capital of the government of Husayn b. 'Ali's son 'Ali, but was forced to submit to the Saudis in 1925.

Jimma: former state, nowadays a town, in southwest Ethiopia. It is a centre of Islamic learning.

Jinn: Arabic term for bodies composed of vapour or flame, which are intelligent, imperceptible to human senses, capable of appearing under different forms and of carrying out heavy labours. They are mentioned in the

Qurʾan, and play an important part in Arabic, Turkish, Indian and Indonesian folklore.

Jinnah, Muhammad ʿAli: founder of the state of Pakistan; 1876-1948. Born in Karachi, he was a lawyer by profession. He became a member of the Indian National Congress, joined the Muslim League in 1913 and negotiated the "Lucknow Pact" which guaranteed the rights of the Muslim community. Before the Second World War, he argued that the Muslims could not expect full justice in a political society with a Hindu majority. In 1940, at the meeting of the Muslim League at Lahore, the so-called Pakistan Resolution was adopted, which stated that a separate state for the Muslims of India was possible and necessary. The state of Pakistan came into existence in August 1947.

Jirga: informal tribal assembly of the Pathans in what are now Afghanistan and Pakistan, with competence to intervene and to adjudicate in practically all aspects of private and public life among the Pathans.

Jisr Banat Yaʿqub ("Bridge of the Daughters of Jacob"): bridge over the Upper Jordan, above the sea of Galilee. The crossing was important for a trade route which was especially frequented in Mamluk times, and it played also a role in the struggle between the Crusaders and the Muslims.

Jisr al-Hadid ("Iron Bridge"): bridge over the lower Orontes. It was of strategic and commercial importance for the route joining Antioch to Chalcis (Qinnasrin) and then Aleppo.

Job (A. *Ayyūb*): the Biblical Job is mentioned in the Qurʾan in lists of those to whom Allah had given special guidance and inspiration. Later Muslim writers amplified the Qurʾanic account.

John the Baptist (A. *Yaḥyā*): the Qurʾan mentions him several times among the just persons who serve as arguments for the Oneness of God. His role as Baptist and the story of his death are not mentioned.

Jolof (Diolof): name of a kingdom in what is now Senegalese territory from the xiiith-xvith c. The inhabitants and their language are called Wolof (Ouolof). According to legend, a Muslim of the Prophet's family converted Senegal to Islam in about 1200. In 1960 ca. 90 % of the population was Muslim.

Jonah (A. *Yūnus b. Mattay*): Sura X of the Qurʾan bears the name of the Biblical prophet, and elsewhere he is mentioned as "The Man of the Fish". Muslim legend later added other material.

Jordan (A. *Urdunn*): the Hashimite Arab kingdom of the Middle East was created in 1923, and recognised by Great Britain in 1946 as an independent state. The first king was ʿAbd Allah b. al-Husayn, until then amir of Transjordan. His son Talal was deposed because of ill health, and was suceeded in 1953 by the present King al-Husayn b. Talal.

Joseph (A. *Yūsuf b. Yaʿqūb*): his story is told in sura XII of the Qurʾan, which is said to be the most beautiful sura. The Shiʿis, however, do not recognise this sura. In later times many legendary details were added to the Qurʾanic story.

Joshua (A. *Yūshaʿ b. Nūn*): he is alluded to in Qurʾan V, 23. Legend has supplied his figure with many new features.

al-Jubbaʾi, Abu ʿAli: famous Muʿtazili of Khuzistan; d. 915. His ideas were refuted by Abu ʾl-Hasan al-Ashʿari, who had been his pupil. His son Abu Hashim ʿAbd al-Salam, d. 933, was one of the very last Muʿtazilis to exercise a direct influence on Sunni thought.

Juči (Joči): eldest son of Genghis Khan and the ancestor of the khans of the Golden Horde, Crimea, Tiumen, Bukhara and Khiva; ca. 1184-1227.

Judaeo-Arabic: usual name for the spoken – or in some cases the written – language of the Jews in the Arabic-speaking countries.

Judaeo-Berber: name for the dialects of the Berber-speaking Jews of the Shleuh and Tamazight regions in Morocco.

Judaeo-Persian: term used for the New Persian language in so far as it is written in Hebrew characters. Judaeo-Persian inscriptions are recorded as early as 752, but Judaeo-Persian literature dates from the xiiith c. during the rule of the Il-Khans over Persia.

Judge (A. *qāḍī*): in theory the head of the community, the caliph, is the holder of all powers; the judge is therefore a direct or indirect delegate, the delegator retaining the power to do justice in person. Justice has always been exercised by a single judge. The objective being the application of the law, which is essentially religious, the function of the judge is a religious one. In theory, his competence embraces both civil and penal cases, and includes the administration of mosques and pious endowments (A. *waqf*). His competence in penal matters, however, is restricted to the very few crimes envisaged by the law, their repression being concurrently undertaken by the police (A. *shurṭa*). Chief-judges (A. *qāḍi ʾl-quḍāt*) were instituted under caliph Harun al-Rashid.

Judi (Jabal Jūdī/Jūdī Dagh): mountain mass north of Jazirat Ibn ʿUmar, Turkey. According to the Mesopotamian tradition it was on this mountain, and not on Mount Ararat, that Noah's ark rested.

Juha: nickname of a person whom popular imagination made the hero of several hundred jests, anecdotes and amusing stories.

Julfa: town on the river Araxes on the northern border of Azerbaijan. In the xvith c. the town became the centre of a flourishing community of Armenian merchants. In 1605 the Safawid Shah ʿAbbas I resolved to depopulate eastern Armenia and to create an empty tract between himself and his enemy the Ottomans. He transferred the major part of the population of Julfa to Persia, where they settled in New Julfa, a suburb of Isfahan. Shah ʿAbbas helped the newcomers to establish themselves, and his support led the Armenian merchants to secure the monopoly of the international silk trade, wresting the privilege from the British. They also traded in spices, cotton goods and porcelain, and built numerous churches.

Jumblat(t) (A. *Jānbulāt*): family of amirs in the Lebanon, Druze in religion, Kurdish in origin. In Kurdish, the word means "soul of steel". They appeared in the xvith c. and are active until the present day. Other modern spellings are Djoumblatt, Jomblatt, etc.

al-Junayd b. 'Abd Allah, al-Murri: one of the governors and generals of the Umayyad caliph Hisham; d. 734. He stabilised the authority of the Muslims in Transoxiana during a strong Turkish counter-movement.

Jurjani: Arabic adjective of origin which means "the man from Gurgan" in Iran.

al-Jurjani, Abu Bakr: philologist and literary theorist; d. 1078. His reputation rests on his theoretical work on stylistics, syntax and poetics.

al-Jurjani, 'Ali b. Muhammad (al-Sayyid al-Sharif): Persian grammarian, philosopher and linguist; 1339-1413.

al-Jurjani, Isma'il b. al-Husayn: physician who wrote in Arabic and Persian; d. 1136. He composed the first medical encyclopaedias in Persian.

Juwayn: name of a district in Nishapur country, Iran, and of a fortified place in Sistan, Iran. Al-Juwayni means "the man from Juwayn".

al-Juwayni, Abu 'l-Ma'ali: theologian and jurist from Juwayn in Nishapur country, Iran; 1028-1085. He owes his honorary name Imam al-Haramayn "Imam of the two Holy Cities" to the fact that he taught at Mecca and at Medina.

Juwayni, 'Ala' al-Din: Persian governor and historian from Juwayn in Nishapur country, Iran; 1226-1283. He visited Mongolia, accompanied the Mongol Il-Khan Hülegü on his campaigns against the Isma'ilis of Alamut and the Baghdad Caliphate, and saved the famous library of Alamut from destruction. He wrote a history of the Mongols and of the dynasty of the Khwarazm-Shahs, which has considerably influenced historical tradition in the East and is a historical authority of the first rank.

Juwayni, Shams al-Din: Persian statesman and brother of 'Ala' al-Din Juwayni; d. 1284. He was a patron of theology, science and art, and wrote Arabic and Persian poetry.

al-Juzjani, Abu 'Amr (Minhaj-i Siraj): historian of the Mu'izzi or Slave kings of India; 1193-ca. 1270.

K

Kaarta: region of Mali, previously part of the empire of Ghana, where missionary activity for Islam was considerable in the xixth c.

Ka'b, Banu: Arab tribe which occupies, at present, parts of Khuzistan in southwestern Iran. Like other Arab tribes inhabiting Iran, they mingled with the non-Arab population and are slowly losing their Arab identity.

Ka'b al-Ahbar: a Yemenite Jew who became a convert to Islam and is considered the oldest authority on Judaeo-Islamic traditions; d. 652.

Ka'b b. al-Ashraf: Jewish opponent of the Prophet at Medina who, by his poetic gifts, incited the Quraysh to fight the Muslims; d. 624.

Ka'b b. Malik: one of the poets supporting the Prophet; d. 673.

Ka'b b. Zuhayr: Arab poet and contemporary of the Prophet. He at first wrote some satirical verses against the Prophet, but later accepted Islam by reciting his famous piece known as "Su'ad has departed", which is an authentic example of the eulogistic poetry of the period.

Ka'ba: the most famous sanctuary of Islam, called "the house of God" (A. *bayt Allāh*). It is situated almost in the centre of the Great Mosque in Mecca. Muslims throughout the whole world direct their prayers to the Ka'ba, and every year hundreds of thousands of pilgrims make here the greater (A. *ḥajj*) or lesser (A. *'umra*) pilgrimage.

The name Ka'ba is connected with the cube-like appearance of the building, which is 15 m high, with a flat roof sloping gently to the northwest corner. The door in the façade, which faces northeast, is at about 2 m above ground level and is accessible by a wooden staircase running on wheels. The Black Stone is in its eastern corner. The Ka'ba is built of layers of the grey-blue stone produced by the hills surrounding Mecca and stands on a marble base. The four walls are covered with a curtain, while there is a special curtain, embroidered in gold and silver, with numerous inscriptions, in front of the door.

In the Qur'an it is said that the foundations of the Ka'ba were laid by Abraham and Ishmael.

At the conquest of Mecca in 629, the Prophet left the Ka'ba as a building unaltered. When he led the pilgrimage in 631, according to tradition not a single idolator was present and thus the Ka'ba had become an exclusively Muslim sanctuary. The building was virtually destroyed when al-Husayn b. Numayr besieged the city, which had been occupied by the anti-caliph 'Abd Allah b. al-Zubayr in 683. The latter's alterations were removed after al-Hajjaj b. Yusuf had reconquered Mecca in 693. The building practically received its previous form again, which has survived to the present day.

Kabakči-oghlu Mustafa: chief of the rebellion which overthrew the Ottoman sultan Selim III in 1807; d. 1808.

Kabards: Muslim people of the Caucasus, completely Islamicized by the end of the xviith c.

Kabou: locality in Togo. Towards the end of the xixth c., when the Europeans arrived, there already existed a Muslim quarter. The German administration followed a pro-Muslim policy, which brought about the conversion of large numbers of the inhabitants.

Kabul: capital of Afghanistan. Its name was known to the Arabs in pre-Islamic times. During Mu'awiya I's caliphate the Muslim governors of Sistan raided as far as Kabul where they captured slaves, but it was only under Ya'qub b. Layth, the founder of the Saffarid dynasty in Sistan (r. 867-879), that Kabul was occupied. The Islamisation of the town and the Kabul region progressed considerably in the xth c. under the Turkish slave commanders of Ghazna. Babur, the later Mughal Emperor, took Kabul in 1504. The city remained firmly within the orbit of the dominions of the Mughal Emperors of India. In 1747 Kabul became the capital of the Durrani kings of Afghanistan.

Kabul is also the name of a river of Afghanistan and the Northwest frontier region of Pakistan, which flows eastwards to the Indian plain where it joins the Indus.

Kabylia: mountainous region in the Algerian Tell. The word, probably from the Arabic *qabā'il* (s. *qabīla* "tribe"), was coined by the French and is not found in the works of Arab historians and geographers. Islam may have been accepted, but it was wholly vested with beliefs peculiar to Berber traditions, and Arabic has not completely supplanted Berber dialects.

al-Kaf (El-Kef): town in Tunisia, conquered by the Muslims in 688. It regained its former importance in the Ottoman era, when it defended the Regency of Tunis against invasion from Algeria. Its decline began with the French occupation of Constantine in 1837.

Kafiristan: the name, which means "land of the unbelievers", was used for a mountainous region of the Hindu Kush massif in northeastern Afghanistan, which was very isolated and politically independent. Since the Afghan conquest of 1896, Islam was introduced and the region is now known as Nuristan "land of light".

Kafur, Abu 'l-Misk: black eunuch who became the dominant personality of the Ikhshidid dynasty in Egypt; d. 968.

Kafur, Malik: eunuch general and minister of 'Ala' al-Din Muhammad Shah I, the Khalji sultan of Delhi (r. 1296-1316); d. 1316.

al-Kahina: the Arabic word means "the sorceress" and indicates the woman who was the guiding spirit of Berber resistance to the Arab invaders who were led into North Africa by Hassan b. al-Nu'man after the collapse of Byzantine power marked by the fall of Carthage in 692.

Kakuyids (Kakwayhids): dynasty of Daylami origin which ruled over part of west-central Persia (Jibal) during the first half of the xith c. as virtually independent sovereigns, and thereafter for more than a century as local lords of Yazd, in Fars, tributary to the Saljuqs. The greatest member of the dynasty was 'Ala' al-Dawla Muhammad (r. 1008-1041).

al-Kalabadhi, Abu Bakr: author of one of the most celebrated manuals on Sufism; d. 994. His *Doctrine of the Sufis* is a basic work for the understanding of Sufism in the first three centuries of Islam.

Kalb b. Wabara: ancestor of the Banu Kalb, the strongest group of the Quda'a. The Banu Kalb played a role of significance in early Islam, together with their rivals the Banu Qays.

al-Kalbi: name of a prominent family from Kufa, known for their swordsmanship and learning. One of the most famous members was Hisham b.

Muhammad, known as Ibn al-Kalbi; 737-819. He was the uncontested master of Arab genealogy.

Kalbids: family of governors, stemming from the Banu Kalb, who ruled over a kind of hereditary emirate in Sicily between 950-1050.

Kalila wa-Dimna: title of an Indian Mirror for Princes, formed by the corruption of the Sanskrit names of two jackals, Karataka and Damanaka, the two principal characters. The Sanskrit original, the Pañcatantra, was translated into Pahlavi by Burzoe by order of the Sasanian king Khusraw Anushirwan (r. 531-579). In the viiith c. Ibn al-Muqaffaʿ translated Burzoe's text into Arabic. The work became widely known in Muslim as well as Christian literatures.

Kalim Allah al-Jahanabadi: one of the leading Čishti saints of his time; 1650-1729. He was responsible for the revival of the Čishtiyya order in the Indo-Pakistan subcontinent.

Kalmuk: Turkish name for a Mongol people, the Oyrat, who in the time of Genghis Khan inhabited the forests to the west of Lake Baykal. After the collapse of the Mongol dynasty in China, they laid the foundations of the Kalmuk nomad empire. Only a small number of Kalmuks ever embraced Islam, the rest remaining actual or nominal adherents of Buddhism.

Kamal al-Din al-Farisi: scientist of Persia who wrote an important revision of the *Optics* of Ibn al-Haytham; xivth c.

Kandi: town in north Dahomey, West Africa. Islam was introduced in the xixth c. by Hausa merchants.

Kanem: at present the name of a prefecture in the Republic of Chad. From the ixth-xth c. it was the name of a trading empire, at various times including southern Chad, northern Cameroon and northeastern Nigeria. Islam was introduced in the xth c. In the xvith c. Kanem became a province of the Bornu Empire, but in the xixth c. the latter was a protectorate of Kanem.

al-Kanemi, al-Hajj Muhammad Amin: scholar of Kanem origin who founded the Shehu dynasty of Bornu; 1775-1837.

Kano: city in northern Nigeria. Islam is said to have been introduced by "strangers" under their leader Bagauda in the xth c. The first Islamic name occurs in the xivth c. The Islamic tradition is focussed on Abu ʿAbd Allah Muhammad al-Tilimsani (d. 1504), a missionary from North Africa. The city is an important centre for Sufi activities.

Kansu: province in the northwest of China. Muslim dominance was established in the xiiith c. by Ananda (r. 1270-1307), a grandson of the Mongol Great Khan Qubilay. In 1953 the Muslim population was estimated at over 1 million.

Kanuri: name of a people and a language in the Chad region. Islam was introduced in the viith c. from the north.

Karachi: the most important commercial and industrial centre of Pakistan, situated on the Indian Ocean. From 1947 to 1960 it was the official capital of the Islamic Republic, but it has gradually been replaced by Islamabad.

Karaites: Jewish sect whose members have lived in several Islamic countries for over 1200 years. They do not recognise the authority of the post-biblical tradition incorporated in the Talmud and in later Rabbinic works.

al-Karak: fortress situated to the east of the Dead Sea in Jordan. It played a role in the time of the Crusades. It was captured by Saladin's brother al-Malik al-'Adil in 1188, and by the Mamluk sultan Baybars I in 1263.

Karakhitai (T. *Qara Khiṭāy*): name of a Mongol people, also called the Western Liao, who were living, from the ivth c. onwards, on the northern fringes of the Chinese Empire. In the first half of the xiith c. they moved into eastern Turkestan, but were defeated by the Ilek-Khans ruling in Kashgharia. In 1137 Mahmud Khan b. Arslan of Samarqand was defeated by the Karakhitai in Farghana and appealed to his suzerain the Saljuq Sultan Sanjar, who invaded Turkestan from Khurasan. In September 1141 both rulers were routed with great losses by the Karakhitai, who then occupied Samarqand and Bukhara. The Khwarazm-Shah Atsiz (r. 1127-1156) was compelled to pay an annual tribute. The news of the Karakhitai victory over the Muslim forces filtered through to the Crusaders and thence to Christian Europe, giving fresh impetus to the legends about Prester John, the powerful Christian monarch who supposedly ruled in Inner Asia and who was attacking the Muslims from the rear. The Karakhitai were defeated by Genghis Khan in 1218.

al-Karaki, Nur al-Din: Imami scholar of al-Biqa' in Lebanon; ca. 1466-1534. Some of his commentaries on earlier legal works became popular books of instruction.

Karakorum (*Qara Qorum* "black boulder"): chain of mountains in the centre of Asia lying north of and almost parallel to the Himalayas. It is the most important watershed in Central Asia. The principal pass is the col of Karakorum (5,574 m.), through which runs the important trade route between Chinese Turkestan and Kashmir.

Karakorum (Qaraqorum): town in Central Mongolia. It was chosen by Genghis Khan as his capital in 1220, and provided with walls by his son Öge-dey in 1235. The capital of the Mongol World Empire was visited by Willem van Ruysbroeck (William of Rubruck) in 1253-1254.

Karamat 'Ali: Muslim religious author of Jaunpur who wrote chiefly in Urdu; d. 1873. He struggled against Hindu customs and superstitions which had crept into the practice of Islam in Eastern Bengal, and against new heterodox schools.

Karay, Refiq Khalid (Refik Halit Karay): Turkish essayist, humorist and novelist; d. 1965. He has been almost unanimously accepted as the unchallenged master of modern Turkish prose.

Karbala': town in Iraq some 90 km to the south-southwest of Baghdad, celebrated for the fact that the Prophet's grandson al-Husayn b. 'Ali was killed and his decapitated body buried there in 680. It is also known as Mashhad (al-)Husayn. Al-Husayn's tomb was destroyed by the 'Abbasid Caliph al-

Mutawakkil in 850, but by 977 there was a large sanctuary with a domed chamber over the tomb. The sanctuary was visited by the Saljuq Sultan Malik Shah, the Il-Khan Ghazan, the Safawid Shah Isma'il and by the Ottoman Sultan Süleyman II. The Safawid Shah 'Abbas the Great won the town for the Persian empire in 1623. Radiyya Sultan Begum, a daughter of Shah Husayn I, presented a large sum of money for improvements, and the gold covering for the dome was given by the founder of the Qajar dynasty, Aga Muhammad Khan. In 1801 the Wahhabis under Shaykh Sa'ud destroyed the shrine, but after the catastrophe contributions poured in from the whole Shi'i world. In 1843 Najib Pasha enforced the recognition of Turkish suzerainty over the town. During the month of Muharram there is a great influx of pilgrims.

Karim Khan Zand: founder of the Zand dynasty and *de facto* ruler of the greater part of Persia; r. 1750-1779.

Karimi: name of a group of Muslim merchants operating from the major centres of trade in the Ayyubid and Mamluk empires, above all in spices.

Karli-ili: the Ottoman name for a district of northwest Greece (Acarnania and most of Aetolia). The word means "land of Carlo", i.e. Carlo Tocco I (1381-1430), count of Cephalonia.

Karnatak: properly the Kanarese-speaking district of southern India, approximately that of the modern Mysore (Mahisur) state.

Karramiyya: sect founded by Muhammad b. Karram (d. 869) which flourished in the central and eastern parts of the Islamic world, and especially in the Iranian regions, from the ixth c. until the Mongol invasions.

Kars: town in Eastern Turkey which, until the xvith c., was in the hands of the Umayyads, the Armenians, the Bagratid Georgians and the Qara Qoyunlu. By 1534 the town was in the possession of the Ottomans and became a fortress of vital importance in the Ottoman-Safawid conflict. In the xixth c. the British considered it as a bulwark against Russian expansion. After a short-lived Armenian control in 1919, it was recaptured by the Turks in 1920.

Karshuni: name of the Syriac script used by the Christians of Syria and Mesopotamia for writing Arabic.

Karun: the largest river in southern Persia, and the only one in the country that admits of navigation. It joins the Shatt al-'Arab at Khorramshahr.

Kasala (Kassala): town and province in the east of the Republic of Sudan. From the xvith c. the province was within the sphere of influence of the Funj sultanate of Sinnar. In the xixth c., under Turco-Egyptian rule, the nomadic tribes were subjugated.

al-Kasani, 'Ala' al-Din (Malik al-'Ulama'): one of the greatest jurists of the Hanafi law school; d. 1189. In his main work he wished to imitate the work of his predecessor and master 'Ala' al-Din al-Samarqandi, but the imitation is far superior to the model.

Kash: town in Uzbekistan on what was once the great trade route between

Samarqand and Balkh. It is the modern Shahr-i Sabz "Green Town", so called on account of the fertility of its surroundings.

Kashan: town of the Jibal in central Persia. The legend of the Magian kings having left from Kashan for Jerusalem was circulated in an early period. The town, said to have been founded by Zubayda Khatun, wife of the 'Abbasid Caliph Harun al-Rashid, enjoyed its greatest prosperity under the Safawids.

Kashani, Ayatollah Abu 'l-Qasim: Iranian *mujtahid* who played a role of some importance after World War II; d. 1962. At first a supporter of Mossadeq, he later supported the coup d'état of Muhammad Reza Shah Pahlavi of 1953.

Kashani, Hajj Mirza Jani: Babi historian; d. 1852. He was one of the disciples of the Bab, Sayyid 'Ali Muhammad of Shiraz.

Kashghar: town in Chinese Turkestan (Sinkiang), of importance under the rule of the Ilek-Khans.

al-Kashghari, Mahmud b. al-Husayn: Turkish scholar and lexicographer; xith c. His *Dīwān of the Turkish language* is one of the most significant records of the Turkish languages and also an important source for the history of the Turkish peoples.

al-Kashi (al-Kashani), Ghiyath al-Din: Persian mathematician and astronomer; d. 1429. He wrote in Persian and in Arabic. He gives a description of the tests undergone by poets when they were admitted to the sovereign's court. He also assisted in the establishment of Ulugh Beg's astronomical tables, and established the value of *pi* with extraordinary exactitude.

Kashif al-Ghita' (Shaykh Ja'far b. Khidr al-Najafi): Imami scholar of al-Najaf; 1751-1812. He led the resistance in al-Najaf during the siege by the Wahhabis in 1805 and became involved in a bloody conflict between two factions of the inhabitants of his native town, which led to a feud lasting over a century.

Kashifi, Kamal al-Din Husayn (*al-wā'iẓ* "the preacher"): Persian writer and preacher; d. 1504. Among other works he wrote a new Persian version of Kalila wa-Dimna. The Ottoman Turkish translation of this work became widely known in Europe; its translation into French is one of the sources of La Fontaine's Fables.

Kashmir: the valley of Kashmir in northern India came for the first time in contact with the Muslims in the viiith c. In 1014 and 1021 Mahmud of Ghazna tried in vain to conquer the country. The dynasty of the sultans of Kashmir was founded by Shah Mir, a soldier of fortune of Turkish origin, who in 1339 ascended the throne under the title of Sultan Shams al-Din. The dynasty ruled till 1561, and was followed by the Čak family, who in 1588 surrendered to the Mughal Emperor Akbar. In 1752 Kashmir passed into the hands of the Durrani dynasty of Afghanistan, and in 1819 to the Sikh ruler of the Punjab. In 1846 the British transferred Kashmir to the Dogra rulers of

Jammu, who gradually ignored the interests of the Muslims. In 1931 the latter, under the leadership of Shaykh Muhammad 'Abd Allah, began to demand openly their rights. In the census of 1941 the Muslims had a majority of 77% of the population.

In 1947 the Maharaja signed the annexation of Kashmir to the Indian Union, and the Indian army took over the country. The popular consultation, however, stipulated by the Indian government, has never taken place. The war which followed between India and Pakistan came to an end in 1949, when an agreement was reached on the demarcation of the ceasefire line, one part coming under Indian control, the other under that of Pakistan. Hostilities broke out again in 1965. In 1966 both countries signed the Tashkent Agreement, but the differences have not yet been resolved.

Kashmiri: the most important member of the Dardic sub-group of Indo-Aryan languages. For writing the language, the Perso-Arabic script is used.

al-Kashshi, Abu 'Amr: Imami transmitter of traditions; xth c. He wrote a work on the reliability of the transmitters from the Imams.

Kasrawi Tabrizi, Sayyid Ahmad: Iranian historian, linguist, jurist and ideologist; 1890-1946. Charges of slander of Islam were brought against him because of his views on religion. He was assassinated by the Fida'iyyan-i Islam.

Kastamonu: town in Northern Turkey. It was seized by the Turks in the aftermath of the battle of Malazgird in 1071, but remained a battleground for the conflicting and successive claims of Byzantine, Danishmend and Saljuq rulers. For a time it was ruled by the Isfendiyar-oghullari, and finally absorbed by the Ottoman state in 1462.

Kastoriá (T. *Kesriye*): town in Macedonia, former Yugoslavia, which came into Ottoman hands ca. 1390. It was known for its fur industry.

Katanga: region in the southeast corner of the Republic of Zaïre, now known as Shaba. The principal highway of Islamic penetration into Africa, from the eastern coast to Lake Tanganyika, continued due east to Maniema and the Luapula valley, where Islam struck its deepest roots in Zaïre. In the 1930s the Qadiriyya order spread among the Muslims, and the first national Muslim Congress met in Kasongo in March 1964.

Ka'ti, Mahmud b. al-Hajj: Songhai scholar; d. 1593. He wrote a work of history concerned with the Songhai.

Katib Čelebi (Hajji Khalifa): historian, bibliographer and geographer; 1609-1657. He was one of the most conspicuous and productive Ottoman scholars of his time, particularly in the non-religious sciences. He wrote some 22 works.

al-Kattani: name of an important and celebrated family of Fez, Morocco, belonging to the Sharifian branch of the Idrisids.

Kavala (T. *Qawāla*): port on the Aegean Sea coast, conquered by the Ottomans in 1383 and ceded to Greece in 1913.

al-Kawakibi, 'Abd al-Rahman: pioneer in the theory of Pan-Arabism; 1849-1902. In 1878 he brought out the first Arabic weekly in his native town of Aleppo.

Kawkaban: name of several places in south Arabia. The best known is the capital of the province which carries the same name, to the northwest of San'a'. For centuries it was the residence of the Imams.

Kaygili, 'Othman Jemal (Osman Cemal Kaygili): Turkish novelist, short story writer and humorous essayist; 1890-1945. His works were inspired by traditional Turkish folk literature and enjoyed by large audiences.

Kaykawus I: Saljuq sultan of Rum; r. 1211-1220. He combined a policy of peace towards the Greeks of Nicaea with interventions against the Armenians of Cilicia in the south, against Sinop on the Black Sea in the north, which he acquired, and against the Ayyubids in the east.

Kay Kawus b. Iskandar: prince of the Ziyarid dynasty in Persia; xith c. He was the author of a well-known *Mirror for Princes* in Persian; xith c.

Kaykhusraw I: Saljuq sultan of Rum; r. 1192-1196, 1204-1210. In 1207 he acquired Antalya, the first real maritime outlet of the Saljuqid state.

Kaykhusraw II: Saljuq sultan of Rum; r. 1237-1245. He was utterly defeated by the Mongols in 1243.

Kaykhusraw III: Saljuq sultan of Rum; r. 1265-1285. He reigned in name only under the tutelage of the Mongols or their lieutenants.

Kayqubad I, 'Ala' al-Din: Saljuq sultan of Rum; r. 1220-1237. His foreign policy made his dynasty one of the most powerful of his time. In the south he occupied a great part of the Cilician Taurus, on the Black Sea in the north he assured a Saljuq protectorate over the Crimean harbour of Sughdaq, and in the east he annexed the Artuqid possessions on the right bank of the Middle Euphrates. He defeated the Khwarazmians and, in 1233, the Ayyubid al-Malik al-Kamil I.

Kayqubadiyya (Kiybad Çiftliği): palace near Kayseri built by the Rum Saljuq Kayqubad I.

Kaysan, Abu 'Amra: prominent Shi'i in Kufa during the revolt of al-Mukhtar b. Abi 'Ubayd al-Thaqafi; d. 686.

Kaysaniyya (Mukhtariyya): name applied by the heresiographers to those supporters of al-Mukhtar b. Abi 'Ubayd al-Thaqafi who recognised 'Ali's son Muhammad Ibn al-Hanafiyya as their Imam and as the Mahdi.

Kayseri (A. *Qaysariyya*): town in central Anatolia, Turkey. The governor of Syria and later Umayyad Caliph Mu'awiya I forced it to pay tribute in 647. It became a royal residence for the Rum Saljuqs, and was destroyed by the Mongols in 1243. The Ottomans brought it under their direct rule in 1474.

Kazaks (T. *Qazaq*): the Özbeg groups who migrated to the West became known there as Cossacks.

Kazan (*Qāzān*): town on the middle Volga, in the xvth and xvith c. capital of the khanate of the same name. The khanate was founded by a descendant of

Genghis Khan, and took an active part in the internecine wars of the Russian principalities. In 1518, after the death of Khan Muhammad Amin, the khanate entered upon a period of anarchy, and in 1552 it was annexed to Muscovy.

Kazaruni, Shaykh Abu Ishaq: founder of a Sufi order variously known as the Murshidiyya, Ishaqiyya and Kazaruniyya; 963-1033. He is known for his charitable concern for the poor which was followed by all the branches of the order.

Kazim Qadri, Husayn (Huseyin Kazim Kadri): Turkish writer and lexicographer; 1870-1934. His major work is a comprehensive Turkish dictionary in four volumes.

Kazim Karabekir: Turkish general and statesman; 1882-1948. In 1919 he was instrumental in organising Turkish nationalist forces to fight the War of Independence. In 1924 he became a chief founder of the republican Progressive Party, and was considered one of the major potential rivals of Mustafa Kemal Atatürk.

Kazim Rashti, Sayyid: leader of the Shaykhi sect in Persia after the death of its founder, Shaykh Ahmad Ahsa'i; 1798-1843.

Kazimayn: one of the most celebrated Shi'i places of pilgrimage, situated near Baghdad. The name, which means "the two Kazims", refers to the seventh and ninth Imams of the Twelver Shi'a buried there, Musa al-Kazim, and his grandson Muhammad al-Jawad (d. 834). Pilgrimage to these tombs is recorded as early as the xiiith c., but already in 947 the Buyid Mu'izz al-Dawla of Kirman (r. 936-949) had domes erected over the two graves. The sanctuary was burnt and plundered in 1051 and 1125, and reduced to ashes by the Mongol Il-Khan Hülegü in 1258. The present faience-covered building is due to the Safawid Isma'il I, and the restoration was completed by the Ottoman sultan Sülayman II in 1534. The covering of the domes with golden tiles was done by the command and at the expense of Shah Aga Muhammad Khan, the founder of the Qajar dynasty.

al-Kazimi, 'Abd al-Muhsin: Shi'i poet of Iraq; 1865-1935. He is known as "the poet of the Arabs", for he derives his images and metaphors from Bedouin life.

al-Kazimi, 'Abd al-Nabi: Imami jurist and traditionist of Kazimayn; 1784-1840. The most important of his numerous works is a biographical dictionary of transmitters of Shi'i Tradition.

al-Kazimi, Haydar b. Ibrahim: Imami scholar of Kazimayn; 1790-1849. He was the ancestor of the Al Haydar, a celebrated learned family of Kazimayn.

Kefe (Kafa, Kaffa): old name of modern Theodosia (Russian Feodosia), on the southeastern coast of the Crimea. It played an important role in the development of the East-West and South-North transit trade. The Genoese were active here from ca. 1266 to 1475, when Kefe was conquered by the Ottomans. It was captured by the Russians in 1783.

Kemakh (T. *Kemah*): small town in eastern Anatolia, Turkey. During the Umayyad and 'Abbasid periods, it was a frontier fortress, possession of which oscillated between the Arabs and the Byzantines. It was occupied by the Ottoman Sultan Bayezid I, by Tamerlane, by the Aq Qoyunlu, briefly by the Safawids and finally fell to the Ottoman Sultan Selim I.

Kemal, Mehmed, Namiq: prominent Ottoman poet, journalist, historian and critic; 1840-1888. Among his many works are monographs about the great men of Ottoman and Islamic history.

Kemal Pasha-zade (Ibn(i) Kemal): Ottoman scholar and Shaykh al-Islam; 1468-1534. He wrote in Turkish, Persian and Arabic in the fields of history, belles-lettres, grammar, theology and law.

Kemal Re'is: Turkish corsair and admiral; d. 1511. He gained great fame through his corsair activities in the western Mediterranean. In 1495 the Ottoman sultan Bayezid II took him and his nephew Piri Re'is into Ottoman service.

Kenya: country in East Africa. Al-Mas'udi (xth c.) relates that the island of Qanbalu, taken to be Pemba or Zanzibar, was ruled by a Muslim family. Immigrants from Persia, known as Banadir (litt. "seaports"), and the so-called Shirazis settled on the coast, while the Nabhani, an Arab family from Oman, formed a dynasty on Pate island, and the Ba 'Alawi, an Arab family of Sharifs from Hadhramaut, established a dynasty on the mainland. Until the arrival of the Portuguese, Mombasa and Malindi knew great prosperity. The Portuguese were succeeded by the Omani Arabs who belonged to the Ibadiyya. However, the coast had evolved as a predominantly Shafi'i region under the influence of the Ba 'Alawi, who also greatly influenced Swahili literature and culture generally.

Islam expanded into the interior of Kenya only in the xixth c., particularly after Sa'id b. Sultan, the Bu Sa'id ruler of Oman and Zanzibar, moved his capital to Zanzibar. Among the Indian Muslims, the Khoja or Nizari Isma'ilis, the Bohoras and the Hanafi Memons predominated. The Twelver Shi'is arrived late in the xixth c. Trade relations with the interior led to at least some seasonal settlements and intermarriage and thus the nuclei of Muslims grew in size and importance. Interaction between the Muslim Somalis and the Oromo tribes led to Islamisation of the latter. From 1886 onwards, most of present-day Kenya came under British influence. Muslim power diminished, but Islam spread inland, despite the hostility of Christian missionaries, due to Indian pioneer members of the Ahmadiyya movement and to the employment of Swahili, Somali and Sudanese troops. After the Second World War, the colonial government, the Aga Khan and the sultan of Zanzibar established the Mombasa Institute of Muslim Education, but in 1951 non-Muslims had to be accepted. At present, some 4% of the population of 12 million (est. 1971) are Muslim.

Kerimba Islands: group of islands off Mozambique. They were possibly Islamicised in the xiith c.

Khabbab b. al-Aratt, Abu 'Abd Allah: Companion of the Prophet; d. 657. He is usually mentioned as the sixth or seventh man who embraced Islam.

Khabur: the larger Khabur is one of the chief affluents of the Euphrates. The lesser Khabur is one of the tributaries of the Tigris.

Khadija: the first wife of the Prophet; d. 619. Before her marriage to the Prophet, she had been married twice, and had engaged in trade. After the Prophet had executed satisfactorily his commission as steward of her merchandise in Bosra (Syria), she offered him marriage, from which at least five children were born. Khadija supported and encouraged the Prophet, fostering his confidence in himself and in his mission.

Khadim al-Haramayn ("Servant of the Two Holy Places", i.e. Mecca and Medina); title used by a number of Muslim monarchs. After the Ottoman Sultan Selim I had conquered Egypt in 1517, the title was said to have been passed to him by al-Mutawakkil III, the last 'Abbasid caliph in Cairo. However, the 'Abbasids, whether in Baghdad or in Cairo, had never used it. The first to adopt it appears to have been Saladin, and several Mamluk sultans used it after him, but it does not seem to have formed part of their standard titulary.

Khadim Süleyman Pasha: Ottoman governor of Egypt and Grand Vizier; d. 1547. In 1538 he was the commander of the campaign against the Portuguese in India, called for by Bahadur Shah of Gujarat (r. 1526-1537). On the way he took the port of Aden.

al-Khadir (al-Khidr): name of a popular figure, who plays a prominent part in legend and story. The majority of the Qur'an commentators identify him with the servant of God mentioned in Qur'an XVIII.

al-Khadir, Muhammad b. al-Husayn: scholar, poet and writer of Tunisian origin; 1876-1958. Between 1952-1954 he was rector of the al-Azhar in Cairo.

Khwafi Khan, Muhammad Hashim: Persian historian; ca. 1664-1732. He is known for his history of the Indian branch of the Timurid dynasties, the most valuable parts being the accounts of the Mughal Emperors Shah Jahan I and Awrangzib.

Khwaju, Kamal al-Din: Persian poet from Kirman; 1290-1352. He attained celebrity as an ingenious and skilful *ghazal*-writer.

Khalaf b. Hayyan al-Ahmar, Abu Muhriz: famous transmitter of ancient Arabic poetry; ca. 733-796. He had a prodigious memory and knew Bedouin life intimately.

al-Khalafiyya: sub-sect of the Ibadiyya, founded in what is now Tripolitania around the beginning of the ixth c. by Khalaf b. al-Samh, a grandson of the Ibadi Imam Abu 'l-Khattab al-Yamani.

al-Khalduniyya: cultural association established in Tunis under the spiritual aegis of Ibn Khaldun, sanctioned in 1896. Its premises were opened in 1897.

Khalid, Banu: Arab tribe in the eastern provinces of modern Saudi Arabia, with its centre at the town of al-Hasa. For the last two centuries, the chieftainship has been in the hands of the ʿUrayʿir family.

Khalid b. ʿAbd Allah al-Qasri: governor for the Umayyads, first of Mecca and later of Iraq; d. 743.

Khalid b. Safwan (Ibn al-Ahtam): transmitter of historical traditions, poetry and memorable orations, famed for his eloquence; viiith c.

Khalid b. Saʿid: according to several transmitters of traditions, he was, if not the fourth Companion of the Prophet, at least one of the second group of three; d. 635.

Khalid b. al-Walid b. al-Mughira: Arab commander at the time of the early Muslim conquests; d. 642. He fought against the Prophet at Uhud (625) but was converted in 627. He is credited with a famous desert crossing, which led to the conquest of al-Hira in 633 and consequently to that of Iraq.

Khalide Edib (T. *Halide Edib Adivar*): prominent Turkish novelist, writer and nationalist; 1884-1964. In May 1919 she made a famous moving and dramatic address at the historic mammoth meeting in the Sultan Ahmed Square in Istanbul against the Turkish policy of the Allies. There was a fundamental conflict between her own liberal views and the radicalism of Mustafa Kemal Atatürk. She is the author of twenty novels and wrote her memoirs in two volumes in English while in exile in England (1924-1928).

Khalifa, Al: the ruling dynasty of Bahrain since 1783, when Ahmad b. Khalifa b. Muhammad wrested control of the Bahrain islands from the Persians.

Khalifa b. Abi ʾl-Mahasin: Arab physician from Aleppo; xiiith c. He wrote a work on ophthalmology.

Khalil, al-Malik al-Ashraf Salah al-Din: Mamluk sultan; r. 1290-1293. His fame rests upon his conquest of Acre in 1291, which put an end to Christian domination of Palestine.

al-Khalil b. Ahmad: important Arab philologist from Oman; d. 791. He was the author of the first Arabic dictionary.

Khalil Allah But-Shikan: Persian mystic of Kirman, active in South India; 1374-1460.

Khalil b. Ishaq (Ibn al-Jundi): Maliki jurist of Egypt; xvith c. His compendium of Maliki law is the most renowned manual in the Muslim West.

Khalil Mutran: Lebanese poet and journalist; 1872-1949. He is remembered for his lyrical and narrative poems.

Khalil Pasha Hajji Arnawud: Ottoman Grand Vizier under Sultan Ahmed I; ca. 1655-1733. In 1717 he was defeated near Belgrade by Prince Eugène of Savoy.

al-Khalisa: former Fatimid citadel in Palermo, built in 937 to suppress a rebellion of the Sicilians against the amir Salim b. Abi Rashid.

Khaljis: Indo-Muslim dynasty which ruled in Delhi from 1290-1320. It was founded by Jalal al-Din Firuz Shah II (r. 1290-1296) of the Khalaj, a Turkish people inhabiting eastern Afghanistan, who took power from the last Mu'izzi or Slave king. The Khaljis were followed by the Tughluqids.

al-Khallal, Ahmad b. Muhammad (Abu Bakr al-Khallal): transmitter of traditions, legal scholar and theologian, and an outstanding figure in the history of Hanbalism; d. 923.

Khalqevi (T. *Halkevi* "People's House"): name for the educational and social centres founded by Mustafa Kemal Atatürk.

Khalwatiyya (T. *Halvetiyye*): highly ramified and widespread mystical order, founded either by 'Umar al-Khalwati (d. 1397) or by Muhammad b. Nur al-Balisi.

Khamis (ibn) Mushayt: the main town in interior Asir in Saudi Arabia, between the Hejaz and Yemen.

Khan (*Khān*): Turkish title, first recorded on the coins of the Ilek-Khans. Today it is a common affix to the names of Muslims of all classes and is often regarded as a surname.

It is also a word of Persian origin designating on the one hand a staging-post and lodging on the main communication routes, on the other a warehouse, later a hostelry in the more important urban centres.

Khanqah: a composite word of Persian origin meaning a building usually reserved for Muslim mystics belonging to a dervish order.

Khansa (Khinsa): town in the Chinese province of Che-kiang, inhabited in the xiiith c. by an important colony of Muslims.

al-Khansa' (Tumadir bint 'Amr): Arab poetess; ca. 575-ca. 640. She is famous for her elegies for her two brothers Mu'awiya and Sakhr, killed in skirmishes. Tradition made her welcome Islam, but her poetry is wholly pagan in feeling.

Khaqan: title meaning "(supreme) ruler". It was applied by the heathen Turks and the medieval Muslim geographers and historians to the heads of the various Turkish confederations, but also to other non-Muslim rulers such as the Emperor of China. In the form *qa'an* it was borne by the successors of Genghis Khan, the Mongol Great Khans in Karakorum and Peking. The Ottoman sultans again carried the title *khaqan*. Early medieval chroniclers in Europe refer to it with the term *kaganus*.

Khaqani, Afdal al-Din Ibrahim: outstanding Persian poet from Shirwan; 1126-1199. He is known for having created a new type of *qasīda* for his panegyrics, but above all for his ascetic Sufi poetry.

Kharana (Qasr): fortified building in the Transjordanian desert to the southeast of Amman, generally identified as Sasanian. There are Arabic inscriptions of the year 710.

Kharg (A. *Khārak*): Iranian island in the Persian Gulf off the coast of Iran, 8 km long and 4 km broad, covered by treeless hills. Four km to the north is the smaller island of Khargu (A. *Khuwayrik*). In classical times Kharg was a port of call on the route from Basra to Oman and India. In the xviith c. the Dutch East India Company made it the main base for its commercial activities in the Persian Gulf. They were, however, driven out by Mir Muhanna of Bandar Rig on the main land. In the xxth c. Kharg became an important terminal for shipping crude oil.

Khargird (Kharjird): place in northeastern Persia, known for two *madrasa*s which are remarkable monuments of Islamic architecture.

Kharijites (A. *al-Khawārij*, s. *Khārijī*): the Arabic term indicates the dissidents who, at the battle of Siffin in 657, refused arbitration between ʿAli and Muʿawiya and "departed" (A. *kharaja*). They in fact facilitated Muʿawiya's victory over ʿAli, and later that of the ʿAbbasids over the Umayyads. They constitute the earliest of the religious sects of Islam. From the point of view of the development of dogma, their importance lies particularly in the formulation of questions relative to the theory of the caliphate and to justification by faith or by works. From the point of view of political history, they disturbed, by means of continual insurrections which often ended in the temporary conquest of entire provinces, the peace of the eastern part of the Muslim empire.

al-Kharj: district in Najd, Saudi Arabia, which is one of the most fertile places of the country. In the xviiith c. its inhabitants were among the principal opponents of the Wahhabiyya. It was recovered from the Al Rashid by ʿAbd al-ʿAzīz Ibn Saʿud in 1902.

al-Kharraz, Abu Saʿid: mystic of the school of Baghdad; d. 899. He strove to combine a doctrine of ecstatic mysticism with orthodox support of the religious law.

Khartpert (T. *Kharput*): stronghold of eastern Anatolia, which passed frequently into the hands of all the powers who transiently ruled the region.

Khartum (A. *al-Khurṭūm*): capital of the Republic of the Sudan, at the confluence of the Blue and White Niles. With the extension of Turco-Egyptian rule, the pacification of the Sudan, and the opening-up of the Equatorial Nile in the xixth c., Khartum developed into a flourishing town.

Kharus, Banu: tribe which has played an important role in the history of the Ibadiyya in Oman. Saʿid b. Khalfan al-Khalil al-Kharusi was largely instrumental in the choice of ʿAzzan b. Qays of the Al Bu Saʿid, the only Ibadi Imam elected in the xixth c.

Khashabiyya: the Arabic word means "men armed with clubs" and was used for the followers of al-Mukhtar b. Abi ʿUbayd al-Thaqafi in Kufa. It was also another name for the Kaysaniyya.

Khathʿam: Arab tribe which inhabited the mountainous territory between al-Taʾif and Najran. They played a part in Abraha's expedition against Mecca and, after initial hostility, recognised the Prophet's mission.

al-Khatib al-Baghdadi, Abu Bakr Ahmad: biographer and critical systematiser of Tradition methodology; 1002-1071. His fame is based on his biographical encyclopaedia of more than 7,800 scholars and other personalities connected with the cultural and political life of Baghdad.

Khattabiyya: extremist Shi'i sect in Kufa, founded by Abu 'l-Khattab al-Asadi (d. 755).

al-Khawlani, Abu Idris: a Muslim of the first generation after the Prophet's time, judge and transmitter of traditions; 629-699.

al-Khawlani, Abu Muslim: a Muslim of the first generation after the Prophet's time, famous for his asceticism; d. 682.

Khaybar: famous oasis about 150 km. from Medina, Saudi Arabi. In 628 the Prophet took the oasis, whose inhabitants were Jewish and Hebraised tribes. Under the terms of the agreement, the Jews could continue to stay on their land and to cultivate it, but were to hand over one-half of the produce to the Muslims.

Khayr al-Din Pasha: Tunisian and Ottoman statesman from the Caucasian tribe of the Abkhaz; 1822-1890. In 1839 he went to Tunis and became in 1857 Minister of the Navy. He was a vigorous proponent of the modernisation of the Tunisian political system and a firm supporter of close links between the Tunisian Bey's official suzerain, the Ottoman sultan, and Tunis. He was made Grand Vizier in 1878 but was dismissed in 1879.

Khayr al-Din (Khidir) Pasha, Barbarossa: famous Turkish corsair and Grand Admiral; ca. 1466-1546. In his fight against the Spanish, he sought help from the Ottoman sultan, whose suzerainty over Algeria was recognised in 1520. From the island of Jerba he ravaged the coasts of the western Mediterranean, and in 1529 took the island of Peñon facing Algiers and still in the hands of the Spanish. In 1534 he conquered Tunis, from where he was driven away by Charles V in 1535. In 1537 the fleet which had been put together by the Emperor, the Pope and Venice, under the command of Andrea Doria, retreated after some skirmishing with Khayr al-Din's fleet. His mausoleum in Istanbul was built by the architect Sinan.

Khayr al-Din (Ustad): Ottoman architect, popularly considered as the founder of Turkish architecture; xvith c. He built complexes of religious and educational buildings in Amasya, Edirne and Istanbul.

al-Khayyat, Abu 'Ali Yahya: Arab astrologer, known in the West as Al-bohali.

al-Khayyat, Abu 'l-Husayn: theologian and jurist; ca. 835-ca. 913. He was a foremost representative of the Baghdad school of the Mu'tazila.

al-Khayzuran bint 'Ata' al-Jurashiyya: former slave of Yemeni origin who, afer being freed, was married to the 'Abbasid Caliph al-Mahdi, to whom she bore the future caliphs al-Hadi and Harun al-Rashid.

Khaz'al Khan, Ibn Hajji Jabir Khan: shaykh of Muhammara, now Khurramshahr, in Iran; ca. 1860-1936. As leader of the Muhasayn tribe, he objected strongly against the proposal of the Persian government to introduce Belgian customs officials into 'Arabistan. He received support from the British diplomatic mission in Teheran, but later lost it. His power was extinguished by Reza Khan (later Shah) Pahlavi.

Khazar: nomadic people in the South Russian steppes who flourished in the early Islamic period.

al-Khazraj: with the al-Aws, one of the main Arab tribes in Medina before and at the time of the rise of Islam. They seem to have been more numerous and more enthusiastic Muslims than the al-Aws.

al-Khazraji, Diya' al-Din: poet from al-Andalus; xiiith c. He wrote a didactic poem which contains a versified treatise on Arabic metres.

Khedive (P. *khidīw*): title of the rulers of Egypt in the later xixth and early xxth c.

Khidash (Khaddash): one of the leaders of the early Hashimiyya movement in Khurasan; d. 736.

Khidr Beg: Ottoman scholar and poet, and the first Muslim judge of Istanbul; 1407-1458.

Khidr-Ilyas (T. *Hidrellez*): in Turkish tradition the name of a popular festival in spring and celebrated on 5-6 May.

Khidr Khan: founder of the "Sayyid" dynasty which ruled at Delhi from 1414 to 1451.

Khilafat Movement: politico-religious movement in British India after the First World War. It had its roots in Pan-Islamism and was stimulated by nationalism. By 1928, it had lost all significance.

al-Khiraqi, 'Umar b. al-Husayn (Abu 'l-Qasim): one of the first and most celebrated of Hanbali jurisconsults; d. 946.

Khirbat al-Bayda': early, probably pre-Islamic, Arab structure in the Syrian desert.

Khirbat al-Mafjar (Qasr Hisham): the modern name for the ruins of an unfinished Umayyad mansion north of Jericho, possibly built during the caliphate of the Umayyad Caliph Hisham.

Khirbat al-Minya: name for the ruins of an apparently unfinished Umayyad mansion on the northern end of Lake Tiberias.

Khirqa-yi Sherif: name of one of the mantles attributed to the Prophet, preserved at the Topkapi Palace in Istanbul, brought there in 1517.

Khiva (*Khīwa*): town and region on the western bank of the river Oxus in Uzbekistan, also known as Khwarazm.

Khiyabani, Shaykh Muhammad: Persian religious scholar and political leader from Azerbaijan; 1879-1920. He played a role in the deposition of the Qajar Shah Muhammad 'Ali in 1909.

Khmer (Cambodia) (A. *Qimār*): Muslim sources mention it as a place on the route to the Far East, where Muslim merchants were welcomed. One single Islamic funerary inscription has been found in Cambodia.

Khoi (Khuy): Iranian town in West Azerbaijan which was of great strategic importance in Safawid and Qajar times.

Khoja: in the strict sense it is the name of an Indian caste consisting mostly of Nizari Isma'ilis; in a looser sense it is the name commonly used to refer to the Indian Nizaris in general. The Khojas were active in the commerce between India and East Africa at least since the xviith c. After 1840, when Sultan Sa'id b. Sultan of Oman and Zanzibar transferred his capital from Muscat to Zanzibar, they settled in large numbers on the island and later in mainland East Africa.

Khoja Efendi, Sa'd al-Din: famous Ottoman Shaykh al-Islam, statesman and historian; 1536-1599. His fame rests on a carefully-written history, based on critical examination of a number of named sources. It deals with Ottoman history from its beginnings to the death of Selim I in 1520.

Khojaev (Faizullah Khoja): revolutionary and nationalist of Bukhara; 1896-1938. The amir of Bukhara was overthrown in 1920, and in 1925 Khojaev became President of the Council of People's Commissars of Uzbekistan. In 1937 he was dismissed, arrested and the next year executed. His name was rehabilitated in 1966.

Khoqand (A. *Khwāqand*): town in Farghana, Uzbekistan. It was the capital of the independent Özbeg dynasty of the Miñ from the xviiith c. to the Russian occupation in 1853. The Muslim peoples of the former khanate played a major role in the anti-Russian rebellion of 1916. In 1918 the town was captured by the Red Army and many inhabitants killed.

Khosrew Beg: beg of Bosnia; 1480-1541. Still well-known among the Bosnian Muslims by the name of Gazi Husrev-beg, he spent his great riches on enlarging Sarajevo.

Khosrew Pasha, Bosniak: Ottoman Grand Vizier; d. 1632. He failed three times to take Baghdad.

Khosrew Pasha, Mehmed: Ottoman Grand Vizier; d. 1855. In 1832, during Muhammad 'Ali's advance on Istanbul, he invited the famous Von Moltke as a military instructor.

Khost: name of various places in Afghanistan, in modern times the most important being the region comprised within the province of Pakhtia.

al-Khubar: town on the Persian Gulf coast of Saudi Arabia. Its importance for the oil industry, started in 1935, diminished when a deep-water pier began operating in al-Dammam since 1950.

Khubayb b. 'Adi al-Ansari: one of the first martyrs of Islam, killed by tribesmen of Lihyan after the battle of Uhud in 625.

Khuda Bakhsh: notable bibliophile of Muslim India; 1824-1908. He was the founder of the celebrated Oriental Public Library at Patna. By 1891, when the collection of manuscripts collected by his father and by himself was made into a pious endowment (A. *waqf*), it had reached the number of 4,000.

Khujand(a): town and district in Central Asia, along the left bank of the middle Iaxartes. The town was captured by the Arabs in 722. It was a place of importance under the Ilek-Khans, and put up a stubborn defence against the

Mongols. At the beginning of the xixth c. the town became part of the khanate of Khoqand, but it fell to the Russians in 1866. Khujand is now an important industrial and cultural centre in Tajikistan.

al-Khujandi, Abu Mahmud Hamid: astronomer and mathematician; d. 1000. He constructed astronomical instruments, the most important among them being the sextant which he made in order to determine the obliquity of the ecliptic.

Khumarawayh b. Ahmad b. Tulun: ruler of the Tulunid dynasty of Egypt and Syria; b. 864, r. 884-896. The 'Abbasid Caliph al-Mu'tamid regarded him as an usurper, but in the end Khumarawayh acknowledged 'Abbasid sovereignty. In return he was granted the *de jure* governorship of Egypt and Syria and Caliph al-Mu'tadid took Khumarawayh's daughter, Qatr al-Nada, as a bride for himself instead of for his son 'Ali. The splendid nuptials lived on in chronicles and folk-literature

Khumayr (Khmir): an element of the population which has given its name to a mountainous massif extending along the north-west littoral of Tunisia. Throughout the medieval period, the historians are completely silent about them. In 1881 the French, trying to put an end to their pillaging their neighbours, marched from Algeria into Tunisia, which was the beginning of the French protectorate over the latter. The Khumayr were routed at Ben Mtir.

Khunji, Fadl Allah b. Ruzbihan: Persian religious scholar and political writer; 1455-1521. He was a staunch Sunni who fiercely opposed the Shi'i Safawid Shah Isma'il, left Persia and fled to Özbeg Transoxiana.

Khurasan: today the north-easternmost province of Iran, with its administrative capital at Mashhad. But in early Islamic times, the term was ill-defined. It frequently covered also parts of what are now the Republics of Central Asia and Afghanistan.

The Arabs appeared in Khurasan already during the caliphate of 'Umar b. al-Khattab, but the permanent pacification of what had been Sasanian territory was a protracted process. During the Umayyad age, authority was exercised by the Arab governors of Basra. Since Khurasani support had been decisive in the rise of the 'Abbasids, the province enjoyed considerable favour from the early 'Abbasid caliphs. Under the dynasty of the Tahirids, who governed Khurasan for the 'Abbasids and had their capital at Nishapur, the province blossomed economically and culturally. Khurasan and the eastern Iranian world in general had a crucial part in the renaissance of the New Persian language and its literature from the ixth century onwards.

In 900 the province was incorporated into the Samanid dominions, but in 994 it passed under the rule of the Turkish Ghaznawids, who ruled there until 1040. Khurasan remained an important province of the Saljuq empire, enjoying stability under Sanjar. The province suffered severely under the Mongols, and never recovered its cultural and intellectual position within Persia as a whole. Under Tamerlane's son Shahrukh Mirza, who ruled there from 1397 till 1446, Khurasan regained a considerable degree of prosperity, which it kept under the Timurid prince Husayn b. Mansur b. Bayqara (r. 1470-1506). In 1510 the province was incorporated by the Safawids into their dominions, but they were unable to hold Balkh against the Özbegs, and frontier towns like Marw oscillated between the two powers.

Under Nadir Shah Afshar, Mashhad became the capital, but after his death northern Khurasan passed into the control of Ahmad Shah Durrani of Afghanistan. Shah Rukh, Nadir Shah's grandson (r. 1748-1796), was the nominal ruler of Khurasan.

Under the Qajar Aga Muhammad, Khurasan came under full control of Teheran but the depredations of the Özbegs and other Turkmen continued to make life in northern Khurasan chronically insecure.

The Russians annexed the oasis of Marw in 1884 and relations with the amirs of Afghanistan remained bad, till the definitive demarcation of the boundary was settled in 1934.

Khurasan, Banu: dynasty which governed Tunis from 1062-1128 and from 1148-1159.

Khurasani, Akhund Mulla: distinguished Shi'i *mujtahid* from Tus in Iran; 1839-1911. Since 1906 his name has been associated with the Persian Constitutional Revolution as one of its most influential supporters.

al-Khurma: oasis in western Saudi Arabia where Ghalib b. Mus'ad, Sharif of Mecca, was defeated by the Wahhabis in 1798. In 1919 the Wahhabis again were victorious here over the troops of 'Abd Allah, son of Husayn b. 'Ali, then king of the Hejaz.

Khurramiyya (Khurramdiniyya): name of the religious movement founded by Mazdak in the late vth c., and of various Iranian, anti-Arab sects which developed out of it under the impact of certain extremist Shi'i doctrines.

Khurramshahr (Khorramshahr): chief town of the district of the same name in the Iranian province of Khuzistan and one of Iran's principal ports-of-entry on the Persian Gulf. Formerly known as Muhammara, the town was ceded by the Ottomans to Persia by the Treaty of Erzerum in 1847 and came firmly under Iranian control in 1925. In 1975 Iran and Iraq signed an agreement whereby the line of deepest water in the Shatt al-'Arab (P. *Arwand-rud*) was taken to be the international boundary.

Khurrem (Khasseki Sultan/Roxelana): the beloved wife of the Ottoman Sultan Süleyman II; d. 1558. According to tradition of Polish origin, she had many pious bequests executed in Istanbul, Edirne, Mecca, Medina and Jerusalem. In 1541 she moved to the Topkapi Palace. With a woman lodged for the first time at the political centre, there began the rule of women, during which the policies of the Ottoman Empire were directed by a succession of foreign favourites, which lasted till the death of Sultan Murad IV's mother in 1651. Due largely to her intrigues, her son Selim remained alone to succeed his father.

Khurshid: Dabuyid prince of Tabaristan; r. 740-761. His rebellion against the ʿAbbasid caliph was subdued in 760.

Khurshid is also the name given in epic romances to a daughter of the emperor of Byzantium as the lover of Jamshid.

Khushhal Khan Khatak: Pathan poet and warrior chieftain; 1613-1689. He is recognized as the national poet of the Pathans.

Khusraw Firuz (al-Malik al-Rahim): the last Buyid ruler of Fars and Khuzistan; r. 1048-1055.

Khusraw (II) Parwiz: Sasanian king (r. 591-628). He was the last great ruler of this dynasty before the invading Arabs overran the Persian Empire. In 602 he overthrew al-Nuʿman III b. al-Mundhir and established direct Persian rule. Shirin, known from the very popular theme of Farhad and Shirin, was his favourite wife.

Khuttalan (Khuttal): region on the right bank of the upper Oxus river in Central Asia. It was fully secured for the Muslims in 750. Under the early Ghaznawids, it was strategically important since it was located in the buffer zone between them and their Ilek-Khanid rivals.

Khuzaʿa: ancient Arab tribe of obscure origin, whose main area of abode was between Mecca and Medina and who had close relations with the Quraysh. A branch of this tribe, the Kaʿb b. ʿAmr, played a decisive role in the struggle between Mecca and the Prophet. Their meritorious attitude is fairly reflected in Muslim tradition.

Khuzistan (ʿArabistan): province in southwestern Iran, which corresponds more or less to the ancient Elam, as is reflected in the names of its present capital Ahvaz, of its ancient capital Susa and of the town of Hawiza. It was conquered by the Muslim Arabs in 640. In the ixth c. the region suffered as a result of the Zanj rebellion, and considerable damage was done to the irrigation systems. During the succeeding four centuries, Khuzistan was governed in turn by the Buyids, the Saljuqs and the Il-Khans. From 1430 till 1508, the region was ruled by the local Arab Shiʿi dynasty of the Mushaʿshaʿ, after which it came under the sovereignty of the Safawid Shah Ismaʿil I. The western portion of Khuzistan became then known as ʿArabistan. In the course of the xviiith and xixth c., the Mushaʿshaʿ dynasty lost ground to Arab tribesmen of the Banu Kaʿb and the Banu Lam. By the xixth c. the name of ʿArabistan was usually applied to the province as a whole, but the name of Khuzistan was restored by Reza Shah Pahlavi in 1925. Due to the oil industry, Khuzistan's prosperity has increased exponentially in the second half of the xxth c.

Khwandamir: surname of the Persian historian Ghiyath al-Din; ca. 1475-ca. 1535. His most valuable work is a general history from the earliest times down to the end of the reign of Shah Ismaʿil.

Khwansari, Sayyid Mirza: Persian religious scholar and writer; 1811-1895. His is best known for a biographical dictionary, which has enjoyed a great reputation.

Khwansari, Sayyid Muhammad Taqi Musawi: Shi'i *mujtahid* of distinguished piety; xxth c. He was recognized as *marja'-i taqlid* and, among other things, sanctioned Mosaddeq's measures towards the nationalization of the Anglo-Iranian Oil Company.

Khwarazm: region lying along the lower course of the Oxus river in Turkestan, in post-Mongol times increasingly known as Khiva. It was conquered by the Arabs in 712 from Khurasan and became a bastion of Sunni orthodoxy and scholarship, attested by the large number of traditionists, jurists, theologians, mathematicians and scientists who are called "al-Khwarazmi", al-Biruni being one of the most outstanding. In 1017 the province passed to the Ghaznawids, becoming wholly Turkish, and in 1077 the line known as Khwarazm-Shahs was founded by Anushtigin Gharča'i. Their extensive empire crumbled before the Mongol onslaught in 1231. Till 1350 Khwarazm was ruled by the khans of the Golden Horde and became again highly prosperous. Tamerlane razed the rebuilt capital Urgenč to the ground in 1388 and Khwarazm never really recovered from this blow. In the xvth c. possession of the province alternated between the khans of the Golden Horde and the Timurids; in 1505 it passed to Muhammad Shaybani, founder of the Özbeg amirate in Transoxiana, and in 1510 briefly to the Safawid Shah Isma'il. The local Özbeg dynasty of the 'Arabshahids ruled here from 1511 to the end of the xviith c., with its centre at Khiva. The best-known ruler of this dynasty was Abu 'l-Ghazi Bahadur Khan. After that, real power was in the hands of the *Inaq* or senior member and military chief of the Qongrat tribe, who in 1804 assumed the title of khan, the remaining khans of Khiva being all from his line. Khiva capitulated to the Russians in 1873, and the last khan, Sayyid 'Abd Allah, was forced to abdicate in 1920. In 1924 the right bank areas of the old Khiva khanate were incorporated in the Uzbek SSR and the left-bank areas in the Turkmen SSR.

Khwarazm-Shah: ancient title of the rulers of Khwarazm, used regularly in the eraly Islamic period until the Mongol invasion, and sporadically thereafter. Until the arrival of the Monghols, the following dynasties have ruled: the Afghirids (305-995), the Ma'munids of Gurganj (995-1017), and, after an intermezzo of Ghaznawid governors (1017-1034), the line of Anushtigin Gharča'i (1077-1231).

al-Khwarazmi, Abu 'Abd Allah: well-known scientist; xth c. His fame rests on his *Keys of the Sciences*, a dictionary of the key terms used by the various groups of scholars, artisans and government officials, in particular those terms which were left out of the current lexica.

al-Khwarazmi, Abu Bakr: Arabic poet and writer; 934-993. He was famed for his prodigious memory.

al-Khwarazmi, Abu Ja'far Muhammad b. Musa: mathematician, astronomer and geographer; ca. 800-ca. 847. His name still lives in the term algorithm. His *Algebra* (A. *al-jabr*) was translated partially by Robert of Chester

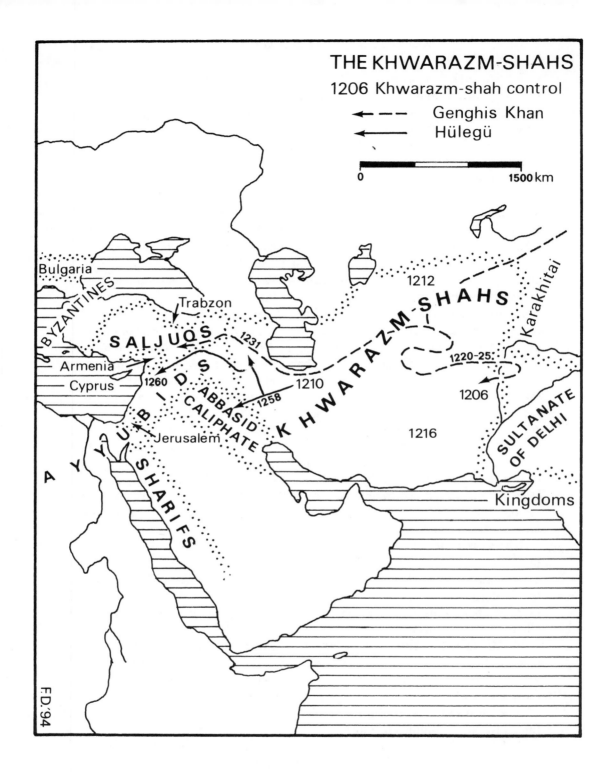

THE KHWARAZM-SHAHS

1206 Khwarazm-shah control

⟵ – – – Genghis Khan
⟵——— Hülegü

0   1500 km

Bulgaria

BYZANTINES

Trabzon

SALJUQS

1231

1212

KHWARAZM-SHAHS

Karakhitai

Armenia

Cyprus

1260

1210

1220-25

1206

Jerusalem

ABBASID
CALIPHATE

1258

1216

SULTANATE
OF DELHI

AYYUBIDS

SHARIFS

Kingdoms

F.D. '94

as *Liber algebras et almucabola*, and shortly afterwards by Gerard of Cremona as *De jebra et almucabola*. In this way, there was introduced into Europe a science completely unknown till then. Almost at the same time an adaptation of his *Arithmetic* on the Hindu-Arabic numerals, which today are called "Arabic numerals", was made known in Spain in a Latin version by John of Seville.

Khyber Pass: one of the principal passes through the mountain barrier separating the Indus valley plains from Afghanistan.

Killing (A. *qatl*): the Arabic term is used in the two principal meanings of the word, sc. the crime of murder and the punishment of execution. As to the first meaning, many verses in the Qur'an forbid unlawful slaying, while in others killing is represented as marking the unbeliever. In the law books two cases of murder are dealt with in particular: the causing of a premature birth or abortion, and killing through giving false evidence. The punishment of execution is applied for cases of murder, for sorcerers, for highway robbers and for the renegade from Islam if his apostasy is proven.

Kilwa: the name of various localities and islands off the east coast of Africa. The best known is Kilwa Kisawani, the Quiloa of the Portuguese, situated on an island near the Tanzanian coast, some 225 km. south of Dar es-Salaam. 'Ali b. al-Husayn, the founder of a dynasty of Shirazi settlers from the Persian Gulf, established a dynasty here in ca. 957. Dawud b. Sulayman was sultan of Kilwa from ca. 1131-1170 and "Master of the Trade" of Pemba, Zanzibar, Mafia and the mainland. After the Omanis captured Mombasa from the Portuguese in 1698, Kilwa also was made tributary to Oman.

Kinda: South Arabian tribal group, whose descent, real or imaginary, from Kahlan correctly identifies them as Arabs and distinguishes them from Himyar and other non-Arab inhabitants of South Arabia. The tribe spread all over Arabia in the vth and vith c., from the south to the centre to the north. Although Kinda had its heyday in pre-Islamic times, it retained some of its power and influence in the time of the Prophet and later. Branches of the Kinda carved out for themselves short-lived principalities in Muslim Spain in the xith c. during the period of the so-called Muluk al-Tawa'if.

al-Kindi, 'Abd al-Masih b. Ishaq: name given to the author, probably a Nestorian Christian, of a defence of Christianity; ixth or xth c. The defence, which is also a refutation of Islam, is presented in the form of a letter written in response to that of a Muslim friend, named 'Abd Allah b. Isma'il al-Hashimi, who invited his correspondent to embrace Islam. The letter was translated into Latin in 1141 by Peter of Toledo and revised by Peter of Poitiers and played a very important role, in the East as well as in the West, in the polemic between Christians and Muslims.

al-Kindi, Abu Yusuf Ya'qub: Arab scholar and philosopher; ca. 801-866. He was a companion of the 'Abbasid Caliphs al-Ma'mun and al-Mu'tasim, and probably had a tendency towards Mu'tazilism. He is known as "the philosopher of the Arabs", and has survived as a universal scholar and as an astrologer.

King (A. *malik*, pl. *mulūk*): the Qur'an mentions several kings, among them Pharaoh and Saul. But Islam presented a new order in which God alone was "the King". *Malik* came to connote the temporal, mundane facet of government – the antithesis of Khalifa and Imam. Considered to be a term of abuse, the word was not officially assumed by Muslim rulers in the early centuries of Islam. However, under Sasanian influence theories on the divine rights of kings were introduced. Towards the middle of the xth c. the Buyids called themselves Malik, as did Samanid, Khwarazmi, Ghaznawid, Saljuq, Fatimid, Ayyubid and Mamluk rulers after them. But the title was also freely applied to princes, viziers and provincial governors, which rendered the term less majestic, the title Sultan being considered superior as it conveyed a sense of independent sovereignty. The Ottomans did not commonly use it. By the time they were in power, the term retained little of its former glory. In the xxth c., however, the title has appeared again in Muslim countries, Husayn b. 'Ali, the Sharif of Mecca, being the first to use it in 1916. But anti-monarchical revolutions and revolts later swept away most kings in the Islamic countries.

King of the poets (A. *malik al-shu'arā'*): honorific title of a Persian poet laureate and the highest distinction which could be given to a poet by a royal patron. During the Middle Ages, he was a supervisor of the poets assembled at the court and passed judgements on poems before they were presented to the patron. Famous poets laureate were 'Unsuri, appointed as such by the Ghaznawid Mahmud b. Sebüktigin, and al-Mu'izzi, appointed by the Great Saljuq Malik-Shah I. In the xixth c. the Qajar Fath 'Ali Shah gave the title to Fath 'Ali Khan Saba (d. 1822). Among the last who received this title was Muhammad Taqi Bahar (d. 1951).

King of the great merchants (A. *malik al-tujjār*): title for an office which existed in Iran from Safawid times until the end of the Qajar period. He was chosen by the prominent merchants of each big town and nominated by the authorities to be the link between the trading community and the authorities. He also settled disputes between the Iranian merchants and their customers, between the merchants themselves, and between local and foreign merchants and trading-firms.

Kirgiz: Turkish people of Central Asia. About 840 they conquered the lands of the Uyghur in Mongolia, and exported musk to the Muslim lands. They were driven out of Mongolia by the Karakhitai, had to submit to Genghis Khan, and afterwards to the Kalmuks and the Russians, who established their rule in 1864.

Kirkuk: city and governorate in northeastern Iraq. In the xiith c. it was dominated by the Begteginid dynasty, who resided in Irbil. After being restored to the 'Abbasid caliphs in the xiiith c., it was conquered by the Mongols, the Aq Qoyunlu, the Safawids and the Ottomans. It fell to the Persians in 1623, and again in 1743, but was in general in the hands of the Ottomans, the local Kurds being the real masters of the region. In 1924 it was incorporated into the kingdom of Iraq and became an important centre of the petroleum industry.

Kirman: city and province in southeastern Iran, known for its carpets. The Arab conquest was begun about 638, and under the Umayyads Kirman became a theatre for the activities of the Kharijites. It was ruled by the Buyids, the Saljuqs, and then by the Oghuz, the Shabankara amirs, the Zangids, the Khwarazm-Shahs and the Qutlugh-Khans, who were under Mongol suzerainty. In 1314 Kirman came under the rule of the Muzaffarids, until the latter were overthrown by Tamerlane in 1393. After the latter's death, Kirman was under the suzerainty of the Timurid Shahrukh Mirza until the Qara Qoyunlu took possession of the province. In 1503 it came into the possession of the Safawid Shah Isma'il. From 1750 till 1794 Kirman was ruled by the Zand dynasty, who were followed by the Qajars.

al-Kirmani, Hamid al-Din Ahmad b. 'Abd Allah: prominent propagandist of the Fatimids; d. after 1020. He was the author of many works on the theory of the Imamate and on Isma'ili philosophy.

Kirmanshah: town and province in western Iran. It was peacefully occupied by the Arabs in 640, and subsequently ruled by the 'Abbasids, the Buyids, the Hasanwayhids and the Saljuqs. With the rise of the Safawids, it became a frontier province facing the Ottomans. About the middle of the xviith c., Kirmanshah was governed by the Zangana family. The province was again occupied by the Ottomans in 1723, but retaken by Nadir Shah Afshar in 1729. In the xixth c. the town became the capital of Persian Kurdistan and the province was one of the most thriving of Persia until the death of its governor Muhammad 'Ali Mirza, son of the Qajar Fath 'Ali Shah. With the opening of the Suez canal, the volume of trade coming through Kirmanshah markedly increased. It also profited from the pilgrim trade, lying as it did on the direct route from Persia to Najaf and Karbala'.

Kirshehir: a town in central Anatolia, Turkey, whose history starts only in the Rum Saljuq period. After the battle of Malazgird in 1071, the town was disputed between the Rum Saljuqs and the Danishmendids. It was taken by the Ottoman Sultan Bayezid I, then by Tamerlane who added it to the territory of the Qaramanids, and finally incorporated into the Ottoman Empire by Sultan Selim I. Among its monuments may be mentioned several madrasas, the "Tulip Mosque", the tomb of the poet 'Ashiq Pasha (d. 1333) and the sanctuary of Akhi Ewran, a semi-legendary Turkish saint. The poet Gülshehri (xivth c.) in all probability originated from Kirshehir.

al-Kisa'i: name of origin given to the unknown author of the famous *Stories of the Prophets*, an Arabic work on the lives of the prophets and pious men prior to the Prophet. The identity of the author remains an enigma.

al-Kisa'i, Abu 'l-Hasan: well-known Arab philologist and "reader" of the Qur'an, of Persian origin; ca. 737-805. He is said to have stayed for some time among the Bedouins in order to become fully conversant in Arabic. He is the real founder of the grammatical school of Kufa. His discussion with Sibawayhi, the prominent grammarian of the school of Basra, has become famous.

Kisa'i, Majd al-Din: Persian poet from Marw; 953-1000.

Kisangani (the former Stanleyville): city in Zaire, and capital of the province of Upper Zaire. At the time of the independence (1960), the Muslims were among the first to form a nationalist party, sc. the "Mouvement National Congolais".

Kish: town of medieval Transoxiana, now Shahr (Shahr-i Sabz) in Uzbekistan. The town was captured by the Arabs in 676, and again in 710. In the viiith c. the Kish district figured prominently in the anti-Muslim religious movement of Hashim b. Hakim, known as al-Muqanna' "the Veiled Prophet of Khurasan". Tamerlane was born in the Kish district in 1336, and he made the town his summer residence and the second capital of his empire after Samarqand. It was captured by the Russians in 1870 and handed over to the khan of Bukhara.

Kitab al-Jilwa ("The Book of Revelation"): one of the two sacred books of the Yazidis. With the *Mushafrash*, it contains the fundamentals of their religion. Though the religious language of the Yazidis is Kurdish, and all their prayers known are in that language, their two sacred books are in Arabic. However, the *Kitab al-Jilwa* might have been originally written in Kurdish.

Konya (A./T. *Qūniya*): city and district in central Turkey, known in antiquity as Iconium. During the centuries of Arab invasion, Konya was a Byzantine military base which the attackers seem for this reason to have avoided and circumvented. The real development of the town dates from the reign of the Rum Saljuq Mas'ud I, who made it his capital. In 1190 the emperor Frederick Barbarossa and the Third Crusaders temporarily occupied the town. From the middle of the xiiith c. the prestige of Jalal al-Din Rumi added to its importance. The progressive establishment of the Mongol protectorate over Saljuq Anatolia in the xiiith c. was prejudicial to the importance of Konya. Political activity was transferred to the Turkmen principalities. The town was definitely annexed to the Ottoman state in 1475 and gradually became a provincial centre.

Konya is famous for its monuments, many of which are heavily restored. They date from the early xiiith c., when the Rum Saljuq sultanate flourished because of the trade relations with the Italian city-states, flourishing after the ports of Antalya and Sinope had been taken.

Köprülü: family of Ottoman viziers who rose to prominence in the latter half of the xviith c. and dominated Ottoman life for much of that period, bringing a halt for some time to the decline of the empire, instituting internal reforms and gaining new conquests. The leading members of the family were Köprülü Mehmed Pasha (?1578-1661); his elder son Fadil Ahmed Pasha (Abu 'l-ʿAbbas) (1635-1676); his younger son Fadil Mustafa Pasha (1637-1691); ʿAmuja-zade Huseyin Pasha, nephew of Mehmed Pasha (d. 1702) and Nuʿman Pasha, the eldest son of Fadil Mustafa Pasha (1670-1719).

Köprülü (Köprülü-zade)**, Mehmed Fuad**: prominent Turkish scholar; 1890-1966. He was the pioneer of Turkish studies in the modern sense.

Korča (Ott. T. *Görije*): urban centre in southeastern Albania, founded by the Ottomans in 1486. During the French occupation in 1916, a short-lived "Republic of Korča" was proclaimed.

Kordofan: region of the Republic of the Sudan lying west of the White Nile. The earliest Arab penetration probably took place in the xivth c. Between the xvith and xixth c. the region was dominated by the Funj, the Musabbaʿat, and by Dar Fur. Turco-Egyptian rule was established in 1821 and lasted until 1885. Events in Kordofan contributed decisively to the success of the Mahdist Revolution between 1885 and 1898. In the latter year the region came under Anglo-Egyptian Condominium rule, which lasted until Sudan became independent on January 1, 1956.

Köroghlu: rebel of the Anatolian Jelali movement in the xvith c. and the hero of a popular romance.

Köse Dagh: land-corridor in Turkey to the north-west of Sivas, where the decisive battle of 1243 took place between the Mongols and the Saljuqs. It opened up Asia Minor to the Mongols and sounded the knell for the Saljuq sultanate of Rum.

Kösem Walide (Kösem Sultan) (Mahpaykar): wife of the Ottoman sultan Ahmed I and mother of the sultans Murad IV and Ibrahim I; ca. 1589-1651. She was Greek by birth, and achieved power in the first place through the harem, exercising a decisive influence in the state during the reigns of her two sons and of her grandson Mehemmed IV.

Kosovo (T. *Qoṣowa*): an upland plain in Serbia. It was the scene of two significant battles in the struggles between the Ottomans and the Christian powers. The defeat in 1389 of the Serbian prince Lazar Gresljanović by the Ottoman sultan Murad I led to the complete encirclement of the Byzantine Empire. The second battle took place in 1448 when an Hungarian army under János Hunyadi was defeated by Sultan Murad II. Between 1775 and 1830, the Kosovo district was involved in various attempts by local governors to break away from control by the Porte. In 1912 the region passed into Serbian hands, the population consisting of a vast majority of Muslim Turks and Albanians. After the First World War, the region came within the new Yugoslavian state, and the Muslim population shrank with the exodus to Albania and Turkey. Since 1945, however, there has been considerable Muslim Albanian immigration.

Kota Kota (Ngotangota): town in central Malawi, on the west side of Lake Malawi (Lake Nyasa). In the xixth c. it was an effective centre for the dissemination of Islam.

Kotoko: people of Black Africa living south of Lake Chad. In the xvith c. the northern principalities, Makari and Afade, were brought under the cultural and Islamic influence of the Kanuri, while the ruler of the southern Kotoko was converted to Islam towards the end of the xviiith c. Most of the Kotoko are now considered Muslims, and the number of those more fully committed to Islam grows steadily.

Kotonou (Cotonou): capital of the People's Republic of Benin (former Dahomey). In the 1920s there was a Muslim minority, consisting of Senegalese, Hausa and Yoruba. In 1955 the Muslim Union of Dahomey was formed.

Kouandé: regional capital in Benin. Islamisation, at the beginning of the xxth c., was very superficial. Only the community of foreign merchants was Muslim. Since then, the influence of the Tijaniyya order has developed considerably.

Krujë: town in northern Albania. Under the Ottoman administration it was officially known as Aq Hisar. Throughout the xixth and early xxth c. it was the scene of various anti-Ottoman rebellions and during the general insurrection of 1912, which led to the proclamation of Albanian independence, Krujë was one of the major centres of anti-Ottoman activities. The town was inhabited by Muslims exclusively, the majority of whom belonged to the Bektashiyya order.

Kubafolo (Bafilo): centre of the administrative region of Northern Togo. When the Germans arrived in 1847, there were already several mosques, and Islamisation has continued ever since.

Kubra, Shaykh Abu 'l-Jannab: eponymous founder of the Kubrawiyya Sufi order; 1145-1220. The order was one of the major ones of the Mongol period in Central Asia and Khurasan.

Kubu: sub-district of Pontianak in Western Kalimantan (Borneo), Indonesia. The family which ruled this area until 1958 was of Arab descent originating from Hadhramaut. The founder of the kingdom was Sayyid Idrus al-Idrus who settled there ca. 1780, shortly after his brother-in-law, the Arab adventurer Sharif 'Abd al-Rahman al-Qadri, had founded the sultanate of Pontianak.

Kučak Khan Jangali, Mirza (Shaykh Yunus): Persian revolutionary from Rasht; 1880-1921. He took an active interest in the idea of Pan-Islamism, and proclaimed the Socialist Republic of Gilan in 1920.

Küčük Qaynarja: village in northeastern Bulgaria which gave its name to the famous Treaty of July 1774 between the Ottoman and Russian Empires. The Treaty brought to an end a disastrous war over the partition of Poland. It contained terms which were uniformly regrettable in their consequences for the Ottoman state and, in particular, for the khanate of the Crimea.

Küčük Sa'id Pasha: Ottoman statesman; 1838-1914. He was seven times Grand Vizier under Sultan Abdülhamid II, and twice in the Young Turk era.

Kufa (A. *al-Kūfa*): city in Iraq, founded by Sa'd b. Abi Waqqas in 638 after the whole of Iraq had been wrested from the hands of the Sasanians. It participated actively in the Islamic expansion into Iranian territory, and, throughout the viith c., was a hotbed of intense political ferment. It took part in the revolt against the Caliph 'Uthman b. 'Affan, supported 'Ali for the battle of the Camel and for that of Siffin, saw the origin of the Khariji movement and witnessed many pro-Shi'i revolts. Kufa was the brain behind the pro-'Abbasid movement, and it was at its Great Mosque that the first 'Abbasid caliph, Abu 'l-'Abbas al-Saffah, was solemnly invested in 749. It remained the capital of the 'Abbasids until the founding of Baghdad in 762. But Kufa equally underwent numerous rounds of Khariji assaults. In the xth c. it was sacked several times by the Carmathians, after which Kufa experienced decline. This abundance of insurrections, of seditious actions and political events earned it the reputation of a turbulent, and, for the later Shi'i consciousness, of a martyr city. Kufa exported its Shi'ism to the Iranian world, to Qumm in particular.

Kufa also held a prominent place in the gestation of Arabo-Islamic civilisation and culture. It gave its name to the monumental writing, known as Kufic script, and the first glimmerings of Law, Tradition and Exegesis took place here. Ascetism and mysticism, canon law, Qur'an "reading" and the study of history and grammar were practised in Kufa.

Today only a few traces remain, mostly of late date or restored.

Kuhistan (A. *Qūhistān* = A. *al-Jibāl*): the Persian name means a mountainous country and has been given to many more or less extensive areas of the Iranian plateau. The principal districts of this name are Kuhistan-i Khurasan, the region which stretches south of Nishapur as far as Sistan; Kuhistan Abi Ghanim and another Kuhistan in the province of Kirman. There is the Kuhistan of Kabul in Afghanistan, and a Kuhistan in the northern part of the native state of Swat in the north-west of India. Finally, Kuhistan is the name of a mountainous region in the eastern part of the district of Karachi.

al-Kulayni (al-Kulini)**, Abu Ja'far Muhammad**: Imami transmitter of traditions; d. 940. His work, known as *al-Kāfī*, is mostly a collection of traditions of the Imams. It gained popularity through the influence of Muhammad b. al-Hasan al-Tusi, and became to be considered one of the most authoritative collections of traditions on which Imami jurisprudence is based.

al-Kumayt b. Zayd al-Asadi: Arab poet of Kufa; 680-743. His renown, maintained by Shi'i circles, rests on his praises aimed principally at the Prophet and at 'Ali and his descendants.

al-Kurani, Ibrahim b. al-Shahrazuri: scholar and mystic of Kurdistan; 1615-1690. Because of his special relationship with the Achehnese 'Abd al-

Raʾūf al-Sinkili, he had an important influence on the development of Islam in what is now Indonesia.

Kurbuqa (Kur-bugha)**, Abu Saʿid**: Turkish commander of the Saljuq period and lord of Mosul; d. 1102.

Kurd ʿAli, Muhammad Farid: Syrian journalist, scholar and man of letters; 1876-1953. He is the author of a monumental history of Syria, and was the first president of the Arab Academy in Syria.

al-Kurdi, Muhammad Amin: one of the leading figures in the recent history of the Naqshbandiyya order, and author of several influential works; d. 1914.

Kurds/Kurdistan: the Kurds are an Iranian people who live mainly at the junction of more or less laicised Turkey, Shiʿi Iran, Arab Sunni Iraq and North Syria, and the former Soviet Transcaucasia. The name "Land of the Kurds" seems to date from the time of the Saljuq Sultan Sanjar. The Kurds played an important part in the history of the Near East. Several dynasties, such as the Marwanids of Diyarbakr, the Ayyubids, the Shaddadids and probably the Safawids, as well as prominent personalities, were of Kurdish origin. The Treaty of Sèvres (1920) had foreseen an independent Kurdistan, but the idea was suppressed by the Treaty of Lausanne (1923).

Kusayla (Kasila) **b. Lamzam**: one of the most eminent figures in the struggle of the Berbers to preserve their independence during the Arab conquest in the viith c.

Kush: the Biblical personage is not named in the Qurʾan. Islamic tradition knows his name but supplies pieces of evidence which do not agree totally with one another or with the evidence of the Bible. From this name the word Cushitic/Kushitic is derived, under which are grouped a body of Hamitic languages spoken by about fifteen million people, the majority of them Muslims. The area in which they live is constituted basically by the Horn of Africa and spreads in the north into Sudanese and Egyptian territory and in the south into Tanzania.

Kushiyar b. Laban: Persian astronomer and mathematician; xth-xith c. His fame rests on his *Roots of the Indian system of calculation*, i.e. of the system of numeration by position, the value of the figures depending on their place in a number. This brought about a revolution in the ways of calculating used in the Near East.

Kutai: regency in the Indonesian province of East Kalimantan. Islam was introduced from Makassar in the first years of the xviith c.

al-Kutubi, Abu ʿAbd Allah: Syrian historian; ca. 1287-1363. His two surviving works are a large history containing valuable observations on Syrian intellectual and religious life, and a biographical work, which contains a wealth of literary information, mainly on Syrian littérateurs.

Kuwait (A. *al-Kuwayt*): capital city of an amirate of the same name, situated on the Arabian shore at the head of the Persian Gulf. At the end of the xviith c. a group of 'Utub Arabs migrated into the area. According to local tradition the three clans of this group, the Al Sabah, the Al Khalifa, and the Al Jalahima, were expelled from their previous settlements near Umm Qasr by the Ottomans. By the middle of the xviiith c., the Al Sabah had achieved a position of local dominance. The Al Khalifa left Kuwait in 1766 and migrated to Qatar before taking control of Bahrain in 1783. The Al Jalahima left Kuwait later and went to Qatar.

The relations of Kuwait with the Ottomans authorities in Iraq were uneasy. Occasionally, the Ottomans were able to exercise some sort of sovereignty. In 1900 Shaykh Mubarak opposed the Germans plans to make Kuwait the terminus of the projected Berlin-Baghdad railway.

In 1913 the Ottomans and the British completed a draft convention in which Kuwait was recognised as an autonomous district within the Ottoman Empire, and in which the land frontiers of Kuwait were laid down. In 1914 the British government recognised Kuwait as an independent government under British protection.

In 1922 a Convention was signed at al-'Uqayr between the clans of Al Sabah and the Al Sa'ud in which a fixed frontier between Kuwait and Saudi Arabia was established, the new territory of Kuwait being much smaller than that mentioned in the draft Anglo-Ottoman convention of 1913.

In April 1923 the British High Commissioner for Iraq recognised the frontier between Kuwait and Iraq as being that of the convention of 1913, which however had not been ratified. In 1961, when Kuwait became a fully-independent state, the government of Iraq claimed that Kuwait was rightfully an integral part of Iraq. The dispute was debated by the Security Council of the United Nations. In the same year 1961 Kuwait was admitted to the League of Arab States and that body resolved to preserve the independence of its new member. In 1963 Kuwait became a member of the United Nations. Iraq's claim to Kuwait resulted in a number of border skirmishes and, on 2 August 1990, the capturing of Kuwait by Iraqi forces. During the Gulf War of 1991 Iraq was defeated and Kuwait liberated by a multinational political alliance that included forces from NATO and several Arab countries.

L

Labid b. Rabi'a, Abu 'Aqil: Arab poet; d. 660. He is said to have become a Muslim in 630 when his tribe, the 'Amir b. Sa'sa'a, made an agreement with the Prophet. One of Labid's *qaṣīdas* was adopted into the collection of the so-called *Mu'allaqāt* and is thought to be one of the best specimens of Bedouin poetry.

Laccadives: group of coral islands in the southeastern Arabian Sea lying off the Malabar Coast of India. Since 1956 they have formed the Indian Union Territory of Lakshadweep. There has been a sustained Arab, particularly Yemeni, influence as the islands lie on the direct sea route between Arabia, South India and the Far East. As a result the islanders write in the Arabic script. They were converted to Islam in the xiiith c.

Lahijan: town in the Caspian coastal province of Gilan in northwestern Iran. Zaydi Shi'ism was introduced by the 'Alid Nasir al-Din al-Utrush (d. 917), the founder of a family who ruled in Biya-pish. They were in turn followed by the local Nasirwands (till 1390), and the Kar-Qiya'i Sayyids (till 1592). The founder of the Safawid dynasty Isma'il I, when a fugitive from the Aq Qoyunlu in 1494, fled to Lahijan, which was incorporated into the Safawid empire in 1592 after the Kar-Qiya'i Sayyid Ahmad b. 'Ali had been intriguing with the Ottomans.

Lahore: principal city of the Punjab, Pakistan. In the xth c. it was subject to the Qurayshite ruler of Multan, and became in the xith c. the second capital of the Ghaznawid empire. In 1241 Lahore was taken and sacked by the Mongols. In the xvith c. it was occupied by the Mughals but soon afterwards it came under Afghan rule. With the restoration of Mughal rule under Humayun in 1555, the city entered the era of its greatest prosperity. The principal monuments, among which can be admired the Fort, mosques, tombs, gardens and gateways, belong to the Mughal period.

Lahut and Nasut: two terms meaning divinity (or deity) and humanity, and forming a pair which plays an important role in the theology of certain Muslim mystics and in the theosophical conceptions of the extremist Shi'is.

Lahuti, Abu 'l-Qasim: Persian Communist poet and revolutionary of Kirmanshah; 1887-1957. He has been rightly acclaimed as one of the founders of Soviet Tajik poetry.

Lak: the most southern group of Kurd tribes in Persia, from which the Zand dynasty arose.

Lakhm: Arab tribe, especially influential in the pre-Islamic period. In Islamic times, the term "Lakhmi" became a title of honour.

Lakhmids: pre-islamic Arab dynasty of Iraq that made al-Hira its capital and ruled it from ca. 300 till 600. They were Sasanian clients and semi-independent kings.

Lakhnawti: ancient city which served as the principal seat of government in Bengal under Muslim rule from ca. 1200 till 1600. In the xvith c. it is described as a large and prosperous town. Its magnificent buildings could still be seen in 1683.

Lalish: valley to the northeast of Mosul in Iraq, famed as the principal pilgrimage centre of the Yazidis.

Lam, Banu: numerous and formerly powerful Arab tribe living on the borders of Iran and Iraq. At the beginning of the xxth c. all members spoke Arabic, but a minority also knew and used Persian. The great majority is Shi'i. In the xviiith c. they joined forces with Nadir Shah Afshar. Many punitive military expeditions were organised against them by the Ottomans. They retained in general a position of autonomy between the Ottoman empire and Persia.

Lamech (A. *Lamak*): in Gen. IX, 21, the invention of music is attributed to Jubal, son of Lamech, but various Arabic sources give primacy to Lamak, of Cain's posterity.

Lamas-su: small river of southern Anatolia where Muslims and Byzantines often assembled for exchanges of prisoners.

Lami'i, Shaykh Mahmud: celebrated Ottoman Sufi writer and poet; 1472-1531. He introduced fresh themes into Turkish literature. Of his works about thirty titles are known.

Lamtuna: great Berber tribe belonging to the branch of the Sanhaja. They already formed a considerable kingdom in the viiith c. and became Muslim, at first only nominally, in the ixth c.

al-Lamtuni, Abu Bakr al-Sanhaji: war leader of the Almoravids and, above all, the real founder of Marrakesh; d. 1075.

Lamu: town, island and archipelago off the East African coast, Kenya. The earliest dedicatory inscription, found in a mosque, is dated 1370. Lamu came under the nominal control of Oman after 1698, but this was not effectively exercised until 1812. In the xixth c. new mosques were dedicated. In the xxth c. it emerged as the most important Islamic religious centre in eastern Africa.

Lanbasar: one of the Isma'ili fortresses in northwestern Iran, which guarded the approaches to Alamut. It surrendered to the Mongols in 1258.

Laq: Muslim people of the Caucasus. Their final conversion to Islam occurred in the xiiith c.

Lar/Larijan: region of northern Iran. At the time of the conquest of Rayy in 643, the Lar agreed conditionally to the payment of the poll-tax and the land-tax. The later governors accorded a warm welcome to the 'Alids.

Lar/Laristan: the name denotes an important town and region of Fars, Iran, and an island and an islet in the Persian Gulf. The inhabitants of Laristan are mainly Sunnis and members of Sunni dervish orders, the Twelver Shi'a being only implanted to a partial extent.

Laranda, modern **Karaman**: provincial town in Anatolia, Turkey. It fell to the Saljuqs after the battle of Malazgird in 1071, then to the Danishmendids, and was retaken by the Saljuq Qilij Arslan II in 1165. Having been in the hands of Frederick Barbarossa and of Leo II of the Armenian kingdom in Cilicia, it was regained by the Saljuqs in 1216. In 1256 it became the capital of the Ilek-Khans who resisted the Saljuqs and the Il-Khans. After 1300 its name was changed into Karaman (Qaraman). In 1397 the Ottoman sultan Bayezid I occupied the town, but Tamerlane restored the Qaramanids to power. In 1468 Laranda/Karaman was definitely conquered by the Ottomans, who destroyed a number of monumental buildings, sacred and profane. The town is yet renowned for its citadel and fortifications, mosques, madrasas, khanqahs, mausolea, baths and fountains.

al-Lari, Muhammad b. Salah (Muslih al-Din): Persian scholar and historian; ca. 1510-1572. He wrote on philosophy and astronomy, on Qur'an and Tradition, and composed a widely-known universal history.

Larin: a silver coin current in the Persian Gulf and Indian Ocean in the xvith and xviith c. It took its name from Lar in Fars, Iran, where it was first struck.

Las Navas de Tolosa (A. *al-'Iqāb*): name under which, in the Spanish annals, is known one of the most decisive battles between Islam and Christendom for possession of the Iberian Peninsula. It took place on July 16, 1212. A large Iberian Christian army, supported by considerable forces from Western Europe and led by Alfonso VIII of Castile, defeated an equally numerous Muslim army led by Almohad Caliph Muhammad al-Nasir.

al-Lat: name of one of the three most venerated deities of the pre-Islamic pantheon, the two others being Manat and al-'Uzza. The deep attachment felt by the Banu Thaqif towards al-Lat, by the Aws and the Khazraj towards Manat, and by the Quraysh towards al-'Uzza, constituted the greatest obstacle in the path of the peaceful implantation of Islam in the regions of the Hejaz.

Latifi, 'Abd al-Latif Čelebi: Turkish biographer, littérateur and poet; 1491-1582. His *Biographies of the Poets* is generally considered, after 'Ashiq Čelebi's, to be the second finest biographical work in Ottoman literature.

Laudatory literature (A. *faḍā'il*, s. *faḍīla*): a genre which elaborates the excellence of individuals, groups, places, things, and regions in order to praise them.

Law, Canon (A. *sharī'a*): the Arabic term can be described as the totality of God's commandments relating to the activities of man. According to the orthodox view, the Shari'a is the basis for the judgement of actions as good and bad, which accordingly can only come from God. According to the Mu'tazila, it only confirms the verdict of the intelligence which has preceded it. The Shari'a regulates only the external relations of man to God and his fellow-men and ignores his inner consciousness; it demands, and is only concerned with, the fulfilment of the prescribed outer forms. It thus stands in contrast to the conscience and religious feeling of responsibility of the individual and his inner relation to God, and it is therefore not sufficient to simply fulfil all the commandments of the Shari'a.

The knowledge of it was originally obtained directly from Qur'an and Tradition, but later among the Sunnis no one was considered qualified to investigate these sources independently. Such a knowledge is authoritatively communicated to later generations through the system of religious jurisprudence (A. *fiqh*). A result of the development of Fiqh has been that there is no codification of the Law in the modern sense. At the same time the Fiqh books are practically "law books" for the orthodox Muslim. God's Law has to be accepted without criticism, as wisdom into which it is impossible to enquire. It is based on God's will which is bound by no principles, therefore evasions are considered a permissible use of means put at man's disposal by God himself. Law thus comprises as an infallible doctrine of ethics the whole religious, political, social, domestic and private life of those who profess Islam.

All the prescriptions of the Shari'a are not to be taken as absolute commands or prohibitions. Five legal categories of prescriptions are distinguished: obligatory, meritorious, permitted or indifferent, reprehensible, and forbidden.

Lawata, Banu: important Berber ethnic group who are known to have been living in Egypt, Barqa (Cyrenaica), Tripolitania, Tunisia, Algeria, Morocco, Mauritania and Sicily.

al-Lawati, Abu Muhammad 'Abd Allah: noted Ibadi historian, transmitter of traditions, biographer and poet; xith c. He wrote a work on the history of the North African Ibadiyya and taught Ibadi history to numerous pupils.

al-Layth b. Sa'd: transmitter of traditions and a jurisconsult of Persian origin in Egypt; 713-791. He is ranked unanimously among the leading authorities on questions of religious knowledge in the early years of the Islamic Empire.

Laz: people of South Caucasian stock, now dwelling in the southeastern corner of the shores of the Black Sea, in the region called in Ottoman times Lazistan.

Lebanon (A. *Lubnān*): middle Eastern country. After their conquest of Syria in 1516, the Ottomans, following the example of their predecessors, had retained the administrative divisions which were based on ethnic distribution. In the xviith c. the Ottomans conducted campaigns against the Druze amir of the leading Ma'n family Fakhr al-Din II. A new *pashalik*, whose governor resided at Sidon, was created. In 1821 amir Bashir Shihab al-Din II sought alliance with Muhammad 'Ali Pasha of Egypt. But in 1840 Muhammad 'Ali's son Ibrahim Pasha had to leave the region with his Egyptian army. With the support of a British military expedition, Turkey re-established its authority, recognised in the Treaty of London. In 1860, after a conflict between Druzes and Christians, Napoleon III sent a French expeditionary force and in an agreement of 1861 the Ottoman sultan declared that Lebanon would be administered by a Christian governor, to be chosen from among the non-Lebanese subjects of the sultan.

The modern State of Lebanon was proclaimed in September 1920 by General Gouraud, High Commissioner of the French Republic to the Levant. In 1923 the Council of the League of Nations placed the Lebanon under a mandate entrusted to France, and in 1941 General Catroux, on behalf of the leadership of Free France, recognised the country as a sovereign and independent State. The National Pact of 1943 was a decisive factor for the position of the Muslims in Lebanon. In 1945 Lebanon was among the founders of the League of Arab States. Civil war broke out in 1975, and in 1976 Syria, under an Arab League mandate, sent troops in order to restore calm.

Lebaran: name generally used in Indonesia for the festival of Breaking the Fast (A. *ʿĪd al-Fiṭr*).

Lemnos (T. *Limni*): Greek island in the northern part of the Aegean Sea. In the Middle Ages it was part of the Byzantine Empire, but suffered the depredations of Arab corsairs from Crete in the xth c. and of the Saljuqs in the xith c. It became an Ottoman fief after the fall of Constantinople in 1453, but remained subject to papal and Venetian attacks. At the Treaty of Lausanne (1923) the island was recognized formally by the Republic of Turkey as not belonging to its territory.

Leo Africanus: the name by which the author of the *Descrittione dell' Africa* is generally known, his original name being al-Hasan b. Muhammad al-Wazzan al-Zayyati (or al-Fasi); 1489-ca. 1555. Returning from the pilgrimage to Mecca, he was captured by Sicilian corsairs. They presented him to Pope Leo X who baptized him in 1520. Before 1550 he returned to Tunis, and probably spent the last years of his life in his ancestral faith. The *Descrittione* remained for centuries a major source on the Islamic world, and is still cited by historians and geographers of Africa.

León (A. *Liyūn*): the medieval kingdom in northeast and central Spain lost much of its lands to the Arabs during the xth c. It is mentioned only rarely by the Arab geographers.

Lepanto (T. *Aynabakhti*): the famous sea-battle near the Oxia islands in the Gulf of Patras, Greece, took place on October 7, 1571.

Leprosy (A. *judhām*): the Qur'an mentions the healing of the lepers by Jesus. According to a tradition attributed to the Prophet, a Muslim should flee from the leper as he would flee from a lion.

Lérida (A. *Lārida*): town to the west of Barcelona. It was taken by the Muslims in the viiith c., and surrendered to Catalan chieftains in 1149.

Lesbos (T. *Midilli* = Mytilene): Greek island in the Aegean Sea. It was raided by Shuʿayb I b. ʿUmar (r. 855-880) of Crete and was under Muslim dominance between 1089 and 1093. It was ruled by the Genoese Gattilusi family until its conquest by the Ottomans in 1462. Ottoman rule ended in 1912 by Greek annexation, and the Turkish inhabitants left as part of the population exchange in the 1920s.

Lewend: name given to two kinds of Ottoman daily-wage irregular militia, one sea-going, the other land-based. The word may derive in its maritime sense from the Italian *levantino*.

Liberia: republic on the West African coast. Muslims account for 15-20% of the population, concentrated mainly between Monrovia and Robertsport on the frontier of Sierra Leone as well as on the frontier of Guinea.

Library (A. *maktaba*; P. *kitāb-khāna*; T. *kütüphane*): the Caliph Muʿawiya I established at Damascus a public library which contained collections of traditions. The library at Baghdad, known by the name of "House of Wisdom" but often called "Treasury of Wisdom", had existed since the times of Caliph Harun al-Rashid and the Barmakids, who had begun to have Greek works translated. The ʿAbbasid Caliph al-Maʾmun had valuable Greek manuscripts purchased in the Byzantine Empire and translated into Arabic. The period of the "House of Wisdom" was followed by that of the "House of Science", established in the style of a public library. They were set up in Baghdad, Mosul, Basra, Damascus, Aleppo and other cities in Syria, and in Egypt. Celebrated libraries were those attached to the Nizamiyya and the Mustansiriyya madrasas in Baghdad. The library of the Fatimid Caliph al-Hakim is stated to have contained 6,500 volumes, and a globe of copper said to have been constructed by Ptolemy.

Under the Spanish Umayyad Caliph al-Hakam I the library at Córdoba is said to have contained some 400,000 volumes. After the conquest of Granada in 1492 the order was given that all useful works of philosophy, medicine and history in the possession of the Moriscos might be retained. Cardinal Cisneros, however, decreed that all books in Arabic should be burnt.

In Persia, libraries are recorded during the ʿAbbasid period at Ram-Hurmuz, Rayy and Isfahan. In Shiraz the Great Saljuq ʿAdud al-Dawla (r. 1063-1072) founded a library which contained a copy of all books written up to that time in all branches of learning. Untold quantities of priceless books were destroyed when the Mongols swept over Persia in the xiiith c.

In India many of the Mughal emperors and their courtiers were dedicated bibliophiles. The imperial library was dispersed after the Indian Mutiny of 1857. Some came to the India Office Library and the Royal Asiatic Society in England, but many remained at Patna and Calcutta.

In Turkey, the Ottoman Sultan Mehemmed II, after the conquest of Constantinople in 1453, assembled manuscripts which now are in the Topkapi Palace. Most of the libraries formerly attached to mosques in the capital are now in the Süleymaniyye Public Library. In 1959 over 135,000 manuscripts were said to be in Istanbul. Most countries in the Middle East now possess a national library which also publishes national bibliographies.

Libya (A. *Lībiyā*): republic of North Africa. The first Muslim attacks into Cyrenaica and Tripolitania took place from Egypt in 642 and the country has remained Muslim ever since. In the xvith c. Libya came under Ottoman domination. Italy invaded the Libyan littoral in 1911, but the Accord of al-Rajma of 1920 recognised Muhammad Idris al-Sanusi as the independent ruler of the interior oases. Italy resumed full-scale war in 1922, but was defeated in 1943. Libya became independent in 1951 under King Idris I al-Sanusi, who was deposed in 1969 by a group of army officers led by Col. Muammar Qadafi. In 1977 the country was renamed "the Masses' Republic".

The name of Libya is also linked to the well-known Libyco-Berber inscriptions, whose alphabet still poses problems.

Lighthouse (A. *manār(a)*): the ancient Arabs used fire to guide caravans, convoys and individuals. Arab geographers mention a more enduring lighthouse near Basra and the famous lighthouse of Alexandria on the islet of Pharos. The Byzantine Greek diminutive *phanarion* led to Turkish *fanār/fener*, which in its turn gave Arabic *fanār*.

Linen (A. *kattān*): until the Middle Ages Egypt remained famous for its flax and linen fabrics. The Persian province of Fars was another important centre for flax and linen industry. A coarse, loose linen (A. *khaysh*) made with flax of poor quality was used in the manufacture of sacks, wrappings and rudimentary tents.

Lipqa (Lubqa): name given to the Tatars who since the xivth c. inhabited Lithuania, and later the eastern and southeastern lands of old Poland up to Podolia, and after 1672 also partly Moldavia and Dobruja.

Liu Chih (Liu Chiai-lien): Chinese Muslim scholar who was active as translator, theologian, philosopher and biographer of the Prophet; xviiith c.

Liyaqat 'Ali Khan: the first Prime Minister of Pakistan; 1895-1951. From 1936-1947 he was honorary secretary of the All-India Muslim league. He became Prime Minister in 1947.

Lodis: Afghan tribe and dynasty which ruled over parts of north India between 1451 and 1526. The first ruler Bahlul (r. 1451-1489) captured Delhi in 1451. He saw himself as a chief of chiefs rather than an absolute autocrat, but his son Sikandar II (r. 1489-1517) considered himself a fully-fledged Sultan. Sultan Ibrahim II (r. 1517-1526) fell in battle, and the sultanate passed into the hands of the Mughals.

Logic (A. *manṭiq*): like the Greeks, the Arab-Muslim thinkers recognised that there is a connection between logic and grammar. It was discussed by Ibn Hazm, by theologians like the Hanbalites and the Ash'arites, and by philosophers like Fakhr al-Din al-Razi and al-Farabi. It is also treated by the Ikhwan al-Safa', and plays a part in the judicial sciences.

Lombok: island belonging to the Indonesian province of the Western Smaller Sunda Islands. Islam was introduced among the Sasaks, the main population group, in the xvith c.

Love poetry (A. *ghazal*; *nasīb*): *ghazal* denotes the independent love poem as distinguished from the amatory prologue (A. *nasīb*) of the *qaṣīda*. In Arabic poetry, the *ghazal* flourished from the vith through the xiith c.

In Neo-Persian lyrics, the *ghazal* was one of the most common themes. Its classical period falls between the xiiith and xvith c. It was followed by the so-called Indian style, which lasted until the xviiith c. and which greatly influenced the *ghazal* in Urdu.

In Turkish literature too, the *ghazal* became the model, both in Chaghatay (Eastern) and Ottoman (Western) Turkish.

Lucknow (A. *Lakhnaw*): capital city of the Indian state of Uttar Pradesh. The known history of the city can be traced to the beginning of the xiiith c. when it was colonised by the Shaykhs. The shrine of Shaykh Muhammad, known as Shah Mina, became a place of pilgrimage. After suffering from frequent Afghan incursions, Lucknow passed into the Mughal dominion under Humayun. The Emperor Akbar had a special fascination for the city. Most of Lucknow's glorious past, however, is connected with the dynasty of the Nawwabs of Awadh. The period of Nawwab Asaf al-Dawla (d. 1797), the extravagance and munificence of whose court passed into a byword, marks the greatest height of Lucknow's prosperity. Next to its gilded domes, mosques, palaces and tombs, Lucknow is famous for its so-called *čikan* embroidery and for the refinement of its contribution to Urdu poetry. The city played a role in the Sepoy Mutiny of 1857, and in 1916 meetings were held there which resulted in the famous Lucknow Pact between the Indian National Congress and the All-India Muslim League.

Luʾluʾ ("pearl"): noun often given to a person of servile origin, a guard, an officer or a leader of a special body of slave servants (A. *ghulām*, pl. *ghilmān*) in the service of a prince. A well-known personality of this name is Luʾluʾ al-Kabir al-Jarrahi al-Sayfi, chamberlain at the Hamdanid court of Aleppo; d. 1009.

Luqman: legendary hero and sage of pre-Islamic Arabia. He appears in the Qurʾan as a monotheist and a wise father giving pious admonitions to his son. In later Islamic lore, he became the creator of fables par excellence and a striking parallel of Aesop.

Luqman b. Sayyid Huseyin: Ottoman poet and historian who wrote in Persian and Turkish; d. 1601.

Lur-i Buzurg: dynasty of atabegs which flourished in eastern and southern Luristan between 1155 and 1423, the capital of which was Idhaj or Malamir.

Luristan (Lorestan "Land of the Lurs"): region in southwestern Iran.

Lurs (P. *Lor*): Iranian people living in the mountains of Luristan. In the xixth c. their religion was considered to be little orthodox, even from a Shiʿi point of view. Their tribes, especially the Bakhtiyaris, have a rich popular literature.

Lute (A. *al-ʿūd*): it is the most important musical instrument of Islamic peoples from the Atlantic to the Persian Gulf. Arabic authors do not discriminate between the *barbaṭ* and the *ʿūd*, but there seems to have been a fundamental distinction between them. The *barbaṭ*, so named by the Persians because it resembled the breast (*bar*) of a duck (*baṭ*), had its sound-chest and neck constructed in one graduated piece, whereas in the *ʿūd* proper the sound-chest and neck were separate. The Arab musician Zalzal (d. 791) invented the lute proper, called the *ʿūd al-shabbūṭ*, so named because it resembled the fish called *shabbūṭ*.

Lutf ʿAli Beg (Adhar): Persian anthologist and poet; 1722-1781. His fame rests primarily on an anthology of the poets of previous times and of the poets of Persia, Turan and Hindustan.

Lutfi: Chaghatay Turkish poet of Harat in western Afghanistan; ca. 1367-1463. He was a great master of the *ghazal* and a close friend of the Persian poet and mystic Jami.

Lutfi Efendi, Ahmed: Ottoman court historiographer and poet; 1816-1907. His most famous work is the continuation of the history of Ahmed Jewdet Pasha. The work, in 15 volumes, covers the events between 1825 and 1876.

Lutfi Pasha: Ottoman statesman and Grand Vizier; ca. 1488-1562. In 1539 he led the negotiations which ended the war with Venice and headed negotiations with the Habsburgs over Ferdinand's claims to territory in Hungary whose issue eventually led to war in 1541.

Lutfi al-Sayyid, Ahmad: Egyptian scholar, statesman and writer; 1872-1963. He campaigned against Pan-Islamism, Pan-Arabism and Pan-Ottomanism and rejected religion as a basis for nationhood.

Lydda/Lod (A. *Ludd*): town in central Israel to the southeast of Jaffa, from ancient times an important station on the eastern branch of the *Via Maris* which runs from Gaza to the Valley of Jezreel. Lydda was conquered by ʿAmr b. al-ʿAs in 637 but was soon overshadowed by Ramla, built by the Umayyad Caliph Sulayman. The town occupies an important place in the Islamic eschatological tradition, perhaps born out of the popular mixture of legends connected with St. George (A. *Jirjīs*) and the false Messiah (A. *dajjāl*).

M

Ma Chung-ying (Ğa Ssu-ling): youngest and best-known of the Chinese Muslim warlords; ca. 1910-ca. 1938. These warlords comprised the "Mu Wa" clique which controlled much of northwest China during the latter half of the Republican Period (1911-1949).

Ma Hua-lung (Ma Ch'ao-ching): Chinese Muslim leader; d. 1871. He was an exponent of the "New Teaching", a neo-orthodox reformist movement in Chinese Islam in northwest China in the latter half of the xviiith c. He played an important part in the great mid-xixth c. Muslim risings against the Ch'ing dynasty.

Ma Huan: Chinese Muslim interpreter and traveller; ca. 1380-1460. He is the author of an account of the Ming Chinese maritime expeditions to Southeast Asia, South Asia, the Arabian Peninsula and East Africa.

Ma Ming-hsin (Muhammad Amin): Chinese Muslim leader; d. 1781. He was instrumental in the development and spread of the "New Teaching".

Maʾ al-ʿAynayn al-Qalqami: scholar and religious and political leader of the Western Sahara; 1831-1910. He organized a desert community, combined the roles of doctor, teacher, arbitrator and avenger, and wrote some 300 books. At least 30 of his major works are about Sufism.

al-Ma'afiri, Abu 'l-Hasan 'Ali: Andalusian Maliki scholar; d. 1208. He is the author of a work called *Biographies of Famous Women* which deals primarily with women from the Umayyad period.

Ma'an (Mu'an): town of the south of Jordan which became a station on the Hejaz railway. The name is said to come from Ma'an, son of Lot.

Ma'arrat Masrin (Misrin): small town in northern Syria. It was conquered by the Muslims in 637, and played a part during the Crusades.

Ma'arrat al-Nu'man: town in northern Syria. Because of its strategic position it was often disputed between various rulers, among them also the Crusaders. During the French mandate in the Levant, the town became an active centre of resistance for the Syrian nationalists. Among its monuments are the city wall, the Great Mosque, madrasas, caravanserais and sanctuaries.

al-Ma'arri, Abu 'l-'Ala' Ahmad: famous Arabic poet and prose author from Ma'arrat al-Nu'man; 973-1058. He lost his eyesight at the age of four, but the defect was more than compensated by his extraordinary retentive memory. The poems of the first half of his life were collected in his *The first spark of the tinder*. Other famous titles are *The self-imposed compulsion*, relating to a peculiarity of rhyme, *Letter of a horse and a mule*, and *The letter of forgiveness*. A great deal of his work is supposed to have been lost during the Crusades.

Ma'bad b. Wahb: one of the great singers and composers in Umayyad times; d. 743. He was the leading musician of the Medinan school of music and figures in Arabic poetry as the musician par excellence.

Macedonia (T. *Māqadūnyā*): central part of the Balkan Peninsula lying astride the frontiers of former southern Yugoslavia, northern Greece and southwestern Bulgharia. Ottoman rule was consolidated after 1430. The region acquired a political significance during the xixth c. as a result of the revival of the Christian nationalities and the rival aspirations of Greeks, Serbs and Bulgarians to establish themselves as the Ottoman Empire's prospective successors.

Madagascar (A. *al-Qumr*): island republic located off the southeast coast of Africa. From ca. 1000, Muslim seafarers of the Persian Gulf and the Hadhramaut took part in migrations and in commerce. The first stone-built mosques appeared between the xiith and xivth c. The xivth and xvth c. constituted a golden age for the Muslim settlements in Madagascar and in the xvith c. the slave trade became important. The Muslim population is confined to the northwest coastal region and the southeast, where a tradition of Arabic-Malagasy manuscript writing is perpetuated.

al-Mada'ini, 'Ali b. Muhammad: early Arabic historian; 752-ca. 843. He wrote more than 200 works, an important part of them dealing with subjects that extend from the origins of Islam until his own days.

Madaniyya: branch of the Shadhiliyya Sufi order named after Muhammad b. Hasan al-Madani (d. 1847). During the xixth c. the order spread in Tripolitania, Cyrenaica, Tunisia and Egypt. Al-Madani initiated the future Ottoman Sultan Abdülhamid II into the order.

al-Madhara'i: family of high officials and revenue officers, originating from Iraq, that held important positions in Egypt and Syria between 879 and 946.

Madhhij: large tribal group in Yemen. They played a considerable part in the early Islamic conquests.

Madrasa: in modern usage, the Arabic word is the name of an institution of learning where the Islamic sciences are taught, i.e. a college for higher studies, as opposed to an elementary school of traditional type (A. *kuttāb*). In medieval usage, it was essentially a college of law in which the other Islamic sciences, including literary and philosophical ones, were ancillary only.

Madrid (A. *Majrīṭ*): capital of Spain. The Arabic sources seldom mention the place during the Muslim period. In the xvth c. it is described as a small town with an impregnable fortress and a Friday mosque.

Madura: island north of East Java. The first Muslim rulers probably date from the xvith c. The Madurese generally adhere to Islam, but customary law still exercises its influence.

Madyan Shu'ayb: town of northwestern Arabia, lying inland from the eastern shore of the Gulf of 'Aqaba on the pilgrimage route between the Hejaz and Syria.

al-Maghazi: term which designates in particular the campaigns and raids organised by the Prophet in the Medinan period. The work on the subject is ascribed to al-Waqidi.

Maghila: Berber tribe belonging to the Butr group who lived, in the early Middle Ages, in Algeria and Morocco.

al-Maghili, Mahammad: reformist jurisconsult of Tlemcen; ca. 1440-1503. He is chiefly known for his persecution of the Jewish community of Tuwat (Touat) in the Algerian Sahara and for the advice he gave to Sudanic rulers.

Maghrawa: major confederation of Berber tribes in Morocco, Algeria and Tunisia, belonging to the Butr group and forming the most powerful branch of the family of the Zanata.

(al-)Maghrib: name given by Arab writers to that part of Africa which Europeans have called Barbary or Africa Minor and then North Africa, and which includes Libya, Tunisia, Algeria and Morocco.

al-Maghribi, Banu: family of Persian origin that performed during the xth and xith c. influential functions at several princely courts in Baghdad, Aleppo, Cairo, Mosul and Mayyafariqin.

Magic (A. *siḥr*): the Arabic term occurs very often in the Qur'an. It is explained by the lexica as the turning of a thing from its true nature or form to something else which is unreal. Magic is considered to be a reality, though it may be a dangerous one. Important Arabic authors such as Ibn al-Nadim, al-Ghazali, Fakhr al-Din al-Razi and Ibn Khaldun developed theories about magic.

Magic square (A. *wafq*): a square divided up like a chessboard, each square of which is inscribed with numerals, letters or words. It is worn as a talisman against illness and for all sorts of other purposes, or can be used for all kinds of magic.

Mahabad (Sawj-Bulaq): town and district in the modern Iranian province of Azerbaijan to the south of Lake Urmiya. The town played a prominent part in recent Kurdish history.

Mahallati, Aga Khan, Sayyid Hasan 'Ali Shah: the last of the Nizari Isma'ili Imams to reside in Iran and the first of them to bear the title of Aga; 1804-1881. In 1836 he rebelled against the central Qajar government, and fled to Afghanistan in 1842. He later acquired great wealth in Bombay.

al-Mahalli, Abu 'Ali Jalal al-Din: Egyptian scholar; 1389-1459. He is known above all as co-author of the famous Qur'an commentary called *The Commentary of the two Jalals*, the other author being Jalal al-Din al-Suyuti, who had been al-Mahalli's pupil and completed the work.

al-Mahdi: the Arabic word means "the rightly guided one" and is the name of the restorer of religion and justice who, according to a widely-held Muslim belief, will rule before the end of the world. Throughout Islamic history there has been a recurrence of Mahdi movements. In early days, the best-known Mahdi was Ibn Tumart, the founder of the Almohad movement; in modern times, the Sudanese Muhammad al-Mahdi. In radical Shi'ism, belief in the coming of the Mahdi of the family of the Prophet became a central aspect of the faith.

al-Mahdi, Abu 'Abd Allah Muhammad: 'Abbasid caliph; b. 743, r. 775-785. His reign was in the main a period of peace and prosperity.

al-Mahdi li-Din Allah Ahmad: title and name of a number of Zaydi Imams of Yemen, occurring in the xiiith, xvth and xviith c.

al-Mahdi 'Ubayd Allah: the first "manifested" Isma'ili Imam and the first caliph of the Fatimid dynasty in Ifrīqiya; b. 873, r. 910-934.

Mahdids: dynasty at Zabid in Yemen, 1136-1176. It took its name from the father of the first leader, 'Ali b. Mahdi (d. 1159).

al-Mahdiyya: town in Tunisia which owes its name to its founder al-Mahdi 'Ubayd Allāh.

al-Mahdiyya: movement in the Egyptian Sudan, launched in 1881 by Muhammad al-Mahdi for the reform of Islam. It was continued by 'Abd Allah b. Muhammad al-Ta'a'ishi and came to an end in 1898 with the battle of Karrari, often called the battle of Omdurman.

al-Mahjar (pl. *al-mahājir*): name given in Arabic to places in North, Middle and South America to which Lebanese, Syrian, Palestinian and other Arabs have emigrated (A. *hājara*).

Mahmal (Mahmil/Mihmal): a richly decorated palanquin, perched on a camel and sent, from the xiiith c. onwards, by sovereigns with their caravans of pilgrims to Mecca in order to bolster their prestige. In 1952 the Egyptian *mahmal*, the last still in service, was suppressed by a governmental decision.

Mahmud: name borne by many Islamic personages, among them a great number of sultans and rulers, especially in India.

In Bengal: Mahmud I Nasir al-Din, r. 1442-1459; Mahmud II Nasir al-Din, r. 1459; Mahmud III Ghiyath al-Din, r. 1533-1538.

In the Deccan: Mahmud Shihab al-Din, ruler of the Bahmani dynasty; b. 1479, r. 1482-1518.

In Delhi: Mahmud I Nasir al-Din, r. 1246-1266; Mahmud II Nasir al-Din, r. 1394-1399.

In Gujarat: Mahmud I Sayf al-Din Begarha (Begra), r. 1459-1511; Mahmud II Nasir Khan, r. 1526; Mahmud III Abu 'l-Futuhat, r. 1537-1554.

In Jaunpur: Mahmud Shah Sharqi; r. 1440-1458.

In Malwa (India): Mahmud Khalji I, r. 1434-1469; Mahmud Khalji II, r. 1511-1531.

In Uttar Pradesh: Mahmud Khan Nasir al-Din, the founder of the Kalpi dynasty which lasted from 1389 to 1443; d. 1410.

Among the Ottoman Sultans: Mahmud I Ghazi, r. 1730-1754; Mahmud II r. 1808-1839.

Mahmud II b. Muhammad b. Malik-Shah: Great Saljuq sultan in western Persia and Iraq; b. 1105, r. 1118-1131. A just ruler, he is known for his Arabic scholarship, rare among the Saljuq rulers, and for his patronising many of the leading poets of his time.

Mahmud Nedim Pasha: Ottoman bureaucrat and Grand Vizier; 1817-1883. In 1872 he was dismissed from the Grand Vizierate by Sultan Abdülaziz as a result of Midhat Pasha's energetic representation to the sultan about the harm he was causing. In 1875 he was re-installed as Grand Vizier to be dismissed again in 1876.

Mahmud Pasha: Ottoman Grand Vizier; d. 1474. He took part in the siege of Constantinople and accompanied Sultan Mehemmed II on several of his campaigns.

Mahmud b. Sebüktigin (Mahmud of Ghazna): sultan of the Ghaznawid dynasty; b. 971, r. 998-1030. During his long reign, he almost ceaselessly campaigned over a vast expanse of southern Asia, particularly in India. He assembled an empire greater than any known in eastern Islam since the decline of the 'Abbasids. His centralised, despotic machinery of state typifies the Perso-Islamic "power-state". His court was a congenial centre for the scientist al-Biruni and for leading poets such as Farrukhi, 'Unsuri and, for a short time, Firdawsi.

Mahmud Shabistari: Persian mystic and writer; ca. 1287-1320. His fame rests entirely on his poem in rhyming couplets, called *The Rose Garden of the Secret*.

Mahmud Shewqat Pasha: Ottoman general, war minister and Grand Vizier; 1856-1913. He was one of the most important military-political figures of the Young Turk period.

Mahmud Taymur: Egyptian writer; 1894-1973. His prolific output includes novels and short stories, theatrical pieces, accounts of journeys, articles and various studies, in particular relating to Arabic language and literature.

Mahmud Yalawač: minister in Central Asia and China; d. 1254. The Mongol Great Khan Ögedey appointed him governor of Peking, an office confirmed by the Great Khans Güyük and Möngke.

Mahmudabad Family: leading Shiʿi landed family of north India under the Mughals, the kings of Awadh and the British; xivth to xxth c.

Mahra: tribe living in the southeastern part of the Arabian Peninsula, in a stretch of land along the coast of the Indian Ocean between Hadhramaut and Oman, and in the hinterland belonging to that region.

Mahsati: Persian female poet. She must have lived at some time between the early xith and the middle of the xiith c. An original collection of her quatrains is not known to exist. The current collections of her poetry are modern compilations from many different sources. Usually, she is represented as a singer, a musician and a court poet.

Mahsud: a Pathan tribe on the northwest frontier of Pakistan. In British Indian times they were the fiercest opponents there of British rule.

Maimonides (A. *Ibn Maymūn, Abū ʿImrān Mūsā*): Jewish theologian and physician of Córdoba; 1135-1204. Apart from his works in Hebrew, he wrote in Arabic a précis of logic, some twelve works on medicine, and a great treatise called *Guide of the Perplexed* on the meaning and value of biblical and rabbinical teachings concerning God, the origin of the world, and the validity and significance of religious law. He drew his greatest inspiration from al-Farabi.

Majd al-Dawla, Abu Talib Rustam: ruler of the northern Buyid amirate of Rayy and Jibal; b. 989, r. 997-1029. The amirate was overrun by the Ghaznawid Mahmud b. Sebüktigin.

Majid b. Saʿid: sultan of Zanzibar of the Al Bu-Saʿid dynasty; b. ca. 1832, r. 1856-1870. After his father Saʿid b. Sultan had died in 1856, Majid's eldest brother Thuwayni, designated by his father as sultan in Oman, attempted to gain control of the African dominions of the sultanate of Oman and Zanzibar, but his armed expedition was turned back at sea by a British man-of-war. The dispute, settled by the Award of Lord Canning, Viceroy of India, and recognised by an Anglo-French Declaration in 1862, led to the independence of Zanzibar from Oman.

Majlisi, Mulla Muhammad Baqir ('Allama Majlisi): authoritative jurist, a most prolific collector of traditions and an unprecedentedly influential author of the Twelver Shiʻa; 1627-1698. Under the Safawid Shah Husayn I he was practically the actual ruler of Iran.

Majlisi-yi Awwal, Muhammad Taqi: prominent Shiʻi religious leader and author; 1594-1659. He was the father of Mulla Muhammad Baqir Majlisi.

Majnun Layla ("the Madman of Layla"): name given to the hero of a romantic love story, the original form of which could date back as far as the second half of the viith c. The tale is known in Arabic, Persian, Kurdish, Pashto, Turkish and Urdu literatures.

Majorca (A. *Mayūrqa*): largest of the Balearic islands in the western Mediterranean. A first Muslim incursion was made in 707. Islamisation began in 902 and Islamic domination lasted until 1231.

Makassar (Ujung Pandang): capital of the Indonesian province of Sulawesi Selatan (South Celebes). About 1512, one year after the conquest of Malacca by the Portuguese, Malays were given permission to build a mosque, but it was only at the beginning of the xviith c. that the Islamisation of the two existing Makassarese kingdoms was officially declared to be completed. Nowadays Muslims form the great majority of the inhabitants.

Makhdum al-Mulk: title of ʻAbd Allah Sultanpuri.

Makhfi (Zib al-Nisaʼ Begum): daughter of the Mughal Emperor Awrangzib; 1638-1702. Competent in Arabic and Persian and skilled in calligraphy, she was a great lover of books.

Makhrama, Ba/Abu: South Arabian Himyarite clan of Shafiʻi jurists and Sufis who lived in Hadhramaut and Aden in the xvth and xvith c.

Makhzum, Banu: clan of Quraysh which achieved a prominent position in pre-Islamic Mecca.

al-Makin b. al-ʻAmid, Jirjis: Arabic-speaking Coptic historian; 1205-1273. His *History*, covering the period from the creation of the world to the accession of the Mamluk Sultan Baybars in 1260, was one of the very first medieval oriental chronicles to become known in Europe.

Makli: the flat hilltop in lower Sind, Pakistan, which, besides being the burial ground for countless thousands of ordinary Muslims, served as necropolis for the local Samma, Arghun, and Tarkhan dynasties in the xvith and xviith c.

Makramids: family which has held the spiritual and political leadership of the Banu Yam and the Sulaymani Ismaʻili community in Najran and Yemen since the xviith c.

Maku: former khanate in the Persian province of Azerbaijan. It is now the name of a town with a very striking site, lying in a short gorge with an incredible mass of rock suspending over it.

Makua: the largest tribal group of Muslims in Mozambique, approximately 30% of the total population of some 12 million. At the end of the xvith c. they were still pagan.

Malabar: name first given by Arab and Persian mariners in medieval times to a pepper-producing coastal region of the southwestern Indian Deccan, approximately co-terminous with the modern state of Kerala. Arab contacts with the Malabar region pre-date the Islamic era by many centuries. The foundations of the present-day Mappila Muslim community of South India were laid within a few years of the Hijra.

Malacca (Melaka): town situated on the west coast of the Malay peninsula. In the xvith c. it was the heart of the Malacca sultanate, which played a key role in the expansion of Islam through the Archipelago.

Málaga (A. *Mālaqa*): major city of southern Spain. It was taken by the Muslims in 711. Ruled by the Hammudids in the first half of the xith c., it was captured by the Zirid of Granada Badis in 1057 who built or rebuilt the famous fortress. The town was very prosperous, known among other things for its figs and excellent wine. In 1238 Málaga was incorporated into the Nasrid kingdom of Granada. In 1487 it was conquered by the Catholic Kings.

Malak Hifni Nasif: pen-name of Bahithat al-Badiya, a pioneer protagonist of women's right in Egypt; 1886-1918. In her ideas on emancipation, she was influenced by the writings of Qasim Amin, though her goals usually remained more moderate and her concern with proper Islamic norms was strong. She defended the veil but was bitterly opposed to polygamy.

Malamatiyya: Islamic mystical tradition, according to which all outward appearance of piety or religiosity, including good deeds, is ostentation. The Malamati has to struggle continuously against his desire for divine reward and for approval by man. The foundation of this tradition has been attributed to Hamdun al-Qassar (d. 884). It was spread in the Arab lands, in Persia and in Ottoman Turkey.

Malatya: town in eastern Anatolia, Turkey, in antiquity at the junction of the Persian royal road and the Euphrates road. Taken by the Arabs in 656, Malatya became one of the frontier fortresses and a base for the summer campaigns into Byzantium. It was captured and re-captured alternately by the two adversaries and by the Armenians until it was conquered by the Danishmendids in 1101. In the xiiith c. Malatya was besieged by the Mongols, came under the rule of the Rum Saljuqs, the Mamluks and finally fell into the hands of the Ottoman Sultan Selim I in 1516.

Malay Peninsula: a long, narrow appendix of the mainland of Southeast Asia, West Malaysia. A Muslim tombstone was found in Kedah bearing the date 903, but organised Arab trade is only attested around the mid-xth c. By the xiith c., Arab trade to Southeast Asia was all but superseded by that of the Muslims from India, and it is to them that the spread of Islam through the archipelago is generally attributed.

Malays: people of Southeast Asia who are Sunni Muslims. The oldest Malay texts which show Muslim influences come from Trengganu in West Malaysia and Atjèh in Sumatra. Both date from the xivth c. The oldest literary manuscripts, written in Arabic letters, date from the last years of the xvith c. Malay as a modern literary language is generally said to begin with the writings of Abdullah bin Abdul Kadir Munshi, known as Munshi Abdullah (d. 1854).

Malazgird/Mantzikert: town in eastern Anatolia, Turkey. The main event in the history of the town was the battle in 1071 between the Great Saljuq of Iraq and Persia Sultan Alp Arslan and the Byzantine Emperor Romanus IV Diogenes (d. 1072). The Byzantines were beaten, the Emperor was captured but honorably treated. The outcome of the battle led to the gradual settlement of Anatolia by Turkish nomads and then townsmen, and to the establishment of the Rum Saljuq sultanate in central and eastern Anatolia.

Maldives: group of islands in the Indian Ocean, some 650 km southwest of Ceylon. The Republic of Maldives, formerly a sultanate, forms an independent Asian state since 1953. The capital and only town of the archipelago is Malé. Probably already known to Arab and Persian mariners even in pre-Islamic times, the Maldives must have been visited by Muslim merchants as early as the viith c. By the late xiiith c. the country was universally Shafi'i Muslim, a situation which remains unchanged today. Amin Didi (1909-1954), Chief Minister and later first President of the Maldives, was a prolific writer.

Mali: landlocked country of West Africa. Islam is said to have been introduced in the ancient kingdom of Mali in the xith c. Visits of the kings of Mali to North Africa, Egypt and Mecca in the xiiith and xivth c. established the fame of Mali as a Muslim kingdom rich in gold. Timbuktu developed into an important commercial town and a cultural centre of Islam since the xivth c.

Malik b. Anas: Muslim jurist and the imam of the law school of the Malikites, which is named after him; ca. 710-796. He is frequently called briefly the Imam of Medina. His great work, the *Book of the Smoothed Path*, is the earliest surviving Muslim law-book. Malik introduced the recognition of the unanimous practice of Medina, which he established as an organised judicial system. He thus created a theoretical standard for matters which were not settled from the point of view of consensus.

Malik b. Nuwayra: Arab poet during the Prophet's lifetime; d. 632. His brother, the poet Mutammim, glorified him in elegies which have come to be counted among the most famous of their kind in Arabic literature.

al-Malik al-'Adil, Sayf al-Din: ruler of the Ayyubid dynasty; b. 1145, r. in Egypt 1200-1218, in Damascus 1196-1218. Called Saphadin by the Crusaders, he was the brother, assistant, and spiritual heir of Saladin. In 1207 he distributed his provinces between his sons: al-Malik al-Kamil in Egypt, al-Mu'azzam in Damascus, al-Ahwad and al-Ashraf in al-Jazira and Diyarbakr, himself moving from place to place as circumstances required.

Malik Ahmad Bahri: the first independent ruler of the Nizam Shahi sultanate of Ahmadnagar in the Deccan; r. 1490-1509.

Malik ʿAmbar: Habshi vizier and military commander who served the Nizam Shahi dynasty of Ahmadnagar; ca. 1548-1626. Purchased as a slave in Baghdad, he supported several Maratha families and thus contributed to the subsequent rise of Maratha power in western India.

Malik Ayaz: Indian Muslim admiral, administrator and statesman in Gujarat; d. 1522. He made the island of Diu into an impregnable fortress.

al-Malik al-Kamil (I), Nasir al-Din: ruler of the Ayyubid dynasty; b. 1177, r. 1218-1238. The eldest son of al-Malik al-ʿAdil, he became viceroy of Egypt in 1207 and, at his father's death, sultan of Egypt and supreme head of the Ayyubid realm. During the fifth Crusade, the Franks took Damietta in 1219 but, with the help of his brothers al-Malik al-Muʿazzam and al-Malik al-Ashraf I, al-Kamil forced them to surrender in 1221. The second period of al-Kamil's reign was marked by the struggle for the leadership with al-Muʿazzam and al-Ashraf. In 1227 al-Kamil offered much of Saladin's conquests to Emperor Frederick II Hohenstaufen in exchange for the Crusaders' withdrawal from Egypt. The Emperor then landed at Acre in 1228. The famous treaty which delivered Jerusalem to the Franks was signed in 1229.

al-Malik al-Kamil (II), Nasir al-Din: Ayyubid ruler of Mayyafariqqin; r. 1244-1260. He was the son of al-Malik al-Muzaffar Shihab al-Din, the Ayyubid ruler of Mayyafariqqin, and a nephew of al-Malik al-Kamil (I). Brought with his brother al-Ashraf before the Il-Khan Hülegü, the latter killed them both personally.

al-Malik al-Muʿazzam, Sharaf al-Din ʿIsa: Ayyubid ruler of Damascus; b. 1180, r. 1198-1227. He was a son of al-Malik al-ʿAdil and brother of al-Malik al-Kamil (I). He concurred in the latter's policy in Palestine, but later struggled with him to secure his own position in Syria.

al-Malik al-Nasir Salah al-Din Dawud: Ayyubid ruler of Damascus; b. 1205, r. 1227-1229. His uncles al-Malik al-Kamil of Egypt and al-Malik al-Ashraf of Diyakbakr opposed him and divided the Ayyubid Empire between themselves. After a three months' siege of Damascus, al-Nasir had to yield. He nevertheless remained loyal to al-Malik al-Kamil when the other Ayyubids combined against him. During the following years he was harassed, put under arrest and not admitted into Baghdad.

al-Malik al-Nasir Salah al-Din Yusuf: the last Ayyubid ruler of Aleppo and Damascus; b. 1230, r. 1236-1260. Until 1242 the regency was in the hands of his grandmother Dayfa Khatun, and the period until 1251 saw the ascendancy of the amir Shams al-Din Luʾluʾ al-Amini. These two periods were successful, but by the time the Mongols appeared in Syria, al-Nasir's regime was on the verge of disintegration. In 1260 the Il-Khan Hülegü captured and sacked Aleppo. Al-Nasir abandoned Damascus, fled to Gaza but lost his nerve and surrendered to the Mongols. After the Mongols had been defeated at 'Ayn Jalut in 1260, they put him to death.

al-Malik al-Salih, 'Imad al-Din: Ayyubid ruler in Damascus; b. 1202, r. 1237-1238, 1239-1245, d. 1250. A son of al-Malik al-'Adil, he repeatedly allied himself with the Khwarazm-Shahs and with the Crusaders out of selfish ambition.

al-Malik al-Salih, Najm al-Din: Ayyubid ruler of Egypt; b. 1207, r. 1240-1249. The eldest son of al-Malik al-Kamil (I), he strengthened his position by the formation of a corps of Mamluks who in the end were to bring about the fall of the Ayyubid dynasty in Egypt.

Malik Sarwar (Khwaja Jahan): founder of the Sharqi Sultanate of Jaunpur in northern India; r. 1394-1399.

Malik-Shah: name of various Saljuq rulers, the most outstanding of whom was the Great Saljuq Malik-Shah I b. Alp Arslan; b. 1055, r. 1072-1092. During his reign, the Great Saljuq empire reached its zenith of territorial extent – from Syria in the west to Khurasan in the east – and of military might. After putting down insurrections by other members of the Saljuq family, Malik-Shah came to a *modus vivendi* with the Ghaznawids of eastern Afghanistan and India and with the Ilek-Khans of western and eastern Turkestan. He defended the northwestern provinces of Azerbaijan, Arran and Armenia against the Georgians and the Turkmen. In the Arab lands of Iraq, Mesopotamia and Syria, Malik-Shah assured Sunni control of major cities such as Aleppo, Damascus, Antioch and Edessa by installing Turkish slave commanders as governors. On Malik-Shah's visit to Baghdad in 1086, the 'Abbasid Caliph al-Muqtadi formally granted him the secular authority. Central policy in the Saljuq state was directed by the great vizier Nizam al-Mulk, who facilitated the revival of Sunni Islam, as the authority of the Shi'i Buyids and Fatimids was waning. This in theory meant harmonious co-operation with the 'Abbasid caliphs, the moral heads of Sunni Islam. Malik-Shah was the patron of such poets as the Arabic al-Tughra'i and the Persians Mu'izzi and 'Omar Khayyam.

Malikites (A. *Mālikiyya*): a juridico-religious group of orthodox Islam which formed itself into a school after the adoption of the doctrine of imam Malik b. Anas. The success of the school is due to Malik's intolerance towards the Qadariyya and the Kharijites. Nor is there *a priori* any place in it for mysticism though a number of Maliki mystics are known. In Medina all trace of the school was lost after the demise of Malik's first disciples. It only returned at the triumph of Sunnism in the xivth c. Malikism is predominant in Morocco, Algeria, Tunisia and Libya. It was the sole official rite of al-Andalus during the viiith and ixth c. At the present time, the majority of the Muslims of the Sudan belong to the Maliki school of law and there are Maliki Muslims in Senegal, Mali, Niger, Togo, Chad and Nigeria.

Malindi: town on the Kenyan coast. Between the xiiith and xvith c., up to the arrival of the Portuguese, Malindi was a Muslim city-state, trading with India and China, and enjoying great cultural and material efflorescence. It was from Malindi that Vasco da Gama set off for India in 1498 under the guidance of the pilot Ahmad b. Majid al-Najji. It was visited briefly by St. Francis Xavier in 1542, when he had a conversation with a Muslim judge, who would seem to have been a Shi'i. Nearby is the Islamic site of Gedi, which was occupied from the xith until the xviith c.

Malkom Khan: Perso-Armenian diplomat, journalist and concession-monger; 1833-1908. He advocated governmental reform and thorough-going westernisation and established the first masonic lodge in Iran. In 1890 he embarked on the publication of a quite successful newspaper, called "The Law".

Mallah: name of the Jewish quarter in the major cities of Morocco.

Malta: the main island of a Mediterranean archipelago that was conquered by the Muslims of Sicily in 870 but lost to the Normans in 1090. Its official language derives from an Arabic dialect, but there are no Muslims left among the population.

al-Ma'luf: Lebanese family name which became renowned throughout the Arab world because of the literary activities of a number of its members, both in Lebanon and in the Americas, during the past 150 years.

Ma'lula: place in Syria to the southeast of Damascus. It owes its fame to the fact that its inhabitants (about 2,000), who have remained Christians, still speak a western Aramaic language.

Malwa: inland district of India, at the crossroads between northern India and the Deccan, and between the western provinces and the seaports of Gujarat. Because of its great strategic and commercial importance, it was invaded by the Mu'izzi king of Delhi Shams al-Din Iltutmish, became a province of the Delhi sultanate under the Khalji 'Ala' al-Din (r. 1296-1316), and was established as an independent sultanate under Hushang Shah Ghuri. In 1436 the Khalji Mahmud Shah I (r. 1436-1469) ascended the throne, but this line ended in 1531 when Malwa was conquered by the Gujarat Sultan Bahadur Shah (r. 1526-1537). In 1570 it passed under Mughal rule and became one of the richest revenue-yielding provinces of the empire.

Malzuza: ancient Berber people belonging to the branch of the Butr, and to the family of the Darisa, who lived in Tripolitania.

al-Malzuzi, Abu Hatim: famous Ibadi Imam; d. 772. His tomb in the Jabal Nafusa is a holy place, surrounded with legends.

Mamluks: sultanate established and maintained by military slaves (A. *mamlūks*) in Egypt (1250-1517) and in Syria (1260-1516). It had its origin in the Bahriyya, a military household of Qipčaq Turkish military slaves, which belonged to the bodyguard of the Ayyubid ruler of Egypt al-Malik al-Salih, Najm al-Dīn. The Bahriyya superseded the Ayyubids under the constraint of the military crises provoked by the crusade of St. Louis in 1249 and by the

Mongol invasion of Syria in 1259. The Bahriyya line (1250-1390) was followed by the Burjiyya or Circassian line, which lasted until the Ottoman conquest of Egypt by the Ottoman Sultan Selim I in 1517. During the Ottoman period, the formation of Mamluk military households, known as Neo-Mamluks and carrying the title of Bey, continued until they were destroyed by Muhammad ʿAli Pasha in 1812.

Under the Mamluks, art and architecture flourished. Mamluk metalwork and glass is well represented in museum collections of Islamic art, and most of the existing monuments in the old quarters of Cairo, Damascus, Tripoli and Aleppo are Mamluk.

The following is a list of the Mamluk sultans:

Bahrī line (1250-1390)

1250	Shajar al-Durr
1250	Aybak, al-Muʿizz ʿIzz al-Din
1257	ʿAli, al-Mansur Nur al-Din
1259	Qutuz, al-Muzaffar Sayf al-Din
1260	Baybars I al-Bunduqdari, al-Zahir Rukn al-Din
1277	Baraka (Berke) Khan, al-Saʿid Nasir al-Din
1280	Salamish, al-ʿAdil Badr al-Din
1280	Qalawun al-Alfi, al-Mansur Sayf al-Din
1290	Khalil, al-Ashraf Salah al-Din
1294	Muhammad, al-Nasir Nasir al-Din (*first reign*)
1295	Kitbugha, al-ʿAdil Zayn al-Din
1297	Lajin, al-Mansur Husam al-Din
1299	Muhammad, al-Nasir Nasir al-Din (*second reign*)
1309	Baybars II al-Jashankir, al-Muzaffar Rukn al-Din
1309	Muhammad, al-Nasir Nasir al-Din (*third reign*)
1340	Abu Bakr, al-Mansur Sayf al-Din
1341	Kujuk, al-Ashraf ʿAlaʾ al-Din
1342	Ahmad, al-Nasir Shihab al-Din
1342	Ismaʿil, al-Salih ʿImad al-Din
1345	Shaʿban I, al-Kamil Sayf al-Din
1346	Hajji I, al-Muzaffar Sayf al-Din
1347	al-Hasan, al-Nasir Nasir al-Din (*first reign*)
1351	Salih, al-Salih Salah al-Din
1354	al-Hasan, al-Nasir Nasir al-Din (*second reign*)
1361	Muhammad, al-Mansur Salah al-Din
1363	Shaʿban II, al-Ashraf Nasir al-Din
1376	ʿAli, al-Mansur ʿAlaʾ al-Din
1382	Hajji II, al-Salih Salah al-Din (*first reign*)
1382	Barquq, al-Zahir Sayf al-Din ʿBurjiʾ
1389	Hajji II, al-Muzaffar/al-Mansur (*second reign*)

Burji line (1382-1517)

1382	Barquq, al-Zahir Sayf al-Din (*first reign*)
1389	Hajji II 'Bahri' (*second reign*)
1390	Barquq, al-Zahir Sayf al-Din (*second reign*)
1399	Faraj, al-Nasir Nasir al-Din (*first reign*)
1405	'Abd al-'Aziz, al-Mansur 'Izz al-Din
1405	Faraj, al-Nasir Nasir al-Din (*second reign*)
1412	al-Musta'in ('Abbasid caliph, proclaimed sultan)
1412	Shaykh, al-Mu'ayyad Sayf al-Din
1421	Ahmad, al-Muzaffar
1421	Tatar, al-Zahir Sayf al-Din
1421	Muhammad, al-Salih Nasir al-Din
1422	Barsbay, al-Ashraf Sayf al-Din
1437	Yusuf, al-'Aziz Jamal al-Din
1438	Jaqmaq, al-Zahir Sayf al-Din
1453	'Uthman, al-Mansur Fakhr al-Din
1453	Inal, al-Ashraf Sayf al-Din
1461	Ahmad, al-Mu'ayyad Shihab al-Din
1461	Khushqadam, al-Zahir Sayf al-Din
1467	Bilbay, al-Zahir Sayf al-Din
1467	Timurbugha, al-Zahir
1468	Qa'it Bay, al-Ashraf Sayf al-Din
1496	Muhammad, al-Nasir
1498	Qansuh, al-Zahir
1500	Janbalat, al-Ashraf
1501	Tuman Bay, al-'Adi Sayf al-Din
1501	Qansuh al-Ghawri, al-Ashraf
1516	Tuman Bay, al-Ashraf

Ottoman conquest

al-Ma'mun, Abu 'l-'Abbas 'Abd Allah: 'Abbasid caliph; b. 786, r. 813-833. He restored the unity of the empire and in 827 proclaimed Mu'tazilism as the official doctrine. One of the logical consequences of this step was imposing the doctrine that the Qur'an was created. This measure inaugurated a period of "trial" (A. *mihna*) which was to last officially during the caliphates of his successors al-Mu'tasim bi-Allah and al-Wathiq bi-'llah. Al-Ma'mun's measure was revoked by the Caliph al-Mutawakkil. This doctrine was strongly opposed by many, the most prominent among them being Ahmad b. Hanbal, whom the caliph had flogged. Al-Ma'mun excelled in Hanafi jurisprudence and was distinguished by his love of knowledge. He encouraged the translation into Arabic of Greek and Syriac works on philosophy, astronomy, mathematics and medicine.

al-Ma'mun, Abu 'l-'Ala' Idris: sovereign of the Almohad dynasty; b. 1185, r. 1229-1232. He was very well-read, and equally versed in profane and religious learning.

Man Singh: Maharaja of Amber, Rajasthan district, India, and outstanding general under the Mughal Emperor Akbar; 1550-1614.

Ma'n, Banu: Arab family of chiefs of the Druze district of the Shuf, in the southern parts of Mount Lebanon. They enjoyed a special political prominence in Syria in the xvith and xviith c.

Manaf: name of a deity of ancient Arabia, whose cult was widespread among the Quraysh.

al-Manama: capital city of Bahrain. In the xixth c. al-Manama became the commercial centre of the archipelago. The development of the modern city began after the First World War.

al-Manar: journal of Muslim thought and doctrine, founded in Cairo by Rashid Rida in 1898. It lasted until 1940.

Manastirli Mehmed Rif'at: Ottoman Turkish officer, writer, poet and playwright; 1851-1907. He is mainly remembered for his contribution to the Turkish theatre by writing, translating and adapting many plays.

Manat: name of one of the most ancient deities of the Semitic pantheon. Like al-Lat and al-'Uzza, Manat was worshipped by the pre-Islamic Arabs. The Prophet ordered it to be destroyed in 629.

Manda: island off the coast of Kenya in the Lamu archipelago.

Mandates: the mandate was essentially a system of trusteeship, instituted by the League of Nations after the First World War, for the administration of territories detached from the vanquished Ottoman Empire. They were instituted in Iraq, Syria and Lebanon, Palestine and Transjordan.

Mande: name of a region situated near the upper Niger but also of the whole of an enormous ethnic family currently inhabiting Guinea, Ghana, Mali, Upper Volta, Niger and Nigeria. The first written information derives from Arabic sources.

Mandil, Banu: chiefly family of the Maghrawa, prominent in the xiiith-xivth c. in what is now western Algeria.

Mandu: fortress and town of central India, once the fortress-capital of Malwa. It is known for its architecture and illuminated manuscripts.

Mandur, Muhammad: leading Egyptian journalist, translator and literary critic; 1907-1965. In intellectual vigour and critical insight he surpassed his teacher Taha Husayn, but did not possess the latter's versatility nor did he acquire the latter's fame.

Maner: former town in Bihar state, India. It was one of the earliest and most important sites of Muslim colonisation in this region.

Mangits: Turkish dynasty which reigned in Bukhara from 1753 to 1920. It was founded by the chiefs of the Özbeg tribe Mangit.

Mangu-Timur (Möngke-Temür): khan of the Golden Horde; r. 1267-1280. Unlike his predecessor Berke, he apparently did not embrace Islam.

Mansa Musa: king (*mansa*) of Mali; r. 1312-1337. In 1324 he made a pilgrimage to Mecca that made a profound impression on the Egyptians. He flooded the market in Cairo with so much gold that its value fell throughout Egypt.

Mansur: miniature painter at the court of the Mughal Emperor Jahangir; d. ca. 1624. He was the only artist who made his reputation by nature painting. Jahangir made animal portraiture one of his primary interests and, having a strong scientific curiosity, he demanded from his artists realistic renderings of a very high standard.

al-Mansur b. al-Nasir: ruler of the Hammadid dynasty; r. 1088-1105. He re-established Hammadid power in Ifrīqiya.

al-Mansur, Abu Ja'far 'Abd Allah: 'Abbasid caliph; b. 709, r. 754-775. He was challenged by Abu Muslim who wished that eastern Persia should be effectively independent, and by Muhammad b. 'Abd Allah al-Nafs al-Zakiyya. A politician of genius, he established the 'Abbasid caliphate as a centralised state under the caliph's control.

al-Mansur, al-Malik Muhammad b. 'Umar: member of the Ayyubid family, local ruler of Hamat, historian and patron of letters; 1171-1220. Among other works, he wrote a chronicle of his time.

al-Mansur bi-'llah (Ibn Abi 'Amir al-Ma'afiri): vizier in Muslim Spain, known in the West as Almanzor.

al-Mansur bi-'llah, Isma'il: caliph of the Fatimid dynasty in Ifrīqiya; b. 914, r. 946-953. He defeated the Khariji rebel Abu Yazid and re-established order in Sicily where rule was entrusted to the Kalbids.

al-Mansur bi-'llah al-Qasim b. Muhammad: eponymous founder of the Qasimi line of the Zaydi Imams in Yemen; b. 1559, r. 1597-1620. In 1597 he started the revolt against the Ottomans who had established themselves in Yemen in the wake of their conquest of Mamluk Egypt.

Mansur al-Yaman Abu 'l-Qasim (Ibn Hawshab): founder of Isma'ili missionary activity in Yemen; d. 914. From there he sent missionaries to Egypt, Bahrain, Sind and Gujarat.

al-Mansura: principal city of the province of Sind under the Arabs. It was founded in 738 to the northeast of modern Haydarabad, India.

al-Mansura: town in Lower Egypt near Damietta, founded in 1219 by the Ayyubid Sultan al-Malik al-Kamil (I) as a fortified camp against the Crusaders.

Mansuriyya: extremist Shi'i sect of the viiith c. named after its founder Abu Mansur al-'Ijli from Kufa; d. ca. 740.

Manučihri, Abu 'l-Najm: the third and last (after 'Unsuri and Farrukhi) of the major panegyrists of the early Ghaznawid court; d. ca. 1041. Unlike his contemporary Persian-writing poets, he was enthusiastic for Arabic poetry, and his engaging lyricism is remarked upon by all commentators.

Mappila: name of the dominant Muslim community of southwest India, located mainly in the state of Kerala, primarily in its northern area, popularly known as Malabar. Mappilas may be regarded as the first settled Muslim community of South Asia. The Muslims of Malabar, estimated at 10 % of the population by the middle of the xvith c., lived generally in harmony with the surrounding Hindus until the arrival of the Portuguese in Calicut in 1498. During the ensuing period of "pepper politics", the Portuguese were replaced by the Dutch (1656), the British (1662) and the French (1725), the position of the Mappilas deteriorating rapidly. The British assumed full power in 1792, which was continued until 1947. In 1921 the Malabar Rebellion, frequently called the Mappila Rebellion, broke out with disastrous results. Theological reform was inaugurated by Wakkom Muhammad Abdul Khader Maulavi (d. 1932), devotion to Islam remaining the key element in Mappila character. At present, many Mappilas are employed in the oil production centres of the Middle East.

Maqam Ibrahim: name of a sanctuary in the Great Mosque of Mecca, surmounted by a small dome. In the Qur'an, the term denotes a place of prayer. The great majority of Muslim scholars identified it with the stone inside the sanctuary on which Abraham is said to have stood, the marks of his feet having miraculously been preserved. The Prophet prayed behind it when he performed the circumambulation of the Ka'ba. The stone itself is 60 cm wide by 90 cm high, placed about three yards above ground level.

al-Maqqari, Shihab al-Din: man of letters and biographer from Tlemcen; 1577-1632. He owes his fame to an immense compilation of historical and literary information, which is of inestimable value for the history of Muslim Spain from the conquest to the last days of the Reconquista.

al-Maqrizi, Taqi al-Din: Egyptian historian; 1363-1442. He appears to have been on familiar terms with Ibn Khaldun. The best-known of his many works, commonly referred to as *Khitat*, deals with the topography of al-Fustat, Cairo and Alexandria and with Egyptian history in general.

Marakkayar: endogamous Tamil-speaking Muslim group of southern India in the coastal districts of Tamil Nadu State. They are Shafi'i Sunnis and read the Qur'an in a Tamil translation written in Arabic characters.

Mar'ash: town in the Taurus Mountains region of southern Anatolia, Turkey, conquered by the Muslims in 637. It played a part during the Crusades, came under Mamluk rule in the xiiith c., was conquered by the Dhu 'l-Qadr in the xivth c. and finally by the Ottomans in 1515.

Mar'ashis: line of sayyids originally from Mar'ash, who formed a dynasty which dominated Mazandaran, Iran, between 1358 and the second half of the xvith c.

Marathas: name of the caste-cluster of Hindu agriculturalists-turned-warriors inhabiting northwest Deccan. Their greatest chief was Sivaji (1627-1680), who challenged the Mughal Emperor Awrangzib.

Marathi: the main Indo-Aryan language spoken by some 40 million people in Bombay and the surrounding state of Maharashtra.

Mardam: affluent and distinguished Syrian family. Renown was achieved by Jamil Mardam (1894-1961), a politician, and by his cousin Khalil (1895-1959), a littérateur.

Mardin: town in southeastern Turkey, in early Islam in al-Jazira. Occupied by the Muslims in 640, Mardin was successively in the hands of the Marwanids, the Saljuqs, the Artuqids, the Mongols, Tamerlane, the Aq Qoyunlu and the Persians until it came under Ottoman rule in 1517.

al-Mardini: name of origin of three mathematicians and astronomers: Abu 'l-Tahir (Ibn Fallus) (1194-1252); 'Abd Allah b. Khalil (d. 1406) and Muhammad b. Muhammad (Sibt al-Mardini) (1423-1506).

al-Marghinani: name of two families of Hanafi lawyers whose native town was Marghinan in Farghana. The most important was Burhan al-Din Abu 'l-Hasan; d. 1197. His principal work is a legal compendium, on which he himself wrote a commentary in eight volumes, and a second celebrated commentary, which later writers repeatedly edited and annotated.

Marib: town in Yemen, some 135 km to the east of San'a', in classical antiquity the capital of the Sabaean realm in southwestern Arabia. The last burst of Marib's famous dam is mentioned in Qur'an XXXIV, 15. The significance of this event has caused Islamic tradition to deal in detail with the catastrophe and its consquences.

Marinids: Berber dynasty of the Zanata group, which ruled in the western Maghrib from 1269 to 1464. The first period of their reign (1269-1358) was characterised by military exploits, urban expansion and governmental stability, the second (1359-1464) by a slow erosion of the political structures, a territorial regression and internal division.

Mariya: a Copt maiden sent by al-Muqawqis of Egypt in 627 to the Prophet as a gift of honour; d. 637. The Prophet was very devoted to her and she bore him a son Ibrahim, who died in infancy.

Marj Bani 'Amir: large plain in Palestine between the mountains of Nabulus and those of Galilee, named after the Arabian tribe 'Amir b. Sa'sa'a. During the British Mandate and in the State of Israel, the name was replaced by the biblical equivalent "the Valley of Jezreel".

Marj Dabiq: plain near Dabiq on the Nahr al-Quwayq in northern Syria. It became famous on account of the battle of August 1516, in which the Ottoman Sultan Selim I defeated decisively the Mamluk Sultan Qansawh al-Ghawri. For the next four centuries Syria then came under Ottoman rule.

Marj Rahit: plain near Damascus famous on account of the battles which took place there. From the xivth c. onwards, the name disappeared in favour of the designation Marj 'Adhra'.

Marj al-Suffar: plain stretching from the south of the irrigated area (A. *ghūṭa*) of Damascus, where many battles were fought.

Marjaʿ-i Taqlid: title and function of a hierarchal nature in the Twelver Shiʿa. It denotes a *mujtahid*, who is to be considered during his lifetime, by virtue of his qualities and his wisdom, a model for reference by every observant Imami Shiʿi (with the exception of other *mujtahid*s) on all aspects of religious practice and law. The first Imami doctrinal formulation was produced in the era of the Buyids. The establishment of Imami Shiʿism as the state religion under the Safawids gave the *mujtahid*s a dominant spiritual and temporal influence. It was supported by their economic power in the Shiʿi shrine cities of Iraq, Najaf, Karbalaʾ, Kazimayn and Samarra, and by endowments received from the Qajar Fath ʿAli Shah. During the xixth c. there existed a precarious equilibrium between the state and the religious authorities, which was apparently also upheld in the early years of the reign of Reza Khan (later Shah) Pahlavi. After the rebirth of Qum as an educational centre in the 1920s, the Imami hierarchy was restructured around the politically neutral Ayatollah Burujirdi, sole Marjaʿ-i Taqlid since 1947. Doubts concerning his succession in 1961 led to discussions, during which Ayatollah Khomayni again politicised the Imami leadership. The publication of these debates led to the imprisonment of Ayatollah Taliqani (d. 1979) and Mihdi Bazargan, following the demonstrations against the "white revolution" of Muhammad Reza Shah Pahlavi, in which Ayatollah Khomayni played a prominent role. The doctrine of the "Rule of the Jurist" (P. *wilāyat-i faqīh*) is enshrined in the Islamic Republic of Iran.

Marmara, Sea of (T. *Marmara Deñizi*): small inland sea partly separating the Asiatic and European parts of Turkey. After the Ottomans had taken Constantinople in 1453, the Sea of Marmara became a Turkish lake. There is, however, a certain limitation on Turkish sovereignty, for the special status of the Straits of the Dardanelles and the Bosphorus affects the Sea as well. The largest island of a cluster of islands in the Sea is called Marmara, the second group being the well-known Princes' Islands.

Marrakesh (A. *Marrākush*): town in Morocco, down to about 1890 known as Morocco. Founded in 1062 as a camp by the Almoravid Yusuf b. Tashufin, the walls were built ca. 1130 to defend the town against the Almohads, who took it in 1147 and made it their capital. Under their rule the town prospered exceedingly. In the xiiith c. it became the scene of the struggle between the royal family and the descendants of the companions of Ibn Tumart. In 1269 Marrakesh was captured by the Marinids, who made Fez their capital. In 1525 the town became the capital of the Saʿdi Sharifs and it prospered again. The famous al-Badiʿ palace was built between 1578 and 1594. The town was occupied by the French in 1912. Marrakesh is famous for its walls, the qasba, the palace, and the Kutubiyya mosque which was built by the Almohad ʿAbd al-Muʾmin. It overshadows the Jamaʿ al-Fna, the mosque of the Almohad

Ya'qub al-Mansur and several madrasas. The Jewish quarter dates from about 1560.

al-Marrakushi, Abu 'Ali: astronomer who worked in Cairo; xiiith c. He compiled a compendium of spherical astronomy and astronomical instruments, which is perhaps the most valuable single source for the history of Islamic astronomical instrumentation.

Marriage (A. *nikāḥ*): Islam reformed the pre-Islamic laws in far-reaching fashion, while retaining their essential features; here, as in other fields of social legislation, the Prophet's chief aim was the improvement of the position of women. Muslim law contains provisions which regulate the marriage. The so-called temporary marriage (A. *mut'a*), known to the pre-Islamic Arabs, is permitted among the Shi'is but prohibited by the Sunnis. The term *'urs* indicates the wedding performed in the tribe or the house of the man, while *'umra* denotes the wedding in the tribe or the house of the woman. The bridal gift (A. *mahr*) plays an important part.

al-Marsafi, al-Husayn: Egyptian scholar and teacher; 1815-1890. Blind from the age of three, he became professor of Arabic linguistic disciplines. He is regarded as the first to have formulated what was to become the attempt at a renaissance (A. *nahda*) in regard to literature.

Martolos: salaried member of the Ottoman internal security forces, recruited predominantly in the Balkans from among chosen land-owning Christians. By 1722 the institution was merged with the Muslim local security police.

Martyr (A. *shahīd*): the term is often used in the Qur'an in the primary meaning of witness, not in that of martyr. Throughout Tradition literature, *shahīd* is the martyr who seals his belief with his death, fighting against the infidels. Martyrs receive the highest rank in Paradise, and can even come back to earth. Martyrdom plays a special role in the Shi'a, where 'Ali's son Husayn is the martyr *par excellence*.

Ma'ruf al-Karkhi: one of the most celebrated of the early ascetics and mystics of the Baghdad school; d. 815. His tomb at Baghdad is still an object of pilgrimage.

Ma'ruf al-Rusafi: leading poet of modern Iraq; 1875-1945. He was extremely audacious and outspoken in expressing his political views, defending the Arab spiritual revival within the framework of the Ottoman Empire. He wrote the most vicious poems against King Faysal I and the British and owes his great fame to his political and social poetry.

Marvel (of a saint) (A. *karāma*): the marvel is a personal favour granted by God to His friends. It should be kept secret, and is in no way the sign of a prophetic mission. The question whether marvels attributed – often in great abundance – to "the friends of God" (A. *awliyā'*, s. *walī*) are to be regarded as authentic, and if so, in what sense, is answered in four different ways by the Mu'tazila, the philosophers (Avicenna), the Ash'aris and the Sufis.

Marw al-Shahijan (Royal Marw) (Merv, modern Mary): ancient city near modern Mary (Bairam Ali) in Turkmenistan. It dominated the rich but notoriously unhealthy oasis region along the lower course of the Murghab river in Khurasan. Conquered by the Muslims in 651, Marw knew great prosperity in the viiith-xiiith c. In 1037 it became the capital of the Saljuq Chaghri Beg Dawud and it was there that the Saljuq Sanjar built his celebrated mausoleum. Marw suffered terribly under the Mongol invasions. In 1406 the Timurid Shahrukh Mirza endeavoured to restore prosperity to the region, but this was brought to an end in 1785 by Ma'sum Khan (Shah Murad) of the Mangit dynasty. It was occupied by the Russians in 1884.

Marwan I b. al-Hakam: Umayyad caliph, the first of the so-called Marwanid branch of the dynasty; b. ca. 623, r. 684-5. He must have known the Prophet and had a considerable reputation for his profound knowledge of the Qur'an. He helped in the recension of the canonical text during the reign of the Caliph 'Uthman b. 'Affan. He acquired extensive personal fortune which he invested in property in Medina. After the battle of the Camel, in which he fought on 'A'isha's side, he somewhat surprisingly gave allegiance to 'Ali. At a meeting of the Syrians at al-Jabiya after the death of Mu'awiya II in 683, Marwan was hailed as caliph. With the help of the Banu Kalb, he defeated the Banu Qays at the battle of Marj Rahit. His short reign was filled with military activity in Egypt and Iraq.

Marwan II b. Muhammad (al-Himar): the last of the Umayyad caliphs of Syria; b. 695, r. 744-750. With the death of the Caliph Yazid III in 744, he refused to accept the authority of the nominated successor Ibrahim, brother of Yazid, and seized power. However, it was only in 746 that he finally established his control over Syria. By 746 he had overcome the Kharijites in Iraq, but by 749 the 'Abbasids had risen in Khurasan and their caliphate had been proclaimed in Kufa. In 750 Marwan was defeated at the battle of the Greater Zab, fled to Egypt but fell in a struggle with a pursuing 'Abbasid force.

Marwan al-Akbar b. Abi Hafsa: great classical Arab poet of a family which included several poets; d. ca. 797. He was a fierce opponent of the 'Alids.

Marwan al-Asghar b. Abi 'l-Janub: grandson of the preceding and a remarkable satirist; ixth c.

Marwanids: the branch of the Umayyad dynasty of caliphs in Syria which began with Marwan I b. al-Hakam in 684 and came to an end with Marwan II b. Muhammad (al-Himar) in 750.

Marwanids: dynasty of Kurdish origin which ousted the Hamdanids and ruled Diyarbakr from 990 to 1085. The greatest ruler was Nasr al-Dawla Ahmad.

Mary (A. *Maryam*): the mother of Jesus. The name occurs frequently in the Qur'an in the combination ('Isa) Ibn Maryam "(Jesus) the son of Mary", no father being mentioned, because, according to Muslim tradition, Jesus had no earthly father. Maryam is much venerated in Muslim folk tradition, often along with Fatima.

Marzban-nama: work in Persian prose containing a variety of short stories used as moral examples and bound together by one major and several minor framework stories.

al-Marzubani, Abu ʿUbayd Allah: one of the most versatile and prolific of Arab scholars in the vast field of belles-lettres; 910-994.

Masarjawayh (Masarjis; P. *Masargoye*): Persian physician; ca. viiith c. He is one of the few physicians from the Umayyad period who are known by name, and probably the first to translate a medical book into Arabic.

Masawwa: island and port in Eritrea, Northeast Africa. It is mentioned as a place of exile in early Islam. In the xixth c. the Egyptians introduced the Hanafi school of law, which has remained predominant in most of the towns on the African coast of the Red Sea.

Ma Sha' Allah: phrase occurring in the Qur'an and widely used in the Islamic lands of the Middle East with the general meaning of "what God does, is well done".

Mashhad: city in northeastern Iran, capital of the present province of Khurasan. Since medieval times it has been the location of the tomb of the eighth Imam ʿAli al-Rida. In the Safawid period, in which Persia became a predominantly Shiʿi land, Mashhad rose in importance, since the holy shrines in Iraq, Karbala' and al-Najaf were often in Sunni Ottoman hands.

Mashrabiyya: Arabic word which designates a technique of turned wood used to produce lattice-like panels, like those which were used in the past to adorn windows in traditional domestice architecture.

al-Masihi al-Jurjani: Christian physician from Gurgan, Iran, who was one of the teachers of Avicenna; xith c.

Masira: island to the north of a gulf of the same name, lying parallel to the eastern coast of Arabia. It is part of the Sultanate of Oman.

al-Masjid al-Aqsa ("The Remotest Mosque"): three meanings are given to these words, which occur in the Qur'an. According to the first, they mean Jerusalem. Muslim consensus on this meaning was established very early, perhaps as early as the year 637. During many centuries the words were also used more specifically for the al-Haram al-Sharif. The most common use of the words, however, is for the large building located on the south side of the al-Haram platform and, next to the Dome of the Rock, the most celebrated Muslim building in Jerusalem. The earliest mosque goes back to the Umayyad period and was either built from scratch or completed under Caliph al-Walid I.

al-Masjid al-Haram: name of the mosque in Mecca. The existing Meccan sanctuary, which then included the Kaʿba, the well of Zamzam and the Maqam Ibrahim, was made a mosque by the Prophet in the year 630. Under the anti-caliph ʿAbd Allah b. al-Zubayr and the Umayyad and the ʿAbbasid caliphs successive enlargements and embellishments were made. The mosque was given a substantial revision in the years 1572-1577, during the reign of the Ottoman Sultan Selim II. Between 1955 and 1978 the mosque underwent its most stupendous expansion in history.

Masjumi: name of two different Islamic organisations in Indonesia, one established during the Japanese occupation (1942-1945), the other after Indonesia became independent in 1949.

Maslama b. ʿAbd al-Malik b. Marwan: son of the Umayyad Caliph ʿAbd al-Malik and one of the most imposing Umayyad generals; d. 738. His siege of Constantinople in 716-718 earned him lasting fame. The failure of the siege was caused mainly by supply difficulties, the plague and the use of Greek fire by the Byzantines against the Arab fleet.

Maslama b. Mukhallad: Companion of the Prophet who took part in the conquest of Egypt; d. 682.

Masmuda (pl. *Masamida*): one of the principal Berber ethnic groups forming a branch of the Baranis. They were converted to Islam in the viith c. by ʿUqba b. Nafiʿ.

Masmughan: Zoroastrian dynasty in the region of Damawand (Dunbawand) to the north of Rayy. The name means "The Great One of the Magians". Their principality was not conquered by the Arabs until 758.

Massa (Berber *Masst*): name of a small Berber tribe of the Sus of Morocco, and of the place where it is settled, some 30 miles south of Agadir. According to legend, it was on the shore there that ʿUqba b. Nafiʿ drove his steed into the waves of the Atlantic, calling God to witness that there were no more lands to conquer in the west.

al-Massisa (Mopsuestis): town of Cilicia to the east of Adana in Turkey. It was conquered by the Arabs in 637. In 965 it was taken by the Byzantines, in 1097 by the Crusaders under Tancred, and in 1266 by the Mamluk Sultan Baybars I. In 1516 it was conquered by the Ottoman Sultan Selim I and has remained in Turkish hands ever since.

Masʿud b. Mahmud: sultan of the Ghaznawid dynasty; b. 998, r. 1030-1040. He was the eldest son of Mahmud b. Sebüktigin. While he was concentrating on India, the Oghuz, led by the Saljuq family, made systematic raids into Khurasan and defeated the Ghaznawid sultan in 1040.

Masʿud b. Mawdud b. Zangi, ʿIzz al-Din: Zangid atabeg of Mosul; r. 1180-1193. His public career was entangled from beginning to end with that of his great adversary Saladin.

Masʿud b. Muhammad b. Malik-Shah: Great Saljuq in Iraq and western Persia; r. 1134-1152. The fortunes of the Saljuq dynasty were regarded as going into steep decline on Masʿud's death.

Masʿud, Sayyid Salar (Ghazi Miyan): legendary hero and martyr of the original Muslim expansion into the Gangetic plain of India. He is alleged to have been born at Ajmer, Rajasthan, India, in 1014 and to have been killed in battle in 1033. His tomb in Bahraič, in northern Uttar Pradesh, is the centre of a wide-spread cult.

Mas'ud-i Sa'd-i Salman: eminent Persian poet of Lahore; ca. 1046-ca. 1121. He is famous for the powerful and eloquent laments he wrote from his various places of incarceration, which lasted some eighteen years.

al-Mas'udi, Abu 'l-Hasan 'Ali: one of the most eminent Arab writers; ca. 893-956. His works comprise geography, history, heresiography, comparativism, general philosophy, science, Muslim law and its principles. He also wrote the history of 'Ali, of the Family of the Prophet, of the Twelver Shi'a, and of the Imamate. The best known among the 36 titles listed are a great history of the world, which is said to have filled 30 volumes; a work containing generalities regarding the universe and information of a historical nature on non-Muslim peoples (including the pre-Islamic Arabs) and the history of Islam, from the Prophet up to the caliphate of the 'Abbasid Caliph al-Mut'i li-'llah, and finally, a work called *Warning and Revision*, which is basically an overall review.

al-Mathamina: name given by the Yemenite historians to eight noble families of southern Arabia who, before Islam, enjoyed important political privileges, either in the kingdom of Himyar (from the end of the iiird c. to 520), or under Abyssinian and Persian regimes.

Mathnawi: name of a poem written in rhyming couplets. In Arabic a poem in which the hemistichs rhyme together two by two is called *muzdawij*. As a rule, the *mathnawī* is used in didactic poems, but it remained of little importance in Arabic literature.

In spite of its Arabic derivation, the word *mathnawī* was probably coined by the Persians, with whom it has been very successful. It is first known from the Samanid period in the xth c., and was used by such great poets as Firdawsi, Sana'i and Nizami. In modern literature it still is a useful medium for the Persian poets.

The Turkish *mathnawī* developed late under the influence of that of Persia and alongside it. It was used in Chagatay, Azeri and Ottoman literatures by poets such as Mir 'Ali Shir Nawa'i and Muhammad b. Sulayman Fuduli. Mystic-didactic *mathnawī*s were introduced into Anatolia by Jalal al-Din Rumi and his son Sultan Walad.

In Urdu the *mathnawī* was intensely used during the Deccan phase of Urdu literature in the xvith and xviith c. In the xviiith c. this form of poetry dealt in particular with love themes based upon personal experience. The predominant theme of the modern Urdu *mathnawī* is social.

Matmata: name of a large Berber people in Tunisia, Algeria and Morocco. There were also some Matmata groups among the Berber tribes who went across to Spain at different periods.

Matrah: largest city and major port of the Sultanate of Oman. The Ya'arubid imam Sultan b. Sayf expelled the Portuguese in 1651. In the early xviiith c.

the town was occupied by Persian troops, who were driven out by Ahmad b. Sa'id of the Al Bu Sa'id dynasty. The construction of the harbour, called Mina Qabus, in the early 1970s has insured the city's commercial importance.

Matraqči, Nasuh al-Silahi: horseman, mathematician, historian, calligrapher, painter, and inventor of some new forms of the game of *matraq*, a contest with a stick, cudgel or rapier for training and knight-errantry; xvith c. Matraqči translated al-Tabari's *History of Prophets and Kings* into Turkish and illustrated a Turkish supplement to this translation, which includes the history of the Ottomans from the beginning to the year 1551.

Matta b. Yunus (Yunan) **al-Qunna'i**: Nestorian Christian who translated Aristotle and commented upon him; d. 940. His Arabic translations were all made from Syriac versions. Al-Farabi was among his pupils.

Matter (A. *hayūlā*): the Arabic word indicates "primary matter" in the philosophical sense (Gr. *hulè*) as opposed to "form" (A. *ṣūra*/Gr. *eidos*).

al-Maturidi, Abu Mansur Muhammad: Hanafi theologian of Maturid in Samarqand, jurist and Qur'an commentator; ca. 873-ca. 944. He was the founder of a doctrinal school which later came to be considered one of the two orthodox Sunni schools of theology (A. *māturīdiyya*), the other being the school of al-Ash'ari. He argued against the positions of the Mu'tazila, of the Karramiyya, of the Imami Shi'a, and of the Isma'ilis. He also refuted the views of Christians, Jews, Zoroastrians, Manichaeans, Bardesanites and Marcionites.

Mauritania (A. *Mūrītāniyā*): Islamic republic in northwest Africa. In the early medieval period, Mauritania contained the pagan kingdom of Ghana, part of an increasingly Islamicised society amongst the Tukulor, and a series of Sanhaja Berber kingships, centred in Awdaghost, west of Timbuktu. After the decline of the Almoravids, who had become established in the Río de Oro, the Banu Ma'qil, of Yemenite stock, entered the Western Sahara and dominated Mauritania. After the so-called "War of Shurbubba", which allegedlylasted from 1645 to 1675, and the amirates of the Awlad Hassan, France took formal possession of the territory in 1817, and in 1920 it was transformed into a French colony. In 1958, the Islamic Republic of Mauritania was proclaimed. The people are divided into Arab-Berber Moors and black African minorities; its entire population, of whatever ethnic origins, is Muslim, the study of the Qur'an always having been at the heart of Mauritanian Islam.

Mauritius: independent state in the southwestern Indian Ocean. Mauritius proper is the central island of the Mascarene group. Muslims from Bihar, Uttar Pradesh, Orissa and Bengal came to Mauritius in large numbers only after the British seizure of power in 1810. Among Indo-Mauritians, approximately 25% (or 16% of the total population of ca. 1,5 million) are of Muslim faith, the great majority being Sunnis of the Hanafi school of law.

Mawdud b. 'Imad al-Din Zangi, Qutb al-Din: atabeg of Mosul and youngest brother of Nur al-Din Mahmud Zangi of Damascus and Aleppo; b. 1130, r. 1149-1169. In the writings of western chroniclers of the Crusades the name of Mawdud is transcribed as Malducus, Maldutus or Manduit.

Mawdud b. Mas'ud, Shihab al-Din wa 'l-Dawla: ruler of the Ghaznawid dynasty; b. ca. 1010, r. 1041-1050. He had to combat the Saljuqs in eastern Khurasan and Sistan.

Mawdudi, Sayyid Abu 'l-A'la' (Maudoodi): journalist, fundamentalist theologian, major influence in the politics of Pakistan and one of the leading interpreters of Islam in the xxth c.; 1903-1979.

Mawlawiyya (T. *Mewlewiyye*; *Mevlevi*): Sufi order which takes its name from the Mawlana "Our Master", the sobriquet of Jalal al-Din Rumi.

Mawlay (Moulay) ("my lord"): honorific title borne by those Moroccan sultans of the Sharifian dynasties, the Sa'dids and the Filalis, who were descended from 'Ali's son al-Hasan. Those who were called Muhammad have the title of Sayyidi/Sidi.

Mawlay Idris, Zawiyat: town in Morocco near Volubilis. Islam came to the region with 'Uqba b. Nafi'. Idris I and Idris II were buried there. The town began to develop during the xvith c. The still existing mausoleum was erected by the Filali Sharif Mawlay Isma'il.

Mawlay Isma'il b. al-Sharif: second ruler of the Sharifian dynasty of the Filalis in Morocco; b. 1666, r. 1672-1727. He vigorously repressed Berber revolts, and raised a professional army, the famous "Black Guard", and the "volunteers of the faith", who waged an unceasing irregular warfare against the Spaniards and the English. Mawlay Isma'il concluded an entente with Louis XIV and the Bey of Tunis against the Turks, which secured to France great commercial benefits. He was also very active as a builder, especially at Mawlay Idris and Meknès.

Mawlay Mahammad al-Shaykh: name of three Moroccan sultans belonging to the dynasty of the Sa'dids, the most important of them being Abu 'Abd Allah (al-Mahdi/al-Imam); b. 1490, r. 1517-1557. He put an end to the dynasty of the Marinids by capturing Fez in 1549 and thus can be considered the true founder of the Sa'did dynasty.

Mawlid/Mawlud: the term denotes the time, place or celebration of the birth of a person, especially that of the Prophet or of a saint (A. *wali*). It is also the name for a panegyric poem in honour of the Prophet.

Mawlidiyya: poem composed in honour of the Prophet on the occasion of the anniversary of his birth and recited as a rule before the sovereign.

al-Mawza'i, Shams al-Din: author of an independent chronicle of early Ottoman Yemen to 1621, particularly of the south and of the city of Ta'izz; d. after 1621.

al-Maydani, Abu 'l-Fadl: Arab philologist of Nishapur; d. 1124. He compiled the most comprehensive and most popular collection of classical Arab proverbs, the only one to be translated into a European language (Latin) under the title *Arabum Proverbia*. He also composed an Arabic-Persian dictionary of common terms and words, and a syntax with Persian notes.

Maymun b. Mihran, Abu Ayyub: early Islamic jurist and Umayyad administrator; 660-735. He is remembered in numerous accounts for his religious and ethical maxims.

Maymun-diz: castle of the Isma'ilis in the Alburz Mountains in northwestern Iran, built in 1097 and reduced in 1256 by the Il-Khan Hülegü.

Maymuna bint al-Harith: the last wife that the Prophet married (629); d. 681.

al-Maysir: game with arrows for the parts of a slaughtered beast. It was forbidden by the Qur'an together with wine.

Mayy Ziyada (Mari Ilyas Ziyada): pioneer essayist, orator and journalist; 1886-1941. She wrote in Arabic, French and English, translated from several European languages, and was a zealous feminist who defended the right of education and freedom for Arab women.

Mayyafariqin: Turkish town to the northeast of Diyarbakr which fell peacefully to the Muslims in 640. It was ruled successively by the Hamdanids, the Buyids, the Marwanids of Diyarbakr, the Artuqids and the Ayyubids. The town was conquered by Hülegü in 1260. It came under Ottoman control in 1515.

Mazandaran: province in Iran, south of the Caspian Sea. Ruled by a series of conquerors, it was finally annexed by the Safawid Shah 'Abbas I in 1596.

al-Mazari, Abu 'Abd Allah: jurist of Ifriqiya, surnamed "al-Imam" on account of his learning and renown; 1061-1141.

Mazata: ancient and powerful Berber people which belonged to the great tribal family of the Lawata. They lived in Egypt, Cyrenaica, Tripolitania, Tunisia and Algeria.

al-Mazati, Abu 'l-Rabi' Sulayman: famous Ibadi historian, theologian and jurisconsult; d. 1070. His collection of biographies of distinguished Ibadis is of particular interest for the history of the sect in North Africa.

Mazin: name of several Arab tribes who are represented in all the great ethnic groupings of the Arabian Peninsula.

al-Mazini, Abu 'Uthman: Arab philologist and Qur'an "reader" from Basra; d. 861. He left a very significant treatise on morphology, which has been transmitted in the form of lecture notes.

al-Mazini, Ibrahim 'Abd al-Qadir: Egyptian writer, translator, poet and journalist; 1890-1949. He was a remarkable storyteller with a great sense of humour.

Mazru'i (pl. *Mazari'*): Arab tribe found in the Gulf States and in East Africa. The most celebrated lineage, which migrated from Oman between ca. 1698 and ca. 1800, provided rulers of Mombasa from 1698 until 1837.

Mazyadids: Arab dynasty of central Iraq, which flourished in the xth-xiith c. They were fervent Shiʿis and may thus have furthered the expansion of Shiʿism in central Iraq.

Mecca (A. *Makka*): city in Saudi Arabia, located in the Hejaz about 72 km inland from the Red Sea port of Jidda. It is the most sacred and celebrated city of Islam, the birthplace of the Prophet where the Masjid al-Haram with the Kaʿba are situated. The city has a population of about 300,000, which during the month of pilgrimage swells to about 1,300,000.

In the first century of Islam, the caliphs were concerned with the danger of flooding and built barrages, dykes and embankments.

Under ʿAbbasid rule, the city was governed by ʿAbbasid princes or individuals closely connected with them. The caliphs, Harun al-Rashid in particular, expended vast sums in Mecca so that the population grew accustomed to living at the expense of others and were ready to give vent to any dissatisfaction in rioting. Occasionally, the ʿAlids caused trouble in the Holy City. After the death of Caliph al-Maʾmun in 833, a period of anarchy began. The appearance of the Carmathians in the xth c. brought further misery.

In connection with the advance of Fatimid rule in Egypt and of Buyid rule in Baghdad, both Shiʿi dynasties, the influence of the ʿAlids increased. From ca. 950 onwards, the Meccan ʿAlids are called by the title of Sharif, which they retained until the end of their rule.

The Sharifian dynasties began with the Musawis (960-1063), who were followed by the Hashimids (Hawashim) (1063-1200), both descendents from the ʿAlid Musa b. ʿAbd Allah. In 1200 Qatada b. Idris, also a descendant of Musa and the ancestor of all later Sharifs, took the city. The rule of his line lasted until 1814, when Sharif Ghalib (r. 1788-1814, d. 1816) had to submit to amir Saʿud b. ʿAbd al-ʿAziz I Al Saʿud (r. 1803-1814). Under his Wahhabi rule, all venerated tombs were destroyed, all tobacco pipes and musical instruments burned, and the call to prayer purged of praises of the Prophet. Muhammad ʿAli Pasha of Egypt took Mecca in 1813 and re-installed the Sharifs. In 1924 Sharif ʿAli b. al-Husayn b. ʿAli was declared King of the Hejaz, but in the same year Mecca submitted to ʿAbd al-ʿAziz II Al Saʿud. Since then, the size and physical appearance of Mecca have changed dramatically.

Medhi: pen-name used by a number of Ottoman poets, among them Mahmud Efendi of Gallipoli, known as Qara Mahmud (d. 1597), and Nuh-zade Seyyid Mustafā Čelebi of Bursa (d. 1680).

Medicine (A. *ṭibb*): one of the branches of science in which the Arabs have attained most fame. They received their knowledge mainly from the Greeks, first through the intermediary of the Syrians and Persians, then directly by the translation of classical works. Hippocrates and Galen were the best-known of the Greek medical authors. At the courts of the caliphs there were Jewish, Christian, Mazdaean, Sabaean and even a few Hindu physicians. This eclectic approach did in general not lead to serious differences in the ideas or

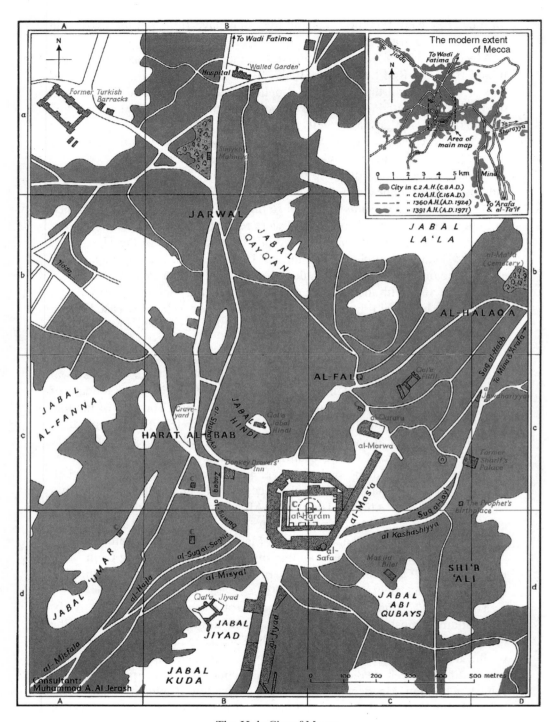

The Holy City of Mecca.

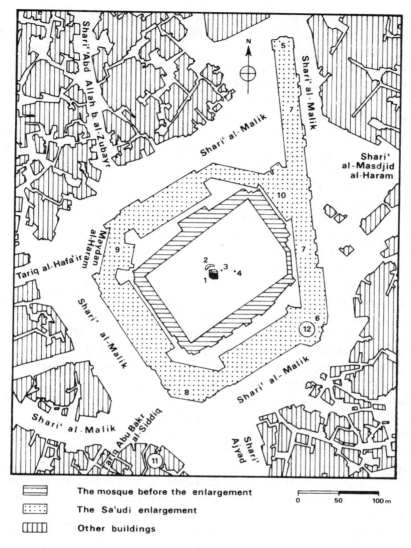

Al-Masjid al-Haram after the Saʿudi enlargement. After Bunduqji.
Key: 1. al-Kaʿba—2. al-Hutaym (semi-circular wall enclosing the Hajar Ismaʿil)—3. Maqam Ibrahim—4. Zamzam—5. al-Marwa—6. al-Safa—7. al-Masʿa—8. Bab al-Malik—9. Bab al-ʿUmra—10. Bab al-Salam—11. al-Haram Library—12. Dome.

practices of the art. Arab medical science had an enormous influence in the western world. It passed first to the Jews, especially to Maimonides, then to the Christians. The Arabs also studied herbs and further developed the knowledge of their medicinal properties, introducing the use of new plants from the Malay archipelago and China. Veterinary science also was the subject of a number of special treatises.

Medina (A. *al-Madīna*): town in the Hejaz, Saudi Arabia, which was the residence of the Prophet after the Hijra in 622 and is the place of his tomb. After Mecca it is the second most sacred city of Islam.

The first three Caliphs Abu Bakr, ʿUmar b. al-Khattab, and ʿUthman b. ʿAffan resided in Medina while the fourth Caliph ʿAli left Medina for Iraq in 656 and never returned. Medina was replaced as capital by Kufa, and, after the acknowledgement of the Caliph Muʿawiya I, by Damascus. Medina then became an important centre of Islamic intellectual life. A wall was built round the central part of the town in 974, which was restored in 1145. A second wall with towers and gateways was built in 1162 and the Ottoman Sultan Süleyman II built walls about 12 m high, which were raised to 25 m by the Ottoman Sultan Abdülaziz. The Wahhabis took the town in 1804 and prevented visits to the Prophet's tomb. In 1813 it was recaptured for the Ottomans by Tusun, a son of Muhammad ʿAli Pasha of Egypt. In 1908 the Hejaz railway from Damascus to Medina was built, and in 1926 the town was incorporated into the kingdom of Saudi Arabia. As at Mecca, the physical appearance of Medina has changed dramatically since then.

Medinaceli (A. *Madīnat Sālim*): town in northeastern Spain, of strategic importance for the Spanish Umayyads from the xth c. onwards.

Meerut: district and town in the modern province of Uttar Pradesh in India. After partition in 1947, many Muslims migrated to Pakistan.

Mehemmed: one of the Turkish forms of the name Muhammad which, having been borne by the Prophet of Islam, is by far the commonest used name in the Islamic world. The name Mehemmed refers here to the relevant Ottoman rulers:

Mehemmed I (*Čelebi*): b. 1386, r. 1413-1421. His success against other pretenders to the throne depended a great deal on his conciliatory and even compliant attitude towards the Byzantine Emperor Manuel II. Under his rule, the Ottoman state, after the defeat in the battle of Ankara in 1402 against Tamerlane, re-emerged as the dominant power in Anatolia and the Balkans.

Mehemmed II (*Fātiḥ* "the Conqueror"): b. 1432, r. 1444-1446, 1451-1481. His father Murad II abdicated in his favour in 1444 but was brought back to power by the Grand Vizier Čandarli Khalil. Mehemmed acceded to the throne for the second time in 1451. He conquered Constantinople in 1453 and immediately declared it his capital. As a consequence he assumed an unprecedented charisma and claimed to be the sole "Holder of the Sword of the Islamic Conqueror " (T./A. *Ghāzī*) even against his Islamic rivals the Anatolian Turkmen rulers, the Aq Qoyunlu Uzun Hasan and the Mamluk sultans of Egypt. The conquest of Rome, symbolised by the Golden Globe (T. *Qizil Elma*), remained as the ultimate goal for the Ottoman ideology. Mehemmed II is the true founder of the classical Ottoman Empire, establishing its territorial, ideological and economic bases.

Mehemmed III: b. 1566, r. 1595-1603. His reign, lying within the Long War (1593-1606) with the Holy Roman Empire, was disastrous, torn by civil and military disturbances, high inflation and insecure government.

Mehemmed IV (T. *Awji* "the hunter"); b. 1642, r. 1648-1687, d. 1693. At his succession, power in the state was divided between the court and the rebellious Janissaries. In 1656 Köprülü Mehmed Pasha became the real strong man, and his son Köprülü Ahmed Pasha after him. The second siege of Vienna in 1683 ended in a Turkish debacle, and in 1687 the Turks were defeated again at Mohács.

Mehemmed V Reshad: b. 1844, r. 1909-1918. In 1909 Turkey lost Bosnia and Herzegovina, and Bulgaria. With the peace treaties with Bulgaria (1913), with Greece (1914) and with Serbia (1914), the Ottoman Empire lost all its European possessions west of the Maritza river, and also the Aegean islands and Crete. During the First World War the Turks fought against the Russians and the English, and succefully defended the Dardanelles.

Mehemmed VI Wahdeddin: the last Ottoman sultan; b. 1861, r. 1918-1922, d. 1926. The landing of Greek forces in Izmir in 1919 led to the growth of a Turkish national resistance movement which opposed the policy of appeasement pursued by the sultan and his government. Mustafa Kemal Pasha (Atatürk) assumed the leadership of this movement. In 1922 the Grand National Assembly at Ankara separated the offices of sultan and caliph, and declared the Ottoman sultanate abolished from 16 March 1920, the date of the Allied occupation of Istanbul. Mehemmed left Turkey on 17 November 1922. The next day the Grand National Assembly divested him of the caliphate, in favour of his uncle Abdülmecid II. Mehemmed's proclamation from Mecca, in which he maintained that the separation of the caliphate from the sultanate was contrary to Muslim law, found hardly any response in the Islamic world.

Mehmed, Mehmet: Turkish form of the name Muhammad, which in this work refers to personages other than Ottoman sultans, who are indicated as Mehemmed.

Mehmed 'Akif (Mehmet Akif Ersoy): Turkish poet, patriot and proponent of Pan-Islamism; 1873-1936.

Mehmed Emin (Yurdakul): Turkish poet and patriot; 1869-1944. He was the pioneer of modern Turkish poetry in spoken Turkish and syllabic metre.

Mehmed Giray, Derwish: member of the Crimean Giray dynasty and historian; xviith c. His chronicle deals with Ottoman and Crimean history from 1682 to 1703.

Mehmed Hakim Efendi: Ottoman literary personality, statesman and official court chronicler; d. 1770.

Mehmed Pasha: name carried by many Ottoman Great Viziers. They are distinguished by their surname, e.g. Čerkes "the Circassian", Gürjü "the Georgian", etc.

Mehmed Pasha, Qaramani, Nishanji: Ottoman Grand Vizier and historian from Konya; d. 1481. He became the main author of Sultan Mehemmed II's legislative policy.

Mehmed Re'is, Ibn Menemenli: Turkish ship's captain and cartographer; xvith c. He is the author of a chart of the Aegean Sea.

Mehmed Yirmisekiz Čelebi Efendi: Ottoman statesman; ca. 1670-1732. He is renowned for his diplomatic mission to France in 1720 and for the account of the mission which he left behind. It is a major contribution to the westernising movement in the Ottoman Empire in its early manifestations.

Mehmed Zaʿim: Ottoman Turkish historian; 1532-? His only known historical book is valuable for the period, for he describes from his own experience events from 1543 to 1578, in which year the work was completed.

Meknès (A. *Miknās*): town in Morocco, 60 km to the southwest of Fez. The Banu Miknasa, a Zanata tribe, vigorously opposed the Idrisids and the Almohads. The Marinids set out to embellish the town, which work was continued by the Filali Sharif Mawlay Ismaʿil.

Memon: name of one of the three Muslim trading communities in Gujarat, the other two being the Bohoras and the Khojas. They claim to have embraced Islam around the xiith c. After the decline of Surat, they moved in the xixth c. to the rising new city Bombay.

Memphis (A. *Manf*): capital of the Egyptian Old Kingdom on the west bank of the Nile, about twelve miles south of al-Fustat. Three verses of the Qur'an are interpreted as referring directly to the city of Manf, and it plays a pivotal role in medieval Arabic geographical and historical writing on Egypt. It was destroyed during the conquest of Egypt by ʿAmr b. al-ʿAs, but continued to dominate the northernmost district of Upper Egypt for some centuries.

Menderes: name of three rivers of Anatolia, usually preceded by the pertinent epithet Büyük "Big", Küçük "Little", and Eski "Old".

Menderes, Adnan: Turkish statesman from Izmir; 1899-1961. He joined Ali Fethi Okyar's Freedom Party in 1930 and, when this was closed down, the People's Party, later called Republican People's Party. Ousted with others from the party in 1945, he founded the Democratic Party in 1946, which won the elections in 1950, 1954 and 1957, Menderes being Prime Minister from 1950 till 1960. He was arrested in 1960 by the military, sentenced to death and executed in 1961. His name was rehabilitated in the late 1980s.

Mengli Giray I: khan of the Crimea; r. 1466-1474, 1475-1476, 1478-1515. He was the real founder of the Crimean state and a patron of the arts.

No more an Ottoman vassal, he generally sought to stay on good terms with Muscovy.

Menteshe-eli: region in the southwestern part of Anatolia corresponding to the classical Caria and today centred on the city of Mugla.

Menteshe-oghullari: Turkish dynasty in southwestern Anatolia, founded by the Turkmen in the xiiith c. It lasted until 1421 when the Ottoman Sultan Murad II captured the territory.

Merjümek, Ahmed b. Ilyas (Mercimek Ahmed): author of a translation into Old Ottoman of a "Mirror for Princes" composed in Persian prose and occasional verse by Kay Ka'us b. Iskandar (xith c.); xvth c.

Mergui: name of an archipelago, district and town in southern Burma, on the eastern shores of the Bay of Bengal. Arab geographical texts of the ixth c. mention the arrival of Muslim merchants from Siraf and Oman. Islamic influences increased with the establishment of the Muslim kingdom of Golconda in the xvith c., but entered into sharp decline in the xviith c. With the Burmese conquest of 1765, Mergui ceased to serve as a channel for Muslim commerce and concepts into Siam, and became instead a Burmese backwater.

Merka (A. *Markah*): settlement south of Mogadishu in the Republic of Somalia. Muslim presence can be traced back to the xvith c.

Mertola (A. *Mīrtula*): town of southern Portugal. In the ixth c. it was the headquarters of an independent chieftain who stood out against the Spanish Umayyad amir 'Abd Allah of Córdoba. Annexed to Seville in 1044, it was the centre of one of the main revolts against the Almoravids. Mertola was conquered by the Christians in the xiith c.

Merzifon: town of north-central Anatolia. In Ottoman times it was the birthplace and scene of the activities of learned men and authors.

Mesih Pasha: Ottoman Grand Vizier; d. 1501. He was a nephew of the last Byzantine Emperor Constantine XI Palaeologus (d. 1453), apparently captured during the conquest of Constantinople.

Mesihi: important Ottoman poet from Pristina, Kosovo; d. ca. 1512. His most original work is a humorous description of the handsome youths of Edirne.

Mesopotamia (A. *al-Jazīra*): region about the lower Tigris and Euphrates rivers, included in modern Iraq. The western part was conquered by the Muslims between 639 and 641, the eastern part in 641.

Messiah (A. *al-Masīḥ*): one can assume with reasonable certainty that al-Masih in the Qur'an is a title of Jesus, but not a messianic one.

Metamorphosis (A. *maskh*): the term occurs in the Qur'an and is understood as indicating "transformation of an exterior form into a more ugly form".

Metaphysics (A. *mā ba'd al-ṭabī'a*): the Arab term is a translation of the Greek *Ta meta ta physika* "the things which come after physical things". The Aristotelian definition of metaphysics as being the science of the being as such is taken up by the great Muslim philosophers Avicenna and Averroes.

Metempsychosis (A. *tanāsukh*): the Arabic term denotes the belief in successive lives and rebirths. The doctrine is widespread in India but also among several sects of the Muslim world. In another sense, the term means the diffusion and distribution of the divine spirit among the beings of this world. In the popular sense of passing from one body to another, the belief is held by several Shi'i sects.

Mewar: name given in the Indian chronicles to the southwestern region of Rajasthan. By the early xivth c. Mewar was seen as a threat to the prestige of Delhi. Its conquest was undertaken by the Khalji Sultan of Delhi 'Ala' al-Din Muhammad Shah I (r. 1296-1316) and later by the sultans of Malwa. In 1527 Mewar lost its independence to the Mughal Emperor Babur.

Mewat: a generally imprecisely defined region of India to the south and southwest of Delhi. The word means "Land of the Me'o", a mixed Indian tribe of largely northeastern Rajput stock, a branch of whom were converted to Islam in the mid-xivth c. Both they and the Hindu Me'o were mostly robbers and freebooters, causing much trouble from the times of the early Delhi sultanates until quelled under the Mughal Emperor Babur.

Mezőkeresztes (T. *Hāčova*): village near Eger in Hungary where the most important encounter occurred between the Habsburg-Hungarian and Ottoman troops in 1596. It ended with the Turkish victory.

Michael (A. *Mīkāl*): the archangel is mentioned in Qur'an II, 92. According to Muslim tradition, Gabriel and Michael "opened the breast of the Prophet", i.e. purified his heart before his night journey to Jerusalem (A. *mi'rāj*). Michael is also said to have come to the aid of the Muslims in the battle of Badr.

Midhat Pasha: Ottoman Grand Vizier, and father of the 1876 constitution; 1822-1884. He was on a collision course with Sultan Abdülhamid II.

Midrarids: minor Berber dynasty which was established in Sijilmasa and which enjoyed relative independence from ca. 784 until 976.

Midyuna: important Berber tribe, belonging to the major branch of the Butr. A significant portion of this tribe moved into Spain in 711. In the Middle Ages they were found in Morocco, Algeria, Tunisia, Spain and Sicily.

Mihna: Arabic term meaning in general usage a "testing" or "trial". More particularly it designates the procedure adopted by the 'Abbasid Caliph al-Ma'mun, and officially applied under his two immediate successors al-Mu'tasim bi-'llah and al-Wathiq bi'llah, for the purpose of imposing the view that the Qur'an had been created. This view was accepted by the jurisconsults and Tradition specialists in Baghdad, with the exception of Ahmad b. Hanbal and Muhammad b. Nuh al-Ijli, who were despatched in irons to Tarsus. At the sudden death of the Caliph al-Ma'mun they were sent back. The Caliph al-Mu'tasim himself seems to have settled for the Mihna as no more than a courtroom formality. Ahmad b. Hanbal, however, was flogged, according to Sunni sources until he actually acknowledged the created

Qur'an. The Caliph al-Wathiq prosecuted the *miḥna* with vigour, but the Caliph al-Mutawakkil put an end to it. Its failure brought to a decisive end any notion of a caliphal role in the definition of Islam and it permitted the unchecked development of what in due course would become recognisable as Sunnism. Henceforward it would be the *'ulamā'*, the religious scholars, who elaborated classical Islam.

Mihrab: the prayer niche in the mosque which indicates the direction of the prayer (A. *qibla*). It is made up of an arch, the supporting columns and capitals, and the space between them. Whether in a flat or in a recess form, it gives the impression of a door or a doorway. The earliest known surviving mihrab, dated 692, is a marble panel in the rock-cut chamber under the Dome of the Rock in Jerusalem. The first concave *miḥrāb* was introduced by the Umayyad Caliph 'Umar b. 'Abd al-'Aziz in the Prophet's mosque in Medina in 706.

Mikalis: Iranian family of Khurasan, prominent in the cultural and social worlds there; xth c. They were also active as local administrators and town officials under the Samanids and early Ghaznawids.

Miletus (A. *Balāṭ*): now a small village in southwestern Anatolia. It came under the control of the Begs of Menteshe in the xiiith c.

Military band (A. *ṭabl khāna*; P. *naqqāra-khāna*): the military band and its quarters in camp and town were called "(kettle)drum house". The band performed a special type of music called *nawba*, which was jealously guarded as one of the attributes of sovereignty and whose performance necessitated respectful silence from auditors. Under the Umayyads, the drum and kettledrum appear to have been introduced into martial music and served as better accompaniments to the reed-pipe (A. *mizmār*) than the tambourine. Persian influences under the early 'Abbasids led to the Persian reed-pipe (P. *surnāy*) being adopted in place of the more primitive *mizmar*. In the xth c. the military band comprised kettledrums, drums, trumpets, horns and reed-pipes. It was part of the insignia of the caliph. With the decline of the caliphate the custom arose that when the caliph conferred regality on subject rulers, a drum or kettledrum usually accompanied the other patents or symbols of authority sent by the caliph, such as a diploma, banner, or standard. The Buyid amir 'Adud al-Dawla Fana-Khusraw is said to have been the first to obtain the coveted musical honours from the 'Abbasid Caliph al-Ta'i'.

Considerable extensions of the privileges of the military band were made under the Saljuqs.

In Yemen the Carmathian al-Mansur b. Hasan (ixth c.) had thirty drums, and the Najahid Sa'id al-Ahwal (d. 1089) had horns and drums.

The Fatimids of Egypt dispensed musical honours upon subject rulers on very much the same lines as the caliphs of Baghdad.

In the Maghrib the nomad Arabs employed an improvisator who sang at the head of the troops just as the Arabs of the Arabian Peninsula did in the pre-Islamic period. The early rulers of western Islamic lands appear to have guarded the regality of the military band as jealously as elsewhere. The loss of the instruments of the band was generally considered a grievous blow, while the capture was prized by the victors. Military bands were equally employed in the Eastern and Western Sudan, at least from the xivth c. onwards.

In the eastern lands the military band was known to the Ghurids in Khurasan, Afghanistan and Northern India, to the Mongol Il-Khans in Persia and to the Mughal Emperors in India.

The Ottoman Turks made a special feature of their military music. Absolute silence was abolished by Sultan Mehemmed I. In the xviith c. the Ottoman bands comprised the large reed-pipe, the small reed-pipe, the flute, the big drum, the ordinary drum, the great kettledrum, the cymbal and the *čaghana*, known in the west as the "Jingling Johnny".

In the Middle Ages Europe borrowed the military band from the Muslims. The percussion instruments in the modern military bands of Europe were adopted from Turkey in the early xviiith c., and when used in orchestral (string band) music they were for a long time called "Turkish Music".

Minaret (A. *manāra*/*manār*): the minaret did not exist during the lifetime of the Prophet. The first one was erected in 665 at Basra. Throughout the medieval period, the role of the minaret oscillated between two polarities: as a sign of power of Islam and as an instrument for calling the faithful to prayer, these functions not being mutually exclusive.

Minbar: the raised structure or pulpit from which solemn announcements to the Muslim community were made and from which sermons are preached. In contrast to the *miḥrāb*, the *minbar* was introduced in the time of the Prophet himself. It has varying architectural features in the Arab, Persian and Turkish lands as well as in India and in East Africa.

Minicoy (Maliku): an isolated coral atoll, the southernmost of the Laccadives, off the coast of Malabar. Hinduism and Buddhism were fairly rapidly eclipsed by the introduction of Islam in the late xiith c., probably some years after the conversion of the Maldivian Sultan Muhammad al-ʿAdil in 1153. In 1956, the atoll was incorporated within the Indian Union Territory of Lakshadweep.

Minorca (A. *Minūrqa*): the easternmost of the Balearic islands, Spain. Under Abu ʿUthman b. Saʿid b. al-Hakam (r. 1231-1282) and his son al-Hakam b. Saʿid (r. 1282-1287), the island was virtually independent under the suzerainty of the kings of Catalonia-Aragon. In 1287 al-Hakam had to surrender to Alfonso III.

Mir: Persian title applied to princes, but also borne by poets and other men of letters.

Mir ʿAli Shir Nawaʾi: outstanding Chaghatay poet; 1441-1501. He also was an important Central Asian cultural and political figure of the reign of the Timurid Husayn Bayqara (r. 1469-1506). He is universally considered as the greatest representative of Chaghatay Turkish literature and exerted profound influence on the development of Azeri, Uyghur, Tatar and Ottoman Turkish literatures.

Mir Jumla, Muhammad Saʿid: prominent minister and military commander in India; d. 1663. He was first in the service of the Qutb-Shahi ruler of Golkonda ʿAbd Allah b. Muhammad and then in that of the Mughal Emperors Shah Jahan and Awrangzib.

Mir Lawhi, Sayyid Muhammad (Naqibi): noted Shiʿi religious scholar; xviith c. He wrote on Shiʿi theology, the Imamate, especially the question relative to the twelfth Imam, and on the refutation of all forms of Sufism. He directed sharp criticism against Majlisi-yi Awwal.

Miracle (of a prophet) (A. *muʿjiza*): the term does not occur in the Qurʾan, which denies miracles in connection with the Prophet, whereas it emphasizes his "signs" (A. *āyāt*), later taken to mean the verses of the Qurʾan. The term denotes the miracles performed by God in order to prove the authenticity of His messengers. Such a miracle is a public act, preceded by a "proclamation" (A. *daʿwa*) and a "challenge" (A. *taḥaddī*), by means of which God's messenger demonstrates inconvertibly the "impotence" (A. *ʿajz*) of his hearers to reproduce likewise the miracle thus brought about.

Miʿraj: originally designating "a ladder", and then "an ascent", the term is used in particular for the Prophet's ascension to Heaven. Qurʾan XVII, 1 reads: "Glory be to Him who transported His servant by night (A. *asrā*) from the Masjid al-Haram to the Masjid al-Aqsa which We have surrounded with blessing, in order to show him one of Our signs." The oldest interpretation detects here an allusion to the Prophet's ascension to Heaven. More modern commentaries interpret al-Masjid al-Aqsa as "Jerusalem". Both interpretations were harmonised by assigning to the term *isrāʾ* the special sense of "Night Journey to Jerusalem". Tradition gives further details of the Prophet's ascension, and the theme has been developed in Arabic, East and West African, and Indonesian literatures.

For the Sufis, it is a symbol of the rise of the soul from the bonds of sensuality to the heights of mystic knowledge. Depiction of the Prophet does not occur in the Semitic environment of Islam, but representations of the *miʿraj* are found in the miniature painting of Persia.

Miranshah b. Timur: third son of Tamerlane; ca. 1367-1408. Babur, the founder of the Mughal dynasty, was his descendent.

Mirdasids (Banu Mirdas): Arab dynasty in Aleppo and northern Syria; r. 1023-1079.

Mirghaniyya (Khatmiyya): dervish order founded by Muhammad ʿUthman al-Mirghani; d. 1851. The main expansion of the order has been in eastern Sudan.

Mirkhwand, Muhammad b. Khwanshah: Timurid historian in Harat; 1433-1498. He wrote a universal history in Persian which enjoyed exceptional popularity throughout the Turco-Iranian regions and was translated several times into Turkish.

Mirza: Persian title, originally meaning "born of a prince". In Persian usage, it was also given to noblemen and others of good birth, thus corresponding to the Turkish Aga. In Indian usage, it is accorded, from Mughal times onwards, to kinsmen of the Mughals, the Timurids, the Safawids, members of other royal houses and to certain Mughal nobles.

Mirza Ahmad Khan: Indian Muslim noble and traveller to the West; xvii-ith c. In 1794 he travelled via Muscat, Istanbul and Marseilles to Paris, where he was well received by the Committee of Public Safety. In gratitude he translated the "Declaration of the Rights of Man" into Persian.

Mirza ʿAziz "Koka": son of the Mughal Emperor Akbar's wet-nurse Jiji Anaga; ca. 1542-1624. He rose to prominence in the Mughal court, army and administration.

Mirzas: turbulent family of Timurid descent in Gujarat, troublesome in the reign of the Mughal Emperor Akbar.

Miskawayh: philosopher and historian from Rayy; 932-1030. Writing in Arabic, he was one of the particularly brilliant intellectual generation who worked in Buyid Persia and Iraq between 961 and 1039. As a philosopher, he is distinguished by the central importance he attached to ethics. His universal history from the Flood to the year 980 is original only in the last part dealing with the Buyids.

Misrata: important Berber tribe belonging to the branch of the Hawwara of the Baranis (Branès) group.

Mizanji Mehmed Murad: Ottoman politician, official and journalist; 1854-1917. Among other works he wrote an Ottoman history in 12 volumes.

Mogadishu (Mogadiscio) (A. *Maqdishū*): capital of the Somali Republic. In the xiith c. an hereditary sultanate was established by Abu Bakr b. Fakhr al-Din. The three principal mosques were founded in the xiiith c. The town reached its highest degree of prosperity in the xivth-xvth c. In the xvth c. the Fakhr al-Din dynasty was succeeded by that of Muzaffar. Separated from the interior by the nomads, Mogadishu began to decline, a process which was hastened by the Portuguese colonial enterprise in the Indian Ocean. In 1585 it fell in the hands of the Ottoman emir ʿAli Bey, but in 1589 the Ottomans were defeated by the Portuguese. Little by little the Somali penetrated into the ancient Arabian town. In 1843 Saʿid b. Sultan of the Al Bu Saʿid dynasty of Oman and Zanzibar appointed a governor. Under Saʿid's son Barghash (1870-1888), Zanzibari authority was established over Mogadishu, only to be ceded to Italy in 1892.

Mogholistan ("The Land of the Mongols"): name used from the time of the Mongols (xiiith c.) onwards to designate the steppe, plateau and mountain region of Inner Asia lying to the north of Transoxiana and the Iaxartes.

Moghols: ethnic and, until recently, linguistic group originally concentrated in west-central Afghanistan, in the modern province of Ghorat; now, however, groups of them have become dispersed throughout northern and central Afghanistan. They number at most 10,000 souls.

Mohács (Ott. T. *Mihāč*): town in southern Hungary where two battles took place. The more decisive of the two was fought in August 1526. The Hungarian army was led by King Louis II of the Jagiellon dynasty, the Ottoman army by Sultan Süleyman II. The Hungarian army was completely defeated, the king lost his life, and the monarchy was destroyed. Although Süleyman did not attach Hungary to his empire, he considered it his own possession.

The so-called second battle of Mohács took place in August 1687 between the Grand Vizier Süleyman Pasha and Charles of Lotharingia, head of the Holy League's army. The fight ended with an Ottoman defeat.

Mohmand: name of a Pathan or Afghan tribe on the boundary between Pakistan and Afghanistan.

Mokha (Mocha) (A. *al-Mukhā*): seaport on the Red Sea in Yemen. It gave its name to the well-known blend of coffee and to a certain type of skins and gloves.

Moldavia (T. *Boghdān*): region in the eastern Balkans. In 1359 prince Boghdan founded a principality between the Eastern flanks of the Carpathians and the Dniestr river. It suffered its first raid by the Ottomans in 1420. Ottoman suzerainty was accepted in 1455 and, after a revolt, again in 1492. The governor was appointed by the Ottoman sultan. In 1775 Austria seized the north-western part of the country (Bukovina), and in 1812 Russia annexed Bessarabia. After the treaty of Aq Qirman of 1826, Ottoman suzerainty became nominal and Russia was recognised as the Protecting Power. In 1859 the twin principalities of Wallachia and Moldavia were united. In 1940 Romania ceded the portion of historic Moldavia east of the Prut river to the Soviet Union.

Molla (Mullah): Persian title, derived from Arabic, indicating in the first instance any Muslim scholar who has acquired a certain degree of religious education and the aptitude to communicate it. In current usage, the title is most often applied to the *'ulamā'*, the religious scholars. Having completed their elementary classes, the students, between the ages of eleven and fifteen years, are admitted to the madrasa, where they pursue a traditional education. Few among them succeed in completing the full cursus of fifteen to eighteen years which will lead them to the superior rank (among the Shi'is) of *mujtahid*. They wear the turban (black for the Sayyids, white for others), a long and ample cloak, sandals, a relatively long beard and a trimmed moustache. Exercising the basic prerogatives in matters of education, ritual functions (prayers, marriages, funerals etc.) and judicial functions, the mollas constitute the basis of what has been called, erroneously in the view of some, a veritable clergy.

Mombasa (A. *Manbasa*; Swahili: *Mvita*): island and town on the east coast of Africa in the Republic of Kenya. The Arabs, Swahili and many Indians inhabitants are Muslims. Al-Idrisi speaks of it as a small place, where the king of the Zanj had his residence. The town was visited by Ibn Battuta in 1331. Between the xiiith and xvith c. Mombasa was, like Malindi, a Muslim city-state, which enjoyed great cultural and material efflorescence because of its trade with India and China. The rule of a queen, called Mwana Mkisi, was followed by a "Shirazi" dynasty founded by Shehe Mvita, who gave his name to the town. This dynasty died out in the late xvith c. The Portuguese then brought from Malindi a sultan of a another "Shirazi" dynasty, and ruled directly from 1631 until 1698, when the town was taken by Arabs from Oman, who ruled until 1890. The British Protectorate began in that year and ended with the proclamation of the Republic of Kenya in 1963.

Monasteries, Christian (A. *dayr*): Christian monasteries continued to function after the Arab conquest of the Middle East, and were very numerous in Iraq, Upper Mesopotamia, Syria, Palestine and Egypt. They were open to virtually all travellers, and often provided a safer stopping-place than elsewhere, even for rulers and princes during their hunting excursions. The buildings were generally surrounded by places of entertainment and even debauchery, and so they figure in bacchic and erotic poetry. Their fortunes varied with the times, and periods of toleration were followed by periods of persecution. The xith c. was the beginning of a period of increasing hardship for the monasteries. They had to contend with successive Saljuq and Mongol invasions, a growing insecurity (e.g. Turkmen raids into Upper Mesopotamia), the worsening of relations with the Muslims at the time of the Crusades, and the progressive disappearance of former small Christian communities.

Monasteries, Muslim (P. *khānqāh*): the term indicates a building usually reserved for Muslim mystics belonging to a dervish order. Rules for communal life were drawn up by the Sufi Abu Sa'id b. Abi 'l-Khayr (d. 1048). Later in the same century, the people of the *khānqāhs* made alliance with the Saljuq ruling power. The ideological linkage of Sufism with Shafi'ism-Ash'arism in Khurasan enjoyed an unprecedented expansion and Nizam al-Mulk's example of founding *khānqāhs* was imitated in Aleppo and Damascus. In Egypt, their foundation, following the Saljuq tradition, began under the Ayyubids after the fall of the Fatimids and continued under the Mamluks. Later they became part of complexes containing several institutions, e.g. mosque-madrasa-mausoleum. From the Ottoman period onwards *khānqāhs* appeared more and more in the form of the Turkish institution of the *tekke*, which, unlike the *khānqāhs*, also reached the Maghrib. Refugees who fled to India before the Mongols founded two new orders, the Čishtiyya and the Suhrawardiyya, who were based upon a widespread network of *khānqāhs* in the Delhi Sultanate. This type of institution, brought from Persia in the xiiith c., prospered right down to modern times and constitutes one of the characteristic manifestations of Indian Islam.

Monasticism (A. *rahbāniyya*): the term occurs in the Qur'an only once and has given rise to divergent interpretations. According to some of the exegists, monasticism is a divine institution while for others it is a purely human one. The expression "no monasticism in Islam", originating from a Prophetic tradition, does not occur in the canonical collections, but allusions to it may be found there.

Monastir: town and port on the eastern coast of Tunisia. The name may indicate the presence of an earlier Christian monastery, but it may also be that the Graeco-Roman term was applied to the first Muslim fortification (A. *ribāṭ*), founded in 796. The area was conquered by the Arabs in the viith c. and the coast fortified by the governor Harthama b. A'yan on instruction of the 'Abbasid Caliph Harun al-Rashid. Monastir's *ribāṭ* was considered the most venerated of the Maghrib.

Mondros (Greek *Mudros*): Turkish name of a harbour on the Aegean island of Lemnos (T. *Limni*). It was the site of the armistice of 1918 which ended the Ottoman Empire's participation in the First World War.

Möngke: fourth Great Khan of the Mongol Empire; b. 1209, r. 1251-1259. He sent his brother Qubilay Khan to begin the subjugation of the Sung Empire in South China, and his other brother Hülegü, the founder of the Il-Khanid dynasty, was commissioned to march west against the Isma'ilis of Persia and the 'Abbasid caliphate. He was notable for his interest in and tolerance of a wide range of religions. The Franciscan missionary Willem van Ruysbroeck (William of Rubruck) visited his court at Karakorum in 1253-4.

Mongolia: the only Muslim communities of the modern Mongolian People's Republic live within the Turkish-speaking Kazakh and Choton groups.

Mongols: name of a tribe whose original home was in the eastern part of the present-day Mongolian People's Republic. In the xiiith and xivth c., under Genghis Khan and his successors, they established by military conquest the most extensive continuous land empire known to history. They invaded the Khwarazm-Shahs' empire in 1219-1223 and sacked the great cities of Khurasan, Harat and Nishapur. The effect of the Mongolian invasion on Persian agriculture, heavily dependent on irrigation by means of underground water channels (A. *qanāt*) was even more serious. South Persia, on the other hand, escaped virtually unscathed. In general, the more long-term effects of the period of Mongol rule in the Islamic world are likely to have been, for the most part, deleterious. The 40 years of pagan Il-Khanid government before the accession of Mahmud Ghazan in 1295 seem to have been characterised by ruthless and short-sighted exploitation. Mahmud Ghazan declared his conversion to Islam, and the Mongols in Persia duly followed his example, at least in name. He introduced administrative reforms, which probably had some beneficial effect.

Monk (A. *rāhib*): in the Qur'an the monks are the religious leaders of the Christians. In one place they are said to live at the expense of other people, in another the Christians' friendship to their fellow-believers is said to be due to their priests and monks.

Monotheism (A. *tawḥīd*): the Arabic term means "making one" and is applied to the Oneness of God. It is the basis of all the articles of the belief of Islam.

Montenegro (T. *Qaradagh*): this Balkan state, part of former Yugoslavia, came under Ottoman rule in 1496. In the xviith c. it became autonomous under Ottoman authority, but revolted and overthrew Ottoman rule in the xviiith c. It was recognized as an independent principality in 1878 and proclaimed a kingdom in 1910. In 1971 the Muslims represented ca. 13% of the population.

Moors (A. *al-Mār*): a rather vague term used in Europe to indicate the ancient Muslims of Spain and the inhabitants of the Mediterranean ports of North Africa.

Morea (T. *Mora*): the peninsula of the Peloponnesus in Greece. By the end of the xivth c. Ottoman suzerainty was acknowledged but after some revolts the region was occupied by Sultan Mehemmed II in 1460. After the Greek War of Independence (1821-1833), Morea formed a part of the kingdom of Greece.

Moriscos: in modern historical terminology the term is used to refer (a) to those Spanish Muslims who under various degrees of duress, were, between 1499 and 1526, converted to Christianity, and (b) to their descendants who continued to live in Spain until the Expulsion of 1609-1614.

Morocco (A. *al-Maghrib/al-Mamlaka al-Maghribiyya*): country in northwest Africa. The name Morocco is a deformation of Marrakush (Marrakesh). The Arabs appeared at the end of the viith c. The Berbers adopted Islam but took up arms in 740 and, having embraced Kharijite doctrines from the east, established principalities. The real conversion to Islam was the work of the dynasty of the Idrisids. The Almoravids added half of Spain to the territory, but the rigid orthodoxy, which had been their strength, relaxed and they were displaced by the Almohads, who conquered all Morocco and Muslim Spain. But separatist tendencies broke up their empire. Local dynasties, such as the Hafsids and the ʿAbd al-Wadids, were set up in Tunis and in Tlemcen. In Morocco proper the Marinids and the Wattasids took over. The threat from the Christian Portuguese and Spanish produced an awakening of religious sentiment, and the coming of the Saʿdi Sharifs meant a regular reconstitution of Morocco. They were succeeded by the Filalis. The Franco-Moroccan war of 1844 and the Spanish-Moroccan war of 1859 were followed by the so-called Moroccan crisis (Algeciras 1906) and the French protectorate, proclaimed in 1912. In 1956 Morocco became independent. All the Muslims are Sunnis and since the Almoravid period have followed the Maliki rite. The duties of religion are most strictly observed in the towns. Religious brotherhoods are fairly numerous and the cult of saints is highly developed.

Mosaddeq (P. *Muṣaddiq*), Muhammad: Persian nationalist politician and Prime Minister; ca. 1882-1967. From 1920 onwards he occupied various short-lived official functions opposing the Pahlavi dynasty. He was elected into the Assembly in 1943 and again in 1947. During the Allied occupation he had formulated the principle of "negative equilibrium", calling for Iran to establish its independence. By 1950 Mosaddeq had established the National Front, a very loose association of many diverse political groups. Supported by Ayatollah Abu 'l-Qasim Kashani (d. 1962), the anti-British sentiment rose. After the assassination in 1951 of the Prime Minister General ʿAli Razmara, the Assembly passed legislation for the nationalisation of the Anglo-Iranian Oil Company and Mossadeq became Prime Minister. In 1952 diplomatic relations with Britain were severed. Economic conditions deteriorated and Mosadeq's position was weakening. Voting was halted and a truncated parliament convened with Mossadeq as Prime Minister. When the Shah Muhammad Reza Pahlavi refused his request to take over the Ministry of War, he resigned but was soon re-appointed and was given full powers for six months by the Assembly. In the same year the Senate was dissolved. With the support of the Communist Tudeh party, Mosaddeq tried to restrict the political powers of the shah, but was arrested by the army under General Fadl Allah Zahidi. The shah, who had fled in panic some days earlier, then returned and Mosaddeq was sentenced to three years' solitary confinement. He spent the rest of his life quietly at Ahmadabad.

Mosaic (A. *fusayfisāʾ*): the Arabic word is ultimately derived from the Greek *psèphos*. Islam preserved the already existing taste for mosaics and the technique for making them.

Moses (A. *Mūsā*): in the Qurʾan, the Biblical prophet is considered as the precursor of, the model for, and the annunciator of the Prophet. Some details differ from the Biblical story. In Islamic tradition he bears the honorific title of "The person who speaks to God" or "The person whom God addresses".

Mosque (A. *Masjid*): the Arabic word means "the place where one prostrates oneself in worship". In the Qurʾan the word is used especially of the Meccan sanctuary (A. *al-Masjid al-Ḥarām*), but the Prophet also worshipped in other places and according to Tradition he said that he had been given the whole world as a mosque. When he came to Medina, a mosque was built in which other activities took place, too. But very soon the building became the political and religious centre of the new community. During the conquest after the time of the Prophet, the first thought of the Muslim generals was to found a mosque as a centre around which to gather. This was the case in Basra, Kufa, al-Fustat, Mosul, al-Madaʾin (Ctesiphon), Damascus, Homs, Qayrawan and Jerusalem. Tribal and sectarian mosques came also into being, and existing sanctuaries were transformed, as was the case in Damascus where the church of St. John was rebuilt. Gradually the sanctity of the mosque increased. Recitation of the Qurʾan, praises of God, sermons etc. took place there, and the Friday prayer could only be performed in the Great Mosque. Finally, mosques became objects of pious visits.

Mosul (A. *al-Mawṣil*): city of Iraq, on the west bank of the Tigris and opposite to the ancient Niniveh. The Muslims took Niniveh in 641 and the existing fortress on the west bank became a camp city. From 906 to 929 the Hamdanids ruled the town as governors of the ʿAbbasid caliph, and from 929 to 991 as sovereign rulers. They were followed by the ʿUqaylids and in 1096 Mosul passed to the Saljuqs. The town developed considerably under the atabeg ʿImad al-Din Zangi, who put an end to Saljuq rule in 1127. In 1185 the Zangid ʿIzz al-Din Masʿud I found himself forced to recognise Saladin as his suzerain. In 1364 the city was incorporated in the kingdom of the Mongol dynasty of the Jalayirids. Tamerlane not only spared Mosul, but gave rich endowments to the tombs of Nabi Yunus and Nabi Jirjis. After their conquest of Baghdad in 1508, the Safawids took over the city, but lost it to the Ottoman Sultan Süleyman II in 1535. In the xviiith c. the town was fairly continuously in the hands of the local family, originally Christians, of ʿAbd al-Jalil. There was a long tradition of French missionary and educational work, largely among the indigenous Eastern Christian churches. In 1918 the town was occupied by British troops, and was awarded to Iraq in 1925.

From the town's name came Eng. muslin.

Mozambique (A. *Musanbīj*): country on the southeast coast of Africa, independent from Portugal since 1975. The name, in origin indicating a town, does not occur in Arabic literature before Ahmad b. Majid. Al-Masʿudi in the xth c. speaks of the Sufalas ("lowlands" or "shoals") of the Zanj. In the xviiith c. there were public schools where the Qurʾan was taught, and the mosques were used daily. In 1980 the number of Muslims was estimated at 13.5% of the population.

Mozarab: the word probably means "arabised" and was used in Christian Spain as a sobriquet against those Christians who preferred to stay rather than flee from the Muslim invader. The Mozarabs were thereby considered a dubious element, having suffered the contagion of the Arabo-Muslim enemy. Their artistic manifestations are also found outside Muslim Spain, and their liturgy is preserved in Toledo.

al-Muʿallaqat: term for a collection of pre-Islamic Arabic poems, generally numbered at seven.

Muʿallim Naji: Ottoman Turkish poet; 1850-1893. He was highly concerned about the Ottoman Turkish language and regretted its deterioration in the name of simplification and modernisation.

Muʿawiya I b. Abi Sufyan: founder of the Umayyad dynasty of caliphs based in Syria; b. ca. 605, r. 661-680. He had been a crypto-Muslim since 628, and made his Islam manifest in 630. His sister Umm Habiba was married to the Prophet. He functioned as a commander against the Byzantines, and in 646 Syria and al-Jazira were under his control. Against the Byzantines he established strong garrisons along the coast and instituted Arab maritime warfare in the Mediterranean. The Caliph 'Uthman b. 'Affan, while being besieged in his Medinan residence in 656, sent word to Mu'awiya asking for help, but the relief force turned back on learning that 'Uthman had been killed. Thereafter Mu'awiya bided his time while the Prophet's son-in-law 'Ali sought to establish himself as leader. After the Battle of the Camel, 'Ali elicited Mu'awiya's oath of allegiance, but, with the support of 'Amr b. al-'As, Mu'awiya decided to fight 'Ali, alleging vengeance for 'Uthman. After the Battle of Siffin in 656 Mu'awiya was recognised as caliph by the Syrians and by 'Amr b. al-'As, who then went to conquer Egypt. While 'Ali's position grew weaker in Iraq fighting the Kharijites, Mu'awiya again bided his time. 'Ali was murdered by a Kharijite in 661, and Mu'awiya became caliph. To posterity his image is ambivalent; he was seen not just as the man who perverted the caliphate into kingship, but also as a clever and successful ruler. He is either cursed or venerated, the legitimacy of his caliphate being a far more important issue than its historical nature.

al-Mu'ayyad bi-'llah Muhammad: name of two Qasimi Zaydi Imams of Yemen, the best-known being al-Mansur bi-'llah al-Qasim: b. 1582, r. 1620-1644. During his reign the Ottoman Turks were expelled from Yemen in 1635 after a continuous presence of a century.

al-Mu'ayyad fi 'l-Din Abu Nasr: eminent Isma'ili missionary; ca. 990-1077. He played a leading role as an intermediary between the Fatimids and al-Basasiri, the military commander of the Buyids, in the campaign of 1057 against the Saljuqs. He left an autobiography which is considered to be the apogee of Isma'ili learning.

al-Mubarrad, Abu 'l-'Abbas: celebrated philologist from Basra; 826-900. The rivalries between him and Tha'lab led to the formation of the two famous schools of philologists at Kufa and Basra. His most famous work deals with an extensive range of themes concerning belles-lettres.

al-Mubashshir b. Fatik: Egyptian historian and savant; xith c. His surviving work, called *Choice wise sayings and fine statements* deals with ancient, almost exclusively Greek, sages. It enjoyed great popularity in the Muslim world. About 1250 it was translated into Spanish.

Mudanya: Turkish town located on the Gulf of Gemlik on the Asiatic shore of the Sea of Marmara. Here an armistice was concluded between the Government of the Grand National Assembly of Turkey and Great Britain, France and Italy in 1922 which brought to an end the Turkish War of Independence.

Mudéjar: term to designate the Muslim who, in return for the payment of tribute, continued to live in territories conquered by the Christians.

Müeyyed-zade: Ottoman theologian and legist; 1456-1516. He encouraged rising young poets, historians and jurists and owned a private library of over 7,000 volumes.

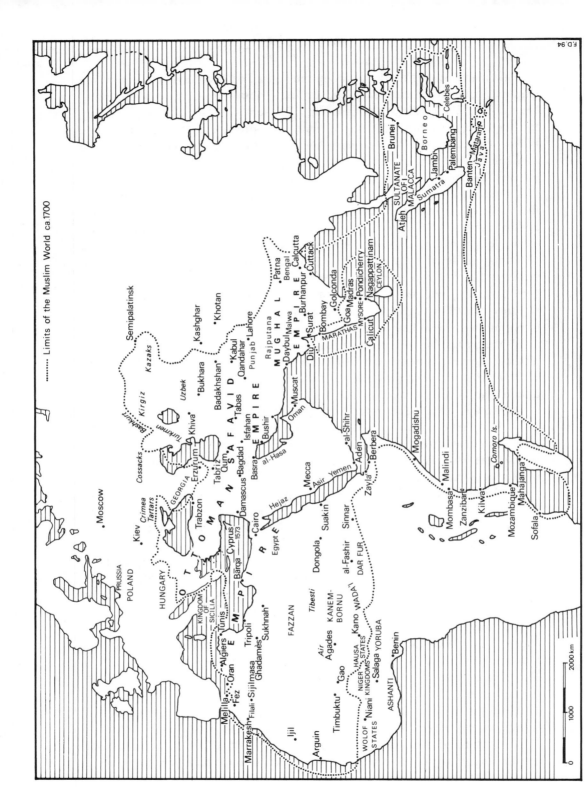

Limits of the Muslim World ca.1700

F.D.94

Moscow

POLAND
PRUSSIA

HUNGARY

Kiev
Crimea
Tartars

Cossacks
Kirgiz
Bashkirt

Kazaks

Semipalatinsk

Turkmen
Uzbek
Khiva
Bukhara
Badakhshan
Khotan
Kashghar

GEORGIA
Erzurum
Trabzon
Tabriz
Qum
Bagdad
Isfahan
Tabas
Qandahar
Kabul
Lahore
Punjab
Damascus
Basra
Bushir
al-Hasa

SAFAVID EMPIRE

OTTOMAN EMPIRE

KINGDOM OF SICILIA
Cyprus
1573
Tunis
Algiers
Tripoli
Bārqa
Cairo
Egypt

Oran
Fez
Melilla
Marrakesh
Filali
Sijilmasa
Ghadamès
Sukhnah

Hejaz
Mecca
Asir
Yemen
Aden
Zayla
Berbera
al-Shihr
Oman
Muscat

Rajputana
MUGHAL EMPIRE
Malwa
Burhanpur
Patna
Bengal
Calcutta
Cuttack
Surat
Diu
Daybul
Bombay
Golconda
MARATHAS
Goa
Madras
Pondicherry
MYSORE
Calicut
Nagappattinam
CEYLON

SULTANATE
LOFI
Atjeh
MALACCA
Brunei
Borneo
Celebes
Sumatra
Jambi
Palembang
Banten
Mataram
Java

Mogadishu
Malindi
Mombasa
Zanzibar
Kilwa
Comoro Is.
Mozambique
Mahajanga
Sofala

Dongola
Suakin
Sinnar
al-Fashir
DAR FUR
WADAI
KANEM-BORNU
Kano
HAUSA STATES
NIGER KINGDOMS
Salaga
YORUBA
Benin
ASHANTI
WOLOF STATES
Niani
Timbuktu
Gao
Agades
Air
Tibesti
FAZZAN

Arguin
Jijil

0   1000   2000 km

Muezzin (A. *mu'adhdhin*): the official who summons the believers by his call (A. *adhān*) to public worship on Friday and to the five daily prayers. He belongs to the personnel of the mosque.

al-Mufaddal b. Abi 'l-Fada'il: Coptic historian; xivth c. His only known work is an account of the Mamluk period from 1260-1348.

al-Mufaddal al-Dabbi: Arabic philologist of the Kufan school; d. ca. 781. His principal work is an anthology of early Arabic poems, mainly pre-Islamic, known as the *Mufaddaliyyāt*. Al-Mufaddal compiled them for his pupil, the future Caliph al-Mahdi.

al-Mufid, Shaykh Abu 'Abd Allah: leading Imami Shi'i theologian and jurist; 948-1032. He was the spokesman of the Twelver Shi'a, and wrote refutations of treatises and views of the Mu'tazili and Sunni traditionalist theologians.

Mughals: Indo-Muslim dynasty which ruled from 1526-1858. They entertained relations with the Safawids of Persia, had a centralised administration, a thriving economy, and an active commerce both internal and external. As for religious life, Emperor Akbar's attempt at reconciliation of the major religious trends inside his vast country was only one in the plethora of religious movements during Mughal times. Mughal architecture created a supremely confident style by synthesising the most heterogenous elements: Central Asian, Timurid, Indian, Persian and European. The manufacture of carpets and textiles flourished, as did painting and the applied arts. Finally, the Mughal period marks the highest point in the development of Persian literature in India.

The following is a list of the Mughal Emperors:

1526	Babur, Zahir al-Din
1530	Humayun, Nasir al-Din (*first reign*)
1540-55	*Suri sultans of Delhi*
1555	Humayun, Nasir al-Din (*second reign*)
1556	Akbar I, Jalal al-Din
1605	Jahangir, Nur al-Din
1627	Dawar Bakhsh
1628	Shah Jahan I, Shihab al-Din
1657	Murad Bakhsh
1657	Shah Shuja' (in Bengal till 1660)
1658	Awrangzib 'Alamgir I, Muhyi al-Din
1707	A'zam Shah
1707	Kam Bakhsh (in the Deccan)
1707	Shah 'Alam I Bahadur Shah I
1712	'Azim al-Sha'n
1712	Jahandar, Mu'izz al-Din
1713	Farrukh-siyar
1719	Rafi' al-Darajat, Shams al-Din

1719	Shah Jahan II, Rafiʿ al-Dawla
1719	Niku-siyar
1719	Nasir al-Din Muhammad
1748	Bahadur, Ahmad Shah
1754	ʿAlamgir II, ʿAziz al-Din
1760	Shah Jahan III
1760	Shah ʿAlam II, Jalal al-Din ʿAli Jawhar (*first reign*)
1788	Bidar-bakht
1788	Shah ʿAlam II, Jalal al-Din (*second reign*)
1806	Akbar II, Muʿin al-Din
1837-58	Bahadur Shah II, Siraj al-Dīn

Direct British rule

al-Mughira b. Saʿid al-Bajali: Shiʿi rebel from Kufa; viiith c. About the time of his revolt in Kufa in 737, he is described as an old man. He was a follower of Muhammad b. ʿAli Zayn al-ʿAbidin and, after the latter's death, of Muhammad b. ʿAbd Allah al-Nafs al-Zakiyya. He taught that he himself was the imam until Muhammad b. ʿAbd Allah's appearance as the Mahdi. He elevated the rank of the ʿAlid imam to divinity. He was put to death by Khalid b. ʿAbd Allah al-Qasri. The extremist Shiʿi sect of the al-Mughiriyya is named after him.

al-Mughira b. Shuʿba: Companion of the Prophet; d. 670. The Prophet sent him to Taʾif to destroy the sanctuary of al-Lat. The Caliph ʿUmar b. al-Khattab appointed him governor of Basra.

al-Muhallab b. Abi Sufra: Arab general and the founder of the influential family of the Muhallabids; 632-702.

al-Muhallabi, Abu Muhammad al-Hasan: chief minister and vizier to the Buyid amir of Iraq Muʿizz al-Dawla; 903-963. His literary circle in Baghdad was frequented by poets and men of letters.

Muhallabids (A. *al-Mahāliba*): kinsmen and clients of Muhallab b. Abi Sufra. They rose to power in the service of the Umayyads, were crashed in 720, but staged a spectacular come-back under the ʿAbbasids and remained politically prominent until the reign of the Caliph al-Maʾmun. They also produced a large number of men of culture, a rebel leader of the Zanj, and the Buyid vizier Abu Muhammad al-Muhallabi.

Muhammad: the Prophet of Islam. Belief that Muhammad is the Messenger of God is second only to belief in the Oneness of God according to the Muslim profession of faith (A. *shahāda*), the quintessential Islamic creed. Muhammad has a highly exalted role at the heart of Muslim faith. At the same time the Qurʾan and Islamic orthodoxy insist that he was fully human with no supernatural powers.

Born ca. 570, he grew up as an orphan. At the age of 25, he married Khadija, and it was at the age of 40 or 43 that he began to have visions and hear mysterious voices. Key themes in his early recitations include the idea of the moral responsibility of man who was created by God, and the idea of judgement to take place on the Day of Resurrection. To these are added vivid descriptions of the tortures of the damned in hellfire and the pleasures of the believers in Paradise. The religious duties that the Qur'an imposed on the Prophet and his followers during the Meccan years were few in number: one should believe in God, appeal to Him for forgiveness of sins, offer prayers frequently, including long night vigils, assist others (especially those who are in need), free oneself from the love of delusive wealth and from all forms of cheating, lead a chaste life, and not expose new-born girls to die in the desert.

When the Meccan merchants discovered that the Prophet attacked on principle the gods of Mecca, they realised that a religious revolution might be dangerous for their fairs and their trade. But during the Meccan years the Prophet had no thought of founding a new religion. His task was only that of a warner, charged with the task of informing the Arabs, to whom no prophet had been sent before, that the Day of Judgement was approaching. The Jews and Christians must also testify to the truth of his preaching, since the same revelation had been sent down to them previously. It is in this context that the meaning of the repeatedly discussed term *ummī*, often translated as "illiterate", is best understood. As applied to the Prophet in Qur'an VII, 157, the term appears to mean "one who has not previously been given the Book of God". After the emigration of some of the Prophet's followers to Abyssinia, a few notables in Mecca were won for the new teaching, but the religious reform of his native city must be regarded as having failed, as also an attempt to establish himself in Ta'if failed. It is at this point that some accounts place the Night Journey to Jerusalem (A. *isrā'*) and the Ascension to Heaven (A. *mi'rāj*). The Prophet persevered in his search for a new sphere of activity outside of Mecca, and found it in Yathrib (later called Medina).

After he had entered into relations with some Medinans who had come as pilgrims to Mecca in 621, the latter began to spread Islam in their native town. After a preliminary conference in al-'Aqaba, he was able to conclude at the same place, during the pilgrimage of 622, a formal agreement with a considerable number of Medinans, in which they pledged themselves to take him into their community and to protect him. These negotiations produced great bitterness in Mecca, and the believers slipped away to Medina, the Prophet and Abu Bakr emigrating last (A. *hijra*). They reached Medina on 24 September 622.

Slowly at first, and then in larger numbers, the Medinans adopted Islam. During his first year in Medina the Prophet devoted considerable attention to the Jews. His relations with any Christians who may have been in Medina can only be surmised from references in the Qur'an. In the so-called "Constitution of Medina" the Prophet established a formal agreement with all of the significant tribes and families and he revealed his great diplomatic skills in his dealings with the Jews. But they would not accept his claims to a new religion, and the Qur'an accuses them of concealing parts of their holy scriptures. The Prophet also came to believe that the Christian scriptures did not preserve the actual message and teachings of the prophet Jesus.

It was at this point that the nascent Muslim community took on a pronounced national character through the adoption of various elements from ancient Arabian worship. This decisive change in the course of Islam occurred in the second year of the Hijra (July 623-June 624), and was signaled by the much discussed "change of the Qibla" from Jerusalem to the ancient sanctuary of the Ka'ba in Mecca. The Prophet came forward as the restorer of the religion of Abraham that had been distorted by Jews and Christians.

Now the inevitable necessity arose of forcing admission to Mecca. The Prophet sent some of his followers to Nakhla, where they succeeded in capturing a Meccan caravan. In 624 the Muslims succeeded in completely routing the far more numerous Meccan enemy in the battle of Badr. The Jewish tribe of Qaynuqa' was forced to leave Medina, while alliances were concluded with a number of Bedouin tribes. At the battle of Uhud in 624, the Prophet was wounded and the Meccans were victorious, but the expected negative consequences of this setback did not materialise in Medina. A second Medinan Jewish tribe, the Banu 'l-Nadir, who were delighted at the Prophet's misfortune, were forced to emigrate to Khaybar.

In 626 the Meccans set out with a large army against Medina. The Prophet had a trench (P. *khandaq*) dug, and after the siege had dragged on, the besiegers gradually began to retire. After that the Prophet declared war on the Jewish tribe of the Qurayza, and all of their men were killed.

He now turned his major attention to the north and led two of the expeditions himself, one against the Banu Lihyan in 627, the other against the Banu Mustaliq. In 628 he felt strong enough to undertake the pilgrimage to Mecca. He encamped at al-Hudaybiya, where he agreed to the proposal of the Meccans that the Muslims would return the following year to perform the so-called "little pilgrimage" (A. *'umra*). He also concluded a ten years' truce with the Quraysh. This so-called "Treaty of al-Hudaybiya" represented a brilliant act of diplomacy on his part, in that he had induced the Meccans to recognise him as an equal. In 628 the fertile oasis of Khaybar, inhabited by Jews, was captured.

At about this time Tradition puts the dispatch of letters from the Prophet to the Muqawqis of Alexandria, the Negus of Abyssinia, the Byzantine emperor Heraclius, the Persian king, and a number of others, in which he demanded that they adopt Islam.

Early in 629 the Prophet performed the pilgrimage to Mecca and accomplished the reconciliation with his family, the clan of Hashim. A few of the most important Meccans, such as the military men Khalid b. al-Walid and 'Amr b. al-'As, became Muslims. In the meantime the Prophet continued his military expeditions. His forces suffered a serious reverse in the battle of

Mu'ta in Transjordan against the Byzantines. The belligerent party in Mecca decided to support one of their client clans, the Banu Bakr, against the Banu Khuza'a, who were allied to the Prophet. This, according to the custom among the Arabs at that time, was seen on both sides as breaking the Treaty of al-Hudaybiya, freeing the Prophet to attack Meccan caravans and even the city itself. In December 629 he set out against Mecca. Not far from the town he was met by some Quraysh, who paid homage to him and obtained an amnesty for all Quraysh who abandoned armed resistance. Thus the Prophet was able to enter his native city practically without a struggle. He acted with great generosity and demanded only the destruction of all idols in and around Mecca. After that he returned to Medina. His forces then routed the Hawazin tribes of central Arabia at Hunayn, but were unable to take Ta'if, which only surrendered in 630.

In the same year many embassies came to Medina from different parts of Arabia to submit to the conqueror of Mecca on behalf of their tribes. Although the Prophet's appeal for a campaign against northern Arabia met with little support, he carried through with his plan. The campaign against Tabuk in 630 was indecisive by itself, but the petty Christian and Jewish states in the north of Arabia submitted to him, as did small groups of Bedouins in regions so far away from Medina as Bahrain, Oman and South Arabia.

In March 632 the Prophet carried through the first truly Islamic pilgrimage, the so-called "Farewell Pilgrimage" or "Pilgrimage of Islam". Only a month before his death he began preparations for a great expedition against Transjordan that he intended to lead himself. At about this time the appearance of rival "prophet's", such as al-Aswad, Musaylima and Tulayha, provoked disturbances.

The Prophet suddenly fell ill and died on 8 June 632. The really powerful factor in his life and the essential clue to his extraordinary success was his unshakable belief from beginning to end that he had been called by God.

Stories about the Prophet, his life and his intercession have permeated popular Muslim thought everywhere, and although he never claimed to have performed any miracle, traditional folk poetry indulges in extensive descriptions of his marvellous attributes and actions.

Muhammad's biography (A. *sira*): immediately after the first Arab conquests, the professional story-tellers began to compose and disseminate stories of the life of the Prophet. A specimen of this sort of literature, which belonged to the historical novel rather than to history, was the "Book of the military campaigns" of Wahb b. Munabbih. The oldest author of a biography of the Prophet was 'Urwa b. al-Zubayr. Oral transmissions by Aban b. 'Uthman (642-723), a son of the third caliph, were collected by 'Abd al-Rahman b. al-Mughira (d. before 742). These earliest productions are given the name "military campaigns". Works of historians like Ibn Shihab al-Zuhri (671-741) and Musa b. 'Uqba (d. 758) also bear this title. The most famous biography of the

Prophet is that of Ibn Ishaq in the recension of Ibn Hisham, who preserved almost intact the primitive text of Ibn Ishaq. Other famous biographers in early Islam were Muhammad b. 'Umar al-Waqidi and Muhammad b. Sa'd (d. 844).

Muhammad III b. 'Abd Allah, Sayyidi/Sidi: Filali Sharif of Morocco; b. 1722, r. 1759-1790. In 1748 he restored his father Mawlay 'Abd Allah b. Isma'il to his throne at Meknès. In 1757 he was proclaimed ruler at Marrakesh and his long reign of serenity was marred only by a limited number of troubles. He repaired the ruins of Fez, and developed great building activities at Marrakesh.

Muhammad b. 'Abd Allah Hassan: the local Somali equivalent of the Sudanese Mahdi; 1864-1920. Called by his British opponents "the Mad Mullah", he preached the puritanical message of the Salihiyya order, and was led to proclaim a "Holy War" against Christian missionary activities and increasing Ethiopian military pressure in the Ogaden. In 1904 he signed a peace treaty (the "Illig Agreement") with the Italians. By 1908 the Dervishes renewed their campaign and were finally defeated in 1920. He was the leading Somali poet of his epoch and was admired for his brilliant command of Somali rhetoric.

Muhammad b. 'Abd Allah al-Nafs al-Zakiyya ("the Pure Soul"): grandson of 'Ali's son al-Hasan; d. 762. Together with his full brother Ibrahim, he rebelled in Medina against the 'Abbasid Caliph al-Mansur and died in battle.

Muhammad (IV) b. 'Abd al-Rahman, Sayyidi/Sidi: Filali Sharif of Morocco; b. ca. 1815, r. 1859-1873. Agreements with European powers and with the United States formed part of the policy of reforms that Sidi Muhammad wished to carry out. He lived in perfect entente with the French in Algeria. The visit of Sir Moses Montefiore in an attempt to improve the lot of Jews, which left much to desire, was an important event, although it did not have spectacular results.

Muhammad 'Abduh: Muslim theologian and founder of the Egyptian modernist school; 1849-1905. Jamal al-Din al-Afghani exercised a profound influence upon him, but Muhammad 'Abduh held that only gradual reform could be successful. He was banished from Egypt in 1882. In 1884 he published in Paris, together with al-Afghani, a paper which exercised a very great influence on the development of nationalism in the Muslim east. In 1889 he returned to Cairo and became in 1899 state *muftī*, the highest clerical post in Egypt. In 1897 he published his most important work, the *Treatise of the Oneness (of God)*. His commentary on the Qur'an remained unfinished. Muhammad 'Abduh's advanced ideas provoked the most vigorous hostility in orthodox and conservative circles. His programme was to reform the Muslim religion by bringing it back to its original condition, to renovate the Arabic language, and to recognzie the rights of the people in relation to the government.

Muhammad b. Abi Bakr: son of the first caliph; d. 658. He was opposed to the Caliph ʿUthman and was defeated by ʿAmr b. al-ʿAs.

Muhammad b. Abi Bakr (Askia al-Hajj Muhammad): founder of the Askia dynasty of Songhai; d. 1538.

Muhammad b. Abi Hudhayfa: Companion of the prophet, born in Abyssinia; d. 657. In 655 he took the functions of the governor of Egypt into his own hands, was confirmed by the Caliph ʿAli but killed by Muʿawiya's troops.

Muhammad b. Ahmad al-Askandarani: Arab physician, who is regarded as the first Qurʾan interpreter in modern times to discuss non-Arab occidental sciences in Qurʾan commentaries; xxth c.

Muhammad ʿAli: political leader, journalist and poet of Rampur, India; 1878-1931. During the First World War he supported the Turkish cause, and was the leader of the popular Khilafat Movement, which died when the caliphate was abolished in 1924.

Muhammad b. ʿAli b. ʿAbd Allah b. al-ʿAbbas: great-grandson of the Prophet's uncle al-ʿAbbas and father of the ʿAbbasid Caliphs al-Saffah and al-Mansur; d. 743.

Muhammad ʿAli Barfurushi Quddus, Molla: outstanding leader of early Babism; 1824-1849. After his execution, his tomb at Barfurush in Mazandaran, Iran, became a Bahaʾi shrine.

Muhammad ʿAli Hujjat-i Zanjani, Molla: leading exponent of Babism in Zanjan, Iran, and chief protagonist of the Babi uprising there; 1812-1851.

Muhammad (Mehmed) ʿAli Pasha: Ottoman governor-general and effective ruler of Egypt; b. ca. 1768, r. 1801-1848, d. 1849. He assumed the title *khedive* (P. *khadiv*, "lord"), granted officially in 1867 by the Ottoman sultan Abdülaziz to his grandson Ismaʿil Pasha. Muhammad ʿAli Pasha's career can be divided into four distinct periods: (1) his rise to the position of governor-general and the consolidation of his power, 1801-1811; (2) the period in which he laid the economic and military foundations for what later became a regional empire centred on Egypt, 1812-1827; (3) the height of Egyptian hegemony and the beginning of the disintegration of Muhammad ʿAli Pasha's economic control system, 1828-1841; (4) the post-heroic phase and the setting in of realism and retrenchment; 1841-1848.

Muhammad b. ʿAli al-Rida: ninth Imam of the Twelver Shiʿa; 811-835. His succession to the imamate as a minor after his father's death in 818 stirred up considerable controversy.

Muhammad ʿAli Shah Qajar: ruler of the Qajar dynasty; b. 1872, r. 1907-1909, d. 1925. The shah wanted to cause the downfall of those who supported the reforms and to restore the power of the royal family. In 1907 he declared the newly-created National Assembly dissolved and the Constitution abolished as it was contrary to Islamic law. In 1909 he was compelled to abdicate in favour of his son Ahmad, still a minor. From Odessa he plotted his return, and in 1911 he landed at Astarabad, but his forces were defeated. In 1912 he went in exile again. Reza Khan (later Shah) Pahlavi got the National Assembly to depose Muhammad ʿAli's successor Ahmad Shah (r. 1909-1924), which brought the Qajar dynasty to an end.

Muhammad b. ʿAli Zayn al-ʿAbidin (al-Baqir): fifth Imam of the Shiʿa; 676-ca. 735. He became Imam upon the death of his father in 712, and refused to support revolts against the Umayyads. He was probably the first to formulate what were to become the basic doctrines of Twelver Shiʿism. He defended the doctrine of dissociation (A. *baraʾa*) from the enemies of the Imams, chief among whom were the majority of the Companions and in particular the first three caliphs. He was opposed to individual reasoning (A. *ijtihad*).

Muhammad(u) Bello: West African "Commander of the Believers" of the Sokoto Caliphate in northwestern Nigeria; b. 1781, r. 1817-1837. He was the son of Shaykh Usman dan Fodio, and wrote a considerable number of works in Arabic, among them a history of Sokoto.

Muhammad Bey: Bey of the Husaynid dynasty in Tunisia; r. 1855-1859. The intervention of Great Britain and France in 1857 caused him to proclaim the "Fundamental Pact", a charter which guaranteed equality and security, and which granted to all, and to foreigners in particular, freedom of trade and the right to own property in the country.

Muhammad Bey ʿUthman Jalal: Egyptian writer; ca. 1826-1898. His importance lies in his endeavour to translate Molière's comedies into the modern vernacular of Egypt, freely adapting them to Arab conditions.

Muhammad Dawud Khan: the first president of Afghanistan; 1909-1978. He served as prime Minister from 1953-1963, pushing a policy of economic development, notably road construction, and of social change. His autocratic style contributed to his resignation. After King Zahir Shah (r. 1933-1973) had been deposed, Dawud Khan was chosen president for six years but was overthrown by a military coup in 1978 in which he was killed.

Muhammad b. Habib, Abu Jaʿfar: Arab philologist of the school of Baghdad; d. 860. He studied especially the history of pre-Islamic and early Islamic times and the genealogy of their leaders and representatives.

Muhammad Ibn al-Hanafiyya: son of the Prophet's son-in-law ʿAli; 637-700. The ʿAlid al-Mukhtar stirred up a movement in Iraq in 685, as champion of Muhammad Ibn al-Hanafiyya's rights, but the latter acted with great restraint. In the end he recognised the Umayyad Caliph ʿAbd al-Malik as the legitimate ruler and visited him in 697 at Damascus.

Muhammad b. al-Hasan b. Dinar (Ibn Dinar al-Ahwal): transmitter of ancient Arabic poetry (A. *rawi*) of Baghdad; d. after 864. His lasting fame is based on a commentary on the *diwan* of Dhu 'l-Rumma.

Muhammad Husayn Haykal: outstanding Egyptian writer; 1888-1956. He played a political role as minister and president of the Senate, but above all he was active in literature and in the study of Muslim religion. His first and best novel is called *Zaynab* (1914), and in his well-known *Life of Muhammad* he defended Islam and Arabism, but without sectarianism.

Muhammad Husayn Tabrizi: famous Persian calligrapher; xvith c. He was a pupil of Mirza Sayyid Ahmad Mashhadi and teacher of Mir 'Imad.

Muhammad b. 'Isa al-Mahani: Persian mathematician and astronomer; ixth c. He wrote commentaries on Euclid's Elements, on Archimedes, and a partial revision of the deficient translation of the Spherics of Menelaus.

Muhammad 'Izzat Darwaza (Darwazeh): advocate of Arab nationalism in Palestine; 1888-1984. He was a close associate of Amin al-Husayni and a prolific author.

Muhammad b. Mahmud b. Muhammad b. Malik-Shah: Saljuq sultan in western Persia; b. 1128, r. 1153-1159. He besieged Baghdad in 1156, but had to raise the siege on hearing news of the appearance at Hamadhan of Ildeñiz, the atabeg of Azerbaijan.

Muhammad b. Mahmud b. Sebüktigin: Ghaznawid sultan in Ghazna and northwestern India; b. ca. 997, r. 1030-1031, 1040-1041. He was deposed by his brother Mas'ud, but after the latter had been defeated by the Saljuqs at Dandanqan in 1040 and his army had mutinied, Muhammad became sultan for a second time. In 1041, however, he was defeated by Mas'ud's son Mawdud near Jalalabad.

Muhammad b. Makki (al-Shahid al-Awwal): Imami Shi'i jurist, traditionist, poet and littérateur; 1333-1384. He was put to death at Damascus at the order of a Maliki judge.

Muhammad I b. Malik-Shah II: Great Saljuq sultan in Iraq and western Persia; b. 1082, r. 1105-1118. In 1104 his half-brother Sultan Berkyaruq agreed to a division of power, with Muhammad to have northwestern Persia, al-Jazira and Syria, whilst Muhammad's full brother Sanjar was to remain in Khurasan acknowledging Muhammad as his overlord. The period after Muhammad's death saw the rise of the Turkish atabegs.

Muhammad b. Marwan: Umayyad commander and governor; d. 719. He was a son of the Caliph Marwan I b. al-Hakam and half-brother of the Caliph 'Abd al-Malik.

Muhammad Murtada: Arabic lexicographer; 1732-1791. He owes his fame to commentaries on al-Firuzabadi's dictionary and on al-Ghazali's *The Revival of Religious Sciences*.

Muhammad al-Qa'im (al-Mahdi/al-Hujja): twelfth Imam of the Twelver Shi'a; ca. 869-941. His death was the beginning of the complete or greater occultation (A. *al-ghayba al-kubrā*) that will last till the reappearance of the twelfth Imam in eschatological times.

Muhammad b. al-Qasim al-Thaqafi: military commander of the Umayyad dynasty and conqueror of Sind; d. 715. He conquered the port of Daybul and, among others, the town of Multan in the Punjab.

Muhammad Reza (Rida) Shah Pahlavi: second and last shah of the Pahlavi dynasty in Iran; b. 1919, r. 1941-1979, d. 1980. In 1941 he took the oath to the Constitution, thus removing the threat of direct rule of Iran by the British and the Soviets. The signature in 1943 of the tripartite Declaration signed by Churchill, Roosevelt and Stalin changed the status of Iran from that of a neutral to that of an ally. The Allied occupation ended in 1946. The Persian Communist Party, reconstituted in 1942 under the name "Tudeh Party", soon became a force to be reckoned with, and the national Assembly was torn by factionalism.

The years 1949-1953 were marked by a continuing struggle for power between the shah and the Assembly, now dominated by Mosaddeq, who compelled the shah to return to the state the crown lands which had been confiscated from private owners for distribution to the peasants. In 1951 Mosaddeq nationalised the Anglo-Iranian Oil Company and in 1953 rejected his dismissal from office by the shah, who then left the country, but returned soon afterwards. Army officers who had joined the Tudeh Party were purged, and many prominent members of the National Front were arrested. Most of the latter were released in 1954 and some formed the nucleus of the National Resistance Movement.

After 1954 the oil revenues started to flow, in 1957 martial law was abolished and the Savak or "State Intelligence and Security Organisation" assumed responsibility for internal security. The shah created two artificial political parties, a "Government Party", and a "Loyal Opposition", but the intelligentsia remained unconvinced about his commitment to constitutional democracy. In 1961 he dissolved the Assembly and delayed new elections. Between 1961 and 1963 he promulgated by decree a series of far-reaching reforms known as the "White Revolution", aiming at land reform, at the enfranchisement of women, and at the campaign against illiteracy.

Opposition came from the National Front and the religious classes and their allies in the bazaar. Violent demonstrations took place in Teheran. Among the religious leaders arrested was Ruhollah Khomayni, who from Najaf in Iraq began to plan the Islamic Revolution. From 1972, the tempo of terrorist activity accelerated sharply.

In foreign policy, the shah signed an agreement with the United States and had a working relationship with Israel, which was the subject of vehement denunciations by Khomayni. He was above all determined to keep open Iran's economic lifeline through the Strait of Hormuz. This concern led him to support the ruler of Oman against the Soviet- and China- supported guerillas in the province of Dhofar. The Algiers Agreement appeared to have decided the dispute with Iraq over the vital Shatt al-'Arab waterway.

From 1975 onwards a series of ill-advised actions set in motion the revolutionary forces which overthrew him: the clearance of the old bazaar around the shrine of Imam 'Ali al-Rida at Mashhad; the promulgation of a new calendar from the date of the accession of Cyrus the Great in 550 B.C.E.; the cancellation of the subsidy which had been paid to the *'ulamā'* since 1965, and a defamatory anti-Khomayni letter published in 1978. In this year Khomayni called for the violent overthrow of the Pahlavi regime, while cancer, which later led to the shah's death, was far advanced. He consistently refused to countenance the use of force against the demonstrators. In January 1979 he left Iran for Egypt, where he was given sanctuary by President Anwar al-Sadat.

Muhammad al-Sadiq Bey: Bey of the Husaynid dynasty in Tunisia; r. 1859-1882. The doubling of the personal tax (A. *majbā*) in 1863 triggered off serious upheavals, which led to pitiless repression by the minister Mustafa Khaznadar. The situation was somewhat redressed by Khayr al-Din Pasha, but the foreign consuls pressed for concessions and privileges. In 1881 Tunisia was occupied by French troops.

Muhammad b. Sahnun: Maliki jurisconsult from Qayrawan; 817-870. He was responsible for the definitive implantation of Malikism in the Maghrib.

Muhammad b. Sam, Mu'izz al-Din: ruler of the Ghurid dynasty; r. 1203-1206. He ruled in Ghazna from 1173 onwards and had helped his brother Ghiyath al-Din (r. 1163-1203) to build an empire stretching almost from the Caspian Sea to northern India.

Muhammad b. Sa'ud: founder of the first Sa'udi state in Najd; 1727-1765. His claim to fame rests on his association with the religious reformer Ibn 'Abd al-Wahhab.

Muhammad Shah: ruler of the Qajar dynasty; b. 1808, r. 1834-1848. During his reign tribal disturbances and outbreaks of religious unrest dominated internal affairs. Persia's foreign relations were dominated by fear and resentment of both Russia and Britain, and Perso-Turkish relations were in a state of tension.

Muhammad Shah b. Jahan-Shah (Rawsan Akhtar): the last of the Mughal emperors in Delhi to enjoy real power; b. 1702, r. 1719-1748. In 1739 Nadir Shah Afshar marched from Afghanistan into India and compelled Muhammad Shah to pay an enormous indemnity, including the famous Peacock Throne of the Mughal Emperor Shah Jahan I.

Muhammad b. Tahir al-Harithi: prominent figure of the Musta'li-Tayyibi Isma'ilis of Yemen; d. 1188. He composed a chrestomathy of Isma'ili literature, which became a classic.

Muhammad b. Tughluq: sultan of the Tughluqid dynasty in Delhi; r. 1324-1351. Under him the Delhi Empire reached its greatest territorial extent.

Muhammad b. Wasif: one of the first known poets to write verse in New Persian according to the rules of the Arabic quantitative metre; ixth c.

Muhammad b. Yusuf (Muhammad V): Filali Sharif and later king of Morocco; b. 1909, r. 1927-1953, 1955-1961. In 1953 he was deposed, but in 1955 his successor Mulay 'Arafa renounced his prerogatives. In the same year Morocco achieved full and unconditional independence and in 1957 it was transformed into a monarchy.

Muhammad b. Zayd: Zaydi Imam who reigned over Tabaristan and Jurjan; d. 900.

Muhammadiyya: term denoting four distinct 'Alid groups: (1) the descendants of Muhammad Ibn al-Hanafiyya; (2) the believers in the Mahdiship of Muhammad b. 'Abd Allah al-Nafs al-Zakiyya, who are divided into the extremist Mansuriyya and the Mughiriyya; (3) the believers in the Imamate of Abu Ja'far Muhammad, son of the tenth Imam al-'Askari; (4) the believers in the divinity of the Prophet, also called Mimiyya.

al-Muharram: the first month of the Muslim year. Specially noted days are the 1st, as the beginning of the year; the 9th, as the fast-day of the Shi'i ascetics; the 10th, as the anniversary of Karbala', the great day of mourning for the Shi'a; the 16th, as the day of the selection of Jerusalem as the Qibla; the 17th, as the day of the arrival of the "people of the elephant" (Qur'an CV).

al-Muhasibi, Abu 'Abd Allah: Muslim mystic; d. 857. His *Book of observance of the rights of God* is meant to enable believers to find the way of life in which they could render to God the service which is His due. Of another work, presented as a vision of the last things, it has been said that it is a "Dies Irae" which ends up in an "In Paradisum".

al-Muhibbi: name of a family of scholars and jurists in Damascus in the xvith-xviith c. of which three members distinguished themselves in literature: Muhibb al-Din Abu 'l-Fadl, 1542-1608; his grandson Fadl Allah; 1621-1671; the latter's son Muhammad al-Amin, 1651-1699. Muhammad's principal work is a collection of biographies of scholars, poets etc. of his time and the period immediately preceding it.

Muhsin-i Fayd-i Kashani (Mulla Muhsin/Fayd): one of the greatest scholars of Safawid Persia; 1598-1679. He wrote on Tradition, philosophy and theoretical Sufism, ethics, jurisprudence, and composed commentaries on the Qur'an, poetry and prayers.

Muhtasham-i Kashani, Shams al-Shu'ara': Persian poet; b. ca. 1500-ca.1587. He wrote panegyrics, convential *qasida*s, enigmatic verses, poetical chronograms, love poetry and elegies.

Muhyi 'l-Din Lari: Persian writer; d. 1526. He is the author of a famous poetical description of the Holy Cities Mecca and Medina.

Muhyi 'l-Din Mehmed (Molla Čelebi): Turkish theologian and historian; d. 1550. He edited the anonymous Ottoman chronicles, which run from the beginnings of the Ottoman Empire and were continued by him down to 1549.

Mu'in al-Din Sulayman Parwana: *de facto* ruler of the Saljuq state of Rum in Anatolia during most of the Mongol Protectorate; d. 1277. Of Persian stock, he attempted to maintain stability both amongst the Turkish emirs and between them and the ever-increasing number of Mongols resident on Anatolian soil. He is said to have enjoyed a close relationship with Jalal al-Din Rumi.

Muʿin al-Din Yazdi: Persian historiographer; d. 1387. He adopted an avowed positive attitude towards the representatives of the despotic Muzaffarids who, after the decay of Mongol power, ruled from 1314 till 1394 in Fars, Isfahan and Yazd.

al-Muʿizz b. Badis: ruler of the Zirid dynasty; b. 1007, r. 1016-1062. In the history of Ifriqiya he remains the artisan of the restoration of Maliki orthodoxy, itself linked to the Hilali invasion of 1057.

Muʿizz al-Dawla, Abu ʾl-Husayn Ahmad: founder of the Buyid rule in Baghdad; b. 915, r. 945-967. Appointed supreme amir by the ʿAbbasid caliph al-Mutiʿ, he made the latter the instrument of his policy. He had to defend himself against the Hamdanids of Mosul and against the Daylami mercenaries, who had helped the Buyids to build their power. He began to rely more and more on Turkish mercenaries and distributed leases without any financial return, which was to become a characteristic of Buyid financial policy.

al-Muʿizz li-Din Allah, Maʿadd: last caliph of the Fatimid dynasty of Ifriqiya; b. 931, r. 953-975. After asserting his control over the central Maghrib against the Kharijites, he turned against the Spanish Umayyad ʿAbd al-Rahman III and his successor al-Hakam II. Hostilities against Byzantium, the ally of the Spanish Umayyads, were resumed in 955. In 963 a Byzantine expeditionary body was destroyed in Sicily and an agreement concluded. In 969 the freedman Jawhar started the famous expedition against Egypt where the Ikhshidids were removed and Cairo was founded. In order to check the Carmathians of Syria, al-Muʿizz transferred the seat of the Imamate to Egypt in 972.

Muʿizzi, Muhammad b. ʿAbd al-Malik: Persian panegyrist of the Saljuq period and poet laureate of the Great Saljuqs Malik Shah II and Sanjar; 1049-ca. 1125.

Muʿizzi or **Slave Kings**: name of a dynasty which ruled in northern India from 1206-1290. It was founded by Qutb al-Din Aybak.

Mujahid, al-Muwaffaq b. ʿAbd Allah: ruler of Denia (A. *Dāniya*) in Spain and of the Balearics; r. 1014-1044. Like many other monarchs of the Muluk al-Tawaʾif, he was a patron of studies, of theology in particular.

Mujir al-Din al-ʿUlaymi: Arab historian; 1456-1522. His principal work is a history of Jerusalem and Hebron.

Mujtahid: the Arabic term denotes one who possesses the aptitude to form his own judgement on questions concerning Islamic law, using personal effort (A. *ijtihād*) in the interpretation of the fundamental principles (A. *uṣūl*) of the law.

In Sunni circles, a consensus was gradually established towards the turn of the xth c. that *ijtihād* could no longer be practised. Only the founders of the four schools of law Abu Hanifa, Malik b. Anas, al-Shafiʿi, Ahmad b. Hanbal, and certain of their contemporaries or immediate successors could be regarded as *mujtahid*s in the strict sense. Like other devout Muslims, jurists were obliged to adopt the utterances of the *mujtahid*s as authoritative (A. *taqlīd*).

In the Twelver Shi'a the Persian term *marja'-i taqlīd* is used.

In India, growing influence was exercised by the *mujtahids* of Lakhnaw during the period of the Nawwabs of Awadh (Oudh) (1714-1856).

In the modern Arab countries, *mujtahids* have played very varied roles, ranging from traditional quietism to political activism.

Mukhammisa: the Arabic word means "Pentadists" and is applied to a doctrinal current among the Shi'i extremists which espoused the divinity of the Prophet, 'Ali, Fatima, al-Hasan and al-Husayn.

al-Mukhtar b. Abi 'Ubayd al-Thaqafi: leader of a pro-'Alid movement which controlled Kufa in 685-687; d. 687. He played a role in the development of Muslim sectarianism.

Mukhtar Pasha: Ottoman Turkish general and statesman; 1839-1919. He became Grand Vizier in July 1912 but had to resign in the following October.

al-Mukhtara: capital of the ephemeral Zanj "state" and centre of the movement which violently shook lower Iraq and lower Khuzistan between 869 and 883.

al-Muktafi bi-'llah: 'Abbasid caliph; r. 902-908. He fought the Carmathians in Syria, put an end to the rule of the Tulunids in Egypt and vigorously pursued the war with the Byzantines.

Mulla Sadra Shirazi: leading Persian philosopher; 1571-1640. His *Secrets* is widely regarded in Iran as the most advanced text in the field of mystical philosophy.

Multan: name given by the Arabs to the ancient city of Mulasthana in the Punjab, Pakistan. It was conquered in 711 and became one of the centres of Muslim rule in western India. It is known for its monuments.

Muluk al-Tawa'if (Sp. *Reyes de Taifas*): the name means "rulers of the factions" or Party Kings and is used for a number of local Muslim dynasties, which ruled in the various parts of al-Andalus between the final collapse of the Spanish Umayyads in the early part of the xith c. and the coming of the Almoravid Yusuf b. Tashufin in 1086.

Mumtaz Mahall: wife of the Mughal Emperor Shah Jahan; 1593-1631. It was for her that the Tāj Mahal was built.

Munajjim, Banu 'l-: name of an extensive family, whose members were active at the 'Abbasid court as scholars, literati and courtiers for six or seven generations; ca. 750-950. Eleven members of the family are mentioned as being of importance.

al-Munafiqun: term used in the Qur'an. It is usually translated as "hypocrites", "doubters" or "waverers", but the term is usually stronger and covers a wide semantic range, such as apostates, those who will never be forgiven and will be punished by eternal hellfire, against whom Holy War is to be waged and who are to be killed. In Qur'an LXIII, which is named after them, they are berated in the strongest terms.

"Dissenters" comes nearest to the totality of the use of the term in the

Qur'an, whereas "hypocrites" most closely fits post-Qur'anic Muslim usage of the term.

al-Munawi, 'Abd al-Ra'uf: Egyptian religious scholar and mystic; 1545-1621. His numerous works enjoyed a great success in his own time, and are still often cited today.

al-Mundhir b. Muhammad: Umayyad amir of Córdoba; b. 844, r. 886-888. His reign was mainly devoted to the war against the rebel 'Umar b. Hafsun.

al-Mundhir b. Sawa (Sawi): chief of the tribal division of Darim of Tamim, who were in close relations with the Persians; viith c. The Prophet is said to have sent a letter to al-Mundhir summoning him to embrace Islam. He played an important role in the Islamisation of Bahrain.

Münejjim Bashi, Derwish Ahmed Dede: Turkish scholar, Sufi poet and, above all, historian; d. 1702. He is the author of a celebrated and important general history in Arabic.

Münif Pasha: prominent Ottoman statesman and educational reformer; 1828-1910. Already in 1862 he pleaded for the reform of the Arabic script.

Mu'nis (Shir Muhammad Mirab): historian, poet and translator from Khiva; 1778-1829. He was one of the first writers who belonged to the period of the flourishing Chagatay literature in Khiva.

Mu'nis al-Muzaffar (Mu'nis al-Khadim): leading 'Abbasid general from 908 to 933, and latterly virtual dictator; d. 933. His example of depriving the caliph of real power was to be followed all too soon by the series of amirs, who were to dominate the successors of the Caliph al-Qahir bi-'llah.

Munqidh, Banu: clan prominent in Syrian (and Egyptian) affairs from ca. 1050-ca. 1300. Many of them perished when in 1157 a massive earthquake destroyed the citadel of Shayzar, northwest of Hamat. A prominent member of the clan was Usama b. Murshid b. 'Ali, known as Usama b. Munqidh.

al-Muntafiq: section of the Arab tribe of the Banu 'Uqayl, which in turn is a subdivision of the great group of the 'Amir b. Sa'sa'a. Mentioned in the history of pre-Islamic Arabia, they appear as ambassadors of the Banu 'Uqayl to the Prophet. In recent times they dominated the area from Baghdad to Basra between the xviith to xixth c. Their might declined through increasingly centralising Ottoman policy.

al-Muqaddasi, Shams al-Din (al-Bashshari): author of the most original and one of most valuable geographical treatises in Arabic literature; xth c. The work is called *The Best Division for the Knowledge of the Regions*. Its object is to treat only the Islamic world, made up of the Arab world and non-Arab world, and that after a division into regions (A. *aqālīm*, s. *iqlīm*), individualised through their physical characteristics.

Muqan (Mughan): steppe lying to the south of the lower course of the river Araxes, the northern part of which belongs to Azerbaijan and the other part to Iran. It was conquered by the Muslims in 642.

al-Muqattam: the limestone plateau that borders the city of Cairo to the east and the Nile to the west. The mediaeval city, therefore, has always grown northwards. In Islamic tradition, the Muqattam is a sacred mountain.

al-Muqawqis: the individual who in Arab tradition played the leading part on the side of the Copts and Greeks at the Muslim conquest of Egypt in 640.

al-Muqtadir bi-'llah: 'Abbasid caliph; b. 895, r. 908-932. His reign was marked by a gradual decline, and it inaugurated a period of unparalleled impotence and disaster for the central power of the caliphate.

Murad, Banu: Arab tribe belonging to the great southern group of the Madhhij. One of their chiefs went to Medina in 631 and concluded a treaty with the Prophet.

Murad I: Ottoman sultan; b. ?1326, r. 1362-1389. He was the first great Ottoman conqueror in the Balkan Peninsula, following the footsteps of his brother Süleyman Pasha and of other Turkish emirs. Under him the state founded by 'Othman rose to be more than merely one of the existing Turkmen principalities in Asia Minor.

Murad II: Ottoman sultan; b. 1403, r. 1421-1444, 1446-1451. In 1422 he began a siege of Constantinople, but this had to be raised. Most of his campaigns were directed to the west. In 1444, he abdicated in favour of his son Mehemmed but had to come back when the Hungarians were preparing a new crusade. He is described as a truthful, mild and humane ruler and was the first Ottoman prince whose court became a brilliant centre of poets, literary men and Muslim scholars.

Murad III: Ottoman sultan; b. 1546, r. 1574-1595. He waged war with Safawid Persia, and his reign was marred by conflicts of rival parties in the palace. He was a keen swordsman, was also deeply involved in popular mysticism and a patron of belles-lettres and of architecture. He spent much time in the harem, and was a minor poet in his own right.

Murad IV: Ottoman sultan; b. 1612, r. 1623-1640. In 1632 he had to suppress an army mutiny. In 1635 the Safawid fortress of Eriwan was taken, and in 1638 Baghdad itself surrendered, followed by a peace treaty with the Safawids in 1639. He possessed some literary talent and was interested in literary debate, Ewliya' Čelebi being his most famous favourite.

Murad V: Ottoman sultan; b. 1840, r. May-September 1876, d. 1904. In 1876 the new Grand Council decided to proclaim a constitution, but this could not be carried through because of Murad's mental state. He was deposed in 1876 and replaced by his brother Abdülhamid II.

Muradabad: district in the northwest of Uttar Pradesh in India with an important Muslim minority.

al-Muradi: name of a family of Sayyids and scholars established at Damascus in the xviith-xviiith c.

Murcia (A. *Mursiya*): town in the southeast of Spain, built about 825 by order of the Umayyad amir 'Abd al-Rahman II. During the period of the Muluk al-Tawa'if it was the capital of a little independent state, which was then conquered by the Almoravids. It was taken by the Christians in 1243 (or 1266).

Murji'a: name of a politico-religious movement in early Islam, derived from the Qur'anic usage of the verb which means "to defer judgement". In later times the name refers to all those who identified faith with belief, or confession of belief, to the exclusion of acts. They generally admitted that God might either punish or forgive Muslim offenders, which punishment, according to some, would be eternal, others affirming that it would be temporal and that all would eventually enter Paradise through the intercession of the Prophet. The latter view agrees with predominant Sunni traditionalist doctrine.

al-Murjibi, Hamid b. Muhammad (Tippu Tip): a personality of Afro-Arab stock who played a role in the history of East Africa and the Congo; ca. 1837-1905. Born in Zanzibar, he led caravan expeditions to the area around Lake Tanganyika and encountered David Livingstone. He was appointed governor of the Stanley Falls District of the Congo Free State in 1887 by King Leopold of Belgium on the advice of Stanley. He returned to Zanzibar in 1891 and remained a highly-respected person.

Murshidabad: district of India in the State of West Bengal, where the Muslims form a majority. Its history is part of the general history of Bengal. In the xviith c. it became an important centre of commerce, and the original name of Makhsusabad was changed into the present one.

al-Murtada, al-Sharif, Abu 'l-Qasim: Imami theologian, grammarian, writer and poet from Baghdad; 967-1044.

Musa, Banu: name of three brothers, Muhammad, Ahmad and al-Hasan, who were among the most important figures of Baghdad in the ixth c. They were skilled in geometry, mechanics, music, mathematics and astronomy. Muhammad (d. 873) played a part in the nomination of the Caliph al-Musta'in (I) bi-'llah. The best known of their books, which is largely the work of Ahmad, comprises descriptions of some 100 small machines.

Musa b. Abi 'l-'Afiya: chieftain of the Miknasa, a prominent Berber tribe of the Zanata confederation; d. 938. His claim to fame rests on his role in the troubled history of the Idrisids of Fez and the politics of the western Maghrib in the xth c.

Musa Čelebi: Ottoman prince and ruler of Rumelia; d. 1413. In 1411 he laid an unsuccessful siege to Constantinople.

Musa al-Kazim: seventh Imam of the Twelver Shi'a; 745-799. He adhered to a quietist policy, devoting himself to prayer and contemplation. Yet he was harassed by the 'Abbasid Caliphs al-Mahdi and Harun al-Rashid. His descendants are known as Musawis.

Musa b. Nusayr: conqueror of the western Maghrib and of Spain; 640-716. In 698 he was given the governorship of Ifriqiya by the governor of Egypt 'Abd al-'Aziz b. Marwan. He crossed to Spain in 712 and left the following year with immense booty.

Mus'ab b. 'Abd Allah: genealogist from Medina; 773-851. His fame rests upon a work on the history of the Quraysh, which is of outstanding importance for the history of the beginnings of Islam, and in particular for that of the first four caliphs.

Mus'ab b. 'Umayr: Companion of the Prophet of the Quraysh clan of 'Abd al-Dar; d. 625 in the battle of Uhud.

Mus'ab b. al-Zubayr: son of the famous Companion of the Prophet al-Zubayr b. al-'Awwam and brother of the anti-caliph 'Abd Allah b. al-Zubayr; d. 691. He defeated al-Mukhtar at Kufa in 687 but was killed near Basra.

al-Musabbihi: Fatimid historian; 977-1030. He is known as a prolific and versatile writer. The only one specimen of his writing which has survived is a chapter of his history of Egypt, recording events of 1023-1024.

Musafirids (Kangarids/Sallarids): dynasty of Daylami origin, which came from Tarum and reigned in the xth-xith c. in Azerbaijan, Arran and Armenia.

Musahib-zade Jelal (Musahip-zade Celal): Turkish classical playwright; 1868-1959. The themes of his plays were mainly taken from the daily lives of the Ottoman people in the xviith and xviiith c.

Musalla: the principal meaning of the word is the open space, usually outside a settlement, used during the sacrificial festival and the festival of breaking the fast.

Musawis: name for the descendants of Imam Musa al-Kazim, who are said to account for some 70% of all the Sayyids in present-day Iran.

Musaylima b. Habib: member of the Banu Hanifa who lived in al-Yamama; d. 632. He claimed to be a prophet, and led a large section of his tribe in revolt during the politico-religious uprisings, known as "apostasy" (A. *ridda*), in various parts of Arabia during the caliphate of Abu Bakr. Khalid b. al-Walid defeated him at the fierce battle of al-'Aqraba', in which many Helpers, invaluable for their knowledge of the as yet unwritten Qur'an, were killed.

Muscat (A. *Masqat*): port on the Gulf of Oman, since 1970 the capital of the Sultanate of Oman. In the late xvth c. the town grew at the expense of Qalhat. In 1507 Afonso d'Alboquerque sacked the town and massacred its population. Muscat then became the basis of Portuguese power in the Persian Gulf. In 1552, it was temporarily taken by the Ottoman admiral Piri Re'is. In 1649 it was stormed by the Ya'rubid Sultan b. Sayf, after which the Imams began to develop trade with India, South Arabia and East Africa. Under Ahmad b. Sa'id Bu-Sa'id (r. 1749-1783), Muscat's trade was directed at south India and close relations developed with Tipu Sultan of Mysore. The port reached its apogee under Sultan b. Ahmad Bu-Sa'id (r. 1792-1806). In 1832 Sa'id b. Sultan transferred the capital to Zanzibar. In the xxth c. Matrah grew in trade and in population at the expense of Muscat. Under Sa'id b. Taymur (r. 1932-1970) the capital of Oman was moved to Salala in Dhofar.

Mush: town and province of eastern Anatolia in Turkey, lying to the west of Lake Van. During the first centuries after the Islamic conquest, it remained a centre of Armenian national life. In Saljuq times, the influence of Islam became stronger. From 1473 it belonged to the Ottoman Empire.

Mushaqa, Mikhaʾil b. Jirjis: Lebanese historian and polemicist, and the most important of modern Arabic writers on the theory of music; 1800-1888.

Mushaʿshaʿ: Shiʿi Arab dynasty of the town of Hawiza (Huwayza) in Khuzistan; xvth-xxth c.

al-Mushatta (al-Mshatta): palatial, ruined structure of early Islamic date, south of Amman in Jordan.

Muslim Brethren, The (A. *al-Ikhwān al-Muslimūn*): Muslim movement, both religious and political, founded at Ismaʿiliyya in Egypt by Hasan al-Banna' in 1927. The Brethren were socially active during the formative period (1928-1936), which was followed by a period of political activity and of expansion, then of troubles (1936-1952). By supporting the cause of the Palestinian Arabs, Hasan al-Banna' was able to spread the movement throughout the Middle East and especially in Syria. After the Arab defeat in 1948, they appeared as an organized army, and the government of al-Nuqrashi dissolved the organization. Al-Banna' was assassinated in 1949. In 1951 the Brethren were able to resume their activities openly. The Revolutionary regime (from July 1952) at first sought their collaboration, but in 1953 a muted but bitter struggle began, and in 1954 the movement was once again dissolved. Shortly afterwards they were again granted the right to exist as a non-political organization. In the same year the future President Nasser narrowly escaped an attempt on his life by a member of the Brethren, who were persecuted but continued to exist clandestinely. Many elements of their doctrine are found in the preaching of Jamal al-Din al-Afghani, but their founder made it the ideological basis of a powerful popular movement. Their main objectives are the struggle against western invasion in all its forms, and the creation of an authentically Muslim state.

Muslim b. ʿAqil b. Abi Talib: leading supporter of al-Husayn b. ʿAli; d. 680. He was killed at Kufa by order of ʿUbayd Allah b. Ziyad.

Muslim b. al-Hajjaj: one of the outstanding early collectors of Prophetic traditions; 817-875. According to the consensus of Sunni Muslim tradition experts, his collection, known as *Ṣaḥīḥ*, forms, together with the *Ṣaḥīḥ* of al-Bukhari, the most reliable one of Prophetic traditions.

Muslim b. Quraysh, Sharaf al-Dawla: the most important ruler of the Bedouin Arab dynasty of the ʿUqaylids; b. 1022, r. 1042-1085. In 1066 he concluded an alliance with the Great Saljuq Alp Arslan, who granted him several towns in al-Jazira. With the help of Alp Arslan's son Malik-Shah I, Muslim took Aleppo, Baghdad, Edessa and Harran. Later, however, he joined forces with the Fatimid Caliph al-Mustansir bi-'llah. After his death, Turkish generals of the Saljuqs became the rulers of Syria and al-Jazira.

Muslim b. ʿUqba: famous commander of the Umayyad Caliphs Muʿawiya I and Yazid I; viith c. He led the expedition against Medina to bring the

Helpers back to obedience, and died before reaching Mecca to deal with 'Abd Allah b. al-Zubayr.

Muslim b. al-Walid al-Ansari: Arab poet; ca. 747-823. He wrote odes, elegies, satires and drinking-songs which describe society and social life in the towns.

Muslims in Europe and in the Americas: the Muslim communities of Europe as a whole can be divided into two distinct groups: the old communities, formed in the distant, or very distant past, and the new communities, established recently in the industrialised countries as immigrants.

1. The first group is found in:

Poland: in the xivth and xvth c. Tatars from the khanate of the Golden Horde and the khanates situated on the Volga arrived in the Grand Duchy of Lithuania. Currently, no more than 2,200 Tatars remain.

Finland: the Muslim community consists of about a thousand "Turko-Tatars" from the Idel Ural and the Volga regions. The majority arrived after the Soviet revolution of 1917.

Hungary: the first Muslim community, formed between 1526 and 1699, disappeared after the reconquest at the end of the xviith c. A new community was established after 1878 by Muslims arriving from Bosnia-Hercegovina, and by Ottoman Turkish citizens. Currently, there is no longer a Hungarian Muslim community.

Rumania: some 50,000 persons of Turkish and Tatar stock live for the most part in the Dobruja.

Greece: the Muslim community numbers between 130,000 and 150,000 persons, belonging to three clearly distinct groups: the Turks (and gypsies) of eastern Thrace, the Bulgarophone Pomaks, and the Turks of Rhodes and Kos.

Albania: in 1945 there were 816,677 Muslims, forming a perfectly homogenised community. The great majority were Sunnis and some 20% Bektashis.

Bulgaria: in 1946 the Muslim population numbered 938,418 persons or 13.35% of the total population, currently, however, some 600,000. They consist of Islamicised Bulgarians, Turks, Tatars and gypsies.

(former) Yugoslavia: the number of Muslims must exceed, to a considerable extent, the figure of three million. They are located in Bosnia-Hercegovina, Kosovo, Macedonia and Montenegro. The Muslim community is composed of four quite distinct strata: the urban intelligentsia, a popular stratum, the Muslim religious intelligentsia, and a still very small stratum of young Islamologists and Muslim "Orientalists". At the time of writing, the Muslim population in Bosnia is forced to defend itself against the "ethnic purity" policy of the Serbs.

2. To the second group belong the migrant Muslims in Western Europe. Before 1945 there were groups of Muslims in Germany because of the links with Turkey, in Britain and France due to the colonial system.

In the 1950s the growing European economies began to seek labour further afield. Muslim communities are now found in:

France: the overall population of Muslim background is about three million, consisting of 800,000 Algerians, 430,000 Moroccans, 190,000 Tunisians and 125,000 Turks.

Great Britain: the Muslim population is estimated at about one million, consisting mainly of people from Pakistan and Bangladesh, and of smaller groups from East and West Africa, Cyprus, Malaysia, Iran, and a variety of Arab countries.

Germany: the total of some two million Muslims (1988) is made up of 1.5 million Turks, the minority being formed by people from Iran, Pakistan, Morocco, Tunisia, and other Arab countries.

Netherlands: there were 337,900 Muslims of foreign origin in 1986. In 1988 the majority was made up of 180,000 Turks and 120,000 Moroccans, the minority being mainly formed by Surinamese of Indian origin, and a few thousand each from Pakistan, Yugoslavia, Indonesia, and Arabs other than Moroccans.

Belgium: in 1986 the total number of Muslims was about 300,000, two-thirds of whom were Moroccans, and the majority of the rest Turks.

Austria: at the end of the 1980s the Muslim population consisted of some 100,000 persons, most of them Turks, and a minority of Yugoslavs and Austrians.

Switzerland: the 1980 census recorded just over 56,000 Muslim residents, and at the end of 1988 estimates suggested a total of about 100,000, half of whom were Turks, about a quarter Yugoslavs, and most of the rest from North Africa.

Scandinavia: the estimates in Sweden vary between 70,000 in 1989 and 100,000 in 1991. Most of the Muslims are of Turkish origin with a smaller group of Yugoslavs. In Denmark the Muslim population approached 50,000 in the late 1980s, over half originating from Turkey. There is also a significant Pakistani population, and about 10,000 Iranians. In Norway there were about 15,000 Muslims in 1984, half of whom were Pakistanis, and the rest mainly from Turkey and Morocco.

Southern Europe: reliable information is lacking, primarily because the vast majority of foreigners are unregistered. In Portugal, most Muslims, possibly two-thirds of a total of 50,000, are stateless immigrants from former Portuguese colonies in India or southern Africa. In Spain, Islam was forbidden under General Franco. Currently, most of the Muslims are immigrants or temporary residents from Morocco or Algeria. In Italy, there may be some 200,000 immigrant Muslims, mostly from North Africa, including a good proportion of Libyans.

3. In North and South America, the majority of the Arabic-speaking emi-

grants to the Americas (A. *Jāliya*) were Christians from Lebanon. Most of the Muslims originated from Palestine, Iraq and the Yemen.

The so-called "Black Muslims" (A. *Bilāliyyūn*), also known as "the Nation of Islam", were founded in Detroit in 1931. Central roles were played by Elijah Muhammad (E. Poole, d. 1975) and Malcolm X (Malcolm Little, d. 1965).

Mustafa: name of several princes belonging to the Ottoman dynasty. Among them may be mentioned Mustafa Čelebi, Düzme, the eldest son of Sultan Bayezid I and counter-sultan or pretender, d. 1422 or 1430; Mustafa Čelebi, Küçük Mustafa, son of Sultan Mehemmed I and counter-sultan, d. 1423; Mustafa, son of Süleyman II, 1515-1553. He was executed at the orders of his father.

Mustafa II: Ottoman sultan; b. 1664, r. 1695-1703. In 1699 peace was concluded with Austria, Poland and Venice at Carlowicz. The sultan abdicated in 1703 and died in the same year. Under him, the imperial cipher (T. *ṭughrā*) appeared for the first time on the Ottoman coins.

Mustafa III: Ottoman sultan; b. 1717, r. 1757-1774. In 1768 a disastrous war with Russia broke out. Mustafa III is praised in the Turkish sources as a good ruler.

Mustafa ʿAbd al-Raziq: Egyptian journalist who became Rector of al-Azhar; 1882-1946. He was a disciple of Muhammad ʿAbduh.

Mustafa Barzani, Mulla: Kurdish leader from Iraq; 1902-1979. His father, Shaykh ʿAbd al-Salam was hanged in Mosul in 1915 for his defiance of the Ottoman state, and his brother Shaykh Ahmad was defeated by the Iraqi army with the help of the British R.A.F. In 1943 Mulla Mustafa raised a revolt in northern Iraq but was expelled into Persia, where the Kurdish Democratic Party (KDP) had been founded in Mahabad. In 1947 he was chased back into Iraq and escaped to the Soviet Union where he stayed until 1948. During his absence, the KPD was led by Ibrahim Ahmad, under whom it gradually developed into a political as distinct from a nationalist party, which led to a rift in the Kurdish movement in later years. After the Revolution of 1958, ʿAbd al-Karim Qasim invited Mulla Mustafa back to Iraq, but by 1961 relations with the government had greatly deteriorated and fighting began. In 1970 a Manifesto for Kurdish autonomy was announced, but by 1973 Mulla Mustafa had come to the conclusion that the Baʿth government of Iraq did not have any serious intention of implementing it. He had resumed his relations with Persia and began a serious dialogue with the United States. In 1975 Saddam Husayn and the Shah of Persia signed the Algiers Agreement, which effectively ended Persian support to the Kurds. Mulla Mustafa went into exile in Teheran, and eventually died in the United States. The leadership of the KPD passed to his son Masʿud. A new movement, the Patriotic Union of Kurdistan, was formed by Jalal Talabani.

Mustafa Kamil Pasha: leader of the second nationalist movement in Egypt; 1874-1908. In 1894 he founded the second Egyptian nationalist party, the first being that of 'Urabi Pasha who had been defeated by the British in 1882. The object was to induce Britain by appeals to justice to abandon the occupation and restore the complete independence of Egypt.

Mustafa Kemal: the founder and first President of the Turkish Republic is generally known under his honorific title Atatürk.

Mustafa Khayri Efendi, Ürgüplü: Shaykh al-Islam of the Ottoman Empire; 1867-1921. In 1914 he issued the ill-famed *fatwā* sanctioning the "Great Holy War" against Russia, Great Britain, France and their allies.

Mustafa Khaznadar: Tunisian official; 1817-1878. He was successively Prime Minister to three Beys, Ahmad (r. 1837-1855), M'hammad (r. 1855-1859) and Muhammad al-Sadiq (r. 1859-1873).

Mustafa Pasha, Bayraqdar ('Alemdar): Ottoman Grand Vizier; ca. 1750-1808. He revived aspects of the modernisation programme envisaged by Sultan Selim III.

Mustafa Pasha, Bushatli: Ottoman statesman of Albanian origin; 1797-1860. He rebelled against the Ottoman power, was defeated in 1831, but rejoined the administration from 1846 onwards.

Mustafa Pasha, Lala: famous Ottoman commander; d. 1580. He conquered Cyprus in 1570-1571 and campaigned in Georgia in 1578.

Mustafa Pasha al-Nashshar: Ottoman governor of Yemen from 1540-1545 and from 1551-1555. In 1542 he supplied troops and weapons to Ahmad Grañ in Abyssinia. He is known for having instituted the first annual pilgrims' caravan to Mecca from Ottoman Yemen.

al-Musta'in (I) bi-'llah: 'Abbasid caliph; r. 862-866. He was made caliph by the Turkish commanders at Samarra after the death of his cousin al-Muntasir.

al-Musta'in (II) bi-'llah: 'Abbasid "shadow" caliph in Egypt; r. 1406-1414, d. 1430. He abdicated as sultan and was deposed as caliph.

al-Mustakfi bi-'llah: 'Abbasid caliph; b. 903, r. 944-946, d. 949. He was forced to recognise the Buyid leader Mu'izz al-Dawla Ahmad as in effect ruler of Iraq, and then was deposed and imprisoned.

al-Musta'li bi-'llah, Abu 'l-Qasim: Fatimid caliph; b. 1074, r. 1094-1101. Throughout his reign, the actual power was entirely in the hands of the vizier al-Afdal b. Badr al-Jamali. His name is connected with the Musta'li Isma'ilis in western India, also known as Bohoras. In 1099 Jerusalem was lost to the Crusaders.

al-Mustanjid (I) bi-'llah, Abu 'l-Muzaffar: 'Abbasid caliph in Baghdad; b. 1116, r. 1160-1170. His reign was dominated by powerful viziers and court officials. Policies aimed at the exclusion of the Saljuqs from Iraq, and al-Mustanjid's reign witnessed the continuing flowering of Hanbalism. The caliph was famous as a poet and had a first-hand knowledge of astronomy.

al-Mustanjid (II) bi-'llah, Abu 'l-Mahasin: 'Abbasid "shadow" caliph of Egypt; b. ?1396, r. 1455-1479. Khushqadam, one of the six successive Mamluk sultans who dominated him, kept him in the Citadel of Cairo until his death.

al-Mustansir (I) bi-'llah, Abu Ja'far: 'Abbasid caliph; b. 1192, r. 1226-1242. At least two major figures at the court were Shi'is. Al-Mustansir's caliphate spans an uneasy lull between Mongol onslaughts. He stands out as a great patron of architecture, among other works through the Mustansiriyya madrasa in Baghdad. He was also a great bibliophile.

al-Mustansir (II) bi-'llah, Abu 'l-Qasim: first 'Abbasid "shadow" caliph of Egypt; r. 1261. When the Mongols captured Baghdad in 1258, he was brought to Cairo, where he was given a ceremonious welcome by the Mamluk sultan Baybars I. The caliph invested Baybars with the black livery of the 'Abbasids and conferred on him the universal sultanate with plenary powers. Baybars sent the caliph to Iraq, to regain his ancestral dominions from the Mongols. He joined forces with a kinsman and rival, who had been proclaimed as the caliph al-Hakim by Aqqush al-Barli, the Mamluk warlord of Aleppo. Al-Mustansir was killed in a Mongol ambush, while al-Hakim made his way to Cairo, where he was installed as caliph in 1262. His descendants continued the titular caliphate until it lapsed after the Ottoman conquest of Egypt in 1517.

al-Mustansir bi-'llah, Abu Tamim: Fatimid caliph; b. 1029, r. 1036-1094. He had the longest recorded reign of any Muslim ruler. The breakdown of the civil administration, the subsequent exhaustion of the treasury and the fightings between the Turkish and Berber troops and the many Sudani slaves led to the neglect of agriculture. The result was a famine, which lasted from 1067-1072. In 1073 the caliph invited the Armenian Badr al-Jamali, who saved the Fatimid caliphate but at the cost of abandoning its temporal authority to a series of military commanders. The success of the Saljuqs affected the position of the Fatimids in the Holy Cities, where the 'Abbasid caliph was acknowledged, in the Hejaz and in Yemen, as well as in the West, where Ifriqiya was lost. Diplomatic relations were entertained with the Georgians, the Daylamis, the khaqan of Turkestan and with Delhi, all hostile to the Saljuqs and the Ghaznawids. It came however to a breach with Constantinople.

The state religion of the Fatimids, Isma'ili Shi'ism, was disseminated in Persia and in Yemen, where it was supported by the Sulayhids.

Müstaqim-zade, Sa'd al-Din: Ottoman scholar and calligrapher; 1719-1788. He composed around 150 books, most of them in Turkish but some also in Arabic and Persian, dealing with religious sciences, belles-lettres and Sufism.

al-Mustarshid bi-'llah: 'Abbasid caliph; b. 1093, r. 1118-1135. He initially juggled with the various factions among the Saljuqs of Iraq and western Persia, depending on one group or another for military support. He finally was defeated by the Saljuq Mas'ud b. Muhammad b. Malik-Shah in 1135 and murdered, allegedly by Assassins. He was a fine calligrapher and an accomplished poet.

al-Musta'sim bi-'llah: the last 'Abbasid caliph of Baghdad: b. 1212, r. 1247-1258. Having refused to meet the demands of the Mongol Il-Khan Hülegü, the caliph was captured and put to death.

al-Mustazhir bi-'llah: 'Abbasid caliph; b. 1078, r. 1094-1118. He was never able to turn the debilitating disputes between the Saljuq sultans Berkya-ruq, Tutush and Muhammad Tapar to his own advantage. The Nizari schism had further weakened the Fatimid caliphate and unleashed the Assassins' campaigns within Saljuq territory.

Mu'ta: town to the east of the southern end of the Dead Sea. It is re-nowned for the defeat of the Muslims there against Christian Arabs in 629.

al-Mu'tadid bi-'llah: 'Abbasid caliph; b. ca. 860, r. 892-902. His strength was the close relations with the army. While forced to acknowledge that Khu-rasan, Syria and Egypt were lost to the 'Abbasids, at least for the time being, he strove to re-establish control over the core territories, Iraq, al-Jazira and western Persia. His reign saw the final return of the 'Abbasid capital from Samarra to Baghdad.

al-Mu'tadid bi-'llah: the most important and most powerful sovereign of the 'Abbadid dynasty in Seville; r. 1042-1069. He very considerably in-creased his territory by making himself the champion of the Spanish Arabs against the Berbers in Spain.

Mutahhari, Ayatollah Murtada: Iranian religious thinker, writer, and close associate of Ayatollah Khumayni; 1920-1979. He was active in foster-ing the intellectual developments that contributed to the Revolution of 1978-1979. He was assassinated in Teheran by adherents of Furqan, a group which espoused a radically modernistic interpretation of Shi'i doctrine.

al-Mu'tamid Ibn 'Abbad: third and last ruler of the 'Abbadid dynasty in Seville; b. 1040, r. 1069-1091, d. 1095. By the middle of the xith c., many Muslim dynasties of Spain were being forced to seek by payment of heavy tribute the temporary neutrality of their Christian neighbours. al-Mu'tamid was defeated by the Almoravid Yusuf b. Tashufin. He was an accomplished poet.

Mutammim b. Nuwayra: poet who was a contemporary of the Prophet; d. after 644. He owes his fame to the elegies in which he lamented the tragic death of his brother Malik b. Nuwayra.

al-Mutanabbi (Abu 'l-Tayyib Ahmad al-Ju'fi): one of the greatest Arab poets; 915-965. Without adhering to Carmathian doctrines, he exploited its principles when in 933 he led a revolt in the Samawa, the region between Kufa and Palmyrene. On this occasion he received the surname al-Mutanabbi "he who professes to be a prophet". After having led a wandering life, he stayed nine years with the Hamdanid Sayf al-Dawla 'Ali I in Aleppo, but fled to Damascus in 957. In Egypt he obtained the patronage of the Ikhshidid regent Kafur but, deprived of moral and material independence, he was forced to sing the praises of a patron for whom in his heart he felt only contempt. In

962 he fled to Kufa and then settled in Baghdad. In 965 he went via Ahvaz to Arrajan in Susiana and from there to Shiraz. On his way back to Baghdad he was killed by marauding Bedouins. The enormous bibliography of al-Mutanabbi's life and work is a striking proof of the eminent place which he occupies in Arabic literature from the xth c. till the present day.

Mutarrifiyya: Zaydi sect in Yemen named after its founder Mutarrif b. Shihab (d. 1067). They constituted a pietist movement which was destroyed by the Zaydi Imam 'Abd Allah al-Mansur b. Hamza (r. 1198-1217) in 1214.

al-Mutarrizi, Burhan al-Din: philologist, jurist and man of letters; 1144-1213. His compendium of Arabic grammar has found the widest circulation.

al-Mu'tasim, Abu Yahya: ruler of the dynasty of the Tujibids of the kingdom of Almería; r. 1051-1091. He took part in the battle of Zallaqa.

al-Mu'tasim bi-'llah: 'Abbasid caliph; r. 833-842. He fought the Khurrami leader Babak, the Byzantines, the Qarinids in Tabaristan and rebels in Damascus, in Palestine and in Jordan.

al-Mutawakkil 'ala 'llah, Abu 'l-Fadl: 'Abbasid caliph; b. 822, r. 847-861. He was determined from the beginning to assert the independence of the caliph and to break the dominance of the Turkish military and the bureaucracy. He broke with the Mu'tazili position which had been the official doctrine of the 'Abbasid government since the Caliph al-Ma'mun had introduced the *mihna*. In its place he stressed his adherence to the doctrines of the Hanbalis and other traditionists. His murder plunged the caliphate into anarchy.

al-Mutawakkil 'ala 'llah, Ibn al-Aftas: last ruler of the Aftasid dynasty in the petty state of Badajoz (1022-1094).

al-Mutawakkil 'ala 'llah, Isma'il: first Qasimi Zaydi Imam to rule Yemen completely independent of the Ottoman Turks; r. 1644-1676. He conducted successful campaigns against Aden and Lahj, al-Bayda' and Yafi', Hadhramaut and even Dhofar in Oman.

al-Mutawakkil 'ala 'llah, Sharaf al-Din: Zaydi Imam in whose time the Ottoman Turks first became established in Yemen; b. 1473, r. 1535-1547, d. 1555.

Mu'tazila: name of a religious movement founded at Basra by Wasil b. 'Ata', subsequently becoming one of the most important theological schools of Islam. The term indicates those who take a position of neutrality in the face of two opposing factions, in particular in the question of how to define a Muslim guilty of a grave sin. For the Kharijites he was an infidel (A. *kāfir*), for the Murji'is a believer in spite of his sinfulness (A. *fisq*), and for Hasan al-Basri, Wasil's teacher, a hypocrite (A. *munāfiq*). The distinctive theses of Mu'tazilism were propounded by Abu 'l-Hudhayl al-'Allaf in the form of the following "five principles": uniqueness of God; justice of God; every Muslim guilty of a serious offence, who dies without repentance, will suffer for eternity the torments of Hell; the same sinful Muslim cannot here on earth be classed either as "believing" or as "disbelieving", but belongs to a separate category, that of the "malefactor" (the theory of an "intermediate state"; A. *al-manzila bayn al-manzilatayn*); every believer has the obligation to intervene in public affairs to uphold the Law and oppose impiety.

For a period of some thirty years, the Muʿtazili school enjoyed the favour of the ʿAbbasid caliphs at Baghdad, until Caliph al-Mutawakkil in 848 revoked the decrees imposing the view that the Qurʾan had been created. But the Muʿtazila continued to be supported in numerous regions of the Islamic world, especially in Persia, and by powerful princes such as the Buyids, during a second period, which lasted from the last quarter of the ixth c. to the middle of the xith c. The most characteristic feature of the first period is the extreme diversity of scholars and of doctrines, whereas in the second period genuine schools were established. Even after the end of the second period, Muʿtazilism did not disappear. Its theses have been adopted by Imami and Zaydi Shiʿis, and in the xxth c. a significant trend of the rehabilitation of Muʿtazilism has been observed, especially in Egypt.

Muʿtazili: name used for an adherent of the religious movement called Muʿtazila.

al-Muʿtazz bi-ʾllah: ʿAbbasid caliph; r. 866-869. His reign marks the beginning of what was in effect autonomy for Egypt under Ahmad b. Tulun and, among other upheavals, the advance into southern Persia of the Saffarid Yaʿqub b. al-Layth (r. 867-879).

al-Muthanna b. Haritha: Arab tribal chieftain and hero of the early Islamic conquest of Iraq; d. 635.

al-Mutiʿ li-ʾllah: ʿAbbasid caliph; r. 946-974. Arab chroniclers regard his reign as the lowest ebb of the caliphate before events began to revive somewhat under his successors al-Qadir bi-ʾllah and al-Qaʾim bi-Amr Allah.

al-Muttaqi li-ʾllah: ʿAbbasid caliph; b. 920, r. 940-944, d. 968. He was deposed by the Turkish general Tuzun.

al-Muwaffaq, Talha b. Jaʿfar (Abu Ahmad): regent and virtual ruler during the time of the ʿAbbasid Caliph al-Muʿtamid ʿala ʾllah (r. 870-892); d. 891. In 883 he extinguished the rebellion of the Zanj.

al-Muwaylihi: name of a well-to-do family of silk merchants in Egypt. Two of its members, Ibrahim (1844-1906) and his son Muhammad (1859-1930), became famous as journalists and writers.

al-Muzaffar, al-Malik, Taqi ʾl-Din: nephew and army commander of Saladin; 1139-1191. He was the founder of the branch of the Ayyubids which ruled in Hamat from 1178 until 1341 and one of the leading military and administrative personalities of the xiith c.

Muzaffar al-Din Shah Qajar: shah of Persia; b. 1853, r. 1896-1907. When he came to the throne, Persia was the focus of intense rivalry between Britain and Russia, and corruption was widespread. In 1897 Belgian officials were employed to re-organise and run the country's Customs service. The shah, who had weak health, made three journeys to Europe.

Muzaffarids: one of the successor dynasties (r. 1314-1393) which arose in Kirman, Fars and Jibal following the disintegration of the Il-Khanid Empire. They took pains to display an unimpeachable orthodoxy, and were patrons of men of letters.

al-Muzani, Abu Ibrahim: "champion" of the Shafi'i school of law; 791-878. He compiled a celebrated compendium of the writings and lectures of his teacher al-Shafi'i.

al-Muzdalifa: place roughly halfway between Mina and 'Arafat where the pilgrims returning from 'Arafat spend the night between 9 and 10 Dhu 'l-Hijja.

Mysore (A. *Mahisur/Maysūr*): former princely state of south India, now the core of a component state of the Indian Union called Karnataka, with its capital at Bangalore. It is also the name of the town which was the dynastic capital of the state. The first contacts with the Muslims were in the xith-xiiith c. In 1310 the region was made tributary to Delhi by the Khalji sultans but did not undergo any Muslim influence of importance. In 1941 the Muslims, overwhelmingly Sunnis, numbered less than 10% of the population of over 7 million.

There are however monuments, such as mosques, tombs and palaces, which show Muslim influence.

Mzab: region of the Algerian Sahara. In early Islam, the Kharijites, many of them Ibadis, founded communities in the Jabal Nafusa. Its architecture is called the jewel of the Sahara.

N

Nabataeans (A. *Nabaṭ*): the Arabs distinguish between the Nabataeans of Syria, installed at Petra towards the end of the Hellenistic imperial era and at the beginning of the Roman one, and those of Iraq.

Nabhan, Banu: name of a tribe in Oman, whose offshoots are found in Pate, in the Lamu archipelago of East Africa, and in Kilwa.

Nabi, Yusuf: highly renowned Ottoman poet from Urfa; 1642-1712. His most famous poetical work is a book of advice from father to son meant as a guide for life.

al-Nabigha al-Dhubyani: one of the most famous poets of the pre-Islamic period; vith c. The collection of his poems has exercised great influence on later poets of renown, among them al-Mutanabbi, who mentions him by name and imitates him in several instances.

al-Nabigha al-Ja'di: poet and Companion of the Prophet; d. ca. 698. He took the part of 'Ali and consequently suffered great harm under Mu'awiya's rule. In his poetry he is influenced by Labid b. Rabi'a.

Nabulus: Muslim town on the West Bank, formerly in Jordan, since 1967 under Israeli administration, with few Jews and Christians and a very small community of Samaritans. From the 1930s onwards it became a centre of resistance to Jewish emigration into Palestine and in 1936 the first "Arab National Committee" was founded there.

Nadhir Ahmad Dihlawi: Urdu prose writer; 1836-1912. He is often described as "the first real novelist" in that language.

Nadhr al-Islam, Qadi (Kazi Nazrul Islam): revolutionary Bengali poet; 1899-1976. He was the greatest Muslim contributor to modern Bengali literature.

al-Nadim, al-Sayyid ʿAbd Allah: radical Egyptian orator and propagandist; 1843-1896. In 1881 he founded a newspaper which became the organ of the movement led by ʿUrabi Pasha.

Nadir, Banu 'l-: one of the three main Jewish tribes of Yathrib (Medina), the others being the Banu Qaynuqaʿ and the Banu Qurayza. They surrendered to the Prophet and some went to Syria, others to Khaybar.

Nadir Shah Afshar: ruler of Persia of the Afsharid dynasty; b. 1688, r. 1736-1747. His rise to power began through his service under the Safawid Tahmasp II, whence the name he adopted of Tahmasp Quli Khan "slave of Tahmasp", known in European sources as (Tamas) Couli-cam. He subdued the Abdali and Ghalzay Afghans, recaptured Hamadan from the Ottomans, denounced Tahmasp's treaties with Turkey and Russia and deposed him in 1732. Acting as regent, he defeated the Ottomans near Kirkuk in 1733. He accepted his proclamation as shah in 1736 upon the condition that the Sunni faith be adopted in place of the Shiʿi cult, introduced by Shah Ismaʿil, in order to facilitate a treaty with Turkey. In 1739 he invaded India, defeated the Mughal Emperor Muhammad Shah and exacted all lands west of the Indus and an enormous sum as reparations, including the Peacock Throne and the Kuh-i Nur diamond. In 1741 he marched against Dagestan. In order to fund his campaigns in the west, he redoubled his exactions from the Persians, which led to rebellion. In 1747 he was killed by a group of Persian, Afshar and Qajar officers.

Nafiʿ b. al-Azraq: leader of an extremist Khariji fraction, known after him as the Azariqa; d. 685. He gave military assistance to anti-caliph ʿAbd Allah b. al-Zubayr, seized control of Basra but was defeated by Muslim b. ʿUbays. He is considered as the first theoretician of Kharijism.

Nafiʿ al-Laythi: one of the seven canonical Qurʾan "readers"; d. 785.

Nafisi, Saʿid: Persian scholar, fiction writer and poet; 1896-1966. He acquired a great love of the French language and its literature and was a prolific writer.

al-Nafusa, Banu (Berber: *Infusen*): name of a Berber tribe, at present dwelling to the south-west of Tripoli in Libya. They are one of the four branches of the large body of the Butr. Their name is recorded for the first time in connection with the capture of the town of Tripoli by ʿAmr b. al-ʿAs in

642. Their greatest activities took place during the Khariji revolts between 739 and the beginning of the era of the Fatimids in the early xth c. They embraced the Ibadiyya and remained ever faithful to it, as they did to their Berber vernacular. They were faithful subjects during the period of Italian rule.

al-Nafusi, Abu Sahl: Ibadi scholar of the Rustamid princes of Tahert; vii-ith c. He is best known as the author of an extensive Berber *dīwān*.

Nafzawa: Berber tribe belonging to the Butr. They are known for having given their name to a region of Tunisia to the south-southeast of the Chott el Jerid.

Nagaur (Nagor) (A. *Nāgawr*): town and district in the Rajasthan state of the Indian Union. Muslim presence dates back to a period preceding the Ghurid conquest in the xiith c. Among its Muslim monuments are inscriptions, a gateway and mosques.

Nagpur: city and district of the state of Maharashtra in the Indian Union. In 1670 the ruler of Deogarh embraced Islam. The most famous ruler was the converted Gond chief Bakht Buland. At present the Muslim community includes Bohora and Khoja Isma'ilis as well as Sunnis.

Nagyvárad (T. *Warād*; German: *Großwardein*): town in Rumania with a considerable Hungarian population. It was taken by the Ottomans in 1660 and in 1692 by Habsburg forces.

Nahj al-Balagha: name of an anthology of dissertations, letters, testimonials and sententious opinions, traditionally attributed to the Prophet's son-in-law 'Ali. Its authorship has been object of constant and lively polemic, from the Middle Ages to the present.

al-Nahhas, Mustafa: Egyptian statesman; 1879-1965. He took over leadership of the Wafd party after the death of its founder Sa'd Zaghlul in 1927.

al-Nahrawali (Nahrawani), **Qutb al-Din**: eminent scholar and chronicler from Lahore who lived in Mecca; 1511-1582. He wrote a well-known chronicle of the Holy City and another of early Ottoman Yemen.

al-Nahrawan: town and canal system in the lower Diyala region east of the Tigris in Iraq. In 658 a battle took place there between 'Ali and the Kharijis, led by 'Abd Alah b. Wahb al-Rasibi, in which 'Ali was victorious.

Na'ili (Piri-zade; Na'ili-yi Qadim): celebrated Ottoman poet; d. 1666. His most important work is his collection of 390 *ghazal*s.

Na'ima: leading Ottoman historian from Aleppo; 1655-1716. His fame rests upon what is generally called *The History of Na'ima*. It is a compilation in largely traditional, annalistic format, covering the years 1591-1660. In 1733 it was one of the first Ottoman printed works.

Na'ini, Mirza Muhammad: prominent Shi'i religious leader; 1860-1936. He was an active supporter of the Persian constitutional revolution of 1906, and a noted constitutional ideologue. In his celebrated *The Admonition and Refinement of the People* (1909) he argued that constitutionalism, despite its being a Western idea, was in harmony with Shi'ism.

Naitias (Na'itas): regional Indian term applied to Muslims of Arab and Persian descent who settled on the coast of Konkan, the coastal plain of Maharashtra, and in Kanara, a region along the Malabar coast of the Arabian Sea. They are the descendants of the earliest Muslim trading communities on the western coast of India.

al-Najaf (Mashhad ʿAli): town and place of pilgrimage in Iraq near Kufa. According to the usual tradition, the Prophet's son-in-law ʿAli was buried near Kufa, but other places also claim his tomb. Under the Hamdanid of Mosul Abu 'l-Hayja' (r. 905-929) a large dome was built, and the Shiʿi ʿAdud al-Dawla built a mausoleum. The sanctuary was burnt down by the fanatical populace of Baghdad in 1051, but must have been soon rebuilt. Illustrious pilgrims were the Great Saljuq Malik-Shah I and his vizier Nizam al-Mulk, the Il-Khan Mahmud Ghazan, the Safawid Shah Ismaʿil and the Ottoman sultan Süleyman II. Al-Najaf was in Persian hands between 1623-1638, when Ottoman control was restored. The town retained a virtual autonomy and revolted several times against Ottoman rule. It was also a focus of anti-British opposition during the Arab revolt of 1920 and subsequently of opposition to King Faysal I. From 1965 to 1978 it was the residence of Ayatollah Khomayni.

Najahids: dynasty of Abyssinian slaves in Yemen who had their capital in Zabid, r. 1022-1158. It is named after Najah, one of the slave governors of Marjan, the independent Abyssinian vizier of the last member of the Ziyadids. Najah was recognised in 1022 by the ʿAbbasid caliph al-Qadir bi-'llah and ruled until 1060, when he was killed by the first Sulayhid ʿAli b. Muhammad (r. 1047-1067). After the death of his son Jayyash (ca. 1107), confusion reigned. In 1159 the Mahdids entered Zabid. Like the Ziyadids before them, the Najahids continually brought over to Yemen shiploads of Abyssinian slaves. They also struck their own coins.

Najd: the plateau region of the Arabian Peninsula lying to the east of the Red Sea lowlands (A. *al-tihāma*) and the mountain barrier running down through the western side of the Peninsula (A. *al-ḥijāz*). The Wadi 'l-Rumma and the Wadi 'l-Dawasir have formed since ancient times the two main routes of traffic in Central Arabia. With the aim of sedentarising the Bedouin, ʿAbd al-ʿAziz II Ibn Saʿud established settlements in Najd. The region, which contains Riyadh, the capital of Saudi Arabia, has benefited from the rapid expansion of the oil industry which began in earnest during the 1950s.

al-Najjar, al-Husayn b. Muhammad: Murji'i theologian of the period of the ʿAbbasid Caliph al-Ma'mun. His opinions influenced the Muʿtazila in their formative period by his keen opposition to some of their views, and paved the way for the Sunni scholars' defence of their doctrine on the basis of reasoned arguments.

Najm al-Din Razi Daya: Sufi of the Kubrawi order and author; 1177-1256. His *Observation Post* treats the major themes of Sufism and exercised wide and lasting influence throughout the lands where Persian was spoken.

Najran: town in southwestern Saudi Arabia along the Yemen frontier. It is thought to be mentioned in Qur'an LXXXV, 4-9. In 630, the Christians sent a delegation to the Prophet in Medina and were permitted to practise their religion against payment of a tribute and the contribution of 2,000 robes. During the caliphate of ʿUmar b. al-Khattab, many Christians emigrated to a locality not far from Kufa, called al-Najraniyya.

Nakhicevan (Nakhčiwan): name of a town and a region in Transcaucasia. The region was conquered under the Caliph ʿUthman b. ʿAffan, and is particularly associated with the family of the Ildeñizid atabegs of Azerbaijan who left many fine buildings. The town was devastated under the Mongols and suffered from the wars between Turkey and Russia under the Ottoman sultan Murad IV. The largely independent khanate was occupied by Russia in 1828. Nakhicevan became an autonomous republic in 1924.

Nakhshabi, Shaykh Diyaʾ al-Din: famous Persian author; xivth c. He used his knowledge of Indian languages to translate Indian books into Persian. The best known of them is the *The Book of the Parrot*.

Name (A. *ism*): in Arabic-Islamic usage the full name of a person is usually made up of the following elements: 1) kunya; 2) ism; 3) nasab; 4) nisba. A certain number of persons are also known by a nickname (A. *laqab*) or a pejorative sobriquet (A. *nabaz*) which, when the name is stated in full, comes after the nisba. From the end of the ixth c., the use of an honorific before or after the kunya became more and more frequent with persons of some importance.

The *kunya* is a name compound with Abu ("father of") or Umm ("mother of").

The *ism* is the name properly speaking. It can be of several types: a) ancient Arab names e.g. Hasan, Ahmad, Muhammad; b) biblical names in their Qur'anic form: Ibrahim (Abraham), Musa (Moses), Ismaʿil (Ishmael); c) compound names in two main patterns: i. ʿAbd (slave (of)), followed by Allah or one of the divine names; ii. Allah, preceded by a construct substantive (e.g. Hibat Allah "Gift of God"); d) Persian names drawn from old Iranian history and legend (e.g. Khusraw, Jamshid, Rustam); e) Turkish names (e.g. Arslan, Tughrul, Timur), which regularly appear as the names of military commanders in the medieval Arabic chronicles of Syria and Egypt. In modern Turkey names of predatory animals and birds are used, or names expressing the parents' wishes.

The *nasab* or pedigree is a list of ancestors, each name being introduced by the word Ibn "son of". The second name of the series is preceded by Bint "daughter of", if the first name is that of a woman.

The *nisba* is an adjective ending in *ī*, formed originally from the name of the individual's tribe or clan, then from his place of birth, origin or residence, sometimes from a school of law or sect, and occasionally from a trade or profession.

The *laqab* is an honorific or descriptive epithet, e.g. "al-tawil (the tall), al-a'war (the one-eyed)".

The *nabaz* is a sobriquet such as al-himar "the ass".

al-Naqqash, Marun b. Ilyas: pioneer of modern playwriting in Arabic; 1817-1855. His five- and three-act plays were inspired by Molière's plays and by the Thousand-and-One Nights.

Naqshbandiyya: important and still active Sufi order, named after Khwaja Baha' al-Din Naqshband from Bukhara (1318-1389). In the extent of its diffusion it has been second only to the Qadiriyya.

In Transoxiana it rose to supremacy in the time of its founder, and spread southward to Harat. In northwestern Persia, however, it was relatively shortlived. With their strong loyalty to Sunnism, the Naqshbandis became a special target of persecution for the Shi'i Safawids. In the xixth c. the Khalidi branch of the Naqshbandiyya, established by Mawlana Khalid Baghdadi (d. 1827), almost entirely supplanted all other branches and wrested supremacy from the Qadiriyya in Kurdistan. At present, the Naqshbandiyya remain strong among the Kurds of Persia, particularly in the region of Mahabad, and in Talish. By contrast, they are now moribund among the Turkmen.

In Turkey, the first implantation took place in the xvth c. It gained the loyalty of the Ottoman Turks with its emphatically Sunni identity and insistence on sober respect for Islamic law. The Mujaddidi branch of the order, established in India by Shaykh Ahmad Sirhindi "the Renewer", was transmitted to Turkey in the xviith c. Soon afterwards a second transmission took place through Mecca, which remained until the late xixth c. an important centre for the diffusion of the Naqshbandiyya. In Turkey too, it was the Khalidi branch which made the Naqshbandiyya the paramount order, a position it has retained even after the official dissolution of the orders.

In India, the Naqshbandiyya was introduced by Khwaja Baqi bi-'llah (1564-1603), and it remained for two centuries the principal order, especially through the Mujaddid branch. Its main characteristic has been its rejection of innovations and its involvement in political struggles.

Naraqi, Hajji Mulla Ahmad: Shi'i religious leader, man of letters, social critic and religious polemicist; 1771-1829. Despite his friendly relations with the Qajar Fath 'Ali Shah, he refused to recognise the legitimacy of his rule. It is only the qualified jurists who carry the authority of the Hidden Imam as his General Agents and are genuinely legitimate rulers of the Muslim community. This line of argument provided an important source of reasoning for Ayatollah Khomayni.

al-Nasafi, Abu 'l-Hasan al-Bazdawi: distinguished philosopher-theologian of the Isma'ilis in Khurasan and Transoxiana; d. 943. He is generally credited with the introduction of Neo-Platonic philosophy into Isma'ili circles.

al-Nasafi, Hafiz al-Din: important Hanafi legist and theologian; d. 1310. He owes his fame to a number of works on Islamic law, among them a concise account of the foundations of law, and a synopsis of another work, used as late as the xixth c. in Damascus and at the al-Azhar in Cairo.

al-Nasa'i, Abu 'Abd al-Rahman: author of one of the six canonical collections of traditions; 830-915.

al-Nasawi, Shihab al-Din: secretary and biographer of the Khwarazm-Shah Jalal al-Din Mingburnu (Mangubirti); d. 1249. He fled with his master before the Mongols from Tabriz into Mughan, in Azerbaijan, and was employed in unsuccessful missions for support against the Mongols. He escaped during the Khwarazm-Shah's final battle with the Mongols in 1231, and died in Aleppo.

Nasikh, Shaykh Imam Bakhsh: leading Urdu poet and arbiter of the language; d. 1838. He aimed at replacing many idioms, current in Delhi, by others considered superior. His reform of the Urdu language included, among others, the elimination of Hindi words and preference for those of Arabic and Persian origin. His reputation as a poet has declined in the xxth c.

al-Nasir: regnal title of five Mamluk sultans:

1. al-Nasir Muhammad b. Qalawun: b. 1285, r. 1293-1296, 1299-1309, 1310-1341. Enthroned in 1293, dethroned in 1296, al-Nasir was enthroned again as sultan in 1299. He participated in battles against the Il-Khan Mahmud Ghazan in 1299 and against a second Mongol invasion in 1303. Ghazan's death marked the virtual end of the threat to the Mamluk sultanate from the Mongols. In 1310 the steward Baybars al-Jashnikir was elected as sultan in Cairo by the Burjiyya, the Circassian Mamluks recruited by al-Nasir's father sultan Qalawun, but in 1310 al-Nasir was again enthroned. The State treasury held a central place in his administrative system.

2. al-Nasir Ahmad: r. 1342, d. 1344. Son of the previous and living in the castle of al-Karak, he was proclaimed sultan in Damascus by the amir Qutlubugha al-Fakhri, went to Cairo for his enthronement but returned to al-Karak and was deposed by the magnates in the same year 1342.

3. al-Nasir Hasan: b. 1336, r. 1347-1351, 1354-1361. In 1351 he was deposed by amirs and his brother al-Salih Salih installed as sultan. During his reign, the Mamluk realm was ravaged by the Black Death. Re-installed in 1354, al-Nasir was defeated by his own Mamluk, Yalbugha al-'Umari, and put to death in 1361. As his chief memorial he left his beautiful madrasa-mosque in Cairo.

4. al-Nasir Faraj: b. 1389, r. 1399-1405 and, after a short interruption, 1405-1412. In 1401 he made a stand at Damascus against Tamerlane. He was indifferent to the importance of a sound and consistent administration.

5. al-Nasir Muhammad: b. 1482, r. 1496-1498. He was a transient and insignificant figure, but his reign is notable for the unprecedented use of firearms and artillery and for the employment of Arab tribal warriors by the factional leaders.

al-Nasir, Abu 'Abd Allah; sovereign of the dynasty of the Almohads; r.

1199-1213. In 1211 he sent an expedition against Spain which ended in disaster for the Muslim troops at Las Navas de Tolosa.

al-Nasir b. 'Alennas: ruler of the Hammadid dynasty; r. 1062-1088. His reign marks the apogee of the little Berber kingdom founded by Hammad. He founded the town of Bijaya (Bougie), where he built the splendid Palace of the Pearl.

Nasir 'Ali Sirhindi: one of the best of the Persian poets of India; d. 1697. His principal work is a version in verse of the love story of Madhumalat and Manuhar, originally written in Hindi.

Nasir al-Dawla, Abu Muhammad al-Hasan: ruler of the Mosul branch of the Hamdanids; r. 920-968. He profited by the rapid decline in the power of the 'Abbasid caliphs, but came into conflict with the Buyid of Iraq Mu'izz al-Dawla. His rule was disastrous because of his exactions and tyrannical seizures of lands.

al-Nasir li-Din Allah, Abu 'l-'Abbas Ahmad: 'Abbasid caliph; b. 1158, r. 1180-1225. After the secular power of the 'Abbasid caliphate had disappeared because of the dominance of the Buyids and the Saljuqs, al-Nasir succeeded in restoring 'Abbasid sovereignty and the former prestige of the caliphate. He tried to achieve a rapprochement of the different opposite dogmatic trends in Islam, and a policy of alliances with Qatada, the Sharif of Mecca, the Zaydi Imams of Yemen and the Ayyubids of Egypt. In the end, he was unable to prevent the impending fall of the 'Abbasid caliphate of Baghdad in 1258.

al-Nasir li-Din Allah, Ahmad Abu 'l-Hasan: third incumbent of the Rassi Zaydi imamate in northern Yemen; d. 927. He defeated the aggressive followers of the Isma'ili Fatimid missionaries, whose unity and influence were shattered.

Nasir al-Din Shah: ruler of the Qajar dynasty; b. 1831, r. 1848-1896. The first phase of his reign (1848-1858) was characterised by a prolonged struggle to assert monarchical authority against the Prime Minister, the Qajar nobility, the European powers and popular and religious dissent. The second phase (1858-1871) was marked by the abolition of the office of Prime Minister and the appointment of ministers to the newly-created ministries, with the shah acting as his own Prime Minister. The third phase (1871-1886) saw the rise of the celebrated reformer Mirza Husayn Khan Mushir al-Dawla and the royal tours to Ottoman Iraq and to Europe. The last phase of the long reign was marked by the shah's personal disillusionment and growing popular discontent.

Nasir-i Khusraw: Persian poet and prose writer, noted traveller, and Isma'ili philosopher and missionary; 1004-ca. 1075. His travel account relates his journeys to Mecca by way of Nishapur, Tabriz, Aleppo and Jerusalem. From Mecca he went to Cairo where he became familiar with the tradition of Isma'ili learning. His Isma'ili writings are the only contributions in Persian by a major Fatimid missionary.

al-Nasir al-Salawi, Shihab al-Din: Moroccan historian; 1835-1897. He wrote a general history of Morocco, which became a much consulted document.

Nasr Allah b. Muhammad (Nasr Allah Munshi): Persian author and statesman; xiith c. His fame rests on his version of the famous Indian Kalila wa-Dimna into Persian prose.

Nasr al-Dawla, Abu Nasr Ahmad: the most important prince of the Marwanid dynasty of Diyarbakr; r. 1011-1061. The ruler of Diyarbakr was regarded as a principal guardian of the frontier of Islam in eastern Anatolia, but Nasr al-Dawla's relations with the Byzantine Emperor were for the most part amicable. His reign, under which Diyarbakr prospered, saw the rise of the Saljuqs from some obscurity to the empire of Persia and Iraq.

Nasreddin Hoca (A. *Naṣr al-Dīn Khoja*): the label of the most prominent protagonist of humorous prose narratives in the whole sphere of Turkish-Islamic influence. He is a legendary character whose historical existence none of the various theories regarding his alleged lifetime has succeeded in proving beyond doubt. The earliest anecdotes about Nasreddin are quoted in a work dating from the xvith c.

Nasrids (Banu 'l-Ahmar): the last major Muslim dynasty in the Iberian Peninsula, which ruled between 1232-1492 from its capital city Granada. The Nasrid kingdom was founded by Muhammad I b. Yusuf al-Ghalib (r. 1237-1273) after Ferdinand III of Castile and León had conquered Córdoba in 1236 and Seville in 1248. In 1237 he accepted the invitation of Granada's notables to assume control of their city. Nasrid art and architecture, having inherited and adapted Almohad artistic forms, reached its apogee in the xivth c., when classically monumental architecture was created and decoration reached its greatest richness. The Alhambra, begun under Muhammad I, owes much to Muhammad V (r. 1354-1359, 1362-1391). In 1492 Granada fell to the Christians, the last Nasrids fleeing to Morocco.

Nasser (A. *Jamāl 'Abd al-Nāṣir*): Egyptian commander, statesman and President; 1918-1970. As a member of the "Free Officers", he took part in the campaign against the new state of Israel in 1948, was the leader of the coup against King Farouk's government in 1952 and became the president of the Revolution Command Council with *de facto* power in 1954. In 1956 he was elected President, with the powers of both head of state and of government. The Suez crisis made him emerge as a victor in defeat, more popular and powerful than before, and a world figure. In 1958 the United Arab Republic came into existence with Nasser as President, but without great enthusiasm by himself. By 1961 a group of Syrian officers unilaterally took Syria out of the United Republic. In the same year, Nasser introduced "Arab Socialism", and in 1962 a new single party, the Arab Socialist Union, was founded. Nasser rejected Communism, but for aid he was dependent on Russia, which in 1960 agreed to finance the construction of the Assuan Dam. From 1962 till 1967

Nasser was trapped into supporting the new Republic of Yemen. In 1966 he joined a pact with Syria and was drawn into the 1967 war with Israel. After the defeat he admitted his failures and resigned from office, resuming it the next day. In 1970 he tried to achieve reconciliation between King Husayn of Jordan and Yaser Arafat, head of the Palestinian Liberation Organization (P.L.O.) after the king had suppressed an attempted Palestinian take-over in Jordan. This was Nasser's last achievement.

Nauplion (T. *Anabolu*): coastal town in the Peloponnesos in Greece. Raids off Nauplion by the Cretan amirate are recorded in the early xth c., while in 1032 the town's Byzantine strategus defeated a fleet of Muslims from Ifrī-qiya. The first Ottoman rule lasted from 1540 to 1686, and the second from 1715 to 1822. From 1823 till 1834 it was the capital of the kingdom of Greece.

Navarino (T. *Anavarin*): seaport of the southwestern Peloponnesos in Greece, in Ottoman hands from 1500 to 1828. It owes its name in history to the naval battle fought in 1827 in its harbour between the combined fleets of England, France and Russia and of Turkey, Egypt and Tunisia, in which the Muslim forces were destroyed.

Navigation (A. *milāha*): the earliest dated pilots were Ahmad b. Tabaruya and Khwash b. Yusuf, both apparently Persians, who sailed in ca. 1009 and were also authors of navigational texts. During the 'Abbasid period, Arab navigation developed in the Mediterranean, and reached its peak in the ixth and xth c. The Muslims invented or improved some important nautical instruments, such as astrolabes which they already used in the xth c., and composed detailed sailing directories and charts. Great Arab navigators were Ibn Majid and Sulayman al-Mahri. Famous among the Turkish navigators and cartographers were Mehmed Re'is and Piri Re'is.

Navy (A. *bahriyya*): after the conquest of Egypt, the Arabs continued the use of the Byzantines' dockyards in Alexandria and Clysma and cleaned Trajan's canal. In Syria, the first dockyards started operating in Acre in 669. In 651 a great naval battle took place between the Arabs and Byzantines, known as "the Battle of the Masts". In general, the Umayyad period is characterised by efforts of the Arabs to construct warships.

In the 'Abbasid period, Byzantine supremacy at sea was seriously challenged at the turn of the ixth c. when there was a gradual development of the Muslim merchant and war fleets, reaching its peak in the xth c. Muslim ships sailed in the Mediterranean but also as far as India, Southeast Asia and China. In Spain, the Muslims had constructed formidable war flotillas as well as merchant ships, but after the reign of 'Abd al-Rahman III, the Spanish Muslim navy declined. By the end of the xiith c. most of the sailing in the Mediterranean had fallen into the hands of the Italians. Saladin was the last medieval Arab ruler who understood the importance of the navy in military affairs, although he gave a personal order to destroy the port of Ascalon (A. *'Asqalān*).

The Mamluks, a military society of horsemen, had a negative attitude towards the sea, to which the scarcity of wood and metals contributed. As a result of the Crusades, the Ayyubids and above all the Mamluks came to realise that the destruction of the Syro-Palestinian ports and coastal fortifications was the only means to stop the Franks from taking profit of their naval superiority. The Egyptian coast, on the other hand, was left almost intact.

The Ottomans, having reached the coast-lands of Asia Minor in the xivth c. under sultan Bayezid I, used the fleets of the occupied principalities of Sarukhan, Aydin, and Menteshe. The first Ottoman sea-battle occurred in 1416 against the Venetians who were superior, but the Ottoman navy progressed. Even the defeat at Lepanto in 1571 was only a temporary setback. In 1770, during the Russo-Turkish war, the Russian fleet virtually annihilated the Ottoman fleet, but in the reign of sultan Selim III great importance was given to equipping the navy by up-to-date methods. Despite the disaster of Navarino in 1827, the navy had a position of strength during the reign of Sultan Abdülaziz, but fell into neglect under sultan Abdülhamid II.

al-Nawaji, Shams al-Din: Arab scholar, poet and man of letters from Cairo; 1386-1455. He is a typical representative of the literature of the post-classical period. His best-known work is an encyclopaedia of wine whose title refers to the poets who vie with one another in descriptions of wine. In spite of vigorous attacks on it, the work has always been very popular.

al-Nawawi, Muhammad b. 'Umar al-Jawi: Arabic writer of Malay origin; xixth c. He wrote a large number of commentaries on popular textbooks.

al-Nawawi, Muhyi al-Din: Shafi'i jurist; 1233-1277. His fame rests on his exceptional knowledge of Tradition and on his standing as a jurist. He was the author of a famous law book, called *Path of the Students*, which became one of the authoritative textbooks of the Shafi'i school of law.

Nazareth (A. *al-Nāṣira*): city in northern Israel, the home of Jesus. Conquered by the Muslims in 636, it was in Christian hands in the xiith c., but taken by Saladin in 1187. In 1263 the Mamluk sultan Baybars I ordered the destruction of Nazareth and particularly of the Church of St. Mary. In 1620 the Druze chief Fakhr al-Din opened the town to the Franciscans. In the xixth c. the great majority of the inhabitants were Christians, the Muslims forming a minority while Jews were not permitted to live there. At present, it is the largest virtually all-Arab town of Israel, and the majority of its population are Christians.

Nazmi, Mehmed: Ottoman poet of Edirne; d. 1555. He collected a vast anthology of Ottoman poems. He is also an exponent of the more simple style of Turkish poetry, which harked back to the earlier stages of Turkish literature.

al-Nazzam, Ibrahim b. Sayyar: Mu'tazili theologian of the school of Basra, poet, philologist and dialectician; d. ca. 840. His theology was dominated by zeal for the strictest monotheism and for the Qur'an, but his dogmatic extravagances brought down upon him the condemnation of almost the whole of the Sunni Muslim community and even of the Mu'tazila.

Nedroma (A. *Nadrūma*): town of the Trara Berbers in northwestern Algeria, 40 miles to the southwest of Tlemcen. These Berbers were the best auxiliaries and the most reliable supporters in the conquests of the Almohads.

Nef'i ('Ömer Efendi): the greatest satirist of the Ottomans; d. 1634. His *Arrows of Fate* are directed against almost every one prominent in politics and society in his time.

Nefta (Nafta): town in southern Tunisia west of Tozeur. In the xth c. the Kharijites survived there, and in the xith c. Shi'ism was professed in Nefta. It used to be an important centre for marabouts, and is known for its palm trees.

Neguib (A. *Muḥammad Najīb*): Egyptian soldier and statesman; 1901-1984. He took part in the 1948 war against Israel and was the official head of the Committee of the Free Officers' Movement during the revolution of 1952. Real power, however, was in the hands of Nasser. Neguib became President and Prime Minister in 1953, but was placed under house-arrest from 1954-1971, and only released by Anwar al-Sadat after Nasser's death.

Negus (A. *al-Najāshī*): the Arabic term is a loanword from Ethiopic and designates the ruler of Abyssinia at the time of the Prophet and in the early period of Islam. He is not mentioned in the Qur'an, but plays an important part in the biography of the Prophet. His name is connected with Islam as early as 615, and the Prophet must have considered him an ally for he gave a number of his followers the advice to emigrate to Abyssinia, the so-called First Hijra. In the famous audience hall at Qusayr 'Amra, however, he is represented among what traditional interpretation calls "the enemies of Islam defeated by the Umayyads".

Nepal: country in the Himalayan region, north of India. The first Muslim merchants coming from Kashmir settled at Kathmandu around 1500. The present Indo-Nepalese dynasty of Gorkha, established since the xviiith c., strengthened the Hindu character of the kingdom. The Muslims were forbidden to proselytise but, unlike the Christians, they were able to practise their religion. They constitute ca. 3% of a population of 19 million, forming a very hierarchical society, an Islamic version of the Hindu caste system. They are almost all Hanafi Sunnites, with a few Twelver Shi'is.

Nergisi (Nergisi-zade Mehmed Efendi): Ottoman stylist, poet and calligrapher from Sarajevo; ca. 1592-1634. His fame is based on his love-stories and stories of liberality, legends, a mirror of princes, and the wars of religion waged by the Umayyad Maslama b. 'Abd al-Malik. He also wrote a historical work on the Bosniak Murtada Pasha, governor of Ofen (d. 1628).

Nesh'et Khoja Süleyman: Ottoman poet from Edirne; 1735-1807. He was an admirable teacher, Ghalib Dede being one of his pupils, and was known for his devotion to Persian.

Neshri, Mehmed: Ottoman historian; d. 1520. He owes his fame to a history of the world in six parts. Only the sixth part, dealing with Ottoman history down to the period of Bayezid II, seems to have survived.

Nesimi, Seyyid 'Imad al-Din: Ottoman poet and mystic; d. 1417. Equally versed in Arabic and Turkish, he was an enthusiastic follower of Fadl Allah Hurufi. His poems were made popular by the wandering Qalandar dervishes.

Nestorians (A. *Nasṭūriyyūn/Nasāṭira*): the term, which derives from Nestorius, bishop of Constantinople, whose Christological doctrine was condemned by the Council of Ephesus in 431, is traditionally applied to the East Syrians, who themselves usually reject it. The Prophet is said to have met Nestorians and is supposed to have signed a treaty with Abu 'l-Harith, the Nestorian bishop of Najran. The Nestorians in Mesopotamia seem to have welcomed the Arab conquerors as liberators from Sasanian persecutions. Dissension within the Church was a contributory cause of the increasing number of conversions to Islam, another being the persecutions which broke out from time to time. In general, however, relations between the Catholicate and the Caliph's court were close, especially after the establishment of the 'Abbasid caliphate in 750. One of the reasons may have been the outstanding role which the Nestorians played in the field of medicine, science and philosophy. The Shi'i Fatimids and Buyids were rather more tolerant than the Sunnis towards the Christians.

After the devastating invasions of Tamerlane, those Nestorians who had survived fled into the Hakkari Mountains to the west of Lake Urmiya. In the xixth c. Westerners regarded them as descendants of the ancient Assyrians, and called them Assyrians, an epithet which they themselves generally accepted.

During World War I they were suspected of supporting the British, and about one-third of them died in the massacres. A new massacre followed in Iraq in 1933 when the British mandate ended.

Nevshehir: town in central Anatolia. The region, known for its monastic caves in the vith-ixth c., became a frontier during the Arab invasions. The well-known cave churches of Göreme and the underground cities of Derinkuyu and Kaymakli are found in the neighbourhood.

New'i, Yahya b. Pir 'Ali: Ottoman theologian and poet; 1533-1599. He is known for his extensive encyclopaedia on the twelve most important branches of learning.

New'i-zade 'Ata'i: Ottoman author and poet; 1583-1634. His fame rests on his biography of scholars and dervish shaykhs from the time of Sultan Süleyman II down to the reign of Sultan Murad IV.

Newres, 'Abd al-Razzaq (Newres-i Qadim): Ottoman poet known for his daring and malicious chronograms; d. 1762.

Newspaper (A. *Jarīda*): the first newspapers in the Middle East were in French, published in Istanbul in the 1790s. The first Arabic newspaper, called al-Tanbih, was published in Egypt in 1800. In 1828 the first real periodical in

Arabic, called al-Waqaʾiʿ al-Misriyya, appeared in Cairo, followed in Istanbul by the Turkish Taqwim-i Weqaʾiʿ in 1832. Algeria saw its first Arabic newspaper in 1847, Tunisia in 1861, Iraq in 1868, Lebanon in 1869, Lybia in 1871, Morocco in 1889, and the Sudan in 1903. In Iran, the first daily newspaper dates from 1898. The Russian newspaper Tifliskie Vedomosti included in 1828 an edition in Persian and, after 1832, in Azeri Turkish. In the sub-continent Muslim newspapers began to emerge in the 1830s, in China in the beginning of the xxth c., and in Japan after the invasion of China in 1937. The first weekly newspaper to appear in Hausa dates from 1939.

Nicosia (T. *Lefqosha*): town in Cyprus. It was sacked by the Mamluk forces of Sultan Baybars and held by the Ottomans from 1571 till 1878. Virtually all the monumental buildings date from the brilliant Lusignan period (1192-1489).

Niebla (A. *Labla*): town in southwestern Spain. It was conquered by the Muslims in 713 and remained under Muslim rule until 1257, when it was taken by Alfonso X.

al-Niffari, Muhammad b. ʿAbd al-Jabbar: Arab mystic from Nippur (A. *Niffar*); d. 965. His most characteristic contribution to mysticism is his doctrine of *waqfa*, a term which implies a condition in the mystic which is accompanied by direct divine audition, and perhaps even automatic writing.

Niğde: town in south-central Anatolia, Turkey. Part of Saljuq territory, it surrendered to the Ottomans in 1390 but was restored to the Qaramanids, who ruled there until 1470. Afterwards it was in Ottoman hands. The town has many notable medieval buildings.

Niger: country of West Africa. Next to Mauritania, Niger is, by repute, the most Islamicised of the territories of former French West Africa, though pockets of paganism survive. The earliest encounters between the Arabs, led by ʿUqba b. Nafiʿ, and the inhabitants of the oases of Kawar, on the Fazzan border, took place in the viith c. The progress of Islam was influenced by the establishment of Berber Sanhaja centres, the foundation of the Agadès sultanate, the penetration of the Qadiriyya and Shadhiliyya orders, the reform movement of Jibril b. ʿUmar (d. after 1784) and the Sokoto Holy War led by Usman dan Fodio. From 1870 onwards, the Sanusiyya penetrated into northern Niger. The country became independent in 1960, and was established as a secular republic.

Nigeria: country of West Africa. The federation of Nigeria, established under British tutelage in 1954, was granted independence in 1960, and became the Federal Republic of Nigeria in 1963. The largest of the more than 250 tribal groups are the Hausa, the Fulani and the Kanuri of Bornu in the north, the Yorubas in the south-west, and the Ibos in the east. Ca. 50% of the population of 90 million are Muslims.

Nihawand: town in the Zagros Mountains of western Persia, now in the province of Khurasan. It is known for the famous battle between the Arabs and the Persians in 640, in which the Arabs were victorious. The battle decided the fate of the Iranian plateau.

Nikopol(is) (T. *Nīkbūlī*): town in northern Bulgaria on the southern bank of the Danube. This important trade centre and military post was captured by the Ottomans after the battle of Nikopolis in 1396, in which the Crusaders were completely routed.

Nilometer (A. *miqyās*): the gauge in which the annual rise of the river Nile could be measured in Cairo. Nilometers were already in use throughout the Hellenistic period. The supervisor reported daily to the sultan the mark reached by the water. Public announcements were made when the level reached 12 cubits/8 m and people rejoiced when the water level reached 16 cubits/11m, since this announced a good year.

Nima Yushij: Persian poet; 1897-1960. His most important work is a long poem, entitled *Myth*, containing a dialogue between a dismayed lover and the Myth which consoles him. The poem may be said to have heralded the beginning of modernism in Persian poetry.

Ni'mat Allah b. Ahmad (Khalil Sufi): author of an important Persian-Turkish dictionary; d. 1561.

Ni'mat Allah b. Habib Allah Harawi: Persian historian; xviith c. His work deals with the history of the Afghans, especially that of the Lodi and Suri sultans of Delhi.

Ni'mat Allah Wali: Persian mystic and eponym of the Ni'mat-Allahiyya order; 1329-1431. He was a descendant of Muhammad b. 'Ali Zayn al-'Abidin (al-Baqir), the fifth Imam of the Shi'a. He is highly esteemed in Iran as a great saint and wonder-worker, and his tomb at Mahan near Kirman is a popular place of pilgrimage. The order was reintroduced into Persia in the late xviiith c. and became the most widely-spread Sufi order in the country.

Nimrod (A. *Namrūd*): Biblical personage. He is not mentioned by name in the Qur'an, but it is clear that his legend was known. Muslim Tradition associates him with the story of the childhood of Abraham.

Nineveh (A. *Nīnawā*): extensive area of ruins on the eastern bank of the Tigris opposite the town of Mosul in Iraq. The tomb of the prophet Jonah (A. *Nabī Yūnus*) is a highly esteemed Muslim sanctuary.

al-Nisaburi, al-Hasan b. Muhammad: littérateur and Qur'anic scholar; d. 1015. He is famous for a collection on intelligent madmen.

Nish: town in Serbia. It was conquered by the Ottomans in 1386 and remained in Turkish hands until 1878, notwithstanding a short-lived capture by the Austrians and the Serbians.

Nishapur (Nisabur/Neyshabur): town in Khurasan, Iran, named after its alleged founder, the Sasanian king Shapur (d. 272). Taken by the Arabs in 651, the town prospered as the capital of the Tahirids. It was under Saffarid rule from 873 to 901, when it passed to the Samanids, under whom it attained its greatest prosperity. Nishapur was sacked by the Mongols under Genghis

Khan in 1221, and it suffered from repeated earthquakes in the xiith and xiiith c. It was known for its pottery and contains the tombs of the astronomer-poet ʿOmar Khayyam and the mystical poet Farid al-Din al-ʿAttar (xiiith c.).

Nisib (T. *Nizip*): town in southeast Anatolia, Turkey. In 1839 Ibrahim Pasha of Egypt defeated there the Ottoman Turks under Hafiz Mehmed Pasha. This defeat led to the speedy proclamation of the reforms in the Ottoman Empire, known as *tanzīmāt*.

Nisibis (Nusaybin) (A. *Nāṣībīn*): town in southeastern Turkey. Having been the intellectual centre of the Nestorian Church from the vth to the viith c., Nisibis was conquered by the Arabs in 639, and knew many vicissitudes until it passed into the hands of the Ottomans in 1515.

Niyazi, Shams al-Din Mehmed (Misri Efendi): Ottoman poet and mystic; 1617-1694. Instructed in the Naqshbandiyya order, he joined the Qadiriyya order and became famous for his sanctity and gifts of prophecy. He was twice banished to Lemnos because of his sermons. His *dīwān* exists in Arabic and Turkish.

Nizam al-Din Ahmad al-Harawi: Persian historian; 1549-1594. His fame rests on a work in which he deals with the history of India from 977 to 1593.

Nizam al-Din Awliya' (Muhammad b. Ahmad al-Bukhari): Indian Muslim saint; d. 1325. He is regarded as one of the most celebrated saints of India, and his tomb near Delhi is visited by many Muslims.

Nizam al-Mulk, Abu ʿAli al-Hasan: celebrated vizier of the Saljuq sultans Alp Arslan and Malik-Shah; 1018-1092. The Ghaznawid sultan Masʿud b. Mahmud having been defeated by the Saljuqs at Dandanqan in 1040, Nizam al-Mulk left the Ghaznawids for the Saljuqs. After the assassination of Alp Arslan in 1072, Nizam al-Mulk, for the next twenty years, was the real ruler of the Saljuq Empire, residing with the young Malik-Shah at Isfahan. His relations with the ʿAbbasid caliphs al-Qaʾim bi-Amr Allah and al-Muqtadi were strained, but after he had been received graciously at Baghdad in 1086, he became a champion of the caliphate, while relations with Malik-Shah and the princely family deteriorated. Nizam al-Mulk was assassinated in 1092, probably by an emissary of the Nizari Ismaʿili al-Hasan b. al-Sabbah, who had obtained possession of Alamut. He was a lavish patron of religious men and of poets. In 1091 and 1092 he wrote a monarch's primer, in which he deals with dangers that threatened the empire, in particular from the Ismaʿilis. After his death, members of his family, known as Nizamiyya, held office under princes of the Saljuqs for the next sixty years, except for a gap between 1123 and 1134.

Nizam Shahis: name of an independent sultanate at Ahmadnagar, which arose out of the ruins of the Bahmanid kingdom of the Deccan; 1490-1633. It was annexed by the Mughals, notwithstanding the attempts of the Maratha leader Shaji Bhonsle to resuscitate the dynasty.

Nizami ʿArudi Samarqandi, Ahmad b. ʿUmar: one of the most remarkable Persian writers of prose; xiith c. He faithfully served the Ghurid princes for 45 years. His fame rests on his *Four Discourses*, each of which deals with one of the classes of men whom the author regards as indispensable in the service of kings: secretaries, poets, astrologers and physicians. Nizami also gives the earliest notice of Firdawsi, and the only contemporary reference to ʿOmar Khayyam.

Nizami Ganjawi, Jamal al-Din Abu Muhammad: one of the greatest Persian poets and thinkers; 1140-1202. His *Quintet* is a collection of five great epic poems. The first, *The Treasury of Mysteries* is a didactic poem strongly permeated by the spirit of Sufism. The second, the famous *Khusraw and Shirin*, is a romantic epic poem, based on historical incidents dealing with the story of the Sasanian Khusraw (II) Parwiz and coinciding in parts with the corresponding sections of the Shah-nama of Firdawsi. The third, the even more famous *Layla (Layli) and Majnun*, is the love story of the Bedouin poet Qays b. al-Muhammad, known as Majnun. It had an astonishing success and stimulated countless imitations, among them some of the pearls of Oriental poetry, such as the work of the same name of the Azerbaijani poet Fuduli. The fourth is the *Sikandar-*(or *Iskandar-)nama*, in which Nizami took the romance of Alexander as the foundation for his poem and treated it very much on the same lines as Firdawsi. The fifth is the *Haft Paykar*, in which the poet goes back to the popular Sasanian hero Bahram Gur and his love for seven kings' daughters. Nizami had a very great influence on later poets.

Nizami, Hasan (Sadr al-Din Muhammad): Persian historian from Nishapur; xiiith c. He is known for a great work which deals with the history of the first three Muʿizzi or Slave Kings of Delhi.

Nizari Ismaʿilis (Nizariyya): a major branch of the Ismaʿiliyya. The Nizaris derive their name from Nizar, the eldest son of the Fatimid Caliph al-Mustansir bi-'llah, to whom they gave their allegiance, rejecting the claims of Nizar's brother al-Mustaʿli bi-'llah. One of their most important figures was Hasan-i Sabbah. After the destruction of Alamut, the various communities in Syria and Persia struggled to survive. They emerged in the Punjab, Sind and Gujarat, where they are known as Khojas. Their present Imam is Aga Khan IV. Nizari communities are found in Asia, Africa (Zanzibar), Europe, the United States and Canada.

Noah (A. *Nūḥ*): in the Qur'an Noah is the first prophet of punishment and an admonisher with whom God enters into a covenant, just as He did with Abraham, Moses, Jesus and the Prophet. Many details about him are worked out in later Tradition.

Novi Pazar (T. *Yeñi Pazar*): town in Serbia, captured by the Ottomans in 1456. It secured communications between Bosnia and Rumelia and at the same time prevented communications between Serbia and Montenegro. It became part of Serbia at the Treaty of Bucharest of 1913.

Novice (A. *murīd*): the Arabic term means "he who seeks" and is used, in Sufi mystical parlance, for the novice or postulant or the seeker of spiritual enlightenment, by means of traversing the Sufi path, in obedience to a spiritual director.

Nubar Pasha: Egyptian statesman; 1825-1899. He conducted negotiations in Istanbul and Paris with the object of securing the territorial sovereignty of Egypt against the Suez Canal Company, which had obtained lands along the Canal. His endeavour to organise a mixed system of justice composed of Egyptian and European elements was opposed by Western Powers who wanted to maintain their privileges. In 1873 he succeeded in obtaining from the Ottoman sultan the decree (T. *firmān*) in which the title of Khedive ("lord") was conferred on the viceroy. In 1876 he appealed to Great Britain to intervene in Egypt because of the enormous debts which had been contracted. In 1878 a European ministry was formed to support European policy and high finance, which was not responsible to the Khedive. This led to the outbreak of 1879, which in its turn caused the deposition of the Khedive and in the end the British occupation of the country in 1882.

Nubia (A. *Nūba*): region in northeastern Africa, extending from the First Cataract of the Nile in Upper Egypt eastward to the Red Sea, southward to Khartum and westward to the Libyan Desert. The Muslims made invasions into the region from Egypt in 641 and 651, the second of which carried them as far as Dongola. Islamisation was brought about by the immigration of Arab tribes, the rise of the Banu Kanz in the xith c., and the intervention of the Mamluk Sultans Baybars I and Qalawun. The first king to bear a Muslim name was ʿAbd Allah b. Sanbu who was installed in 1316. With the coming of the negroid Funj in the xviith c. the history of Nubia is merged in that of the Sudan.

Nuh (I) b. Nasr: Samanid amir of Khurasan and Transoxiana; r. 943-954. During his reign, which showed unmistakable symptoms of decline, much trouble was caused by the rebel governor of Khurasan Abu ʿAli b. Muhtaj.

Nuh II b. Mansur b. Nuh: Samanid amir; b. 964, r. 977-997. Rebellions separated Khurasan from the direct authority of Bukhara, the Samanid capital. In the end, Ahmad I Arslan Qara Khan, the founder of the Ilek-Khans, and Nasir al-Dawla Sebüktegin, the founder of the Ghaznawids, divided the Samanid territories among themselves.

Nukkaris: one of the main branches of the Ibadiyya in North Africa, also known under other names. It was founded by Abu Qudama Yazid b. Fendin al-Ifreni in 784. The Nukkaris acquired preponderance among the Ibadis after ʿUbayd Allah al-Mahdi (r. 909-934) had established the Fatimids in North Africa, but they revolted under Abu Yazid al-Nukkari (d. 947), and again in the xth and xith c. Remnants of the sect have survived on the island of Jerba.

al-Nuʿman b. Abi ʿAbd Allah: Ismaʿili jurist and protagonist of the early

Fatimids in Egypt; d. 974. He was a prolific and versatile writer. His greatest work is *The Pillars of Islam*, the official *corpus iuris* in the Fatimid Empire.

al-Nuʿman (III) b. al-Mundhir: the last Lakhmid king of al-Hira; r. 580-602. He was a vassal of Sasanian Persia and is often mentioned by Arab poets, according to circumstances a subject of panegyrics or of lampoons. He was imprisoned by the Sasanian king Khusraw (II) Parwiz.

Numerals, Arabic (A. *ʿIlm al-Ḥisāb* "the science of reckoning, arithmetic"): the traditional assertion by medieval Arabic scholars that the "Arabic numerals" are of Indian origin is now generally accepted, although there remain questions about their ultimate source and their diffusion. In the Islamic world the numerals existed and have continued to exist mainly in two forms, one in the East and the other in the West. Usually the Eastern numerals are called "Indian", whereas the others, the immediate parents of the modern European numerals, were called "dust" (A. *ghubār*) numerals. Both forms were known to the Arabs by 733, if not earlier. However, up to now no reference to Indian authors and titles has been found in Arabic treatises on arithmetic – unlike the situation in Arabic astronomical writings. On the other hand, some Arabic phrases are clearly the equivalent of Sanskrit terms.

Nur al-Din Arslan Shah (al-Malik al-ʿAdil): Zangid atabeg of Mosul; r. 1193-1211. In 1199 he defeated the future Ayyubid ruler of Egypt al-Malik al-Kamil, but was himself routed in 1204 by his cousin Qutb al-Din, who ruled in Sinjar. An alliance, first with and later against the Ayyubid of Egypt al-Malik al-ʿAdil, was abandoned.

Nur al-Din Mahmud b. ʿImad al-Din Zangi (al-Malik al-ʿAdil): Zangid atabeg of Damascus and Aleppo; b. 1118, r. 1146-1174. In 1144 he captured Edessa from Count Joscelyn II, which made him the hero of the Sunnis, but which also provoked the Second Crusade. Nur al-Din continued to fight the Franks and captured Damascus in 1154. He made peace with Baldwin III of Jerusalem, but war broke out again and Baldwin suffered a disastrous defeat in 1157. In 1158 the Franks inflicted a severe defeat on Nur al-Din on the Jordan. Around 1160 his attention was drawn to the declining Fatimid rule in Egypt, and his history then became closely linked up with that of Saladin. In 1173 he invaded Asia Minor and took several towns from the Rum Saljuq Qilij Arslan II. The ʿAbbasid caliph al-Mustadiʾ bi-Amr Allah recognised him as lord of Mosul, al-Jazira, Irbil, Khilat, Syria, Egypt and Konya. Nur al-Din was a pious Muslim, a lover of justice, and Damascus shows his great activity as a builder. His constant aim was the expulsion of the Christians from Syria and Palestine, and he paved the way for Saladin's career and the constituting of the Ayyubid Empire.

Nur Jahan: name given to Mihr al-Nisaʾ, the famous queen of Jahangir, the Mughal Emperor; 1577-1645. An extraordinarily beautiful woman, well-versed in Persian literature, she entirely dominated her husband.

Nur Muhammadi ("the light of Muhammad): technical term for the preexistence of the soul of the Prophet. The predestined essence of the Prophet is said to have been created first of all, in the form of a dense and luminous point. Among the Sunnis, the idea began to dominate popular worship from the ixth c. onwards. Among the Shi'is, it appeared earlier, and it is a fundamental dogma of the Isma'ilis.

Nurbakhshiyya: religious Shi'i order named after its founder Muhammad b. Muhammad b. 'Abd Allah from Qa'in in Kuhistan, called Nurbakhsh "light-gift"; 1392-1464. The founder received the title Mahdi in virtue of his supposed descent from the seventh Imam Musa al-Kazim, and was proclaimed caliph by a number of his followers, reason for the Timurid ruler in Samarqand Shahrukh Mirza to arrest him. In his poems he emphasizes Sufi pantheism.

Nuri al-Sa'id: Iraqi statesman; 1888-1958. During the First World War he was on the side of the British and of Sharif Husayn of Mecca against the Turks. He was fourteen times Prime Minister of Iraq and remained Britain's most faithful servant, until he was killed at the hands of a hostile crowd in Baghdad on the day after the revolution of 1958.

Nusayris (*'Alawites*): name of a Shi'i sect in western Syria and in the southeast of present-day Turkey. In 859 Ibn Nusayr, a notable of Basra, proclaimed himself the Bab of the tenth Shi'i Imam al-'Askari and of his eldest son Muhammad al-Qa'im. Husayn b. Hamdan al-Khasibi (d. 957) conveyed the doctrines of the sect to northern Syria. From the xiith c. onwards, their political history has been a series of persecutions by invaders, such as the Crusaders, the Mamluk sultan Baybars I, the Ottoman sultan Selim I, and of civil wars, amongst the various clans themselves and against the Isma'ilis. They have their own religious teaching on cosmogony, eschatology, revelation, on catechesis and initiation. In 1924 the name Nusayris was changed into that of 'Alawites because of their reputation for being heretics.

al-Nuwayri, Shihab al-Din Ahmad: Egyptian encyclopaedist and historian; 1279-1333. His fame rests on an encyclopaedia in which he wishes to sum up all the knowledge that was indispensable for a first class secretary, the greater part being devoted to Muslim history. His work was known in Europe in the xviith c. Al-Nuwayri was also a fine calligrapher.

O

Oath: the oath in general is designated by the term *qasam* (or *yamīn*). It is the oath by which a person binds himself to do or not to do a certain specific physical or juridical act, by invoking the name of God or one of the divine attributes. The term *li'ān* designates the oath which gives the husband the possibility of accusing his wife of adultery without legal proof and without his becoming liable to the punishment prescribed for this, and the possibility also of denying the paternity of a child borne by the wife. *Muhābala* implies swearing a conditional curse (e.g. "may God's punishment hit me if...") and a purifying oath, while *munāshada* designates a set form of oath, at the beginning of a prayer of petition, sometimes involving a threat or coercion, directed at God.

Oath of allegiance (A. *bayʿa*): in Sunni doctrine, the oath of allegiance to a caliph is the act by which one person is proclaimed and recognised as head of the Muslim State. The first caliph, Abu Bakr, was designated by the oath of an assembly which took place in 632. It is a contractual agreement between the electors and the elected. In Shiʿi doctrine, on the other hand, the only method of designating the Imam is appointment by testament (A. *naṣṣ*) of one in the legitimate line of descent. In the Zaydi branch of the Shiʿa, however, the Imamate is acquired by election from within the ʿAlid family, and so the oath was practised here in the sense of an act of election. The binding effect of the oath is personal and life-long, but it is made on condition that its recipient remains faithful to the divine prescriptions.

Obelisk (A. *misalla*): when ʿAbd al-Latif al-Baghdadi visited Heliopolis (A. *ʿAyn Shams*) around 1195, one of the two mighty obelisks had already collapsed. They were unanimously counted among the outstanding marvels of Egypt.

Observatory (A. *marṣad*): the first astronomical observations carried out in the Islamic world seem to date back to the end of the viiith c., i.e. to the period when Indo-Persian astronomical materials were introduced and the first Ptolemaic data appeared. The first systematic programme of observations was implemented under the ʿAbbasid Caliph al-Maʾmun. Official patronage of astronomy was revived under the Buyids in the xth c. An observatory was founded at Isfahan by the Great Saljuq Malik-Shah I, another one by the Il-Khan Hülegü near Maragha, at the suggestion of Nasir al-Din al-Tusi, and still another one at Samarqand in 1420 by the Timurid Ulugh Beg, then governor of the region. Thanks to the patronage of the Ottoman Sultan Murad III, the Samarqand observatory was imitated at Istanbul in 1575. The last large Islamic observatories are those which were founded by Jay Singh, Maharaja of Amber (d. 1743).

Og (A. *ʿŪj*/*ʿĀj b. ʿAnaq*): the king of Bashan in modern Syria, mentioned in the Old Testament. The Qurʾan does not mention him, but the giant king is described by Abu Jaʿfar al-Tabari, Abu Mansur al-Husayn al-Thaʿalibi and Abu ʾl-Hasan al-Kisaʾi.

Ögedey: third son of Genghis Khan and second Great Khan of the Mongol Empire; b. 1186, r. 1229-1241. During his reign, the empire continued to expand in China, Persia, Russia and Eastern Europe.

Oghuz (A. *Ghuzz*): name of an eastern Turkish people, the best-known tribes being the Uyghurs, the Saljuqs, the Artuqids and the Ottomans. In the ixth c. some groups spread to the west and are known to have settled around

Diyarbakr. In the xth c. they occupied a territory the southern border of which was formed by the Aral Sea and the Iaxartes, where they came in touch with the Muslim world. By the end of the xth c. Islam had become general among them. By that time, those of the Oghuz who had become Muslim were indicated with the name Turkmen, but later the name Oghuz was also used for the Muslims. In the third and fourth decades of the xith c. a group, under the leadership of Chaghri-Beg and Tughril-Beg of the Saljuq family, expanded westwards, and defeated the Ghaznawid Mas'ud in 1040. The greater part of Persia and Iraq was conquered on behalf of the so-called Great Saljuqs. Most of the Oghuz concentrated in Azerbaijan, from where a section spread to Asia Minor and converted it into what from then on was known as Turkey. Oghuz tribes who had remained behind in Central Asia were driven back by the Karakhitai and settled in Khurasan. They defeated the Great Saljuq Sanjar in 1153, but were subdued by the Khwarazm-Shahs. After the foundation of the Mongol Empire in the xiiith c., the name Oghuz is no longer found, whereas that of Turkmen has survived until the present day. The epic of the Oghuz is called Oghuz-nama.

Öljeytü (A. *Ūljāytū*) **Khudabanda, Ghiyath al-Din**: Mongol Il-Khan of Persia; b. 1282, r. 1304-1316. He was baptized as a Christian but became a Buddhist, and afterwards embraced Islam. Showing at first preference for the Shi'a, he became an adherent of the Sunna, and finally joined the Shi'a again. He continued the traditional warfare of his predecessors with the Mamluks and their friendly relations with European Christian powers. He established his chief seasonal residence at the recently founded town of Sultaniyya, where his mausoleum is still to be seen.

Oman (A. *'Umān*): sultanate on the southeastern coast of the Arabian Peninsula, until 1970 called Oman and Muscat. Islam penetrated in the region during the Prophet's time. Towards the second half of the viith c., the inhabitants became fervent admirers of the Khariji leader Mirdas b. Udayya (d. 680). Under the influence of Ibadi jurists from Basra, the Khariji movement took on an Ibadi character, and in the viiith c. Oman became the spiritual centre of the Ibadiyya. At the end of the ixth c. began a period of discord and internecine strife between the descendants of 'Adnan, the ancestor of the Northern Arabs, known in Oman as Nizaris – called Ghafiris since the early xviiith c., the Banu 'l-Duru' being the best known among them – and the descendents of Qahtan, the ancestor of the Southern Arabs, known in Oman as Hinawis or Banu Hina. At that time the Rustamids of western Algeria were recognised as universal Imams of the Ibadiyya, though the Ibadi rulers in Oman were elected locally. In 893 Oman was conquered by the 'Abbasid general Muhammad b. Nur, but the Ibadi imamate continued to exist without interruption.

From 962-1055 Oman was a Buyid possession, after which it was seized by Qawurd Qara Arslan Beg, the founder of a line of Saljuq amirs in Kirman.

In 1521 Husayn b. Saʿid, a member of the Jabrid dynasty in eastern Arabia (r. xvth-xvith c.) and field commander in Oman, joined the Portuguese in expelling the Persian garrison. By the time the Portuguese were dislodged from Hormuz in 1622, Oman was ruled by the Yaʿrubid Imam Nasr b. Murshid (r. 1624-1649), who took Suhar in 1643. His successor Sultan b. Sayf (r. 1649-1679) expelled the Portuguese from Muscat in 1649, from Matrah in 1651, and began to build up trade with India, South Arabia and East Africa. The Dutch and English East India Companies, however, were not allowed to establish a factory in Oman. Under the fourth Yaʿrubid Imam Sayf b. Sultan (r. ca. 1692-1711), Oman became a formidable maritime power. Following the death of the Yaʿrubid Imam Sultan II b. Sayf in 1718, civil strife between the Hinawis and the Ghafiris encouraged Persian intervention, summoned by the Yaʿrubid Imam Sayf b. Sultan (r. 1722-1724, 1727-1738).

About 1749 the governor of Suhar Ahmad b. Saʿid (d. 1783) was recognised as Imam of Oman. He became the founder of the Al Bu Saʿid dynasty which ruled in Oman and Zanzibar. After the death of Saʿid b. Ahmad (ca. 1820), the title of Imam was no longer used in the Al Bu Saʿid dynasty. Lord Canning's Award of 1861 consolidated the separation between Oman and Zanzibar, which had risen after Saʿid b. Sultan's death in 1856. Oman was attributed to Sultan Thuwayni b. Saʿid (r. 1856-1866), and Zanzibar to Majid b. Saʿid. During disorder following the assassination of Thuwayni, the Persians resumed in 1868 the lease of Bandar ʿAbbas, which had been in the hands of the sultan of Oman since 1793. A prominent Ibadi leader of the Banu Hina in the xixth c. was Salih b. ʿAli al-Harithi (1834-1896). In 1913 a new Ibadi Imam was elected in Inner Oman in opposition to sultan Taymur b. Faysal (r. 1913-1932). Sultan Saʿid b. Taymur (r. 1932-1970) was succeeded by Sultan Qabus b. Saʿid, b. 1940, r. since 1970.

ʿOmar Khayyam (P. *ʿUmar Khayyām*): famous Persian scientist and poet from Nishapur; d. 1132. He was appreciated by the Great Saljuq Malik-Shah I but Sanjar had a grudge against him. He met Abu Hamid al-Ghazali. As a scientist, he worked on the reform of the calendar and wrote on algebra and physics. As a poet he became very popular in the west after Edward Fitz-Gerald (d. 1883) published his free translation of the *Quatrains*. Of the 1,000 quatrains originally attributed to him, 102 are considered authentic, the rest being added in the manuscripts in the course of time.

Omdurman (A. *Umm Durmān*): town on the west bank of the Nile at the confluence of the Blue and White Niles, now linked with Khartum and Khartum North. It was captured from the British in 1885 by the Sudanese Muhammad al-Mahdi. Under his successor ʿAbd Allah b. Muhammad al-Taʿaʾishi (ʿAbdullahi), the early settlement grew into a town, which was captured by Sir Herbert (later Lord) Kitchener in 1898. During the Anglo-Egyptian Condominium (1899-1955), the speech of Omdurman became the standard Sudanese colloquial Arabic.

'Ömer Efendi: Ottoman historian from Bosnia; xviiith c. He wrote a vivid account of the events in Bosnia between 1738-1739.

Oneness (of God) (A. *tawhīd*): the word does not occur in the Qur'an. According to al-Taftazani, the *Science of the Oneness and of the Qualities* is the basis of all the articles of the belief of Islam. In this definition the Mu'tazila would exclude the qualities and make the basis Oneness alone.

Opium (A. *Afyūn*): in Islamic times it was used as medicine and as a narcotic. The cultivation of the poppy and the preparation of opium flourished in Egypt until the beginning of the xixth c. In Asia Minor it spread after the Crusades, and the town of Qara Hisar received the nickname of Afyun Qara Hisar. In Persia it is often called "antidote". Yazd and Isfahan used to export opium to India, where it played a considerable role. The knowledge of preparing opium is said to have come to the Chinese from medieval India.

Oran (A. *Wahrān*): sea-port town on the coast of Algeria. Founded at the beginning of the xth c. by émigrés from al-Andalus, it was held alternately by the Fatimids of Qayrawan and the Spanish Umayyads. In 1081 it was taken by the Almoravid Yusuf b. Tashufin, and by the Almohads in 1146. The port continued to remain prosperous under the 'Abd al-Wadids of Tlemcen and under the Marinids. It was taken by the Castillians in 1509. Remained confined within the walls, they held the town until 1708, when it came under the Dey of Algiers. The Spanish returned in 1732, but in 1791 it was again surrendered to the Dey. The French entered it in 1831.

Order, Religious (A. *ṭarīqa*): the Arabic term means "road, way, path". In Muslim mysticism it first denoted, in the ixth-xth c., a method for the practical guidance of individuals who had a mystic call. After the xith c. it came to indicate the whole system of rites for spiritual training laid down in the various Muslim religious orders which began to be founded at this time.

Orkhan b. 'Othman: eldest son of 'Othman I Ghazi; b. ca. 1288, r. 1326-1362. Between 1326 and 1344 he established Ottoman power in Asia Minor, and from 1344 he was preparing to extend his rule on European soil. He laid the foundations for the later empire of the Ottomans and is to be regarded as its real founder.

Ossetians: Iranian-speaking people who live in the central part of the North Caucasus. They are divided into Orthodox Christians and Sunni Muslims. The latter constitute between 20 to 30% of the population. Both faiths form only a thin veneer over a strong residual influence of the ancient polytheist and animist beliefs.

'Othman I Ghazi: eponymous founder of the Ottoman dynasty; xivth c. According to unanimous tradition, he was a son of Ertoghrul. There are a number of Turkish traditions on his conquests, but they are, in general, clearly unhistorical and should be understood as belonging to the literary genre of folk-epic.

'Othman II: Ottoman sultan; b. 1603, r. 1618-1622. In 1620, war broke out with Poland, and the Polish army was annihilated in the battle of Yassy. Next year, however, the Turks and Tatars were checked and a preliminary peace was signed. The people, the army and the religious men were opposed to him on account of his avarice, his brutal treatment of the Janissaries and his wish to take four legitimate wives. The Grand Vizier Dawud Pasha had him put to death in 1622.

'Othman III: Ottoman sultan; b. 1699, r. 1754-1757. His reign was uneventful, but is remembered for the great fires in Istanbul in 1755 and 1756. His name is associated with the great mosque of Nuruosmaniyye.

'Othman Pasha, Özdemir-oghlu: Ottoman Grand Vizier and celebrated commander; 1526-1585. A son of Özdemir Pasha, he was *beglerbegi* of Habesh from 1561-1567 and then served as governor of San'a' till 1569. In 1578 he scored two decisive victories over the Safawids, and another in 1583.

'Othman-zade, Ahmed Ta'ib: Ottoman poet, scholar and historian; d. 1724. The most important of his many works is a collection of lives of the first ninety-two Grand Viziers of the Ottoman Empire.

Ottomans (Othmanli): name of a Turkish dynasty, ultimately of Oghuz origin, which ruled from 1281 to 1924 over Anatolia, the Balkans and the Arab lands.

The family probably stemmed from the Qayigh clan and seems to have led a nomadic group in Asia Minor. They had been attached to the Rum Saljuqs in Konya, who had gradually relapsed into anarchy after the victory of the Mongols over Kaykhusraw II in 1243. Several principalities arose in Asia Minor: the Qarasi-oghlu in Mysia, the Sarukhan-oghlu in Lydia, the Aydin-oghlu in Ionia, the Menteshe-oghlu in Caria, the Teke-oghlu in Lycia, the Germiyan-oghlu in Phrygia, the Hamid-oghlu in Pisidia and the Qaraman-oghlu in Cilicia. These regions were never part of the territory administered by the Mongols in the xivth c.

Ottoman history may conveniently be divided into four consecutive periods: the foundation and expansion of the Ottoman Empire (xiiith c.-1500); the empire at its zenith (1500-1650); the period of decline (1650-1840); the beginnings of reform and westernisation, and the end of the dynasty (1840-1924).

The father of 'Othman I, Ertoghrul, is said to have established himself with his little tribe in the neighbourhood of Sögüd near Eskişehir. 'Othman's successor Orkhan took Izniq, Izmid and Bursa (Brusa), which became the capital. At his death the Saqarya river was practically the eastern boundary of the state, and to the south it had reached Eskişehir. He had also acquired the Turkmen principality of the Qarasi-oghlu. Both he and 'Othman had close relations with the Christian chiefs and commanders in the neighbourhood. In 1353 began the military occupation of the European side of the Hellespont; Gallipoli was taken in 1357, and in 1362 Adrianople (Edirne) became the European capital of Murad I. The greater part of what is now Bulgaria was assured and Serbian power was crushed in the battle of Kosovo in 1389. Sultan Bayezid's military expeditions extended over Hungary, Bosnia and southern Greece, but the conquests were not yet permanent. Constantinople became a mere vassal town. Ankara fell in 1359 and the territories of the Germiyan-oghlu and the Hamid-oghlu were acquired by marriage and sale.

After the battle of Ankara in 1402, in which Bayezid I was crushed by Tamerlane, Sultan Mehemmed I was able to restore Ottoman power, which in general was realised without much bloodshed. Trebizond was conquered in 1461 and in 1468 the Qaraman dynasty was extinguished. The Ottomans survived the dangerous raid of the Aq Qoyunlu Uzun Hasan in 1472, but their frontier wars with the Mamluk forces in Syria were not glorious.

During the xvth c. the chief military activity of the Ottomans took place in Europe. A conflict with Venice broke out with the advance into Albania and Morea, and Hungary became the other Christian opponent through Ottoman raids and conquests in Serbia and Wallachia. The capture of Constantinople in 1453 by Mehemmed II was only the realisation of a part of his political scheme.

The xvith c. brought wars with the Shi'i Safawids of Persia. At the end of the reign of Süleyman II, the Ottoman Empire found itself between two powerful continental neighbours, the Austrian monarchy and the Safawids. The defeat at Lepanto in 1571 is considered to be the first great military blow inflicted on the Ottomans, and the impossibility of further military expansion brought about a further inner weakening of the Empire. Baghdad was lost in 1623 but reconquered in 1638. In 1639 a long period of peace with Persia began.

During the xviiith c. Austria and Venice diminished in power, but another formidable enemy had risen in the now much enlarged Russia. By the end of the century the Ottoman Empire began to be a factor in the new imperialistic schemes of the Western Powers. Bessarabia was lost to Russia, and Ottoman authority in Egypt was weakened. The Greek independence brought further humiliation. But the existence of the Ottoman Empire was considered as a political necessity, and treaties were concluded with several Western Powers. The Capitulations (*Imtiyāzāt*), however, brought a form of international servitude which, at the end of the xixth c., had taken the character of a collective tutelage, the Empire being dismembered more and more.

During World War I Turkey had joined the Central Powers and had to sign the Treaty of Sèvres in 1920. Under the growing successes of the Nationalists, the Government at Istanbul was dissolved and the Sultan deposed, by which the Ottoman Empire and its dynasty came to an end.

The following is a list of the Ottoman sultans:

	Ertoghrul (d. ca. 1280)
1281	'Othman I
1324	Orkhan

1362	Murad I
1389	Bayezid I Yildirim ("the Lightning-flash")
1402	*Timurid invasion*
1403	Mehemmed I Čelebi (at first in Anatolia only, after 1413 in Rumelia also)
1403	Süleyman I (in Rumelia only until 1411)
1421	Murad II (*first reign*)
1444	Mehemmed II Fatih ("the Conqueror") (*first reign*)
1446	Murad II (*second reign*)
1451	Mehemmed II Fatih (*second reign*)
1481	Bayezid II
1512	Selim I Yavuz ("the Grim")
1520	Süleyman II Qanuni ("the Law-giver"/"the Magnificent")
1566	Selim II
1574	Murad III
1595	Mehemmed III
1603	Ahmed I
1617	Mustafa I (*first reign*)
1618	'Othman II
1622	Mustafa I (*second reign*)
1623	Murad IV
1640	Ibrahim
1648	Mehemmed IV
1687	Süleyman III
1691	Ahmed II
1695	Mustafa II
1703	Ahmed III
1730	Mahmud I
1754	'Othman III
1757	Mustafa III
1774	Abdülhamid I
1789	Selim III
1807	Mustafa IV
1808	Mahmud II
1839	Abdülmecid I
1861	Abdülaziz
1876	Murad V
1876	Abdülhamid II
1909	Mehemmed V Reshad
1918	Mehemmed VI Wahdeddin
1922-4	Abdülmecid II (as caliph only)

Republican regime of Mustafa Kemal Atatürk.

Ottoman arts can be divided into several branches. Architecture developed in the xivth c. The great name here is Mi'mar Sinan. Glazed pottery and tiles are found at Konya in the xiith-xiiith c., and later Izniq became the great centre. Carpets and textiles were produced since the xvth c. Flourishing were also metalwork, bookbinding, glass-making, manuscript illustrations, royal portraiture and numismatics.

Ottoman literature may be divided into three great periods: from the xiiith to the end of the xviith c; the period after 1600; the so-called "European type" as well as national literature, arising out of the development of the national movement, to the end of the dynasty.

Ottoman social and economic history can be studied under the following headings: the governing class and its subjects; peasant status and power in the countryside; peasant production; nomads and other herdsmen; trade; monetary developments; urban artisans; urban society and spatial structure; social dynamics.

Religious life under the Ottomans had a two-fold aspect. First, there was the official religious institution of the *'ulemā'* and *fuqahā'*, in varying extents connected with the ruling dynasty and headed by the Shaykh ül-Islam (Shaykh al-Islam) in Istanbul. Second, there had always been a strong current of Sufi mysticism.

Oxus (Amu-Darya): large river in Central Asia, flowing like its sister stream, the Iaxartes, into the Aral Sea.

Özbeg (Uzbek): term which had a variety of uses in pre-modern times.

As a generic term, it was applied to the Turco-Mongol nomadic tribal groups in Central Asia, especially in Trans- and Cis-Oxania and Khwarazm. From the mid-xvth c. onwards they comprised the military support for the Shaybanids and the Janids. By the xvith c. there were two well-established traditions listing 32 and 92 distinct Özbeg tribes.

More specifically, the term was also used as part of a proper name, perhaps designating urbanised Turkish-speakers. Contemporary indigenous sources often applied the term to uncultured and unlettered individuals.

Finally, in the late xixth and early xxth c. the term was used by the Durrani Afghans for long-term residents in northern Afghanistan. The khanates of Bukhara, Khiva and Khoqand were Özbeg. They are Sunni Muslims who follow the Hanafiyya legal tradition, while Naqshbandiyya Sufism is a social and political force.

In the present day the Özbeg are found in the Republics of Turkmenistan (Turkestan), Uzbekistan, Tajikistan, Kirghiziya, Kazakhstan, across northern Afghanistan, in Kabul and in China. The Özbeg language was traditionally written in Arabic script, but since 1940 Cyrillic script has been used in the former Soviet Republics.

Özbeg b. Muhammad Pahlawan: last atabeg of the Ildeñizids; r. 1210-

1225. Before his accession to the throne of Azerbaijan, the centre of his activities was at Hamadhan where he was attacked by his ruling brother Nusrat al-Din Abu Bakr (r. 1195-1210), by the Khwarazm-Shah 'Ala' al-Din Muhammad (r. 1200-1220), the 'Abbasid Caliph al-Nasir li-Din Allah and various ambitious slaves. After 1210 he was attacked by the Georgians and the Mongols, and he was finally dispossessed by the Khwarazm-Shah Jalal al-Din Mingburnu.

P

Padishah: title of Persian origin, employed for the Ottoman sultans and the Mughal Emperors.

Padri (Padries, Padaries): name given in Dutch literature to the Padari i.e. men from Pedir in Atjeh who, in the early decades of the xixth c., wished to carry through by force in Minangkabau (Central Sumatra) the reformation of Islam initiated by the Wahhabis. The local chiefs felt their power jeopardized, and the Dutch authorities supported them. The so-called Padri War lasted from 1821 till 1837.

Pakistan: country in southern Asia. The name, which means "land of the pure", is said to have been constructed in 1933 by Chaudhri Rahmat 'Ali, an Indian Muslim student at Cambridge, Great Britain, from letters taken from the names of its component provinces: Punjab, Afghaniyya (North-West Frontier), Kashmir, Sind and Baluchistan.

The country achieved independence on 14 August 1947, the great instigator having been Muhammad 'Ali Jinnah. It was the first modern state to be set up on the grounds of religion.

After Liyaqat 'Ali Khan had been assassinated at Rawalpindi in 1951, martial law was imposed by General Ayyub Khan, who in 1965 had to hand over responsibility to General Yahya Khan. The decisive victory of the East Pakistani Awami League at the elections of 1970 led East Pakistan, separated from West Pakistan by over 1,600 km of Indian territory, to break away in 1972 to form Bagladesh. In Pakistan power came in the hands of Zulfikar Ali (Dhu 'l-Fiqar 'Ali) Bhutto, leader of the Pakistan People's Party. In 1977 General Zia-ul Haq (Diya' al-Haqq) took over power. Bhutto was hanged in 1979. Zia proclaimed himself President and embarked on his programme of Islamisation. He was killed in an unexplained aircrash in 1988. Benazir Bhutto, daughter of Zulfikar Ali, had returned from exile in 1986, became Premier in 1988 but was dismissed by President Ghulam Ishaq Khan in 1990, and Nawaz Sharif, leader of the Islami Jumhuri Ittihad, was sworn in as Prime Minister.

Palermo (A. *Balarm*): city-port of Sicily, Italy. It surrendered to the Aghlabid Ziyadat Allah I (r. 817-838) in 831. The local dynasty of the Kalbids, under Fatimid suzerainty, was established by al-Hasan b. ʿAli al-Kalbi in 948 and lasted till about 1050. The city surrendered to the Normans in 1072. By the end of the xiith c., the Arab colony had almost ceased to exist, although some Muslims of rank remained at the court of Emperor Frederick II.

Palestine (A. *Filasṭīn*): territory on the eastern Mediterranean coast. ʿAmr b. al-ʿAs invaded the region of Ghaza in 634 and conquered most of the towns of the Byzantine province. In 640 Muʿawiya, the future Umayyad Caliph, completed the conquest by occupying Ascalon (A. *ʿAsqalān*). The Arab capital first was at Ludd, then at al-Ramla, founded by the later Umayyad Caliph Sulayman, in which he continued to reside after he had become caliph.

In the ʿAbbasid period Palestine reverted, with Syria, to the rank of a mere province. Immediately after having taken Egypt, the Fatimids occupied Palestine in 969, but their rule was never firmly established. In the xth c. it was one of the most fertile regions of the province of al-Sham, but became the scene of battles during the period of the Crusades. When the Franks were expelled in 1291 after Acre had been taken by the Mamluk sultan al-Ashraf al-Khalil, all Palestine was again under Muslim rule.

After the battle of Marj Dabiq in 1516, in which the Ottoman sultan Selim I defeated the Mamluks, Palestine fell under Ottoman rule, which was to last almost without interruption until 1917. From the late xvith c. there was a noticeable decline, but from the xviiith c. onwards Palestine became a subject of increasing interest to the Great Powers of Europe, on economic as much as religious grounds.

Throughout the period of Islamic rule, there were some Jewish inhabitants in Palestine, though their numbers were much reduced during the Crusades. They were from time to time reinforced by immigration, notably in the xvith c. A new type of immigration began in the late xixth c., with the establishment of the first Zionist agricultural settlements. Despite attempts by the Ottoman government to restrain it, this movement gained force. The number of Jews resident in Palestine rose from 25,000 in 1880 to 80,000 in 1914.

After the collapse of the Ottoman Empire, Palestine was occupied by the British in 1917, and in 1923 Great Britain was given the Mandate which covered the areas on both sides of the Jordan. In fact, however, British administration was established only in the region to the west of the river. That to the east formed the Amirate of Transjordan, with an autonomous government under Emir ʿAbd Allah b. al-Husayn. The policy of the British mandatory government in Palestine was from the beginning influenced by the promises made by Britain to the Jews to establish a Jewish National Home in Palestine, the so-called Balfour Declaration of 1917. The British Government also declared that Palestine was excluded from the territories promised to the Arabs for their independent States. The Arabs, disturbed by the massive immigration of Jews, who in 1939 already numbered 400,000, refused to cooperate with the Palestine administration and reacted with violence. Bloody disturbances broke out in 1928, 1929, 1933, 1936 and 1939. In spite of the Arab reaction, the Zionists consolidated their international position by the creation of the "Jewish Agency". Great Britain, faced with unshakeable opposition from the Arabs, was forced to give an ever more restricted interpretation to the Balfour Declaration. The White Paper, published by the British Government in 1939, excluded the establishment of the Jewish National Home, and an outburst of Jewish violence followed. During the Second World War the British authorities began to force the Jews, who during the Holocaust gazed with hope towards Palestine, back. The Jewish secret organizations entered on a campaign of terror against the British, who in 1946 proclaimed martial law.

In 1947 the U.N. General Assembly adopted a plan envisaging the creation of two independent States, Arab and Jewish, and of an international zone covering the Jerusalem area under U.N. control. The plan was accepted by the Jews but rejected by the Arabs and fighting broke out. Britain gave up the Mandate on 15 May 1948. The day before, David Ben Gurion had proclaimed the birth of the State of Israel. The Arab armies advanced, but the Jews confronted them everywhere. The Security Council imposed a truce, accepted by both Arabs and Jews, but the United Nations' efforts at conciliation ended in failure. In December 1948, the battle recommenced, Egypt being the only Arab state prepared to fight. A ceasefire was imposed by the Security Council. The armistice between Israel and Egypt, signed at Rhodes on 24 February 1949, and those signed successively thereafter between Israel and Lebanon, Jordan, and Syria, established the partition of Palestine.

Pan-Arabism: name of an ideology advocating an overall union of Arabs. This ideology has consistently recommended such union on the basis of language and culture, history, ethnic origins, and territorial contiguity from the coast of Morocco to Iraq and Saudi Arabia. Notwithstanding various moves for unification, starting with Egypt and Syria in 1958, soon joined by Yemen, the Iraqi-Jordanian unification, several similar moves in North-Africa, the influence of President Nasser and of the Baʿth movement in Syria since 1963 and in Iraq since 1970, Pan-Arabism failed to achieve any meaningful results. Nevertheless, the outpouring of emotional support among Arab masses in several countries for Saddam Husayn and his policies in 1990-1992 is an indication that the latent ideal of Pan-Arab unity is maintained among Sunni Arabs.

Pan-Islamism: name of the ideology which aims at a comprehensive union of all Muslims into one entity, thus restoring the situation prevalent in early Islam.

As a political movement, Pan-Islamism came into being during the last third of the xixth c., when European colonialism reached its peak. Its aim was to save all Muslims from foreign, non-Muslim domination by uniting them. At first, it was centred around the Ottoman Sultan Abdülhamid II.

During the inter-war period, Pan-Islamic congresses were convoked at

Mecca 1924, Cairo 1926, Mecca 1926, Jerusalem 1931 and Geneva 1935, but Pan-Islamism receded to Russia, India and Turkey. After the Second World War, the more extreme Pan-Islamists still advocated a religio-political union of all Muslims, while numerous others more moderately argued for solidarity among the new Muslim states. Three of the most important organisations were the Muslim World Congress, set up in Karachi in 1949, which now comprises some thirty-six member states, the Muslim World League, founded in Mecca in 1962, and the Organisation of the Islamic Conference, established in 1969 as an association of some forty-five Muslim states complementary to the Muslim World League.

Pan-Turkism: an ideology originating in the late xixth c. It expressed strong nationalist interest in the welfare of all Turks and members of Turkic groups and addressed itself chiefly to those in Turkey, Cyprus, the Balkans, the former Soviet Union, Syria, Iraq, Iran, Afghanistan and Sinkiang (East Turkestan). The ideology was worked out by intellectuals from the Tatars, Azeris and other Turkic groups in Tsarist Russia, the leading figure being Isma'il Gaspirali. Mustafa Kemal Atatürk, however, was very critical of such universalist ideologies as Pan-Turkism and Pan-Islamism, replacing them with his own popular brand of local nationalism, focused on Turkey and its Turks.

Pandore (A. *ṭunbūr*): the pandore may be generally distinguished from the lute by its smaller sound-chest and longer neck. It was the most favourite instrument in Persia, and by the late ixth and early xth c. had become so popular with the Arabs as to threaten the supremacy of the lute.

Panipat: town in the eastern or Indian part of the divided province of the Punjab, situated at some 80 km north of Delhi. The plain of Panipat witnessed three major battles, deciding at the time the fate of what was then called Hindustan. In 1526 the Mughal ruler Babur defeated and killed Ibrahim Lodi, the sultan of Delhi. In 1556 the Mughal Emperor Akbar defeated the usurping Hindu minister Hemu. In 1761 the Marathas were put to flight by Ahmad Shah Durrani of Afghanistan.

Panthay: term applied to the Chinese Muslims of Yunnan province in south-west China, and to their rebellion in the xixth c. Islam took root in Yunnan after the Mongol conquest of the whole of China in 1279. Under the Manchus (1644-1911), Muslims found it increasingly difficult to uphold their religious freedom in the face of oppressive Confucianisation and Han chauvinism. Chief among the factors contributing to the Yunnanese Muslim rebellion of 1855-1873 were religio-cultural and economic conflicts and institutionalised oppression by Han officials. A Muslim sultanate was established at Tali, seeking military assistance from Western Powers. This was however turned down by Great Britain, and the sultanate collapsed. Many Muslims who refused to assimilate further into Confucian society fled to Burma and became the forebears of the present-day Chinese Muslims in that country.

Paradise (A. *janna* "garden"): the Qur'an describes Paradise in concrete details, especially in the Suras of the first Meccan period. Throughout the centuries the so-called traditional exegesis, which multiplies concrete details about life in Paradise, has co-existed with the attempts of believing philosophers and mystics, who retain the obvious meaning of the Qur'anic texts, but emphasize the primacy of the spiritual over the carnal order.

Parliament (A. *majlis*): the first Ottoman parliament was inaugurated in 1877, and Turkey's Grand National Assembly opened as a Constituent Assembly in 1920. The first Persian parliament was established in 1906. Parliamentary history in Iraq commenced with the inception of the British Mandate in 1922, and the first Chamber of independent Syria was elected in 1947. The Lebanese parliament was first initiated by the French Mandatory authorities in 1922. A Legislative Council was set up in Jordan in 1928, in Kuwait in 1938, where the first elections were held in 1963. In Bahrain, elections for the Constituent Assembly were held in 1972, while in the same year an amended Provisional Constitution was promulgated in Qatar. In the United Arab Emirates legislative authority is vested in the Federal National Assembly. In former North Yemen a Consultative Assembly was established in 1970, and in the same year a constitution was promulgated in former South Yemen. In Egypt the khedive Isma'il Pasha established a representative assembly in 1866. After independence in 1952, a new constitution was promulgated in 1956, providing for a National Assembly. In Sudan an Advisory Council was inaugurated in 1944, and in Libya a National Constituent Assembly met in 1950. Independence in Tunisia was proclaimed in 1957 by the Constituent Assembly, established in 1955, for which elections had been held in 1956. The king of Morocco inaugurated the Consultative National Assembly in 1956, the year of independence. Elections to the National Assembly of independent Algeria took place in 1964. After independence had been achieved in 1960, the Mauritanian Assembly adopted a new constitution in 1961. Afghanistan received its first constitution in 1923, revised several times until the revolution of 1978. After the partition of the Indian subcontinent in 1947, the Indian Constitution of 1950 abolished the old Muslim safeguards of separate electorates and reserved seats. The Congress Party has come to be seen as the best protector of Muslim interests. In Pakistan, a Constituent Assembly was elected in 1947 by the old provincial legislatures inherited from the British period, and the first general elections were held in 1970. In Bangladesh, created in 1971, a Constituent Assembly met and adopted a constitution in 1972.

In Isma'ili usage, the term *majlis* refers to a formal session of religious instruction, and to the lecture or sermon read in it to the faithful. In Indian Shi'i usage the term is especially used for the Shi'i mourning assemblies held during the month of Muharram to commemorate the tragedy of Karbala'.

Parsis: Persian term, meaning "inhabitants of Fars", and given to those descendants of the Zoroastrians who, after the Arab conquest, refused to adopt Islam and migrated to India, mostly to Gujarat. From India, where they form a high-status social group, they have migrated to China, Great Britain, the United States, Australia, Pakistan, in particular to Karachi, and East Africa.

Pasha: Turkish term for the highest official title of honour in the Ottoman Empire and in modern Turkey until 1934. It survived even longer in some former Ottoman provinces like Egypt and Iraq. It always followed the proper name. Military rather than feudal in character, it was however also given to certain high civil officials, but not to religious people. It was not hereditary, did not give any rank to wives, and was not attached to territorial possession.

Passarowitz (T. *Pasarofča*): town to the southeast of Belgrade, former Yugoslavia, famous for the treaty signed in 1718 between the Ottomans and Austria and Venice. By its terms the Ottomans lost substantial territories to Austria.

Passion play of the Shiʿites (A. *taʿziya*): term used for the lamentation for the martyred Imams and in particular for the mourning for Husayn b. ʿAli. It is performed during the first third of the month Muharram, especially on the 10th. The plays performed on that occasion, which vary in the various regions, include the street processions such as the cavalcade with Husayn's horse, the wedding procession of Husayn's son al-Qasim with Fatima, the daughter of his brother Hasan, and the procession to the cemetery with a copy of al-Husayn's tomb in Karbalaʾ. The term finally also denotes the actual performance of the passion play itself on a stage.

Patani: region on the northeastern coast of the Malay peninsula, formerly a Malay Sultanate but since 1909 included in Thailand. The royal court was reportedly converted to Islam in the mid-xvth c. Patani is known for its lengthy and continuing tradition of Islamic texts written in Malay using Arabic script, called Jawi. The region was also famous as the home of a distinct tradition of Islamic education and earning as conducted in the so-called *pondok* ("hut") schools.

Pecewi, Ibrahim: Ottoman historian; 1574-ca. 1649. Born in Pécs, Hungary, he wrote a history which covers the period from the accession of Süleyman II in 1520 to the death of Murad IV in 1640. It is one of the principal sources for Ottoman history, particularly for the period ca. 1590-1632.

Persians: the Arabic term *ʿajam*, used by the Arabs to denote the Persians, is parallel to the Greek word *barbaroi* i.e. those who have an incomprehensible and obscure way of speaking. To the Arabs, the barbarians were primarily their neighbours the Persians. During the whole Umayyad period the superiority of the Arabs over the conquered *ʿajam* was uncontested. The coming to power of the ʿAbbasids brought the victory of the *ʿajam* over the *ʿarab*. The Persians, having obtained political and social supremacy, soon laid claim to the supremacy of their cultural and spiritual values in the so-called Shuʿu-

biyya movement. Another term used by the Arabs to denote the Persians is
al-Furs.

Peshawar: city and district in the North-West Frontier Province of Pakistan, near the Khyber Pass. The town and district were captured by the Muslims in 988. Laying athwart the route of invading armies from the direction of
Central Asia, much of its history resembles that of the Punjab. It was only
nominally incorporated in the Mughal Empire, and later became part of the
Durrani Empire founded by Ahmad Shah Durrani.

Pharaoh (A. *Firʿawn*): the figure of Pharaoh is mentioned in the Qurʾan
and is seen in relation with the Prophet's own mission i.e. with the determined
rejection of the divine message by the unbelievers who in the end are severely
punished, while the believers are saved.

Philippines: Islam was probably introduced as early as the ixth c. along
the trade routes which linked Arabia and China through Southeast Asia. A
Muslim grave, dated 1310, has been found on Jolo, the largest island in the
Sulu archipelago. The sultanate of Sulu was founded around 1450 by an Arab
visitor, Sayyid Abu Bakr. Islam on Mindanao is believed to have come from
Johore around 1515, and to Mindoro and southern Luzon from Borneo. By
the xvith c. Islam was well established in Sulu and western Mindanao. When
the Spanish arrived in 1521, they resumed the crusades. After several wars
during the xviith and xviiith c., the sultan of Sulu acknowledged Spanish
sovereignty in 1878. In 1898 the Philippines were ceded by Spain to the
United States. Resistance to American rule resulted in a series of military
confrontations, until in 1915 the sultan of Sulu surrendered his temporal authority to the US government. Several uprisings occurred again in the 1920s
and 1930s. The Philippines became independent in 1946, but what came to be
referred to as "the Moro Problem" remained unsolved. A feeling of grievance
among Muslim communities promoted a heightened sense of Islamic identity.
In 1968 the Muslim Independence Movement was formed with the objective
to create an independent Islamic Republic of Mindanao, Sulu and Palawan.
A more radical Muslim separatist group, the Moro National Liberation Front,
was established in 1969. Increasing Christian-Muslim tension followed after
the elections of 1971, and over 100,000 Muslims took refuge in Sabah. Negotiations under the government of President Aquino broke down, but Philip-
pine governments appear to be showing greater sensitivity to the demands of
the Muslims.

Pilgrimage to Mecca (A. *ḥajj*): it is a duty obligatory on every Muslim
man or woman who has reached the age of puberty and is of sound mind to
perform the pilgrimage to Mecca once in his or her life provided that they
have the means to do so. The pilgrimage always takes place during the first
two weeks of the last month of the Muslim year, which is therefore called
Dhu ʾl-Hijja. Ever since Islam suppressed the intercalary month (A. *nasiʾ*),
which every three years corrected the discrepancy between the solar and the

lunar year, the Muslim festivals, and consequently the pilgrimage, fall each year ten to eleven days earlier than the preceding year.

When the pilgrim passes through one of the places prescribed for this by tradition, or before he boards the plane for Jidda, he puts on the sacred garment in order to be in a state of ritual purity (A. *ihrām*).

The rites consist of walking seven times round the Ka'ba, praying while facing the Maqam Ibrahim and the Ka'ba, and finally traversing seven times (four times going and three times returning) the distance between Safa and Marwa (A. *sa'y*).

These observances are carried out individually, but the visits to the Holy Places in the vicinity of Mecca are made collectively in a traditional order, between 8 and 12 Dhu 'l-Hijja. It is generally on the 8th that an immense crowd moves towards the east and enters a desert valley. The night from 8th to 9th is spent at Mina or already at 'Arafat (25 km from Mecca). The central event of the pilgrimage is the halting (A. *wuqūf*) on the 9th, in front of the Jabal al-Rahma, a small rocky eminence in the valley of 'Arafat itself. The halting begins at noon with the joint recital of the midday and afternoon prayers brought forward, and it lasts until sunset. Tents are erected as a shelter from the sun. The mass of pilgrims leaves 'Arafat on the evening of the 9th, when the sun has set. Then there begins the running, in which the pilgrims retrace the road by which they have come. The evening and night prayers are recited together at Muzdalifa, and the night is passed here.

On the morning of the 10th, after the recital of the morning prayer, the crowd proceeds to Mina, which for three days will be the place where the pilgrims gather. They first proceed to throw seven small stones at a construction which stands against the mountain at the western exit from the valley of Mina and which now in the thoughts of the pilgrims symbolizes the Devil. Next follow the sacrifices which have given this day its name of Feast of Sacrifices. The pilgrims themselves consume a part of the meat from the slaughtered animals, mainly sheep and goats, then the poor take what they want and the rest is abandoned. This offering of a victim in memory of that of Abraham is not absolutely obligatory. It is usual after the sacrifice to have the head ritually shaved or the hair cut short. Then the pilgrims return to Mecca to walk again seven times round the Ka'ba, which forms an indispensable part of the pilgrimage.

The 11th-13th are days of social relations, and of visits in company to Mina. Each day, normally between midday and sunset, every pilgrim has to throw seven stones at each of the three constructions, ending with that of 'Aqaba, the only one which had been stoned on the 10th. It is permitted to leave Mina on the 12th and thus to omit the three ritual stonings still prescribed for this day. It appears that the pilgrims usually take advantage of this permission and so return to Mecca.

When they are about to leave the town for good, it is the custom for them to walk again seven times round the Kaʿba.

The pilgrims take advantage of their presence at Mecca to visit the places which are connected with memories of the Prophet and his family.

Pilgrimage, the little (A. *ʿumra*): the ceremonies of the little pilgrimage show great similarity to those of the *ḥajj*, the distinction lying in the fact that the first is of a personal nature, especially when it is undertaken separately and not together with the *ḥajj*, and that it is therefore not necessarily performed during Dhu 'l-Hijja. The Little Pilgrimage, like the *ḥajj*, can only be performed in a state of ritual purity. On assuming this state, the pilgrim must make up his mind whether he is going to perform the *ʿumra* by itself or in combination with the *ḥajj* and must express his intention. If he combines the two, he can assume the *iḥrām* for both pilgrimages at once; in the other case, the *iḥrām* must be especially assumed for the *ʿumra* in the unconsecrated area outside of the sacred area of Mecca.

The actual ceremony of the *ʿumra* begins with the utterance of the formula "at Your service" (A. *labbayka*). The pilgrim enters the mosque of Mecca through the north door of the north-east side, goes to the Black Stone and, turning right, begins the sevenfold circumambulation of the Kaʿba. The first three circumambulations are performed at a rapid pace, the four last at an ordinary rate. He then presses himself against the part of the Kaʿba which lies between the Black Stone and the door of the Kaʿba. He prays behind the Maqam Ibrahim, drinks a draught of the holy Zamzam water and touches once again the Black Stone. Leaving the mosque through the great al-Safa door, he then performs the second essential part of the *ʿumra*, namely running seven times between al-Safa and al-Marwa. After having his hair cut or shaved, the ceremony of the *ʿumra* is completed.

For centuries the *ʿumra*, when dissociated from the *ḥajj*, was preferably performed in the month of Rajab, the seventh of the Muslim calendar. In comparatively modern times, the individual *ʿumra* is rather performed during the last ten nights of Ramadan. The different law schools give different answers to the question whether the Muslim is bound to perform the *ʿumra* in the same degree as he is with regard to the *ḥajj*. The question is however rather theoretical, in as much as every Muslim who performs the *ḥajj* as a rule performs the *ʿumra* at the same time.

Pillars of Islam (A. *arkān*; s. *rukn*): according to the view that has come to prevail among the Sunni Muslims, Islam is based on five pillars: the profession of faith (A. *shahāda*); the ritual prayer (A. *ṣalāt*); alms-tax (A. *zakāt*); pilgrimage to Mecca (A. *ḥajj*), and fasting in the month of Ramadan (A. *ṣawm*).

Piri Reʾis b. Hajji Mehmed: Turkish mariner, cartographer and author; d. 1553. He learned the trade of seaman with his uncle, Kemal Reʾis. After the latter's death in 1510 he devoted himself to marine cartography and science of navigation. His fame rests on a world map of which only a part has survived. No less an achievement was his *Book on Seafaring*, which surpassed his Italian and Catalan models. Of another map of the world only a fragment has survived. Aside from writing and cartographical work between 1523 and 1529, Piri Re'is may have on accasion accompanied Khayr al-Din Barbarossa to North Africa. In 1547 he re-emerges as commander of the Ottoman fleet based at Suez. He carried out the reconquest of Aden in 1549, but raised the siege of Portuguese-held Hormuz, withdrew to Basra and from there to Suez. This led to a death sentence which was carried out at Cairo.

Piyale Pasha: Ottoman Grand Admiral; d. 1578. His greatest exploit at sea was the capture of the island of Jerba in 1560. His siege of Malta in 1565 failed.

Planets: following the Ptolemaic system, Arabic astrology knows seven planets. Jupiter (A. *al-mushtarī*) "the larger star of good fortune", and Venus (A. *al-zuhara*), "the smaller star of good fortune", are considered as the two auspicious planets (A. *al-sa'dān*) in contrast to the two inauspicious planets (A. *al-nahsān*) Saturn (A. *zuḥal*), "the larger star of misfortune", and Mars (A. *al-mirrīkh*), "the smaller star of misfortune". Mercury (A. *'uṭārid*) is called "the hypocritical", because in conjunction with an auspicious planet it brings good fortune and with an unlucky one ill-luck.

Sun (A. *al-shams*) and moon (A. *al-qamar*) are of particular importance for Muslim religious ceremonies. The time of daily prayer is closely connected with the different stages of daylight, and the first appearance of the crescent moon indicates the beginning of the fast of Ramadan.

Plato (A. *Aflāṭūn*): most Arab thinkers subordinated Plato to Aristotle, but they were aware of a basic agreement between the two philosophers. Interpretations of Plato, untinged by Neoplatonism, found their way to the Arabic philosophers and were studied by them, but, in general, they looked at him through the eyes of his Neoplatonic interpreters, Plotinus, Porphyry, Proclus and others. The mystical aspects of Platonism, or rather Neoplatonism, were emphasized by al-Suhrawardi al-Maqtul and the Sufis now became followers of Plato. He was also made the author of alchemical works.

Plotinus (A. *al-Shaykh al-Yūnānī*): the father of Neoplatonism, who deeply influenced the thought of the Islamic world, was known to the Arabs as "the Greek Shaykh".

Poet (A. *shā'ir*): in ancient Arabia the poet was considered to be possessed by some special knowledge, communicated to him by a kind of familiar spirit which inspired him. He had in his company one or more real persons (A. *rāwī*, pl. *ruwāt*) whose business it was to remember his verses and to recite them in other camps. In many cases the *rāwī* himself became a poet of note. The poet stood for the honour of his tribe; he had to mourn his relations or the valiant men of his clan or sing the defiant diatribe (A. *hijā'*) against the enemy. In the viiith c. the poets began to beg for favours from the mighty and the rich, to add lampoons against rivals and to use new themes such as poems on boys and obscene ditties. The Prophet condemned the poets "whom follow the beguiled" (Qur'an XXVI, 224), although Hassan b. Thabit is considered as his poet laureate.

Poetry (A. *shi'r*): formally, Arabic poetry consists of metre and rhyme. With the exception of the *rajaz*, all metres consist of a double line with the rhyme at the end only. Metre is quantitative and considerable freedom is allowed in the substitution of long for short syllables and vice versa. The rhyme may include as many as three syllables. Throughout a poem all the double lines have the same rhyme and the opening line has it also in the single line.

Poitiers, Battle of (A. *balāṭ al-shuhadā'*): in Ramadan 114/October 732 the Frankish ruler Charles Martel defeated near Poitiers the governor of al-Andalus 'Abd al-Rahman b. 'Abd Allah al-Ghafiqi. From the Muslim point of view, the battle did not have the importance it has been given in Western sources.

Poland (T. *Leh*): a large number of Tatar families were settled in Lithuania, after 1385 united with Poland. When the Crimea, ruled by the Giray Khans, became a vassal state of the Ottomans in 1475, the country came in contact with the world of Islam. During the xvth-xviith c., the Tatars took part in Ottoman invasions of Poland, supported Poland in her war in the Ukraine in 1654, but again took part in the Ottoman war against the country. In the xviiith c., the danger presented by the Tsarist empire to Poland and the Crimea reconciled the two countries once again. Islamic material culture shed an oriental influence on Polish national costume, domestic furniture, the conduct of war, and arms and equipment.

Police (A. *shurṭa*; T. *karakol* "police-station"): in the 'Abbasid period, the title "commander of the bodyguard" was reserved for a special official who was responsible for order and public security. Under the 'Abbasids, the Spanish Umayyads and the Fatimids, he was empowered to take action on mere suspicion. Only the lower classes, however, were under his power. In the Ottoman Empire the maintenance of security and order was entrusted mainly to the Janissaries. After the suppression of the latter in 1826, public security became the responsibility of an official called *ser-'asker*.

Polytheism (A. *shirk*): the Qur'an uses the term in direct contrast to the profession of the Oneness of God and expressly declares polytheism to be the sin for which God has no forgiveness. Tradition literature reflects the hostile feeling against the polytheists (A. *mushrikūn*), who in the law books are in general regarded as outlaws. In a later period it was recognised that all unbelievers are not the same and are not to be treated alike.

Pomaks: name given to a Bulgarian-speaking group of Muslims in Bulgaria and Thrace, now divided amongst Bulgaria, Greece and western Macedonia. Adoption of Islam in these regions was gradual and at different periods. The process of conversion began at the end of the xivth c. and lasted until the xixth c.

Port Said (A. *Būr Saʿīd*): Mediterranean seaport of Egypt at the entrance of the Suez Canal, mainly man-made. It was founded in 1859 during the reign of the Khedive Saʿid Pasha and named after him.

Potiphar (A. *Qiṭfīr*): Biblical personage who in the Qurʾan is merely referred to by his title al-ʿAziz. Little is related about him in Islamic tradition.

Prayer (A. *duʿāʾ*; *ṣalāt*): Arabic *duʿāʾ* means appeal, invocation addressed to God, and thus has the general sense of personal prayer. *Ṣalāt* indicates the ritual prayer or divine service.

Prayer-rug (A. *sajjāda*): term, not found in the Qurʾan or in the canonical Tradition, which indicates the rug on which the *ṣalāt* is performed.

Price regulations (P. *narkh*): the Persian term was used in Ottoman Turkish for the prices determined by official authorities for almost all commodities, but in particular for foods, shoes and other basic goods.

Primary schools (A. *kuttāb*; pl. *katātīb*): primary schools were already wide-spread in early ʿAbbasid times. Boys formed the overwhelming majority of pupils, while girls studied, if at all, separately. Emphasis was generally laid on memorising, and independent thinking was frowned upon. The Qurʾan was initially taught in Arabic, later difficult passages were sporadically explained in the local language. Reforms were introduced from the mid-19th century, the study of the Qurʾan and of Islam remaining a standard part of the core curriculum.

Principles (A. *uṣūl*): among the various terminological uses of the Arabic word, three are prominent as terms for branches of Muslim learning. "Principles of religion" (A. *uṣūl al-dīn*) are synonymous with theology (A. *ʿilm al-kalām*); "Principles of Tradition" (A. *uṣūl al-ḥadīth*) indicate the terminology and methods of the science of Tradition; "Principles of Muslim jurisprudence" (A. *uṣūl al-fiqh*) generally indicate the science of the proofs which lead to the establishment of legal standards. These proofs, according to the view which finally prevailed, are the Qurʾan, the Sunna, the unanimous agreement of the Muslim community (A. *ijmāʿ*), and the reasoning by analogy (A. *qiyās*).

Printing (A. *maṭbaʿa*): printing was introduced in Lebanon in 1610, and in Syria the first press operated in 1706. In other Arab countries, the practice emerged in the beginning of the xixth c. In Persia wood-block printing for paper money was introduced under the Mongols in 1294 in imitation of Chinese practice. In Turkey the first press was established in 1727 by Ibrahim Müteferriqa. In Muslim India the earliest known specimen of Arabic printing also dates from 1727, but Arabic, Persian and Urdu printing really began in Calcutta from the 1780s onwards.

Processions (A. *mawākib*; s. *mawkib*): ʿAbbasid ceremonial was almost certainly of a static and non-processional character, while the Fatimids had, perhaps, the most elaborate processions of any of their contemporaries, staging them at the New Year, on the first of Ramadan and on the last three Fridays of that month, the Major and the Minor Festivals and the inundation of the Nile.

In Muslim Spain, the processions of the Almohads were rich and complex, while those of the Nasrids probably were very simple, due to the exiguousness of their territories.

In Persia, processions, on the whole, do not appear to have been highly organised. Only in the immediate vicinity of the ruler was there a certain order and discipline, but the scenes often were of great splendour.

The Ottoman court knew the so-called Imperial procession, organised when the Sultan or the Grand Vizier started for or returned from a campaign, and thirteen further different processions are described. There was also a special code for processions and a kiosk for spectacles.

Processions in India were, and still are, of a great popular appeal, from the panache of the simple wedding ceremonies to the pomp of royal ceremonial. The royal hunt, which was highly esteemed since it kept the army ready and exercised, called for very large processions.

Proclus (A. *Buruqlus*): head of the pagan philosophical school at Athens; 410-485. The outstanding scholastic systematizer of Neoplatonic thought was mainly familiar to Arabic thinkers as proclaiming the eternity of the world.

Prognostications (A. *khawāṣṣ al-Qurʾān*): letters, words, names of angels, prophets or God, drawn from suitable Qurʾan verses, are widely used in treatises of popular medicine.

Prostitution (A. *bighāʾ*): the Qurʾan forbids any woman being compelled to practise prostitution. The institution as such is regarded as incompatible with Muslim ethics. At certain times prostitution was oppressed severely, but it was in general tolerated and often subject to a tax payable to the public treasury.

Proverbs (A. *mathal*): the Arabic term includes proverbs, proverbial sayings, adages, set turns of speech, and parables or fables. There exist a great number of Arabic collections, and the genre is also practised in Persian, Turkish, Urdu and Swahili.

Psalms (A. *zabūr*; pl. *zubur*): in the Qurʾan, the singular *zabūr* occurs exclusively in connection with David, while the plural *zubur* denotes the revealed books. There exists an Arabic translation of Psalm lxxviii, 20-31, 51-61 which dates from the viiith c.

Ptolemy (A. *Baṭlamiyūs*): more than any other Greek scientist he dominated medieval Islamic astronomy, astrology, geography, harmonics and optics.

Public treasury (A. *mīrī*): throughout Ottoman history, the term, which is a shortened form of *amiri*, was used as a noun meaning lands belonging to the government, land tax levied from them, as well as the public treasury. Upon the conquest of a given area by the Ottomans, its agricultural lands, the most promising source of income, were declared governmental property.

Punishment (in the tomb: A. *'adhāb al-qabr*): the idea is based on the conception that the dead had a continued and conscious existence of a kind in their grave. So arose the doctrine of the two judgements, one which involves punishment or bliss in the grave and a subsequent judgement on the Day of Resurrection.

The Qur'anic term *barzakh*, which means obstacle, hindrance, is interpreted either as a prohibition by God to the godless who want to return to earth to accomplish the good they have left undone during their lives, or as a barrier between Hell and Paradise or else as the grave which lies between this life and the next.

Punjab (Panjab): the word means "land of the five rivers" and denotes a province of the northwestern part of the Indo-Pakistan subcontinent, divided between India and Pakistan at the partition in 1947. The Punjab was first invaded by the Arabs in 711, when Muhammad b. al-Qasim al-Thaqafi captured Multan. The area was annexed in 1006 by the Ghaznawid Mahmud b. Sebüktigin, followed by the Ghurid Ghiyath al-Din Muhammad (r. 1163-1206) in 1186. In 1206 the Punjab became a province of the sultanate of Delhi under Qutb al-Din Aybak, and remained so until 1626 when Ibrahim Lodi was defeated by the Mughal Emperor Babur. Under Awrangzib's intransigeant policy, Sikh political power grew. In 1739 the Punjab was invaded by Nadir Shah Afshar of Persia, and in 1761 by Ahmad Shah Durrani of Afghanistan. The province was annexed by the British in 1849 after two Sikh wars.

Purification (A. *istinjā'*): the believer has to purify himself after the fulfilment of his natural needs. The practice is obligatory and must be carried out either immediately, or before performing the *ṣalāt* or any other act which requires a state of ritual purity.

Pyramid (A. *haram*; pl. *ahrām*): in Muslim literature, the pyramids are pre-eminently those of Cheops and Chephren, or sometimes also of Mycerinos, west of Giza. The account of the Arab geographers as a rule have little value as original documents.

Pythagoras (A. *Fīthāghūras*): no true distinction was made between the Greek philosopher of the vith c. B.C. and the school, or schools, bearing his name. It was constantly repeated that he had coined the word "philosophy", and that he was the inventor of the science of music and the propagator among the Greeks of arithmetic, geometry, physics, and metaphysics. The "Golden Words" which are ascribed to him enjoyed a wide circulation in their Arabic translation, and the Pythagorean "Symbola" were often cited. The influence of Pythagoras and Pythagoreanism on Muslim civilization must be rated rather high.

Q

Qabid: heretic molla from Persia, who was educated in Istanbul; d. 1527. He maintained that the Qur'an depended in large measure upon the Old and New Testaments, and that Jesus was superior to the Prophet. After a trial, he was invited to recant and when he again refused, he was sentenced to death.

al-Qabisi, 'Abd al-'Aziz: Arab astrologer, known in the West as Alcabitius.

Qabus b. Wushmagir b. Ziyar: ruler of the Ziyarid dynasty. Despite his reputation for cruelty, he achieved a great contemporary renown as a scholar and poet in both Arabic and Persian. He was also an expert calligrapher and an authority on astrology. Avicenna took refuge at his court and al-Biruni, who came to Gurgan in 998, dedicated one of his works to him.

Qadariyya: name commonly used by Islamists to denote a group of theologians, not in itself homogeneous, who represented in one form or another the principle of free will in the early period of Islam, from about 690 to the definitive consolidation of the Mu'tazila at the beginning of the ixth c. The word was always derogatory, never applied to oneself.

Qaddur al-'Alami: name by which the famous Moroccan popular poet 'Abd al-Qadir al-'Alami al-Hamdani is known; d. 1850. His most popular poem is devoted to the saints of Meknès.

al-Qadi al-Fadil, Abu 'Ali al-'Asqalani: famous counsellor and secretary to Saladin; 1135-1200. His reputation is mainly based on the exceptional quality of his private and official epistolary style. Many examples of his official writings have survived.

Qadi Muhammad: head of the leading Kurdish family of Mahabad in Azerbaijan; c. 1895-1947. On 22 January 1946 the Autonomous Kurdish Republic was proclaimed with Qadi Muhammad as president, but in December of the same year the Republic collapsed and Qadi Muhammad was put to death.

al-Qadir bi-'llah: 'Abbasid caliph; b. 947, r. 991-1031. His main preoccupation was the struggle against Shi'ism in all its forms, against Mu'tazilism and even against Ash'arism. He worked effectively for the restoration of threatened Sunnism and at his death the caliphate had won a considerable amount of prestige.

al-Qadiri, Abu 'Abd Allah: Moroccan historian and biographer; 1712-1773. His fame is based on his dictionaries of the celebrities of the xviith and xviiith c.

Qadiriyya: order of dervishes called after 'Abd al-Qadir al-Jilani. Theoretically both tolerant and charitable, the order spread from Baghdad to North Africa and is known for its symbols and rites.

al-Qadisiyya: name of several places in Iraq and in al-Jazira, the most famous being that near al-Hira, in the plain where Kufa was later founded. It was the site of the resounding victory of the Muslims over the army of the Sasanian king Yazdagird III in 637, which opened up the route to Ctesiphon-Seleucia (A. *al-Madā'in*). After the victory at Jalula' in 637 which led to the conquest of all of Iraq, the campaign of the Iranian plateau could be undertaken.

Qahraman-nama: popular romance in prose, existing in both Persian and Turkish, in which themes from the Iranian epic tradition are developed.

al-Qahir bi-'llah: 'Abbasid caliph; r. 932-934; d. 950. He had the amir Mu'nis al-Muzaffar put to death, and was deposed by his former vizier Ibn Muqla.

Qahtaba b. Shabib: Arab general and one of the most prominent leaders of the 'Abbasid propaganda in Khurasan; d. 749. When Abu Muslim was sent to Khurasan in 745 to organize the decisive campaign against the Umayyads, Qahtaba was appointed to lead the army. In 749 he defeated the armies of the Umayyad generals 'Amir b. Dubara al-Murri and Ibn Hubayra, thus sealing the fate of the Umayyads in the Near East.

Qahtan: according to the consensus of opinion among Muslim genealogists, historians, and geographers, and in popular tradition, he was the ancestor of all the South-Arabian peoples, whence he is sometimes known as "father of all Yemen". He thus corresponds to 'Adnan, the common ancestor of the northern Arabs.

Qa'im Al Muhammad ("the Qa'im of the family of Muhammad"): term used in Shi'i terminology for the member of the family of the Prophet who was expected to rise against the illegitimate regimes and restore justice on earth. Among the Imamiyya, the twelfth, Hidden Imam was identified with the Qa'im. In the Isma'ili doctrine, the "Qa'im of the Resurrection" shall act as the judge of mankind.

al-Qa'im bi-Amr Allah: 'Abbasid caliph; b. 1001, r. 1031-1075. His rule corresponded with the end of the Buyid period and the beginning of the Saljuq period in Iraq.

al-Qa'im bi-Amr Allah (Abu 'l-Qasim Muhammad): Fatimid caliph; r. 934-946. Having re-established his authority in the south of Ifrīqiya, he resumed hostilities against the 'Abbasids in their Egyptian province and intensified "Holy War" in the Byzantine territories in eastern Sicily and Calabria. He lacked in both energy and foresight in fighting the Khariji agitation.

Qa'im-maqam (T. *kaymakam*): title borne by a number of different officials in the Ottoman Empire. The *kaymakam* enjoyed almost all the authority of the Grand Vizier, issuing firmans and nominating functionaries, but he was not allowed to intervene in the area where the army was operating. In 1864 the *kaymakam* became the governor of an administrative district, called *qaḍā'*, and under the Republican regime he continued to be the administrator of such a district. In Ottoman Egypt, the term was applied to the acting viceroy before Muhammad 'Ali Pasha, and under the latter to specific grades in the military and administrative hierarchies.

Qa'it Bay, al-Malik al-Ashraf: Mamluk sultan of Egypt and Syria; r. 1468-1496. His chief political problem was his relations with the Ottomans. He granted new privileges to the Italian merchants and made no attempt to monopolize the spice trade, but also introduced measures to protect the interests of native merchants. However, the seemingly rich and powerful Mamluk state was heading for disaster and was no match for Ottoman Turkey.

Qajar: name of a dynasty in Persia, which ruled from 1779 till 1923. The Qajar were a tribe of Turkmen which had probably been settled near Astarabad since Mongol times. In the early xvith c. they supported the Safawids and formed one of the Qizil-Bash tribes. Under the Safawids Tahmasp I and Shah 'Abbas I, Qajar khans held important offices. Fath 'Ali Khan (d. 1726) plotted against the Safawid Tahmasp II. His grandson Aga Muhammad Khan was the real founder of the dynasty. He made himself master of Gurgan, Mazandaran and Gilan, took Isfahan and Kirman, made Teheran his capital and invaded Georgia. He was crowned in Teheran in 1796 but was murdered in 1797 while marching against Georgia. By that time the Qajar had ceased to be tribal leaders and became absolute rulers, seeking to emphasize the high, almost sacred, character of their rule. Aga Muhammad's nephew Fath 'Ali Shah decreased the power of the tribes apart from the Qajars. But rebellion was facilitated by the fact that there was no clear dividing line between the provincial governor, the tribal leader, the landowner and the military commander. Besides, the Qajars never succeeded in establishing family solidarity. The next ruler Muhammad Shah kept several Qajar princes in captivity in Ardabil. After his death riots and disorders erupted in Teheran. His successor Nasir al-Din was supported by the merchant community of Tabriz.

In the second half of the xixth c. the influence of the bureaucracy grew. Hostilities with Russia, which had been intermittent from about 1805, ended in 1828 with a treaty of peace that was unfavourable for Persia. The hostilities with Turkey, which had started in 1821, were first brought to an end by the Treaty of Erzurum of 1823 but a second Treaty of Erzurum had to be signed in 1847. Persia's geographical situation on the frontiers of Russia on the one hand, and of India and the Persian Gulf on the other, involved her in the struggle between Russia and Great Britain. Shah Nasir al-Din encouraged foreign powers to invest in Persia, which led to the grant of monopolies and concessions, among them the so-called Tobacco Regie of 1890 and the establishment of the Anglo-Persian Oil Company in 1909. The increasing dominance of non-Muslim nations over Persia led to pro-Islamic and anti-foreign hostility against the government. New intellectual currents also contributed to the progressive dissolution of the old institutions of government and society.

In 1879 a Russian mission arrived to organize the Cossack Brigade, which became the most efficient regiment in the Persian army. The intrusion of France, Russia and England acted first as a stimulus to modernization, but from the middle of the xixth c. onwards, it added to the prevailing insecurity and intrigue. The press and the *'ulamā'* played a prominent part in the events leading to the grant of the Constitution in 1906. But under Russian pressure the Constitution was suspended in 1911, the leadership having passed into the hands of the bureaucracy and the landowning classes. In 1921 Reza Khan Pahlavi organized a *coup d'état* which brought an end to the Qajar dynasty. Ahmad Shah was deposed and the crown of Persia conferred by a Constituent Assembly upon Reza Khan as Reza Shah Pahlavi.

The following is a list of the Qajar Khans and Shahs:

Tribal chiefs in Mazandaran:

1721	Fath 'Ali Khan
1750	Muhammad Hasan Khan
1770	Husayn Quli Khan

Shahs:

1779	Aga Muhammad
1797	Fath 'Ali Shah
1834	Muhammad
1848	Nasir al-Din
1896	Muzaffar al-Din
1907	Muhammad 'Ali
1909-25	Ahmad

Pahlavi Shahs

Qalandar/Qalandariyya: name given to the members of a class of dervishes, which existed within the area extending from Turkestan to Morocco, especially in the xiiith c. Its spread westward is due to the activities of Jamal al-Din al-Sawi (d. 1223). They adopted Malamatiyya doctrines and distinguished themselves by their unconventional dress, behaviour and way of life.

al-Qalasadi, Abu 'l-Hasan: Muslim mathematician, jurist and scholar of Spain; d. 1486. He was a prolific author and compiler. Some of his works enjoyed considerable renown both in East and West.

Qal'at al-Najm: fortress in northern Syria on the right bank of the Euphrates. The bridge over the river was constructed at the order of the Caliph 'Uthman b. 'Affan and played an important role from the earliest years of Islam.

Qalawun al-Alfi, al-Malik al-Mansur: Mamluk sultan of Egypt and Syria; r. 1279-1290. In 1281 he defeated the Mongols at Homs. Following the example of Sultan Baybars I in pursuing the holy war against the Crusaders in Syria, he took the offensive against the Christian Armenians, and subdued Nubia. He maintained good relations with the Golden Horde, Byzantium, Castile, Sicily and with Rudolf I of Habsburg. In Cairo he erected a hospital, which is perhaps the most remarkable building of the Mamluk era.

Qal'a-yi Safid: fortress in Fars built on the flat top of a mountain, which can only be reached by cliff-paths. It was spared by Hülegü in 1264, but stormed by Tamerlane in 1393.

Qalhat: the chief coastal settlement of the Banu Salima and Malik b. Fahm tribes of southeastern Oman.

al-Qali, Abu 'Ali Isma'il al-Baghdadi: great Arab philologist; 901-967. In 942 he went to Córdoba and became the key figure in the Iraqi tradition in the West. The best-known of the few works which have survived deals with every conceivable question of Arabic philology .

al-Qalqashandi: gentilic of several Egyptian scholars, the most important of them being Shihab al-Din Abu 'l-'Abbas; 1355-1418. He was a legal scholar, secretary in the Mamluk chancery and author. He owes his fame mainly to the multi-volumed *Dawn of the Night-Blind One*, in which he gives a very detailed conspectus of the theoretical sciences and the practical skills required by a secretary concerned with official correspondence.

Qamaran: coralline island in Yemeni territorial waters. In the second part of the xixth c. Turkey established there a quarantine station for pilgrims to Mecca arriving through Bab al-Mandab. It was closed in 1952.

Qandahar: city and province in southeastern Afghanistan, of strategic and commercial importance all through recorded history. The whole area round the city is a rich agricultural one, and water is brought by a complex system of underground channels. As opposed to the capital Kabul, Qandahar is the centre of a strongly Pashto-speaking region.

Qandiya: Ottoman name of a town on the north coast of the island of Crete, the Herakleion of antiquity. The fortress was taken by the Ottomans in 1669. The port was progressively silting up, and Qandiya lost ground to Canea (Hanya), although it remained the capital of the island until 1855. By 1923, it had ceased to exist as a Muslim town.

Qansawh al-Ghawri: penultimate Mamluk sultan of Egypt; r. 1501-1516. Having been governor of Tarsus and Malatya, and secretary of state to sultan al-'Adil Tuman Bay (r. 1501), he was compelled by a junta of high amirs to become sultan in 1501. He was confronted by fiscal problems and the growing maritime power of the Europeans, the Portuguese seeking to exclude Muslim shipping from the Red Sea. He organized a unit armed with handguns and established a cannon-foundry, weapons despised by the genuine mamluks. After the battle of Chaldiran in 1514, the principality of Dulgadir (A. *Dhu 'l-Qadr*), a dependency of the Mamluk sultanate, came under Ottoman domination. Alarmed, the Mamluk sultan organized an expedition. At Aleppo conciliatory messages were exchanged with the Ottoman ambassadors, but the Ottoman Sultan Selim I, who intended another campaign against the Safawids, decided to end the danger to his flank. The Mamluks were decisively beaten at Marj Dabiq in 1516, and Qansawh al-Ghawri died on the battlefield.

Qapi Aghasi: senior officer in the Ottoman sultan's palace who had the authority to petition the sultan for the appointment, promotion and transfer of palace servants. He had his office at the Inner Gate of the palace, called "Gate of Felicity".

Qara Bagh: recent name, meaning "black garden", of the mountainous region lying to the north of the middle course of the Araxes river in Transcaucasia. In the xixth c. it was a buffer-region between Qajar Persia and the expanding Russian empire. The modern population, mostly Armenian, with some Shi'i Azeri Turks, is concentrated in the deep valleys.

Qara Hisar ("Black Castle"): name given to at least twelve localities in Asia Minor. They are distinguished from one another by means of other names or epithets, but are nevertheless frequently confused.

Qara Mustafa Pasha, Merzifonlu, Maqtul: Ottoman Grand Vizier; 1634-1683. Brought up in the household of Köprülü Mehmed Pasha, his political fortunes steadily improved. In 1665 he was put in charge of naval preparations for the planned final reduction of Crete, and took part in the Polish campaign of 1672. He became Grand Vizier in 1676. Although animated by xenophobia, he showed deep interest in, and knowledge of, the affairs of Europe. After his successful second Russian campaign in 1678, he turned his attention to the affairs of Hungary and to the planning of offensive warfare against Austria. After the unsuccessful siege of Vienna in 1683, his political enemies turned Sultan Mehemmed IV against him, and he was executed at Belgrade.

Qara 'Othman-oghlu: important family active in Manisa, Turkey, from the end of the xviith c. until 1861.

Qara Qoyunlu ("Black Sheep"): Turkish dynasty of the Oghuz, which ruled over parts of Eastern Anatolia, Iraq, al-Jazira and most of Iran from 1380 till 1468, when all these territories passed into the hands of the Aq Qoyunlu.

Qaragöz ("black eye"): name of the principal character in the Turkish shadow play, and also of the shadow play theatre itself. The theatre is played with flat, two-dimensional figures, manipulated by the shadow player, which represent inanimate objects, animals, fantastic beasts and beings, and human characters. The two central figures are Qaragöz, who combines within himself all the minor vices, and Hajivad, the petit bourgeois and educated man. It is generally recognised that the shadow play spread from eastern and Southeast Asia towards the Near East and Europe.

Qarakhanids: name under which the Ilek-Khans are also known.

Qaramanids (Qaraman-oghullari): Turkish dynasty which was opposed to the Ottomans and ruled over the regions of Konya and Niğde from ca. 1262 to 1475. Various groups in the Qaramanid state took part in the foundation of the Safawid state in Persia.

Qaramanli: family of Turkish origin, several members of whom governed Tripolitania, Libya, from 1711 to 1835, constituting themselves into a real dynasty. They supported the Arabs against the Turks, without however rejecting Ottoman suzerainty.

Qaraqush, Baha' al-Din al-Asadi: officer of Saladin; d. 1201. Described as the ablest man of his day, he built the citadel of Cairo, and the bridge at Gizeh out of stones from the pyramids at Memphis. He also extended the city walls and fortified Acre, where he was taken prisoner at the fall of the town in 1191. Saladin ransomed him for a high sum.

Qarasi: name of a Turkish chief in Asia Minor and of the dynasty arising from him. His territory, comprising the ancient Mysia, the coastland and hinterland of the Asiatic side of the Dardanelles, has retained this name until the present time. The territory was incorporated into the Ottoman Empire ca. 1360, but the history of the dynasty, the first of those which were to be suppressed by the Ottomans, is wrapped in obscurity.

Qarasu-bazar: important commercial centre in the Crimea, particularly under the Giray dynasty of the Crimean Tatars.

Qarata: small Ibero-Caucasian people akin to the Avars and living in Dagestan. Islam was introduced in the Avar country at the end of the xith c.

al-Qarawiyyin: the celebrated mosque and Islamic university at Fez in Morocco. The mosque is an eminent witness of the Hispano-Moorish art in architecture and in the decorative arts. The university attained its apogee in the xivth c. An important reform was introduced in 1931-1933, and a thorough reorganisation in 1963. The library was created in 1349 by the Marinid Abu 'Inan Faris. After a period of neglect, it now holds more than 4,000 manuscripts, among which some very valuable or very rare ones.

Qarluq: Turkish tribal group in Central Asia from whose ranks the Ilek-Khans may have come. Together with the Uyghurs they brought about the disintegration of the eastern Turkish Empire in 743-745. They were in turn defeated by the Uyghurs and compelled to move westwards towards Transoxiana. In the ixth c. they became disposed to reception of Islamic faith and culture.

Qarqisiya: town in Syria on the left bank of the Euphrates. It was occupied by the Muslims in 640, and is often mentioned in the history of the wars of medieval Islam.

Qasab, Teodor (T. *Teodor Kasap*): Ottoman Turkish writer, journalist and playwright; 1835-1897. In Paris he became the private secretary of Alexandre Dumas *père*, and later published in Istanbul the first humorous magazine in Turkish. He bitterly criticized the patently pro-Russian policy of the Grand Vizier Mahmud Nedim Pasha and in 1879 was sentenced to imprisonment by Sultan Abdülhamid II. He fled to Paris but was pardoned.

Qasida (A.): a polythematic ode which numbers at least seven verses, but which generally comprises far more. It consists essentially of an amatory prologue (A. *nasib*), in which the poet sheds some tears over what was once the camping place of his beloved now far off; of the poet's narrative of his journey to the person to whom the poem is addressed; and of the central theme, constituted by the panegyric of a tribe, a protector or a patron, or by a satire of their enemies. The Arabic *qaṣīda* is a very conventional piece of verse, with one rhyme and in a uniform metre.

The Persian *qaṣīda* is a lyric poem, most frequently panegyric. It is first and foremost a poem composed for a princely festival, especially the spring festival and the autumn one. It was connected with courtly life in Persia.

The Muslim Turks adopted and developed the *qaṣīda*, a verse form very different from their own traditional poetry, under the influence of classical Persian literature.

al-Qasim: district in northern Najd in the central part of the kingdom of Saudi Arabia, known for the fine quality of its horses. It was the bone of contention between Al Saʿud of Riyadh and Al Rashid of Hayil in Jabal Shammar until ʿAbd al-ʿAziz Al Saʿud defeated Al Rashid in the early xxth c.

Qasim b. Asbagh al-Bayyani: famous traditionist, philologist, historian and genealogist of Muslim Spain; 859-951.

Qasim (Kassem), **ʿAbd al-Karim**: officer and dictator of Iraq; 1914-1963. Opposed to the Western-orientated monarchy, he became chairman of the Free Officers Central Committee. At the revolution in 1958 King Faysal II, the crown prince ʿAbd al-Ilah and the Prime Minister Nuri al-Saʿid were killed and the Republic proclaimed, Qasim becoming commander-in-chief and Prime Minister. Vis-à-vis Arab unity, he jealously maintained Iraq's independence. Through a working alliance with the Communists, he withstood the revolt of March 1959 by the commander of the Mosul garrison, Brigadier ʿAbd al-Wahhab al-Shawwaf. In January 1960 a law was promulgated in which political parties were legalized. But its effects soon petered out, and only a phantom pseudo-Communist Party was tolerated. All genuine political life degenerated, and open warfare with the Kurds began in 1961. After Kuwait had become independent in 1961, Qasim made an inept attempt to seize it. A combination of Baʿthist and nationalist anti-Communist officers put a bloody end to him and his regime in February 1963. Qasim's Agrarian Reform Law of 1958 is a milestone in the social history of Iraq. His Personal Status Law of 1959, applicable to Sunnis and Shiʿis alike, was repealed after his overthrow.

Qasim Aga: architect-in-chief at the Ottoman court; ?1570-?1670. His mastery as an architect is apparent from the Činili Jamiʿ and the ʿAtiq Walide Jamiʿ in Üsküdar, opposite Istanbul.

Qasim Amin: Egyptian Arab publicist; 1863-1908. He wrote on social topics and was the promoter of the emancipation of the Arab woman. He was in contact with the two great reformers of modern Islam, Jamal al-Din al-Afghani and his disciple Muhammad ʿAbduh. His patriotic feeling is found in his *Les Égyptiens* (in French), and his dedication to the social advancement of women in his *The Emancipation of Women* and in *The New Woman*.

Qasim-i Anwar (Muʿin al-Din Tabrizi): mystic, poet and leading Safawid missionary; 1356-1433. His successful missionary activities became an embarrassment to the Timurid political and religious authorities. He was banished from Harat, resided at Samarqand and later returned to Khurasan.

Qasim Pasha, Güzelje: Ottoman vizier in the reign of Süleyman II; d. ca. 1552. He started reconstructing the quarter of Istanbul which is named after him.

Qasimids: line of Zaydi Imams of Yemen, founded by al-Mansur bi-'llah al-Qasim b. Muhammad. The dynasty, which dominated much of Yemen, lasted until the outbreak of the republican revolution in 1962.

Qasimov: chief town of a district of the province of Ryazan in Russia. It was the capital of a Tatar khanate, founded ca. 1452, which lasted until 1678 as a feudal vassal of Moscow.

Qasiyun (Jabal): mountain which forms part of the Anti-Lebanon. It has a sacred character because God is said to have spoken to it. Three grottoes mark the place where the blood of Abel is said to have been shed.

Qasr al-Hayr al-Gharbi: Umayyad castle in the Syrian desert at 60 km south-south-west of Palmyra. The Umayyad Caliph Hisham had a residential palace constructed in 728. The site was abandoned during the 'Abbasid period, but was reoccupied under the Ayyubids and the Mamluks.

al-Qasr al-Kabir (Alcazarquivir): town in northern Morocco, known for its pre-Almohad Great Mosque and for the veneration of several marabouts.

al-Qasr al-Saghir: town in northern Morocco, now in ruins, on the south bank of the Straits of Gibraltar. In the xvth c. the inhabitants, forced by economic pressure, turned to piracy. Al-Qasr therefore became one of the first towns to be captured by King Alfonso V of Portugal.

Qasr-i Shirin: town in the southwestern part of Persian Kurdistan, known for its extensive system of ruins dating from the Sasanian period. It was the scene of the unhappy love-story of Shirin, the favourite wife of Khusraw (II) Parwiz (560-628), and the royal architect Farhad. In the Muslim period the palaces seem no longer to have been inhabited.

al-Qastallani, Abu 'l-'Abbas Ahmad: an authority on tradition and theologian from Cairo; 1448-1517. He owed his literary fame mainly to his exhaustive commentary on the *Sahih* of al-Bukhari. His history of the Prophet enjoyed great popularity in the Muslim world.

Qat (A.): name of a shrub, whose leaves and young shoots contain an alkaloid which produces a euphoric, stimulating, exciting but finally depressing, effect when chewed or drunk in a concoction. It is widely used in Ethiopia, Jibuti, East Africa and Yemen.

Qa'taba: small town in the administrative district of Ibb in Yemen. As a border stronghold, it played a role in the advance of Ottoman forces against Aden during World War I, and during the struggle following the evacuation of Aden by the British in 1967.

Qatada b. Di'ama: a Successor; ?680-?735. Blind from birth, he became proverbial for his prodigious memory and his knowledge about genealogies, lexicography, historical traditions, Qur'anic exegesis and the readings, and Tradition.

Qatada b. Idris (Abu 'Uzayyiz): ancestor of the Sharifs of Mecca; d. 1221. Having united his tribe with the other tribes of the district of Yanbu', he captured Mecca and killed Muhammad b. Mukaththir, the last Sharif from the ruling family of the Hawashim. Although he was a Shi'i, he acknowledged the suzerainty of the 'Abbasid caliph al-Nasir li-Din Allah, but the relations were strained. His descendants were ruling Sharifs in Mecca until 1916, when Husayn b. 'Ali converted the sharifate into a kingdom.

Qatar: independent Arab state on the Arabian peninsula, jutting out into the Persian Gulf. The modern period begins with the immigration of the Al Khalifa clan of the 'Utub from Kuwait in 1766. Zubara, on the western shore, became the centre of the pearl trade. In the xixth c. the Banu Yas caused much friction between Qatar and Abu Dhabi, while relations with Bahrain were also uneasy. In 1868 began the rule of the Al Thani. In 1913 a convention was concluded by which Turkey renounced any claims to Qatar. Oil was discovered in 1940, and the country became independent in 1971.

Qatari b. al-Fuja'a: the last chief of the Azraqi Kharijis; d. ca. 697. Representing the type of a Khariji intransigeant, he had a real talent as orator and poet, with Kirman as the centre of his power. He was defeated by Sufyan b. al-Abrad, sent against him by al-Hajjaj.

al-Qatif: large oasis in Saudi Arabia on the southern shore of the Gulf. During the last decades of the viith c. it was held by the Kharijites, and in 899 invaded by the Carmathians, whose power was brought to an end in the xith c. by the 'Uyunids. Having been ruled by the Salghurid atabeg of Fars, by the 'Usfurids of 'Ukayl and the king of Hormuz, al-Qatif came in the hands of the Jabrids, whose rule was overthrown by Shaykh Rashid b. Mughamis of Basra in 1524. In 1551 the Ottomans built a new citadel, and in the xviith c. the oasis became an important centre for Portuguese trade in the Gulf. Towards the end of the xviiith c. al-Qatif was subdued by Sa'ud b. 'Abd al-'Aziz Al Sa'ud, who posed a threat to Ottoman suzerainty. After the Turco-Egyptian evacuation of central Arabia, Turki b. 'Abd Allah reintroduced the rule of the Al Sa'ud. In 1838 a Turco-Egyptian force was quartered in al-Qatif, but Faysal b. Turki restored Sa'udi rule. Between 1871 and 1913 al-Qatif was again ruled by the Ottomans, but then it became part of the domains of the Al Sa'ud. In 1938 oil was first discovered at Dhahran not far south of al-Qatif.

Qatran al-'Adudi: poet from Azerbaijan; xith c. He was the first Azerbaijani poet to write in the Persian of Khurasan. He also composed a Persian lexicon, which has not survived.

al-Qawasim (s. *Qasimi*): the ruling family of Sharjah (al-Shariqa) and Ra's al-Khayma. In the first half of the xviiith c. Rashid b. Matar, the first

Qasimi to be mentioned in the historical records, may have been the ruler of Ra's al-Khayma, the older name of which was Julfar. In 1737 a Persian garrison stayed in Ra's al-Khayma, but by 1763 the Persians had left. Almost all Rashid's subjects were Hanbalites, and so would be open to Wahhabi proselytism. In 1778 a long conflict arose between the Qawasim and the British, who took to using the Arab name in the corrupted form Joasmee as a generic term for all Arabs in the Gulf who harassed their shipping. In 1809 the British plundered Ra's al-Khayma and set it on fire, but in 1819 a treaty of peace was signed with Sultan Sultan b. Saqr (d. 1866). In 1835 a maritime truce for six months was signed, and renewed repeatedly. The stretch of coast to which it applied, formerly called the Pirate Coast by the British, came to be known as the Trucial Coast. In 1904 British intervention prevented Persia from taking the islands of Abu Musa and Tunb. After 1866 the position of leadership slipped away into the hands of Dubayy and Abu Dhabi. Oil was discovered in 1959. In 1971 Iran occupied the islands of Abu Musa and Greater and Lesser Tunb. As the British moved out in 1971, the seven Trucial States banded together in the new United Arab Emirates.

Qawurd b. Chaghri Beg Dawud (Qara Arslan Beg): Saljuq amir; d. 1074. He was the founder of a line of amirs which endured for some 140 years in Kirman.

Qayghusuz Abdal: Turkish mystical poet and writer; d. 1415. He is generally considered the founder of the Bektashi dervish literature.

Qayi: one of the Oghuz tribes to which, according to some Turkish chroniclers, the Ottoman dynasty belonged.

Qaynuqa', Banu: one of the three main Jewish tribes of Yathrib, the others being the Banu Qurayza and the Banu 'l-Nadir.

Qayrawan: town in central Tunisia. The name refers to the garrison camp which was set up by Mu'awiya b. Hudayj in 654. The town went through many vicissitudes, suffering severely under the early Fatimids, during the reign of the Zirid al-Mu'izz b. Badis, and under the pillage of Khalil, Bey of Tripoli (1700). The Great Mosque, rebuilt into its present form by the Aghlabid Ziyadat Allah (r. 817-838), is the oldest and most prestigious religious building of the Muslim West. The town is also reputed for its hand-produced "long-wool" carpets.

Qays b. al-Khatim b. 'Adi: the most important poet of Yathrib. His poetry is a very important source for the conditions in Yathrib just before the coming of Islam.

Qayyum Nasiri: one of the first and greatest modernist reformers amongst the Tatars of the Volga; 1825-1902. He created a Tatar literary language, based on the dialect spoken in Kazan, the town on the middle Volga.

Qazdughliyya: with the Dhu 'l-Faqariyya and the Qasimiyya, the third of the great neo-Mamluk households of Ottoman Egypt. Its eponym, Mustafa al-Qazdughli, rose to power in the xviith c. In the xixth c. the factious households were incapable of resisting the growing strength of Muhammad 'Ali Pasha.

Qazwin (Kazvin): town and district northwest of Teheran. It was conquered by the Muslims in 644. The town wall was completed in 868. In the first half of the xth c. it fell to the Buyids, and in 1030 passed into Ghaznavid hands. In the xiith c. the inhabitants were molested by the Isma'ilis of Rudbar. In 1220 the Mongols are alleged to have carried out a massacre of the inhabitants, and Qazwin suffered decay. In 1555, during the reign of the Safawid Tahmasp I, the town, situated on the main route from Azerbaijan to Khurasan, became the capital until 1597, when Shah 'Abbas built a new capital in Isfahan. At the beginning of the xixth c. Qazwin was beginning to flourish once more. It played little part in the events leading up to the grant of the constitution in 1906, and it declined under the reign of Reza Khan (later Shah) Pahlavi.

The earliest surviving Islamic building is the dome chamber of the Masjid-i Jami' of the early xiith c. Apart from the Haydariyya mosque, there is the so-called mausoleum of Hamd Allah Mustawfi and the much-ruined palace of Shah Tahmasp I.

al-Qazwini, Abu Hatim Mahmud: Shafi'i jurist; xith c. He is the author of one of the oldest works on legal devices (A. *ḥiyal*).

al-Qazwini (Khaṭīb Dimashq), Jalal al-Din: author of two famous compendiums on rhetoric; d. 1338.

al-Qazwini, Zakariyya' b. Muhammad: famous Arab cosmographer and geographer; ca. 1203-1283. He met Diya' al-Din Ibn al-Athir, and the Persian historian and statesman 'Ala' al-Din al-Juwayni was his patron. His Cosmography, entitled *Prodigies of things created and miraculous aspects of things existing*, is the first systematic exposition of the subject in Muslim literature. It enjoyed great popularity. The oldest version of his Geography is entitled *Prodigies of the Countries*, and the second one is called *Monuments of the Countries and History of their Inhabitants*.

Qerri (Gerri): site on the east bank of the main Nile in the Sudan, about 44 miles north of the confluence of the Blue and White Niles. From the xvith to the xviiith c. it was politically important as the seat of the 'Abdallabi shaykhs, who were regarded as the overlords of the Arab tribes.

Qibla: the Arabic term indicates the direction of Mecca, towards which the worshipper must direct himself for the *ṣalāt*. More specifically, the *qibla* is the direction of the Ka'ba or the point between the water-spout (A. *mīzāb*) and the western corner of it. It may be considered established that the Prophet and his community, during the early years of the Hijra, turned at the *ṣalāt* towards Jerusalem. The question what his *qibla* was before the Hijra is treated in Tradition. The adoption of the *qibla* is a necessary condition for the validity of a *ṣalāt*. Only in great danger and in a voluntary *ṣalāt* on a journey can it be neglected.

The determination of the *qibla* was an important problem for the scientists of medieval Islam. Although essentially a problem of mathematical geography, it can also be considered as a problem of spherical astronomy. Thus most Islamic astronomical handbooks (A. *zīj*) contain a chapter on the determination of the *qibla*.

Qilburun (Qinburun): a sharp cape or headland at the mouth of the Dniepr on the Black Sea coast of Ukraine. In the xviith c. a fortress was built by the Ottomans against Cossack raids. It was demolished by Russia in 1860.

Qilij Arslan I: Rum Saljuq prince of Asia Minor; r. 1092-1107. He crushed the Peasant Crusade of Peter the Hermit, but was forced to give up the capital Nicaea to the Barons' Crusade. In 1101, in cooperation with Danishmend, he annihilated the rearguard of the Crusaders. He was defeated by the Great Saljuq Muhammad I b. Malik Shah.

Qilij Arslan II: one of the most important Rum Saljuqs; b. 1115, r. 1156-1192. He had a form of allegiance with the Byzantine Emperor Manuel Comnenus, and was alternately allied and at odds with the Zangid Nur al-Din Mahmud. On the latter's death, he annexed what remained of the Danishmendid territories and thus accomplished the political unity of Asia Minor. In 1176 he crushed Manuel Comnenus at Myriokephalon. In 1190 he was inclined to promise free passage to Frederick Barbarossa, but his son Qutb al-Din's Turkmen attacked the Germans, who converged on Konya.

Qilij Arslan IV (Rukn al-Din): Rum Saljuq; d. 1265. After the death of the Rum Saljuq Kaykhusraw II in 1246, the sultanate was shared jointly by his three minor sons 'Izz al-Din Kaykawus II, Rukn al-Din Qilij Arslan IV and 'Ala al-Din Kayqubad II. Rukn al-Din and his party wanted to submit to the Mongols, while 'Izz al-Din sought to organize resistance with the aid of the Turkmen of the West and in alliance with the Byzantines. Both brothers participated in a campaign against Syria under the orders of the Il-Khan Hülegü, but 'Izz al-Din then fled to Constantinople. Qilij Arslan remained sole sultan but was put to death by Mu'in al-Din Sulayman, the favourite of the Mongols.

Qinalizade, Hasan Čelebi: Ottoman scholar and biographer; 1546-1604. His fame rests on his biographical dictionary of the Ottoman poets.

Qinnasrin: town and military district in Syria. It was taken by the Muslims in 638. The Umayyads installed a military headquarters, and in the xth c. it became the object of contention between the Byzantines and the Hamdanids.

Qipčaq (Kipchak): Turkish people and tribal confederation. In the middle of the xith c., the Qipčaq tribes moved to the Russian steppes and were exposed to the influence of both Islam and Christianity. Qipčaq military played an important role in Egypt as the so-called Bahri Mamluks.

Qisas al-Anbiya' ("Legends of the pre-Islamic prophets"): title of several works relating the lives of the prophets of the Old Testament, the story of

Jesus, and some other events in which pious heroes or enemies of God are involved.

Qishn: small town of Yemen. Formerly it was the mainland capital of the Mahri sultanate of Qishn and Socotra.

Qizil-Bash (T. "Red-head"): in its general sense, the word is used loosely to denote a wide variety of extremist Shi'i sects, which flourished in Anatolia and Kurdistan from the late xiiith c. onwards, including such groups as the 'Alawites. The common characteristic was the wearing of a red headgear. In its specific sense, the word was a term of opprobrium applied by the Ottoman Turks to the supporters of the Safawid house, and adopted by the latter as a mark of pride. In the Safawid state, established in 1501, the Qizil-Bash constituted the military aristocracy, for they had been largely responsible for bringing the Safawids to power. This brought them in immediate friction with the Persian elements in the administration, whom they called contemptuously "Tajiks". The Qizil-Bash were the only troops in the Islamic world who had earned the grudging respect of the Ottoman Janissaries. Shah 'Abbas reduced their strength, which ultimately undermined the military power of the Safawid Empire.

Qizil Elma (T. "Red Apple"): an expression in Turkish tradition, referring to a legendary city which was to be the ultimate goal of Turkish Muslim conquests. In the Ottoman period the term tended to be identified with the large cities associated with Christianity: Constantinople, Budapest, Vienna and Rome. Another tradition identifies Qizil Elma with Dagestan.

Qizil Irmaq (T. "Red River"): the ancient Halys. Nearly 600 miles long, it is the largest river in Asia Minor, rising near Sivas and finally reaching the Black Sea.

Qizil Qum (T. "Red Sand"): desert between the Iaxartes and the Oxus rivers, falling within the modern Uzbekistan and Kazakhstan. At the southeastern extremity lay the Qatwan Steppe where the Great Saljuq Sanjar was defeated by the Karakhitai in 1141.

Qizil Üzen (Azeri T. "Red River"; P. *Safid Rud*): river of northern Iran which flows through Azerbaijan and enters the Caspian Sea. It was known to the Arabs as "White River".

Qoči Beg (Görijeli Qoja Mustafa Beg): Ottoman writer of treatises on statecraft; xviith c. He is famous for his memoranda to the sultans Murad IV and Ibrahim. He was also tutor to the historian Na'ima. His best-known work deals with an analysis of the causes of Ottoman decline and contains suggestions for remedies.

Qoja Eli (Kocaeli): region between the Black Sea and the Sea of Marmara, Turkey, with Izmit as capital. It was one of the earliest Ottoman administrative districts, formed during the reign of Orkhan in the years 1327-1338.

Qoshma: originally a general term for poetry among the Turkish peoples, it was later applied to the native Turkish popular poetry, in contrast to the classical poetry taken from the Persian.

Qozan-Oghullari: family of Derebeys in Ottoman southern Anatolia. From the beginning of the xixth c. until 1878 they acted as virtually independent local rulers in Qozan.

Quatrain (A. *rubāʿī*, pl. *rubāʿiyyāt*): the quatrain consists of two distichs or four hemistichs rhyming together with the exception of the third; the two hemistichs of the first distich must rhyme. The vogue of the quatrain seems to have reached its height in the Saljuq period.

Qubači: people of the eastern Caucasus. Their artisans are still famous for their fine jewellery and gold and silver smithing.

Qubadabad: residence of the Rum Saljuq Kayqubad I on the west bank of Lake Beyshehir, southwest of Konya.

Quban: one of the four great rivers of the Caucasus, about 450 miles long. Rising near Mount Elburz at a height of 13,930 feet, it enters the plains at a height of 1,075 feet. Its lower course divides into two branches, one of which flows into the Sea of Azov and the other, the main one, into the Black Sea. The territory of Quban was for a long time disputed between the Russians and the khans of the Crimea.

Qubilay: Mongol Great Khan; b. 1215, r. 1260-1294. He transferred the capital of the Empire from Karakorum to Peking. Like most of the Great Khans, he was favourably disposed to Islam and the Muslims; only during the years 1282-1289, as a result of the events connected with the assassination of the minister Ahmad, did the Muslims fall into disfavour with him.

Qučan: town of northern Khurasan, Iran, between Teheran and Mashhad. It constituted the granary of Nishapur, and cotton was also grown. The town suffered badly during Genghis Khan's attack on Khurasan. ʿAlaʾ al-Din al-Juwayni persuaded the Il-Khan Hülegü to rebuild it. After a revolt of the inhabitants against the Qajar Fath ʿAli Shah, the town was almost destroyed and later severe earthquakes increased the devastation. In the later xixth c. the three Kurdish principalities of Qučan, Bujnurd and Darreh Gaz lost their military importance, due to the subjection to Imperial Russian rule of the formerly predatory Turkmen. Qučan has remained the centre of an important wheat-growing area.

Qudaʿa: group of Arab tribes who, at the beginning of Islam, controlled the coastal route of the caravans between Syria and Mecca. The most important divisions were the Juhayna and the Bali, to the north of Juhayna. The Prophet concluded a treaty with them. Tribesmen of Bali (A. *balawī*) took part in the battles between the Prophet and Quraysh on the side of the Prophet, who is said to have sent a letter to a Balawi group, the Banu Juʿayl. Both groups participated in the conquest of Egypt.

Qudama b. Jaʿfar al-Katib al-Baghdadi: philologist and historian from

Baghdad; ?873-?932. He was one of the first scholars to introduce the systematic study of the figures of speech in Arabic literature.

al-Quduri, Abu 'l-Husayn/al-Hasan Ahmad: Hanafi jurist of Baghdad; 972-1037. He wrote a concise legal manual which had a great scholarly reknown.

Queen of Sheba: according to tradition the queen ruled in southwest Arabia in the xth c. B.C. She is connected with King Solomon and plays an important role in Ethiopian folklore. In Arabic literature she is known under the name Bilqis.

Quetta (Kwatta): town and district of northern Baluchistan, Pakistan. In medieval Islamic times, the history of this very mountainous region was closely connected with that of Qandahar. After a brief Safawid occupation from 1556-1559, the region was incorporated in the Mughal empire, but after 1622 it came under Safawid control again. In the xviiith c. it was controlled by the khans of Kalat (Kilat), Baluchistan. In recent times, Quetta was an emporium for trade between southern Afghanistan and the lower Indus valley, but it had above all a strategic position, as became clear in the Second Afghan War (1878-1880). The population is largely Pathan.

al-Qulzum: Egyptian town and seaport, at the mouth of the canal which led from the Nile to the Red Sea. This canal, begun by Pharaoh Necho and finished by Darius of Persia, was later restored by Ptolemy II Philadelphus and by Trajan. In the Muslim period labour was repeatedly spent on it. The Arabs call the Red Sea Bahr al-Qulzum. The town was a source of salt.

Qum (A. *Qumm*): city of central Iran, 150 km. to the south of Teheran. The city and its region became one of the first bastions of Shi'ism. In 816 Fatima al-Ma'suma, sister of the eighth Imam 'Ali b. Musa al-Rida, died and was buried in Qum. Her sanctuary and the town's reputation as a centre of theological education contributed most to its fame. Patronised by the Buyids, the inhabitants were massacred in 1224 at the time of the Mongol conquest. In the xivth c. Qum was mostly in ruins, but there was an attempt at revival under the Il-Khans. Although a massacre was perpetrated under Tamerlane, the Timurids showed respect to the holy city. The Qara Qoyunlu and Aq Qoyunlu sultans, as well as the earlier Safawids, used it as a kind of winter capital. Qum was endowed with an unprecedented glamour by Shah 'Abbas I. After the terrible depression of the xviiith c., the Qajars revived the practice of building royal monuments, but under their rule Qum was also a haven of refuge for political opponents of the regime. In June 1963 Ayatollah Khomayni was arrested there. In January 1978 the troubles, which convulsed the whole of Iran, began at Qum, and in March Khomayni returned to the city.

Qumis: Arabic transcription of Latin *comes*, a title which in Muslim Spain denoted the Christian responsible to the state for the Christian Mozarabs. It is also the name of a small province of medieval northeastern Persia.

Qum(m)i, Qadi Ahmad Ibrahim Husayni: Persian chronicler and chancery clerk; 1546-?. He wrote a chronicle in five volumes, of which the fifth volume only has been preserved. It describes the history of the Safawids down to the first years of Shah 'Abbas I. He is also the author of a treatise on calligraphers and painters.

Quna (Qena): town in Upper Egypt, on the east bank of the Nile, noted for its porous pottery and for the tomb of 'Abd al-Rahim b. Ahmad b. Hajjun (d. 1196), twelfth descendant of the twelfth Imam Ja'far al-Sadiq.

Qunbi Salih: important cluster of ruins in southern Mauritania. The place probably was the capital of the Sarakoli kingdom of Ghana from around the vith c. until ca. 1076.

Qungrat: name of first a Mongol and then a Turkmen tribe of Central Asia, and of a settlement on the lower Oxus.

Qur'an (A. *al-Qur'ān*): the Muslim scripture, containing the revelations recited by the Prophet and preserved in a fixed, written form. The word is based on the Arabic verb which, in the Qur'an itself, means "to recite", occasionally "to read (aloud?)". The orthodox view is that God is the speaker throughout, that the Prophet is the recipient, and that the angel Gabriel is the intermediary agent of revelation – regardless of who may appear to be the speaker and addressee.

The most widely accepted story of the "first collection" of the Qur'an places an official, written copy of the entire text in the reign of the first caliph, Abu Bakr. The complete consonantal text is believed to have been established during the reign of the third caliph, 'Uthman b. 'Affan. The general view is that 'Uthman canonised the Medinan text tradition and that this one was most likely the closest to the original revelation. Other text traditions, attributed to several Companions of the Prophet, are said to have flourished at Kufa, Basra and in Syria. The final vocalised text is believed to have been established in the early xth c.

The Qur'an consists of 114 sections of widely varying length and form, called *sūra*s, which are divided into a number of verses (A. *āyāt*), ranging from three to 287. After the first *sūra*, called "The Opening" (A. *al-fātiḥa*), the others are arranged roughly in order of descending length. All of them, except *sūra* IX, start with the formula "Bismi 'llāhi 'l-raḥmāni 'l-raḥīm", the so-called *basmala*, of which at least three interpretations or translations are given. All *sūra*s also have their own name, while at the beginning of 29 of them stands a letter or group of letters, which have intrigued Muslim scholars for 14 centuries. The *sūra*s are designated as "Meccan" or "Medinan" i.e. revealed before or after the Hijra.

The traditional Muslim dating of the *sūra*s is based on the assumption that the present *sūra*s were the original units of revelation, that their chronological order can be determined, and that Tradition provides a valid basis for dating them. Western scholars, on the other hand, have proposed a variety of dating systems.

Most medieval Muslim scholars believed that the Qur'an was in the spoken language of the Prophet, the dialect of the Quraysh, which was also the language of the "Classical Arabic" poetry of the Prophet's day. Most western Arabists now accept the view that the language of the Qur'an, far from being the spoken dialect of the Quraysh or a *Hochsprache* of the entire Hejaz, as maintained by Th. Nöldeke and others, is the "poetic *koine*" of the Classical Arabic poetry, with some adaptation to the Meccan speech. The earliest exegetes, and many after them – with al-Shafi'i as a notable exception – recognised and discussed freely a large number of non-Arabic words in the Qur'an. Al-Suyuti classifies them as words borrowed from Ethiopic, Persian, Greek, Indian, Syriac, Hebrew, Nabataean, Coptic, Turkish, Negro and Berber.

A distinctive feature of Qur'anic style, closely related to its oral nature, is that it is all rhymed or assonanced prose (A. *saj*). As to the literary forms found in the Qur'an, they may in general be distinguished in oath and related forms; passages in which certain phenomena of nature and human life are spoken of as "signs" of God; so-called "say-passages" in which a short statement or question is introduced by the imperative verb "Say"; narratives, such as versions of ancient Near Eastern myths, prophetic and punishment-stories, parables, and regulations.

The Qur'an was not originally intended for non-Arabs, but as a result of the Arabic-Islamic conquests the question arose whether non-Arabs were permitted to recite the texts in their native language. Several solutions were proposed and accepted, but a "translation" of the whole of the Qur'an in the true sense of the word was not considered as possible, because the wording of the Holy Book is a miracle incapable of imitation by man. Instead, a translation in the sense of a commentary might be used and so translations made by Muslims are printed beside the Arabic text. The Qur'an has been "translated" into most of the languages of Asia and Europe, and into some African ones.

Quraysh: tribe inhabiting Mecca in the time of the Prophet and to which he belonged. At the present day there are many Quraysh living as Bedouin in the neighbourhood of Mecca, while in the city itself the key of the Ka'ba is held by a clan of Quraysh called Shayba.

Qurayza, Banu: one of the three main Jewish tribes of Yathrib (Medina), the others being the Banu Qaynuqa' and the Banu 'l-Nadir. The Prophet besieged them in their forts for twenty-five nights. After negotiations they agreed to surrender unconditionally. At the decree of Sa'd b. Mu'adh, chief of the clan of 'Abd al-Ashhal who had been brought to give judgement, all the men were put to death and all the women and children sold as slaves.

Quriltay: Arabic orthography of a Mongol term which means an assembly of the Mongol princes summoned to discuss and deal with some important question such as the election of a new khan.

Qurrat al-ʿAyn, Fatima Umm Salma (Janab-i Tahira): Persian poetess and Babi martyr; 1814-1852. Her way of life was extremely emancipated for her time, and she has remained a symbol of women's emancipation ever since.

al-Qurtubi, Abu ʿAbd Allah Muhammad: Maliki scholar from Córdoba; d. 1272. His fame rests on his commentary on the Qurʾan, which contains a very great number of traditions, many of which are not mentioned by Abu Jaʿfar al-Tabari.

Qus: town of Upper Egypt situated on the eastern bank of the Nile, some 30 km. to the north of Luxor.

al-Qusantini (Ksentini), **Rashid** (Ibn al-Akhdar): Algerian dramatist, comic actor and song-writer; 1887-1944.

Qusayr ʿAmra: audience hall and bath in Jordan, built by the future Umayyad Caliph al-Walid II, remarkable for its paintings.

Qusayy: ancestor of the Prophet in the fifth generation and restorer of the pre-Islamic cult of the Kaʿba in Mecca.

al-Qushashi, Safi ʾl-Din Ahmad: Sufi mystic and scholar of Medina; 1583-1660. He attracted numerous students, among them the Sumatran ʿAbd al-Raʾuf of Singkel.

al-Qushayri, Abu ʾl-Qasim ʿAbd al-Karim: theologian and mystic of Khurasan; 986-1072. In all his works he tried to reconcile mystical practices with the principles of Muslim law.

Quss d. Saʿida al-Iyadi: semi-legendary character of Arab antiquity pictured as the greatest orator of all the tribes, whose eloquence has become proverbial.

Qutadghu Bilig ("Knowledge that brings happiness"): the first long narrative poem in Turkic literature, written in the xith c. by Yusuf Khass Hajib of Balasaghun. It is also the oldest monument of Turkic Islamic literature, written in Qarakhanid, the earliest variety of eastern Middle Turkic and the first literary language of the Muslim Turks.

Qutayba b. Muslim: Arab commander; 669-715. His governorship of Khurasan contributed much to the extension of Islam in what is now Afghanistan and Central Asia.

Qutb al-Din Aybak: Turkish commander of the Ghurid Muʿizz al-Din (r. 1173-1206) and founder of the dynasty of the Muʿizzi or Slave Kings in Delhi; r. 1206-1210. After the death of Muʿizz al-Din, Qutb al-Din moved from Delhi to Lahore. He was the first ruler of the Indo-Muslim state which was subsequently to be based at Delhi. He achieved renown as the builder of the Qutb Minar near Delhi.

Qutb al-Din Shirazi, Mahmud b. Masʿud: Persian astronomer and physician; 1236-1311. In his two comprehensive astronomical works he has given what is conceivably the best Arabic account of astronomy (cosmography) with mathemetical aids.

Qutb Minar: a lofty tower, 238 feet in height, of red sandstone near Delhi, erected in 1193 by Qutb al-Din Aybak and named after the saint Khwaja Qutb al-Din Bakhtiyar Kaki (d. 1235).

Qutb Shahids: Indo-Muslim dynasty, which ruled from 1496 till 1687, when it was conquered by the Mughal Awrangzib. It dominated the eastern Deccan plateau as one of the five successor states to the Bahmanid kingdom. Their power was based on the city and hill-fort of Golkonda. The founder of the dynasty, Sultan-Quli Qutb al-Mulk, was a Turkmen adventurer of the Qara Qoyunlu, who declared Shi'ism the official creed. The kingdom was engulfed in constant warfare with Bijapur, Ahmadnagar and the Hindu state of Vijayanagar. But it also formed a composite culture that combined Islamic and Indian styles, as reflected in the nature of its rule, in the flourishing of Telegu, Persian and Dakhni literature, and in painting and architecture. In the xviith c. Golkonda was the world's most important diamond market.

Qutham b. al-'Abbas b. 'Abd al-Muttalib al-Hashimi: Companion of the Prophet, son of his uncle and of Umm al-Fadl Lubaba al-Hilaliyya, herself the Prophet's sister-in-law. After his death at the siege of Samarqand in 677, his supposed tomb there became a shrine and pilgrimage place.

Qutuz, al-Malik al-Muzaffar Sayf al-Din al-Mu'izzi: Mamluk sultan of the Bahri dynasty and nephew of the Khwarazm-Shah Jalal al-Din; r. 1259-1260. Proclaiming a Holy War, Qutuz led an army from Egypt into Palestine. He first secured the neutrality of the Franks at Acre and then met, and defeated, the Mongol army at 'Ayn Jalūt. He was murdered shortly afterwards.

R

Rabah: chief lieutenant of Sulayman b. Zubayr Pasha, the Egyptian governor of Bahr al-Ghazal; d. 1900. Sulayman, who had joined Harun, the dethroned sultan of Dar Fur, in order to rebel against Egypt, was defeated by Ghessi Pasha, sent by Gordon. Rabah then began a series of raids in Central Sudan, and was finally defeated by Commandant Lamy.

Rabat (A. *Ribāṭ al-Fatḥ*): the capital of Morocco on the estuary of the Bu Regreg, founded by the Almohads. After the final subjugation of the Banu Berghwata, the Almohad 'Abd al-Mu'min made the fortified Muslim monastery (A. *ribāṭ*) into the place of mobilisation for the troops intended to carry Holy War into Spain. Ya'qub al-Mansur (r. 1184-1199) ordered the building of a colossal mosque which was never finished; its enormous minaret, also unfinished, still stands. It is related to the minarets of the Kutubiyya at Marrakesh and of the Giralda at Seville. In 1248 Rabat passed into the hands of the Marinids. The expulsion of the last Moriscoes in 1610 brought an important colony of Andalusian fugitives who, unlike in other Moroccan towns, never mingled with the inhabitants and devoted themselves to piracy. Rabat, known in Europe as "New Salé" in contrast to neighbouring Sala, soon became the centre of a regular little maritime republic in the hands of the Spanish Moors, who hardly recognised the suzerainty of the Sharifs of Morocco. In 1757 Muhammad III b. ʿAbd Allah endeavoured to organise the piracy himself. After the bombardment by a French fleet in 1765, Rabat declined. It was occupied by French troops in 1911.

Rabiʿa and Mudar: the two largest and most powerful combinations of tribes in ancient northern Arabia. Legend records very old connections of the Mudar with the Meccan sanctuary, while Christianity was widespread among the Rabiʿa in the Prophet's time. Later, the tribes of Rabiʿa and Mudar are mentioned as important contingents in the Muslim armies.

Rabiʿa al-ʿAdawiyya: famous mystic and saint of Basra; d. 801. She gathered round her many disciples, and miracles were attributed to her.

Race (A. *ʿirq*): the ancient Arabs made much of the purity of their genealogy (A. *nasab*). In the Qurʾan, the Prophet struck a blow at the old preoccupations concerning race by advising his followers to marry a believing slave rather than a woman of the polytheists. But these preoccupations lived on among the Bedouins, while Sharifs and Sayyids also showed concern about the nobility of their stock.

Rachel (A. *Raḥīl*): the wife of Jacob is referred to in the Qurʾan, and is spoken of in Tradition. She also plays a role in the story of Joseph.

al-Radi bi-ʾllah: ʿAbbasid caliph; b. 909, r. 934-940. Government was in the hands of Muhammad b. Yaqut, and after the latter's fall in 935, Ibn Muqla gained control but only for a year. Power then passed into the hands of Muhammad b. Raʾiq. In 938 he was replaced by Bejkem, a manumitted slave of Turkish origin (d. 941), who had to fight the advancing Buyids while in Baghdad fanatical Hanbalis were harassing the population.

Radiyya, Jalalat al-Din Begum: female ruler of the Muʿizzi dynasty of Delhi; r. 1236-1240. She was a daughter of sultan Iltutmish, and was proclaimed queen by the people of Delhi. She favoured the "Abyssinian" (A. *ḥabashī*) Malik Jamal al-Din Yaqut, which led the Turkish amirs to depose and kill her. She was the only woman to succeed to the throne of Delhi during the period of Muslim rule and, with the exception of the Mamluk Shajar al-Durr of Egypt, the only female sovereign in the history of Islam.

al-Raghib al-Isfahani: Arab theological writer; d. 1108. He compiled a dictionary of the Qurʾan arranged alphabetically according to the initial letters.

Raghib Pasha: Ottoman Grand Vizier; 1699-1763. He was also one of the classical authors of Turkish literature.

Rahmaniyya: religious order in Algeria. It is a branch of the Khalwatiyya order and is named after its founder Muhammad b. ʿAbd al-Rahman al-Gushtuli (d. 1793).

Raid (A. *ghazw*): in its most common sense, the word signifies a small expedition set on foot by Bedouins with the acquisition of camels, or booty in general, as its object, and also the force which carries it out. Very little blood was ordinarily shed, mercy being freely granted.

Rain, supplication for (A. *istisqā'*): the Arabic term denotes a rogational rite during periods of great drought, dating back to the earliest Arab times and still practised at the present day, notably in Jordan and Morocco. While still a small boy, the Prophet is said to have played a part in the rogations celebrated at Mecca. Subsequently, Islam tried to remove the astral and magical features of the rite, and a precise ritual was established.

In Turkey, some magico-religious practises are employed to produce rain.

Rainbow (A. *qaws quzaḥ*): the term is the Arabic variation of the name of a divinity found among the peoples moving round the region between Central Arabia and the river Jordan. Arabic literature knows many descriptions of rainbows.

Rajaz: name of an Arab metre. Whereas in other metres the lines of verse consist of two symmetrical half-lines, separated by a caesura, the line of verse of the *rajaz* is in one part only and has no caesura.

Rajputs: large group of tribes and clans in India who claim to be the modern representatives of the Kshatriyas. The term has no racial significance. After the Muslim conquest of the eastern Punjab and the Ganges valley, the Rajputs maintained their independence in Rajasthan. In the xviith c. they accepted Mughal overlordship and, after the Maratha wars, submitted to the British in 1818. In 1947, the Rajput states formed the state of Rajasthan within the Indian Union.

Ramadan: the ninth month of the Muslim calendar which is the month of fasting. Abstention from food, drink, and sexual intercourse from dawn until dusk is prescribed. A part of the day is passed in sleeping, and the nights are given up to all sorts of pleasures. As important days of the month, Muslim scholars mention: the 6th, birthday of Husayn b. 'Ali; the 10th, death of Khadija; the 17th, the battle of Badr; the 19th, the Prophet's occupation of Mecca; the 21st, death of 'Ali and of the Imam 'Ali al-Rida; the 22nd, birthday of 'Ali; and the night of the 27th, the so-called Laylat al-Qadr, in which, according to Qur'an LXXXVII,1, the Holy Book was sent down.

Ramadan-oghullari: petty Anatolian dynasty of Turkmen origin. They ruled over southwestern Anatolia from 1379 till ca. 1600.

Ramadan-zade Mehmed Pasha (Küčük Nishanji): Ottoman historian; d. 1571. At the bidding of the Ottoman Sultan Sülayman II he compiled a history of the Ottoman Empire down to 1561. It became one of the most widely used handbooks of Ottoman history.

al-Ramadi, Abu 'Umar Yusuf: poet from Córdoba; d. 1013. His life was dominated by his attachment to Abu 'Ali al-Qali, by his devotion to the cause of the chamberlain Abu 'l-Hasan al-Mushafi, and by his love for Khalwa.

Ram-Hormuz (Ramuz): town and district in Khuzistan, Iran. The Buyid ʿAdud al-Dawla built a magnificent market there, and the town was a centre of Muʿtazili teaching.

al-Rami, Hasan b. Muhammad: Persian stylist; xivth c. He wrote a treatise on the most common poetical figures for describing the different parts of the human body.

Rami Mehmed Pasha: Ottoman Grand Vizier and poet; 1654-1707. He was one of the plenipotentiaries at Carlowicz.

al-Ramla: town in Israel. It was founded by the future Umayyad Caliph Sulayman, who continued to live there after becoming caliph. It was made a bishopric by the Crusaders, who built a church which is now the Jamiʿ al-Kabir mosque. In 1187 the town was destroyed by Saladin. In 1789 it was Bonaparte's headquarters.

Rampur: town and district in Rohilkhand, now Uttar Pradesh, India. Its early history is that of the growth of Rohilla power, founded by Dawud Khan, an Afghan adventurer who arrived in India after the death of the Mughal Awrangzib in 1707. In 1774 the Rohillas were defeated by the Nawwab of Oudh Shujaʿ al-Dawla, who was assisted by the British. During the Mutiny of 1857, Muhammad Yusuf ʿAli Khan, the ruler of Rampur, rendered services to the British.

al-Raqqa: town in Syria near the Euphrates. It surrendered to the Arabs in 639. In 772 the ʿAbbasid Caliph al-Mansur built alongside al-Raqqa a new town, al-Rafiqa, planned in the shape of a horse-shoe and modelled on the round city of Baghdad. The name of al-Raqqa came to be transferred to this new town. The high walls of the "horse-shoe town" still stand. The town is known for the so-called Raqqa ware, produced between the ixth and xivth c.

Raqqada: residential city of the Aghlabid amirs, about six miles north of Qayrawan. It was founded by the Aghlabid Ibrahim II but razed to the ground by the Fatimid al-Muʿizz.

Rashid, Mehmed: Ottoman imperial historiographer; d. 1735. He wrote a history of the Ottoman empire from 1660 to 1721.

al-Rashid b. al-Sharif, Mawlay: Sharif of Morocco and the real founder of the so-called Filali Sharifian dynasty; b. 1630, r. 1664-1672. He was born in Tafilalt in southern Morocco where his family, the Hasani Sharifs, was acquiring political influence during the decline of the Saʿdi Sharifs. He conquered Fez in 1666 and extended his possessions west- and southwards.

Rashid al-Din Sinan: leader of the Syrian Nizari Ismaʿilis; d. 1193. He played a prominent part in Syrian and Egyptian politics, successfully defending his people against Sunni Muslim rulers, especially Saladin, and against the Crusaders.

Rashid al-Din Tabib: Persian physician and historian; ca. 1247-1318. Under the Il-Khans Mahmud Ghazan and Öljeytü Khudabanda he rose to great political power and played a role as a builder. In the end, however, he was executed. He owes his fame to his history of the Mongols. The first volume contains the history of the Turkish and Mongol tribes, of Genghis Khan, his predecessors and successors down to Ghazan. The second volume deals with Adam, the Muslim and Hebrew prophets, the old Persian kings, with the Prophet and the caliphs down to the capture of Baghdad by the Mongols in 1258.

Rashid Rida: Syrian Arab scholar; 1865-1935. His life was devoted to the reconciliation of the Islamic heritage to the modern world. He was influenced by Jamal al-Din al-Afghani and Muhammad 'Abduh, of whom he wrote a well-known biography. He founded the newspaper al-Manar and published it throughout his life.

Rasht (Resht): capital of the province of Gilan in Iran. The town, famous for its silk, was sacked by Stenka Razin in 1636. From 1722 to 1734, Rasht was occupied by the Russians, but later restored to Persia. It played a role again after World War I.

Rashidis: dynasty in Ha'il, Najd, Saudi Arabia. In 1835 the house of Ibn Rashid became firmly established as rulers under the suzerainty of the Al Sa'ud. Under Muhammad Ibn Rashid, who ruled Ha'il between 1872-1897, Jabal Shammar was independent and trade relations existed with al-Najaf in Iraq. After the death of Muhammad, the House of Rashid was weakened by dynastic disputes. Ha'il was taken by 'Abd al-'Aziz Al Sa'ud in 1921.

Rassids: line of Zaydi Imams of Yemen, ruling from ca. 860 to 1281. The name is taken from a property near Mecca, called al-Rass, which belonged to the grandfather of the first Imam, al-Qasim al-Rassi, who was a descendant of Hasan b. 'Ali. The Rassids ruled from Sa'da, but their reign was disturbed by several other dynasties, such as the Sulayhids, the Ayyubids, the Rasulids and the Tahirids of Lahij. The Rassids were followed by the Qasimids.

Rasulids: dynasty of Yemen, ruling from 1229 to 1454. Rasul, who gave his name to the dynasty, was a Turkmen of Oghuz origin. After the departure of Mas'ud, the last Ayyubid, Rasul's grandson Nur al-Din 'Umar (r. 1229-1250) made himself independent at Zabid, captured many places from the Zaydi Imams, among them San'a', and in 1240 took Mecca, which remained in Rasulid hands for fifteen years. The kingdom stretched from the Hejaz to Hadhramaut, making the Rasulids a power of international significance in the Islamic world. After al-Malik al-Nasir's death in 1424, internal strife set in, and in 1454 the last Rasulid abdicated before the Tahirids of Lahij and Aden.

Ratan, Baba Hajji Abu 'l-Rida: Indian saint; xiiith c. His shrine near Bhatinda in the Punjab is a place of pilgrimage visited by Muslims and Hindus. There has been much discussion in Muslim circles about his claim that he was a long-lived Companion of the Prophet.

Rawalpindi: capital of Pakistan from 1959 to 1969, lying 14 km southwest of Islamabad, the national capital.

al-Rawda: large island in the Nile before it divides into the Damietta and Rosetta branches. It was used as the site for the Nilometer, as a dockyard, and as a natural fortified refuge. The Bahri Mamluks ruled Egypt from there for nearly a century and a half.

Rawshaniyya: Afghan sect founded by Bayazid b. 'Abd Allah, who took the title Pir-i Rawshan (1525-1585). The sect, whose doctrine is said to have been extreme pantheism, was suppressed in 1637.

Rayy: ruined city near Teheran, the ancient Rhaga, Latin Ragae (modern Shahr Rey). It was conquered by the Arabs in 641. In 750 the passing of power from the Umayyads to the 'Abbasids took place at Rayy. The 'Abbasid Caliph al-Mahdi rebuilt the city under the name of Muhammadiyya. In 908 the Samanid Ahmad II b. Isma'il (r. 907-914) received there investiture from the 'Abbasid Caliph al-Muqtadir. All Arab authors emphasize the importance of Rayy as a commercial centre. After a Daylami intermezzo, the Buyids established themselves in Rayy in 925 and it remained in their hands for about one hundred years. In 1042 the town fell into the power of the Saljuqs until 1217. Already in 1186 civil war had broken out between the Sunnis and the Shi'is, and the town fell in decay. The final blow was delivered by the Mongols in 1220.

Rayy was famous for its decorated silks and ceramics. The Arabic word "al-Razi" means: originating from Rayy.

al-Razi, Abu Bakr Muhammad b. Zakariyya': the greatest physician of Islam, alchemist and philosopher; 864-925. A number of his works, among them his large medical encyclopaedia in Arabic, called *al-Hawi*, were translated into Latin and down to the xviith c. his authority was undisputed. In chemistry, al-Razi rejected all occult and symbolical explanations of natural phenomena. Of his metaphysical works only a few fragments have been preserved in later authors. He was an opponent of the Aristotelians and relied on the authority of Plato and the pre-Socratic philosophers. He had a critical attitude to established religion, refuted the Mu'tazila, the extreme Shi'a and the Manichaeans, and denied the possibility of a reconciliation between philosophy and religion. One of his writings was read among the Carmathians, and seems to have influenced the famous theme of the "De Tribus Impostoribus".

al-Razi, Ahmad b. Muhammad b. Musa: the first in date of the great historians of al-Andalus; 888-955. He was surnamed "The Chronicler". His description of al-Andalus is of great importance for the period of 'Abd al-Rahman III.

Razi, Amin Ahmad: Persian biographer; xvith c. He owes his fame to a great collection of biographies of famous men, which is arranged geographically according to the seven climes.

al-Razi, Fakhr al-Din: one of the most celebrated theologians and exegetists of Islam; 1149-1209. One of his numerous works is his *Testament*, which is a true profession of Sunni faith and an example of total resignation to the will of God.

Readers/Reciters of the Qur'an (A. *qurrā'*): the Arabic term occurs in Arabic historiography to indicate a group of Iraqis who rose against the Caliph 'Uthman and later against 'Ali after he had accepted the arbitration with Mu'awiya at Siffin. In European research, the term has been usually rendered as "readers/reciters of the Qur'an". Recently, the term has been interpreted as "villagers", denoting those participants in the wars against the Sasanian Empire who had occupied the vacated estates of southern Iraq and whose privileges had been threatened since 'Uthman's reign.

Reed-pen (A. *qalam*): it is a tube of reed cut between two knots, sliced obliquely, or rendered concave, at the thicker end and with the point slit, like the European quill and the later steel pen. Each kind of script needed a special pen, and the cutting of the nib was an art in itself. It is kept in a metal box, to which an inkwell is attached, or in a papier-mâché box adorned with lacquerwork.

Refi'i: Ottoman poet and Hurufi; xvth c. In his *Message of Joy* he explains the teachings of the Hurufiyya and deals with the life of its founder Fadl Allah Hurufi (1340-1394).

Reforms, Ottoman (A. *Tanẓīmāt*; T. *Tanẓīmāt-i Khayriyye*): the term is used to denote the reforms which were introduced into the government and administration of the Ottoman Empire from the beginning of the reign of Sultan Abdülmecid I, and which ended with the absolute rule of Sultan Abdülhamid II. These reforms were carried out by the Grand Viziers Mustafa Rashid Pasha (d. 1858), 'Ali Pasha (d. 1871), Fu'ad Pasha (d. 1869) and Midhat Pasha (d. 1883). In the rescript of Gülkhane, known as the *Khaṭṭ-i Sherif*, the sultan expressed the wish that the farming out of taxes should be abolished, the army recruited more regularly, all criminals tried in public, and all subjects, to whatever religion they belonged, be equal before the law. The greatest difficulties lay with giving the Christian and Jewish subjects equal rights to the Muslims, thus depriving the former of considerable autonomy, the latter of their rights of jurisdiction and administration, and with taking away from the foreigners the liberties and privileges granted by the Capitulations. The rescript of 1856 confirmed the promises made in 1839 regarding the equality of treatment of non-Muslim subjects. Foreign Powers were given the right to possess landed property in Turkey, and continued to interfere in Ottoman affairs. The promulgation of the Ottoman Constitution of 1876 during the "European Conference" at Istanbul did not gain the success anticipated, since the Turco-Russian War (1877-1879) brought the beginning of disintegration. The period of the Reforms did not bring economic revival. After the financial catastrophe of 1879, the International Council of the Ottoman Debt was established in 1881. On the other hand, during this period the foundations for a new Turkish culture were laid by Ibrahim Efendi Shinasi, Ahmed Wefiq Pasha, Ahmed Jewdet Pasha, Ziya Gökalp and Khalide Edib.

Repentance (A. *tawba*): the word, often used in the Qur'an, originally means "return" and is used either in connection with God, Who turns with forgiveness to the penitent, or for someone who turns to God with repentance. Its validity depends on three conditions: a conviction of sin, remorse, and a firm resolution to abstain from sin in the future. Sin being an offence against God, repentance is indispensable for salvation. To the Sufis, the term denotes the spiritual conversion which is the necessary starting-point for those entering the Path (A. *ṭarīqa*), the new orientation of the entire personality.

Resmi, Ahmed b. Ibrahim: Ottoman statesman and historian; 1700-1783. He wrote descriptions of his embassies to Vienna (1757) and Berlin (1763), an eye-witness account of the Russo-Turkish war of 1769-1774, and some biographical collections.

Resurrection (A. *qiyāma*): in the Qur'an, the term is always found in the expression *yawm al-qiyāma* "the Day of Resurrection". The resurrection of bodies follows the annihilation of all creatures and precedes the Day of Judgement (A. *yawm al-dīn*), which will be the Last Hour (A. *al-sā'a*). These concepts, taken as a whole, constitute one of the "necessary beliefs" which determine the content of the Muslim faith.

Rewani (Ilyas): Ottoman poet; d. 1523. In a poem written in rhyming couplets he describes the drinking bouts of his time in detail.

Reza Khan (later Shah) **Pahlavi**: general and the first Pahlavi Shah of Iran; b. 1878, r. 1925-1941, d. 1944. Born in Mazandaran province, he rose through army ranks and organized in 1921 a revolution against the incompetent Qajar Ahmad Shah and his weak government. Reza Khan became minister of war, strengthened the army and became Prime Minister in 1923. Ahmad Shah, who was in Europe for a lengthy cure, refused to come back to Iran and was deposed in 1925 by the parliament, which elected Reza Khan as shah. He tried to introduce social reforms, and in foreign politics to play the Soviet Union off against Great Britain. In 1941 both powers occupied Iran in order to be able to supply the Soviet Union with war material. Reza Shah then abdicated in favour of his son Muhammad Reza Shah Pahlavi.

Rhodes: the most easterly island of the Aegean Sea, Greece. The island was invaded by the Arabs in 672, but evacuated soon afterwards and recovered by the Byzantines. In 1308 it was seized by the Knights Hospitallers after they had been expelled from Acre in 1291. The Order of Saint John of Jerusalem now came to be known as the Knights of Rhodes. Under their rule the island became one of the strongest outposts of Latin Christianity in the Levant. Between 1440 and 1444 three attacks by the Mamluks of Egypt were beaten off. The Knights were overthrown by the Ottoman Turks in 1522. In 1912, during the Turco-Italian war, the island came under Italian rule until it was assigned to Greece in 1943.

Rida Quli Khan (Hidayat): Persian scholar and man of letters; d. 1871. He wrote lyrical poetry and works of a historical nature.

Rida'i, Aqa: Indo-Persian miniature painter from Harat; xviith c. He worked at the court of the Mughal Emperor Jahangir.

Ridwan b. Tutush: Saljuq ruler in Aleppo; d. 1113. He waged war with his brother Duqaq, conquered Edessa and was recognised as lord of Damascus, where he was joined by his step-father Tughtigin. He failed to take Jerusalem, which had fallen into the hands of the Fatimids. In 1100 he was defeated by the Crusader Bohemond of Antioch and in 1105 by Bohemond's successor Tancred. Ridwan was accused of favouring the Isma'ilis.

Ritual impurity: the so-called major ritual impurity (A. *janāba*) is caused by marital intercourse, to which religious law assimilates any *effusio seminis*. Ritual purity is obtained by the so-called major ritual ablution (A. *ghusl*). Minor ritual impurity (A. *hadath*) is incurred by contact with an unclean substance like sperm, pus, urine, fermented liquor, and by the emission of any substance whether solid, liquid or gaseous. Ritual purity is regained by the simple ablution (A. *wudū'*).

Riyadh (A. *al-Riyād*): the capital of Saudi Arabia, lying in the Najd region. The then oasis was conquered in 1762 by the founder of the Al Sa'ud, Muhammad b. Sa'ud, but it remained in the hands of the local ruler Dham Ibn Dawwas until 1772. Al-Dir'iyya remained the capital of the Al Sa'ud until it was destroyed by Ibrahim Pasha of Egypt in 1818. Turki b. Sa'ud (r. 1823-1834) transferred his capital to Riyadh in 1824. The history of the town remained troubled until 1902, when 'Abd al-'Aziz II Al Sa'ud retook it from the Rashid family of al-Ha'il and made it the centre for his conquest of Arabia. Riyadh was designated as capital in 1932, when the unified kingdom of Saudi Arabia was proclaimed.

Riyah, Banu: Arab tribe. It was the most powerful of the tribes that left Upper Egypt and invaded North Africa in the middle of the xith c.

Riyal: the Arabic word is derived from the Spanish "real (de plata)", given in the Muslim world to the large European silver coins which formed the international currency of the xviith and xviiith c. In the late xviiith and xixth c. the name was given to the Austrian Maria Theresa thaler.

Robe of honour (A. *khil'a*): the practice of bestowing garments of honour became an almost daily occurrence in 'Abbasid times, and the custom remained widespread throughout the Muslim world until recent times.

Ronda (A. *Runda*): almost impregnable natural fortress and town west of Málaga, southern Spain, in the mountain massif called Serrania de Ronda (A. *Tākurunnā*). On the fall of the Spanish Umayyads in 1031, it became the capital of a little independent state of the Berber Banu Ifran. It was taken by the Catholic Kings in 1485.

Rosary (A. *subha*): it consists of three groups of beads made of wood, bone, mother of pearl, etc. The groups are separated by two transversal beads of a larger size, while a much larger piece serves as a kind of handle. The number of beads within each group varies, but the sum total is one hundred in accordance with the number of Allah and His 99 beautiful names. The rosary serves for the enumeration of these names, but it is also used for the counting of eulogies and the formulae at the end of the *ṣalāt*.

Rose (P. *Gul*): in eastern Islamic literature the (red) rose plays a very important part, its image recurring in all manner of similes, metaphors and other figures of speech, in set phrases, idioms and puns. With the nightingale (P. *bulbul*) it constitutes an old established pair of lovers. "Rose and Nightingale" are the titles of Persian, Indian and Turkish *mathnawī*s. The thorn is used as rival claimant for the rose, occasionally also as its protector.

Rosetta (A. *Rashīd*): town in Egypt on the western bank of the Rosetta branch of the Nile. It remained a rather unimportant town until the Ottoman conquest of Egypt in 1517 and the decay of European trade through Alexandria. It then became a centre for trade with Istanbul and continued to flourish until Muhammad 'Ali Pasha reconstructed the Mahmudiyya canal for navigation between Alexandria and the Nile. The famous Rosetta Stone was discovered in the neighbourhood of the town.

Ru'ba b. al-'Ajjaj al-Tamimi: Arab poet of *rajaz* verses; ca. 685-762. His poems are among the most difficult in Arabic literature as they are full of words unknown from elsewhere.

Rudaki, Abu 'Abd Allah Ja'far: one of the great Persian poets; d. 940. He was a master of the panegyric, excelled in bacchic poetry, and was remarkable for his original similes and his descriptions of nature.

Rudhrawar: district in Iran between Hamadhan and Nihawand. It produced many kinds of fruit and was widely renowned for its saffron.

al-Rudhrawari, Zahir al-Din Abu Shuja': 'Abbasid vizier; 1045-1095. He is praised for his piety, his eloquence and poetical gifts.

Ruhi: Ottoman historian; xvith c. His history of the Ottomans ends in 1511.

Rukn al-Dawla, Abu 'Ali al-Hasan b. Buya: second in age of the three brothers who founded the Buyid dynasty; d. 976. When his elder brother 'Ali, later 'Imad al-Dawla, occupied Fars in 934, he was given the governorship of Kazarun. But shortly afterwards 'Imad al-Dawla sent him as a hostage to the Ziyarid Mardawij, their former overlord, whom he wanted to conciliate. On Mardawij's assassination in 935, Rukn escaped, took Isfahan but was ejected from this city in 939 by Washmgir, Mardawij's brother. Soon afterwards, however, he succeeded in recovering Isfahan and, when the Samanid Nasr b. Ahmad died in 943, he was able to drive Washmgir out of Rayy, and so gained control of the whole Jibal. His contest with Washmgir lasted until the latter's death in 965. In 949, at 'Imad al-Din's death, he became the head of the family. The remarkable Abu 'l-Fadl Ibn al-'Amid was Rukn al-Dawla's vizier for thirty years.

Rukn al-Din Mas'ud I: Rum Saljuq ruler; r. 1116-1156. He was a son of Qilij Arslan I and succeeded in founding a securely established dominion in Konya, which he gradually extended.

Rukn al-Din Sulayman II b. Qilij Arslan II: Rum Saljuq ruler; r. 1196-1204. In his old age Qilij Arslan II divided his kingdom among his many sons, who set up as independent rulers. In the course of time, Rukn al-Din was able to bring the whole kingdom under his sway.

Rum: name used in Arabic, Persian and Turkish for the Byzantine Empire, and later for Europeans in general. The term means the land and people of the Rhomaeans (Romaioi). A branch of the Saljuqs, ruling from Konya, are known as Rum Saljuqs.

Rumeli(a): the name means "Land of the Rhomaeans" and was given by the Ottomans to the province which comprised Thrace and Macedonia. Philippopolis, in Turkish Filibe (now Plovdiv), was conquered by Lala Shahin Pasha in 1363. Political dissensions and the mixture of peoples favoured in Rumeli the formation of sects.

Rupee (P. *rupiyya*): Indian silver coin, introduced by Shir Shah Sur, the Afghan sultan of Delhi. The silver tanga then became a copper denomination. It continued to be struck by the Mughals and the English East India Company. The rupee became current in British East Africa and in the shaykhdoms along the Persian Gulf.

Ruqayya bint Muhammad: one of the daughters of the Prophet; d. 624. She is said to have married a son of the Prophet's uncle Abu Lahab. After her divorce, she married the future Caliph 'Uthman b. Affan and went with him to Abyssinia. After her return she accompanied the Prophet to Medina and died in 625, the year of the battle of Badr.

Rus: name first used for the Northmen, then for the Scandinavian-Slav adventurers who founded the principality of Kiev.

al-Rusafa (Rusafat al-Sham): town in the Syrian desert near Palmyra. The Umayyad caliphs occasionally lived in al-Rusafa, and Hisham b. 'Abd al-Malik died there in 743. In 1269 the inhabitants fled for fear of the Mongols, and the town remained uninhabited. The imposing ruins date almost entirely from ancient times.

Ruse (T. *Rusčuk*): port on the Danube in Bulgaria. The town developed under Turkish rule and became an important trade centre. The Ottoman architect Sinan built a mosque for the Grand Vizier Rustem Pasha. The town suffered heavily during the Turco-Russian Wars of 1811 and 1877. The Russians ceded it to Bulgaria in 1881.

Rustamids: dynasty of Ibadis of Tahert in Algeria. It was founded by 'Abd al-Rahman b. Rustam (d. 784), who was of Persian origin. The dynasty lasted until 908.

Rüstem Pasha: Ottoman Grand Vizier and historian; 1500-1561. Born near Sarajevo, he became very wealthy and erected many mosques in various parts of the empire, employing the great architect Sinan. His reputation as an historian is based on his *History of the Family of 'Othman*, which is important for the events of his time.

Ruyan: district comprising the western half of Mazandaran, Iran. From the Mongol period onwards, the geographical term Rustamdar is found. The princes of Ruyan, known as Ustundar, retained their autonomy down to the time of the Safawids.

S

Saba': name of a people and kingdom in southwestern Arabia in the first millennium B.C. At the period of the rise of Islam, Saba' was beginning to disappear from the memory of the Arab world. The most valuable items of information about Saba's geography, history and architecture are given by Abu Muhammad al-Hamdani. The legendary Queen of Sheba (A. *Bilqīs*) is said to have reigned in Saba'.

Sabaeans (A. *al-Ṣābi'a*): the name has been given to two quite distinct sects. One is that of the Mandaeans or Subbas, a Judaeo-Christian sect practising the rite of baptism in Mesopotamia, the so-called Christians of John the Baptist. The other is that of the Sabaeans of Harran, a pagan sect which survived for a considerable time under Islam.

The Sabaeans mentioned in the Qur'an are apparently the Mandaeans. The Sabaeans of Harran believed in a creator of the world, who is reached through the intermediary of astral spirits. They were persecuted by the 'Abbasid Caliph al-Qahir bi-'llah. After the middle of the xith c. all traces of the Sabaeans of Harran are lost. Some great scholars belonged to this sect, among them Thabit b. Qurra and Sinan b. Thabit, the physician of the Caliph al-Muqtadir (r. 908-932).

Sabbath (A. *sabt*): the Prophet definitely rejected the Jewish Sabbath commandment. In Tradition the reproach of anthropomorphism, continually made against the Jews, is very frequently based on the alleged "rest of God". The seventh day even acquired an unfavourable character.

al-Sabi, Abu Ishaq Ibrahim: member of the Sabaeans of Harran and a high official under the Buyids; d. 994. He was chief secretary of the Department of State documents under the Buyids of Iraq Mu'izz al-Dawla and his son 'Izz al-Dawla (r. 967-978), but was put in prison by the latter's uncle 'Adud al-Dawla Fana-Khusraw. His official letters have been preserved as well as his poems.

al-Sabi, Hilal b. al-Muhassin: secretary to the Buyid vizier Abu Ghalib Muhammad Ibn Khalaf (d. 1016); d. 1056. Only some fragments of the nine works which he composed have been preserved.

Sabur b. Ardashir, Abu Nasr: vizier of Baha' al-Dawla, the Buyid of Fars and Khuzistan; d. 1025. In the first period of his vizirate he had founded a great library. In 1000 he witnessed the mutiny of the Turkish mercenaries at Baghdad.

Sabzawar: name of a town to the south of Harat in western Afghanistan, and of another in Khurasan, Iran. With the latter many legends of the heroic age of Persia are associated, among others the combat between Rustam and Suhrab. This town was captured in 1186 by Sultan Shah b. Il-Arslan, brother of the Khwarazm-Shah 'Ala' al-Din Tekish, and destroyed by the Mongols. In 1337 a certain 'Abd al-Razzaq founded there the dynasty of the Sarbadars.

Sabzawari, Hajji Hadi: Persian philosopher and poet; 1797-1878. He disseminated and clarified the doctrines of Mulla Sadra Shirazi. The Qajar Shah Nasir al-Din ordered a mausoleum to be built for him at Mashhad.

Sa'd b. Abi Waqqas: Arab general; d. 671. He was one of the oldest Companions of the Prophet and took part in the battles of Badr and Uhud and in the following campaigns. He defeated the Persians at the famous battle of al-Qadisiyya and captured Ctesiphon-Seleucia (A. *al-Mada'in*). He also built a strong military camp, which was to be the town of Kufa. On his death-bed, the Caliph 'Umar appointed him as one of the six Companions to choose a new caliph. He refused to pay hommage to 'Ali.

Sa'd b. Mu'adh b. al-Nu'man: contemporary of the Prophet; d. 627. He showed great zeal for the new faith and was appointed the Prophet's deputy in Medina. Mortally wounded, he decreed that all the men of the Banu Qurayza were to be put to death.

Sa'd b. 'Ubada b. Dulaym al-Khazraji: contemporary of the Prophet; d. ca. 636. He was one of the few persons in the Arabia of his time who were able to write. He played a role at al-'Aqaba, and at Uhud he tended the wounded Prophet. He proved himself an exceedingly energetic champion of Islam, and distinguished himself by great liberality. At the Prophet's death, he was proposed as his successor. After Abu Bakr had received homage as Caliph, Sa'd went to al-Hawran, where he died.

Sa'd I b. Zangi, 'Izz al-Din Abu Shuja': Salghurid atabeg of Fars; r. 1203-1231. He waged war with his cousin and predecessor Tughril b. Sunqur during the latter's reign (r. 1194-1203). Under his rule Fars enjoyed considerable prosperity, although he had to acknowledge the suzerainty of the Khwarazm-Shahs.

Sa'd al-Din Köpek (Göbek): high official at the time of the Rum Saljuq Kaykhusraw II; xiiith c. He built the large khan still standing near Konya.

Sa'da: town in Yemen. It lies on the pilgrim road from Mecca to San'a', and was known for its leather and excellent lances. The Zaydi Imam Yahya al-Hadi ila 'l-Haqq made it the base of Zaydi power.

Sadaqa b. Mansur b. Dubays: ruler of al-Hilla; d. 1108. He founded the town in 1102 from Kufa, which he had occupied in 1101. In the fight between the Great Saljuq Berkyaruq and his brother Muhammad I, he stood on the latter's side. In 1103 Sadaqa extended his power over a great part of Iraq, and took Hit, Wasit, Basra and Takrit. He was finally defeated by Muhammad I.

al-Sa'di, 'Abd al-Rahman: historian of the Songhai kingdom in the

Sudan; 1596-ca.1656. His history of the Sudan contains the early history of the tribes of the Songhai, the Melli and the Tuareg, as well as of the towns of Dienné and Timbuktu.

Sa'di, Shaykh Muslih al-Din: one of the greatest Persian poets; 1184-1283. Born in Shiraz, he studied Sufi mysticism at the Nizamiyya madrasa at Baghdad, with Shaykh 'Abd al-Qadir al-Jilani and with Shihab al-Din Suhrawardi. He made the pilgrimage to Mecca many times, travelled to Central Asia, India, the Saljuq territories in Anatolia, taking part in Holy War in these regions, to Syria, Egypt, Arabia, Yemen, Abyssinia and Morocco. His best-known works are *Garden* and *Rose-garden*, also known as *Sa'di-nama*. The former is a collection of poems on ethical subjects, the latter a collection of moral stories in prose. He also wrote a volume of odes, and collections of poems known as *Pleasantries*, *Jests* and *Obscenities*. He is regarded as the master of the *ghazal*. His influence on Persian, Turkish and Indian literatures has been very considerable, and his works were often translated into European languages from the xviith c. onwards.

Sa'dids (Banu Sa'd): name of the dynasty of Sharifs of Sus in southern Morocco which in 1544 replaced the Wattasid dynasty on the throne of Fez. They reigned until 1659, when they were replaced by the Filali Sharifs from Tafilalt.

Sa'diyya (Jibawiyya): order of dervishes in Syria, named after Sa'd al-Din al-Jibawi (d. 1300). The order spread to Turkey and Egypt, where in the xixth c. the so-called *dawsa* ceremony was practised, in which the shaykh rode on horse-back over the backs of the dervishes without allegedly inflicting any harm.

al-Safa: mound at Mecca opposite the eminence al-Marwa. During the pilgrimage, Muslims perform the ritual running (A. *sa'y*) between al-Safa and al-Marwa in memory of the fact that Hagar ran backwards and forwards seven times between these two eminences to look for a spring for her thirsty son Ishmael.

Safad: town in Israel, north-east of the Lake of Tiberias. The Crusaders built a fortress which served as a point of support for the hinterland of Acre. It was captured by Saladin in 1188, ceded to the Templars in 1220 by the ruler of Damascus Salih Isma'il, and conquered by the Mamluk Baybars in 1266. It surrendered to the Ottoman Sultan Selim I in 1516, and to Bonaparte in 1799. The town suffered greatly from earthquakes in 1819 and 1837. In the middle of the xixth c. a great influx of Moroccan, Algerian and Persian Jews took place, which was increased since 1880 by Zionist immigration.

al-Safadi, Salah al-Din Khalil b. Aybak: head of the treasury at Damascus and a prolific author; d. 1362. All his works practically are compilations from earlier authors, a fact which he frequently states faithfully.

Safar: name of the second month of the Muslim year, considered to be unlucky.

Safawids: the dynasty which ruled Persia from 1501 till 1786. Turkish-speaking and quite probably of Kurdish origin, the dynasty took its name from Shaykh Safi al-Din al-Ardabili and was founded by Isma'il I in 1501. He made Shi'ism the state religion and virtually extinguished the Sunnis in Persia. To the great rulers of this dynasty belong, besides Isma'il, Tahmasp I, 'Abbas I the Great and Sulayman I. They had to face the hostility of their Sunni neighbours, the Ottomans in the west and the Özbegs in the northeast. They moved their capital from Ardabil to Tabriz, then to Qazwin and finally to Isfahan.

The following is a list of the Safawid rulers:

1501	Isma'il I
1524	Tahmasp I
1576	Isma'il II
1578	Muhammad Khudabanda
1588	'Abbas I
1629	Safi I
1642	'Abbas II
1666	Sulayman I (Safi II)
1694	Husayn I
1722	Tahmasp II

Nominal rulers in certain parts of Persia only:

1732	'Abbas III
1749	Sulayman II
1750	Isma'il III
1753	Husayn II
1786	Muhammad

Qajar rule

Saffarids: dynasty which reigned in Sistan, Persia, from 867 till ca. 1495. During that period Sistan fell under the suzerainty of the Samanids and the Ghaznawids, and came under that of the Mongols in 1221.

Safi (Asfi): port in Morocco on the Atlantic Ocean. In 1507 it became the centre of Portuguese operations, but was taken by the Sa'dids in 1541.

Safi, Fakhr al-Din 'Ali: Persian author; d. after 1533. Among other works, he wrote a narrative work which contains anecdotes regarding individuals of various classes of society.

Safi al-Din, 'Abd al-Mu'min b. Yusuf: one of the best-known Arabic writers on the theory of music; d. 1294. He was at the service of the last 'Abbasid Caliph of Baghdad al-Musta'sim bi-llah. Because of his performances on the lute, his life and that of his family was spared by the Mongol Il-Khan Hülegü when he conquered Baghdad in 1258.

Safi al-Din al-Ardabili, Shaykh: ancestor of the Safawids; 1252-1334. He was the founder of the dervish order of the Safawis, whose members later wore as a badge a twelve-gored cap of scarlet wool, from which comes the Turkish name Qizil-Bash.

Safid Kuh (Sefid Koh "The White Mountain"): the most prominent mountain range of northern Afghanistan. In its northern and western spurs are the Khyber Pass between Peshawar and Jalalabad, and the passes between Jalalabad and Kabul through which India from time to time has been invaded.

Safiyya bint Huyayy b. Akhtab: the Prophet's eleventh wife; d. ca. 670. She belonged to the Jewish tribe of the Banu 'l-Nadir and was married to the Prophet after the fall of Khaybar in 628.

Sahara (A. *al-Ṣaḥrā'*): the Arab name means "of a fawn colour", and is applied to areas covered with moving sands and absolutely devoid of water. Arab penetration took place in the viith c. when they first arrived in Fazzan, and was intensified by the Hilali invasion, by the expulsion of the Muslims from Spain and by the conquest of Sudan by the Sharifian Saʿdids of Morocco. On the other hand, the black empires of Soninke of Ghana, of the Mande, of the sultans of Kanem and of the Askia of Gao also extended over the Sahara. As a consequence, there are a white and a black element, either pure or altered by mixture in different degrees. The first, numerically the most important, is represented by the Arabs and the Touareg. The intermarriage of Blacks of various origins seems to have given birth to a particular type, the "Hartani" (pl. *Harratin*), who play an important part in the economy of the Sahara. Islam was spread by Arab traders and nomad Berbers, like the Lamta and the Lamtuna. The western Sahara is under the influence of the Qadiriyya and the Tijaniyya orders, the eastern Sahara under that of the Sanusiyya.

Saharanpur: town and district in Uttar Pradesh in northern India. It was founded about 1340 and was named after a local saint, Shah Haran Čishti. Muslim influence gained much by the proselytizing zeal of ʿAbd al-Quddus, who ruled the district under the reign of the Mughal Akbar I. It was conquered by the British in 1803.

Sahir, Jelal: Ottoman poet and author; b. 1883. He actively championed the simplification of the language, but in prosody he adhered strictly to the classical form. His main theme was women and love, in a noble and ideal way, and with the Turkish constitution he became a champion of women's rights.

Sahl b. Harun: Arab author and poet; ixth c. He held high offices in the chancellery at the court of several caliphs. He was a fanatical adherent of the so-called Shuʿubiyya. His greatest admirer was his younger contemporary al-Jahiz, and his name often occurs in the Thousand-and-One Nights.

Sahl al-Tustari, Abu Muhammad: Arab Sunni theologian and mystic; 818-896. His *Thousand Sayings* gave rise to the theological school of the Salimiyya.

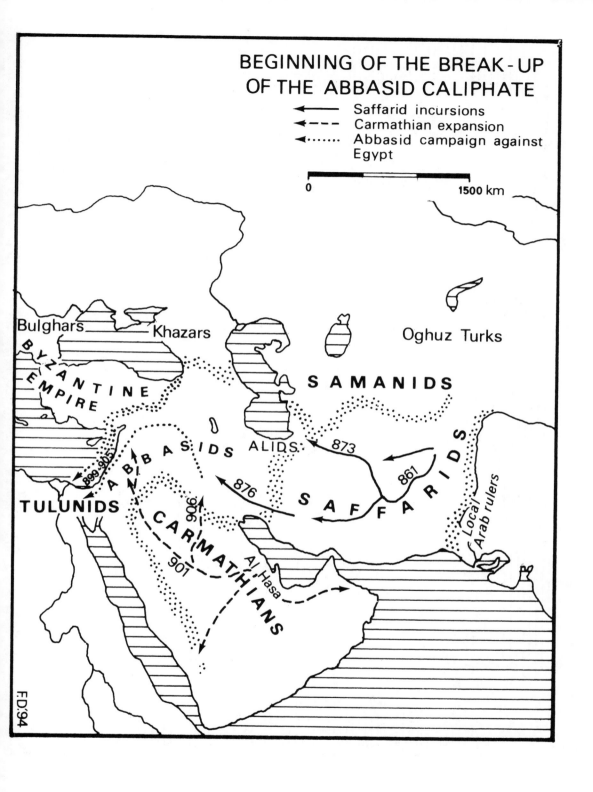

BEGINNING OF THE BREAK-UP
OF THE ABBASID CALIPHATE

⟵⟶ Saffarid incursions
⟵--- Carmathian expansion
⟵···· Abbasid campaign against
Egypt

0 _____ 1500 km

Bulghars   Khazars   Oghuz Turks

BYZANTINE
EMPIRE   S A M A N I D S

                    ALIDS   873
                                        861

ABBASIDS   S A F F A R I D S

TULUNIDS   Local
                                            Arab rulers
      CARMATHIANS
                876
            906
                    Al Hasa
            907

F.D.'94

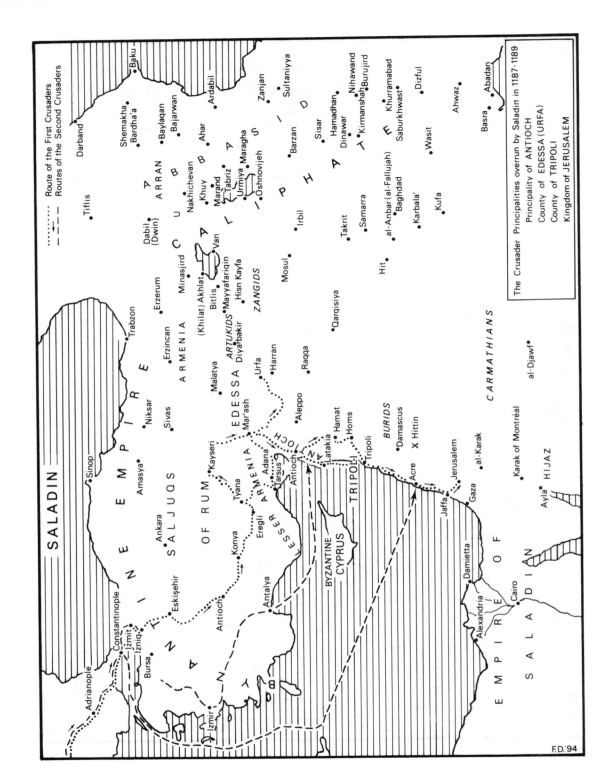

SALADIN

BYZANTINE EMPIRE

SALJUQS OF RUM

LESSER ARMENIA

BYZANTINE CYPRUS

EMPIRE OF SALADIN

ARMENIA

EDESSA

ARTUKIDS

ZANGIDS

CAUCALPHIA

ARRAN

BURIDS

CARMATHIANS

HIJAZ

Baku
Darband
Shemakha
Bardha'a
Baylaqan
Bajarwan
Ardabil
Zanjan
Sultaniyya
Nihawand
Burujird
Khurramabad
Dizful
Abadan
Ahar
Maragha
Barzan
Sisar
Hamadhan
Dinawar
Kirmanshah
Saburkhwast
Ahwaz
Basra
Tiflis
Khuy
Marand
Tabriz
Urmiya
Oshnovijeh
Barzan
Irbil
Samarra
al-Anbar (al-Fallujah)
Baghdad
Karbala'
Wasit
Nakhichevan
Dabil
(Dwin)
Van
Minasjird
(Khilat) Akhlat
Bitlis
Mayyafariqin
Hisn Kayfa
Mosul
Takrit
Hit
Kufa
Erzerum
Erzincan
Trabzon
Niksar
Sivas
Malatya
Diyarbakir
Harran
Raqqa
Qarqisiya
Sinop
Amasya
Ankara
Kayseri
Tyana
Eregli
Adana
Tarsus
Antioch
Aleppo
Mar'ash
Urfa
Latakia
Hamat
Homs
Damascus
X Hittin
Tripoli
al-Karak
Karak of Montréal
al-Djawf
Eskişehir
Konya
Antalya
Antioch
Acre
Jaffa
Jerusalem
Gaza
Ayla
Damietta
Alexandria
Cairo
Adrianople
Constantinople
İzmit
İzniq
Bursa
İzmir

F.D.'94

Sahnun, ʿAbd al-Salam: Maliki jurist from Qayrawan; d. 854. He was responsible for the spread of the Maliki school of law in the West, to which his monumental work, called *Mudawwana*, made a large contribution.

Saʾib, Mirza Muhammad ʿAli: Persian poet; 1603-1677. He was one of the most prolific poets of his time, and is highly praised by Oriental critics.

al-Saʿid (Saʿid Misr): the Arabic name for Upper Egypt. It extends from the south of Cairo to the cataract of Aswan.

Saʿid b. al-ʿAs b. Saʿid: governor of Kufa and Medina; ca. 623-678. He was nominated by the Caliph ʿUthman as a member of the committee to establish a definite text of the Qurʾan.

Saʿid b. Sultan: member of the Al Bu Saʿid dynasty and the greatest ruler of the united sultanate of Oman and Zanzibar; b. 1791, r. 1806-1856. Under strong British pressure he restricted the slave trade. In 1832 he made Zanzibar the capital of his empire. His greatest achievement was the extension of his African dominions into a commercial empire. He asserted his authority over the Arab and Swahili colonies from Mogadishu to Cape Delgado, including Mombasa. In 1854 he ceded the Kuria Muria Islands to Great Britain.

Saʿid Pasha: khedive of Egypt; b. 1822, r. 1854-1863. He relieved the economic position of the people by promulgating an agrarian law, attempted to abolish the slave trade, and in 1856 granted to Ferdinand de Lesseps the permit to construct the Suez Canal. The town of Port Said is named after him.

Sajʿ: name given to a peculiar mode of rhetoric in which at short intervals words occur in rhyme. It is distinguished from poetry (A. *shiʿr*) by not being bound by a regular rhythm or metre. The most striking example of *sajʿ* is the Qurʾan, especially in the older *suras*.

Sajah, Umm Sadir bint Aws b. Hikk: prophetess and soothsayer; viith c. She is said to have joined the forces of the prophet Musaylima b. Habib and to have married him.

al-Sajawandi, Abu ʾl-Fadl: "reader" of the Qurʾan; d. ca. 1164. He is mainly known by his work on the recitation of the Qurʾan.

al-Sajawandi, Siraj al-Din: Hanafi jurist; xiiith c. His work on the law of inheritance is regarded as the principal work in this field.

Sajids: name of a family which ruled in Azerbaijan under the nominal suzerainty of the ʿAbbasid caliph at the end of the ixth and the beginning of the xth c. It took its name from the founder of the dynasty, Abu ʾl-Saj (d. 879) and comprised five rulers.

al-Sakkaki, Abu Bakr Yusuf: Turkish rhetorician from Transoxiana; d. 1160. His fame rests upon his *Key to the Sciences*, the most comprehensive book on rhetoric written up to his time.

Saladin (al-Malik al-Nasir Salah al-Din Yusuf): the great Ayyubid ruler; b. 1138, r. 1169-1193. In 1154 he went with his uncle Shirkuh to the court of the Zangid Nur al-Din Mahmud at Damascus, accompanied him on his military mission to Egypt in 1164, and again in 1168, when he withstood the siege of Alexandria by Amalric I, king of Jerusalem. When the latter besieged Cairo, the last Fatimid Caliph al-ʿAdid li-Din Allah sent for assistance to Nur al-Din, while his vizier Shawar negotiated with Amalric. Shirkuh and Saladin were hailed at Cairo as rescuers, and Saladin had Shawar executed as a traitor. The caliph appointed Shirkuh as vizier and, when the latter died after two months, he appointed Saladin as such and gave him the title "al-Malik al-Nasir".

His aims were to secure power for himself and his family, to put down Shiʿism and to fight the Crusaders to the utmost. He attained these aims to a great degree.

He put down a rebellion of the caliph's black guards and in 1169 resisted the siege of Damietta by Amalric, who was assisted by a fleet from Constantinople and an auxiliary force from southern Italy. Saladin then had the name of the Shiʿi Fatimid Caliph omitted in the Friday ṣalāt, and that of the Sunni Caliph of Baghdad al-Mustadi bi-Amr Allah mentioned. Thus the Fatimids and Shiʿism came to an end in Egypt.

In 1173 Saladin sent his brother Turan-Shah to Yemen, which was subjected. The relations between Saladin and Nur al-Din meanwhile had become strained, but the latter died in 1174. Saladin then defeated the Normans of Sicily, who had landed at Alexandria, and captured an enormous booty. He now turned his attention to Syria, where he defeated the troops of Nur al-Din's son al-Salih Ismaʿil (r. 1174-1181) at Qurun Hamat, but left him in the possession of Aleppo and gave Hamat, Homs and Baʿalbek, which had surrendered, to relatives as fiefs. In 1175 he was granted by the caliph rule over Egypt, Nubia, Yemen, North Africa from Egypt to Tripoli, Palestine and Central Syria. After a final attempt by the Zangids against him in 1176, he made peace with them. He was however unable to take the fortress of Masyad in central Syria from Shaykh Rashid al-Din al-Sinan, the leader of the Syrian branch of the Ismaʿilis and known to the West as "the Old Man of the Mountain". The latter promised Saladin that he would not attack him.

In 1177 he met at Ramla the troops of Baldwin IV, reinforced by many Knights under the leadership of Raynald de Chatillon of al-Karak. Saladin suffered a crushing defeat. But the next year he was able to defeat Baldwin, and again in 1179. In the following years he gained suzerainty over Mesopotamia. In 1183 he signed a four years' peace with Baldwin V, who was soon succeeded by Guy de Lusignan. But when Raynald de Chatillon fell upon a large caravan and refused to give any satisfaction, fight became inevitable. At Hittin the Crusaders were utterly defeated. Saladin gave Guy de Lusignan a friendly reception, but slew Raynald with his own hand, and had all the Templars and Knights of St. John executed. He now was master of Palestine, including Tiberias, Nazareth, Samaria, Sidon, Beyrouth, Acre, Ramla, Gaza. Hebron also fell into his hands, and on October 2, 1187 Jerusalem was conquered. The inhabitants who could not pay the ransom were sold into slavery, but many were released at the intercession of Muslim and Christian persons of standing, as were a large number of poor people by Saladin himself. Only Antioch, Tripolis, Tyre and a number of smaller towns and castles remained in the possession of the Christians. At the siege of Tyre, Saladin suffered a severe reverse. He had Acre rebuilt, and in 1188 went to Damascus from where he captured many places.

The fall of Jerusalem led to the Third Crusade. The Franks began the siege of Acre in 1189, which ended with its capitulation in 1191. Peace was concluded in 1192 and the Crusaders were allowed to make pilgrimage to the Holy Places unarmed. They kept only a small strip of land along the coast.

Saladin was fanatical against the Crusaders as a body but not as individuals and not against the subjected Christians of his empire. He remained a popular figure in the East, and in Europe he was in general considered the pattern of chivalry.

Salafiyya: name of an orthodox reformist movement in xxth c. Islam. The term is connected with the Arabic word for forefathers, i.e. the predecessors whose perfect orthodoxy, piety, holiness, and religious knowledge make them worthy of being taken as models and guides. Inaugurated by Jamal al-Din al-Afghani, Muhammad 'Abduh and 'Abd al-Rahman al-Kawakibi, the idea of reform (A. *iṣlāḥ*) spread in Syria, Egypt, Tunisia, Algeria, Iran, Turkey, India and Pakistan.

Salamanca: capital of León in west central Spain. It was taken by the Muslims in 712, but never became a true Muslim possession. It was definitely conquered by the Christians in 1055.

Salamiyya: town in Syria. Conquered by the Arabs in 636, it became the secret centre of Isma'ili propaganda in about 864. The first Fatimid Caliph, 'Ubayd Allah, was born here. It was virtually wiped out by the Carmathians. At the time of the Crusades, it was a meeting-place for the Muslim armies. In 1299 the Egyptian army was defeated near Salamiyya by the Mongols under the Il-Khan Mahmud Ghazan.

Salar Jang (Mir Turab 'Ali): Indian statesman of Persian descent; 1829-1883. During the Sepoy mutiny in 1857, he was on the British side and strengthened the hands of his master the Nizam of Haydarabad.

Salat (A. *ṣalāt*): the Arabic word for the ritual prayer. Every Muslim who has attained his majority is bound to observe the five daily *ṣalāt*s: of midday, of the afternoon, of sunset, of late evening and of dawn. The obligation is suspended for the sick, but *ṣalāt*s omitted must be made up. According to Muslim tradition, the establishment of the number five dates back to the beginnings of Islam and is connected with the Prophet's ascension to Heaven.

Salé (A. *Salā*): town in Morocco on the Atlantic coast at the mouth of the Bu Regreg, opposite Rabat.

Salghurids: name of a dynasty of atabegs in Fars, Iran. Salghur, the founder of the dynasty, was the chief of a band of Turkmen who migrated into Khurasan and attached themselves to the first Great Saljuq Tughril I. One of his descendants, Sunqur b. Mawdud, rose against the Saljuqs and in 1148 established his independence in Fars. The dynasty was to rule until 1270, remaining however tributary to the Saljuqs of Iraq, the Khwarazm-Shahs and lastly the Mongols. The great Persian poet Sa'di derived his pen-name from the Salghurid Sa'd II (r. 1260).

Salih: a prophet who was sent to the Arab Banu Thamud. He is mentioned several times in the Qur'an and presented as a sign and a warning in the style of the Prophet.

al-Salih, Nur al-Din Isma'il: Zangid ruler of Damascus and Aleppo; r. 1174-1181. He was the son of Nur al-Din Mahmud b. Zangi, and resisted Saladin's efforts to conquer Aleppo.

Salim, Mehmed Emin (Mirza-zade): Ottoman jurist and biographer of poets; d. 1739. He is the author of commentaries on theological works, of a Turkish-Persian dictionary and of a book on Holy War.

Salimiyya: a school of dogmatic theologians with mystical tendencies which was formed among the Maliki Sunnis of Basra in the ixth-xth c. It was based on the sayings of Sahl al-Tustari, collected by the latter's pupil Muhammad Ibn Salim (d. 909).

Saljuqs (Seljuqs): Turkish princely family which ruled over wide territories in Central Asia and the Near East from the xith to the xiiith c. For Islam the rise of the Saljuqs meant the victory of the Sunni creed, as far as their power stretched, over the Shi'i tendencies which had been gaining more and more ground under the Buyids and the Fatimids. The following dynasties are distinguished: the Great Saljuqs of Iraq and Persia; the Saljuqs of Syria; the Saljuqs of Kirman ; the Rum Saljuqs of Anatolia.

The Great Saljuqs of Iraq and Persia (1038-1194) (I):

1038	Tughril I, Rukn al-Dunya
1063	Alp Arslan, 'Adud al-Dawla
1072	Malik-Shah I, Jalal al-Dawla
1092	Mahmud I, Nasir al-Din
1094	Berqyaruq, Rukn al-Din
1105	Malik-Shah II, Mu'izz al-Din
1105	Muhammad I, Ghiyath al-Din
1118-57	Sanjar, Mu'izz al-Din (ruler in eastern Persia 1097-1157; after 1118 supreme sultan of the Saljuq family)

The Great Saljuqs in Iraq and western Persia only:

1118	Mahmud II, Mughith al-Din
1131	Dawud, Ghiyath al-Din
1132	Tughril II, Rukn al-Din
1134	Mas'ud, Ghiyath al-Din

1152   Malik-Shah II, Mu'in al-Din
1153   Muhammad II, Rukn al-Din
1160   Sulayman Shah, Ghiyath al-Din
1161   Arslan, Mu'izz al-Din
1176-94 Tughril III, Rukn al-Din
Khwarazm-Shahs

The Saljuqs of Syria (1078-1117) (II):

1078   Tutush, Taj al-Dawla
1095-1113 Ridwan (in Aleppo)
1095-1104 Duqaq (in Damascus)
1113   Alp Arslan al-Akhras (in Aleppo)
1114-17   Sultan Shah (in Aleppo)
Burids in Damascus
Il Ghazi (Artuqid) in Aleppo

The Saljuqs of Kirman (1041-1186) (III):

1041   Qawurd, 'Imad al-Din
1073   Kirman Shah
1074   Husayn
1074   Sultan Shah, Rukn al-Dawla
1085   Turan Shah I, Muhyi al-Din
1097   Iran Shah, Baha' al-Din
1101   Arslan Shah I, Muhyi al-Din
1142   Muhammad I, Mughith al-Din
1156   Tughril Shah, Muhyi al-Din
1170   Bahram Shah
1175   Arslan Shah II
1176   Turan Shah
Oghuz occupation

The Saljuqs of Rum (1077-1307) (IV)

1077   Sulayman b. Qutlumish
1086   *interregnum*
1092   Qilij Arslan I
1107   Malik-Shah
1116   Mas'ud I, Rukn al-Din
1156   Qilij Arslan II, 'Izz al-Din (division of territories amongst his sons during the latter part of his reign)
1192   Kaykhusraw I, Ghiyath al-Din (*first reign*)
1196   Sulayman II, Rukn al-Din
1204   Qilij Arslan III, 'Izz al-Din
1204   Kaykhusraw I, Ghiyath al-Din (*second reign*)

1210	Kaykawus I, 'Izz al-Din
1219	Kayqubad I, 'Ala' al-Din
1237	Kaykhusraw II, Ghiyath al-Din
1246	Kaykawus II, 'Izz al-Din
1248	Kaykawus II and his brother Qilij Arslan IV, Rukn al-Dīn jointly
1249	Kaykawus II, Qilij Arslan IV and Kayqubad II, 'Ala' al-Din jointly
1257	Qilij Arslan IV
1265	Kaykhusraw III, Ghiyath al-Din
1282	Mas'ud II, Ghiyath al-Din (*first reign*)
1284	Kayqubad III, 'Ala' al-Din (*first reign*)
1284	Mas'ud II (*second reign*)
1293	Kayqubad III (*second reign*)
1294	Mas'ud II (*third reign*)
1301	Kayqubad III (*third reign*)
1303	Mas'ud II (*fourth reign*)
1305	Kayqubad III (*fourth reign*)
1307	Mas'ud III, Ghiyath al-Din

Mongol occupation

(I) Tughrïl I ruled over Gurgan, Tabaristan, Khwarazm, the territory of what is now Iran, Iraq, Mosul and Diyarbakr. Under his brother Alp Arslan the Saljuq conquests reached the Iaxartes river, and their empire also comprised Syria and almost the whole of Anatolia. Under Malik Shah even Aden and Yemen were conquered, although Saljuq rule was hardly effective there. According to the Turkish view, the right to rule belonged to the whole family, the oldest member having only a certain right as primus inter pares to the obedience of his male relatives. Malik Shah thus came in conflict with the Rum Saljuq Sulayman b. Qutlumish, and Berkyaruq with the Saljuq of Syria, Tutush. The Great Saljuqs had their residences in Isfahan and Baghdad. Sanjar, after handing over Iraq, Fars, Khuzistan and the western provinces to the sons of his brother Muhammad, had his residence at Marw. He died childless, and with him the line of the Great Saljuqs came to an end.

(II) After the episode of Atsiz b. Uvak, Tutush could establish himself only after the Great Saljuq Malik Shah had died. Under Duqaq, the real power lay in the hands of his atabeg Tughtigin b. 'Abd Allah, the founder of the Burids.

(III) Qawurd submitted to the Great Saljuq Alp Arslan, but revolted under Malik Shah, by whom he was defeated. The line came to an end by the devastating invasions of the Oghuz.

(IV) Notwithstanding their fights with the Byzantines and the Danismendids, the Saljuqs of Rum succeeded in establishing their rule in Konya. The territory became fragmented under the sons of Qilij Arslan II, and in 1190

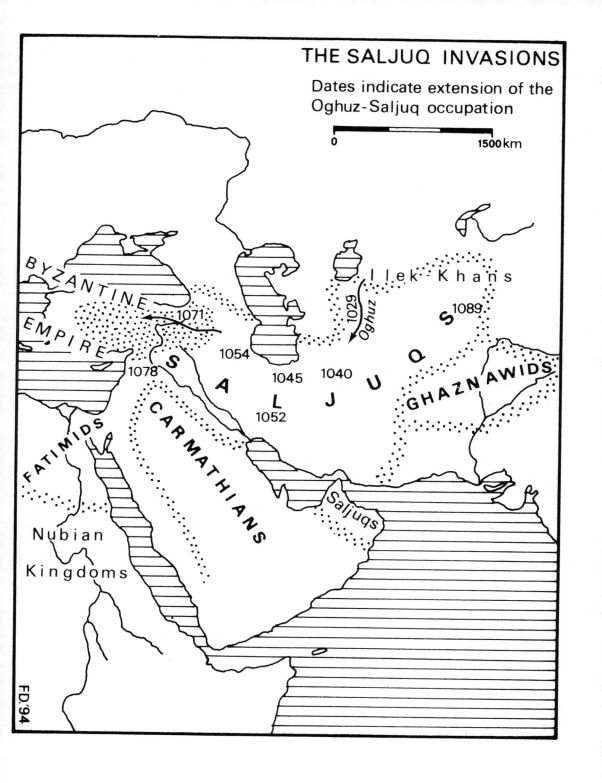

THE SALJUQ INVASIONS

Dates indicate extension of the
Oghuz-Saljuq occupation

0   1500 km

BYZANTINE

EMPIRE

Ilek-Khans

1071

1029

Oghuz

1089

1054

S A L J U Q S

1045   1040

GHAZNAWIDS

1078

1052

FATIMIDS

CARMATHIANS

Saljuqs

Nubian

Kingdoms

F.D.'94

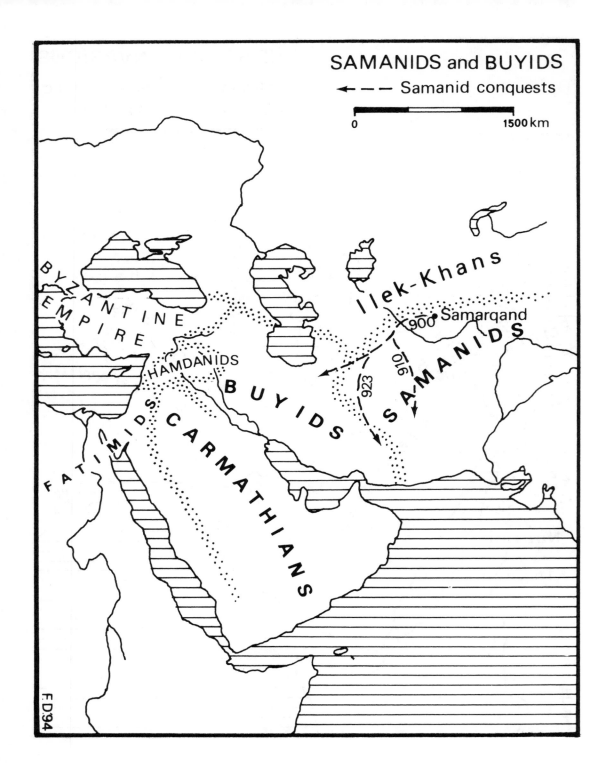

SAMANIDS and BUYIDS

←--- Samanid conquests

0   1500 km

BYZANTINE EMPIRE

Ilek-Khans

×900 • Samarqand

SAMANIDS

910

923

HAMDANIDS

BUYIDS

FATIMIDS

CARMATHIANS

F.D.94

Frederick Barbarossa and the Third Crusaders occupied Konya temporarily. The Latin conquest of Constantinople in 1204 gave the Rum Saljuqs the opportunity to re-establish their power. They took Antalya and Sinop and were thus able to open up relations with the Italian city-states. Trade brought wealth, as is testified by the architectural and artistic glories of Saljuq Konya. But the arrival of the Mongols, who defeated Kaykhusraw II at Köse Dagh in 1243, decided the future of the sultanate of Konya. It retained its independence, but had to pay heavy tribute to the Mongols, and remained internally divided. A number of Turkmen dynasties arose on its ruins.

Salman al-Farisi: Companion of the Prophet of Persian origin; viith c. He has become one of the most popular figures of Muslim legend, the national hero of Muslim Persia and one of the favourite personages of the Shuʿubiyya. He is venerated as the patron of barbers.

Salonika (Thessaloniki) (T. *Selānīk*): town in Greece. In 904 it was sacked by a fleet from Tripolis in Syria. In 1385 it was taken by Khayr al-Din Pasha, restored to the Byzantine Emperor Manuel and taken again by the Ottoman Sultan Bayezid in 1394. After having changed hands several times between the Ottomans and the Venetians, it fell to the Ottomans in 1430. In the second half of the xixth c. Salonika became the centre of the troubles in Macedonia. As a result of European control, it became less subject to the direct influence of Istanbul and thus a hotbed of Young Turk propaganda. Mustafa Kemal Atatürk was born at Salonika in 1881. The Committee of Union and Progress held its meetings there and in 1908 the Constitution was proclaimed at Salonika. Sultan Abdülhamid II, deposed in 1909, remained there until the Balkan War. In 1913 the town was incorporated into Greece, and, with the Turks, a great many Jews migrated to Istanbul.

Salur: name of an Oghuz tribe, who migrated from the banks of the Iaxartes into Transoxiana and finally to eastern Anatolia. The Salghurid dynasty arose from them and they played a role in the history of the Saljuqs in Anatolia. Under the general name of Turkmen, a certain number of them went eastwards and settled in Kansu, northwestern China. They are Hanafi Sunnis and in recent times have always been Naqshbandis.

Sam Mirza: Persian poet; 1517-1576. He was a son of the Safawid Shah Ismaʿil I and compiled an anthology of contemporary poetry.

Samanids: Persian dynasty from Balkh in northern Afghanistan, who ruled from 819 to 1005 in Khurasan and Transoxiana. They were descended from a certain Saman-Khuda, who adopted Islam in the viiith c. at the hands of Asad b. ʿAbd Allah al-Qasri, governor of Khurasan. His four grandsons played a political role in the eastern caliphate under the ʿAbbasid Caliph al-Maʾmun, and were a kind of sub-governors of the Tahirids. The reign of Nasr b. Ahmad (r. 864-892), the patron of Rudaki, marked the zenith of the dynasty. The turbulence of the military aristocracy and the danger from the northern Turkish tribes caused the decline of the dynasty. It is from their epoch that New Persian language and literature took their rise with Rudaki and Firdawsi.

Samarqand: city in Uzbekistan. Islam started to enter Central Asia after Qutayba b. Muslim had become governor of Khurasan. The Samanids made Samarqand into their capital, which became famous because of the theologian Abu Mansur al-Maturidi (d. ca. 944) and because of its paper manufacture. It was then ruled by the Ilek-Khans and, after the defeat of the Saljuq Sanjar by the Karakhitai in 1141, by the Gurkhans. The latter were overthrown by the Khwarazm-Shah Muhammad b. Tekish in 1209, but the city surrendered to Genghis Khan in 1220. The revival of prosperity began when Tamerlane in 1369 chose Samarqand as the capital of his empire, and the city continued to prosper under the Timurids who reigned in Samarqand until 1500. The Čihil Sutun palace and the famous astrological observatory were built by Tamerlane's grandson Ulugh Beg. After two brief occupations by the Mughal Babur, Samarqand was left to the Özbegs and fell behind Bukhara. The famous Samarqand rugs were produced in Khotan, Kasghar and Yarkand, lying along the old silk route across Chinese Turkestan.

Samarra: town in central Iraq on the east bank of the Tigris, about 100 km. north of Baghdad. On the coins of the caliphs is written *surra man ra'ā* "delighted is he who sees (it)", which is often given as the etymology of the town's name. However, the original form is probably Iranian. Samarra was founded in 836 by Ashnas, a Turkish general of the 'Abbasid Caliph al-Mu'tasim bi'llah, who felt threatened in Baghdad by the mutinies of his Turkish and Berber mercenaries. It remained the capital of the empire until 889, when the Caliph al-Mu'tamid 'ala Allah transferred it back to Baghdad.

Samarra was one of the richest and most prosperous cities of the 'Abbasid period. The vast area of ruins still shows the walls of the Great Mosque built by the Caliph al-Mutawakkil and the imposing minaret, called al-Malwiyya, with its spiral staircase on the outside. Beside the Great Mosque, Shi'is locate the tombs of the tenth and eleventh Imams, Abu 'l-Hasan 'Ali al-'Askari and Abu Muhammad al-Hasan al-'Askari, and the cave where the twelfth Imam, Muhammad al-Qa'im, entered the state of greater occultation in 941 and where he is destined to reappear at the end of time.

al-Samaw'al b. Gharid b. 'Adiya: Jewish-Arab poet; vith c. He owes his fame to his devotion to his guest Imru' al-Qays b. Hujr, which has become proverbial: "more faithful than al-Samaw'al".

al-Samhudi, Nur al-Din Abu 'l-Hasan: Arab historian; 1440-1505. He is known for his history of the city of Medina.

Sami, Shams al-Din: Turkish author and lexicographer from Albania; 1850-1904. He wrote a French-Turkish/Turkish-French dictionary, a six volume general encyclopaedia and a Turkish dictionary, which is a true picture of the educated Turkish of his time. However, he does not seem to have had any traceable influence on the development of the Turkish language.

al-Samiri ("the Samaritan"): name given in the Qur'an to the man who tempted the Israelites to the sin of the golden calf.

Samma: name of a Rajput clan who accepted Islam and ruled Sind from 1333 till 1520.

Samos (T. *Sīsām adasi*): Greek island in the Aegean Sea. It was raided by the Arabs in 889 and 911 and by the Saljuqs. Many Turks fled there at Tamerlane's invasion of Anatolia. The Turkish admiral Qilij 'Ali Pasha had it given to him by Sultan Süleyman II in 1562. During the Greek War of Independence the island obtained autonomy, and in 1913 it was united with Greece.

Samsam al-Dawla, Abu Kalijar al-Marzuban: Buyid ruler in Persia and Iraq; r. 990-998. He was a son of 'Adud al-Dawla. During his reign civil strife within the dynasty began.

Samsam al-Dawla, Shahnawar Khan: Indian statesman and historian; 1700-1758. He wrote a biographical dictionary of all the important statesmen under the Mughals from Akbar I down to his own day.

Samsam al-Saltana, Najaf Quli Khan: Bakhtiyari chief in Persia. Born in 1846, he formed a new cabinet in 1911 but came in conflict with the American advisor Morgan Shuster. His second cabinet of 1918 lasted only for a year.

Samsat (A. *Sumaysāt*; Gr. *Samosate*): ancient town in southeastern Turkey on the right bank of the Euphrates. It was conquered by the Muslims in 639 and, as a frontier town, was often ravaged by the Arabs and the Byzantines. It was taken by Saladin in 1188.

Samsun (A. *Ṣāmsūn*): harbour on the Turkish coast of the Black Sea. From the time of the Rum Saljuq Mas'ud II Ghiyath al-Din, Samsun was a mint of the Saljuqs and later of the Il-Khans. Occupied by the Isfendiyar-oghlu of Kastamonu, it surrendered to the Ottoman sultan Mehemmed I.

Samum: extremely hot whirlwind in Arabia and the Sahara. It blows in Mecca in August, and is mentioned in Qur'an and Tradition.

San Stefano (T. *Aya Stefanos*): little town on the Sea of Marmara, known for the preliminary peace treaty signed in 1878 between Turkey and Russia. In 1909 the National Assembly was constituted at San Stefano.

San'a': capital of Yemen. In 631 the fifth Persian governor Badham adopted Islam. In 869 the town came under the rule of the Ya'furids, and in 901 under that of the Zaydis and the Carmathians. The Sulayhids ruled in San'a' from 1061 to 1098, and were followed by the Hamdanids, who reigned until the invasion by Saladin's brother Turan-Shah in 1174. However, the town was almost destroyed in 1187 by the Hamdanid 'Ali al-Wahid b. Hatim, and held twice, in 1199 and in 1214, by the Zaydi Imam 'Abdallah al-Mansur. The suzerainty of the Rasulids began in 1229, but Zaydi power was restored at the end of the xivth c. The Ottoman general Özdemir Pasha entered the town in 1546, but in 1628 the Ottoman governor Haydar Pasha capitulated to the Zaydi Imam al-Mu'ayyad bi-'llah. San'a' remained in the hands of the Zaydis till 1676, after which followed a period of fighting among rival Imams. The early xixth c. was marked by devastating Bedouin invasions, which induced Imam al-Nasir in 1849 to admit the Turkish general Qibrisli Tewfiq Pasha to the town. But the latter's troops were massacred, and in 1850 the Meccan Sharif Muhammad b. 'Awn intervened. During the Ottoman conquest by Mukhtar Pasha, San'a' was taken by storm in 1871, but the Zaydis remained. Between 1905 and 1910 the Ottomans had great difficulty in restoring their position. In 1920 the Zaydi Imam Yahya Mahmud al-Mutawakkil (r. 1904-1948) was recognised as lord of San'a' and of Yemen in the Treaty of Sèvres.

Sana'i, Abu 'l-Majd Majdud b. Adam: one of the most famous poets at the court of the later Ghaznawids; d. 1131. He left Ghazna for Marw, where he led the life of a mystic. Returning later to Ghazna, he continued to lead a religious life. He composed a *dīwān*, which comprises all his poems written in other than the *mathnawī* form. The popularity of his poetry has been both wide-spread and long-lived.

Sanhaja, Banu: one of the great confederations of the Berbers, the other being the Banu Zanata. The Touaregs of Hoggar belong to the Sanhaja confederation. They reached their zenith in the xth-xiith c.

Sanjar b. Malik Shah, Mu'izz al-Din: Great Saljuq in Iraq and Persia; 1086, r. 1097-1157. He ruled in eastern Persia from 1097, taking the part of his brother Muhammad I against his other brother Berkyaruq. After 1118 he was the supreme Sultan of the Saljuq family, ruling in Iraq, Persia, Khurasan, Afghanistan and Northern India. He came into conflict with the Ghaznawid Arslan Shah b. Mas'ud III (r. 1115-1118), was involved in a long struggle with the Khwarazm-Shah Atsiz b. Muhammad (r. 1127-1156) and was defeated in 1141 by the Karakhitai, led by the Gurkhan Yeh-lü Ta-shih, who endeavoured to take Samarqand. Sanjar then lost Transoxiana. He also had to fight the Ghurid 'Ala 'l-Din Husayn (r. 1149-1161) and the Oghuz.

Santarém (A. *Shantarīn*): town in Portugal on the right bank of the Tagus, northeast of Lisbon. An important fortress town between Christians and Muslims, it fell under Muslim domination from 928 until 1147, when it was definitively taken by the first king of Portugal, Alfonso Henriquez. In 1184 the Almohad Abu Ya'qub Yusuf I had to raise the final Muslim siege of the town.

Santiago de Compostela (A. *Shant Ya'qūb*): town of pilgrimage in northwestern Spain. It was burned to the ground in 997 by Almanzor, only the tomb of St. James being spared. It was recaptured by the king of Galicia, Bermudo II, at the end of the xith c.

al-Sanusi, Abu 'Abd Allah Mahammad: learned Ash'ari theologian of Tlemcen; ca. 1427-1490. Some of his works have acquired great authority in North Africa.

Sanusiyya: Muslim mystic and military brotherhood established in Cyrenaica in 1837 by Sidi Muhammad b. ʿAli (1791-1859). It was a reform movement which aimed at a return to early Islam. In 1951 the head of the movement, Idris, was proclaimed king of Libya. He was overthrown in 1969 by a military coup, led by Colonel Muʿammar al-Qaddafi.

Saqarya: river in Anatolia, rising in the northeast of Afyun Qara Hisar. It is known for the battle of 1921, when the Greek army was defeated in a last great effort to reach Ankara.

Saracens: name used by the Christians to indicate their opponents, both Arabs and Turks. In the first three centuries A.D. the term refers to an Arab tribe living in the Sinai Peninsula, called *Sarakènoi*. After the foundation of the Arab Empire, the Byzantines used the term for all the Muslim peoples subject to the caliph, not however for the Saljuqs and the Turks, who were called Persians or Hagarenes. Through the Crusades, the term spread to the West.

Saragossa (A. *Saraqusṭa*): town in Spain, formerly capital of the kingdom of Aragon. It fell into the hands of the Arabs in 712. Charlemagne besieged the town in 778, but was summoned away. On his return, he was ambushed by the Basques in the pass of Roncevaux. At that time a Saragossa family, the Banu Kasi, attained great power in Aragon. They were succeeded by the Tujibids and the Hudids. The town was taken by Alfonso I of Aragon in 1118.

Sarajevo: capital and cultural centre of Bosnia and Hercegovina, former Yugoslavia. It became the military centre of Bosnia after the Ottomans had captured it in 1463. Numerous mosques, *madrasa*s and baths give evidence of its Muslim character. The Turks were ousted in 1878 and the town was taken over by the Austrians. In 1914 Archduke Franz Ferdinand, heir apparent of the Austro-Hungarian Empire, was assassinated in Sarajevo. During World War II, the city suffered considerable war damage, and at the time of writing, Sarajevo is being pounded mercilessly by the Serbs.

al-Sarakhsi, Shams al-Aʾimma Abu Bakr: Hanafi jurist from Transoxiana; d. 1090. He was thrown into prison by the Ilek-Khan Hasan b. Sulayman (r. 1073-1102) for having stigmatised as illegal the ruler's conduct when he married his manumitted *umm al-walad* without observing the period of abstention (A. ʿ*idda*). His most important, multi-volumed law books he dictated entirely from memory to his pupils, who sat before his prison. He also wrote several commentaries, especially on Abu ʿAbd Allah al-Shaybani's works.

Sarbadars: name of a line of Shiʿi robber chiefs; r. 1335-1387. They made themselves masters of a considerable part of Khurasan after the death of the Il-Khan Abu Saʿid (r. 1317-1335).

Sardes (T. *Ṣart*): town near Izmir, Turkey. It was incorporated into the Ottoman empire by Sultan Bayezid I in 1390, and probably destroyed by Tamerlane in 1402.

Sardinia (A. *Sardāniya*): island in the western Mediterranean, Italy. It was invaded several times by the Arabs, first in 710, and again in 760. In 841 they used it as the basis for their attack on Rome. The island was plundered again under the first Fatimid Caliph al-Mahdi 'Ubayd Allah. The last Arab endeavour to conquer Sardinia was made in 1015 by Mujahid, the ruler of Denia (A. *Dāniya*). He was quickly ejected by the combined fleets of Pisa and Genoa.

Sarèkat Islam: the first nationalist political party in Indonesia, founded in 1910, working for the self-government of the Dutch East Indies.

Sari (A. *Sāriya*): town in Mazandaran, Iran. It was rebuilt and embellished in the viiith c. by al-Farrukhan Gilan Shah, military governor of Tabaristan, and became the capital of Tabaristan under the Tahirids.

Sari 'Abd Allah Efendi: Ottoman poet and man of letters; d. 1660. He wrote a commentary in Turkish on the first volume of the *mathnawī* of Jalal al-Din Rumi, and composed several original works.

Sari Saltiq Dede: Turkish dervish and Bektashi saint from Bukhara; xiiith c. He is said to have led a large body of people to the western coast of the Black Sea.

Sarliyya: name of a sect in northern Mesopotamia to the south of Mosul. Their language is said to be a mixture of Kurdish, Persian and Turkish. They are said to be monotheists, believing in certain prophets, paradise and hell, but are not obliged to fast or pray.

Saruj: town in southern Turkey, between the Euphrates and Urfa. It has attained great fame in literature because the hero of the *Sessions* of al-Hariri, Abu Zayd, belonged to it.

Sarukhan: a Turkmen dynasty, which made itself independent in Anatolia on the collapse of the Rum Saljuqs in the early xivth c. Their capital was Maghnisa. The principality was conquered by the Ottoman Sultan Bayezid I in 1390 but, like other petty dynasts, the ruler Khidr Shah Beg was restored to power by Tamerlane. The dynasty came to an end under the Ottoman Sultan Mehemmed I. Its governorship formed a stepping-stone to influence and power, and so the position of governor was sometimes given to eldest sons of the House of 'Othman.

Sasan, Banu: name for wanderers and vagrants, such as jugglers, beggars, conjurers, and those who go up and down the country accompanied by animals, who show real or feigned diseases and mutilations, gipsies etc. Sasan (P. "beggar") is their patron saint.

Sasanians: Persian dynasty which ruled from 226-651. The rulers who belong to Islamic times are: Khusraw (II) Parwiz (r. 591-628); Kawadh II (r. 628); Ardashir III (r. 628-630); several ephemeral rulers; Yazdigird III (r. 632-651).

Satan (A. *Shayṭān*): the word is common in the Qur'an, where Satan is the chief of the evil spirits, made of fire. His punishment for resisting God is postponed to the end of the world when he will receive his reward in hell-fire.

In the Qur'an it is not Satan but Malik who is the lord of hell. In religious thought he is the power that opposes God in the hearts of men, but he has no real power over man, owing his success to craft alone.

Saʿud, Al: name of the ruling house of Saudi Arabia. It was founded by Muhammad b. Saʿud, the chieftain of al-Dirʿiyya in Najd. His successors ruled over much of Arabia from 1780 to 1880 and, beginning with ʿAbd al-ʿAziz Ibn Saʿud, over Saudi Arabia as absolute monarchs since 1932. Their history is closely connected with that of the Wahhabiyya movement.

Saudi Arabia (A. *al-Mamlaka al-ʿArabiyya al-Saʿūdiyya*): country in southwestern Asia. Muhammad b. Saʿud, who had associated himself with Ibn ʿAbd al-Wahhab, and his son ʿAbd al-ʿAziz I (r. 1765-1803) in 1747 became involved in an eight years' war with the Shaykh of Riyadh, Dahham b. Dawwas. In the captured places they built a fort and garrisoned it with well-paid believers. In 1773 ʿAbd al-ʿAziz took Riyadh. Relations with the Sharif of Mecca were friendly at first, but Sharif Surur later forbade the Wahhabis access to the city as pilgrims. In 1785 this prohibition was withdrawn. In the 1790s the Wahhabis subdued al-Hasa and raided the border of Iraq. The Turkish pasha of Baghdad received orders to deal with the movement, but the force of Thuwayni, chief of the Banu Muntafiq, dispersed after his assassination in 1797. An attack by the Sharif of Mecca, Ghalib, also came to nothing, as did a second expedition from Baghdad. In 1801 the Wahhabis sacked Karbala' and massacred the inhabitants. In revenge, ʿAbd al-ʿAziz I was murdered in 1803 at al-Dirʿiyya by a Shiʿi from Karbala'. His son and successor Saʿud (r. 1803-1814) purged Mecca, which had been evacuated by Ghalib, but failed to conquer Jidda and Medina. Meanwhile, his garrison at Mecca was massacred by the inhabitants. A fresh attack from Baghdad again petered out, and Saʿud took Medina in 1804, Mecca and Jidda in 1806. When the Wahhabis attacked al-Najaf and Damascus, Muhammad ʿAli Pasha of Egypt was autorized by the Ottoman government to intervene. His son Tusun took Medina in 1812 and Mecca in the following year, but Muhammad ʿAli, who took the command in 1813, suffered a serious defeat. Tusun made a treaty with ʿAbd Allah I b. Saʿud, who was to acknowledge the suzerainty of the Ottoman sultan, while the Egyptians were to evacuate Najd. But Muhammad ʿAli denounced the treaty and organized a fresh expedition under his eldest son Ibrahim Pasha. In 1818 the latter took al-Dirʿiyya, and ʿAbd Allah was sent to Istanbul, where he was beheaded. This terminated the first Wahhabi empire.

In 1821 Turki (r. 1823-1834), a cousin of ʿAbd Allah, established himself at Riyadh, but was assassinated in 1834. His son Faysal (r. 1834-1837, 1843-1865) rewarded the Shammar chieftain ʿAbd Allah b. Rashid (d. 1847) by the governorship of al-Ha'il for having assisted in finding the murderer of his father. ʿAbd Allah III b. Faysal (r. 1865-1871) was dethroned by his brother Saʿud in 1871, but on the latter's death in 1877 he returned to Riyadh as ruler

(1877-1887). Meanwhile, relations with the Rashid dynasty had become strained, and in 1883 Ibn Rashid won a complete victory over the Saʿudis. When Saʿud b. Faysal's sons revolted in 1884, Ibn Rashid invaded Riyadh and despatched ʿAbd Allah to al-Haʾil. In 1891 he defeated a great Saʿudi alliance and became ruler of desert Arabia until his death in 1897. Soon afterwards his nephew ʿAbd al-ʿAziz b. Mitʿab was involved in a struggle with the Shaykh of Kuwait, who was providing refuge for ʿAbd al-Rahman b. Saʿud. In 1901 the latter's son ʿAbd al-ʿAziz Ibn Saʿud, the founder of Saudi Arabia, succeeded in entering Riyadh.

Saul (A. *Ṭālūt*): the Biblical king is mentioned in the Qurʾan, which contains some memories of the Biblical story. Muslim legend adds many details, in particular about his relations with David.

Sawa (Sawaj): town and district in Central Persia between Qazwin and Qum. It was noted for its camels and camel-drivers and for its fortifications and baths. Its pomegranates are renowned to this day. In 1220 the town was sacked by the Mongols and its fine library, which also contained astronomical instruments, burnt. Among the antiquities of Sawa are the barrage on the Qaračay, the fortress of Qiz Qalʿa, two mosques and an old minaret, perhaps dating from the early xiith c.

According to a frequently quoted tradition, a lake in the neighbourhood of Sawa sank into the ground in the night in which the Prophet was born.

Sawakin (Suakin): seaport in northeastern Sudan, on the west coast of the Red Sea, built on an island. The old connections of the Mekkans with the African coast brought about the settlement of Arab merchants who intermarried with the local Beja. Sawakin was the starting place of pilgrims to Jidda. It was occupied by the Ottomans in the early xvith c. and governed by the pasha of Jidda through an aga until 1821, when it was leased to Egypt. During the Mahdist period (1883-1898) trade died away owing to the closing of the Sawakin-Berber caravan road.

Sawda bint Zamʿa b. Qays: the Prophet's second wife; d. 673. She accompanied her first husband al-Sakran b. ʿAmr to Abyssinia, where the latter became a Christian. The pair returned to Mekka before the Hijra, and al-Sakran died there. Sawda was married to the Prophet about a month after the death of Khadija in 619.

Sawda, Mirza Muhammad Rafiʿ: Urdu poet and satirist; 1713-1781. He is recognised as one of the masters of Urdu poetry.

Sawji: a younger brother of ʿOthman I, the founder of the Ottoman dynasty. It is also the name of the eldest son of the Ottoman sultan Murad I who rebelled against his father; d. 1385.

Sayabija (Sayabiga): name of a people living on the coasts of the Persian Gulf. They are considered descendants of ancient Malaysians who migrated to India, then to Iraq and to the Persian Gulf where there is evidence of their existence before Islam.

Sayf b. Dhi Yazan: member of the Himyarite royal line, who played a part in the expulsion of the Abyssinians from South Arabia about 570. The existing version of the romance which bears his name very probably dates from the xvth c., being composed in Cairo.

Sayf b. ʿUmar al-Asadi: Arab historian. Al-Tabari used his two works for the period of the "apostasy" (A. *ridda*) and of the early conquests.

Sayf al-Dawla, ʿAli I Ibn Hamdan: ruler of the Aleppo branch of the Hamdanid dynasty; b. 915 r. 945-966. In 944 he took Aleppo from the ruler of Egypt al-Ikhshid (r. 935-946), captured Damascus but was defeated by the Ikhshidid, who kept Damascus while Aleppo was retained by Sayf al-Dawla. In 948 he started his struggles with the Byzantines, which were to last until his death. He was a poet in his own right, and surrounded himself with such celebrities as al-Mutanabbi and al-Farabi (Alfarabius).

Sayfi, Mawlana: poet from Bukhara; d. 1504. His fame rests on his *Sayfi's Prosody*, one of the best works on Persian prosody.

Sayhan: one of the large mountain rivers in Anatolia. It rises on the Qoramaz Daghi near Kayseri and enters the Mediterranean below Tarsus. It was considered one of the rivers of Paradise. Under the Umayyads it was one of the frontier rivers with Byzantium where prisoners were ransomed.

Sayyid (lit. "Lord, Master"): term used throughout the Muslim world of the descendants of the Prophet. It was sometimes conferred upon others, like in the case of Rudolph Said-Ruete, son of Princess Salme bint Saʿid b. Sultan, who was given the title by Sultan Khalifa b. Harub of Zanzibar in 1932.

al-Sayyid al-Himyari, Abu Hashim: Arab poet from Basra; 723-789. He became a Shiʿi, held the doctrine of metempsychosis and proclaimed himself the reincarnation of the prophet Jonah. He enjoyed the favour of the ʿAbbasid Caliph al-Mansur.

Sbeitla (A. *Ṣubayṭila*; ancient Sufetula): town in Tunisia to the southwest of Qayrawan. It was conquered by the Muslims in 646.

Secunda (A. *Shaqunda*): little town opposite Córdoba. In 747 a decisive battle was fought there between the Maʿaddi clan under Yusuf al-Fihri and the Yemeni clan commanded by Abu ʾl-Khattar, who was defeated. It later became one of the richest suburbs of Córdoba.

Segovia (A. *Shaqūbiyya*): town to the northwest of Madrid. It was taken by the Arabs in the beginning of the viiith c., captured in 757 by Alfonso I of Castile, and conquered for a short time by Almanzor in the second half of the xth c.

Segu: town on the right bank of the Niger in Sudan. It was taken in 1862 by the Tukulor al-Hajj ʿUmar Tal, and by the French in 1890.

Sehi Čelebi: Ottoman poet and biographer of poets; d. 1549. His biographical collection is the oldest work of this kind in Turkish.

Selaniki, Mustafa: Turkish historian from Salonika; d. 1599. His history of Salonika covers the period from 1563 to 1599.

Selim I: Ottoman sultan, known as Yavuz "the Grim"; b. 1467, r. 1512-1520. With the support of the Janissaries, he rebelled against his father Bayezid II, whom he dethroned, and exterminated his brothers and nephews. He then began a systematic persecution of the Shi'is in the Ottoman Empire which made war with the Safawid Shah Isma'il inevitable. In 1514 he crushed the Persian army in the plain of Chaldiran between Lake Urmiya and Tabriz. The next year he conquered eastern Anatolia and Kurdistan. In Istanbul he constructed a new fleet and arsenal under the direction of Piri Re'is and re-organised the corps of the Janissaries. His annexation of the lands of the Dhu 'l-Qadr caused the Mamluk Sultan of Egypt Qansawh al-Ghawri to march against him in order to support Shah Isma'il and to retake Mar'ash. The armies met on Marj Dabiq, north of Aleppo. In a short battle the Egyptians were routed, and Qansawh fell. Selim then took Damascus. The new Mamluk Sultan in Egypt Tuman Bay refused to recognise Ottoman suzerainty. In 1517 the Egyptians were defeated again at Raydaniyya near Cairo and many inhabitants massacred. Tuman Bay was executed, which meant the end of Mamluk rule.

Barakat, the Sharif of Mecca, submitted to Selim, who took the title of "Servant of the Two Holy Places", i.e. Mecca and Medina, a title henceforth borne by all the Ottoman sultans. The last 'Abbasid caliph al-Mutawakkil III, who had been staying at the court of the Mamluks in Cairo, was sent to Istanbul where he remained in prison until Selim's death, after which he is said to have returned to Cairo. The tradition, according to which al-Mutawakkil renounced the caliphate in favour of Selim, is spurious, but became an article of general belief in Turkey. Selim's nickname "Yavuz" expresses horror for the numerous executions ordered by him, but also admiration for his achievements. The sultan, who was fond of the society of poets, is celebrated himself as a poet. His *dīwān* is entirely in Persian.

Selim II: Ottoman sultan; b. 1524, r. 1566-1574. He was the first Ottoman sultan to spend his life in the seraglio, and dissipated habits spread under his reign. In 1571 Yemen was reconquered and Cyprus taken. His most famous building is the Selimiyye mosque in Edirne, built by Sinan from 1567 to 1574. Selim II was a poet in his own right, and surrounded himself with poets such as Mahmud 'Abd al-Baqi and Mehmed Fadli.

Selim III: Ottoman sultan; b. 1761, r. 1789-1807. The war against Austria was continued but the Ottomans were beaten in Moldavia in 1789. In 1791 the peace of Zistowa was concluded. The disastrous war with Russia was ended by the Treaty of Jassy in which the Crimea was definitively lost to the Ottomans. Immediately after the war, the sultan took up the question of the reforms which he considered inevitable to restore the strength of the Empire. The finances were reorganised as well as the army, artillery in particular. Bonaparte is said to have had in 1794 the intention to put himself at the head of the Turkish artillery. There was much less opposition to the reforms in

Asia than in the European part of the Empire. The French expedition against Egypt led to a declaration of war against France in 1798. In 1800 the Ottomans were defeated near Heliopolis by General Kléber but a combined fleet of Turkey and Russia expelled the French from the Ionian Isles. Peace with France was signed in 1802. Troubles then arose in Serbia in 1803, which in 1805 had its own constitution and took control of the citadel of Belgrade. In the same year 1803 Mecca fell to the Wahhabis and Muhammad ʿAli Pasha came to the front in Egypt. Opposition in the capital against the reforms led to the deposition of the sultan in 1807. Selim III wrote poems under the pen-name Ilhami and is said to have had musical talents.

Semnan (Simnan): town in northern Iran. Often visited by armies passing by on the road to Khurasan, the town was known for its manufacture of cotton goods.

Senegal: name of a country and a river of West Africa. The name is said to be that of the Berber tribe of the Sanhaja or Zenaga, but early geographers and travellers mention a black kingdom called Sanaghana. Islam entered the region about 1040 under the Almoravids, who won over the king of the Tukulor. Towards 1770 the Tukulor waged a Holy War against the Fulani of Futa. From here several great campaigns of conquest and Islamisation started about 1800, led by Usman dan Fodio, which brought about the foundation of the Muslim empire of Sokoto.

Sepoy: the word is the English corruption of the Persian *sipāhī*, the adjective formed from *sipāh* "army". In Persian, Turkish and French (Spahi), it invariably means a "horse-soldier". In India, the French and the British applied it since the beginning of the xviiith c. to natives of India trained, armed and clad after the European fashion as regular infantry soldiers. The Indian Mutiny of 1857-1859 is also called Sepoy Mutiny because it was started by the Sepoys.

Seraglio (P. *sarāy*): in Persian the word is often compounded with another sustantive to indicate a particular kind of building, like *kārwān-sarāy* "caravanserai". In the Turkish lands the word has come to mean the residence of a prince, a palace. The *sarāy* par excellence was the *Sarāy-i Humāyūn*, the imperial palace of Topkapi in Istanbul. The meaning "harem" is a non-Oriental limitation of the word.

Serbia (T. *Ṣîrb*): part of former Yugoslavia. The first encounter between the Ottomans and the Serbs under king Vukašin, who ruled over what had been left of the great Serbian Empire under Stephan Dušan (r. 1331-1355), took place in 1371 in the battle of Čirmen. The Ottomans were victorious and the Serbian princes in Macedonia had to acknowledge the suzerainty of the Ottoman Sultan Murad I. The Bosnian Ban Tvrtko, having become king of Serbia, together with Prince Knez Lazar, the most powerful of the Bosnian rulers, and his son-in-law Vuk Branković led a new force against the Muslims but were utterly defeated by the Ottomans in the battle of Kosovo in 1389.

During the battle Sultan Murad was killed, but his son Bayezid I assumed the leadership. The Ottoman victory was the death-blow to the Serbian state although it was able to survive for another 70 years. Lazar's son and successor Stephan Lazarević took part as Sultan Bayezid's vassal in the battle of Ankara against Tamerlane in 1402, but after the Ottoman defeat exchanged the sultan's suzerainty for that of Sigismund of Hungary. His nephew and successor George Vlković or Branković (r. 1427-1456) was the last ruler of Serbia of any note.

One year after his capture of Constantinople in 1453, Sultan Mehemmed II laid Serbia waste in dreadful fashion, and in 1459 changed the Serbian despotate into a province of the Ottoman Empire, ruled by a Turkish pasha. Many Serbs emigrated into southern Hungary, southwest Bosnia and into the marches of Croatia. Well-armed bands, usually in Austrian service, fought inceasingly against the Ottomans. Large numbers of Serbs took part as volunteers in the offensive of the Holy League against the Ottomans after Qara Mustafa had been defeated before Vienna in 1683.

After the Peace of Passarowitz of 1718, Serbia came under Austrian rule, which lasted till 1739, when the peace of Belgrade restored the former Ottoman province to the Empire. In 1804 the Serbs, harassed by the atrocities of dismissed Turkish mercenaries, rose in revolt, led by George Petrović. They took Belgrade and were about to come to an accomodation with the Ottomans, when in 1806 the Russo-Turkish war broke out. Petrović had to submit to a Russian protectorate. After the war Serbia remained an Ottoman possession. During a new Russo-Turkish war in 1809, a Russian garrison was established in Belgrade, but by the peace of Bucarest in 1812 the Serbs were again delivered over to the Ottomans. In 1815 Miloš Obrenović rose in revolt, which in the end led to the Ottoman sultan recognising Serbia as an autonomous principality under Ottoman suzerainty.

In 1875 war was declared on the Ottomans, but the Serbians were defeated twice. At the Berlin Congress of 1878, the provinces of Bosnia and Hercegovina were allocated to Austria, and in 1908 they were occupied by the Danube monarchy. In 1912 Serbia, together with Bulgaria, Montenegro, and Greece, declared war on the Ottomans. It led to Serbia obtaining northern Macedonia, thus more than doubling its territory. The Sarajevo assassination of 1914 was planned by Greater Serbian revolutionary organisations, but World War I cost Serbia about one quarter of its population. In 1918 the new kingdom of the Serbs, Croats and Slovenes was proclaimed under King Alexander I (r. 1921-1934). In 1929 the regions thus united took the name of Yugoslavia. After the presidency of Josip Broz Tito (d. 1980), Serbia developed a strong nationalism, which in 1991 led to the secession of Slovenia, Croatia, Bosnia and Hercegovina, and Macedonia. In 1992 Serbia and Montenegro re-formed into a new rump Yugoslavia.

Seth (A. *Shīth*): the Biblical personage is mentioned in Muslim tradition.

The Sabaeans of Harran had several writings attributed to him, and the Druzes always associate him with Adam.

Seven (A. *Sabʿ/Sabʿa*): the number seven has a special significance for the Muslims, as it has for many other peoples. There are the sevenfold circumambulation of the Kaʿba, the sevenfold running between al-Safa and al-Marwa, the sevenfold casting of stones at the pilgrimage, and the seven "readers/reciters" of the Qurʾan. The number also plays a role in Tradition.

Seveners (A. *Sabʿiyya*); term used in the West to indicate the Ismaʿiliyya, referring to those Shiʿis who restrict the number of visible Imams to seven. The first six Imams ʿAli b. Abi Talib, al-Hasan b. ʿAli, al-Husayn b. ʿAli, ʿAli b. al-Husayn (d. 714), Muhammad b. ʿAli Zayn al-ʿAbidin and Jaʿfar al-Sadiq are accepted as such by both the Seveners and the Twelvers. Confusion came upon the legitimist Shiʿa, who believe that the character of Imam is transmitted by divine providence from father to son, when about 762 Ismaʿil, the (eldest?) son of the sixth Imam Jaʿfar al-Sadiq died before his father. The majority replaced Ismaʿil by another son of Jaʿfar, Musa al-Kazim, who is the seventh in the series of the twelve visible Imams of the Twelvers. Others attached themselves to Jaʿfar's otherwise less prominent sons, Muhammad, ʿAbd Allah and ʿAli. The strictest legitimists, however, remained faithful to Ismaʿil, denying that he died before his father. The Ismaʿiliyya, which is named after him, believes that Ismaʿil was the last Imam, that he entered major occultation and will reappear as the Mahdi.

The Sevener movement split up in several subdivisions, among them the Nizaris and the Mustaʿlis, related to the Fatimids Nizar b. al-Mustansir bi-'llah and al-Mustaʿli bi-'llah b. al-Mustansir bi-'llah. The Druzes and the Nusayris may also be traced back to the old Sevener movement. However, the name as a rule is used identically with the Ismaʿiliyya, which comprises the Carmathians, the Fatimids, the Assassins and the Ismaʿilis of India, Persia and Central Asia.

After the middle of the ixth c., the Ismaʿili movement appeared as a secret revolutionary organization carrying on intensive missionary efforts in Kufa, great parts of Persia, Yemen, and western Algeria, where the foundation for Fatimid rule was laid. In 899 a Carmathian state was founded in Bahrain, from where al-Qatif, Oman and al-Yamama were conquered. The movement was centrally directed from Salamiyya in Syria. At present, the Ismaʿiliyya is represented by the Bohoras, the Khojas, the Nizaris and the Nusayris (ʿAlawites).

Seville (A. *Ishbīliyya*): city and a province in southwestern Spain. It fell into the hands of the Muslims in 712. In 1023 Seville became the capital of the ʿAbbadids, who ruled till 1091, when the city was conquered by the Almoravids. During the reign of Muhammad II al-Muʿtamid, Seville became the centre of the best scholars of the period. Under the Almohad Abu Yusuf

Ya'qub a Great Mosque was built on the site where now the cathedral stands, of which only the celebrated minaret, the Giralda, survives. The city was taken by Ferdinand III in 1248.

Seza'i, Shaykh Hasan: Turkish poet; d. 1738. His work is of a mystical and allegorical nature and remarkable for the beauty of the language.

Sfax (A. *Ṣafāqis*): town in central Tunisia. Its Great Mosque was built in 849. During the anarchy that followed the Hilali invasion, Sfax was from 1095 till 1099 the capital of a little independent principality, renowned for the cultivation of the olive. It was occupied for a short time by the Normans of Sicily in the xiith c. and by the Spaniards in the xvith c.

Shabak: religious community of Kurdish origin near Mosul. They are related to the Yazidis, and show a particular devotion to the Prophet's son-in-law 'Ali. They are also associated with the Shi'i Ahl-i Haqq.

Sha'ban: name of the eighth month of the Muslim year. It is particularly devoted to the commemoration of the dead.

Sha'ban II al-Ashraf Nasir al-Din: Bahri Mamluk sultan; r. 1363-1376. His reign was marked by frequent attacks by Frankish fleets on Alexandria and Tripolis. Peace was concluded in 1370. In 1374 the Egyptians attacked Little Armenia, which became a permanent Muslim possession. The frontier town of Aswan was destroyed by the rebellious Nubians.

Shabankara: name of a Kurdish tribe and region between Fars, Kirman and the Persian Gulf, whose capital was the stronghold Ig. Their most glorious period fell between 1168 and 1200. In 1220 Ig was destroyed by Hülegü, and in 1354 the region became part of the Muzaffarid state.

al-Sha'bi, Abu 'Amr 'Amir b. Sharahil: transmitter of traditions; 640-ca. 728. He is said to have been sent by the Umayyad Caliph 'Abd al-Malik on missions to Constantinople and Egypt. Judged as trustworthy, he was the teacher of Abu Hanifa.

Shabib b. Yazid b. Mu'aym: Kharijite leader; 646-697. In his struggle with al-Hajjaj, he showed himself to be a master of guerilla warfare.

Shabistari, Sa'id al-Din Mahmud: Persian mystical poet; ca. 1252-1320. He is known for his *mathnawī* in which he explains the descent and ascent of the "Perfect Man" (A. *al-insān al-kāmil*).

Shabwa: town in Yemen. It was the centre of the frankincense trade between Egypt and India. The ancient ruins have given rise to many legends.

Shaddadids (Banu Shaddad): dynasty of Kurdish origin who ruled over Arran and eastern Armenia between 951 and 1174.

al-Shadhili, Abu 'l-Hasan: mystic of Moroccan origin and founder of the religious brotherhood named afer him; 1197-1258. He is said to be the originator of coffee-drinking.

Shadhiliyya: Sufi sect which, apart from the mysterious knowledge of its leaders, claimed to be strictly orthodox. When a revelation conflicted with the *sunna*, the latter had to prevail. The members of the sect claimed that they were all predestined to belong to the "well-guarded Tablet" (A. *lawḥ maḥfūẓ*), that ecstasy does not permanently incapacitate them from active life, and that "the most perfect human being" (A. *quṭb*) will throughout the ages be one of them. The main seat of the brotherhood is Algeria and Tunisia. Many other communities have sprung from it.

al-Shafiʿi, al-Imam Abu ʿAbd Allah Muhammad: founder of the Shafiʿi school of law; 767-820. He belonged to the tribe of Quraysh and was a Hashimi, thus remotedly connected with the Prophet. He acquired a thorough knowledge of the old Arab poets, knew the *Muwaṭṭa* of Malik b. Anas by heart, and remained with him in Medina till the latter's death in 796. In Yemen he was involved in ʿAlid intrigues and was imprisoned in Raqqa by the ʿAbbasid Caliph Harun al-Rashid in 803. After his release he became intimate with the celebrated Hanafi Muhammad al-Shaybani, went via Harran and Syria to Egypt and in 810 to Baghdad where he set up successfully as a teacher. In 814 he returned to Egypt. Saladin had a great madrasa built in his honour at the foot of the Muqattam Hills in al-Fustat. Al-Shafiʿi may be described as an eclectic who acted as an intermediary between the independent legal investigation and the traditionalism of his time. He is regarded as the founder of the "Principles of Jurisprudence" (A. *uṣūl al-fiqh*), laid down in his *Treatise*. Unlike the Hanafis he sought to lay down the rules for reasoning by analogy (A. *qiyās*) and rejected human interpretation (A. *istiḥsān*).

Shafiʿites (A. *al-Shāfiʿiyya*): the Sunni school of Islamic law, derived from the teachings of al-Shafiʿi. In the ixth and xth c. the school won many adherents in Baghdad, Cairo, Mecca and Medina, although their position in Baghdad was difficult because of the so-called "partisans of personal opinion" (A. *aṣḥāb al-ra'y*). In the xith and xiith c. there were frequent street fights with the Hanbalis in Baghdad. Under the Ottoman sultans the school was replaced by the Hanafis, while in Persia they had to cede to the Shiʿa under the Safawids. The school is still dominant in South Arabia, Bahrain, Malaysia, East Africa, Dagestan and some parts of Central Asia.

Shah: title given in the past to the head of state in Persia, and the usual word for king in Muslim lands where Persian is spoken. It was also used in proper names, as in that of Turan-Shah, the Ayyubid ruler of Yemen.

Shah ʿAlam II, Jalal al-Din ʿAli Jawhar: Mughal emperor; r. 1760-1788, 1788-1806. Throughout his long reign he was a puppet in the hands of others. He gave half-hearted support to Mir Qasim, the Nawwab-Nazim of Bengal, who was defeated by the British in 1764. After that, Shah ʿAlam became a pensioner of the latter.

Shah Jahan I, Shihab al-Din: Mughal emperor; b. 1592, r. 1628-1657, d. 1666. In 1632 he compelled the kingdoms of Ahmadnagar, Golkonda and Bijapur in the Deccan to submit. In 1657 his son Awrangzib defeated his three brothers, imprisoned his father and ascended the throne. Shah Jahan I had the Tāj Mahal built at Agra over the remains of his wife Mumtaz Mahall and ordered the famous Peacock Throne to be constructed, which took seven years in the making.

Shah Mir: an adventurer who founded the first dynasty of Muslim rulers in Kashmir; d. 1349. He settled in Kashmir in 1315, compelled the widow of the deceased ruler Adnideva to marry him, had her killed and ascended the throne in 1341. He limited the demands of the treasury and his rule was tolerant and beneficent. The forcible conversion of the inhabitants to Islam was not effected until the reign of his grandson Sikandar Butshikan.

Shah Shuja', Jalal al-Din: ruler of the Muzaffarid dynasty in southern Persia; r. 1364-1384. He was involved in disputes with his brother Mahmud, governor in Isfahan, and waged war with the Jalayirid Husayn b. Uways. He submitted to Tamerlane. The poet Hafiz lived at his court.

Shahara: town in Yemen in the district of San'a'. It was the source of the red onyx with white veins, used in rings. The town became the capital of the Zaydi Imam al-Mu'ayyad bi-'llah Muhammad I after he had expelled the Ottomans from San'a' in 1629. It was reconquered by the Turks in 1871.

Shahrastan: name of several towns in Persia, the best-known of which is that in Khurasan, the birth-place of the historian al-Shahrastani.

al-Shahrastani, Muhammad b. 'Abd al-Karim: principal Muslim historian of religions in the Middle Ages; 1076-1153. In his most famous work, a treatise on religions and sects, he passes in review all the philosophic and religious systems that he was able to study and classes them according to their degree of remoteness from Muslim orthodoxy. After the Muslim sects, the Mu'tazila, the Shi'a and the Batiniyya, follow the Christians and the Jews, then the Magi and the Dualists, and finally the Sabaeans. The author then goes back to pagan antiquity and gives articles on the principal philosophers and sages of Greece, and then gives an exposition of Arab scholasticism as a derivative from Hellenism; the last part of the book is devoted to the religions of India.

Shahrizur: district in Iraq, east of the Little Zab river. It is closely associated with the beliefs of the sect of the Ahl-i Haqq, whose initiates believe the Last Judgement to take place in the plain of Shahrizur.

Shahrukh Mirza: ruler of the Timurid dynasty in Transoxiana and Persia; b. 1377, r. 1405-1447. The fourth son of Tamerlane, he became governor of Samarqand around 1394, took part in the expeditions against Persia, Syria and Anatolia, and held important commands at the siege of Aleppo and at the battle of Ankara of 1402. On the death of Tamerlane in 1405, he was recognised as sovereign of Khurasan and fought his brother Khalil Sultan, whom he nevertheless accepted as ruler. Rebellions having deprived Khalil of any authority, Shahrukh gave his lands to his son Ulugh Beg and conquered Mazandaran in 1406. In 1420 he defeated the army of Qara Yusuf, the Qara Qoyunlu ruler of Azerbaijan and Iraq. Praised by historians as a munificent sovereign, he rebuilt Marw, fortified and embellished Harat and was a patron of writers, artists and scholars. During his reign Turkish poetry began to rival Persian.

Shamil: popular leader in Dagestan; d. 1871. He was the head of the local Naqshbandiyya and the last and most successful leader of the rising against Russian rule.

Shammar: name of a plateau in Saudi Arabia and of a confederation of tribes in this region. The Banu Shammar have been some of the most devoted champions of Wahhabi doctrines.

Shams al-Dawla, Abu Tahir b. Fakhr al-Dawla: member of the line of the Buyids who ruled in Hamadan and Isfahan; r. 997-1021. He was in permanent conflict with his brother Majd al-Dawla.

Shams al-Din, Ibn ʿAbd Allah al-Samatrani: Malay mystical author from North Sumatra; ca. 1575-1630. His radical mysticism brought him, together with his contemporary Hamza Fansuri, in conflict with the more orthodox Nur al-Din al-Raniri. He has exercised a considerable influence on Javanese mystic literature.

al-Shanfara: pre-Islamic black Arabian poet. Associated with the poet and Bedouin hero Taʾabbata Sharran, he was a terror to tribes. One of his poems, in which he celebrates a committed murder, is known for its amatory introduction (A. *nasīb*). Another poem, generally known as *Lāmiyyat al-ʿArab* and attributed to him, is acknowledged as one of the finest products of Arabic poetry.

Shapur (Sapor; A. *Sābūr*): name of several members of the Sasanian dynasty. The following were known to the Muslim historians: Shapur I b. Ardashir (A. *Sābūr al-Junūd*) (r. 241-272). Muslim sources, based on older Persian traditions, give his biography, which is for a large part legendary but contains a number of historical details otherwise unknown; Shapur II b. Hurmizd (Dhu ʾl-Aktaf) (r. 310-379). He is said to have waged war against several Arab tribes; Shapur III (r. 383-387).

Sharaf al-Din, ʿAli Yazdi: Persian poet and historian; d. 1454. He was the companion of the Timurid Shahrukh and his son Mirza Sultan Muhammad, who summoned him to Qum. Sharaf al-Din wrote the history of Tamerlane.

al-Shaʿrani: name carried by several individuals. The best-known among them is Abu ʾl-Mawahib ʿAbd al-Wahhab; 897-973. A Sufi of the Shadhiliyya order, he was a very prolific author, whose works have been quite popular because of his easy style. He exaggerated his own value, but was a champion of justice.

Sharif (pl. *ashrāf/shurafāʾ*): Arabic title which means primarily a free man, who can claim a distinguished position because of his descent from illustrious ancestors. Although the Qurʾan teaches the equality of all believers, the old reverence for a distinguished genealogy never quite disappeared. Under the influence of Shiʿa views and the increasing veneration for the Prophet, membership of the so-called "People of the House" became a mark of distinction. In many Muslim countries, the title *sayyid*, like *sharīf*, came to be applied only to descendants of the two sons of ʿAli, Hasan and Husayn. The green turban, which became usual as a mark of the *sharīf*s, especially in Egypt, owes its origin to an edict of the Mamluk sultan al-Ashraf Nasir al-Din Shaʿban II. It did however not become the general headgear of the *sharīf*s throughout the Muslim world.

Sharif also used to be the regnal title of the rulers of Mecca, and, under the term Shorfaʾ, it still is the title of the rulers of Morocco.

Sharif Pasha: Egyptian statesman of Turkish origin; 1823-1887. He was sent to Paris for higher education together with the future khedives Saʿid Pasha, Ismaʿil Pasha and ʿAli Mubarak Pasha, and served for some time in the French army. After the inauguration of constitutional government in Egypt in 1878, he formed three cabinets. After the defeat of ʿUrabi Pasha he came into conflict with the British and resigned in 1884.

Sharja: one of the United Arab Emirates, ruled by the al-Qawasim. The capital al-Shariqa (Sharja town) was long a commercial centre in the Persian Gulf, and from 1823 till 1954 the station of a British agent. British protection ended in 1971 and the United Arab Emirates came into being.

Sharqawa: name of a marabout family in central Morocco. They were members of the Shadhiliyya order and were active in the xviith and xviiith c. Their religious centre was in Boujad (A. *Abu 'l-Jaʿd*) in the Tadla. It became one of the most frequented sanctuaries in Morocco.

Shatt al-ʿArab: the tidal estuary formed by the confluence of the Euphrates and the Tigris rivers at al-Qurna in southern Iraq. On the right Iraqi bank lie Basra and al-Faw, on the left Iranian bank Khorramshahr and Abadan. At Khorramshahr the Shatt al-ʿArab is joined by the Karun river, which flows from Khuzistan. Because of the bar at the mouth, which is an obstacle to navigation, the estuary was known in the Middle Ages as "the Blind Tigris" (A. *dijla al-ʿawrā*) and, in Persian, as Bahmanshir. The status of the Shatt al-ʿArab waterway remained the major sticking point in the peace negotiations in 1988 between Iran and Iraq after their eight-year-old conflict. Iraq refused to acknowledge the so-called Algiers Arrangement made by Shah Muhammad Reza Pahlavi in 1975.

Shawar, Abu Shujaʿ: vizier of the last Fatimid Caliph al-ʿAdid li-Din Allah; d. 1169. He had to flee from Cairo in 1163, returned with the support of Nur al-Din Mahmud Zangi but came into conflict with Nur al-Din's general Shirkuh. Shawar appealed for help to Amalric I, king of Jerusalem, who forced Shirkuh to return to Syria. In 1167 Shirkuh invaded Egypt for a second time and defeated Shawar, but the latter, again allied to the Franks, succeeded in getting Shirkuh to leave once more. In 1168 Nur al-Din sent Shirkuh into Egypt for the third time with the avowed object of driving out the Franks, whose demands had provoked a rupture with Shawar, who purchased their departure. When the Caliph al-'Adid made a personal appeal to Nur al-Din for help, Shirkuh's entourage, notably his nephew Saladin, decided upon Shawar's death.

al-Shawbak: fortress of the Crusaders in Syria. It was built by Baldwin I of Jerusalem in 1115. Besieged several times by Saladin, it surrendered after the battle of Hittin.

Shawwal: name of the tenth month of the Muslim calendar. The law recommends fasting during six days following the minor festival.

Shayba, Banu: name of the keepers of the Ka'ba.

al-Shaybani, Abu 'Abd Allah Muhammad: Hanafi jurist; 749-804. At an early age he studied under Abu Hanifa in Kufa. The Hanafi school owes its spread of popularity to al-Shaybani and to Abu Yusuf Ya'qub al-Ansari (d. 798).

al-Shaybani, Abu 'Amr Ishaq: the foremost of the grammarians of Kufa; ca. 719-820. He compiled a large collection of poetry and linguistic data, gathered among the nomad Arabs. His *Book of the (letter) Jīm*, the unfinished part of an Arab dictionary, is one of the earliest books in the Arabic language.

Shaybani Khan (Shah Beg Khan Uzbek): khan of the Özbegs; b. 1451, r. 1500-1510. He conquered Transoxiana from the last Timurids, defeated the future Mughal Emperor Babur in 1499 and starved Samarqand into surrender. In 1509 he was defeated by the Safawid Shah Isma'il.

Shaybanids: Özbeg dynasty of descendants of the Mongol Prince Shayban, a brother of Batu b. Juči. They ruled in Transoxiana from 1500 till 1598. They were Sunnis and waged war with the Shi'i Safawids of Persia.

Shaykh: among the Bedouins the word indicated one who bore the marks of old age, i.e. one who was over fifty. The shaykh was the patriarch of the tribe or family, and had a considerable moral influence. It was also the title of the governor of Medina. At present, the title is a term of polite address, given to high dignitaries of religion and to all persons respected for their office. In the Muslim religious orders, the title indicates the master of the order.

Shaykh al-Islam: honorific title, at first given to respected religious authorities. It was more particularly applied to the Mufti of Istanbul, whose office acquired religious and political importance from Sultan Selim I onwards. The last Mufti who held his position for a long series of years was Abu 'l-Su'ud (1545-1574). After that time the Muftis succeeded one another at intervals averaging three to four years. The eminence of the position of the Shaykh al-Islam is found in the ceremonial, only the Grand Vizier being higher in rank. Great importance was attached to the *fatwā*s or legal opinions issued by the Shaykh al-Islam relating to questions of policy and public discipline.

Shaykhi: name of dissenting Shi'i theologians in Persia, followers of Shaykh Ahmad al-Ahsa'i (d. 1826). The sect was founded by Sayyid Kazim of Rasht. They were opposed to the doctrines of the Akhbariyya. According to them, the twelve Imams are the effective cause of creation, all the acts of the divinity being produced by them. Their doctrines prepared the way for those of the Bab.

Shayzar: town in northern Syria. Conquered by the Arabs in 638, the fortress changed hands many times in the Middle Ages because of its citadel. It also suffered from a number of earthquakes.

Shefiq Mehmed Efendi (Musarrif-zade): Ottoman imperial historian and stylist; d. 1715. He describes only the events of the year 1703, which witnessed the fall of Sultan Mustafa II and the accession to the throne of Sultan Ahmed III.

Sheker Bayram (lit. "sugar festival"): term used in Turkey for the festival of the breaking of the fast (A. *ʿīd al-fiṭr*) on 1st Shawwal and following days.

Shella (Chelle): necropolis of the Marinid sultans of Morocco, to the south-east of Rabat. The first member of the Marinids to be buried there was Umm al-ʿIzz (d. 1284), wife of Sultan Abu Yusuf Yaʿqub (r. 1258-1286). Once a simple construction, it was rebuilt in 1339 as a splendid sanctuary by Abu ʾl-Hasan ʿAli I (r. 1331-1348), who was the last Marinid sultan to be buried there. The enclosure however continued to receive the remains of members of the family.

Sheykhi: pen-name of a considerable number of Turkish poets. The most important was Sheykhi Čelebi, alias Mevlana Yusuf Sinan Germiyani (xvth c.). His best-known poem is the Turkish version of Abu Muhammad Nizami's *Khusraw and Shirin*.

Sheykh-oghlu (Shaykh-zade): patronym used for several Turkish writers. One is that of the author of the *Khurshid-name*; b. ca. 1340. The work describes the loves of Khurshid, the daughter of the king of Persia Siyawush and of Ferahshad, son of the king of the Maghrib. Another is that of the author, or rather the translator (xvth c.), of the *History of the Forty Viziers*, related to the *History of the Seven Viziers* (*Sindibad-name*).

Shiʿa: the term means "party", in particular "party of ʿAli" (A. *shīʿat ʿAlī*), and is used as the general name for a large group of very different Muslim sects, the starting point of all of which is the recognition of the Prophet's son-in-law ʿAli as the legitimate caliph after the death of the Prophet. Much more than the blood of ʿAli, who was murdered in 661, it was that of his son al-Husayn, killed in 681 by government troops, that was the seed of the Shiʿa. It restored to religion the motive of passion, which has thoroughly penetrated Shiʿism. To this was added the idea of the manifestation of the divine in man, namely in the Imam, who is especially chosen by God as the bearer of a part of the divine being and the leader to salvation. His death is rendered void by the idea of "return" (A. *rajʿ*), by belief in "concealment", and by parousia, which led to the concept of the Mahdi.

The particular character of the Shiʿa offered so much incentive to dogmatic speculation that it never, like the Sunna, attained any far-reaching uniformity.

In general, three main forms may be distinguished: the Zaydis, who limit the manifestation of God in the Imam to mere divine "right guidance"; the extremists, the so-called Ghulat i.e. "those who go beyond all bounds" in maintaining that the mortal in the Imam is entirely swallowed up by union with God (A. *ḥulūl*); and the intermediate Imamis, for whom the Imam remains mortal but who believe that a divine light-substance is inherent in him by partial union with God.

Each of these three groups knew many sub-divisions. The Zaydis, who believe in five Imams, formed small principalities in Tabaristan and Daylam (from 864) and in Yemen (from 901); the Ghulat found very varied expression in the Carmathians, the Isma'ilis (Seveners), the Druzes, the Nusayris and many other groups; the Imamis (Twelvers), finally, who believe in twelve Imams.

The consolidation of the separate groups began with the separation of the Isma'ilis from the Imamis (ca. 800), followed by the Zaydis (ixth c.) and various dynasties like the Bawandids, the Musafirids, the Fatimids and the Carmathians (early xth c.).

Political aspirations were further opened up by the Samanids, who were themselves not Shi'is, the Hamdanids of Mosul, the Buyids, the Mazyadids, the Mirdasids, the Sulayhids, the Kakuyids, the Isma'ilis at Alamut and in Syria. In later time there were the Safawids, the Qajars and now the Islamic Republic in Iran. In India, the first Shi'i state was that of the 'Adil Shahs of Bijapur, and, the most important, that of the Qutb Shahs of Golkonda. Growing influence was exercised by the *mujtahids* of Lakhnaw during the period of the Nawwabs of Awadh (Oudh).

Shibam: name of several towns in Yemen, of which Shibam Kawkaban and Shibam in Hadhramaut are the best known.

Shibl al-Dawla Nasr I: member of the Mirdasid dynasty of Aleppo and northern Syria; r. 1029-1038. He defeated the Byzantines, but came to terms with the emperor. His reign ended with a temporary conquest by the Fatimids.

al-Shibli, Abu Bakr Dulaf: Sunni mystic of Baghdad; 861-945. After the execution of his friend al-Hallaj in 922, he led an eccentric life. His tomb was venerated at Baghdad.

al-Shihr: port and district on the southern coast of Yemen, from where frankincense was exported.

Shilluh: name given to the Berber-speaking peoples of Sus, of the High and Anti-Atlas in Morocco, renowned for their poets.

Shinasi: pen-name of a number of Turkish poets, the best-known of whom is Ibrahim Efendi; 1826-1871. While in Paris, he is said to have hung the Republican flag on the Pantheon during the Revolution of 1848. In 1860 he founded a journal, which was to exist until its suppression in 1925. He attempted to write a poem with Turkish words only, tried his hand at a comedy, and collected Turkish proverbs.

Shir ʿAli, Barakzay: amir of Afghanistan; r. 1863-1865, 1867-1879. In 1865, his eldest brother Afdal Khan was proclaimed amir at Kabul, but he died almost immediately. In 1867 Shir ʿAli returned from Afghan Turkestan where he had fled, and entered Harat, Qandahar and Kabul. He sought assistance from the British against the Russians who in 1873 had conquered Khiva. Rebuffed, he entered into relations with Russia. In 1878 the British Government declared the second Afghan War. Shir ʿAli placed his son Muhammad Yaʿqub Khan on the throne (r. 1879-1880) and fled to Turkestan but died during the journey.

Shir Shah Sur, Farid al-Din: founder of the Sur or Afghan dynasty who ruled in Delhi from 1540 till 1555; r. 1540-1545. In 1539 he defeated the Mughal Emperor Humayun, and again in 1540. In 1545 he was killed during the siege of the fortress of Kalinjar.

Shiraz: town in central Iran, capital of the province of Fars in a vast plain to the south of Isfahan. It was conquered by the Muslims ca. 644. Taken by the Afghans in 1724, the Zand Muhammad Karim Khan (r. 1750-1779) made it his capital and erected fine buildings, notably the great bazaar. Shiraz was laid in ruins by the earthquakes of 1813 and 1824. The town was known for its wine and possesses many tombs of saints.

al-Shirazi, Abu ʾl-Husayn ʿAbd al-Malik: mathematician from Shiraz; fl. ca. 1150. He prepared a synopsis of the Conic Sections of Apollonius of Perge, which is of great value since the last three of the seven books of this work only survive in Arabic.

al-Shirazi, Abu Ishaq Ibrahim: Shafiʿi jurist; 1003-1083. He was greatly honoured during his lifetime and wrote a legal compendium on which commentaries have frequently been written.

Shirazis: name of a dynasty established at Kilwa by ʿAli b. Husayn ca. 957. They were immigrants from Persia, known as Banadir (lit. "seaports"), who intermarried with Bantu-speaking groups on the east coast of Africa. A second so-called Shirazi dynasty was founded by Shehe (Shaykh) Mvita, who gave the island and town of Mombasa their Swahili name. This dynasty died out in the late xvith c. and was followed by another Shirazi dynasty, which ruled from 1631 until 1698, when the Yaʿrubids from Oman began to extend their influence over the towns on the east coast of Africa.

al-Shirbini, Yusuf b. Muhammad: Egyptian moralist and poet; xviith c. He describes the peasants of the Nile valley.

Shirkuh, Abu ʾl-Harith Asad al-Din: uncle of Saladin; d. 1169. He entered the service of the Zangid Nur al-Din Mahmud of Aleppo, who in 1163 sent him to Egypt to assist Shawar in gaining the vizierate. Dirgham, the vizier of the Fatimid Caliph al-Adid li-Din Allah, was defeated, but then Shawar turned against Shirkuh. With the help of the Franks, Shirkuh was defeated in 1164 and returned to Damascus. In 1167 he again invaded Egypt, installed Saladin as governor in Alexandria, but was ousted by Shawar. In

1169 he was recalled to Egypt, this time by the caliph himself. After Shawar had been assassinated, Shirkuh became vizier, but died after only two months.

Shirwan: district in the republic of Azerbaijan, former Soviet Union. At the time of the ʿAbbasid Caliph Harun al-Rashid, it was ruled by Shammakh b. Shujaʿ, who is said to have given his name to the later capital Shamakhi. The Shirwan-Shahs were displaced by the Safawids, and Shirwan became a province of Persia. In 1578 it was taken by the Ottomans. In 1722 Husayn ʿAli, the Qaytaq khan of the principality of Quba, submitted to the Russian Czar Peter the Great, and the territory along the western coast of the Caspian Sea with the city of Baku was occupied by the Russians, while Shirwan remained Turkish. After a short Persian interval under Nadir Shah Afshar, several independent principalities arose, and the name Shirwan was limited to the territory of the khan of Shamakhi (Russian *Shemakha*). In 1805 the khan submitted to the Russians and in 1820 his territory was incorporated into Russian territory. Shirwan is known for its rugs.

Shorfaʾ (*Shurafaʾ*): the term, which is the dialectical plural form of the title Shrif (Sharif), is used throughout North Africa, and especially in Morocco, for the descendants of the Prophet or for those who regard themselves as such. All the Shorfaʾ of Morocco, with the exception of two branches, claim descent from al-Hasan b. Ali. These so-called Hasanid branches comprise three groups: the Idrisids, with several sub-divisions; the Qadirids, who came from Spain after the Christian conquest and settled in Fez; the Saʿdids and the Filalis, who came to power after the fall of the Berber dynasties of the Almoravids, the Almohads and the Marinids. The founder of the Idrisids, Idris I, was a great-grandson of al-Hasan b. Ali, while the Saʿdids and the Filalis trace their descent from al-Hasan's grandson Muhammad b. ʿAbd Allah al-Nafs al-Zakiyya. Two less important branches of the Shorfaʾ in Morocco, who claim descent from al-Husayn b. Ali, belong to the so-called Husaynid groups: the Sicilians (A. *Ṣāqilliyūn*) and the Iraqis (A. *ʿIrāqiyyūn*).

Shurat: Qurʾanic term which means "those who sell their life to God". It was adopted by the extreme Kharijites who vowed to fight to death against their enemies.

Shushtar (A. *Tustar*): town in Khuzistan, Iran, on the Karun river, famous for its irrigation constructions. Conquered by the Arabs ca. 635, it became a stronghold of the Kharijites during the Umayyad period. Under the ʿAbbasids, many merchants and notables from Shushtar took up residence in Baghdad. In the xvith c. it became a centre of Shiʿism, and in the xixth c. a considerable number of Mandaeans were living there.

Shushtari, Abu ʾl-Hasan ʿAli b. ʿAbd Allah: mystic poet of Muslim Spain; ca. 1203-1269. He is known for a collection of short, poignant poems written in vulgar Arabic.

Shushtari, Sayyid Nur Allah: Shiʿi writer from Lahore; d. 1610. He defended the Imamiyya against the Sunnis, and mysticism against the majority

of the Imamis. He wrote a fully documented biographical collection of the
principal martyrs of Imami and mystic Islam, and a treatise on Imami apo-
logetics.

Shuʿubiyya: name of a movement in early Islam of non-Arabs who objected to the privileged position of the Arabs and their pride towards them,
who exalted the non-Arabs over the Arabs or who, in general, despised and
depreciated the Arabs. The term is derived from the Qurʾan XLIX, which
teaches the brotherhood and equality of all Muslims without regard to tribe
and race.

Sibawayhi: pen-name of a prominent grammarian of the school of Basra;
ixth c. Sibawayhi, who died young, left a large work on Arabic grammar
which has remained the basis of all native studies on the subject. It is known
as *The Book*.

Sicily (A. *Ṣiqilliya*): Italian island in the Mediterranean. It was first raided
by the Muslim Arabs from Alexandria in 652, and again in 813, this time
from North Africa. A pact was concluded with the patricius Gregory, but in
827 the Aghlabid Ziyadat Allah I (r. 817-838) invaded the island again, and
by 840 a third of its territory was in Muslim hands. In 878 Syracuse was conquered, and Pope John VIII paid tribute for two years. By 1042 many cities
had been recaptured by the Christians, and towards the end of the xith c. the
island was in the hands of the Normans.

Sidon (A. *Ṣaydāʾ*): old city on the Mediterranean, Lebanon. It was taken
by the Arabs about 637. Conquered by the Crusaders in 1111 but recaptured
by Saladin in 1187, it then changed hands several times and was sacked by
the Mongols. Its defences finally were razed by the Ayyubid of Damascus and
Diyarbakr al-Malik al-Ashraf I. The Druze ruler Fakhr al-Din II erected a
market for European traders, still existing under the name Khan Fransawi.

Siffin: place not far from the right bank of the Euphrates, west of Raqqa,
Syria. It became famous by the battle fought there in 657 between ʿAli and
Muʿawiya, the founder of the Umayyad dynasty. Muʿawiya, then governor of
Syria, refused to recognise ʿAli as caliph after the murder of his kinsman the
Caliph ʿUthman b. ʿAffan in 656. ʿAli then invaded Syria. The two armies
met at Siffin where many skirmishes took place but no decisive battle was
fought. ʿAmr b. al-ʿAs is said to have suggested to Muʿawiya to attach manuscripts of the Qurʾan to lance-heads to express symbolically that the decision
should be left to the Holy Book. A considerable number of ʿAli's followers
declared that such an appeal could not be rejected and agreed to Muʿawiya's
proposal to indicate two arbitrators, who were to meet at a later date and to
decide whether ʿUthman had been guilty of abusing the divine law or not. If
his murder was justified, ʿAli's position would be secure; if not, Muʿawiya's
attempt to dislodge him would be legal. The Syrians chose ʿAmr b. al-ʿAs,
while ʿAli had Abu Musa al-Ashʿari forced upon him. The agreement was
signed in 657 and the armies went home, ʿAli's troops very much dejected. In

658 the arbitrators decided on 'Uthman's innocence, a verdict denounced by 'Ali. Each of the two parties retained their partisans, but Mu'awiyah's authority grew while that of 'Ali was limited to Kufa. After the latter's assassination in 661, the road was free for Mu'awiya.

Sijilmasa: ancient town of Morocco at the edge of the Sahara. Refounded in 757 by the Miknasa Berbers of the Banu Midrar, it was taken in 976 by Khazrun b. Falfal al-Maghrawi, the leader of the Zanata Berbers, who was fighting on behalf of the Umayyad Caliph of Córdoba. Later the Banu Khazrun declared themselves independent, but in 1055 the town was taken by 'Abd Allah b. Yasin, the promoter of the Almoravid movement. Henceforth the town was, theoretically at least, a dependency of the empire of Morocco, but it had a troubled history. During the siege of 1274 by the Marinid Abu Yusuf Yaqub (r. 1258-1286), artillery was employed for the first time in Morocco. In the Middle Ages, Sijilmasa was the starting point for caravans to Ghana and the Sudan and it was known for its fruits and wool. The present dynasty of the Filali Sharifs founded their dynasty at Sijilmasa in the first half of the xviith c.

Silves (A. *Shilb*): small town in southern Portugal, the former capital of the province of Algarve and an important metropolis under Arab rule. The town was ruled from 1048 till 1063 by an ephemeral dynasty of the Banu Muzayn. It was captured by the king of Portugal Sancho I in 1190.

Sinai, Mount (A. *Jabal al-Ṭūr/Jabal Mūsā*): granitic peak of the south central Sinai Peninsula, Egypt. The name occurs once in the Qurʾan as Tur Sinin. The monks of the monastery possess a copy of what is said to be a letter from the Prophet granting protection. There are genuine documents from Mamluk sultans granting protection against marauding Bedouins. The monastery also contains a mosque, whose pulpit was presented in the time of the Fatimid Sultan al-'Amir bi-Ahkam Allah.

Sinan, Mi'mar: the greatest architect of the Ottomans; 1489-1578. Born at Kayseri in Anatolia of Christian origin, he became a Janissary and took part in several campaigns, during which he attracted attention by devising ferries and building bridges. From ca. 1540 he was exclusively engaged in building mosques, palaces, schools and public baths from Bosnia to Mecca. His three most famous works are the Sheh-zade Mosque and the Süleymaniyye in Istanbul, and the Mosque of Sultan Selim II in Edirne. The list of his buildings is given by his biographer, the poet Mustafa Sa'i (d. 1595).

Sinan Pasha: name of several viziers of the Ottoman Empire, mostly of Christian origin. The most important are Khadim Sinan Pasha, Grand Vizier under Sultan Selim I; d. 1517. He was killed in personal combat with the Mamluk Sultan Tuman Bay II; Khoja Sinan Pasha, vizier under Sultan Mehemmed II; ca. 1438-1486; Khoja Sinan Pasha, five times Grand Vizier; d. 1596. As governor of Egypt in 1568, he conquered Yemen and in 1574 incorporated Tunis in the Ottoman Empire. During his third grand vizierate he concluded the Hungarian campaign and captured many castles and strong-holds.

Sind: name of the southeastern province of Pakistan, which consists of the lower valley and delta of the river Indus. The city of Karachi is the provincial capital. The country was invaded in 711 by Muhammad b. Qasim al-Thaqafi by the order of the Umayyad Caliph al-Walid I. The successive Muslim governors left the administration chiefly in the hands of the natives, and around 871 two Arab chiefs founded independent states at Multan and Mansura. The Carmathian governor Abu 'l-Fath Dawud was replaced when the Ghaznawid Mahmud b. Sebüktegin led his raids into India. During the xiiith and xivth c. the Rajput tribes of the Sumras and the Sammas tried to throw off the suzerainty of the Delhi sultans. The greatest ruler of the Samma line was Jam Nanda Nizam al-Din, who reigned for forty-six years and died in 1509. The last of the Sammas, Jam Firuz, was driven into Gujarat in 1520 by Shah Beg, member of the Arghun dynasty which ruled at Qandahar from 1479-1591. The later Mughal Emperor Akbar I, the son of Humayun who had been expelled from India by Shir Shah Sur, was born in Sind. Akbar annexed Sind in 1592, incorporating it into Multan, but local affairs remained much the hands of the Kalhoras (r. 1700-1782). After the death of the Nadir Shah Afshar, Sind passed into the hands of the Afghan Ahmad Shah Durrani, but the local ruler Muhammad Murad Yar Khan appeased the Afghan and retained his possessions. His brother and successor Ghulam Khan founded Haydarabad. In 1783 Fath 'Ali, the first of the Talpur Mirs of Baluchistan (r. 1782-1843), established himself as ruler of Sind, but his successors were divided into three branches. The army of the Mirs, who themselves remained faithful to the British, rose in rebellion but was defeated in 1843. During the Mutiny of 1857 the province remained tranquil. Established as a separate province in 1937, Sind was integrated into the province of West Pakistan from 1955 to 1970, when it was re-established as a separate province.

Sindibad-name: a collection of stories around Sindbad the Wise, also known as *The History of the Seven Viziers*. It became incorporated in the Thousand-and-One-Nights, but also retained an independent existence.

Singapore: city-state at the southern tip of the Malay Peninsula. Though mainly non-Muslim in population, the city used to be an important link in the pilgrim traffic to Mecca.

Sinnar (Sennar): town on the Blue Nile in the Sudan south of Khartum. Formerly the name was extended to the triangular territory between the Blue and the White Nile with undefined borders in the south. This country now forms the Blue Nile Province and the Funj Province. The town was the seat of the Funj kingdom from the xvith through the xixth c. According to tradition, Islam was introduced when the Umayyads took refuge there from the 'Abbasids. The region became a dependency of Egypt after Muhammad 'Ali Pasha's expedition in 1821.

Sinop (A. *Sīnūb*): town and seaport on the southern coast of the Black Sea in Turkey. The town was taken in 1214 from the Byzantines by the Rum Saljuq 'Izz al-Din Kaykawus I. Some time later Sinop was given as a hereditary fief to the vizier Mu'in al-Din Sulayman Parvana, but in 1300 it passed to the lords of Kastamonu. It was the last refuge of the Isfendiyar-oghlu, who abandoned the port to the Ottoman Sultan Bayezid I in 1394. They were restored by Tamerlane in 1402. In 1458 the Ottoman Sultan Mehemmed II incorporated Sinop into his territory. It suffered from an invasion of the Don Cossacks in 1614, and in 1853 the Turkish fleet was defeated by the Russians in its roadstead. The town still shows its citadel and the enormous walls dating from the Byzantine period. The marble minbar of the Mosque of the Rum Saljuq 'Ala' al-Din Kayqubad I, a marvel of art, cracked when the Ottoman Sultan Süleyman II wanted to have it transported to Istanbul for the Süleymaniyye Mosque.

Sipihr: pen-name of the Persian historian and man of letters Mirza Muhammad Taqi; d. 1878. One volume of his *Effacement of the Chronicles* contains the official history of the Qajar dynasty up to 1851, and has been much used by later historians.

Sirafi, Abu Sa'id al-Hasan: grammarian and Hanafi jurist from Siraf, a town on the Persian Gulf in Iran; 903-978. Among other works he wrote a commentary on *The Book* of Sibawayhi, a biography of grammarians of the school of Basra, and a geographical work.

Sistan (P./A. *Sīstān/Sijistān*): border district between eastern Iran and southwestern Afghanistan which, for its water-supply and cultivation, depends on the Helmand river. The population consists chiefly of Tajiks. Sistan was subdued by the Arabs between 644 and 651, and from 867 to 911 ruled by the Saffarids, whose founder was a Sistani. After that it belonged successively to the empire of the Samanids, the Ghaznawids and the Saljuqs, but had its own native rulers. The region suffered greatly from the Mongols, and then again at the hand of Tamerlane. The Safawid Shah Isma'il conquered Sistan in 1508, and the princes remained vassals to the Persian Empire till the invasion of the Afghans in 1722. After 1838 the authority was exercised by local chiefs until in 1862 the Sarbandi chief Taj Muhammad submitted to Persia, being in fear of Dust Muhammad Khan, the amir of Afghanistan. In 1872 British arbitration led to the limitation of the border between Persia and Afghanistan.

Sistan is the home of Rustam, the greatest Persian epic hero.

Sitt al-Mulk (Sayyidat al-Mulk): sister of the Fatimid Caliph al-Hakim bi-Amr Allah; d. 1024. According to a popular but unreliable account, she killed her brother the caliph, became regent and brought back stability and order.

Sivas: city and province in central Turkey. It was Islamicised under the Saljuqs after the battle of Malazgird in 1071 and passed into the hands of Turkmen dynasts until 1172, when it was conquered by the Rum Saljuq Qilij

Arslan II. Ca. 1398 it was taken by the Ottoman Sultan Bayezid I, sacked by Tamerlane in 1401 but recaptured by the Ottomans. The National Congress called by Mustafa Kemal Atatürk was held at Sivas in 1919. The town contains fine remains of xiiith c. Saljuq architecture.

Skanderbeg (George Kastriota): the national hero of Albania; ca. 1404-1467. Of Serbian origin and brought up as a Muslim, he became a more or less faithful local governor after 1436, but was negotiating with the Venetians and the Hungarians. After the victory of the Hungarians over the Turks in 1443 at Nish, he returned to Christianity, captured Krujë and gathered the Albanian chiefs of clans around him. In 1449 and 1450 the Ottoman Sultan Murad II ordered expeditions against Albania. Skanderbeg, supported by the king of Naples, the Pope and the Hungarians, held out until 1460 when he was forced to conclude a treaty and to pay tribute to the Ottomans. Soon afterwards he resumed a guerilla warfare until the Ottoman Sultan Mehemmed II started to conquer Albania in 1466.

Skopje (T. *Üsküb*): principal city of Macedonia. It was occupied by the Ottomans in 1392 and became the capital of the district of Kosovo. Turkish rule ended with the Balkan War in 1912. The city was hit by an extreme earthquake in 1963.

Slave (A. *'Abd*): Islam has never preached the abolition of slavery as a doctrine, but it has endeavoured to moderate the institution and mitigate its legal and moral aspects. Spiritually, the slave has the same value as the free man, and the same eternity is in store for his soul. The Qur'an makes the emancipation of slaves a meritorious act. Muslim ethic, expressed in Tradition, follows the same line of Qur'anic teaching.

Slavs (A. *Ṣaqāliba*, s. *Ṣaqlab*): the word is probably taken from the Greek *Sklabènoi, Sklaboi*. The Arabs met the Slavs during their first campaign against Constantinople (715-717) and are said to have taken many of them. As early as the viith c. their red (or reddish) hair and complexion are mentioned, but they were classed with the Turks as descendants of Japhet. The fullest notices of the Slavs in Europe are found in the travels of the Spanish Jew Ibrahim b. Ya'qub in 945. From the xiith c. onwards the word gradually disappears from Muslim literature. The Slavs were sometimes introduced into Muslim lands as slaves, as white eunuchs in particular, and special regiments were formed from them by the Fatimids in Egypt and in Muslim Spain.

al-Slawi (al-Salawi), **Shihab al-Din Abu 'l-'Abbas**: Moroccan historian from Salé; 1835-1897. Among other works he wrote a survey of the heresies and schisms in Islam and a monograph on the Nasiriyya brotherhood to which he himself belonged. His reputation is founded on his general history of Morocco.

Socotra (A. *Suquṭrā*): island in the Indian Ocean on the east side of the Gulf of Aden, belonging to Yemen. Its name goes back to the Sanskrit "island abode of bliss", and was known in classical antiquity as the island of Dioscorides. In various legends it is mentioned as "the fortunate frankincense island", excellent kinds of frankincense being indeed found. In the Middle Ages it was notorious as a nest of pirates. The last traces of Christianity date from the xviith c. For a long period the Imam of Muscat extended his suzerainty over the island, followed by the sultan of Qishn. In the early xixth c. Socotra was touched by the Wahhabi movement. In 1886 the island became a British protectorate as a dependency of Aden. In 1967 the sultanate came to an end, and Socotra became part of independent Yemen.

Sofala: port in Mozambique, called "Sofala of the Zanj" by the Arab geographers to distinguish it from Sofala in India, the ancient Surparaka, near Bombay. According to al-Masʿudi it produced gold in abundance and was the limit of navigation for ships from Oman and Siraf.

Sogdiana (Soghd): ancient name for a region in Uzbekistan. For the Arab geographers it comprised the lands east of Bukhara.

Söğüd: town near Eskishehir in central Turkey. It is famous in Ottoman history for having been the cradle of the Ottoman dynasty. The tomb of Ertoghrul, the father of ʿOthman I, lies in the neighbourhood. After the fall of Constantinople in 1453 the town lay on the main route of pilgrimage to Mecca. The country around it is noted for a preserve made of grapes steeped in vinegar.

Sokoto (Sakatu): town in the Hausa country of northwestern Nigeria. In 1801 it became the capital of the Fulani Empire established by the Tukulor Usman dan Fodio, founder of the Torodo dynasty. The empire included almost all the lands to the south of the Sahara between the eastern course of the Niger and Chad, with the exception of Bornu. On the death of Usman in 1815, the empire broke up into three allied states, his son Muhammad(u) Bello succeeding him in Sokoto (r. 1815-1837). The inhabitants everywhere abjured Islam and rebelled, supported by the Touaregs and the sultan of Bornu. Muhammad(u) Bello was succeeded by his brother Atiku (r. 1837-1847) who made himself very unpopular by prohibiting music and dancing. His successor was Aliyu (r. 1847-1860), a son of Muhammad(u) Bello. The Torodo dynasty lasted until 1904, when the British under Sir Frederick Lugard entered Sokoto. The town was famous for its leather products, made from the skin of the Sokoto red goat, the source of the moroccoleather.

Solomon (A. *Sulaymān b. Dāwūd*): in the Qur'an, the Biblical king is frequently mentioned as a divine messenger and prototype of the Prophet. Among other things, he is said to have corresponded with Bilqis, the Queen of Sheba, who accepted his summons to Islam. He is an outstanding personality in Muslim legends, which lay special emphasis on his wonderful powers of magic and divination.

Somalia: country in northeast Africa which occupies the greater part of the Horn of Africa. Islam is the official religion, most of the Somalis belonging to the Shafi'i school of law and adhering to the Salihiyya order, founded by Shaykh Muhammad Salih from Mecca, and the Qadiriyya order. From the viith c. onwards, merchants from Arabia and Persia settled on the coast, founding the towns of Zayla', Berbera, Merca, Brava and Mogadishu. They created Muslim sultanates, in which the nomadic Somalis first served as soldiers but which they gradually took over. In the xixth c. Britain, Egypt, France and Italy controlled the country. From 1899 until 1920 Muhammad b. 'Abd Allah Hassan waged war against Britain. In 1960 British and Italian Somaliland were united to form the independent republic of Somalia.

After nine years of parliamentary rule, a military revolution brought General Muhammad Siad Barre to power. In 1988 the rebellion in the north of the country by the Somali National Movement, which had smoldered for seven years, flared into a full-scale civil war. In 1989 an agreement was reached with Ethiopia over the disputed Ogaden region, but the civil war continued. In 1991 Siad Barre fled from the capital Mogadishu but tried to establish a base in his own territory near Gedo in the southwest. A conference in Jibuti of all the main Somali groups was boycotted by Barre's new grouping, the Somali National Front, and by General Muhammad Farah Aydid, chairman of the United Somali Congress. In Mogadishu fighting broke out between the supporters of interim president Ali Mahdi Muhammad and those of Aydid. In 1992 Siad Barre sought refuge in Nigeria, Somalia being effectively divided into separate regions, the northwest, the northeast, and the south. By the end of the year nearly all of the south was controlled by Aydid and his grouping, now called Somali National Alliance. At the time of writing the international food airlift and the intervention of UN forces have not achieved their goals.

Somay: Kurdish district in Iran near the Turkish frontier, ruled in the xth and early xith c. by the Hasanwayhids. In the xixth c. it was gradually occupied by the Shakak Kurds. The region contains some interesting monuments.

Somnath (A. *Sūmanāt*): ancient ruined town in southwestern Gujarat, India. Its temple, dedicated to Shiva, was desecrated by the Ghaznawid Mahmud b. Sebüktigin in 1025 who sent one piece of the idol to Mecca, another to Medina, to be trodden underfoot by the faithful. The town fell into the hands of the Rajputs, who revived the former temple, but it was desecrated again during the reign of 'Ala' al-Din Muhammmad Shah I (r. 1296-1316), the Khalji sultan of Delhi. Having been included in the dominions of the Rajas of Girnar, it passed into the possession of the sultan of Gujarat under Mahmud I Begra. It was finally conquered by the Nawwabs of Kathiawar.

Songhai (Songhoy): Negroid people in Mali. The state of Songhai is said to have been founded by Berbers in the viith c., the capital being at first at Gungiya or Kukiya in the island of Bentia, then, at about 1000, at Gao or Gaogao. Prince Kosoy, who reigned in the xith c., was the first to adopt Islam. In 1325 Songhai was annexed to the Mandingo or Mali empire. In 1464

Prince 'Ali (d. 1492) delivered the country from Mandingo suzerainty, captured Timbuktu and founded a powerful empire. The throne was seized in 1493 by Muhammadu Ture (d. 1528) who founded a new dynasty. He made the pilgrimage to Mecca, met Jalal al-Din al-Suyuti and received investiture as sultan for the lands of Takrur (i.e. of the Sudan) at the hands of the Sharif of Mecca. During his reign Songhai assumed the place previously occupied in the western Sudan by the Mali empire. In 1590 the Sa'di Sharif of Morocco, Ahmad al-Mansur al-Dhahabi, captured Gao and put an end to the state of Songhai.

Soqollo, Mehmed Pasha (Tawil, "the Tall"): one of the most famous Ottoman Grand Viziers; d. 1579. Born in Bosnia, he took part in several campaigns, and conquered Temesvár in Hungary in 1552. He was appointed Grand Vizier in 1568 and held the office until his death, being the real ruler of the empire, especially during the reign of Selim II. During his vizierate the empire, and especially the capital, passed through the richest and most glorious period in its history. Soqollu maintained peace with Persia, assisted Muslim rulers in India, and the khans of Transoxiana against the Russians. With the support of France and Poland, he was on his guard against Austria and Spain. He had a new fleet built in less than a year after the disaster suffered by the Ottomans at Lepanto in 1571.

Soso (Susu): place in Mali to the north-northeast of the capital Bamako. Its kingdom became independent in 1076, when the Almoravids took Kumbi, the capital of the empire of Ghana, of which Soso had been a dependency. In 1180 a soldier by the name of Jara Kante overthrew the ruling Muslim family. His successor Samanguru Kante took Kumbi in 1203 and persecuted the Muslims who fled to Biru. In 1235 he was defeated by Sun Jata, the king of Mali, who destroyed Kumbi, putting thus an end to the ephemeral state of Soso.

At present the Soso people, living in parts of Guinea and Sierra Leone, are largely Muslim.

Sri Lanka (Ceylon; A. *Sarandib*): island-state in the Indian Ocean, just off the southeast coast of India, independent since 1947. Ceylon was renamed Sri Lanka in 1972. It is believed that the first Muslims arrived in the early part of the viiith c. At present, the Muslims constitute some 7% of the island's populations.

Subki: name of a large family of Shafi'i scholars and judges in Egypt from the xivth through the xxth c. The name of origin is derived from the place Subk in the region of Memphis.

Successor (A. *tabi'*): term used for those Muslims who belong to the generation coming after that of the Companions of the Prophet.

Sudan, The (A. *al-Sudan*): the term is derived from the Arabic *bilad al-sudan* "Land of the Black Peoples" and was used by the medieval Arabic writers for the area of West and Central Africa south of the Sahara. It was only in the xixth c. that the name came to be applied to the countries of the Nile basin, which were conquered by the troops of Muhammad 'Ali Pasha of Egypt in 1820-1822. Thereafter they were known as the Egyptian Sudan until 1899 when it became the Anglo-Egyptian Sudan, re-affirmed by the Anglo-Egyptian treaty of 1936. In 1956 the Sudan was proclaimed independent under the name The Democratic Republic of the Sudan.

Islam must have spread very early among the Nubians of the Nile valley. The eastern Sudan was Islamicised towards the xvith c. only by tribes of Arabic origin. The Western Sudan came in contact with Islam through Berbers of the Sahara when they launched the Almoravid movement in the xith c. In 1042 the Berber reformer 'Abd Allah b. Yasin left his monastery on an island of the Lower Senegal and began to preach Islam to the Berbers of the Adrar and to the Blacks of Takrur (Futa Toro) who wanted to cast off the yoke of the Sarakolle of Kumbi in Ghana. The kings of Takrur, Mali and Songhai became converts, Awdaghost was taken in 1054 and Kumbi in 1076. The Sarakolle now also converted to Islam and began to spread it further. At about 1224 a religious and commercial centre was organised at Walata and soon Timbuktu and Dienné were reached, Timbuktu becoming the Muslim metropolis of the Western Sudan. In 1325 mosques began to be built by an Arab of a Granada family under Gongon Musa, the ruler of Mali.

As a result of the policy of the Songhai ruler Muhammadu Ture, Islam spread even more rapidly at the end of the xvth c. However, it suffered a considerable setback in Senegal in the middle of the xvith c. as a result of the conquest of Takrur by the Fulani, who established a pagan monarchy which held power from 1559 to 1776. The new religion had made its converts mainly among kings and high dignitaries; the mass of the population remained pagan.

It was in the xviiith and xixth c. that Islam made most progress in the western Sudan, due to the theocracy of the Muslim Tukulor caste of the Torodbe (s. Torodo) of Takrur, begun in 1720 at Futa Jallon. In 1776 the Fulani were defeated by the Tukulor, and Futa Toro was founded. The majority of the Fulani and the Wolof of Lower Senegal were gradually converted. In 1802 Usman dan Fodio established the empire of Sokoto. At his death in 1864, the Tukulor al-Hajj 'Umar left a vast empire in which Islam was a sort of official religion but this empire was to collapse before the French conquest (1890-1893). An attempt to set up another Muslim empire between the Senegal and the Upper Volta, begun by the conquering Mali Samori Ture, was checked by the French troops.

In the central Sudan, Islam first appeared in the xiith c. when in 1194 a Muslim dynasty of native origin, the May, overthrew the reign of Ume in Kanem. The capital was transferred to Bornu in the xvth c. At this time Islam took firm root on both sides of Lake Chad. At the end of the xvith c. it reached Baghirmi and in the xviith c. a certain Salih brought Islam to Waday. At the end of the xixth c. Islam spread southwards under the stimulus of the adventurer Rabah.

In the eastern Sudan, Dar Fur was partly converted to Islam in the xvith c. by the founder of a new dynasty named Solun-Sliman. One of his successors, Teherab, conquered Kordofan in the xviiith c. and converted the Koldaji.

In an edict granted to Muhammad 'Ali Pasha in 1841 by the Ottoman sultan Abdülmecid I, the territory committed to his rule is described as comprising Nubia, Dar Fur, Kordofan, and Sennar with their dependencies. Subsequently, Egyptian rule was extended to the countries of the Upper Nile and the Bahr al-Ghazal. An administration was set up staffed largely by Turks and Albanians, and supported by troops of the same nationalities. The countries were devastated and large numbers of the natives carried off into slavery. In 1869 the khedive Isma'il Pasha entrusted Sir Samuel Baker with the task of establishing administrative stations and curbing the activities of the slave-traders. He was succeeded in 1870 by Colonel (later General) C.G. Gordon, who resigned in 1880.

Meanwhile Islam was making rapid progress under the influence of Muhammad al-Mahdi, who in 1881 had launched the al-Mahdiyya movement and conquered Kordofan, Dar Fur, Bahr al-Ghazal, Sennar and Khartum. Islamisation continued under his successor 'Abd Allah b. Muhammad al-Ta'a'ishi, whose activities came to an end in the battle of Omdurman in 1898. Sudanese nationalism, supported by the Egyptian nationalists, had began to develop in the early xixth c.

Since independence in 1956, successive regimes have been unable to placate the fears and suspicions of the southern tribes, and guerilla warfare continued throughout the south until a settlement was reached in 1972, granting the southern provinces a certain measure of autonomy. But the religious differences between the Muslims, who constitute some 70% of the population, and the non-Muslims in the south intensified. In 1982 the Sudan People's Liberation Army began a civil war, and in 1988 the Sudanese army pressed Prime Minister Sadiq al-Mahdi to implement the peace arrangements made privately with the SPLA, led by Col. John Garang. In 1989 General Omar Hassan Ahmad al-Bashir became the fourth military leader to overthrow a civilian government since 1956. In 1990 three coups by military officers were thwarted. In 1991 a government proposal to divide the country in nine states was rejected by Garang, because, according to him, it was based on sectarianism. The promulgation of a new code of Islamic law was equally unpopular with the rebels, though the government said it would be enforced only in the Muslim north. A split in the SPLA between John Garang and Riek Machar along tribal lines led to vicious fighting in the south. In 1992 the government declared that it was prepared to recognize the nation's plural society and to guarantee freedom of belief and religious observance. However, the question whether Islamic law would form the basis of the country's legal system was not solved. Sudan, which had supported Iraq during the Gulf war, strengthened its relations with both Iraq and Iran and underlined its commitment to the Arab and Islamic cause.

Suez (A. *Sūways*): Egyptian port at the southern terminal of the Suez Canal. Under early Muslim rule the town flourished, but declined under the Mamluks and diminished further on the discovery of the Cape Route. After the conquest of Egypt by Selim I in 1517 it revived as a naval station. By the beginning of the xixth c. the town had once more fallen into decay, but began to flourish again when the overland mail route was opened in 1837 between England and India, and still more after the construction of the Suez Canal.

Sufism (A. *taṣawwuf*): the Arabic term refers to the practice of wearing a robe of wool (A. *ṣūf*) and denotes the act of devoting onself to the mystic life.

Sufyan al-Thawri, Abu ʿAbd Allah: celebrated theologian, traditionist and ascetic from Kufa; 715-778. As a jurist he was the founder of a law school which however later disappeared.

Sughdaq: town in the Crimea. It was sacked by the Tatars in 1223 and 1238, but they were forced by the Byzantines to leave in 1249. It was occupied during the reign of Özbeg, a khan of the Golden Horde (r. 1302-1340), taken by the Genoese in 1365 and conquered by the Ottomans in 1475.

Suhar (Mazun): seaport in Oman on the Gulf of Oman. In 629 envoys of the Prophet handed his message to the two princes of the town, and in 634 it was taken by the Muslims. In the early viiith c. al-Hajjaj b. Yusuf al-Thaqafi conquered Oman and united it to Iraq. By the xth c. Suhar had attained considerable prosperity, being a depot for wares from China and the centre for trade with Iraq and Yemen. The language of business was Persian. The port was destroyed in the Carmathian troubles, but was rebuilt again. In 1041 it was taken by a Persian army sent to Oman by the Buyid Abu Kalijar. By about 1225 the port was destroyed and its trade had passed to Hormuz, but it seems to have been revived again. In 1506 the Portuguese occupied it and built a new fortress in 1588. The Yaʿrubid Nasir b. Murshid b. Sultan besieged it, and by 1650 the Portuguese had to leave. In 1724 it was taken by Khalaf b. Mubarak but later surrendered to the Yaʿrubid Sayf b. Sultan. Suhar's governor Ahmad b. Saʿid defeated the Persians after their conquest of Muscat. British intervention led in 1819 to a naval battle between the pirates and the British navy off Suhar, after which a treaty with the pirates was concluded. During the absence in East Africa of Saʿid b. Sultan, piracy was revived and the pirate chief Hamud b. ʿAzzan seized Suhar, but was blockaded by Saʿid in 1836 with the help of Faysal b. Turki of the Al Saʿud. The British forced Hamud to hand over the rule to his son Sayf, but the latter was murdered in 1849 by his father, who himself was imprisoned by Saʿid. He was succeeded by his brother Qays b. ʿAzzan, who had to hand over the port to Saʿid b. Sultan in 1852. From that date Suhar has formed part of the sultanate of Oman.

al-Suhrawardi, Shihab al-Din Abu Hafs 'Umar: Sufi theologian of the Shafi'i school of law; 1145-1234. He wrote a treatise on ethics and practical mysticism and a polemical work directed against the study of Greek philosophy.

al-Suhrawardi, Shihab al-Din Yahya (al-Maqtul): mystic theologian and philosopher; ca. 1155-1191. His best-known work is called *Knowledge of Illumination*, in which he develops the Neoplatonic theory of light, which serves as a symbol of emanation but at the same time is regarded as the fundamental reality of things. He was also the founder of a sect, called "the Illuminates". Suspected of pantheism, he was put to death (A. *al-maqtul*) in Aleppo in 1191 by Saladin's son al-Malik al-Zahir.

Sulayb: Arab pariah tribe living in Central Arabia. They used to be hunters and breeders of the highly esteemed Sulayba ass. Their customs showed traces of ancient Christian and Sabaean elements.

Sulayhids: Shi'i dynasty which ruled over Yemen as nominal vassals of the Fatimids from 1047 till 1138. It was founded by 'Ali b. Muhammad, who chased the Abyssinian slave dynasty of the Najahids from Zabid, fought the Zaydi Imam al-Qasim b. 'Ali and took San'a' in 1063, Zabid in 1064 and Aden in 1065. He restored order in Mecca and appointed Abu Hashim Muhammad (r. 1063-1094) as Sharif. He was killed by the Najahid Sa'id b. Najah (d. 1088) in 1067. His son al-Mukarram (r. 1067-1091) again conquered Zabid from the Najahids and rescued his mother Asma' bint Shihab (d. 1086). In the same year 1086 he instituted a new coinage called "Maliki Dinars", but left state affairs to his wife al-Sayyida Arwa (b. 1052, r. 1084-1138), who transferred her residence from San'a' to Dhu Jibla in winter, making the castle of Ta'kar, where the treasures of the Sulayhids were stored, her residence in summer. In 1119 the Fatimid Caliph al-'Amir sent Ibn Najib al-Dawla as an emissary to Yemen. He reduced the smaller principalities to obedience but Queen Arwa was able to resist his endeavours. At her death the Sulayhid dynasty came to an end, and power passed to the Zuray'ids, who were to hold it until the arrival of the Ayyubid Turan-Shah in 1174.

Sulaym b. Mansur: name of a powerful tribe belonging to the Banu Qays 'Aylan. They commanded the road to Medina as well as the access to Najd and the Persian Gulf, possessing mineral wealth of gold and silver. At first hostile to the Prophet, they adopted Islam around 630. The Sulaymi Abu 'l-A'war was one of the lieutenants of the Umayyad Caliph Mu'awiya I. They refused to recognise Marwan I b. al-Hakam and supported the anti-caliph 'Abd Allah b. al-Zubayr. Later they took the side of the Carmathians. In 1052 the Fatimid Caliph al-Mustansir sent the Egyptian branch, together with the Banu Hilal, to conquer North Africa.

Sulayman, Mawlay Abu 'l-Rabi' b. Muhammad: Sharifian Filali of Morocco; r. 1792-1822. After many campaigns inside his country and against the Ottomans of Algiers, the learned and pious Sulayman was able to assure his authority by 1803. After several years of peace and prosperity, he had to take the field again, especially against the Berbers of the central Atlas.

Sulayman b. ʿAbd al-Malik: Umayyad Caliph; b. 680, r. 715-717. He founded al-Ramla, where he continued to live after becoming caliph. In 715 Maslama b. ʿAbd al-Malik besieged Constantinople.

Sulayman al-Mahri: Arab navigator and author of five *Sailing Instructions*; d. 1553. Besides all the various aspects of navigation, they contain some detailed itineraries which are remarkably accurate, like that from Diu to Malacca.

Sulayman b. Qutlumish: ancestor of the Rum Saljuqs; d. 1086. He became chief of the Saljuqs after the death of his father in the battle against his relative Alp Arslan in 1064 and founded an independent kingdom. He defeated the Byzantine general Isaac Comnenos, weakened by a mutiny of his Norman mercenaries, and concluded a treaty with Emperor Michael VII. In 1081 he conquered Izniq (Nicaea) and made it his capital. He defeated the ʿUqaylid Muslim b. Quraysh in 1085.

Sulayman b. Surad al-Khuzaʿi (Yasar): early Shiʿi; d. 685. Having adopted Islam in the time of the Prophet, he showed himself an ardent supporter of al-Husayn b. ʿAli but did nothing to support him when he approached Kufa. Later he led the so-called "Penitents", the people of Kufa who regretted not having supported al-Husayn. In the battle at ʿAyn al-Warda against Husayn b. al-Numayr al-Sakuni, Sulayman was killed and the Shiʿa cause routed.

al-Sulaymaniyya: town and district in northeastern Iraq, known from the earliest times. In the Muslim period it had a more or less autonomous existence from the late xviith c. till 1850 under a local dynasty called Baban, who maintained their position between the Ottoman Empire and Persia. In 1850 it came under Ottoman rule. In the treaty of Sèvres of 1920, Sulaymaniyya was to be included in "Southern Kurdistan", but in 1925, after insurrections led by Shaykh Mahmud Barzanja, it became part of the new state of Iraq. The ancestor of the Barzanja family, Hajji Kaka Ahmad, is buried in Sulaymaniyya.

Süleyman II (Qanuni/the Magnificent): the greatest of the Ottoman sultans; b. 1494, r. 1520-1566. Peace-loving by nature, he took part in thirteen great campaigns in Europe and Asia. In 1521 he conquered Belgrade and the next year the island of Rhodes. In 1526 the Hungarians were defeated at Mohács and Buda was temporarily occupied. 1529 saw the siege of Vienna, which was however raised soon. The various embassies to Austria had no success, and in 1532 Süleyman started upon what the Turkish sources call "the German campaign against the king of Spain". However, in 1533 an armistice was concluded with Austria.

Süleyman's next campaign was directed against Persia, which avoided the battle. In 1534 the sultan made his ceremonial entrance in Baghdad, where he stayed for four months and built the mausoleum of Abu Hanifa. He also visited Najaf, Kufa and Karbala'. In 1541 and 1543 he was again in Hungary, where Turkish administration was introduced. The war against Persia was resumed in 1548 but without success, and in 1555 a treaty was concluded at Amasia, where Süleyman received the Austrian embassy under Ogier Giselin de Busbecq. It could only obtain an armistice. The sultan died during the siege of Szigeth.

Süleyman was a pious man, and must have been a born ruler. As a poet, he used the pen-name of Muhibbi. Following the principles of his predecessors, he elaborated the system of state institutions by promulgating the "Canon", which deals mainly with the organisation of the army, the laws of landed property, the police and the feudal code. During his reign, the Ottoman Empire established its place in international affairs. The Christian states had lost all hope of driving the Turks out of Europe, and King Francis concluded an alliance with the Ottoman sultan. The Turkish fleet began to be active in the Mediterranean, in the Red Sea and in the Indian Ocean. The possession of Aden and Yemen was secured for the empire.

Under Süleyman, Ottoman civilisation gained its own special character in the field of literature and especially in that of architecture with the works of Sinan in Istanbul, Baghdad, Konya, Jerusalem and Mecca.

Süleyman III: Ottoman sultan; b. 1642, r. 1687-1691. During his reign the Ottomans suffered defeat after defeat in Hungary and Dalmatia. They lost the battle of Nish in 1689, but recaptured it in 1690, along with Semedria and Belgrade.

Süleyman Čelebi (Süleyman Dede): Ottoman poet from Bursa; d. 1421. He is the earliest Ottoman poet of whom an original poem written in Turkish has survived. It is the *Hymn on the Prophet's nativity*, often recited at religious ceremonies, in particular at the festival of the Prophet's birthday (A. *mawlid*).

Süleyman Pasha: eldest son of the Ottoman sultan Orkhan; 1316-1359. He was the first to cross to the European shore of the Dardanelles with permanent results by taking Gallipoli and the whole of Rumelia. He was buried in Bulayr, a symbol of the firm resolve never again to abandon the new won ground. His tomb became a place of national pilgrimage.

Süleyman Pasha (Khadim, "the eunuch"): Turkish general and Grand Vizier; d. 1548. From 1524 till 1534 he was governor of Egypt, and the first to send the yearly revenue, the so-called Egyptian treasure, to Istanbul. In reply to the appeal of Bahadur, the sultan of Gujarat (r. 1526-1537), he was ordered by Sultan Süleyman II to equip a fleet to strengthen Turkish power in the Red Sea and to drive the Portuguese out of India. On his way out, he conquered Aden and Yemen, but failed in India for lack of support.

al-Suli, Abu Bakr Muhammad b. Yahya: chess-player, historian and man of letters of Turkish origin; d. 946. At the court of the 'Abbasid Caliph al-Muktafi bi-'llah he defeated the leading chess-player of his time al-

Mawardi. He wrote a history of the 'Abbasids, a handbook for clerks in the chancelleries, and compiled a collection from 'Abbasid poets. Criticized for his plagiarism and vanity, his compilations nevertheless had influence on later literature.

Sultan (A. *sulṭān*): the term occurs frequently in the Qur'an with the meaning of a moral or magical authority. In Tradition literature it has exclusively the sense of power, usually governmental. As a personal title, the word was used for the first time by the great usurpers of power of the caliph such as the Buyids, the Ghaznawids and the Saljuqs. In 1051 the Great Saljuq Tughril I received from the caliph the title al-Sultan Rukn al-Dawla. It was with the Saljuqs that *sulṭān* became a regular sovereign title, to which such titles as *malik* and *shāh* were subordinate. It was later adopted by the Mamluks and the Ottomans. Jurists and historians then set themselves to construct theories to find a justification for the existence of potentates for whom the old conception of the Muslim caliphate had no place.

Sulṭān is also the title given to Sufi shaykhs from the xiiith c. onwards, especially in Anatolia and countries influenced by Ottoman civilisation.

Sultan al-Dawla Abu Shuja': Buyid ruler; r. 1012-1021, d. 1025. He ruled in Fars, Khuzistan and Iraq, but had to fight his brothers Jalal al-Dawla and especially Abu 'l-Fawaris, the governor of Kirman (d. 1028).

Sultan Walad: eldest son of Jalal al-Din Rumi; 1226-1312. In 1285 he succeeded Čelebi Husam al-Din, the first successor to Jalal al-Din as head of the Mawlawi order. His works are written in Persian, including some verses in Turkish and Greek. He is said to have been the first representative of the school of Turkish poetry under Persian influence, that of popular mystic poets being represented by Yunus Emre.

Sultaniyya: town in northwestern Iran, near Zanjan. It was constructed by the Il-Khan Arghun (r. 1284-1291), and made the chief seasonal residence of the Il-Khan empire by his successor Öljeytü Khudabanda, who was buried in the mausoleum which still exists. After the fall of the Il-Khans in 1336, the town often changed hands between the Jalayirids and the Muzaffarids. It was taken by Tamerlane in 1384. After the Safawid Tahmasp I had removed the capital to Isfahan, and trade had gone back to Tabriz, the town became forgotten.

al-Sumayl b. Hatim Abu Jawshan al-Kilabi: famous Arab chief in Muslim Spain; d. 759. In 749 he commanded the district of Saragossa and took the part of Yusuf b. 'Abd al-Rahman, the governor of Córdoba, against 'Abd al-Rahman I, who had him strangled.

Sumatra: the second largest island of Indonesia and the fifth largest in the world. The first mention of Islam in Sumatra is made in 1292 by Marco Polo. Ibn Battuta visited part of the island in 1345. The first king who embraced Islam in Atjeh, the northern extremity of the island, is said to have been 'Ali Mughayat Shah (r. 1507-1521), but Islam was probably brought there by Arab traders in the early centuries of the Hijra. Learned men may have come to the archipelago from southern India, as did Muslim traders from Gujarat. Islam however adapted itself to the native creed, and made large concessions to Hinduism since Sanskrit words are until this day used for religion (*agama*), Muslim fasting (*puwasa*), teacher (*guru*) and disciple (*sasiyan*).

During the xixth and xxth c. the Bataks of central Sumatra responded with enthusiasm to Islam, as was the case on the island of Nias.

Islam may have come to the Minangkabau, the largest ethnic group on the island, around the middle of the xvith c. During the so-called Padri War, the Padri tried by violent means to introduce orthodox Islam against the unorthodox matriarchal form of society and its original Malay laws of inheritance.

The southern part of Sumatra, the Lampong-districts, seem to have been Islamicised from Banten on western Java.

Sünbül-zade Wehbi: Turkish poet and scholar from Marʿash; d. 1809. He is known for his good-humoured but ribald lampoons against his close friend Sayyid ʿOthman Süruri. His works are important for the impression made by Persia on an intelligent Turk.

Sunna: the Arabic word means custom, use, statute, and is found in the Qurʾan and in Tradition. According to the usual explanation, the Prophet's *sunna* comprises his deeds, utterances and his unspoken approval, but the word occurs also in a negative meaning. The word *al-Sunna* i.e. "the Sunna" has become the characteristic term for the theory and the practice of the orthodox Muslim community who refrain from deviating from dogma and practice. As such it is particularly used in opposition to Shiʿa. In the system of Islam it became a standard of conduct alongside of the Qurʾan. The relation between Qurʾan and Sunna is fully discussed in the law books. It was propagated by the Prophet's Companions, and fixed orally and in writing in the Tradition. The followers of the *sunna* are known as Sunnis or Sunnites.

Suqman b. Artuq Muʿin al-Dawla: first ruler of the line of the Artuqids in Hisn Kayfa and Amid (Diyarbakr); d. 1104. He received Jerusalem as a fief from the Saljuq Tutush b. Alp Arslan, but it was taken from him by the Fatimids in 1096. He then took Saruj and Hisn Kayfa. Together with his old enemy Chekirmish, the lord of Jazirat Ibn ʿUmar, he defeated the Franks and took Count Baldwin of Edessa and Joscelin prisoners.

Sur: name of a clan of Afghans. They are a subdivision of a clan of the Lodi, whose sultans ruled at Delhi between 1451 and 1526 and attracted many Afghans to India. The Suris ruled as sultans of Delhi from 1540 till 1555, their strongest ruler being Farid b. Muhammad, known as Shir Shah Suri. After his death, the internecine strife was not restrained any more. The last Suri ruler, Ahmad Khan Sikandar Shah III was defeated by the Mughal Akbar.

Sura: name given to the chapters of the Qurʾan. In the Qurʾan itself, the word means the separate revelations which were revealed to the Prophet from time to time. The authorised Qur'an contains 114 *sura*s of which the first and the two last are conjurations. They are said to have been lacking in the Qur'an as edited by Ibn Mas'ud.

Surakarta (Solo): name of a former kingdom on central Java, Indonesia. It arose out of the kingdom of Mataram, which was founded by Senapati about 1575 as the third Muslim kingdom after the decline of Demak and Pajang. The Javanese prince, called the Susuhunan, was officially recognised as Muslim ruler by the authorities in Mecca and received the title "Arranger of the Religion".

Surat: town on the south bank of the Tapti River in Gujarat. The Tughluqid Firuz Shah III built a fort there, but the modern town is said to have been started by a Hindu merchant. The town was burned three times by the Portuguese in the first half of the xvith c. The present fort was founded in 1540 by Khudawand Khan, a Turkish officer in the service of Mahmud III of Gujarat. It was taken by the Mughal Emperor Akbar I. The British and Dutch founded factories there in the early xviith c. It was plundered by the Maratha Shivaji b. Shaji Bhonsle, and from 1669 an annual Maratha raid was almost a matter of course. In 1687 it was superseded by Bombay, and it became a British possession in 1800.

Süruri: name of several Ottoman poets. One of the most notable is Muslih al-Din Mustafa Efendi, a distinguished philologist; d. 1562. He was perhaps the greatest authority on Persian language and literature that Turkey has ever produced, and he had also a perfect command of Arabic. He wrote well-known commentaries on the works of Hafiz, a text book of prosody and rhyme and a synopsis of Qazwini's Cosmography.

Another poet known under this name is Sayyid 'Othman (Süruri-yi Mü'errikh); 1751-1814. He was an intimate friend of Sünbül-zade Wehbi and is considered the greatest Ottoman writer of chronograms.

Susa (A. *al-Sus*): ruined site in the Khuzistan region of Iran. It fell into the hands of the Arabs in 638 and remained for several centuries a flourishing city, known for its silk. By the xvth c. it had become deserted. The tomb-mosque of the prophet Daniel outside Susa was visited by Muslims, Jews and Mandaeans.

al-Sus al-Aqsa: district in the south of Morocco near Agadir. It was conquered and converted to Islam in 735, played a dominant role in the early days of the Almohad movement and again in the history of Sa'di Sharifs, the town of Tedsi in al-Sus being the cradle of this dynasty.

al-Su'udi, Abu 'l-Fadl al-Maliki: Arab theologian; xvith c. He is known for a polemical work against the Christians and the Jews.

al-Suwaydiyya: the harbour of Antioch which knew a period of great prosperity during the so-called Christian Principality of Antioch, which lasted from 1098 till 1277, when the town was conquered by the Mamluk Sultan Baybars I.

al-Suyuti, Jalal al-Din: the most prolific Egyptian writer in the Mamluk period and perhaps in Arabic literature; 1445-1505. The list of his writings contains 561 works, but it includes numerous quite short treatises. His compilations are of great value as compensating for lost works.

Syria (A. *al-Shām*): after the Byzantines had been defeated by the Arabs in the battles of Araba, Dathina, al-Ajnadayn and Fihl, Palestine was definitively lost to the empire. Damascus fell in 635 and the battle on the Yarmuk in 636 settled the fate of Syria. Jerusalem surrendered in 638 and Caesarea in 640. Syria was divided into military districts from which the conquerors controlled the country and collected the taxes. Mu'awiya I, the governor of Damascus, was acclaimed caliph at Jerusalem by the troops and amirs of Syria, and took up his residence in Damascus, making the Syrian Arabs supreme during the Umayyad period. After Abu 'l-'Abbas al-Saffah had himself proclaimed caliph at Kufa in 749 and the Umayyads had been defeated at the battle of the great Zab in 750 and were persecuted everywhere, the Syrians tried in vain to raise the "white flag" against the "black flag" of the 'Abbasids.

With the fall of the Umayyads and the transfer of the capital to Baghdad, Syria lost its privileged position and became a province, carefully watched on account of its attachment to the old regime. During the period of the early 'Abbasids, lines of forts were built in the Syrian military marches to check Byzantine invaders. The short-lived dynasties of the Tulunids and the Ikhshidids, ruling in Egypt, tried in vain to get a permanent foothold in Syria. Meanwhile, the Carmathians had devastated the country and left the germ of Isma'ili doctrine. After the rule of the Shi'i Hamdanids at Aleppo, Syria fell to the Fatimids of Egypt from 969 till 1171, but their direct authority was limited to the presence of their military. From 963-1025 the Byzantine Emperors held northern Syria but in the end kept only Antioch until 1084. Aleppo was in the hands of the Mirdasids from 1023 till 1079. The origin of the Druzes is connected with the Fatimid Caliph al-Hakim. After 1084, Syria was divided into the Saljuq sultanates of Aleppo and Damascus.

In 1097 the Crusaders appeared before Antioch, which they entered in 1098. In 1099 they took Jerusalem, which became the capital of the Latin kingdom, comprising the counties of Edessa and Tripoli and the principality of Antioch. Strong castles like Castellum Peregrinorum (A. *'Athlīth*), Crac des Chevaliers (A. *Ḥiṣn al-Akrād*), Chastel Blanc (A. *Ṣafītā*), Maraclea (A. *Maraqīya*), Margat (A. *Marqab*), Beaufort (A. *Shaqīf Arnūn*) in southern Lebanon, and Crac and Montréal in Transjordan, defended the Crusaders' possessions. The great cities of Aleppo, Hamat, Homs, Baalbek and Damascus remained independent. The Franks, the Byzantines and the Armenians enfeebled one another while the Muslims gathered around remarkable leaders like the Zangid Nur al-Din Mahmud and Saladin. In 1187 the latter defeated the Christians at Hittin and took Jerusalem, only Antioch, Tripoli and Tyre remaining in the hands of the Crusaders. Acre, conquered in 1191, became the capital of the Latin kingdom. Taking advantage of the discord among Saladin's numerous heirs, Emperor Frederick II negotiated with al-Malik al-Kamil, the Ayyubid of Egypt, about the cession of Jerusalem, but the alliance of Saladin's sons with the Franks was defeated by al-Malik al-Kamil near Ghaza in 1244 and enabled the Egyptians to occupy Jerusalem, Damascus and Homs. The fall of Acre and of Castellum Peregrinorum in 1291 brought the period of the Crusaders to an end.

Syria now came under Mamluk rule, but, fearing the ambitions of their deputies (A. *nā'ib*) in Damascus, the Mamluks changed them continuously so that unrest remained. In 1299 the Il-Khan Mahmud Ghazan routed the Mamluks near Homs, but was defeated by them at Marj al-Suffar in 1303. The Burji Mamluk Nasir al-Din Faraj began the reconquest of Syria no less than seven times, but in 1401 Tamerlane conquered Aleppo and Damascus, which was thoroughly devastated.

In 1516 the Ottoman Sultan Selim I invaded Syria and defeated the Mamluk army at Marj Dabiq. Aleppo, Damascus and other towns opened their gates to the new conqueror. Syria was now divided into three great districts, Damascus, Tripoli, and Aleppo, each governed by a pasha. The pashas collected the taxes and left the interior of the country to the old feudal tenants: Bedouin amirs, Turkmen, Druzes and Nusayris. The pashas were changed continuously – Damascus saw 133 pashas in 180 years – and so the Druze leader of the house of Maʿn, Fakhr al-Din II, was able to lay the foundations of modern Lebanon. The Ottoman pashas invoked the help of one of his successors, Bashir Shihab II, but neither was able to prevent Muhammad ʿAli Pasha's son Ibrahim from taking over Syria temporarily in 1833. In 1840 the whole of Lebanon was stirred up by the British, and Ibrahim had to agree to evacuate Syria, amir Bashir going into exile and the country returning to Ottoman rule.

The struggle for power between the Druzes and the Christians led to the intervention of France in Lebanon in 1860. In 1888 the rest of Syria was divided into three provinces, Damascus, Aleppo and Beirut. The Ottoman Sultan Abdülhamid II instituted a system of turkicising, which was continued by the Young Turks and provoked nationalistic feelings. During World War I, Syria was invaded by the British, with a French contingent. In March 1920 a Syrian congress meeting in Damascus elected Faysal, son of Sharif Husayn of Mecca, king of a united Syria including Palestine, but shortly afterwards it was decided at San Remo that France should have the mandate for Syria. The French dethroned Faysal, who was made king of Iraq, and organized Syria in four provinces: Aleppo, Damascus, the ʿAlawite country of Latakia and Jabal al-Duruz to the south of Damascus. The Syrian nationalists, however, rejected the mandate, and in 1925 the first major rising began in Jabal al-Duruz, which was subdued in 1927. Meanwhile, the Lebanese Republic had been proclaimed in 1926. The Franco-Syrian Treaty of 1936, by which the ʿAlawite and the Druze states, as well as the Alexandretta country, were included in the Syrian Republic, was never ratified by France. In 1938 Alexandretta was proclaimed the autonomous Republic of Hatay. In 1946 Syria and Lebanon became completely independent.

T

Taʾabbata Sharran: nickname of the old Arab poet and Bedouin hero Thabit b. Jabir b. Sufyan of the tribe of Fahm. He was associated with al-Shanfara, for whom he wrote a lament.

Tabala: place in the region of Asir in western Saudi Arabia, which used to be a station between Mecca and Sanʿaʾ.

al-Tabari: Arabic word indicating someone originating from Tabaristan. Most bearers of this name come actually from Amul, a town in Mazandaran, Iran, south of the Caspian Sea. Next to the great Arab historian Abu Jaʿfar al-Tabari, there are two Shafiʿi jurists known under this name: Abu ʾl-Tayyib Tahir b. ʿAbd Allah; 959-1058, and Muhibb al-Din Abu ʾl-ʿAbbas Ahmad; 1219-1294. The latter is the author of a well-known collection of traditions.

al-Tabari, Abu Jaʿfar Muhammad b. Jarir: the greatest of the Arab historians; 839-923. He is said to have known the Qurʾan by heart by the time he was seven. He visited Rayy, Baghdad, Basra and Kufa, Egypt and Syria, his homeland Tabaristan, and settled in Baghdad where he died. His main subjects were history, Muslim law, recitation and exegesis of the Qurʾan, but also poetry, lexicography, grammar, ethics, and even mathematics and medicine. He belonged to the Shafiʿi school of law but then founded a school of his own, known as Jaririyya, which differed from the Shafiʿi school less in principle than in practice. After his death it soon fell in oblivion. He recognised Ahmad b. Hanbal only as an authority on Tradition but not on Law, and thus brought upon himself the hostility of the Hanbalis. His Commentary on the Qurʾan is a standard work, but his most important contribution to Muslim scholarship is his *History of Prophets and Kings*, in fact a history of the world up to the year 915. It is known in the West as *Annals*.

Tabaristan: name applied by the Arabs to the Persian province of Mazandaran, Iran. After several unsuccessful attempts, the region was conquered in the early viiith c. by Yazid b. Muhallab. The inhabitants however remained rebellious for a long time to come. Shiʿism was introduced in the ixth c.

Tabarka: town on the Tunisian coast, which from 1540 till 1741 belonged to the Lomellini of Genoa. It was a market for the exchange of European merchandise and a depot of Christian slaves awaiting their ransoms. In 1741 it was taken by ʿAli Pasha, the Bey of Tunisia (r. 1735-1756). The French landed there at the beginning of the Tunisian expedition in 1881.

Tablet, the carefully preserved (A. *lawḥ maḥfūẓ*): the term, which occurs in the Qur'an, denotes the tablet kept in heaven, which is the original copy of the Qur'an as well as the record of the decision of the divine will. In Sufi mysticism and in esoteric philosophy and cosmology, the tablet occupies an important place.

Tabriz: capital of the province of Azerbaijan, Iran. One feature of the town is the frequent earthquakes, recorded for the years 858, 1042, 1641, 1727, 1780, 1854 and 1856. According to a Muslim legend, Tabriz, which dates from pre-Islamic times, was "built" by Zubayda, wife of the 'Abbasid Caliph Harun al-Rashid. Its possession was disputed by the Ziyarids, the Kurds and the Musafirids. Under the Ildeñizid Qîzîl Arslan 'Uthman (r. 1186-1191), Tabriz became the capital of Azerbaijan and was confirmed in this role by the Il-Khan Abaqa (r. 1265-1282). It reached its greatest splendour under the Il-Khan Mahmud Ghazan. His successor Öljeytü Khudabanda created a new capital at Sultaniyya.

The fortunes of the Jalayirid dynasty were also closely connected with Tabriz. In 1392 the town was conquered by Tamerlane and after his death in 1405 it became the capital of the Qara Qoyunlu Qara Yusuf (r. 1389-1420). Under the Qara Qoyunlu Jihan Shah (r. 1438-1467) the famous Blue Mosque was built. In 1468 the Aq Qoyunlu Uzun Hasan, whose reign is described by Venetian merchants, made the town his capital. Isma'il I, the founder of the Safawid dynasty, occupied Tabriz in 1500 and imposed Shi'ism on the Sunni inhabitants. The road to the town was opened to the Ottomans after their victory at the battle of Chaldiran in 1514. However, Sultan Selim I had to return due to the refusal of the Janissaries to continue the campaign. Yet, the Safawid Tahmasp now transferred his capital to Qazwin. Tabriz was occupied by the Ottomans for a second time in 1534, and again in 1548, the Ottoman Sultan Süleyman II making efforts to spare the town from plundering by his military. In 1585 Tabriz was again occupied by the Ottomans, and by the disastrous peace of 1590 the Safawid Shah 'Abbas I had to cede the town to them. But the shah retook the town in 1603, a great number of the Turkish troops being killed by the Shi'i inhabitants. In 1612 a new peace treaty was signed, but the struggle continued. Tabriz was plundered under the Ottoman Sultan Murad IV. By the Treaty of 1639 the Persians secured for themselves the frontier with Turkey which has survived in its main lines to the present day.

In 1729 Nadir Shah Afshar entered Tabriz. The Qajar Aga Muhammad added the town to his fief, but the incorporation of Georgia into Russia in 1801 made Tabriz the centre of Persian preparations for war. The former splendour had gone. The town was occupied by the Russians in 1827, but the Peace Treaty of Turkmančay in 1828 put an end to the Russian occupation. Since 1799 Tabriz had been the official residence of the heir to the throne 'Abbas Mirza, son of the Qajar Fath 'Ali Shah. The transfer of the British and

Russian diplomatic missions to Teheran in 1834 reduced the importance of Tabriz, although the movement of goods from Russia via Trebizond-Tabriz encouraged the northern Persian markets.

In 1908 open rebellion broke out as part of the Persian nationalist and revolutionary movement. Tabriz was occupied by the Russians in 1909 until 1914, when the town was taken by the Kurds. In 1918 the Ottomans again entered the town. Order was finally established by Reza Khan (later Shah) Pahlavi.

Tabriz is known for its carpets and its school of miniature painting, founded by the Il-Khans and active until the early xvith c.

Tabuk: town on the pilgrim road from Damascus to Medina. In 630 the Prophet started there his campaign against the north, but the great heat dispirited his followers.

Tadla (Tadila): region in Morocco between Fez and Marrakesh which, from the xiith c. onwards, became the battleground of rival dynasties in the country.

al-Taff: the desert region in Iraq that lies west of Kufa along the alluvial plain of the Euphrates. It was the scene of the first encounter between the Arabs and the Persians and of the battle of al-Qadisiyya. Karbala' is also located in this region.

Tafilalt: name of a district in southeastern Morocco. Its historical capital is Sijilmasa. It is known as the cradle of the Filali Sharifs of Morocco.

al-Taftazani, Sa'd al-Din Mas'ud: celebrated authority on grammar, rhetoric, logic, metaphysics, theology, jurisprudence, Qur'anic exegesis and philology; 1322-1389. He was treated with great honour by Tamerlane at Samarqand, where he met 'Ali b. Muhammad al-Jurjani, which led to rivalry between the two old acquaintances.

Taha Husayn: famous Egyptian author; 1889-1973. As a modernist, he was often at odds with religious conservatives. His best-known work is *The Days*, his autobiography.

Tahert (Tagdempt): town in Algeria, founded in 761 by the Rustamid 'Abd al-Rahman b. Rustam (r. 777-784), Imam of all the Ibadis in North Africa. It was utterly ruined by Abu 'Abd Allah al-Shi'i in 908.

Tahir b. al-Husayn: founder of the Tahirid dynasty in Khurasan; b. 775, r. 821-822. Having been given by the 'Abbasid Caliph al-Ma'mun all the lands east of Baghdad, he died suddenly in his capital Marw, shortly after he had omitted the mention of the caliph in prayer, thus committing an act of open rebellion.

Tahirids: dynasty of governors which ruled in Khurasan from 821 till 873 under the suzerainty of the 'Abbasid caliphs. Their capital was Nishapur. The last ruler, Muhammad b. Tahir (r. 862-873, d. 908), surrendered the capital to the Saffarid Ya'qub b. Layth (r. 867-879). The Tahirids were noted for their high education and literary activities in Arabic.

Tahirids is also the name of a Sunni dynasty of Lahij and Aden, Yemen, which ruled from 1454 to 1517, when the Ottomans conquered Yemen.

Tahmasp I: ruler of the Safawid dynasty; b. 1514, r. 1524-1576. In the wars with the Ottomans, the Persians were on the defensive. In 1541 the Mughal Humayun took refuge with Tahmasp at Isfahan, as did Bayezid, son of the Ottoman Sultan Süleyman II, after his rebellion in 1556. Tahmasp, however, ordered or allowed him to be put to death for 400,000 pieces of gold. The last years of his reign were marked by Özbeg invasions of Khurasan and by a famine followed by the plague. Tahmasp wrote an autobiography, which ends in the year 1561.

Tahmasp II: ruler of the Safawid dynasty; r. 1722-1732. He escaped from Isfahan while it was besieged by the Afghans in 1722, made a treaty with Peter the Great of Russia, and was supported by Nadir Shah Afshar. Nadir Shah defeated the Afghans, and was given the governorship of Khurasan, Sijistan, Kirman and Mazandaran. Tahmasp himself was defeated by the Ottomans in 1731. His treaty of peace was not recognised by Nadir Shah, who imprisoned his sovereign and in 1736 had himself proclaimed ruler of Persia.

al-Ta'i' li-Amr Allah: 'Abbasid caliph; b. 929, r. 974-991, d. 1003. His physical strength seems to have been extraordinary, but political power was in the hands of the Buyids. He was deposed in 991 by the Buyid Baha' al-Dawla.

Ta'if: town in Saudi Arabia, ca. 100 km. to the southeast of Mecca. It is mentioned in the Qur'an. At the eve of the Hijra, this urban centre of the Banu Thaqif was regarded as the second city of western Arabia. It had close relations with Yemen. The Prophet laid siege to Ta'if in 629, but without success. Next year the inhabitants accepted Islam after lengthy negotiations. Members of the Banu Thaqif held high positions under the Umayyads, and consequently were not favoured by the 'Abbasids or the Shi'is. During the centuries, the town was under the jurisdiction of the Meccan Sharifs. Ta'if was taken by the Wahhabis in 1802, in 1813 by the Egyptians. In 1924 it was incorporated into Saudi Arabia.

Ta'izz: town in Yemen, linked by tradition with 'Ali and with the legend of the Seven Sleepers after whom a mosque is named. The Ayyubid Turan-Shah moved his capital from Zabid to Ta'izz. It was also the capital of the Rasulids, one of whem, al-Malik al-Mu'ayyad Dawud (r. 1296-1322), left a library of 100,000 volumes. The Tahirids moved their capital to San'a'. The town was captured by the Ottomans in 1545 and remained in their hands, with some intervals, until 1918, when it came under the rule of the Zaydi Imams.

Tāj Mahal: name of the mausoleum erected at Agra, northern India, by the Mughal Shah Jahan for his wife, Arjumand Banu Begum, of whose title Mumtaz Mahall the name is a corruption. She died in 1631. The design is the work of Ustadh 'Isa, a native either of Turkey or of Shiraz, and the structure was not completed for twenty-two years.

Tajik: name of a people living in Tajikistan, Turkestan and Afghanistan. The word is derived from the Arab tribal name of Tayy, the nearest Arab tribe to the Iranians. It was originally used with the meaning "Arab", afterwards with that of "Iranian" in contrast to "Turk". The Muslim conquerors seem to have been known to the Iranian population of central Asia by the Pahlavi word *Tāčīk*. As, in the view then prevailing, an Iranian convert to Islam became an Arab, the word reached the Turks with the meaning "a man from the land of Islam" and as the majority of the Muslims known to the Turks were Iranians, the word Tajik came to mean Iranian in Turkic.

Takrit: town on the right bank of the Tigris to the North of Samarra in Iraq. It was conquered by the Muslims in 637, and again in 640, but in the early centuries of Islam it remained almost exclusively Christian. It was the birthplace of Saladin.

Tala'i' b. Ruzzik al-Malik al-Salih: Fatimid vizier; 1101-1161. He was vizier to the child caliph al-Fa'iz and his successor al-'Adid. He ransomed his predecessor 'Abbas from the Crusaders in Palestine and had him killed.

Talha b. 'Ubayd Allah: Companion of the Prophet; d. 656. He was one of the earliest converts to Islam and one of the most intimate friends of the Prophet, whom he defended with his body as a shield at the battle of Uhud. He became immensely wealthy and was a candidate to the succession to the caliphate after the death of 'Umar b. al-Khattab in 644. Bitterly disappointed about 'Uthman's election in 644, he joined the party of 'Ali and al-Zubayr b. al-'Awwam, and in 656 was near becoming caliph when 'Ali was proclaimed. With al-Zubayr he fled from Medina to Mecca where he joined the Prophet's favourite wife 'A'isha in her opposition to 'Ali. The three allies went to Basra, but were defeated by 'Ali in the Battle of the Camel, in which Talha and al-Zubayr lost their lives.

Tamerlane (Timur Lang): the Turkic conqueror of Asia; b. 1336, r. 1370-1404. Born near Samarqand in a family that claimed descent from Genghis Khan, he established dominion over Transoxiana during ten years of fighting. On the partition of the Qipčaq in 1375, he took the part of Ghiyath al-Din Toqtamish, khan of the Crimea (r. 1376-1395), who afterwards became his opponent.

His conquest of Persia began in 1380 with the occupation of Khurasan, followed by that of Gurgan, Mazandaran and Sistan. During the years 1386-1387 Fars, Iraq, Luristan and Azerbaijan were conquered, Isfahan being severely punished for rebellion by the massacre of 70,000 inhabitants. Tamerlane is said to have had a lively disputation with Hafiz in Shiraz.

In 1392 he set out on what is known as the "five years' war", the main episodes being the massacre of heretics in the Caspian provinces, the destruction of the Muzaffarid dynasty, and the Mesopotamian campaign. The Jalayirid Ghiyath al-Din Ahmad fled into Syria, where he became a vassal of the Burji Mamluk Barquq. When the latter refused to extradite him, Tamerlane invaded western Asia and took Edessa, Takrit, where he erected a pyramid of skulls, Mardin and Amid (Diyarbakr). Attacked by Toqtamish, he invaded Qipčaq territory in 1395, occupied Moscow for over a year, invaded Georgia and suppressed several risings in Persia.

Convinced that the Muslim rulers of India were much too tolerant, he set out in 1398, crossed the Indus and took Delhi, which was plundered and destroyed. A rebellion which had broken out in Syria, and the invasion of Azerbaijan by the Jalayirid Ahmad, who had returned to Baghdad, made Tamerlane turn westwards again. He ravaged Georgia and took Sivas, Malatya, Aleppo, Hamat, Homs and Baalbek. He defeated the Mamluk Faraj (r. 1399-1412), sacked Damascus, where he met Ibn Khaldun, and in 1401 took Baghdad by surprise. Here he wrought a great massacre.

Meanwhile, the Ottoman Sultan Bayezid I attacked the Byzantine emperor, an ally of Tamerlane's, and molested the Turkish princes of Anatolia. Returning from Georgia, Tamerlane defeated Bayezid at the battle of Ankara in 1402. The Ottoman fell into his hands, but he treated him with respect. In 1404 Tamerlane returned to Samarqand, where he received, among others, Ruy Gonzalez de Clavijo, ambassador of Henry III of Castile, who has left a valuable account of the court of Samarqand.

A new campaign was planned, this time against China, which belonged to Tamerlane's suzerainty. In 1404 he crossed the Oxus on the ice, granted pardon to Toqtamish, but died soon afterwards. He is buried in the Gur-i Mir at Samarqand, which can still be admired. Tamerlane favoured the new Naqshbandiyya order, and on his campaigns he was accompanied by religious men, artists and men of letters.

al-Tamgruti, Abu 'l-Hasan 'Ali: Moroccan author; d. 1594. He left an account of the embassy which he led to the Ottoman sultan Murad III.

Tamim b. Murr: name of an Arab tribe. By the vith c. they appear to be very numerous, but were divided into many different clans who often were opposed to each other. The two Tamimi poets al-Farazdaq and Jarir b. 'Atiyya insulted each other's clans in their poetical duels. The Tamim had relations with the Sasanian kings of Persia, and were in continual rivalry with the 'Amir b. Sa'sa'a. They sent a delegation to Medina in 629 but without becoming converts. During the so-called "apostasy" (A. *ridda*), they were subdued by Khalid b. al-Walid. They settled at first in the camps of Kufa and Basra, and later formed the majority of the Arab population in Khurasan. The most fanatical of the Kharijites were found among these true Bedouins, who were by nature rebels against all authority. On the other hand, some of the most illustrious poets of all old Arabic literature are found among them.

Tamim b. al-Mu'izz: ruler of the Zirids of Ifriqiya; r. 1062-1108. He fought his relatives the Hammadids and tried to prevent the conquest of Sicily by the Normans.

Tamim al-Dari: Companion of the Prophet; d. 660. He came to the Prophet from Hebron after the Tabuk campaign of 630, embraced Islam and settled at Medina. He is said to have been the first narrator of religious stories, among others those of the end of the world and the coming of Antichrist (A. *al-dajjāl*) and the Beast (A. *al-jassāsa*). He is also said to have asked the Prophet to give him the district of Hebron as a fief, although Palestine was still under the Byzantines. The grant allegedly was confirmed by a document, which is said to have been drawn up by 'Ali and to have passed to the Ottoman Sultan Murad III or Murad IV, who put it in their library. The keepers of the sanctuary at Hebron claimed to be descended from Tamim al-Dari.

al-Tanasi, Muhammad b. 'Abd Allah: North African author; d. 1494. He left a history of his patrons, the 'Abd al-Wadids of Tlemcen.

al-Tanawuti: name of many spiritual shaykhs of the Ibadis of North Africa, the best-known of whom is Abu 'Ammar 'Abd al-Kafi; d. ca. 1174. He wrote a *Refutation of all enemies of truth*, in which he tried to show that the Ibadis were distinct from all other schools.

Tanga (Tanka): name of a small silver coin which formed the main currency of the Mongol world from the end of the xivth to the beginning of the xvith c. It was struck by the later Il-Khans, the khans of the Golden Horde, the earlier khans of the Crimea and the early Timurids. It survived as a somewhat heavier silver coin, and as a gold coin, struck till the xixth c. by the Mu'izzi sultans of Delhi, the shahs of Persia, the khans of Khoqand and the amirs of Bukhara. Under Shir Shah Sur it came to be called rupee, and as such it has continued as the monetary unit of India.

Tangier (A. *Ṭanja*): town in Morocco on the Strait of Gibraltar. It was captured by Musa b. Nusayr at the beginning of the viiith c. From 740 till 785 it was in the hands of the Berber Maysara, then in those of the Idrisids. Tangier fell to the Almoravids in 1077, to the Almohads in 1147, and came under Marinid suzerainty only in 1274. The town attracted the covetousness of the Portuguese, who occupied it in 1471 and remained there until 1661. In this year it passed into the hands of the British, who fortified the town but became very unpopular. After a siege of six years, Tangier was captured by the Filali Sharif Isma'il al-Samin (r. 1672-1727) in 1684. Until the xixth c. the governors of the town occasionally threw off the authority of the Sharifs. In 1844 Tangier became French, but under a special status. Tangier was an international city from 1923 till 1956, when it was integrated with the Kingdom of Morocco.

Tanta: town in the Egyptian delta, famous for the tomb and mosque of the most celebrated Muslim saint of Egypt, Ahmad al-Badawi.

al-Tantawi, Muhammad 'Ayyad (al-Marhumi): Egyptian scholar; 1810-1861. He taught at the Azhar mosque and in St. Petersburg, where his large collection of manuscripts is kept.

al-Tanukhi, Abu 'Ali al-Muhassin: Arab writer; 939-994. He left a collection of proverbs, anecdotes and sayings, called *Joy follows Sorrow*, which became very popular and played a part in Persian, Turkish and Jewish literatures.

Taqi-Khan, Mirza (Amir-i Nizam): Prime Minister of Persia; d. 1851. He undertook to remedy the abuses, reorganized the finances and persecuted the Babis.

Tarafa b. ʿAbd al-Bakri: pre-Islamic poet, whose name is found in all the different lists of poets put forward as authors in the collection of pre-Islamic Arabic poems known as *al-Muʿallaqāt*. His description of the camel has become famous.

Taranci: Turkic term for agriculturists, given to the colonists transported by the Chinese government in the middle of the xviiith c. from Kashghar in Sinkiang to the Ili valley. An independent principality arose in 1863 which lasted until 1871 when it was conquered by the Russians.

Tari: name of a gold coin, a quarter-dinar, struck in Sicily by the Fatimids, who introduced it in Syria. It was continued to be struck by the Normans.

Tarif, Abu Zurʿa b. Malik: client of Musa b. Nusayr and leader of the first Muslim forces to reconnoitre Spain in 710. His name survives in the town of Tarifa on the north shore of the Strait of Gibraltar.

Tarim: ancient town in Hadhramaut, formerly a centre of textile industry. It belonged to the Kathiri tribes and had its own silver and copper coins. It is also the name of a fortress on the road from Jizan on the Red Sea to Saʿda.

Tariq b. Ziyad b. ʿAbd Allah: Berber chief and leader of the Muslim forces in the conquest of al-Andalus. He crossed the Straits in 711 and concentrated his troops on a hill which took his name: Jabal Tariq (Gibraltar). The Muslims were victorious in the decisive battle fought with the Goths at the mouth of the Wadi Bekka (Sp. *Rio Barbate*). Tariq was joined by his commander Musa b. Nusayr in 712 and the Muslim forces took Madina Sidonia, Carmona, Seville, Merida, Ecija, Toledo, Córdoba, Archidona and Elvira and soon reached Saragossa and the highlands of Aragon, León, the Asturias and Galicia. In a very short time Muslim Spain had practically attained its extreme geographical limits.

Tarragona (A. *Tarrākūna*): town in northeastern Spain, occupied by the Muslims in 714. It was taken from them by Alfonso IX el Batellador, king of León, in 1220.

Tarsus (A. *Ṭarsūs*): ancient town of Cilicia, Turkey. After the Muslim conquest, it became one of the frontier towns which formed a protective line against the Byzantines. It was restored, populated by Arabs and given a mosque by the ʿAbbasid Caliph Harun al-Rashid in 788. The ʿAbbasid Caliph al-Maʾmun was buried there. It was ruled for a short time by the Tulunids and passed into the hands of the Hamdanids, but in 965 the large, prosperous town was taken by the Byzantines. It fell to the Mamluks of Egypt in 1275.

Tartus: town on the Syrian coast. It was taken by the Muslims in 638. The

Qur'an of the Caliph 'Uthman is said to have been kept at Tartus. The town was taken by the Byzantines in 995, and in 1102 by the Crusaders. Saladin occupied Tartus in 1188, but one of the towers, defended by the Templars, resisted the siege. In 1270 the Templars concluded a treaty with the Mamluk Baybars I, but in 1291 the town was taken by the Mamluk Khalil. After a short Templar interval (1300-1302), Tartus was finally taken by the Mamluk al-Nasir Muhammad. The town was known for its Church of the Virgin.

Tarum (A. *Ṭarm*): district on the Qizil-üzen river in Azerbaijan, which was ruled by the Musafirids from the fortress of Shamiran, and later by the Mongols, the Timurids and the Aq Qoyunlu. Tarum is also the name of a town in Fars.

Tashkent: district and town in Uzbekistan. It was conquered by the Arabs in 751 after Ziyad b. Salih, sent by Abu Muslim, defeated the Chinese on the river Talas. Tashkent was then regarded as the frontier of Islam against the Turks. It was ruled by the Samanids from 819 till 996, when it was ceded to the Turks. After the period of the Chagatay Mongols in the xiiith and xivth c., Tashkent belonged to the Timurid empire (1370-1506), and after 1503 it fell sometimes under the Shaybanids, sometimes under the Kazaks. In 1814 it was annexed by the khanate of Khokand and in 1865 captured by the Russians. The town was replaced as capital by Samarqand in 1924, but became the capital of Uzbekistan in 1930.

Tashköprü-zade: name of a family of Turkish scholars from Tashköprü near Kastamonu. The best-known among them are Mustafa b. Khalil al-Din (1453-1528), who wrote a number of commentaries on law books; Ahmad b. Mustafa (1495-1561), who compiled in Arabic an encyclopaedia of arts and sciences and the biographies of 522 jurists and shaykhs of orders divided into ten classes according to the reigns of ten Ottoman sultans, 'Othman to Süleyman II (xiiith-xvith c.); Kemal al-Din Mehmed b. Ahmed (1552-?), who was a poet and a translator and composed a history of the Ottoman Empire down to Sultan Ahmed I.

Tashriq: Arabic name for the three last days of the pilgrimage to Mecca (11th-13th Dhu 'l-Hijja), during which the pilgrims stay in Mina and have to throw seven stones daily on each of the three piles of stones there.

Tatars (Tartars): at present a Turkic-speaking people living along the central course of the Volga River. With the foundation of the empire of the Kara-khitai, the Turks were driven out of Mongolia and went to the lands of the Tatars who, together with the Turks, moved westwards. Mahmud al-Kash-ghari noted that their language was different from Turkish. The Khwarazm-Shah Tekish campaigned against the Tatar Yusuf in 1218. In the accounts of the Mongol conquests of the xiiith c., the conquerors are everywhere called Tatars, and the peoples of Mongol origin and language had apparently always called themselves thus. Genghis Khan introduced the word Mongol to supplant the word Tatar. In the most western parts of the Mongol empire, the word Mongol never became predominant, although it was also introduced there officially. The people of the Golden Horde are always called Tatar, as are the Turkish-speaking peoples of the Crimea, who also apply the name to themselves. The descendants of the Mongols in Anatolia, leading a nomadic life between Amasya and Kayseri, were called "Black Tatars". Later, in Russia and Western Europe, the name Tatars was applied to all Turkish peoples with the exception of the Ottomans, and then extended to the Mongols and especially to the Manchus in China.

Tawakkul b. Bazzaz: a dervish; xivth c. He wrote the biography of Shaykh Safi al-Din of Ardabil, the ancestor of the Safawid dynasty. The historical and geographical details, important for the history of northwestern Persia, are overlaid with miraculous elements.

Tawfiq Pasha: khedive of Egypt; b. 1852, r. 1879-1892. In 1880 the nationalist revolt of 'Urabi Pasha broke out. The international financial troubles brought about an anti-foreign feeling in the country, which culminated in the massacre of 1882 in Alexandria, followed by the bombardment of that town by the British fleet. The nationalistic movement was crushed by the British, and Tawfiq Pasha had to fall in with their wishes. During his reign also occurred the Mahdist rebellion in the Sudan and the abandonment of that province by Egypt.

al-Tayalisi, Sulayman b. Dawud: collector of traditions; 750-818. He handed down traditions on the authority of well-known traditionists, laid down in a work called *Musnad*. He was an authority for Ahmad b. Hanbal.

Tayy, Banu: tribe in early Arabia of Yemenite origin. With the Banu Azd they joined the migration which tradition connects with the breaking of the dam of Marib and settled to the south of the desert Nafud. They were in friendly relations with the Persians. In 630 they sent an embassy to the Prophet, to which belonged Qays b. Jahdar who is said to have been the first of the Banu Tayy to embrace Islam.

Taza: town and province in north central Morocco to the east of Fez. It was founded as a frontier post against the Almoravid forces by the Almohad 'Abd al-Mu'min in 1133. It was taken by the Marinids in 1216. The citadel was used by several rebels in the xvith and xviith c., and lastly in 1902 by the agitator Abu Hamara. The town was occupied by the French in 1914.

Tébessa: town in Algeria not far from the Tunisian frontier. The Roman town passed into the hands of the Berbers in 597 and into those of the Arabs in 682. It shared the destinies of this part of North Africa, and belonged to the Aghlabids, the Fatimids, the Zirids, the Almohads and the Hafsids. The Turks took it at the end of the xvith c., and the French established a permanent garrison there in 1851.

Teheran (Tehran): capital of Iran since 1786, lying on the southern slopes of the Elburz mountains. The earliest reference dates from 1116. The town grew after the Mongols had destroyed neighbouring Rayy in 1220. In the xvth c. it was governed by Tamerlane's son-in-law, the amir Sulayman-Shah. The prosperity of Teheran dates from Shah Tahmasp I who built a city wall and a bazaar. Under Shah Tahmasp II the town fell to the Afghans, but in 1728 the shah was able to return. Under Afsharid rule, Teheran did not play a role. In 1759 the Zand Muhammad Karim Khan (r. 1750-1779) occupied the town, but finally decided on Shiraz as his capital. It was from Teheran, which became his capital in 1786, that the Qajar Aga Muhammad led the expeditions which united all Persia under his rule. During the xixth c. the tranquillity of the town was disturbed by epidemics and the periodical migrations caused by famine, major events being the persecution of the Babis, and the movement against the concession to the Tobacco Monopoly Corporation in 1891. After the Persian revolution of 1906 the capital became the political and intellectual centre of the country. In 1921 Teheran was occupied by Persian Cossacks under Reza Khan Pahlavi, who was crowned as the first Pahlavi Shah in 1924.

Teke-eli: district in southern Turkey, where many 'Alid risings have taken place. Its two ports Antalya and Alanya were important centres of export. The first passed into the hands of the Ottomans in 1450, the second in 1472.

Teke-oghlu: Turkmen dynasty in south Anatolia, ruling over Teke-eli in the xivth c. In 1392 the Ottoman Sultan Bayezid I incorporated the principality in the Ottoman empire. The last-known ruler, 'Othman Čelebi, was defeated and killed in 1424.

Tekish (Takash) **b. Il-Arslan, 'Ala' al-Din**: a Khwarazm-Shah; r. 1172-1200. In 1187 he took Nishapur, the capital of Khurasan, and in 1194 destroyed the Saljuq rule in Iraq and western Persia by defeating the Great Saljuq Rukn al-Din Tughril III. Rayy and Hamadhan passed into his hands, and in 1196 he defeated an army of the 'Abbasid Caliph al-Nasir li-Din Allah. Fighting against the Karakhitai, he took Bukhara but nevertheless remained their vassal.

Teküder (Tagudar)**, Ahmad**: Il-Khan ruler of Persia; r. 1282-1284. He is said to have been baptised in his youth, but immediately after his accession he was converted to Islam. His approach to the Bahri Mamluk Qalawun al-Alfi did not prevent the Egyptians from occupying two Il-Khanid fortresses.

Tell al-'Amarna: site on the right bank of the Nile in Upper Egypt, north of Asyut, famous for having been the residence of Amenophis IV and for the cuneiform tablets discovered in 1887. Its antiquities seem to have been scarcely known to the Arab writers.

Tell Bashir: fortress in Northern Syria, north of Aleppo. In 1097 it was taken by Count Baldwin of Bourg, Godfrey's brother, and made part of the county of Edessa. In 1151 the Franks were defeated at Tell Bashir by the Great Saljuq of Iraq and western Persia Ghiyath al-Din Mas'ud and his ally Nur al-Din Mahmud Zangi, and the fortress surrendered to Nur al-Din. In 1176 it submitted to Saladin. During the xiiith c. it changed hands several times. The Mamluk Sultan Baybars I is said to have destroyed its fortress.

Tenes (Ténès): coastal town in Algeria, built in 875 on the ruins of the Roman Cartennae by sailors from Muslim Spain. Under the Spanish Umayyads the town was a place of exile, and from the xth c. onwards it passed under the dynasties of central North Africa: the Fatimids, the Sanhaja, the Maghrawa, the Almoravids and the Almohads. It then came in the hands of the Ziyanids of Tlemcen, and in the second half of the xvth c. it formed a little independent principality. In the early xvith c. the Turkish corsair and admiral Khayr al-Din Pasha established Turkish power there. In 1843 the inhabitants submitted to the French.

Ternate: small volcanic island, west of Halmahera in the eastern part of the Malay Archipelago. According to tradition, Islam was introduced in the xvth c.

Tétouan (A. *Tiṭṭāwīn*): town in northern Morocco. When the empire of Idris II was partitioned, Tétouan fell to his son al-Qasim, who ruled it from Tangier. An important fortress was constructed in 1286 by the Marinid Abu Ya'qub Yusuf (r. 1286-1307), around which a town was built by his successor Abu Thabit 'Amir (r. 1307-1308). In 1400 the town was destroyed by Henry III, king of Castile. Abu 'l-Hasan al-Mandari, one of the defenders of Granada against Ferdinand of Castile, built a fortress after 1492. In the xvith c. Tétouan was a town of trade, the supremacy being in the hands of the al-Naqsis family, which was exterminated by the Filali Sharif Isma'il (r. 1672-1727). At the end of the Spanish-Moorish war of 1859-1860, Tétouan was captured by the Spanish, who made it the capital of their protectorate.

Tewfiq Fikret (Mehmed Tewfiq; Tewfiq Nazmi): Ottoman Turkish poet and metricist; 1867-1915. In 1896 he published his principal work *The Broken Lute*, followed by *Mist*, a vigorous poem directed against the despotic rule of Sultan Abdülhamid II. He created a new language of poetry.

Tewfiq Mehmed (Tewfiq Nazmi): Ottoman Turkish author; 1843-1893. He owes his reputation to his literary activities in the field of anecdote.

al-Tha'alibi, 'Abd al-Rahman b. Muhammad al-Ja'fari: theologian from Algiers; 1386-1468. His principal work is a commentary on the Qur'an.

al-Tha'alibi, Abu Mansur 'Abd al-Malik: compiler in the fields of poetry, lexicography and rhetoric; 961-1038. His most famous and, for posterity most important, work is an anthology of the poets of his own and the preceding generation, arranged under countries. Another part of his compilations deals with entertaining literature and proverbs. Finally there are his philological works, the most famous of them being a work on Arabic synonyms.

al-Tha'alibi, Abu Mansur al-Husayn al-Marghani: Arab historian; xith c. He wrote a history of mankind from Adam down to the period of the Ghaznawid Mahmud b. Sebüktigin. In the introduction he gives the sources used by Firdawsi for his *Shāh-name*.

Thabit b. Qurra: mathematician, physician and philosopher from Harran; 836-901. The 'Abbasid Caliph al-Mu'tadid bi-'llah appointed him as one of his astronomers at Baghdad. The greater part of his life was spent in translating and expounding Greek mathematicians, in composing his own mathematical works, in philosophical studies and in the practice of medicine. He wrote in Syriac on the doctrine and worship of the Sabaeans, his co-religionists of Harran.

Thabit ('Ala' al-Din): Ottoman poet from Bosnia; ca. 1650-1712. His Turkish vocabulary is very rich, expecially for idioms.

Thailand: except for Patani, Islam does not seem to have made early converts in the country. The Muslims are immigrants from Malaysia, Java, Afghanistan and India, and now form an estimated 3% of the population.

al-Tha'labi, Ahmad b. Muhammad al-Nisaburi: theologian and Qur'an exegist; xith c. His commentary on the Qur'an was once widely used. His *History of the prophets* is quite popular.

Thamud, Banu: an old Arab people who had disappeared some time before the coming of the Prophet. Their fate is mentioned in the Qur'an as a warning.

Thanisari, Mawlana (Ahmad): learned and pious Sufi from Delhi; d. 1417. He met Tamerlane and wrote the so-called *Qaṣīda Dāliyya* which became very famous.

Thaqif, Banu: tribe in the district of Ta'if on the eve of the rising of Islam. The common ancestor is said to have been Qusayy, Thaqif being a surname. A malicious tradition has identified him with Abu Righal, the traitor who guided Abraha's Abyssinian army to Mecca, and whose tomb on the road from Ta'if to Mecca used to be stoned.

Thousand-and-One Nights (A. *alf layla wa-layla*): title of the most famous Arabian collection of fairy-tales. There are stories of Arab caliphs and viziers, of sultans, of King Solomo, of the kings of ancient Persia and of Alexander the Great. Some of the material was borrowed from India, but there are also stories in which guns, coffee and tobacco are mentioned.

Thumama b. Ashras (Abu Ma'an al-Numayri): Arab theologian; ixth c. He was a representative of the liberal movement under the early 'Abbasids and sharply criticized conservative views.

Thüreyya, Mehmed: Ottoman biographer; d. 1909. He has earned fame as the compiler of an Ottoman Dictionary of National Biography.

Tiberias (A. *Ṭabariyya*): town on the western side of the lake of Tiberias (Sea of Galilee). It surrendered to the Muslims in 635, broke the agreement with them during the caliphate of 'Uthman but was conquered again by 'Amr b. al-'As and yielded on the old terms. A new chapter of its history began during the Crusades. While in the possession of Raymond of Tripoli, it was captured by Saladin in 1187. In 1240 Tiberias was taken by Odo of Montbelliard, but in 1247 it came into the hands of the Khwarazm-Shahs and remained

Muslim right down to the end of Turkish rule. In 1560 the Ottoman Sultan Süleyman II granted the town to Joseph Nasi, duke of Naxos, a Jewish statesman and financier. In 1759 and in 1837 it suffered much from earthquakes, and in 1799 was occupied for a short time by Bonaparte's troops. Tiberias is described by Arab geographers and by the Persian traveller Nasir-i Khusraw who visited it in 1047. The hot medicinal baths played an important part in the life of the town.

Tibet (A. *Tubbat/Tabbut*): in the Chinese annals Arabs are often mentioned as allies of the Tibetans and vice versa, while Arab sources only refer to contacts between Tibet and the caliphs during the viith-ixth c. Probably the first campaign of the Muslims against Tibet was that of 1205 by Muhammad Bakhtiyar Khalji, a general of the Ghurid Mu'izz al-Din Muhammad (r. 1173-1206). After the final triumph of Islam in central Asia and northern India in the xvth c., Tibet, the so-called Little Tibet or Baltistan in particular, was invaded by Muslim rulers during the xvith c. Islam then became a political force in Little Tibet. In 1841 it came under the suzerainty of Kashmir.

al-Tibrizi, Abu Zakariya' Yahya: celebrated Arab philologist from Tabriz; 1030-1109. He wrote commentaries on the *Hamāsa* of Abu Tammam.

Tibrizi (Shams-i Tibrizi): Sufi from Tabriz; d. 1245 (?). He was the spiritual guide of Jalal al-Din Rumi.

Tibu (Tubu): Berber-speaking people of the eastern and central Sahara, who are very distinct from the Sudanese on the one side, and from the Arabs and Berbers on the other. The name has been given by Europeans to a great variety of peoples living beteen the Libyan desert on the east, the Haggar on the west, Fazzan in the north and Chad in the south. It is particularly applied to the natives of Tibesti. They are Muslims of recent date, influenced by the Sanusiyya order and seem to have played a fairly important role in the history of Kanem.

al-Tifashi, Shihab al-Din: author of one of the best-known works on jewels; d. 1253. He describes 25 kinds according to their origin, provenance, natural and magical properties, defects and merits, price and appreciation of particular varieties.

Tiflis (Tbilisi): capital of Georgia. Having conquered Armenia, Habib b. Maslama took Tiflis in 645 and the inhabitants were soon converted to Islam. In the viiith c. the town was attacked by the Khazar Turks, and conquered in 852 by the Turkish military leader Bugha al-Kabir al-Sharabi. During the xth c. Tiflis was dominated by the Musafirids. In 1121, during the reign of the Great Saljuq Mahmud II b. Muhammad, it was taken by the Christian king of Georgia, Dawid II the Restorer. In 1226 the town was occupied by the last Khwarazm-Shah Jalal al-Din Mingburnu, but conquered by the Mongols in 1235. However, the Georgian kings continued to rule under the patronage of the Mongols and Il-Khans. In 1386 Tiflis was taken by Tamerlane, and again in 1400. In 1453 the town surrendered to the Aq Qoyunlu Uzun Hasan, in

1501 to the Safawid Isma'il I, and in 1540 again to the Safawid Tahmasp I. In 1578 Tiflis was taken by the Ottomans, who ruled there until 1603, when it was retaken by the Safawid Shah 'Abbas I, during whose reign the worst misfortunes fell upon Georgia. Yet the Georgian rulers in general followed a pro-Persian policy, some of them becoming converts to Islam. From 1723 till 1734 Tiflis was again in the hands of the Ottomans as a result of the Russo-Persian Treaty. In 1734 the town passed into the hands of Nadir Shah Afshar, while still serving the Safawid Tahmasp II. After Nadir Shah's death, there was some respite for Georgia. After the Qajar Aga Muhammad had pillaged Tiflis in 1795, Georgia was annexed by Russia in 1801. In 1918 three republics were formed in Transcaucasia: Georgia, Armenia and Azerbaijan, Tiflis becoming the capital of Georgia. German troops appeared in the town, to be replaced by British troops after the armistice. In 1921 Georgia, including Tiflis, passed to the Soviet Union.

Tigris (A. *Dijla*): the river rises in the southern slopes of the main Taurus in Turkey, is joined in Iraq by the Greater Zab below Mosul and by the Lesser Zab some 100 km. to the south, and is drained, together with the Euphrates, into the Persian Gulf by the Shatt al-'Arab.

Tihama: narrow strip of low land along the coast which runs from the Sinai Peninsula along the west and south side of Saudi Arabia, lying between the mountains to the east and the Red Sea. Mecca is usually included in the Tihama.

al-Tijani, Abu Muhammad 'Abd Allah: Arab author of Tunis; xivth c. He wrote an account of his travels through North Africa and a compendium on love and marriage.

Tijaniyya: name of an order in Algeria founded by Abu 'l-'Abbas Ahmad al-Tijani; 1737-1815. The reputation of the order was vastly increased when they held out for eight months in 1838 against amir 'Abd al-Qadir b. Muhyi 'l-Din (r. 1832-1847).

al-Tilimsani: the Arabic word means "the man from Tlemcen". Many Arabic scholars are known by this name, among them Abu Ishaq Ibrahim: a jurist; 1212-1291. Among other subjects, he wrote on the law of inheritance; 'Afif al-Din Sulayman: a Sufi; 1219-1291. He was a pious man of affable manners, but was accused of being an adherent of the Nusayris. He was an ardent follower of Ibn al-'Arabi and left several works; Shams al-Din Muhammad, son of 'Afif al-Din; 1263-1289. He wrote short amatory poems.

Timar: term used in Ottoman Turkey to denote a kind of fief, the possession of which entailed upon the feudatory the obligation to go mounted to war and to supply soldiers or sailors in numbers proportionate to the revenues of the appanage.

Timbuktu (Tombouctou): town in Mali. It was founded in the xith c. by the Maghsharen Touareg. The first dynasty, which came from Mali, reigned there from 1336-1433. When Ibn Battuta visited the town in 1352, the people were Muslim. The Maghsharen Touareg then ruled for 40 years and were followed by the Songhai dynasty, founded by Sunni 'Ali (r. 1468-1492), who is described as a libertine. The Songhai, whose most prominent ruler was al-Hadi Muhammad, raised the town to a high degree of prosperity. They ruled until 1528, when the town came under Moroccan domination, which lasted until 1750. Timbuktu was an important stage on the trans-Saharan caravan route and a centre of Islamic culture. When the trade with Florence was cut off after the xvith c., the town was talked of as mysterious and inaccessible, but said to be very beautiful and rich. The Touareg regained the town in 1792, the Fulani took it in 1827, followed by the Tukulor. In 1893 Timbuktu was incorporated in the French colonial system. The best-known author of Timbuktu is Ahmad Baba (d. 1626), who compiled a biographical dictionary.

Timurids: the term is sometimes used for all the descendants of Tamerlane, but it means more specifically the princes of his family who ruled in Persia and central Asia in the xvth c. Tamerlane's sons and grandsons ruled in two great kingdoms, one in western Persia and Iraq, the other in Khurasan and Transoxiana. Under their rule the eastern Islamic world, notwithstanding many political troubles, was a splendid cultural unity. The so-called Timurid art covers the fields of architecture, music, miniature painting in the schools of Harat, Shiraz and Tabriz, leatherwork, bookbinding and calligraphy. Some of the princes were artists and scholars themselves, like Ulugh Beg, an astronomer in his own right; Ghiyath al-Din Baysunghur (d. 1433), the son of Shahrukh Mirza, a calligrapher of the first rank; and Husayn Bayqara (r. 1470-1506), an artist and poet. All rulers were great patrons of letters and science. Zahir al-Din Babur, the last Timurid ruler of Farghana, survived the conquest of the dynasty by the Shaybanids in 1506 and founded in 1526 the line of the Mughal emperors in India.

Timurtash, Husam al-Din: prince of the Artuqid dynasty which ruled in Mardin and Mayyafariqin; b. 1104, r. 1122-1152. His great opponent was Imad al-Din b. Aq Sunqur Zangi, although they joined in the siege of Diyarbakr in 1132.

Timurtash Pasha: Ottoman general and vizier; d. 1405. In 1375 he became governor of Rumeli and led many campaigns in the European part of the Ottoman empire. In 1386 it was his intervention which brought the Ottoman victory over the Ilek-Khan 'Ala' al-Din b. Khalil (r. 1381-1403) in the plain of Konya. In the battle of Ankara of 1402 he fell into the hands of Tamerlane, but was released.

Tipu Sultan: ruler of Mysore, western India; b. 1753, r. 1783-1799. Having first concluded peace with the British, he became their bitter enemy. In 1792 Lord Cornwallis attacked Seringapatam, Tipu's capital, and compelled him to submit. He was in communication with the French at Pondicherry in southern India and was admitted as a citizen of the French Republic under the title of "Citizen Tipu". He was killed in 1799 fighting against the British who again attacked his capital.

Tirana: capital of Albania. The town was founded about 1600 by the Turkish general Barqin-zade Süleyman Pasha. The story that he called the place after the Persian capital Teheran in memory of his Persian campaigns is not worthy of credence, because "il borgo di Tirana" is already mentioned as early as 1572. The region belonged to the Toptan family from Krujë, whose best-known member is Qaplan Ahmed Pasha (ca. 1800).

al-Tirimmah b. Hakim al-Ta'i: celebrated poet of the first c. of Islam. He was an opponent of the poet al-Farazdaq.

Tirmidh (Termez): town in Uzbekistan, on the north bank of the Oxus river. From 689 till 704 it was in the hands of Musa b. 'Abd Allah b. Khazim, who had thrown off Umayyad authority. In the xith c. it was ruled by the Ghaznawids and passed into the hands of the Karakhitai in the xiith c. In 1205 it was taken by the Ghurids, in 1206 by the Khwarazm-Shah 'Ala' al-Din Muhammad (r. 1200-1220) and in 1220 by the Mongols who destroyed the town, which was later rebuilt. From the xvith c. Tirmidh belonged to the kingdom of the Özbegs, and in the xviith c. it was occupied by Sa'adat Khan, prince Awrangzib's general.

al-Tirmidhi, Abu 'Abd Allah (al-Hakim): Sunni theologian from Khurasan, a jurist of the Hanafi school of law, and a mystic; d. 898.

al-Tirmidhi, Abu 'Isa Muhammad: author of one of the canonical collections of traditions; d. 892. He travelled widely in order to collect traditions, which are brought together in the work which made him famous. Nearly one half is devoted to such subjects as dogmatic theology, popular beliefs, devotion, manners and education, and hagiology.

Tirmidhi, Sayyid Burhan al-Din: a Sufi; xiiith c. He was the teacher of Jalal al-Din Rumi.

Tlemcen (A. *Tilimsān*): town in northwestern Algeria. Sunni Islam was definitively established in the region at the time of the founder of the Idrisid dynasty Idris I, who built a mosque in 790. The Almoravid Yusuf b. Tashufin founded the military settlement named Tagrart, which merged with the existing town. Under the Almoravids, the Great Mosque and the citadel (Méchouar) were built and Tlemcen was a centre of theological and legal studies. In 1197, under the Almohads, the mystic Abu Madyan of al-Andalus was buried at Tlemcen and became the patron saint of the town. The rising of the Zanata tribes under Yaghmurasan b. Zayyan in 1236 led to the foundation of the independent 'Abd al-Wadids, under whom Tlemcen became a centre of trade. During the xiiith and xivth c. it was continuously attacked by the Marinids. In 1555 Salah Re'is, the Turkish pasha of Algiers, occupied Tlemcen, which entered upon a period of decay. The Qulughlis, descendants of Turks and Arab women, formed an important ethnical element in the town. The French entered Tlemcen in 1836 and secured it in 1842. In

1962 the town served as a headquarters for the nationalist leader Ahmad Ben Bella.

Toledo (A. *Ṭulayṭula*): town in south central Spain. It was conquered by Tariq b. Ziyad in 714. After the establishment of the Umayyad amirate of Córdoba, Toledo became a hotbed of sedition, the greater part of the inhabitants remaining Mozarabs. In 797 their spirit of rebellion was fanned by the poet Ghirbib. In 807 a renegade from Huesca, called 'Amrus, was appointed governor of Toledo by al-Hakam I, the Umayyad amir of Córdoba. He had the notables of the town killed on what became known as "the day of the ditch", but rebellion continued. In 854 the Toledans even defeated the troops sent by the Umayyad amir Muhammad I and made an alliance with Ordoño I, king of León, but suffered a crushing defeat. Toledo was finally subjected by the Umayyad 'Abd al-Rahman III in 932. During the period of troubles which ended in the fall of the caliphate of Córdoba, Toledo no longer played a part. The town became the capital of the Dhu 'l-Nunids, who brought prosperity, especially under Yahya al-Ma'mun (r. 1043-1075). Under his successor Yahya al-Qadir, Alfonso VI, the king of Castile and León, took the town in 1085. More than anything else, the fall of Toledo determined the invasion of Spain by the Almoravids in 1086. After this date, the town never again passed into Muslim hands, although it remained one of the great objectives of their armies.

Toqtamish, Ghiyath al-Din: khan of the Golden Horde; r. 1376-1395, d. 1406. Before his accession to the throne, he went to Tamerlane at Samarqand, who lent him his support against his brothers. In 1381 he sacked and destroyed Moscow, imposing another century of Tatar rule. His first hostile act against Tamerlane dates from 1383, when he had coins struck in his own name in Khwarazm, and in 1386 he sent an army against Tabriz, which was laid waste in a terrible fashion. The next year he invaded Azerbaijan, but Tamerlane continued to show much restraint. In this year 1387 Toqtamish invaded the heart of Tamerlane's empire, reached the Oxus and besieged Bukhara. In 1391 Tamerlane reacted, defeated the khan at Qunduzča, advanced as far as the Volga but did not attack the kingdom of the Golden Horde. In 1393 Tamerlane had sent a mission to Egypt but the Mamluk Sultan Barquq had his ambassador murdered. In 1394 and 1395 Toqtamish sent missions to Egypt to form an alliance against Tamerlane. From Mahmudabad the latter again sent an envoy to Toqtamish, but the reply proved unsatisfactory. In 1395 the khan was defeated on the Terek river in Georgia, and Tamerlane sacked Azov, Astrakhan and Saray. The next year he went back to Azerbaijan, and Toqtamish returned to his throne, but he had to flee to the prince of Lithuania. He sent the assurance of his penitence and an appeal for pardon. Tamerlane promised to come to the land of the Golden Horde after his campaign against China and to restore his throne to Toqtamish. But Tamerlane died in 1404, and Toqtamish in 1406.

Topal 'Othman Pasha: Ottoman Grand Vizier; 1692-1733. In 1733 he defeated Nadir Shah Afshar and drove him out of Baghdad. Some time later Topal was severely defeated and lost his life in the battle.

Topal 'Othman Pasha: Ottoman governor of Bosnia; 1804-1874. He resided at Sarajevo where he built the so-called Cengič villa, a splendid country house. His governorship from 1861 till 1869 may be described as a golden period in the history of Bosnia under the Ottomans. He deprived the powerful Begs of their influence, placed Bosnian notables in public offices, raised the status of artisans and small traders, and protected the common people. He devoted special attention to education, endowed the mosque of Ghazi Khosrew with a splendid library and instituted printing-works.

Torah (A. *Tawrāt*): the term is used in the Qur'an to denote a holy scripture revealed after the time of Abraham and Jacob and afterwards confirmed by Jesus. The *Tawrāt* also contains a prophecy of the coming of the Prophet. It is frequently mentioned in Tradition.

Tortosa (A. *Ṭurṭūsha*): town in northeastern Spain. In 809 Tortosa was taken by Louis the Fair, who held it for a short time. His army was then defeated by the Spanish Umayyad 'Abd al-Rahman II during the reign of his father al-Hakam I. In 945 the Spanish Umayyad 'Abd al-Rahman III ordered wharves to be built, and a Great Mosque was constructed in 956. As a frontier town of the caliphate of Córdoba, it was a place of exile from the Córdoban court. On the formation of the small kingdoms after the dismemberment of the Umayyad caliphate, Tortosa became the capital of the little principality of the 'Amirid "Slavs", the best known of whom is a certain Nabil, who in 1060 handed the town over to the ruler of Saragossa, al-Muqtadir Ibn Hud. It was captured in 1148 by Raymond Berenger IV, count of Barcelona. Tortosa seems to have been a brilliant centre of Muslim studies.

Touareg (Tuareg): Berber-speaking pastoralists, inhabiting an area ranging from Algeria and Libya to northern Nigeria and from Fazzan to Timbuktu. They are Muslim, but retain a matriarchal organization and an unusual degree of female freedom.

Tozeur (A. *Tūzer*): town and oasis in southern Tunisia, known for its palm trees. It fell to the Arabs at the end of the viith c. During the following centuries, the inhabitants of Tozeur endeavoured, often successfully, to remain virtually independent.

Trabzon (Trebizond; T. *Tarabzun*): town in northeastern Turkey on the southeastern shore of the Black Sea. After the Arab conquest had deprived Byzantium of large parts of Armenia, Trabzon became an important trading port between the lands of Rum and the northern parts of the Muslim empire. After the Saljuq conquest of Anatolia, the port became isolated until 1204, when the empire of the Comneni was founded which came under the suzerainty of the Rum Saljuq Qayqubad I. Trabzon was spared the Mongol invasion and became the corridor to Anatolia, through which ran the trade-route to the Far East which the Mongols had opened. Trade was in the hands of the Venetians and especially of the Genoese. In the xivth c. the Saljuqs were replaced by Turkmen states such as the Isfendiyar-oghullari, the Dhu 'l-Qadr and the Aq Qoyunlu. The xvth c. saw the decline of the Genoese and the rise of the Venetians, and in 1460 the port capitulated to the Ottoman Sultan Mehemmed II. After that the town never again became important. In 1916 it was occupied by the Russians for two years.

Trade (A. *tijāra*): the Prophet was favourably disposed to trade, but he raised a warning voice against the evils which at Mecca were associated with it. The Qur'an emphasizes that trade had to be conducted according to law and justice, that it should not detain believers from the worship of God and from performing the *ṣalāt* and that it was prohibited during the Friday service. It was however permitted during the pilgrimage. Tradition, on the whole also well disposed to trade, vigorously attacks speculation and other dishonest dealings, and forbids a whole series of branches of business and practices on account of the element of uncertainty which they imply. The fundamental principles of Muslim commercial ethics have found their classical expression in Abu Hamid al-Ghazali's *Revival of the Religious Sciences*.

Tradition (A. *al-ḥadīth*): the Arabic term denotes the account of what the Prophet said or did, or of his tacit approval of something said or done in his presence. Traditions from the Prophet, and sometimes from Companions or Successors, are also indicated with the term "news, information" (A. *khabar*). Traditions from the Companions and Successors are also referred to with the term "traces" (A. *athar*, pl. *āthār*). After a lengthy process, Tradition came to be considered as an authoritative source of guidance, second only to the Qur'an itself. Books of traditions were compiled in the viiith c. They had two necessary features: the chain of authorities (A. *isnād*) going back to the source of the tradition, and the text (A. *matn*) of the tradition in question. The first to arrange traditions according to subject matters was Malik b. Anas. Among the Sunnis, the works by al-Bukhari, Muslim b. al-Hajjaj, Ibn Maja, Abu Dawud al-Sijistani, Abu 'Isa Muhammad al-Tirmidhi and al-Nasa'i, the so-called "Six Books", became the most authoritative, the first two in particular. The Shi'is have books of their own, accepting only traditions traced through 'Ali's family. The most authoritative Shi'i works are those of al-Kulayni, Ibn Babawayhi and Muhammad b. al-Hasan al-Tusi. Traditions are divided into sound, good, weak or infirm, each of these categories having its own sub-divisions.

Transoxiana (Transoxania) (A. *mā warā' al-nahr*): the Arabic term means "the land which lies beyond the river", i.e. beyond the Oxus. It is used in contrast to "the lands lying this side of the river (Oxus)" (A. *mā dūn al-nahr*), a term which often, but not always, indicates Khurasan, the latter being not infrequently used vaguely to designate all the eastern Islamic lands beyond western Persia.

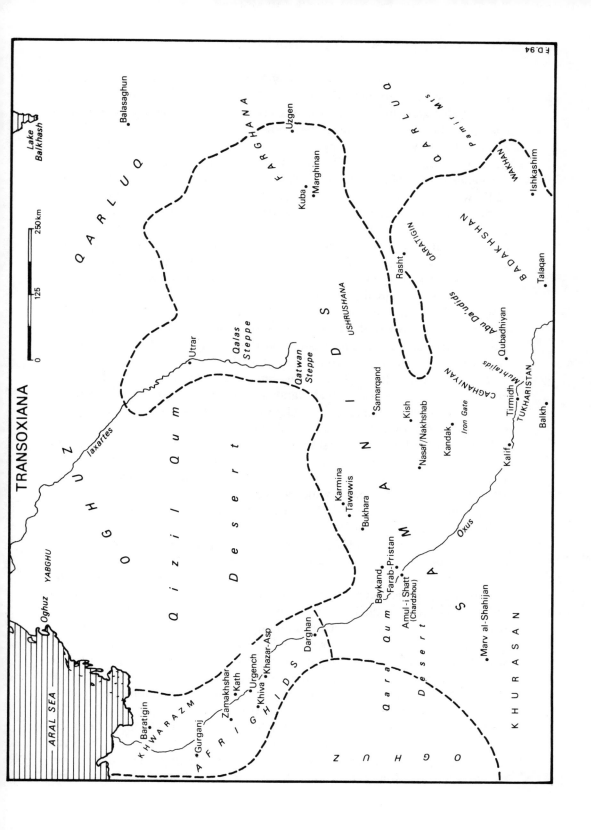

F.D.94

TRANSOXIANA

Lake Balkhash

ARAL SEA

250 km
125
0

• Balasaghun

QARLUQ

FARGHANA

Uzgen •

• Marghinan

Kuba •

QARATIGIN

Rasht •

QARLUQ

Pamirs

WAKHAN

• Ishkashim

BADAKHSHAN

• Talaqan

Abu Da'udids

Qubadhiyan •

USHRUSHANA

QALAS Steppe

Qatwan Steppe

Utrar •

OGHUZ

Iaxartes

YABGHU

Qizil Qum Desert

D

Samarqand •

• Kish

Nasaf/Nakhshab •

Kandak •

Iron Gate

CHAGHANIYAN

Muhtajids

Tirmidh •

TUKHARISTAN

Balkh •

Kalif •

N

A

Karmina •

• Tawawis

• Bukhara

Oxus

M

A

S

Baykand •

Farab-Pristan •

Amul-i Shatt
(Chardzhou) •

Oghuz

• Marv al-Shahijan

KHURASAN

Qara Qum Desert

Darghan •

AFRIGHIDS

KHWARAZM

• Baratigin

• Gurganj

Zamakhshar •

Kath •

Urgench •

Khiva •
Khazar-Asp •

Tripoli (A. *Ṭarābulus al-Gharb* = Western Tripoli): town in northwestern Libya on the Mediterranean coast. It was first reached by the Muslims in 642 and by 665 a garrison was permanently established there. Throughout the ixth and xth c. the town was troubled by the political-religious revolt of the Ibadis. Aghlabid rule was followed by that of the Zirids of Ifriqiya and that of the Banu Khazrun Berbers (1000-1145). Between 1146 and 1158 Tripoli was in the hands of the Normans, after which it was held by the Almohads until 1247, who were followed by the Hafsids until 1324. In 1354, during the rule of the almost autonomous dynasty of the Banu Thabit (or 'Ammar) Berbers which lasted until 1400, Tripoli was sacked by the Genoese Filippo Doria. In the xvth c. it was almost independent under its own rulers until the Spanish conquest in 1510. The Knights of Malta held the town from 1530 to 1551, when it was taken by Khoja Sinan Pasha (d. 1596) and passed under Ottoman suzerainty. Spain and the Order of Malta tried many times to take Tripoli from the Turks. A domineering oligarchy was developed by the Janissaries and marriages between the Turks and Arab women led to the ethnic group of the so-called Qulughlis. Under Mehmed Pasha Saqizli (1632-1649) and his son-in-law 'Othman Pasha (1649-1669), both from Chios, the corsair navy of Tripoli was very active, which led to English and French bombardments in 1676 and 1685. In 1711 Ahmad Qaramanli founded a dynasty which ruled, with the consent of Istanbul, until 1835. In 1784-1785 Tripoli was hit by a terrible famine and by the plague. Capitulations were renewed on England's behalf, and established for the first time on behalf of the Kingdom of Sardinia in 1816. In 1835 direct Turkish rule was re-established, which lasted until 1911, when Italian troops landed there. From 1943 until Libya's independence in 1951 the town was occupied by the British.

Tripoli (A. *Ṭarābulus al-Shām* = Eastern Tripoli): town and port in north Lebanon. During the caliphate of 'Uthman, the town was taken by Sufyan b. Mujib al-Azdi after the inhabitants had left on Byzantine ships. Mu'awiya I, then governor of Syria, made a considerable number of Jews settle there to populate the empty town. A county of Tripoli was created in the Crusading period and given to Raymond of Saint-Gilles, count of Toulouse, who began the siege in 1101 but died in 1105 without having attained his goal. The town was conquered in 1109. It remained an important base for the Crusaders until 1289, when it surrendered to the Mamluk Sultan Qalawun al-Alfi. The town was destroyed, and a new Tripoli built on the so-called Pilgrims' Hill. The town was incorporated into the State of Greater Lebanon in 1920, was occupied by the British and Free French during World War II, and became part of the independent Republic of Lebanon in 1943.

Tudela (A. *Tuṭīla*): little town in Spain on the right bank of the Ebro, ca. 75 km to the northwest of Saragossa. Founded under the Spanish Umayyad amir al-Hakam I, it was the headquarters of rebel Muslim leaders, and the fief of Musa b. Musa Ibn Qasi, who declared war on the Spanish Umayyad amir

'Abd al-Rahman II. Its name is connected with the famous Jewish traveller Benjamin of Tudela (xiith c.).

Tughluqids: dynasty which ruled in northern India from 1320 till 1413. It was founded by Ghiyath al-Din Tughluq Shah I.

Tughra: Turkish term for the cipher or calligraphic emblem of the Oghuz, then of the Saljuqs and finally of the Ottoman sultans. In course of time it became the coat of arms or escutcheon of the state, and was placed by the rulers not only on rescripts and firmans but on title-deeds of property, coins, official monuments and ships-of-war. In more modern times it is found on documents of identification, passports, postage stamps, sheets of stamped paper and goldsmith's marks. The official use ceased in Turkey with the dethronement of the last Ottoman Sultan Abdülmecid II in 1922.

al-Tughra'i, Mu'ayyid al-Din: Arab poet, calligrapher and alchemist from Isfahan; 1061-ca. 1121. He is known for a poem in which he complains about the evil times in which he lived. It was perhaps the earliest specimen of Arabic poetry accessible to wider circles in Europe.

Tughril I (Tughril Beg), **Rukn al-Dunya wa 'l-Din**: the first Great Saljuq ruler of Iraq and Persia; r. 1038-1063. He entered Nishapur in 1038 at the request of the 'Abbasid Caliph al-Qa'im bi-Amr Allah, who had complained about the robberies of the Oghuz, but he was driven out of the town by the Ghaznawids. After his defeat at Dandanqan in 1040, the Ghaznawid Mas'ud I was forced to withdraw from Khurasan and leave this province to the Saljuqs. Tughril, who had a certain pre-eminence among the Saljuqs, submitted the Ziyarids of Tabaristan and Gurgan in 1041, conquered Khwarazm and Rayy, and defeated the Buyid Majd al-Dawla, who had still been holding out in the stronghold of Tabaraq. The Buyid Abu Kalijar al-Marzuban made peace with the Saljuqs in 1047. The Marwanids of Diyarbakr submitted to Tughril, and in 1051 he took Isfahan, which he made into his residence. Tabriz and Ganja in Azerbaijan submitted in 1054. Meanwhile, the Buyid Khusraw-Firuz had made secret arrangements at Baghdad with the Fatimids of Egypt, and the 'Abbasid caliph invited Tughril to march against the capital. Tughril entered Baghdad in 1055 and brought an end to Buyid rule. While he was away in 1058 to fight the Saljuq Ibrahim Inal, who had joined the pro-Fatimid policy of al-Basasiri, the military commander of Baghdad, the latter re-entered the capital, upon which the caliph left the city. Tughril returned in 1059, brought the caliph back and defeated al-Basasiri.

Tughril II b. Muhammad, Rukn al-Din: Great Saljuq ruler in Iraq and western Persia; b. 1109, r. 1132-1134. He plotted against his brother the Great Saljuq Mahmud II and sought refuge with the Great Saljuq Sanjar who installed Tughril as sultan in 1132. The latter however was not a match for his brother Mas'ud.

Tughril III b. Arslan, Rukn al-Din: last of the Great Saljuqs in Iraq and western Persia; b. 1168, r. 1175-1194. He made arrangements with a number of Turkish amirs and seized the Saljuq capital Hamadhan. In 1188 he defeated an army sent from Baghdad, led by the vizier Ibn Yunus, but was taken prisoner by the Ildeñizid Qizil Arslan ʿUthman (r. 1186-1191) of Azerbaijan. Tughril III fell in a battle against the Khwarazm-Shah Tekish.

Tughril-Shah b. Qilij Arslan II: Rum Saljuq; d. 1225. When his father divided his kingdom among his many sons, Tughril-Shah received the town of Elbistan. In 1200 his brother Rukn al-Din Sulayman II conquered Erzurum, which he handed over to Tughril-Shah. He was a vassal of the Georgian king Georgi III Lasha in Tiflis.

Tughtigin b. ʿAbd Allah, Amin al-Dawla: founder of the Burid dynasty; r. 1104-1128. He became actual ruler after the death of the Saljuq Duqaq (r. 1095-1104), thrusting aside the latter's brother Ertash, who entered into negotiations with king Baldwin I of Jerusalem. He is described by historians as an able and just ruler, and as one of most dreaded enemies of the Christians.

Tujibids (A. *Banu Tujib*): name of an Arab family, who ruled in Saragossa between 1019-1029. They became divided into the Banu Hisham of Saragossa and the Banu Sumadih of Almería.

Tukulor (Toucouleur) (A. *Takrūr*): Muslim theocracy of the xixth c. in the western Sudan. The name is a corruption of the local Tokoror or Tokolor and denotes, strictly speaking, the Futa of Senegal. Islam penetrated to the Futa ca. 1050 under the influence of the Almoravid movement, and Tukulor became synonymous with Muslim.

The theocratic Tukulor state was founded by Sulayman Bal, who succeeded in casting off Futa suzerainty in 1775. In 1841 a treaty of friendship was signed with France. The state lasted until 1890, when it was annexed to the French colony of Senegal.

In 1801 the Tukulor Usman dan Fodio founded the state of Sokoto. Another Tukulor state was founded by al-Hajj ʿUmar Tal. It was destroyed by the French in 1893.

Tulayha b. Khuwaylid b. Nawfal: one of the tribal leaders who headed the so-called "apostasy" (A. *ridda*) under Caliph Abu Bakr after the Bedouin tribes had renounced their personal allegiance to the Prophet. Tulayha was defeated in the expedition of Qatan in 625, took part in the siege of Medina in 626, but submitted to the Prophet in 630. In 631 he rebelled again, assuming the role of prophet. After the Prophet's death he was defeated by Khalid b. al-Walid in 632. On ʿUmar b. al-Khattab's election as caliph in 634, he came to pay homage, and later took a valiant part in the battles of al-Qadisiyya, Jalula and Nihawand.

al-Tulaytili, Abu ʾl-Qasim Saʿid (al-Qadi Saʿid): Spanish Muslim jurist, historian, mathematician and astronomer; 1029-1070. He was judge at Toledo during the rule of the Dhu ʾl-Nunids, and compiled a history of the sciences, later considered as a first-hand source of information.

Tulunids: name given to the first Muslim dynasty of independent governors of Egypt, whose rule lasted from 868 till 905. The founder, Ahmad b. Tulun (r. 868-884), created a strong army and a naval base at Acre and succeeded in uniting Egypt and Syria under his rule, in virtual independence of the caliphate in Baghdad. The Tulunid period was one of marked material prosperity and progress, and was in afterdays recalled as a golden age. The dynasty was brought to an end by the caliphal general Muhammad b. Sulayman.

Tuman Bay II, al-Ashraf: the last of the Mamluk sultans; r. 1516-1517. After the defeat of his predecessor Qansawh al-Ghawri by the Ottoman Sultan Selim I at Marj Dabiq in 1516, he restored order and was unanimously elected sultan. Sultan Selim offered peace, wanting only to be recognised as suzerain. Tuman Bay wished to submit, but Selim's envoys were put to death by the Egyptian amirs, making the continuation of the war inevitable. The Mamluk army was defeated and Cairo plundered. Tuman Bay fled to Upper Egypt, again entered into negotiation with Selim I, who promised to retire provided his name was put on the coins and mentioned in the Friday service. But the Ottoman envoys again were put to death, and the war continued. After an initial Mamluk success, Tuman Bay's forces were crushed by the Turkish artillery, a new weapon despised by the Mamluks. The Mamluk sultan finally was betrayed by a Bedouin chief. Selim I was impressed by his noble bearing and was inclined to give him his life, but had him hanged at Bab Zuwayla in Cairo on the advice of the Egyptian amirs who had gone over to him.

Tunis (A. *Tunus/Tunis*): capital of the Republic of Tunisia. After Hasan b. al-Nu'man had destroyed Carthage in 698, he constructed a naval base and an arsenal in the existing little town. The construction of the Great Mosque al-Zaytuna is attributed to the Umayyad governor Ibn al-Habhab (732), who also rebuilt the arsenal. During the viiith-xth c. Tunis was renowned as a centre of legal and religious teaching; the patron saint of the town, Sidi Mahriz (Muhriz b. Khalaf) died in 1029. Disaster came in the xith c. with the invasion of the Hilali Arabs from Lower Egypt, who overran the Zirid dynasty. From the time of the Almohad 'Abd al-Mu'min, Tunis has been the capital of Ifriqiya. It was ruled by the Hafsids from 1228 till 1574, being besieged in 1270 by King Louis IX of France during the Eighth Crusade. In 1534 the town was sacked by Khayr al-Din Barbarossa, and in 1535 by Charles V. In 1574 Turkish rule began and in 1609, under the Dey 'Othman, there was a great influx of Moriscoes from Spain. At the end of the xviith and the beginning of the xviiith c. Tunis was twice occupied by the Algerians. In the xixth c. European influence increased and the town was occupied by the French in 1881. Tunis was occupied by the Germans in 1942, liberated in 1943 by the Allies, and in 1956 it became the capital of Tunisia.

al-Tunisi, Muhammad b. 'Umar b. Sulayman: Tunisian Arab scholar; 1789-1857. Born in Tunis, he stayed for a number of years in Dar Fur and returned to Tunis in 1813. From there he moved to Cairo where he entered the service of Muhammad 'Ali Pasha. He left valuable descriptions of Dar Fur and Wada'i.

Tunisia: the region of present-day Tunisia was raided in 647 by 'Abd Allah b. Sa'd b. Abi Sarh, the governor of Egypt, and again in 665 by Mu'awiya b. Hudayj. The real occupation began with the victories of 'Uqba b. Nafi' over the Berbers and the Byzantine governors. By 698 Hassan b. al-Nu'man had taken almost the whole of modern Tunisia from the Berbers and the Byzantines. The viiith c. was marked by uprisings of the Kharijites. Ifrīqiyya was ruled by the dynasty of the Muhallibids, Yemenis by origin, from 772 till 794. They were followed by the Aghlabids, who pursued a policy of pacification, organisation and expansion.

Meanwhile, the Shi'i propaganda of Abu 'Abdallah al-Shi'i had a powerful effect on the Ketama Berbers, preparing the arrival of the Fatimid Mahdi 'Ubayd Allah, who established the Fatimid dynasty in 909. By the time of his death in 934, the Khariji Rustamids of Tahart, the Idrisids of Fez and the Sufris of Sijilmasa had recognised Fatimid suzerainty.

Before leaving for Egypt, the Fatimid al-Mu'izz al-Din Allah had entrusted the government to the Berber amir Yusuf Buluggin I b. Ziri (r. 972-984), the founder of the Zirids of Ifrīqiya. The Zirid al-Mu'izz b. Badis, supported by the Malikis of Qayrawan, transferred his homage to the 'Abbasid caliphs in Baghdad and broke openly with the Fatimids. In 1051 he was twice defeated at Qayrawan by the nomad Hilali Arabs, quartered to the east of the Nile. As a consequence, the country became arabicised and the Berbers were driven back, but, as central power was broken up, insecurity set in and agriculture was ruined. Al-Mahdiyya, the stronghold of the Zirids, was taken first by the Pisans and Genoese in 1087, then by Roger II of Sicily in 1148.

Political unity was restored by the Almohads. In 1228 the Hintata Berber Abu Zakariya' Yahya I (r. 1228-1249) founded the Hafsid dynasty, which was to rule over Tunisia till 1574. In the xvith c. Tunis was twice occupied by the Marinids and under Sultan Abu 'Abd Allah Muhammad al-Hasan (r. 1526-1543) it was conquered temporarily by Khayr al-Din Barbarossa in 1534.

After the sultan had been a vassal of the Emperor Charles V until 1574, Tunisia fell to the Ottoman troops of Sinan Pasha and became a Turkish province under the rule of a pasha, at first under Algiers, from 1587 directly under Istanbul. In 1591 a bloody revolution brought power to the Deys, the title borne by the heads of the 40 sections of the militia, the pasha holding only a honorary position. The third Dey, 'Uthman (r. 1594-1610), set up a code of laws and maintained order through a Bey, who collected taxes. The Deys ruled until 1702, generally as puppets in the hands of the Beys, who had succeeded in supplanting them. The Bey Murad (1612-1631) founded the line of the Muradid Beys, which lasted until 1702, when Husayn b. 'Ali Turki established the Husaynid dynasty of Beys, which lasted until 1957, when the Bey Lamine (al-Amin) was deposed and a Republic proclaimed in Tunisia.

al-Tur: town on the Gulf of Suez, to the southwest of Jabal Musa. Until about 1047, when 'Aydhab took its place, al-Tur was the most important Egyptian harbour for the pilgrimage to Mecca.

Tur 'Abdin: name of a mountainous plateau between Mardin and Jazirat b. 'Umar, Turkey, known for its many Christian monasteries. It passed into the hands of the Muslims in 639. The Muslim part of the present-day population consists mainly of Kurds.

Turan: Iranian term applied to the region lying to the northeast of Iran and ultimately indicating very vaguely the country of the Turkic peoples. The term Pan-Turanianism was used on the one hand as synonymous with Pan-Turkism, and on the other to denote the tendency to a rapprochement among the so-called "Turanian peoples".

Turan-Shah b. Ayyub: founder of the Ayyubid dynasty of Yemen; r. 1174-1176, d. 1180. His brother Saladin sent him to Yemen, where he conquered Zabid, Aden and San'a'. Not feeling comfortable there, he urgently requested Saladin for a transfer, and became governor of Damascus in 1176, where he spent three years. He died at Alexandria.

Turban: the headdress of males, consisting of a length of cloth wound round the head or a cap. In Islam the turban has developed a threefold significance, a national for the Arabs, a religious for the Muslims and a professional for civil professions in contrast to the military. It was only in later days that non-Muslims were not permitted to wear a turban and had to limit themselves to a cap. Over the centuries the colour of the turban was not at all uniform. White was the commonest colour, but the Prophet is said to have worn a black one on entering Mecca, and the 'Abbasids claimed that this turban had been handed down to them. Although Tradition is unanimous that the Prophet never wore a green turban, this colour became quite popular.

Turkestan: town in Kazakhstan, on the middle course of the Iaxartes river. In the xivth c., and perhaps as early as the xiith c., it was called Yasi. Tamerlane erected here a splendid mausoleum in honour of the Muslim poet and saint Ahmad Yasawi (d. 1166).

Turkestan (P. *Turkistān*): the Persian word means "the land of the Turks". For the Arab geographers of the ixth and xth c., Turkestan began north of the area of Arab culture, i.e. in Transoxiana. Later, the name was formally employed to designate the regions between Siberia on the north and Tibet, India, Pakistan, Afghanistan, and Iran on the south, the Gobi desert on the east, and the Caspian Sea on the west. In 1924 the principle of nationality having been carried through in the Soviet Union, the name Turkestan had to give way to terms formed of the names of the various peoples such as Kazakhstan, Turkmenistan, Tajikistan, Kirghizistan and Uzbekistan. These vast regions are sometimes indicated as West Turkestan, East Turkestan being formed by the Sinkiang Uyghur Autonomous Region of China.

Turkmanchay (T. *Türkmen-čayı*): village in northern Iran on the road from Tabriz to Teheran. It is known in history for the treaty signed there between Russia and Persia in 1828, which ended the Russo-Persian War of 1826-1828. It replaced the treaty of 1813 and was the origin of the Persian capitulations.

Turkmen (Turcoman/Turkoman): Turkish people, the majority of whom nowadays live in Turkmenistan, while there are large groups in northern Iran, in northeastern and northwestern Afghanistan, in central Turkey, and small groups in northern Iraq and Syria. From the xth c. onwards, the name is applied to a large section of the Oghuz peoples, more specifically to those who were the descendants of the groups which followed the Saljuqs to the west in the xith c. They played an important part in the rise of dynasties such as the Rum Saljuqs and the Great Saljuqs, the Artuqids of Diyarbakr, the Salghurids of Fars, the Danishmendids and the Qaramanids of central Anatolia, the Ottomans, the Qara Qoyunlu and the Aq Qoyunlu. There were also many Turkmen tribes in the empire of the Mamluks from Diyarbakr to Gaza. In the xviith and xviiith c. the Turkmen suffered a great deal from the attacks of the Kalmuks, the founders of the last great nomad empire in central Asia. The nomadic Turkmen did not form a state of their own, but maintained their independence in various kingdoms, such as Persia, Khwarazm, Bukhara, and still in xviiith c. Afghanistan. The treaties following the Russian conquests in central Asia (1869-1885) settled the distribution of the Turkmen in Russia, Persia and Afghanistan. The literature of the Turkmen, previously only oral, consists of lyric poems and epics, poetry of a religious and didactic nature as well as popular romances. Well-known poets like Ahmad Yasawi (d. 1166), Nesimi, Mir 'Ali Shir Nawa'i, Fuduli and Makhdum Quli "Firaqi" (d. 1782), who all wrote in Chagatay Turkish, were of Turkmen origin.

Turks: the word Turk first appears as the name of a nomad people in the vith c. The two brothers Bu-min and Istemi founded two empires stretching from Mongolia and the northern frontier of China to the Black Sea, distinguished by the Chinese as the Northern and Western Turks. In the viith c. both empires had to submit to the nominal suzerainty of the Chinese T'ang dynasty (r. 618-907).

Between 682 and 744 the Northern Turks were again independent, and it is to this empire that belong the so-called "Orkhon inscriptions", named after the river Orkhon in Mongolia, which are the oldest monument of the Turkish language.

The kingdom of the Western Turks, led by the Türgesh tribe, was ended by the Arabs under Nasr b. Sayyar in 739. In the Arab geographical literature of the ixth and xth c. five Turkish peoples are mentioned who spoke one language and could understand each other: the Toghuzghuz, the Kirgiz, the Kimek, the Oghuz and the Karluk. The lands on the Upper Yenisei marked the limits of the world as known to the Arabs.

Islam was adopted by the Turks in the xth c. of their own free will. The spread of Islam in Central Asia was not checked by the foundation of the non-Muslim Karakhitai around 1130. Turkish culture was brought to Asia Minor and Azerbaijan by the Saljuqs in the xith c., while Saladin brought bodies of Turkish troops to Egypt whence some of them found their way to North Africa and Spain.

The Mongol Empire, and especially the foundation of the Golden Horde, was of great significance for the Turks. From the latter were formed the "Tatar" kingdoms of Qazan, Astrakhan and of the Crimea. In the first half of the xvith c. all the lands from the Balkan Peninsula to the Chinese frontier were under the rule of Muslim Turks, but they could not cope with the rising power of Russia. On the other hand, Islam as a religion and Turkish as a language have made new progress under Russian rule.

Different literary languages began to develop in the xivth and xvth c., the most important being Chagatay and Ottoman Turkish. The former developed in the lands of the Timurids, which consisted of the domain of Chagatay, the second son of Genghis Khan, while the latter has been intimately connected with the political and cultural development of the Ottoman Empire.

At present, there are some 70 million speakers of a Turkic language.

Tursun Beg (Lebibi): Ottoman historian; xvith c. He wrote a history of the reign of Mehemmed II and of the first years of his successor Bayezid II.

Tus (A. *Ṭūs*): district in Khurasan, Iran, and also a town near Mashhad, where Firdawsi died in 1020. The site of his tomb is still remembered. Abu Hamid al-Ghazali was born and died in Tus. The town was destroyed by Tamerlane in 1389, never to be rebuilt.

al-Tusi, Muhammad b. al-Hasan: Shi'i scholar; 995-1067. He studied with Shaykh al-Mufid and al-Sayyid al-Murtada. Public agitation drove him from Baghdad to al-Najaf, where he died. He wrote a commentary on the Qur'an, and works on Tradition, Shi'i law and creed, and on prayers and pious rites. He is considered as one of the great Shi'i scholars.

al-Tusi, Nasir al-Din Abu Ja'far: astronomer and Shi'i politician; 1201-1274. In 1256 he lured the Assassin leader Rukn al-Din Khurshah into the hands of the Il-Khan Hülegü, accompanied the latter to Baghdad and founded the observatory of Maragha. He had a strong sympathy with the Twelver Shi'a, to whom a certain degree of mercy was shown during the Mongol holocaust and whose sanctuaries were spared. He wrote on dogmatics, logic and philosophy, law and belles-lettres, and above all on the sciences, in particular on astronomy.

Tutush b. Alp Arslan, Taj al-Dawla: Saljuq ruler of Syria; b. 1058, r. 1079-1095. Syria was allotted to him by his brother the Great Saljuq Malik-Shah I. He had to fight the Turkmen Atsiz who had taken the whole of Palestine including Jerusalem from the Fatimids, who however continued to claim the country. While making conquests around Aleppo, the 'Uqaylid Muslim b. Quraysh drove the Mirdasids out of the town and got his rule recognised by

Malik-Shah. Muslim b. Quraysh fell in a battle with Sulayman b. Qutlumish, the founder of the Rum Saljuqs, who now became Tutush's rival for Aleppo. After Sulayman's death, Malik-Shah gave the town to the amir Aqsunqur, and Edessa to the amir Buzan. Together with them, Tutush made notable conquests in Syria. After the sudden death of Malik-Shah, the amirs had to pay homage to Tutush, and supported him in the conquest of Nisibis, Diyarbakr, Mayyafariqin and Mosul. When Malik-Shah's son Berkyaruq came forward as his father's rightful heir, the amirs joined him. They were defeated by Tutush in 1094, but the latter was conquered by Berkyaruq in 1095. Aleppo then passed to Ridwan, and Damascus to Duqaq, both sons of Tutush.

Twelvers (A. *Ithnā 'Ashariyya*): the name of that branch of Shi'ism that believes in twelve Imams. According to the Twelvers, the first six Imams, given under "Seveners", were followed by Musa al-Kazim; 'Ali al-Rida; Muhammad al-Jawad al-Taqi (d. 835); Abu al-Hasan 'Ali al-'Askari (al-Naqi); Abu Muhammad al-Hasan al-'Askari, and Muhammad al-Qa'im (al-Mahdi/al-Hujja).

Principal among the basic doctrines of Twelver Shi'ism, as formulated by the fifth Imam Muhammad b. 'Ali Zayn al-'Abidin (al-Baqir) are: the belief that the imamate passes on from one Imam to the next by virtue of a divine command which is revealed in an explicit divinely-inspired designation (A. *naṣṣ*) made first by the Prophet, who listed all the Imams, and then by each Imam in turn designating his successor; that all the Imams are descendants of the Fatimid line; that they possess special knowledge of a kind denied to ordinary mortals; that they have absolute spiritual authority and should also have absolute political authority.

Within the whole body of Shi'ism, the Twelvers are both the most numerous in terms of adherents and theologically the most balanced between the exoteric and esoteric elements of Islam. Their religious history can be divided into the period of the twelve Imams; the period from the great occultation after Muhammad al-Qa'im to Nasir al-Din al-Tusi; the period from al-Tusi until the Safawid revival around 1500; the period from Safawid times to the present.

U

'Ubayd Allah b. Ziyad: Umayyad governor; d. 686. A son of Ziyad b. Abihi, he was appointed governor of Khurasan and advanced as far as Bukhara. In 675 he became governor of Basra, where he subdued the Kharijites, and in 679 also of Kufa. It was he who sent troops against al-Husayn b. 'Ali, who lost his life at the battle of Karbala' in 683. 'Ubayd Allah had to flee from Kufa and went to Syria. At the battle of Marj Rahit in 684, he commanded the left wing of the Umayyad Caliph Marwan I b. al-Hakam and in the following year he was sent to Qarqisiya in order to subdue Iraq. In 686 he suffered near Mosul a disastrous defeat against al-Mukhtar b. Abi 'Ubayd al-Thaqafi.

'Ubayd Zakani, Nizam al-Din: Persian poet from Qazwin; 1300-1371. He was a satirical and erotic poet, who wrote such works as *The Morals of Aristocracy* and *The Book of the Beard*, a dialogue between the poet and the beard, regarded as a destroyer of youthful beauty.

Ubeda (A. *Ubbada*): little town in the southeast of Spain, renowned in the Muslim world for its crops of saffron. It was taken by the Christians in 1212.

'Udhra, Banu: Arab tribe belonging to the great subdivision of the Quda'a and established in the north of the Hejaz in the Wadi 'l-Qura. They exercised control over the road between the Hejaz and Syria. In 623 the Prophet sent them a letter and in 630 they despatched an official embassy to Medina. They played no part in politics and did not give any personage of note to the history of Islam. They achieved however a fame without equal for their love of poetry, giving their name to the so-called "'Udhri love".

'Udhri love: named after the Banu 'Udhra, "'Udhri love" is, in the history of Islamic thought, a literary and philosophical theme, related to the "platonic love" of the Greeks. The theme celebrates an ideal Bedouin tribe in which lovers "die of love" rather than "place a hand" on the beloved object. The 'Udhri ideal is Jamil b. 'Abd Allah. The theme was taken over into mysticism by Abu Hamza al-Baghdadi (d. 882), Ahmad al-Ghazali and 'Ayn al-Qudat al-Hamadhani (d. 1131).

Uhud: mountain about five km north of Medina, well-known for the battle fought in 624 between the Prophet and the Meccans. The latter, eager to avenge their defeat at the battle of Badr, were led by Khalid b. al-Walid. The Prophet's archers were unable to restrain themselves when they saw the Meccan camp being pillaged, and the rumour spread that the Prophet had fallen, though he was only wounded. Some of his followers succeeded in concealing him in a ravine. The Meccans did not know how to follow up their victory. The Prophet particularly lamented the death of his uncle Hamza, and afterwards went every year to Uhud, which thus became a prominent place of pilgrimage. A mosque was built over Hamza's tomb.

'Ukaz: oasis situated between Ta'if and Nakhla, primarily celebrated for its annual fair, which was held on the 1st-20th Dhu 'l-Qa'da, the eleventh month of the Muslim calendar. This fair was also an official occasion for a gathering of groups and individuals belonging to the same tribe where individuals competed for honours and for the honour of the tribe.

'Ulama' (A.): the learned of Islam, i.e. the religious teachers, canon lawyers, judges, and high state religious officials like the Shaykh al-Islam. They came to have, in a wide and vague fashion, the ultimate decision on all questions of constitution, canon law and theology. They might be government functionaries, either controlled by the government or keeping the government in a certain awe; or they might be private and independent students of canon law and theology.

Ulugh Beg, Muhammad Turghay: Timurid ruler in Samarqand; b. 1393, r. 1447-1449. A son of Shahrukh Mirza, he became governor of a part of Khurasan and Mazandaran in 1407, and in 1408 of Turkestan. But he was first of all a man of letters, an artist and a poet. Being able to recite the Qur'an by heart according to all seven "readings", he was also a great bibliophile and a learned mathematician, fond of poetry and history. He enriched Samarqand with superb buildings. Above all he was an astronomer, who built an observatory and invented new and powerful instruments for researches he carried out with other astronomers. He sought to correct Ptolemy's computations, and compiled an astronomical almanac, known as "the new almanac of the sultan", which became celebrated in Europe in the xviith c. Less happy in war and politics, he had to fight his son 'Abd al-Latif, who in the end defeated his father and had him executed.

Uluj 'Ali (It. *Ochialy*): Turkish corsair and admiral; ca. 1500-1587. Born in Calabria, he was captured and became a galley slave. Having converted to Islam, he was lieutenant to the Turkish admiral Turghud 'Ali Pasha (d. 1565) during Charles V's expedition against the island of Jerba, became Turghud's successor as viceroy of Tripolis and later of Algiers. He took part in maritime expeditions against the Venetians and the Maltese, and commanded the left wing of the Ottoman fleet at the battle of Lepanto in 1571. He brought a part of the fleet safely back to Istanbul and became Grand Admiral until his death.

'Umar b. 'Abd al-'Aziz b. Marwan: Umayyad caliph; b. 682, r. 717-720. In 706 he became governor of the Hejaz and settled at Medina where he formed an advisory council. He became famous for his piety and frugality, feeling no obligation to spread Islam by the sword. He preferred peaceful missionary activity, which method proved successful among the Berbers and in Sind. He adopted a kindly attitude towards the 'Alids, the Christians, the Jews and the Zoroastrians. His most important measure was the reform of taxation. The ever-increasing conversion to Islam of non-Arabs led to more and more subjects being exempt from taxation. Furthermore, agriculture suffered to a great extent as a result of many converts settling in the cities. Al-Hajjaj therefore had imposed the land-tax (A. *kharāj*) also upon Muslim landowners and prohibited immigration to the cities. 'Umar, however, adhered to the principle that Muslims should pay no tribute and propounded that conquered land was the common property of the Muslim community and could not be transformed into immune private property by sale to individual Muslims. In 718 he forbade Muslims to buy land which should pay tribute and permitted immigration of new converts into the cities. In course of time a whole cycle of pious legends gathered round his name. Even the historians of the 'Abbasid period give him the highest praise, and his tomb at Dayr Sam'an near Aleppo was left undisturbed after the 'Abbasid triumph.

'Umar b. Abi Rabi'a: the greatest love poet of the Arabs; 644-712. He was from a wealthy family in Mecca, and served for a time as governor in Yemen. He was the first townsman poet in Arabic.

'Umar b. 'Ali al-Misri (Ibn al-Farid): celebrated Sufi poet; 1181-1234. The outer and inner meanings of his poems are so interwoven that they may be read as love poems or as mystical hymns. But the collection of his works also contains two purely mystical odes, one on divine love, the other on "the Pilgrim's Progress".

'Umar b. Hafs: governor of Ifriqiya; d. 771. He was appointed by the 'Abbasid Caliph al-Mansur in 768 to subdue the Kharijites who rose in a general insurrection under the Sufri Abu Qurra.

'Umar b. Hafsun: leader of a famous rebellion in Muslim Spain; d. 918. After his conversion to Islam, he spent some time at Tahert, Algeria. Upon returning he established himself in the almost impregnable fortress of Bobastro and exercised complete authority over the mountainous region between Ronda and Málaga. In 883 he submitted to the Umayyad amir Muhammad I b. 'Abd al-Rahman II (r. 852-886), but in the following year recaptured Bobastro. He now became the champion of the malcontents, whether Christians or neo-Muslims, repudiated Islam openly, took the name Samuel and began to lead a regular crusade against Islam. Bobastro was captured by the Umayyad amir 'Abd al-Rahman III in 928.

'Umar b. al-Khattab: second caliph and founder of the Arab empire; b. 592, r. 634-644. At first he was a declared enemy of the Prophet's message. Tradition places his conversion to Islam in 618 when he was 26 years old. He belonged to the Banu 'Adi b. Ka'b who enjoyed no political influence at Mecca. Due to his strength of will, his influence began in Medina after the Hijra, in perfect agreement with Abu Bakr. He became the Prophet's father-in-law when the Prophet married his daughter Hafsa. He took part in the battles of Badr, Uhud and later ones, although his part was that of a counsellor rather than of a soldier.

After the death of Abu Bakr he was recognised as the latter's successor by the majority of the Companions, there being dissatisfaction only on the side of the party of 'Ali and of the "Helpers", who had already suffered defeat when Abu Bakr became caliph two years earlier.

During the great expansion of Muslim conquests, which had already begun, 'Umar never lost control of his generals. He dismissed Khalid b. al-Walid and treated 'Amr b. al-'As with tact. He also made use of the powerful family of the Umayyads. All the political institutions by which the Muslim state was later to be ruled had their origin in his caliphate. The regulations for the non-Muslim subjects, the institution of a register of those having right to military pensions, the founding of military centres out of which were to grow the future great cities of Islam, the creation of the office of judge, they were all his work. Religious ordinances, such as the prayer of Ramadan and the obligatory pilgrimage, as well as civil and penal ordinances, such as the era of the Hijra, the punishment of drunkenness, and stoning as a punishment for adultery, go back to him. 'Umar is said to have substituted in 640 the title of "Commander of the Believers" (A. *amīr al-mu'minīn*) for that of *khalīfa* "deputy". He fell in 644 by the dagger of Abu Lu'lu'a. As a motive for the murder, tradition gives the very heavy tax against which the slave had appealed in vain to the caliph. 'Umar really was the second founder of Islam, but the Shi'a has never concealed its antipathy to him because he was the first to thwart the claims of 'Ali.

'Umara b. Abi 'l-Hasan: Arab man of letters from Yemen; 1121-1174. He studied and taught at Zabid, and was engaged in trade, which brought him in contact with the Najahids. After 1157 he settled in Egypt, where he dedicated his poems to the autocratic viziers Tala'i' b. Ruzzik, Ruzzik b. Tala'i', Dirgham (d. 1164) and Shirkuh. His sympathies inclined to the Fatimids, for whom he wrote a *qaṣīda* of lament. He took part in a conspiracy to restore them, and as a result was put to death by Saladin. He wrote a history of the Egyptian viziers, and one of Yemen.

Umayya b. 'Abd Shams: ancestor of the Umayyads, who were the principal clan of the Quraysh in Mecca. Like his father, he commanded the Meccan army in time of war.

Umayya b. Abi 'l-Salt: Arab poet, contemporary of the Prophet; d. 629. He is said to have refused to recognise the Prophet's claim to be God's Messenger. There are similarities, and divergences, between the Qur'an on the one hand and the recognition of one personal God, the eschatological conceptions of the Last Judgement, Hell and Paradise, and the appeals for a moral life found in Umayya's poems on the other. The agreement between the Qur'an and Umayya's poems may be explained from the fact that before and at the Prophet's time currents of thought related to the concept of monotheism had attracted wide circles, especially in Mecca and Ta'if.

Umayyads (Banu Umayya): dynasty of caliphs which ruled the Islamic world from 661 till 750. The Banu Umayya were the principal clan of the Quraysh of Mecca, represented by two main branches, the A'yas and the 'Anabisa. 'Affan, the father of the Caliph 'Uthman, was descended from the A'yas, as were the Caliph Marwan I b. al-Hakam and the caliphs who came after him until the end of the dynasty. Marwan and his descendants formed the Marwanid line of the Umayyads. The amirs, later caliphs, of Muslim Spain were also desended from the A'yas. The most illustrious family of the 'Anabisa branch was that of Harb, whose son Abu Sufyan was the father of the first Umayyad Caliph Mu'awiya I. His line became extinct with the death of Caliph Mu'awiya II, the son of the Caliph Yazid I, and was followed by the Marwanid line.

If tradition, as established after their fall under the influence of the ideas dominant in pietist circles, has cursed the memory of the Umayyads, it nevertheless remains true that it was precisely under their regime and partly under their stimulus that Islam established itself as a universalist religion. The Umayyad caliphs, as descendants of the Meccan aristocracy which had fought Islam in its early stages, must have believed in good faith that the propagation of the Muslim faith and the expansion of their temporal power were one and the same thing. They must have been convinced that the enemies of their policy, whether Shiʿis or Kharijites, were also enemies of the true tradition of the Prophet.

The Umayyad party triumphed under the third caliph ʿUthman b. ʿAffan at the expense of the first converts, of the Prophet's son-in-law ʿAli in the first place. The opposition between Muʿawiya and ʿAli raised an exceedingly delicate constitutional problem: that of the assumption of supreme power over the believers by one who was not among the earliest Companions of the Prophet. Rather than being the continuators of the *sunna* of the Prophet, the Umayyads became in fact, if not in official title, "kings" or rather "tyrants" in the Greek sense of the word. The Umayyad period is marked by a strong opposition between Syria and Iraq, due to Ziyad b. Abihi's merciless suppression in Iraq, so different from the policy practised by Muʿawiya himself. The Iraqi population seems to have been justified in thinking that the Umayyad caliphate really represented the hegemony of Syria over the rest of Islamic territory and the memory of ʿAli, which legend soon seized upon, was in a way bound up with the nationalism of Iraq.

The most tangible success of Muʿawiya's policy was that he made the caliphate hereditary after having succeeded in extracting from the tribal chiefs the oath of allegiance (A. *bayʿa*) for his son Yazid. This principle was continued under Marwan I b. al-Hakam. The caliphate of the latter's son ʿAbd al-Malik, under the driving power of al-Hajjaj b. Yusuf al-Thaqafi, was an attempt to establish an absolute monarchy. Al-Hajjaj reduced the Kharijite movement to temporary impotence, while Shiʿism, defeated in the open field, took refuge in secret propaganda which was only to bear fruit much later. The vast conquests of Qutayba b. Muslim in the east, begun in 705, brought about the conversion to Islam of the Turks, while in the west the Berbers, notwithstanding their opposition to the Arab conquerors, gradually also accepted the new religion. It was to these two races, placed at the two extremes of the Arab empire, that Islam owed the greater part of its future successes but also a profound change in its civilisation.

The Caliph al-Walid I was the great builder of the dynasty, and the fiscal reforms of ʿUmar II b. ʿAbd al-ʿAziz paved the way for the equal treatment of Arabs and non-Arab "clients" and contributed more than anything else to the fusion of the descendants of the conquerors and conquered.

Under the Caliph Hisham b. ʿAbd al-Malik, the Umayyad caliphate experienced another period of splendour. But Hisham had exploited to the limit the fiscal reforms of ʿUmar II and exhausted his Muslim and non-Muslim subjects alike. The scandalous conduct of the Caliph al-Walid II played also an important part in the collapse of the established order. Misery brought about a revival of Kharijism, and the Shiʿa movement began again to show itself openly in Iraq. Neither Yazid III b. al-Walid nor his brother Ibrahim b. al-Walid succeeded in checking the anarchy which was spreading throughout the empire. Marwan II b. Muhammad, the governor of Armenia, proclaimed himself caliph and subdued Syria, Egypt and Iraq. But in 747 the forces of Abu Muslim rapidly conquered Khurasan and Fars, and in 748 occupied Iraq where the ʿAbbasids suddenly put forward their claims and proclaimed Abu 'l-ʿAbbas al-Saffah caliph at Kufa. Marwan II was killed in 750.

It can be said that the intellectual and moral unification of the Muslim world, accomplished by the ʿAbbasids, had already begun under the Umayyads.

The following is a list of the Umayyad caliphs of Syria:

661	Muʿawiya I b. Abi Sufyan
680	Yazid I b. Muʿawiya
683	Muʿawiya II b. Yazid
684	Marwan b. al-Hakam
684	ʿAbd al-Malik b. Marwan
705	al-Walid I b. ʿAbd al-Malik
715	Sulayman b. ʿAbd al-Malik
717	ʿUmar II b. ʿAbd al-ʿAziz b. Marwan
720	Yazid II b. ʿAbd al-Malik
724	Hisham b. ʿAbd al-Malik
743	al-Walid II b. Yazid II
744	Yazid III b. al-Walid I
744	Ibrahim b. al-Walid I
744-750	Marwan II b. Muhammad al-Himar.

ʿAbbasid caliphs

Umayyads of Spain: dynasty which reigned from 756 till 1031 in the Iberian peninsula with Córdoba as their capital. ʿAbd al-Rahman I al-Dakhil, "the Immigrant", was recognised as amir in 756 in Córdoba, the traditional residence of the Arab governors. The main task of all his successors was to be the pacification of the new amirate. The Maliki law school was introduced at the end of the viiith c. Amir ʿAbd Allah gradually consolidated Umayyad authority. The most glorious period in the history of Muslim Spain was the reign of ʿAbd al-Rahman III. The decline and fall of the Spanish Umayyads became evident under the successors of Hisham II. Between 1009 and 1031 no less than nine caliphs are listed, their reigns being continuously interrupted by the Hammudids of Málaga. From this time onwards civil war reigned in

Córdoba and the caliphate, the Berber element playing a more and more disastrous part in the troubles. All the provinces of Muslim Spain proclaimed their independence under a Spanish, Slav or Berber chief. These rulers, known as Party Kings (A. *muluk al-tawā'if*), lasted until the end of the xith c., when the Almoravids conquered Muslim Spain.

The following is a list of the Spanish Umayyads:

756	'Abd al-Rahman I al-Dakhil
788	Hisham I
796	Hisham II
822	'Abd al-Rahman II
852	Muhammad I
886	al-Mundhir
888	'Abd Allah
912	'Abd al-Rahman III
961	al-Hakam II
976	Hisham II al-Mu'ayyad (*first reign*)
1009	Muhammad II al-Mahdi (*first reign*)
1009	Sulayman al-Musta'in (*first reign*)
1010	Muhammad II al-Mahdi (*second reign*)
1010	Hisham II al-Mu'ayyad (*second reign*)
1013	Sulayman al-Musta'in (*second reign*)
1016	*Hammudid 'Ali al-Nasir*
1018	'Abd al-Rahman IV
1018	*Hammudid al-Qasim al-Ma'mun (first time)*
1021	*Hammudid Yahya al-Mu'tali (first time)*
1022	*Hammudid al-Qasim al-Ma'mun (second time)*
1023	'Abd al-Rahman V
1024	Muhammad III
1025	*Hammudid Yahya al-Mu'tali (second time)*
1027-31	Hisham III
Muluk al-Tawā'if	

Umm al-Kitab (A.): name for the original copy of the Book with God in heaven, from which the revelations of the Qur'an come and from which God, according to the Qur'an, abrogates and confirms what He pleases. This original copy is written in the Tablet.

Umm Kulthum: daughter of the Prophet; d. 630. She is said to have married 'Utba, a son of Abu Lahab, the enemy of Islam, but to have been divorced by him at his father's orders before the marriage was consummated. After the death of her sister Ruqayya, her brother-in-law 'Uthman b. 'Affan, later the third caliph, married her during the battle of Badr.

Umm al-Walad (A.): the Arabic term means "mother of children" and was applied to a slave-girl who has borne her master a child. In the Qur'an her position is not defined. According to the Law, every slave-girl, even a non-Muslim, who has borne her master a child, becomes *ipso iure* free, and a legacy set aside by her master in her favour is therefore valid.

'Unayza: town in southern Najd in Saudi Arabia. It was on the caravan route from Basra to Mecca, and played a role in 1815 during the campaign of Tusun, the second son of Muhammad 'Ali Pasha, against the Wahhabis. It was incorporated in the Wahhabi state of Najd in 1862.

Unsuri, Abu 'l-Qasim Hasan: Persian poet; d. 1049. He owes his fame to a collection of poetry, which contains love-poems and panegyrics. Among the latter, many are written in praise of the Ghaznawid Mahmud b. Sebüktigin.

'Uqaylids (Banu 'Uqayl): dynasty in Mosul, with other lines in Jazirat ibn 'Umar and Nisibis; r. ca. 990-1096. They belonged to the great Beduin tribe of the 'Amir b. Sa'sa'a. From Central Arabia they spread in different directions. The dynasty was founded by Abu 'l-Dhawwad Muhammad (d. 996). His grandson Mu'tamid al-Dawla Qirwash reigned from 1001 till 1050. After the reign of Sharaf al-Dawla Muslim (r. 1061-1085), 'Uqaylid power declined rapidly. Ibrahim (r. 1085-1093) was defeated and put to death by the Saljuq of Syria Tutush. The last ruler 'Ali b. Muslim had to give up Mosul in 1096. Another branch of the 'Uqaylids was established between 1036 and 1056 in Takrit.

'Uqba b. Nafi' b. 'Abd Qays: famous Arab commander; ca. 630-683. Shortly before his death in 663 his uncle 'Amr b. al-'As, the conqueror of Egypt, gave him the supreme command in Ifriqiya. In 670 he founded the military stronghold of Qayrawan. He was dismissed in 675 but restored to his post in 682. He defeated the Berbers but did not secure his conquests. He was defeated by the Berber chief Kusayla.

'Urabi Pasha, Ahmad: Egyptian nationalist; 1839-1911. Under the slogan "Egypt for the Egyptians" he led a movement directed against foreign control. The khedive Tawfiq Pasha requested the assistance of the French and the British, and the latter defeated him in 1882.

Urdu: name of one of the official languages of Pakistan. The word is Turkish, meaning "camp". This refers to the royal camp of the Ghaznawids Mahmud b. Sebüktigin and his son Mas'ud I b. Mahmud, where soldiers of Turkish, Persian and Hindi origin were living together. Their mixed language was called "the language of the urdu", and after some time the term came to be used for this type of language. Urdu cannot strictly be called a branch of Hindi, the common language, or an offshoot of Persian, the court language of the Muslim rulers in India, but is a distinct language of a mixed character. It was cultivated as a literary language at the courts of the sultans of Gujarat, the Qutb Shahis at Golkonda, and the 'Adil-Shahs at Bijapur. Urdu is written in a modified form of the Persian Arabic alphabet.

Urfa (Edessa; A. *al-Ruhā'*): town in south-eastern Turkey. It surrendered to the Muslims in 639. In 750 it was the scene of fighting between the followers of the last Umayyad Caliph Marwan II and the later 'Abbasid Caliph al-Mansur. In 943 the picture of Christ, called *al-Īqōnat al-Mandīl* (Gr. *Mandulion*) was handed over to the Byzantines in return for the release of 200 Muslim prisoners. The town was burned in 971 and again in 1030. From Urfa/Edessa the Crusaders ruled the "County of Edessa" from 1098 till 1144, when it was taken by 'Imad al-Din Zangi I. This conquest led to the Second Crusade. In 1182 the town fell to Saladin, in 1234 to the Rum Saljuq Qayqubad I, and in 1260 to the Il-Khan Hülegü. By 1400 Edessa had been rebuilt, and it was taken by the Ottoman Sultan Murad IV in 1637.

'**Urfi, Jamal al-Din**: Persian poet from Shiraz; d. 1591. He emigrated to India where the Mughal emperor Akbar I took him into his service. He enjoyed great popularity in his time in India, especially for his *qaṣīda*s.

Urmiya: name of a lake, a district and a town in the Iranian province of Azerbaijan. The district, inhabited by Kurds, was conquered by Sadaqa b. 'Ali in the ixth c., according to others by 'Utba b. Farqad in 640. It changed hands many times. It is not known at what period the Aramaic-speaking Christians, who after World War I called themselves "Assyrians", appeared in Urmiya.

'**Urwa b. al-Zubayr b. 'Awwam**: one of the earliest and foremost authorities on tradition in Medina; ca. 645-ca. 710. His mother Asma' was a daughter of Abu Bakr, and his father a nephew of the Prophet's wife Khadija. The famous anti-caliph 'Abd Allah b. al-Zubayr was his brother.

Usama b. Munqidh: Arab knight, courtier and man of letters; 1095-1188. Throughout his life he was in constant relations with the Franks, sometimes hostile, sometimes friendly; quite a number of the Templars were among his friends. He spent nine years (1129-1138) in the army of 'Imad al-Din Zangi I, and six years (1138-1144) at the court of the Burids in Damascus. Between 1144-1154 he was in Egypt, becoming involved in political intrigues during the last phase of Fatimid rule. On the way from Cairo to Damascus, he lost his entire library, which contained over 4,000 manuscripts. From 1154-1164 he undertook many campaigns against the Franks with Nur al-Din Mahmud Zangi. Another ten years (1164-1174) were spent in Hisn Kayfa, ruled by the Artuqid Qara Arslan of Diyarbakr (r. 1144-1167). The fame of Saladin brought him for the third time to Damascus. His fame rests above all on his Memoirs, called *Book of Instruction by Example*, composed or dictated in 1183. It gives a vivid picture of his time.

Usama b. Zayd b. Haritha al-Kalbi: son of the Abyssinian freedwoman Baraka Umm Ayman, he is reckoned among the Prophet's freedmen; d. ca. 673. Tradition records many instances of the Prophet's fondness for him as a child. He was among those who prepared the Prophet's body for burial. The election of 'Uthman b. 'Affan to the caliphate in 644 took place in the house of his wife Fatima bint Qays al-Fihriya, and after the murder of 'Uthman in 656, Usama refused homage to 'Ali.

Ushrushana (Usrushana): district in Transoxiana to the northeast of Sa-marqand. It was invaded by Qutayba b. Muslim in 712, and again in 822 during the reign of the ʿAbbasid Caliph al-Maʾmun by Haydar b. Afshin Kawus (d. 841), who subdued the region. Ushrushana was ruled by the Sajids of Azerbaijan until 893, when it became a province of the Samanid empire.

Usman dan Fodio (ʿUthman b. Fudi): founder of the state of Sokoto; 1754-1815. He was a Tukulor shaykh from Senegal, belonging to the Torodo (pl. Torodbe) caste, a Sufi, philosopher and revolutionary reformer. He founded the state of Sokoto in 1801 and led a Holy War between 1804-1808.

Ustadsis: name of the leader of a religious movement in Khurasan, directed against the ʿAbbasids. The rising began in 767 and spread rapidly. Ustadsis represented himself as a prophet and exhorted the people to unbelief (A. *kufr*). The movement was suppressed by Khazim b. Khuzayma.

Usuliyya: term which, in the Twelver Shiʿa, denotes those who, in contrast to the Akhbariyya, admit a larger share of speculative reason in the principles (A. *uṣūl*) of theology and religious law.

ʿUtayba, Banu: large Bedouin tribe in central Saudi Arabia, which traces its genealogy back to Mudar and claims to belong to the Qays ʿAylan.

ʿUtba b. Ghazwan b. al-Harith: one of the first Companions of the Prophet; d. ca. 636. He is best known as the founder of Basra.

al-ʿUtbi, Abu Nasr Muhammad: Arab historian from Rayy; ca. 961-1036. He was the author of a history of the reign of the Ghaznawid Nasir al-Dawla Sebüktigin, the governor of Khurasan on behalf of the Samanids, of his son Mahmud and of the early years of his grandson Masʿud I.

al-Utrush, Abu Muhammad al-Hasan: ruler in Tabaristan and recognised as Imam by the Zaydis, including those of Yemen; ca. 844-917. He went from Medina to Tabaristan where al-Hasan b. Zayd b. Muhammad had founded the Zaydiyya. He conducted ʿAlid propaganda from Gilan and, having defeated the troops sent by the Samanid Ahmad II b. Ismaʿil (r. 907-914), he established a little ʿAlid state at Amul in east Mazandaran, which lasted till 1126.

ʿUthman Abu Bakr Digna (Diqna): governor and general of the Mahdiyya in the Eastern Sudan; ca. 1840-1926. He was a slave trader who joined Muhammad al-Mahdi in 1883.

ʿUthman b. ʿAffan: the third caliph; r. 644-656. He belonged to the Banu Umayya and accepted the teaching of the Prophet several years before the Hijra. He was a rich merchant, and married the Prophet's daughter Ruqayya. He is believed to have taken part in the migration to Abyssinia and in the Hijra to Medina, but he did not take part in the battle of Badr. After the death of Ruqayya, he married Umm Kulthum, another daughter of the Prophet. After the murder of ʿUmar b. al-Khattab in 644, he was elected caliph by a council of the six oldest Companions, perhaps as being a member of the Prophet's family through his marriages, as being an Umayyad and as being the most outstanding candidate, since ʿAli, al-Zubayr b. al-ʿAwwam, Talha b. ʿUbayd Allah, Saʿd b. Abi Waqqas and ʿAbd al-Rahman b. ʿAwf ruled one another out. During his caliphate many serious grievances were uttered, the first and perhaps gravest charge being that he appointed members of his family to the governorships in the provinces of Syria and Egypt. He also assigned the booty of the expeditions not entirely to the soldiers, but reserved a share for his governors and family by developing the system of fiefs. Cutting down the military pensions because of the economic crisis following the sudden enriching of the Arab masses also increased the number of malcontents. One of the steps which contributed very greatly to stirring up the religious element against ʿUthman was the official edition of the Qurʾan, the destruction of the provincial copies being considered most odious.

In 650 the first movements of rebellion began in Iraq, which was suffering most from the economic crisis, especially in Kufa, and spread to Egypt. In 655 bodies of rebels advanced on Medina. ʿUthman gave in to all their demands, but on returning the Egyptians found a letter from the caliph to his foster brother ʿAbd Allah b. Saʿd (Ibn Abi Sarh), the governor of Egypt, containing an order to put to death or mutilate the leaders of the movement. ʿUthman denied that the letter was genuine, but his house became besieged. The Companions, including ʿAli, maintained an attitude of neutrality and ʿAʾisha, the widow of the Prophet, who was opposed to ʿUthman, left for Mecca. ʿUthman refused to abdicate. It is not known whether it was Muhammad b. Abi Bakr, the son of the first caliph and brother of ʿAʾisha, or another who gave the coup de grâce. ʿAli was then elected caliph, but he was destined to be challenged by Muʿawiya, the Umayyad governor of Syria. The political, and soon also the religious unity of Islam was at an end and the period of schisms and civil wars had begun.

ʿUthman b. Mazʿun b. Habib: one of the earliest Companions of the Prophet; d. 625. He took part in the emigration to Abyssinia and in the battle of Badr. In Tradition ʿUthman is the most characteristic representative of the ascetic tendencies in early Islam, and he is said to have asked the Prophet's permission to castrate himself.

Utrar: town on the right bank of the Iaxartes. At the time of Genghis Khan, it was a frontier town of the empire of the Khwarazm-Shah ʿAlaʾ al-Din Muhammad (r. 1200-1220). In 1218, a great caravan of 450 Muslims arrived, sent by the Mongols to open up commercial and peaceful relations with the Muslim Empire. They were all massacred by the commander Inalciq, and when Genghis Khan sent an envoy to ʿAlaʾ al-Din, the latter refused to hand over the commander and had the envoy put to death. The town was taken by the Mongols in 1219 and it was from Utrar that they set out to conquer the empire of the Khwarazm-Shah. Tamerlane died at Utrar in 1404.

Uways I: ruler of the Jalayirids; b. 1341, r. 1356-1374.

Uyghurs: Sunni Muslim, Turkic-speaking people in Sinkiang, western China. Their Manichaean kingdom was destroyed around 840 by the Kirgiz.

Uzun Hasan: ruler of the Aq Qoyunlu; r. 1453-1478. From 1453 he was prince of Diyarbakr, and from 1467 until his death sovereign of a powerful state comprising Diyarbakr, eastern Anatolia and Azerbaijan. In the west he made alliance with the Qaramanids against the Ottomans. In 1467 he defeated the Qara Qoyunlu Jihan Shah and conquered the Timurid Abu Saʿid. He entered into negotiations with Venice against the Ottomans, but the latter routed him in 1473. He thrice invaded Georgia, and succeeded in coming to an agreement with the Burji Mamluks about the frontier between Egypt and his own lands.

al-ʿUzza ("the Powerful"): ancient Arabian goddess, who was especially associated with the Banu Ghatafan, but whose principal sanctuary was in the valley of Nakhla on the road from Taʾif to Mecca. She gradually acquired a predominant position among the Quraysh, and formed with al-Lat and Manat a trinity, called "Allah's daughters" by the Meccans. Al-ʿUzza was also worshipped by the Lakhmids of al-Hira. After the taking of Mecca, the Prophet sent Khalid b. al-Walid to destroy the sanctuary of al-ʿUzza.

V

Valencia (A. *Balansiyya*): town in eastern Spain, also called Valencia del Cid. During the period of the Spanish Umayyads it was one of the most active centres of Muslim Spain, but in the political history it seems to have been a place of minor importance. In the xith c. however, it became one of the principal objectives of the Christian reconquista. In 1021 a Muslim kingdom was founded here by the ʿAmirids, which lasted till 1096. The reign of ʿAbd al-ʿAziz al-Mansur (r. 1021-1061), who recognised the authority of the caliph of Córdoba, brought prosperity. He was succeeded by his son ʿAbd al-Malik al-Muzaffar (r. 1061-1065), who sought the assistance of the Dhu 'l-Nunid Yahya al-Maʾmun of Toledo (r. 1043-1075) against Ferdinand I of Castile and León. Yahya dethroned ʿAbd al-Malik and incorporated his principality in the kingdom of Toledo. From 1089-1099 it was in the hands of El Cid and was taken by the Almoravids in 1102. In 1147 Ibn Mardanish was proclaimed king of Valencia, and in 1238 it fell into the hands of James I of Aragon.

Van (A. *Wān*): name of a town and a lake in eastern Turkey. The whole of Armenia was overrun in 852 by the Turkish military leader Bugha al-Kabir, but the ʿAbbasid Caliph al-Muʿtamid recognised the Baghratid Ashot as king of Armenia. The region fell to the Great Saljuq Alp Arslan after his victory over the Byzantines in the battle of Malazgird in 1071. In the Mongol period authority was in the hands of the Kurds of Hakkari. Towards the end of the xivth c. the rule of the Qara Qoyunlu was extended over Van, but the direct administration remained in the hands of the Kurds. In the first decades of the xvith c. the town and the region were alternately under Ottoman and Persian rule, but they were finally annexed by the Ottomans in 1543. In 1896 there were troubles on a large scale between Armenians and Muslims. The Russians occupied Van from 1915-1917.

Varna: Bulgarian town on the Black Sea. The first Turkish attack on Varna took place in 1388 under the Ottoman Sultan Murad I and in 1393, under Sultan Bayezid I, the whole of Bulgaria became an Ottoman province. In 1444 the Christian armies under Wladislaw III, king of Poland and Hungary, were routed by the Ottoman Sultan Murad II. This victory formed a stepping stone to the conquest of Constantinople in 1453. In the following centuries, Varna several times was the scene of battles between Russians and Ottomans. It was conquered by the Russians in 1828 but was restored to the Ottoman empire at the peace of Edirne. The Crimean campaign of 1854 began from there. At the Congress of Berlin in 1878 Varna was definitely allotted to Bulgaria.

Veil (A. *lithām*): a strip of cloth with which the Bedouins cover the lower part of the face, the mouth and sometimes also part of the nose. According to the Arab dictionaries, the term *lifām* indicates a mouth-veil which also covers the top of the nose and is worn by women. From the purely religious point of view, the veil has no considerable importance for Islam; it is forbidden along with other garments for the person who has adopted the state of temporary consecration (A. *iḥrām*).

Vijayanagar: Hindu town and kingdom of southern India, whose history is largely a record of intermittent warfare with the Muslims on its northern frontier, first with the Bahmanids, and later with the Muslim states which rose on the ruins of the Bahmanid sultanate. In 1564 the allied sultans of Bijapur, Ahmadnagar, Golconda and Bidar made an end to the Hindu kingdom.

Vine (A. *karm*): notwithstanding the official attitude of Islam towards wine, the vine was incontestably cultivated in the majority of medieval Muslim countries, as is attested by the very considerable and exceptional place accorded to it by Muslim agronomists. At the end of the Middle Ages the vine declined, as much through the growth of strictness and conversions as through the interference of nomad invasions.

Vizier (A. *wazīr*): title of ministers of state and of the highest dignitaries in several Near Eastern kingdoms, especially in the Ottoman empire. The Arabs took over the term from Sasanian Iran, and in later times the Persians took it back as if it were really Arabic. The signet-ring was the visible badge of the office. Under the Ottomans the first vizier is said to have been 'Ala' al-Din, brother of Sultan Orkhan b. 'Othman. The so-called "dome viziers" sat with the Grand Vizier under the dome in the palace, assisted him and replaced him during his absence. The office disappeared with the Ottoman empire in 1923.

W

Wada'i: region to the west of Dar Fur, Sudan. Islam is said to have been introduced in 1615. About 1635 'Abd al-Karim, also known as Muhammad al-Salih, preached Holy War against the pagan dynasty of the Tunjur princes and founded a new dynasty which retained the throne till 1912. He transferred the capital from Kadama to Wara, from where it was moved to Abeshe. In 1912 Wada'i became part of the French colony of Chad.

Wadi 'l-Qura: valley between al-'Ayla' and Medina on the ancient trading route from Yemen to Syria, usually called Wadi Deidibban. At the beginning of Islam the Wadi 'l-Qura supported a considerable Jewish population who, like their co-religionists in Medina, were hostile to the Prophet. In 626 they joined the defensive alliance formed by the Jews of Tayma', Fadak and Khaybar. In 628 they were forced to surrender to the Muslims.

Wadi Nun (Wadi Nul): name of a great plain in southwestern Morocco. In the xth c. the Lamta Berbers had a town there, called Nul Lamta. It was conquered by the Almoravids in the xith c., and became known to Europe under the name Tagaost (modern Qsabi). For trade with the Niger, the Sa'di Sharifs favoured their native town Tagmadart in the upper Dar'a over the oases of Wadi Nun, and the Filali Sharifs the route by Tafilalt for similar reasons. Consequently, there was always enmity between the Wadi Nun and the Filali Sharifs. In the xixth c. Wadi Nun formed a practically independent state under Shaykh Bayruk (d. 1859), whose capital Awgelmim supplanted Tagaost. The direct relations of the Bayruk family with Europe forced the Filali Sharif al-Hasan I b. Muhammad in 1866 to conquer Tazerwalt and the Wadi Nun, and to force the English merchants to depart.

Wafd: name of a political party organized in Egypt by Sa'd Zaghlul (1857-1927). In 1918 he led a delegation (A. *wafd*) which demanded that the British protectorate in Egypt be abolished. After much unrest, the British created some form of independence for Egypt in 1922, and the *Wafd* organized itself as a political party in 1923, calling for internal autonomy, constitutional government, civil rights, and Egyptian control of both the Sudan and the Suez Canal. After Egypt gained complete independence in 1936, Wafd governments were in constant conflict with the monarchy. In 1952 the Revolutionary Command Council under Nasser put an end to both the monarchy and the *Wafd*.

al-Wafrani (al-Ifrani), Abu 'Abd Allah Muhammad: Moroccan biographer and historian; 1669-1727. He is best known as the author of the great chronicle of the Sa'di Sharifs of Morocco, covering the period from 1511 to the end of the xviith c.

Wahb b. Munabbih, Abu 'Abd Allah: story-teller of Persian descent from Yemen; 654-728. He is celebrated for his *Book of the military cam-*

paigns, describing the Prophet's campaigns. He was also an authority on the traditions of Jews and Christians.

Wahhabism (A. *Wahhābiyya*): Muslim puritan movement founded by Ibn ʿAbd al-Wahhab. The name was given to the movement by its opponents in the founder's lifetime, and is used by Europeans; its members call themselves "Unitarians" (A. *Muwahhidūn*) i.e. those who emphasize the absolute One-ness of God (A. *tawḥīd*). They are Sunnis, following the school of Ahmad Ibn Hanbal, as interpreted by Ibn Taymiyya. The history of the movement is closely linked with that of Saudi Arabia.

Wahhabi doctrine was introduced into India by Sayyid Ahmad Brelwi (1786-1831). He established a permanent centre in Patna, marched against the Sikh cities of the Punjab and took Peshawar in 1830. His adherents started an insurrection in Lower Bengal. In 1870 the older Muslim communities of India, both Shiʿi and Sunni, dissociated themselves from the Wahhabi doctrine of Holy War.

al-Walid I b. ʿAbd al-Malik: Umayyad caliph; r. 705-715. He was the great builder of the Umayyad dynasty. In 706 he began the reconstruction of the basilica of St. John the Baptist at Damascus into a magnificent mosque. He also built the Great Mosques at Mecca and Medina. Other striking features of his reign were the arabisation of the administration and the progress of conquests. In his reign the Arab empire attained its greatest extent from Transoxania to Spain.

al-Walid II b. Yazid II: Umayyad caliph; r. 743-744. He was remarkably cultivated, but also a libertine. In 743 he sold Khalid al-Qasri, the former governor of Iraq, to the latter's mortal enemy Yusuf b. ʿUmar al-Thaqafi, which raised the Yemenis in Syria against him. Before being caliph, he had built the hunting lodge Qusayr ʿAmra, and as a caliph he began with the construction of al-Mushatta.

al-Walid b. al-Mughira b. ʿAbd Allah: opponent of the Prophet; d. 622. He was the head of the numerous and prosperous Banu Makhzum at Mecca.

al-Waqidi, Muhammad b. ʿUmar: Arab historian from Medina; 747-822. A moderate Shiʿi, he owes his fame to the *Book of the campaigns (of the Prophet*, the only one of his many writings that has survived as an independent work. His merit lies mainly in his transmission of a very large amount of material and in fixing its chronology.

Walide Sultan: title borne in the Ottoman empire by the mother of the reigning sultan and only for the duration of her son's reign.

Wanquli, Mehmed b. Mustafa al-Wani: famous Ottoman jurist from Van; xvith. c. His translation of the Arabic lexicon of Abu Nasr Jawhari was printed in 1728 by Ibrahim Müteferriqa, as one of the first books printed in Turkey.

Waraqa b. Nawfal b. Asad: cousin of Khadija; viith c. He is said to have belonged to the Meccan group of monotheists (A. *ḥanīf*).

Waramin: town about 60 km to the south-southwest of Teheran, which shows ruins of a citadel and of a mosque built in 1322 under the Il-Khan Abu Sa'id (r. 1317-1335).

Wargla (Ouargla): oasis in the Algerian Sahara. At the time of the Arab conquest the land was occupied by Zenata Berbers. They adopted Ibadi doctrines so thoroughly that after the destruction of the Rustamid kingdom by the Fatimids in 909, many Kharijites came to settle there. Abu Yazid, the "man with the ass", who had rebelled against the Fatimids, recruited many followers in this region. In the xivth c. Wargla, although under the suzerainty of the Hafsids, was practically independent under the rule of sultans belonging to the family of the Banu Abi Ghabul. At the end of the xvith c. these sultans were extremely wealthy, and so Wargla was plundered by the Turks under Salah Re'is in 1540. French authority was imposed in 1872.

al-Warka': ruined site in southern Iraq where the first encounter between Arabs and Persians took place at the beginning of the Muslim campaigns against the Sasanian Empire. It marks the site of Uruk.

Washmgir (Wushmaghir) **b. Ziyar Abu Talib**: ruler of the Ziyarid dynasty in Tabaristan and Gurgan; r. 935-965. Under his brother Mardawij (r. 927-935) he conquered Isfahan and drove from there 'Ali b. Buya, the founder of the Buyid dynasty, who had taken it when he was in Mardawij's service. In 940 he was defeated by the Samanids who were in alliance with the Buyids. Later Washmgir fled to the Samanid Nuh I b. Nasr, who assisted him against the Buyids, Tabaristan thus becoming a buffer state between the Samanids and the Buyids.

al-Washsha', Abu 'l-Tayyib Muhammad: Arabic philologist and bel esprit; xth c. He wrote a handbook of rules of good society for the aristocrats of Baghdad.

Wasi' 'Alisi ('Ali): Ottoman author, scholar and poet, stylist and calligrapher; d. 1543. His fame is based on his Turkish translation of the Persian version of the *Kalila wa-Dimna*.

Wasif, Ahmed: official historian of the Ottoman empire; d. 1806. His four state chronicles, called appendices because they follow on to 'Izzi's work, cover the greater part of the period from 1783 to 1805. He also wrote an account of Bonaparte's invasion of Egypt.

Wasil b. 'Ata', Abu Hudhayfa al-Ghazzal: chief of the Mu'tazila; 699-748. He migrated to Basra where he belonged to the circle of Hasan al-Basri, and entered into friendly relations with Bashshar b. Burd. His wife was a sister of 'Amr b. 'Ubayd Abu 'Uthman, next to himself the most celebrated of the earliest Mu'tazila. His deviation from the views of Hasan al-Basri is said to have become the starting point of the Mu'tazila. Four theses are ascribed to him: denial of God's eternal qualities; the doctrine of free will, which he shared with the Qadarites; the doctrine that the Muslim who commits a mortal sin enters into a state intermediate between that of a Muslim and that of an unbeliever; the doctrine that one of the parties who took part in the murder of ʿUthman, in the battle of the Camel and in that of Siffin, was wrong.

Wasit: once one of the most important towns of Iraq, lying on the west bank of the Tigris, half-way between Basra and Kufa. It was founded as a garrison town by al-Hajjaj b. Yusuf in 702 to separate the Syrian troops from the Iraqis and to keep the military colonies of Basra and Kufa in check. Al-Hajjaj died here in 714. The ʿAbbasids put an end to the dominating position of Wasit, but the town continued to be of great strategic importance. It was also a centre of theological studies. The decline began in the xvth c. as a result of a change in the channels of the waters of the Tigris.

al-Wathiq bi-'llah, Abu Jaʿfar Harun: ʿAbbasid caliph; r. 842-847. His reign was marked by troubles caused by an alleged descendant of the Umayyads, named Abu Harb, usually called al-Mubarqaʿ. He also had to send the general Bugha al-Kabir to Medina in order to subdue the rebellious Bedouins around the town. The Kharijites and the Kurds were also causing trouble. al-Wathiq was an ardent Muʿtazili.

Wattasids (Banu Wattas): Moroccan dynasty which ruled from 1428-1547. In the xiiith c. the Banu Wattas established themselves in the Rif of eastern Morocco. They became practically independent rulers when their relatives, the Marinids, had replaced the Almohads. Their history is at first linked with that of the Marinids and afterwards closely connected with the Christian attempts to conquer territory in Morocco and with the accession of the Saʿdi Sharifs. The founder of the dynasty Abu Zakariyaʾ Yahya (r. 1428-1448) took control of Morocco as vizier after it had lapsed into anarchy following the assassination of the Marinid Abu Saʿid ʿUthman III (r. 1399-1420). He fought successfully the Portuguese who had landed on the Moroccan coasts. His son ʿAli, however, could not prevent the fall of al-Qasr al-Saghir, and the third Wattasid vizier, Yahya, was assassinated in 1458 with most of his family. The last Marinid Abu Muhammad ʿAbd al-Haqq II (r. 1428-1465) then tried to govern directly, but he was killed in 1465. In 1472 the Wattasid Muhammad I al-Shaykh (r. 1458-1470) was able to take Fez, now under Idrisid government, and was proclaimed sultan. The successors of Muhammad II al-Burtuqali ("the Portuguese") (r. 1470-1525) were unable to check the rising power of the Saʿdi Sharifs, who in 1524 seized Marrakesh.

Watwat, Rashid al-Din: Persian poet; d. 1182. He left a Persian translation of the 100 sayings of ʿAli, and a treatise on rhetoric.

Wehbi, Sayyid: Ottoman Turkish poet; d. 1736. With Ahmed Nedim (d. 1730), Mehmed Emin Beligh (d. 1729) and ʿAbd al-Razzaq Newres, he is reckoned among the most important representatives of the romantic group in the reign of Sultan Ahmed III.

Wejihi, Husayn: Ottoman poet and historian from the Crimea; d. 1660. His history comprises the years 1637-1656.

Weysi (Uways b. Mehmed): famous Ottoman scholar and poet; 1561-

1628. He was one of the best prose writers of his time, using a particularly fine persianising style. He wrote a biography of the Prophet, which only comes down to the battle of Badr.

Y

al-Yafi'i, 'Abd Allah b. As'ad: Sufi author from Yemen; 1300-1367. He compiled several biographical works on the lives of saints and Sufis.

Ya'furids (Hiwalids): name of a dynasty which ruled in San'a' from 861 till the beginning of the xth c. It was founded by Ya'fur b. 'Abd al-Rahman al-Hiwali.

Yaghma Jandaqi (Abu 'l-Hasan Rahim b. Hajji Ibrahim Quli): Persian poet; 1782-1859. He wrote funeral chants and slanderous and obscene satires.

Yahya: Turkish poet of Albanian origin; d. 1572. In Istanbul he became a bitter enemy of the court poet Khayali Bey and wrote a satirical lament upon the Grand Vizier Rüstem Pasha.

Yahya b. Adam b. Sulayman: Muslim student of religion from Kufa; ca. 757-818. He was primarily a traditionist and legist, and wrote a work on land-tax (A. *kharaj*).

Yahya b. 'Ali: one of the best-known theorists of music of the old Arabian school; 856-912. His grandfather Yahya b. Abi Mansur al-Munajjim (d. 831) was the famous astronomer at the court of the 'Abbasid Caliph al-Ma'mun, and his father 'Ali b. Yahya b. Abi Mansur and his uncle Muhammad had particular skill in music. He wrote a *Treatise on Music*.

Yahya b. Khalid: member of the Barmakid family; d. 805. He was imprisoned by the 'Abbasid Caliph al-Hadi, but the Caliph Harun al-Rashid, whose tutor he had been, appointed him as vizier with unlimited power. In 803 his son Ja'far b. Yahya, the favourite of Harun al-Rashid, was suddenly executed, and Yahya imprisoned until his death.

Yahya b. Zayd al-Husayni: regarded as Imam by the Zaydis; d. 743. After his father's death in 740 at Kufa, he fled to Khurasan but was imprisoned by the governor Nasr b. Sayyar. Released at the order of the Umayyad Caliph al-Walid II, he defeated the commander of Nishapur but fell in the fight against Salm b. Ahwaz, sent by Nasr. His death deeply affected the Shi'a of Khurasan, and vengeance for him became the watchword of the followers of Abu Muslim, the leader of the 'Abbasid movement in Khurasan.

al-Yamama: district in central Arabia. It became notorious in early Islam because of the revolt there of Musaylima b. Habib.

Yanbu' (Yenbo): a port and a town in the Hejaz. The port is also known as Yanbu' al-Bahr or Sharm Yanbu', and serves as main port for Medina. The town, at some distance to the north-northeast of the port, is called Yanbu' al-Nakhl. The Prophet is said to have conducted the *salat* in the town, whose date-palms and henna have been known since ancient times.

al-Yaʿqubi, Ahmad b. Abi Yaʿqub b. Wadih: renowned Arab historian and geographer; d. 897. He was a Shiʿi of the moderate Musawis. His fame is based on his *Book of the countries*, a geographical work for which he had been collecting material by research in literature and making inquiries of travellers. His style is simple and his text free from fables. He also wrote a history of the world, which he brought down to the year 872.

Yaqut al-Mustaʿsimi, Jamal al-Din: famous calligrapher; d. 1298. He composed an anthology and a collection of aphorisms.

Yaqut al-Rumi (Shihab al-Din Abu ʿAbd Allah): famous Arab encyclopaedist; 1179-1229. A trader in the Persian Gulf, he travelled widely and ransacked libraries wherever he went. He wrote on the Arab genealogies and composed a work containing biographies of men of letters. His fame rests upon his *Lexicon of the countries*, which contains not only geographical information but also, under each place-name, astrological and historical data, quotations from poems and a list of eminent natives of the place.

Yarbuʿ: name of an important group of the tribe of Tamim, whose territory stretched between al-Yamama to below the Euphrates. On the death of the Prophet, they were the first to rebel, the prophetess Sajah being one of them. They lent considerable support to the Kharijites, and counted a number of remarkable poets.

al-Yarmuk: perennial tributary of the river Jordan which, for most of its course, forms the boundary between Syria and Jordan. It has become famous in Islamic history for the battle in 636 of the Muslims under Khalid b. al-Walid against a superior force of the Byzantines. The Muslim victory led to the annexation of Syria.

Yaʿrub b. Qahtan b. Hud: grandson of the prophet Hud, who is regarded as the ancestor of the Himyar kings.

Yaʿrubids: dynasty of Oman; r. 1624-1741. They are named after their ancestor Yaʿrub b. Malik and ruled in al-Rustaq, Yabrin and al-Ham. They were followed by the Al Bu Saʿid.

Yasawi, Ahmad: Muslim saint from Turkestan; d. 1166. He is regarded as having converted the Turks to Islam. Tamerlane erected a splendid mausoleum in his honour in the town of Turkestan.

Yazd: town in the province of Fars, known for its beautiful Great Mosque, built in 1375.

Yazid I b. Muʿawiya: Umayyad Caliph; b. ca. 642, r. 680-683. As a prince he had commanded the Arab army at the siege of Constantinople. At his accession to the throne, al-Husayn b. ʿAli and ʿAbd Allah b. al-Zubayr refused to recognise him and took refuge in Mecca. From there al-Husayn left for Iraq, where in 680 he met his death at Karbalaʾ. At Medina Yazid was declared deposed, but the town was taken by Muslim b. ʿUqba. Yazid is described as a generous patron, who was a poet himself, fond of music. Alone among the caliphs he earned the title of "water engineer". He completed his father's administrative organisation, and reorganised the finances.

Yazid b. al-Muhallab b. Abi Sufra al-Azdi: governor of Khurasan; 672-720. He had strained relations with his brother-in-law al-Hajjaj b. Yusuf, who had him imprisoned in 705. In 708 he found support with the future Caliph Sulayman at al-Ramla. In 715 he was appointed governor of Khurasan while retaining the supreme command in Iraq. He made himself generally hated by his extortions, and was arrested at the orders of the Caliph ʿUmar II b. ʿAbd al-ʿAziz. In 720 he preached open war on the Umayyads, seized Wasit but was defeated by Maslama b. ʿAbd al-Malik.

Yazidis (A. *Yazidiyya*): name of a Kurdish tribal group and of their peculiar religion. They are found in the districts of Mosul, Diyarbakr, Aleppo and in Armenia. Their religion includes pagan, Zoroastrian, Jewish, and Muslim elements, but also features from Christian sects, especially the Nestorians, from Sufism, from the Sabaeans and from the Shamans. They possess two Sacred Books: *The Book of Revelation* and *The Black Book*. God is only the Creator, not the Preserver of the world. The active organ of the divine will is Malak Tawus or "the peacock angel", who is the denial of evil. Satan is the fallen angel who has been restored to God's favour. The Yazidis do not believe in hell, but they do accept transmigration. Their most concrete expressions are the figures of peacocks, called *sanājiq*, who are seven in number, corresponding to the seven angels who took part in the creation of the world. They consider themselves completely separated from the rest of mankind and have a high level of morality. The annual pilgrimage to the tomb of Shaykh ʿAdi, located north of Mosul, is a strict religious duty. Marriage is endogamous, and as a rule monogamous, except for the amir. They practise baptism and circumcision, and have burial ceremonies of their own. The structure of Yazidi society is theocratic, consisting of laity and clergy, which is divided into six different classes. Muslim theologians hold the view that the Yazidis at one time were Muslims. They have withstood numerous attempts at conversion and extermination by Turkish pashas and Kurdish tribes.

al-Yaziji, al-Shaykh Nasif b. ʿAbd Allah: Arab poet and philologist from Lebanon; 1800-1871. He contributed to the popularity of al-Mutanabbi in Syria, and obtained fame as the last representative of the *Session* genre. He also exercised great influence on modern Arabic literature. His sons Ibrahim (1847-1906) and Khalil (1858-1889), and his daughter Warda (1838-1924) also contributed to the revival of the Arabic language.

Yaziji-oghlu Ahmed (Ahmed Bijan): Turkish poet, brother of the Mehmed Yaziji-oghlu; d. ca. 1456. He was the author of several much esteemed mystical works.

Yaziji-oghlu (Yaziji-zade) **Mehmed**: Turkish poet; d. 1451. He is known as the author of a long didactic poem, which contains a lengthy expression of the doctrines and traditions of Islam based on Qurʾan and Tradition.

Yazuri, Abu Muhammad al-Hasan: vizier and chief judge of the Fatimid Caliph al-Mustansir bi-ʾllah. When the Zirid al-Muʿizz b. Badis rebelled against the Fatimids in 1051, Yazuri sent the Banu Hilal and the Banu Sulaym to ravage Ifrīqiya. In the east Yazuri gave considerable financial assistance to the Turkish military leader Arslan al-Basasiri in his rebellion against the ʿAbbasid Caliph al-Qaʾim.

Yemen (A. *al-Yaman*): country in the southeastern and southwestern part of the Arabian Peninsula. The Republic of Yemen was formed in 1990 by the union of the former Yemen Arab Republic (North Yemen, Sanʿaʾ) and the People's Democratic Republic of Yemen (South Yemen, Aden).

At the time of the Prophet, the Persian governor of Yemen Badham was converted to Islam. ʿAli b. Abi Talib is said to have preached Islam in Yemen in 631.

In 632 al-Aswad b. Kaʿb, like several other Bedouin chiefs during the period of the "apostasy" (A. *ridda*), reacted against the political system established by the Prophet, but he was subdued. In 692 Khariji control in Yemen ended, but the tendencies persisted. The ʿIbadis, whose movement had been introduced by ʿAbd Allah b. ʿIbad, took Mecca and Medina in 746, but were defeated by an army sent by the Umayyad Caliph Marwan II.

The first of the many dynasties that have ruled in different parts of Yemen over the centuries were the Ziyadids. In 879 Ismaʿilism was introduced by Mansur al-Yaman and ʿAli b. al-Fadl (d. 915). Both at first remained faithful to al-Mahdi ʿUbayd Allah, but in 913 ʿAli made war on Mansur al-Yaman. After ʿAli's death, his party disintegrated rapidly.

The ixth c. saw also the rise of the Zaydis and the Yaʿfurids. The rule of the Sulayhids ended in 1138, when power passed to the Zurayʿids, while the Hamdanids ruled over Sanʿaʾ. The Ayyubids ruled from 1174 until 1229, when they were followed by the Rasulids.

From 1454 onwards, the Sunni Tahirids held much of Yemen until 1517, when power passed to the Ottomans in the wake of Sultan Selim's conquest of Mamluk Egypt, Khadim Süleyman Pasha being the first governor. The Ottomans were driven out in 1635 by Imam al-Muʾayyad bi-ʾllah. In 1732 the ʿAbdali sultans of Lahj made themselves independent from the Zaydi Imams. In 1872 Yemen came again under Ottoman suzerainty, which lasted until 1918.

In 1958 North Yemen joined with Egypt and Syria in a United Arab Republic, but in 1962 a revolution against the Imam touched off a five-year civil war, in which the revolutionaries were supported by President Nasser of Egypt. A military coup followed in Sanʿaʾ in 1974. Meanwhile, the People's Democratic Republic had been established in 1967 upon the departure of the last British troops from Aden.

Yildiz Kiosk (T. *Yıldız Köshkü/-Sarāyî*): the residence of the Ottoman sultans in Istanbul from the xixth c. onwards. The earliest buildings date from the period of Sultan Mahmud II.

Young Turks: name of a revolutionary group, whose centre was the *Itti-*

had we Teraqqi Jem'iyyeti. They initiated the rebellion against the regime of Sultan Abdülhamid II.

Yunus al-Katib (al-Mughanni): musician and writer on music; viiith c. He is mentioned in the Thousand-and-One Nights and composed verses extolling the beauty of Zaynab bint 'Ikrima b. 'Abd al-Rahman, which became the rage under the name of *Zayanib*.

Yunus b. 'Umar b. Muhammad: governor of Iraq; d. 744. A relative of al-Hajjaj b. Yusuf, he governed Yemen from 725-738. As governor of Iraq, residing at al-Hira, he acquired the reputation of a bloodthirsty tyrant.

Yusuf b. Tashufin: Sanhaja Berber who was the first independent ruler of the Almoravids; r. 1061-1106. In 1062 he founded Marrakesh as his capital. After Toledo had fallen to Alphonso VI of Castile in 1085, he was summoned by the Muluk al-Tawa'if to save Islam in the Iberian Peninsula. He defeated Alphonso in the battle of Zallaqa in 1086 and suppressed almost all the Tawa'if.

Yusuf Khass Hajib: Turkish author; xith c. He wrote a "Mirror of Princes" for the Ilek-Khanid prince of Kashghar Bughra-Khan (d. 1102). It is the first classic of Turkish poetry of Central Asia.

Yusufi, Mawlana: secretary to the Mughal Emperor Humayun. He acquired a place in Indian literature with his epistolary manual.

Z

Zab: region around Biskra in Algeria. The country suffered greatly from the Arab invasions of the xith and xiith c. The Hafsids entrusted the government of Zab to the Banu Mozni, who made themselves almost independent in the xivth c. From the end of the xvith c. effective power was for two centuries and a half in the hands of the chief of the Arab family of Bu Okkaz, to whom the Turks allowed the title of Shaykh al-'Arab. Biskra was occupied by the French in 1844.

al-Zab: name of two left bank tributaries of the Tigris. The Upper or Great Zab rises near Lake Van and joins the Tigris south of Mosul. Here the last Umayyad Caliph Marwan II was defeated in 750. The Lower or Little Zab rises near Lake Urmiya and empties in the Tigris near Kirkuk. The valley of the Little Zab is the richest oil field of Iraq.

Zabid: town in the Tihama of Yemen, on the road from Mecca to Aden, about 16 km from the Red Sea coast. It adopted Islam in 631, and did not take part in the "apostasy" wars. The town became important under the Ziyadids, who were followed by the Najahids. At the end of the ixth c. it was burned by the Carmathians and in 989 it was taken for a time by 'Abd Allah b. Qahtan of the Ya'furids, who recognised the Fatimid caliphate, as did the Sulayhids. The latter interrupted the rule of the Najahids between 1060 and 1080. After

the interlude of the Khariji Mahdis, the town was in the hands of the Ayyubids, who were followed by the Rasulids. The Tahirids then ruled the town
until 1517, when it passed to the Ottomans, who had governors there until
1635, when the Zaydi Imam al-Mu'ayyad bi'llah drove them out. After the
second Ottoman occupation, which ended in 1918, the Zaydi Imams again became masters of the town after fighting the Idrisids of Asir.

Zacharias (A. *Zakariyyā'*): father of John the Baptist. In the Qur'an he is
reckoned along with John, Jesus and Elias among the righteous. His story is
expanded by later legend.

Zafar: name of a group of ruins in southern Yemen, to the southwest of
Yarim, celebrated in ancient times as the capital of the Himyar kingdom (ca.
115 B.C.E.-ca. 525 C.E.). It is also the name of a ruined site to the south-west
of San'a', and of a fortified hill about 30 km to the north-west of San'a' near
Kawkaban.

al-Zahawi, Jamil Sidqi: Arab poet, scholar and philosopher of Kurdish
descent from Iraq; 1863-1936. He associated with the Young Turks, was opposed to the Wahhabis and an ardent champion of the emancipation of
women. He is also celebrated as a Persian poet.

al-Zahir Ghazi, al-Malik: Ayyubid prince; 1172-1215. He was the second
son of Saladin, who made him ruler of Aleppo in 1186. During the wars with
the Crusaders he loyally assisted his father and later his brother al-Malik al-
Afdal, the ruler of Damascus, and his uncle al-Malik al-'Adil, the ruler of
Egypt and, after al-Afdal had been deposed, of Damascus. He played an energetic part in the fighting for Acre and Jaffa. In 1198 he recognised al-'Adil's
suzerainty.

Zahir al-Din al-Mar'ashi, Sayyid: Persian statesman and historian; xvth
c. He composed a chronicle of Tabaristan from the earliest times to 1476.

al-Zahiriyya: name of a school of law, which would derive the law only
from the literal text (A. *ẓāhir*) of Qur'an and Sunna. Founded by Dawud b.
Khalaf, it spread in Iraq, Persia and Khurasan. In Spain it was codified by Ibn
Hazm, who remained practically isolated. Only in the reign of the Almohad
Abu Yusuf Ya'qub al-Mansur was the Zahiri school recognised as the state
code.

Zallaqa: name given by the Muslim historians to the place near the town
of Badajoz, Spain, where the armies of the Almoravid Yusuf b. Tashufin inflicted in 1086 a severe defeat on the troops of Alfonso VI of Castile. The battlefield is now known as Sagrajas.

al-Zamakhshari, Abu 'l-Qasim Mahmud: Persian-born Arabic scholar,
theologian and philologist from Khwarazm; 1075-1144. As a theologian he
followed the teachings of the Mu'tazila and as a philologist, in spite of his
Persian descent, he championed the absolute superiority of Arabic. His principal work is a commentary on the Qur'an. At the very beginning of the work
he declares the Qur'an created, but notwithstanding this clearly Mu'tazila

point of view, it was widely read in orthodox circles. He also wrote grammatical works, a collection of old proverbs, and composed a series of moral discourses.

Zamzam (Zemzem): name of the sacred well at the Kaʿba in Mecca. Muslim tradition connects its origin with the story of Abraham. It was opened by the angel Gabriel to save Hagar and her son Ismaʿil, who were dying of thirst in the desert. The pilgrims drink its water as health-giving and take it home with them to give to the sick.

Zanata, Banu: name given by the Arab historians of the Middle Ages to one of the two great confederations of the Berbers, the other being the Banu Sanhaja.

Zands: name of a dynasty which ruled over Persia between 1750-1794. It was founded by Muhammad Karim Khan after the death of Nadir Shah Afshar. In 1794 the whole of Persia fell to the Qajars.

Zangids: dynasty of Turkish origin, which ruled in Mosul and Aleppo from 1127 till 1222, in Damascus and Aleppo from 1146 till 1181.

Zanj (pl. Zunūj): name of the black tribes of the east coast of Africa. It was given by the Arab historians to the rebel slaves who, having previously rebelled in 694, for fifteen years (868-883) terrorised Lower Mesopotamia. They were led by a man called "the veiled". They took al-Ubulla, now part of Basra, Abadan, Ahvaz, now the capital of Khuzistan, and finally Basra itself. They were in the end defeated by the ʿAbbasid regent al-Muwaffaq.

Zanjan: town in northwestern Iran, where the Babis in 1850 offered armed resistance to the government.

al-Zanjani, ʿIzz al-Din ʿAbd al-Wahhab (al-ʿIzzi): Arab grammarian; xiiith c. Besides grammatical works, he wrote on the use of the astrolabe and made a collection of Arabic poems.

Zanzibar (A. *al-Zanjabār*): town and port of the island of the same name, which lies off the east coast of Africa and is part of the Republic of Tanzania. The town lies on the west side of the island. The island became a possession of Oman and Muscat in the late xviiith c. It owes its rise to the Al Bu Saʿid sultan Saʿid b. Sultan, who made it his capital in 1832. In 1856 it was separated from Oman and Muscat and became an independent sultanate under Majid b. Saʿid b. Sultan. Under Sultan Barghash (r. 1870-1888) Zanzibar came under British and German influence, and in 1890 the British proclaimed it a protectorate. In 1963 the sultanate regained its independence and became a member of the British Commonwealth, but after the revolution of 1964 Zanzibar became part of the sovereign state of Tanzania, formed by the union of the Republic of Tanganyika with the islands of Zanzibar and Pemba. Independence marked the end of the rule of the Al Bu Saʿid dynasty in Zanzibar.

Zaranj: ruined capital of Sistan, to the south of Harat in western Afghanistan. It was taken in 651 by al-Rabiʿ b. Ziyad al-Harithi, who left it to the Persian satrap Parwiz in return for a substantial payment. His successor ʿAbd al-

Rahman b. Samura raised the siege upon an even higher payment. The town, fortified with a ditch and five iron gates, was the residence of the founder of the Saffarid dynasty Ya'qub b. Layth (r. 867-879) and his brother and successor 'Amr b. Layth (r. 879-901). It was taken by Tamerlane in 1383 and destroyed.

al-Zarnuji, Burhan al-Din: Arab philosopher; xiiith c. He composed a vademecum for students to teach them the ethical outlook of the man of learning, which became very popular.

Zawiya: Arabic term used in North Africa to indicate a building or group of buildings of a religious nature, which resembles a monastery and a school. The term was also applied to a small mosque or praying room.

Zayd b. 'Ali Zayn al-'Abidin: Shi'i leader of a rebellion against the Umayyads; viiith. c. He was a grandson of al-Husayn b. 'Ali and placed himself at the disposal of the people of Kufa as Imam. He was mortally wounded during street fighting against the troops of the governor Yusuf b. 'Umar al-Thaqafi. The Zaydiyya, to which he gave his name, revere him as a political and religious martyr.

Zayd b. 'Amr b. Nufayl: member of the Quraysh at Mecca, and a seeker of the original and true monotheistic religion (A. *hanif*). He died before the beginning of the Prophet's mission, but tradition considers him a true believer.

Zayd b. Haritha: a slave from Syria whom Khadija presented to the Prophet as a gift before his mission; d. 629. The Prophet freed and adopted him. He was one of the very first converts to Islam, perhaps the first.

Zayd b. Thabit b. al-Dahhak: Companion of the Prophet; d. 665. He became the Prophet's secretary, and is best known for his part in the editing of the Qur'an.

Zaydan, Jirji: Christian Arab scholar, journalist and man of letters from Egypt; 1861-1914. He wrote many novels, the majority of which deal with the history of Islam from the Arab conquest to the beginning of the Mamluk dynasty. They were translated into several languages. Their main value lies in the popularising of history. His best-known works are the *History of Muslim Civilisation* and the *History of the Arabic Literature*.

al-Zaydiyya: a group of the Shi'a which is distinguished from the "Twelvers" and the "Seveners" by the recognition of Zayd b. 'Ali Zayn al-'Abidin as Imam. The essential demands on the Zaydi Imam are membership of the Family of the Prophet, ability to resort to the sword if required, and the necessary learning. There was thus no dynastic tradition, individual success being in the end the deciding factor.

The Zaydiyya was founded as a united community in Tabaristan by al-Hasan b. Zayd Muhammad and lasted there until 1126, after which date it became merged in the little sect of the Nuqtawis.

In Yemen the Zaydiyya was founded by al-Hadi ila 'l-Haqq I Yahya, grandson of al-Qasim al-Rassi, founder of the Rassids. The Rassid line lasted until 1281, and their successors, the Qasimi line, founded by al-Mansur bi-'llah al-Qasim, until 1962.

Zayla': port in Somalia on the Gulf of Aden. The medieval Arab geographers describe it as the port of Abyssinia for trade with Yemen and the Hejaz. In 1516 it was captured by the Portuguese, and after the episode of Ahmad Grāñ in Abyssinia, it came into the hands of the Sharifs of Mocha. Between 1870 and 1884 it was occupied by the Egyptians, and in 1885 by the British.

Zaynab bint Jahsh b. Ri'ab: one of the Prophet's wives; d. 640. First he had given her in marriage to his freedman and adopted son Zayd b. Haritha. She was a friend of 'A'isha's, and, next to her, the Prophet's favourite. She became celebrated for her charity.

Zaynab bint Khuzayma: one of the Prophet's wives; d. 625. He married her in 625, but she died in the same year.

Zaynab bint Muhammad: one of the Prophet's daughters; d. 629. Her daughter Umama was married to 'Ali after Fatima's death.

al-Zaynabi, Abu 'l-Qasim 'Ali: vizier under the 'Abbasid Caliphs al-Mustarshid, al-Rashid, and al-Muqtafi; d. 1144. He was on particularly good terms with the Great Saljuq Mas'ud b. Muhammad b. Malik-Shah.

Zaytun: town in southeastern Turkey. Mostly inhabited by Armenians, the town was able to maintain a certain independence until 1864. During the xixth c. many troubles took place. Following the general persecution of the Armenians, it was taken by the Turkish governor of Mar'ash, and secured peace and amnesty through French intervention.

al-Zayyani, Abu 'l-Qasim: Moroccan statesman and historian; 1735-1833. He wrote a general history of Islam and a full account of his various journeys, among which is a description of his visit to Istanbul of 1786.

Zenta (Senta): town in Serbia, on the right bank of the Theiss river. It is celebrated in history because of the victory in 1697 of the so-called Holy League (Austria-Poland-Venice-Russia) led by Prince Eugène of Savoy, over the Ottoman army led by the Sultan Mustafa II. The defeat forced the Ottomans to sign the Treaty of Carlowicz in 1699 and made Austria the foremost power in Central Europe.

Zeybek: Turkish tribe in the region of Izmir, which distinguished itself by a peculiar dress. They were subdued under the Ottoman Sultan Murad II. Mustafa Kemal Atatürk endeavoured to make the dance peculiar to this tribe into a Turkish national dance.

Zikrawayh b. Mihrawayh: Carmathian missionary; d. 907. Having disposed of 'Abdan, Zikrawayh conquered Kufa in 906 but had to return to the district of al-Qadisiyya. In the same year he fell upon the great pilgrim caravan returning from Mecca. In the next year he was defeated by an 'Abbasid commander.

Zinda-rud: one of the principal rivers of central Iran. It rises in Khuzistan, flows through Isfahan and empties in a large brackish swamp. It separates Isfahan proper on its north bank from its southern suburb New Julfa.

Zirids: name of two mediaeval dynasties in the Muslim west.

The Zirids of Ifrīqiya (r. 972-1152) were Berbers of the Sanhaja confederation. Ziri b. Manad had founded Ashir about 940 as a bulwark against the Zanata Maghrawa, allies of the Umayyads of Córdoba. He thus rendered service to the Fatimids, especially by relieving al-Mahdiyya when it was besieged by the Khariji Abu Yazid. When the Fatimid al-Muʿizz li-Din Allah left for Egypt, he appointed Yusuf Buluggin I b. Ziri governor of Ifrīqiya. He became the founder of the Zirid dynasty. Under Badis (r. 996-1016) an amicable division of the Zirids into two kingdoms took place, one in the west, which went to the Hammadids who lived on the Qalʿa, and the other in the east to the Zirids with Qayrawan as capital. Al-Muʿizz (r. 1016-1062) threw off Fatimid suzerainty, but he was defeated by the Arab nomad tribes of the Banu Hilal and the Banu Sulaym, sent by the Fatimid Caliph in Cairo al-Mustansir bi-'llah. His successors made repeated attempts to retake command of the sea from the Normans of Sicily, who in 1148 took al-Mahdiyya.

The Zirids of Granada (r. 1012-1090) were a secondary branch of the Zirids of Ifrīqiya. They founded an independent principality with Granada as capital at the time of the dismemberment of the Umayyad caliphate of Córdoba. The founder of this dynasty was Zawi b. Ziri. His nephew and successor Habbus b. Maksan (r. 1025-1038) appointed the Jew Samuel Ibn Naghzala as vizier, a thing unprecedented in Muslim Spain. The latter's son Joseph Ibn Naghzala endeavoured to establish a Jewish principality in Granada but was killed in 1066, together with several thousand Granada Jews. The citadel of the town was built by Habbus and enlarged by the latter's son Badis (r. 1038-1073). Almoravid governors were installed at Granada and Málaga in 1090.

Ziryab, Abu 'l-Hasan ʿAli: the greatest musician of Muslim Spain; ixth c. He was first at the court of the ʿAbbasid Caliph Harun al-Rashid, then entered the service of the Aghlabid Ziyadat Allah I (r. 817-838), afterwards went to the court of the Spanish Umayyad al-Hakam I, and was on intimate terms with the latter's successor ʿAbd al-Rahman II.

Ziyad b. Abihi: viceroy of Iraq; d. 675. His name "Ziyad son of his father" indicates that the name of his father was not known. He was a member of the Banu Thaqafi. Having at first served ʿAli b. Abi Talib, he caught the eye of the Umayyad Caliph Muʿawiya I and when Ziyad rejected the first advances, Muʿawiya recognised him as a son of Abu Sufyan, thus making him his half-brother. He was given the governorship of Basra, and in his famous inaugural speech announced a strict programme. This having led to order in town and province, Muʿawiya entrusted him also with Kufa, where he restored order as well. To checkmate the ʿAlid opposition and that of the Arab tribes settled in Iraq, he moved 50,000 Bedouins to Khurasan.

Ziyadids: Yemeni dynasty which ruled from 819-1018 with its capital at Zabid. The dynasty was founded by Muhammad b. Ziyad. His grandson Abu 'l-Jaysh Ishaq b. Ibrahim ruled for an extremely long period (r. 904-981). In 989 'Abd Allah b. Qahtan, who restored the power of the Ya'furids for a short time by taking and burning Zabid, put an end to the dynasty of the Ziyadids. The actual ruler by that time was the Abyssinian slave vizier al-Husayn b. Salama who, by making pilgrim roads with mosques and wells, secured a long-lasting fame. He was followed by his slave Marjan as independent vizier, who in turn divided the government between his two slaves Najah, who founded the dynasty of the Najahids who were to rule in the northern provinces, and Nafis (or Anis) who was to rule in the southern provinces, including the capital.

Ziyaniyya: branch of the Shadhili order, with its headquarters at Qenadha to the southwest of Figuig in Morocco. It was founded by Muhammad Ibn Abi Ziyan (d. 1733). At the end of the xixth c. their speciality was the guiding and protection of caravans through the Sahara.

Ziyarids: dynasty of vassals of the Samanids, founded by Mardawij b. Ziyar. They reigned over Tabaristan and Gurgan from 927-1090. Their adherence to Sunni and not Shi'i Islam marks them off from almost all the other Daylami dynasties.

Zubayda bint Ja'far: wife of the 'Abbasid caliph Harun al-Rashid; 762-831. She is famous for her love of splendour, her liberality to poets and scholars, and for the public works she carried out.

al-Zubayr b. al-'Awwam (al-Hawari "the Apostle"): cousin of the Prophet and nephew of Khadija; d. 656. He was one of the earliest converts to Islam. With his wife Asma bint Abi Bakr he had three sons who also became known in early Islam: 'Abd Allah, 'Urwa, and Mus'ab. He took part in all the battles and campaigns of the Prophet, and was renowned for his gallantry. His epithet "the Apostle" was given him by the Prophet on account of his services as a spy in the conflict with the Banu Qurayza. In the conflict between 'A'isha and 'Ali, he was on the side of the Prophet's widow, but withdrew from the Battle of the Camel and was treacherously killed.

Zuhayr b. Abi Sulma: pre-Islamic Arab poet. With Imru' al-Qays b. Hujr and al-Nabigha al-Dhubyani, he is considered one of the great poets of the pre-Islamic period.

al-Zuhri, Muhammad b. Muslim (Abu Shihab): a celebrated traditionist; 670-ca. 737. He collected a great amount of traditions and is described as the first to fix Tradition in writing. He also dealt with chronology, was a critic of poetry and was one of the chief authorities for the biography of the Prophet, written by his pupil Ibn Ishaq.

Zuhuri, Nur al-Din Muhammad: Persian poet of the school of Harat; d. 1615. His poetry is admired in India where he lived for a long time.

Zuray'ids (Banu 'l-Karam): dynasty from Aden, which was in power in Yemen from 1138 till the arrival of the Ayyubids in 1174.

Khalid ibn Mashᶜan, great-grandson of the famous Bedouin raider and poet Shlewih al-ᶜAtawi, praying in the *majlis* of the house his father built in the desert west of ᶜAfif, Saudi Arabia. Photo courtesy of P. Marcel Kurpershoek.

The Inal al-Ajrud complex (Sufi monastery, madrasa and mausoleum), built 1451-1460, Cairo, Egypt. Photo courtesy of Heinz Halm.

Ince Minareli medrese, built 1260-1265, Konya, Turkey. Photo courtesy of Heinz Halm.

Badshahi mosque, built 1673-1674, Lahore, Pakistan. Photo courtesy of Heinz Halm.

The sanctuary of Fatima al-Maʿsuma, xviith c., Qum, Iran. Photo courtesy of Heinz Halm.

The madrasa of Shir-dar, built 1619-1636 by the Uzbeg Yalangtush Bahadur, Samarkand, Uzbekistan. Photo courtesy of Heinz Halm.

Giralda. Minaret of the Almohad mosque, built ca. 1197-1198, Seville, Spain. Photo courtesy of Heinz Halm.

Bastion-mosque and tomb of Ibn Tumart, built ca. 1153, Tinmal, Morocco. Photo courtesy of Heinz Halm.